DRUGS AND SOCIETY

DRUGS AND SOCIETY

A BIOLOGICAL PERSPECTIVE

Patricia Jones-Witters, Ph.D.

Weldon L. Witters, Ph.D.

OHIO UNIVERSITY

Department of Zoological and Biomedical Sciences

WADSWORTH HEALTH SCIENCES

MONTEREY, CALIFORNIA

Wadsworth Health Sciences Division
A Division of Wadsworth, Inc.

Printed in the United States of America

10   9   8   7   6   5   4   3   2   1

Library of Congress Cataloging in Publication Data

Jones-Witters, Patricia.
   Drugs and society.

   Bibliography: p.
   Includes index.
     1. Drugs.   2. Drugs—Toxicology.   3. Medication
abuse.   4. Substance abuse.   5. Pain—Chemotherapy.
I. Witters, Weldon L.   II. Title.   [DNLM: 1. Drug
therapy—Drugs. 2. Drugs—Adverse effects. 3. Sub-
stance abuse. QV 55 J79d]
RM300.J58   1983   615'.1   82-21738
ISBN 0-534-01412-7

ISBN 0-534-01412-7

Drug charts on inside covers by arrangement with the Catalyst Group, Gwynedd Valley, Pennsylvania.

Cartoons appearing on pages 4, 65, 347, and 371 are reprinted by permission.
© Sidney Harris: American Scientist Magazine.

Subject Editor: James Keating
Signing Representative: Miriam Nathanson
Production: Ron Newcomer & Associates, San Francisco, California
Interior Design: Ron Newcomer
Cover Design: Bill Agee
Illustrations: Irene Imfeld and Dale Johnson
Typesetting: Graphic Typesetting Service
Production Services Manager: Stacey C. Sawyer

PREFACE

Background

We developed this text from a human biology course designed to provide a biological background on drugs. Much of the material was selected for inclusion based on weekly evening discussion groups held in college residence halls. The information is directed to those students who are not majoring in biology and who have had a modest scientific background, but who have questions about the therapeutic drugs that have been prescribed for them and about the recreational drugs they take. We have discovered from these informal meetings and from students bringing drugs for analysis that many people have a rather general knowledge of drugs but do not have the necessary biological background to make the informed decisions they want to make. To meet these needs, we decided to treat the topic in a general college text covering social developmental patterns and the behavioral aspects of drug use.

Scope and Sequence

We treat the material from the biologist's point of view, rather than that of the psychologist or the sociologist. We describe the history, composition, use, and the reactions of drugs relative to their therapeutic values, their known and potential injurious effects on the human body, and their potential for inducing drug dependence. Discussions of unwanted side effects, such as those that alter sexual functioning, are included.

First we briefly cover the important psychological and biological reasons people take drugs, because humans are unique among animals in the extent of this behavior. Because so many drugs exert their effects through the nervous system, a chapter (directed to the nonscience student) is devoted to a description of the concept of homeostasis and how the nervous system works. This section leads into a description of how a drug, as a biochemical substance introduced into the body, can produce an effect on the body. It also describes the different dosage forms and the effect of time, tolerance, and dependence. The fascinating role of the placebo, or inactive "drug," is discussed. Drugs seldom are ingested one at a time, so the student needs to know not only the effects of the major classes of drug that are widely used but also how they can interact with one another in surprising ways.

The text begins its discussion of drug abuse with an examination of various societies' early and continuing use of the many plant-derived hallucinogens. Marijuana and the synthetic LSD are discussed in detail. In contrast to the hallucinogens, the stimulant and the depressant drugs, especially amphetamine diet pills and tranquilizers, are much more widely abused by the adult middle class.

Tobacco use, which led to the first drug controversy of global dimensions, is so widespread that it is often not perceived as the addiction it is. Alcohol, probably the first psychoactive drug widely used and abused, continues to be an important medical, social, and economic problem in all classes of society. The narcotics, such as heroin, are likely to be more devastating than alcohol and tobacco, but affect far fewer people.

The text also devotes several chapters to special drug-related topics not necessarily involving abuse—for example, the treatment of chronic pain, which is a major health problem today. The role of drugs in treating pain is described along with other medical approaches to controlling pain. Because we have noted considerable interest in drug interactions with human sexuality, a chapter is devoted to the effects of therapeutic drugs, recreational drugs, and the so-called aphrodisiacs on sexuality. Another chapter discusses the contraceptive drugs that have made such an impact on the structure of society. This material includes discussions of oral contraceptives, medicated intrauterine devices, and spermicidal products in terms of how they work and what the important risks and side effects are. Still another chapter covers special problems associated with medication of the elderly, who constitute an increasing proportion of the population.

Our treatment of over-the-counter (OTC) drugs centers on the consumer's point of view, and it also introduces the history of OTC drug legislation. A separate chapter describes the checkered history of the regulation of opiate narcotics, marijuana, and cocaine and discusses the present legal approach to this problem. Although it is not intended as a substitute for medical consultation, a brief guide to first aid in abused-drug emergencies and withdrawal is included.

A subsequent section describes, along with some analysis of their limitations, prevention approaches directed at drug abuse and treatment and rehabilitation programs for the more difficult types of drug dependence. The final chapter develops the theme that, although a desire to alter one's state of consciousness seems to be a part of human nature, using drugs to accomplish this is neither necessary nor the best way. Alternatives are discussed in this context.

Learning Aids

Each chapter begins with a study outline, or Chapter Objectives. These items emphasize the major points and key definitions. The glossary defines terms that are likely to be new to a non-science student. The reference section lists the specific sources we have used in developing this text. This section is intended to be a starting point for the examination of the extensive literature on the topic of drug use and abuse.

Finally, we have tried not to moralize but to provide accurate, up-to-date information gleaned

PREFACE

from current thinking and research. We realize that the ultimate choice in handling drugs must be an individual one—that an informational program alone will not prevent people from making faulty decisions. Nevertheless, we believe that possessing accurate information and an understanding of human biology and drug use will provide a basis for making intelligent decisions—with less chance of errors in judgment—now and in the future.

We gratefully acknowledge the invaluable assistance and boundless patience of Dr. Marvin Fletcher, Dr. Craig Farrar, and the staff of the Ohio University Computer Center. David D. Mowry, Ohio University, William J. Pizzi, Northeastern Illinois University, and John Leach, Western Illinois University, painstakingly reviewed the manuscript and made many helpful suggestions.

Patricia Jones-Witters
Weldon L. Witters

CONTENTS

4

PHARMACODYNAMICS: THE MECHANISMS OF DRUG ACTION   49

5

THE CLASSIFICATION OF DRUGS AND DRUG INTERACTIONS   67

9

TOBACCO *149*

10

DEPRESSANT DRUGS *171*

CONTENTS

11

ALCOHOL 195

12

OPIUM AND ITS DERIVATIVES 229

CONTENTS

CHAPTER 1

WHY DO PEOPLE TAKE DRUGS?

CHAPTER OBJECTIVES

1. List the four classes of drugs that alter consciousness, mood, or awareness; define *psychoactive drug*.
2. Formulate a hypothesis to explain why a person who has an immature personality is more likely to take drugs than a mature person.
3. Discuss whether or not a person's potential to abuse drugs can be predicted according to that person's behavior in childhood.
4. Give the reasons that any behavior may persist; then relate these reasons to drug-taking behavior.
5. Compare primary and secondary psychological drug dependence.
6. Describe how positive reinforcement and rewards might affect psychological dependence on drugs.

FREQUENCY OF DRUG USE

Why is there such an increase in drug use today? In analyzing a question like this you will find there are a number of possible answers, none of which by itself offers a satisfactory solution to this complex problem. Practically all of us are drug users, and the definition of drug abuse is just a matter of degree.

We are a drug-oriented culture. We use a host of different drugs for a variety of purposes: to restore health, to reduce pain, to induce calmness, to increase energy, to create a feeling of euphoria, to induce sleep, and to enhance alertness. A multitude of substances are available to swallow, drink, or inhale in order to alter mood or state of consciousness. Youngsters are bombarded with many commercials exhorting them to use a chemical to solve almost any problem. The message is: Why cope with an uncomfortable problem? Try our tablet, and the problem will go away.

An incredible amount of money is spent each year for legal chemicals that alter consciousness, awareness, or mood. There are four classes of these legal chemicals (1979 and 1980 data from the Census Bureau and the *33rd Annual Report on Consumer Spending*):

1. Social drugs—$50.9 billion for alcohol, $21.7 billion for tobacco, and about $5 billion for coffee, tea, and cocoa.
2. Prescription, or ethical, drugs—$12.7 billion.
3. Over-the-counter (OTC), or patent, drugs—$3.4 billion, including cough and cold items, external and internal analgesics, antacids, laxatives, antidiarrheals, and sleep aids/sedatives.
4. Miscellaneous drugs—aerosols, nutmeg, morning-glory seeds, and others. (The amount of such drugs diverted to alter consciousness is unknown.)

Studies from the Social Research Group of George Washington University, the Institute for

TABLE 1-1 Use of coffee and sleeping pills[*]

Item	Coffee			Sleeping pill	
	Male	*Female*		*Male*	*Female*
Total persons (millions)	64.6	72.9		64.6	72.9
Nonusers (millions)	10.6	14.9		51.8	60.2
Users (millions)	46.1	54.9		4.5	9.4
percent of total (users)	71.4	75.3		7.0	12.9
1 cup or less daily	18.2	21.8	less than		
2–5 cups daily	40.5	42.9	once/week	3.3	6.2
6 cups or more daily	12.7	10.6	once a week		
			or more	3.7	6.7

[*] *Statistical Abstracts of the United States.* 1980. 101st ed. U.S. Department of Commerce, Bureau of the Census, p. 130.

Research in Social Behavior in Berkeley, California, and others have given us detailed, in-depth data showing that drug use is universal. A major purpose of these investigations was to determine the level of psychoactive drug use in the population aged 18 through 74, excluding those persons hospitalized or in the armed forces. Tables 1-1 and 1-2 are based on data for the specific categories of drugs used: caffeine, sleeping pills, nicotine, alcohol, and other psychoactive drugs. Note that persons in the 18 to 25 age group are by far the heaviest users and experimenters.

Over 80% of respondents in the previously mentioned studies reported that they drank coffee, and over 50% said that they drank tea during the previous year. One of the surprising findings from these data showed that nearly a third of the population was drinking more than five cups of caffeine-containing beverage each day. In 1979, 250 billion doses of caffeine were consumed in the United States. These figures exclude caffeine sources such as chocolate, cocoa, cola drinks, NoDoz®, and other over-the-counter tablets such as Empirin®, APCs, and others.

The number of cigarettes smoked in the United States in 1979 was about 600 billion. Almost 22 gallons of beer were consumed for each man, woman, and child, as were more than 2 gallons of wine and more than 2.8 gallons of distilled spirits. Studies indicate that large numbers of persons have tried or routinely use marijuana:

TABLE 1-2   Drug use, by type of drug and by age group[*]

Type of drug	% of youths (12–17 yr)		% of young adults (18–25 yr)		% of adults (26 yr and older)	
	Ever used	Current user	Ever used	Current user	Ever used	Current user
Alcohol	70.3	37.2	95.3	75.9	91.5	61.3
Cigarettes	54.1	12.1	82.8	42.6	83.0	36.9
Marijuana	30.9	16.7	68.2	35.4	19.6	6.0
Inhalants	9.8	2.0	16.5	1.2	3.9	0.5
Hallucinogens	7.1	2.2	25.1	4.4	4.5	<0.5
Cocaine	5.4	1.4	27.5	9.3	4.3	0.9
Heroin	0.5	<0.5	3.5	<0.5	1.0	<0.5
Analgesics	3.2	0.6	11.8	1.0	2.7	<0.5
Stimulants	3.4	1.2	18.2	3.5	5.8	0.5
Sedatives	3.2	1.1	17.0	2.8	3.5	<0.5
Tranquilizers	4.1	0.6	15.8	2.1	3.1	<0.5

[*] *Statistical Abstracts of the United States.* 1980. 101st ed. U.S. Department of Commerce, Bureau of the Census, p. 129.

51% of those between 16 and 17 years of age, and 68% of those in the 22 to 25 year range (Petersen, 1980). It is estimated that as many as 40 million or more people have tried marijuana or use it on a regular basis.

The average household has about 30 drugs, of which one out of five is a prescription drug and the other four are over-the-counter drugs. Of the many prescriptions written by physicians, approximately one-fourth are for drugs that in one way or another modify mood or behavior. Gallup polls show that over half of all adults in the United States report that at some time in their lives they have taken a psychoactive drug (one that affects mood and/or consciousness). Over a third of all adults have used or are using tranquilizers.

Men are most likely to report use of stimulants in their 30s, tranquilizers in their 40s and 50s, and sedatives from age 60 on. Women, however, are most likely to report use of stimulants from age 21 through age 39 and frequent use of tranquilizers in their 30s. Women use sedatives in a pattern similar to that of men, the frequency of use increasing with age. Women tend to use pills to cope with problems, whereas men tend to use alcohol. In addition, persons over 35 are more likely to take pills, whereas younger people prefer alcohol. Among those using pills, younger persons and men are more likely to use stimulants than older persons and women, who take sedatives (Chambers & Griffey, 1975).

The true figures for use of all psychoactive drugs are probably 35% higher than reported. This discrepancy exists partly because a large number of people get their psychoactive drugs on the black market and from friends and rel-

"HE'S THE TYPICAL AMERICAN MOUSE— LIKES A DRINK BEFORE DINNER, SMOKES A LITTLE, WATCHES TV..."

atives who have legitimate prescriptions. An estimated 70% of all psychoactive prescription drugs used by people under 30 years of age are obtained without the user having a prescription. Pharmacists' records show that about 400 million psychoactive drug prescriptions were written in 1979, and the rate of increase is about 7% per year. Statistics such as these indicate that it should be harder to find persons who do not use psychoactive drugs than those who do.

WHY DO PEOPLE USE AND ABUSE DRUGS?*

Many people think that drug abuse is new and that we have new problems facing us in the use of drugs today. As one reads about ancient cultures, however, one realizes that drug use has always been part of our history. For example, the Grecian oracles of Delphi used drugs, Homer's Cup of Helen induced sleep and provided freedom from care, and the mandrake root supplied hallucinogenic belladonna compounds. In Genesis 30:14–16, the mandrake is mentioned in association with lovemaking:

> In the time of wheat harvest Reuben went out and found some mandrakes in the open country and brought them to his mother Leah. Then Rachel asked Leah for some of her son's mandrakes, but Leah said, "Is it so small a thing to have taken away my husband, that you should take my son's mandrakes as well?" But Rachel said, "Very well, let him sleep with you tonight in exchange for your son's mandrakes." So when Jacob came in from the country in the evening, Leah went out to meet him and said, "You are to sleep with me tonight; I have hired you with my son's mandrakes." That night he slept with her. [New English Bible, 1970]

There are numerous descriptions in ancient literature of the use of mushrooms, datura, hemp, marijuana, opium poppies, and so on. Under the influence of some of these drugs many people experienced extreme ecstasy or terror. Some old pictures of demons and devils look very much like those described by modern drug users during so-called "bummers" or bad trips. Witches' beliefs that they could fly may have been drug induced, because many of the natural preparations used in "witches' brews" induced the sensation of dissociation from the body—in other words, flying or floating.

Some drug use led to attempts to regulate it legally. For instance, problem drinking is addressed in the code of Hammurabi (2240 B.C.) and is described as a problem of men with too much leisure time and lazy dispositions. Nearly every culture has as part of its historical record laws controlling the use of a wide range of drugs, including tobacco.

As we have seen, human beings have always experimented with natural drugs. Why does this experimentation occur? Like the Assyrian who sucked on opium lozenges or the Roman who ate hashish sweets about 2000 years ago, many users claim to be bored, in pain, frustrated, unable to enjoy life, or alienated. They turn to drugs in the hope of finding oblivion, peace, togetherness, or euphoria. The fact that few drugs actually cause the effects for which they are taken—or if they do, they do so for only a brief time—seems to be no deterrent. People continue to take drugs for other than medical reasons because:

1. They are searching for pleasure. Drugs may make them feel good.

---

*This section is largely taken from Lettieri, Sayers, & Pearson, 1980.

2. Drugs may relieve stress or tension, or provide a temporary escape.

3. Peer pressure is strong, especially for young people. The use of drugs has become a "rite of passage" in some parts of our society. Sometimes it is part of the thrill of risk taking.

4. From an early age we are "programmed"; the media tell us that drugs are part of the technology that can help make life a little bit better. They urge us to seek "better living through chemistry." One national commission studying the drug-abuse problem estimated that by the age of 18 the average American has seen 180,000 television commercials, many of which give the impression that pleasure and relief are to be found in sources outside oneself (Resnik, 1979).

5. In some cases the drugs may enhance religious or mystical experiences. A few cultures teach their children how to use specific drugs for this purpose.

The Difference Between Use and Abuse

There is a distinction between use and abuse of drugs. Almost everyone uses a psychoactive substance, even if it is a socially accepted substance such as coffee, but not everyone misuses or abuses drugs. Misusing a drug means using it in a way that can have detrimental effects. Getting drunk may be a misuse of alcohol, but it does not necessarily mean the drunk person is an alcoholic or that he or she has sustained bodily damage from the episode. There are many definitions of *abuse* of a drug. The National Institute on Drug Abuse (NIDA) defines *drug abuse* as drug use that results in the physical, mental, emotional, or social impairment of the user. There are other definitions linked more to social relationships—that is, use becomes abuse

if the drug has a negative effect not just on the user, but on others with whom the person is in contact. The reasons for abusing a drug vary widely, but most drug abusers have at least one thing in common: they use drugs as a substitute for something they lack—good feelings about themselves, a sense of competency and peace of mind, the feeling of being liked just for themselves, or other aspects of what are generally regarded as universal human needs (Resnik, 1979).

What do we mean by "needs?" Many scholars have tried to understand how we develop our personalities and identities. Abraham Maslow was a humanistic psychologist who postulated a hierarchy of needs, or basic goals, that motivate a person. He believed there are at least five sets of goals (Maslow, 1973):

1. The *physiological needs*, including food and water, are essential to life. These are the prepotent needs, meaning that when a person is extremely hungry or thirsty everything else is unimportant. Only when the person is not chronically hungry or thirsty do the higher needs emerge. If a person's physiological requirements are not met, especially during the first two years of life, that person may lose the ability to develop the higher needs. He or she may never be capable of giving or receiving love, for example, even though later in life his or her physiological requirements are met.

2. The *safety needs* may be defined in terms of a stable reference framework, of some kind of undisrupted routine, and of the absence of both danger and the threat of the completely unfamiliar. Small children find loud noises and strangers threatening not because they are actually being harmed, but because these things disrupt their world. In order to cope as adults, we need to feel that somewhere there is a familiar environment we can retreat to.

3. The *love needs* emerge if both the physiological and safety needs are fairly well satisfied. People with love needs crave friends, affection, and a place in their group, and they are strongly motivated to achieve these goals.

4. The *esteem needs* fall into two subcategories: (a) the need for strength, confidence, and independence; and (b) the need for the respect of others.

5. The *need for self-actualization*, or self-fulfillment—to become everything that one is capable of becoming—occurs in people who have satisfied their physiological, safety, love, and esteem needs.

The five basic goals just listed are shown in order of importance, but each need does not have to be 100% satisfied before the next need emerges. However, only when the physiological needs, such as hunger, are at least partially satisfied does a person show some need for safety and perhaps a little need for love (see Figure 1-1). The satisfaction of these needs is not mutually exclusive—the average person is most often partially satisfied and partially unsatisfied in all of his or her wants. "Thus man is a perpet-

ually wanting animal!" (Maslow, 1973). Maslow considers any obstacle—real or imagined—to the achievement of these basic human goals as a psychological threat that can lead to psychopathology.

Drugs might be used as a substitute for the achievement of a goal, such as the satisfaction of the need for affection and a sense of belonging or for a feeling of self-confidence. If the drug satisfies the need to some extent, the user may not learn how to give and receive affection or develop a sense of self-worth and confidence. Such a person would be stunted in his or her personality development and may continue to turn to drugs as a way to satisfy his or her needs.

Maslow's work is widely but not universally accepted. Some find his goal of self-actualization too vague; others have their own theories of motivation (Madsen, 1974). People do, nevertheless, appear to share a basic need to feel worthwhile: "I am a human being; do not fold, spindle, or mutilate!" But such a statement can be difficult to make in an ever more complex world, where economic, political, and technological pressures are bringing about changes in our lives at an accelerating rate. The structure of the family unit has been altered.

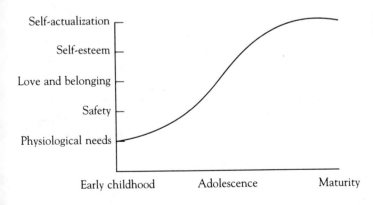

FIGURE 1-1
Gratification of the hierarchy of human needs: Maslow's theory of motivation.

More than half of all women in the United States work outside the home now, largely for economic reasons; how this fact affects the quantity and quality of child care and nurturing is difficult to assess. Also, increasing numbers of children are being raised in single-parent households due to separation and divorce. Mobility of the population is thought to be a contributing factor to the lack of a feeling of self-worth in many people. Children are moved from one location to another and have difficulty establishing a sense of permanence about anything. Often one's community is a mass of strangers. There may be little pride in home or community and no commitment to the society one lives in (Resnik, 1979).

Another major factor thought to be involved in drug dependence is a feeling of powerlessness due to discrimination based on race, sex, social standing, or other attributes. Groups subject to discrimination have a disproportionately high rate of unemployment and below-average income. The Carnegie Council on Children estimated that 17 million children grow up in poverty and feel powerless in their situation. The adults they have as role models are unemployed and also powerless. There are higher rates of delinquency and drug addiction in such settings.

Drug Abuse Among Teenagers

Studies have shown us that the majority of young drug users come from homes in which drugs are used extensively. Mom needs something to wake up in the morning, to stay on her diet, and often something to relax her during the day. Dad has his relaxing drinks, perhaps something for his nervous stomach, and a stimulant to get started at work. Both parents often take sleeping pills to end the day. Pills are taken in almost unbelievable volume. Sometimes one wonders if these people could make it through a typical day without chemical props. This chemical "cop-out" is more prevalent than many people believe, and the phrase "better living through chemistry" is becoming more fact than fiction.

Dr. Robert Petersen at the National Institute on Drug Abuse has pointed out that:

> Society lacks meaningful alternatives for more than a fraction of our youth. At the same time that they have an unparalleled awareness of the problems of the society and are frequently very perceptive about it, teenagers are denied a meaningful role in shaping it. They are instead encouraged to be part of the teenage market—to consume without producing. Despite their many material advantages, they are commonly "put down" as human beings along with the aging, and given an unenviable sense of uselessness. [1974]

Drug use provides an easy way of rebelling against parents and against a social culture whose values many young people disdain. Brought up in an affluent society, many middle-class students are not motivated by the forces that drive their parents toward seeking economic security. They question the values of the compulsive work ethic and the "treadmill" existence. Although many may go along with the system because it will get them where they want to go, their hearts are often not in it. Drug use may be an unconscious expression of this lack of commitment.

A more dangerous reason for taking drugs, psychiatrists point out, is to escape the psychic pain of growing up. Young people who take drugs because they ease the stress of coping with life's difficulties are the people most likely to become chronic users.

THE BEHAVIORAL ASPECTS OF DRUG USE

We have discussed why people take drugs. We have seen that drug use is as old as recorded history and has occurred in all civilizations. The important point to remember is that drug use is a part of human behavior, and as such it follows the same rules and principles of any other behavioral pattern. One basic behavioral principle is that behavior persists when it either increases the individual's pleasure or reduces his or her discomfort (psychic or physical). People do not take just any drug—they take only those that affect them pleasurably or that make a situation less intolerable. Further, of those drugs that do increase pleasure or decrease discomfort, the ones chosen must be acceptable within the user's cultural setting.

Behavior, including drug use, is nurtured in several ways. Thus there is no single cause of drug abuse. Studies with animals show that susceptibility to narcotics addiction is partially genetically determined. Strains of laboratory animals have been bred that are either susceptible or resistant to induced addiction (Nichols & Hsiao, 1967). Similarly, strains of laboratory animals have been developed that prefer alcoholic solutions over water for drinking, whereas most animals will select tap water if given the choice (Segovia-Riquelme, Hederra, Anex, Barnier, Figuerola-Campo, Campos-Hoppe, Jara, & Mardones, 1970). This suggests that alcoholism in humans may be partly based on hereditary predisposition (Goodwin, 1979).

Drug use, whether influenced by genetic factors or not, is the result of a complex interaction of past experiences and present environment. This is true of any behavior. It is possible to group some persons together because of a common history and environment and to predict whether or not they will probably use drugs as well as the class of drug they will most likely use. This fact does *not* mean that potential users can be readily identified; rather it means that some groups of individuals can be identified according to the *probability* of their becoming drug users. Various types of drug user may also be classified according to differences in personality and background. For example, narcotics addicts usually start drinking alcoholic beverages in their early teens, before their age and social-class peers do. After experimenting with alcohol, narcotics addicts often try marijuana or inhalants, such as those found in glue. The average age of first narcotic use is the late teens. As one drug becomes more acceptable in society—for example, marijuana—the next drug selected is usually less socially acceptable than the previous one. The family pattern often found in the male narcotic addict is (1) presence of a dominant, overprotective mother and a detached, uninvolved father (or absence of the father) and (2) a tendency to continue living with the mother or other female relatives long past the usual age (Nurco, 1979).

Social Development Patterns

A number of social development patterns are closely linked to drug use. Based on the age at which an adolescent starts regular alcohol consumption, predictions can be made about his or her sexuality, academic performance, lying, cheating, fighting, and marijuana use. The same holds true of marijuana use. This represents a point of departure toward less conventional behavior, greater susceptibility to peer influence, increased delinquency, and lower school achievement. There are a number of characteristics that drug abusers have in common (Blum & Richards, 1979):

1.   Their drug use usually follows clear-cut developmental steps and sequences. Use of one of the legal drugs, such as alcohol, almost always precedes use of illegal drugs.

2.   The dysfunctional attributes of drug use usually appear to precede rather than to derive from drug use. In other words, the "amotivational syndrome" often attributed to a person's heavy marijuana use was probably part of that person's personality *before* he or she started the drug.

3.   Immaturity and maladjustment usually *precede* the use of marijuana and of other illicit drugs.

4.   Those who will try illicit drugs usually have a history of poor school performance.

5.   Delinquent and deviant activities usually precede involvement with illicit drugs.

6.   A constellation of attitudes and values that facilitate the development of deviant behavior exists before the person tries illicit drugs.

7.   There is a process of anticipatory socialization during which youngsters who are going to try drugs first develop attitudes favorable to the use of legal and illegal drugs. A social setting favorable to drug use usually reinforces and increases individual predisposition to use.

8.   Drug behavior and drug-related attitudes of peers are usually among the most potent predictors of subsequent drug involvement.

9.   Parents' behaviors, attitudes, and closeness to their children usually have varying influence at different stages of their children's involvement in drugs.

10.   Highly deviant children start using drugs at a younger age than less deviant children.

11.   The older one is when one starts using drugs, the less the involvement and the greater the probability of stopping drug use. The period of greatest risk of initiation into illicit drug use is usually over by the mid-20s.

A certain amount of rebelliousness is not unusual in youngsters as they try to assert themselves and gain self-identity. Some experiment with drugs to annoy and upset their parents. Lewis Carroll alludes to this type of behavior in *Alice's Adventures in Wonderland,* when one of the characters says: "Speak roughly to your little boy, and beat him when he sneezes: he only does it to annoy, because he knows it teases." The use of illegal drugs symbolizes a rejection of the social standards and moral codes of the parent, and, because many parents live for the future through their children, the threat of losing this link by drug abuse is seriously agitating.

So, drug-taking behavior is not unique, but is like other behaviors. An appreciation and understanding of this fact is important in the prediction of drug behavior. Another type of behavior that approximates drug-taking behavior in motivation and effect is the neurosis. Examples of neuroses are anxiety, compulsive types of speech or action, fatigue with no physical cause, various types of fear with no basis, such as fear of open spaces, and many others. These behaviors have similar characteristics, and possibly some of the classic neurotic symptoms will gradually be replaced by drug use. It may be that drug use will just be superimposed on neurotic behavior, or vice versa. It follows that the same kinds of concern should be shown about drug use as about neurotic patterns of behavior.

As is true of neurotic behavior, illegal drug use offers the individual both benefits and disadvantages. The benefit is usually a short-term gain, such as increased positive feelings or a decrease in discomfort. The disadvantages are multiple but usually remote. For example, there is a decrease in the chance of reaching long-term, permanent solutions to underlying problems. There is also, in our society, a probable decrease in the rewards an individual can obtain if he or she persists in drug use.

Development of Drug Dependence*

Dr. Maurice Seevers believed that the only means by which drug dependence could be eliminated in human society is for people never to come in contact with particular drugs. The reason is that, having once experienced certain drug effects, a majority of the world population would inevitably become drug dependent. Many drugs are such powerful, immediate reinforcers that, if all the population were allowed to try every major psychoactive drug and then were permitted free access to the drug of their choice, the effect on society would be disastrous. Part of Seevers's basis for this statement is animal research. If a monkey or a rat is allowed to self-administer a drug such as cocaine, it will do so until it dies of starvation, because it ignores its food.

Some people have looked on the drug addict as a depraved person, but from research with animals, one realizes that susceptibility is a relative condition and that almost everyone can be made drug dependent in the fullest sense of the term, even against his or her will. This fact has long been recognized by persons wanting to elicit admissions of some act, and induced drug dependence is one of the types of so-called brain washing that works on almost any person.

A diagram of how drug dependence is thought to develop is shown in Figure 1-2. If the first

*This section is largely based on Seevers, 1968.

drug trial is a rewarding experience, a few more rewarding trials follow until drug use becomes a conditioned pattern of behavior. Continued positive reinforcement with the drug, in the psychological sense, leads in time to primary psychological dependence. Primary psychological dependence is all that is needed to lead to uncontrollable compulsive abuse of any psychoactive drug in certain susceptible persons. The effect of drug dependence on the particular person is related to the nature of the psychoactive substance, the quantity used, and the characteristics of that person and of his or her environment. It is often not possible to draw a sharp line between use and abuse, because there are all shades of gray between the total abstainer and the drug "addict."

Even strong psychological dependence on some psychoactive substances does not necessarily result in injury or in social harm. For example, typical dosages of mild stimulants such as coffee do not induce harmful reactions. Even though the effects on the central nervous system are barely detectable by subjective or objective analysis, strong psychological dependence on mild stimulants like tobacco, caffeine-containing beverages, and betel may develop, such that withdrawal may be difficult. Ask a five–ten-cup-a-day coffee drinker to stop drinking, or a two-pack-a-day cigarette smoker to stop smoking for three days, and you may observe minor withdrawal symptoms. Although this type of dependence is partly psychological, it is nevertheless real. The heavy coffee drinker deprived of the stimulant probably will report feeling jittery and will have headaches and even muscular fatigue. Many of us know friends or relatives who are a real nuisance when they are in the early stages of their latest attempt to stop smoking. Thus even the mild stimulants may cause some dependence. But the fact that their use does not typically induce antisocial behavior distin-

PSYCHOPHARMACOLOGICAL ELEMENTS OF DRUG DEPENDENCE

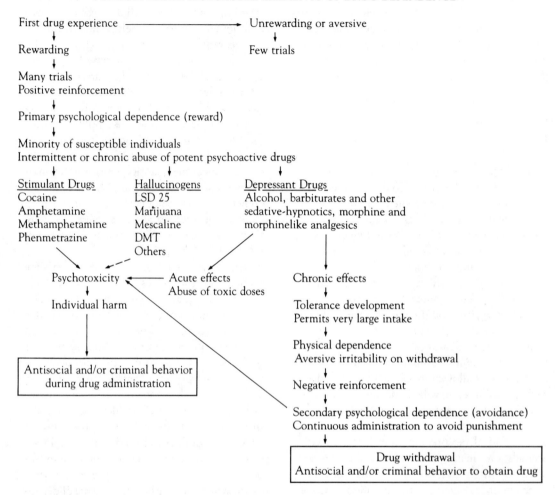

FIGURE 1-2

Steps in the process of drug abuse or drug rejection. (From "Psychopharmacological Elements of Drug Dependence," by M. H. Seevers, *Journal of the American Medical Association*, 1968, 206(6), 1263–1266. Reprinted by permission of the American Medical Association.)

guishes them from all other forms of dependence-producing drugs.

Possibly 70% of the U.S. adult population are able to use alcohol—a potent psychoactive agent—in moderation, even to the point of strong psychological dependence, with minimal personal injury and social consequence. Many persons use other powerful psychoactive drugs under the supervision of a physician without becoming drug dependent. The study of the use of these powerful psychoactive drugs is fascinating and surprising. Morphine, for example, produces no significant pain relief in as much as 25% of persons given it; in fact, it may produce unfavorable reactions. Some people can take small amounts of heroin for years without becoming dependent on it, whereas a few become physically addicted after one intravenous dose. Perhaps 5%–10% of the population would be or could be classified as susceptible to these powerful psychoactive agents; drugs dominate these people's lives. Stimulated by their need for drugs, some of these people become directed toward one goal only—obtaining the money to buy their drug. After talking to many such people, one has the feeling that they could have been successful in almost any legitimate endeavor if they had applied to it only half of their drive to obtain drugs.

The user of depressants may develop secondary psychological dependence (see Figure 1-2). This dependence is related to the fact that depressants cause two separate phenomena: *tolerance* and *physical dependence*. Tolerance develops as the drug's action on the vital organs typically affected, such as the nervous system, the cardiovascular (heart and circulatory) system, and the respiratory system, is lessened. In other words, the same dose has less effect, so the dose must be increased. Not all parts of the body become tolerant at the same rate, and the brain is exposed to larger and larger drug concentra-

tions as tolerance develops in various bodily systems (cardiovascular, respiratory, and so on). Not enough is known about brain changes under these conditions.

Continuous exposure of the nervous system to large concentrations of depressant drugs induces physical dependence (see Figure 1-2). This condition is characterized by increased nervous activity but is evident only when the drug is discontinued. The complex of symptoms following cessation of drugs is often referred to as *withdrawal*, or the *abstinence syndrome* (which means literally that certain symptoms occur after administration of the drug is stopped).

To make matters a bit more complicated, there are two types of abstinence syndrome: the morphine type and the alcohol-barbiturate type. The morphinelike drugs may be used interchangeably to give the same effects and to block withdrawal symptoms. The dosage of morphine and morphinelike drugs must be increased as tolerance builds and physical dependence develops. Finally a dose is reached above which further increases will not have any effects on drug dependence. Morphine withdrawal, or morphine abstinence syndrome, is not life threatening and can usually be accomplished without too much difficulty. Alcohol-barbiturate dependence and the subsequent withdrawal syndrome is different from the morphine type in that it usually takes prolonged and continuous administration of large doses over a period of time to develop dependence when the drug is taken orally. Intravenous administration is, however, different—this way a drug user can become physically dependent in a few weeks. The alcohol-barbiturate type of abstinence syndrome is intense, and the severe convulsions associated with it can kill. Because withdrawal is a risky process, it is usually accomplished slowly. Withdrawal from alcohol, the barbiturates, and the minor tranquilizers (Valium, Librium)—but not the major tranquilizers (Thorazine, Stelazine, and so on)—cause this condition, and these drugs may be given interchangeably to suppress withdrawal symptoms (see Chapters 10 and 11).

The interchangeability of alcohol, barbiturates, and the minor tranquilizers suggests that these drugs work by a common mechanism, but the mechanism is not understood. When a person who is physically dependent on a depressant drug stops taking the drug, symptoms occur that are very similar to those induced by a stimulant. The resulting state of agitation, or hyperexcitability, is apparently due to some action of the central nervous system and is often called the *rebound effect,* or the *paradoxical effect.* Some authorities believe that the rebound effect might be due to release of inhibitory centers in the brain; others believe that it is induced by direct stimulation of neural centers (see Chapter 3).

Let us sum up the facts about drug dependence. All drug dependence has as a basis psychological conditioning to the effects of the various drugs. The first characteristic that encourages drug taking is primarily psychological dependence resulting from the positive reinforcement of the reward. In other words, the experience is good, or pleasurable, or it temporarily covers some painful feelings. This is what we mean by a rewarding experience. Each time the person takes the drug in question the experience is rewarding, and the behavior is positively reinforced. In the case of depressants that may cause physical dependence following repeated use, a second type of behavior, secondary psychological dependence, results. Secondary psychological dependence is a negative experience, or *avoidance,* as it is sometimes called. It is also called *aversive reinforcement* because the feelings of withdrawal from the depressant are very unpleasant, and the particular depressant drug is taken to prevent the occurrence of withdrawal symptoms. For example, once an alco-

holic starts to experience the symptoms of withdrawal, he or she is motivated to drink to avert the symptoms. The use of depressants is especially difficult to stop because of the buildup of tolerance to the dose taken. As tolerance builds, the dosage needed must be increased, and the reward of taking the drug becomes less important. Then the need to prevent the occurrence of withdrawal, or secondary psychological dependence, becomes the most important factor that will encourage use of the drug.

Psychological conditioning to drug use involves more than the pharmacological actions of the various drugs. The drug user's environment and physiological characteristics are also involved. Further, the individual psychological makeup of the person will respond differently to various types of peer pressure and social use of drugs. Such abstract emotions as the desire to belong, to prove one's bravery by taking chemicals, and to experiment with a special group can greatly affect one's drug use. These types of emotion influence the decision either to try or not to try drugs. The motives for drug use are obviously different in some ways for the ghetto dweller, the inmate in a penal institution, and a middle-class suburbanite. Yet these people share many motives for drug use once the drugs are tried, because the same conditioning forces are at work on all of them. However, people will respond differently to drugs because of their different behavioral makeup.

As we have seen, drugs have multiple effects that vary with the amount of the drug used and the personality of the user, as well as the user's expectations of the drug's effects. The reason people initially take drugs recreationally varies considerably, but it is either to obtain a pleasurable experience or to reduce unhappiness. Whether or not a person decides to use drugs to solve problems depends on his or her background, present environment, and the availability of the drugs. The availability of drugs is both a major and a minor problem. On the one hand, if drugs were not available, obviously no one would be using them; on the other hand, if the availability of drugs alone were the problem, we could solve it by simply shutting off the supply. The biggest problem, however, is people, not drugs. People look for rapid solutions to problems, and drugs are one of the options our society makes available.

WHO IS A DRUG ABUSER?

Is it the Black or Hispanic from the ghetto, the Vietnam veteran, the youngster from an emotionally turbulent family, or the skid-row bum in a large city who is the most likely drug abuser? What setting most encourages drug abuse? The physician's office, the suburban home, the business office, the assembly line, the construction business, the nursing home for the elderly? A person with some insight would say that all of these places foster addiction to some mind-altering substances, and he or she would be right. Addicts and drug abusers are found among housewives, automobile assembly line workers (especially on Monday and in the mornings), in the operating rooms and nursing stations of hospitals, among business people enjoying three-martini lunches, in the priesthood, in the law profession, and in all stations of life. There is no place where drug dependence has not been found. Addiction is found in all races, religions, and social levels of life. Addiction is the "equal opportunity" affliction. The only difference is that some social classes have greater percentages of addiction to various types of drug.

Many people do not realize that well-educated members of the professions have addictions just as do young people in the ghettos and from broken homes in nice locations. We have come to expect addiction in the latter group but not in the former. Many professional organizations have started rehabilitation programs for those members who have alcohol and other drug problems. These organizations represent the medical, legal, and teaching professions, the ministry, and others. Once you realize that some highly intelligent persons become addicts—and in fact some of them carry out their job function for years without too many people realizing that they are impaired—you have to change your conception of how addicts get "hooked" on various drugs.

Alcohol addiction is the drug dependency that affects the greatest number of professionals (as well as laymen). A study by the American Medical Association estimated that 400 doctors are lost from the medical profession each year because of alcoholism. That does not sound like a significant number until you realize that it is the equivalent of the graduating classes from four large medical schools each year. All that effort, time, and money gone to waste! This figure does not include those doctors lost because of use of narcotics and other drugs. Of the professionals addicted to drugs other than alcohol, physicians have one of the highest addiction rates. This is partly due to their access to narcotics and other potent drugs and partly due to the stress of the medical profession (Hall, Stickney, & Popkin, 1978).

The nursing profession has had comparable problems with certain kinds of addiction, particularly tranquilizers, narcotics (to a lesser extent than physicians), and stimulants. Nurses have the opportunity to divert drugs prescribed for patients, and this diversion appears to provide the major supply. Nurses often receive little professional respect and may be the object of contempt by physicians, which, combined with irregular working schedules, leads to considerable job-related stress. It becomes an easy matter to pop a prescription tranquilizer when one cannot scream back at a surgeon having a bad day, or a stimulant to keep going through a double shift.

The Catholic Church has for years had special rehabilitation centers for priests with alcohol problems. The use of alcohol as a drug for socialization and the psychological stresses and pressures of handling the problems of the congregation are usually given as causes of alcoholism. The legal profession has developed programs to help lawyers who are having difficulty performing well because of heavy use of alcohol and other drugs. In the past decade the armed forces have finally admitted to themselves that there are many service people with serious drug problems. Part of the drive to develop treatment programs began with the realization that many of the service personnel in Vietnam were using the readily available narcotics. A great deal of money was funneled into the Veterans' Administration (VA) hospitals to help treat addicts.

Another area of society that is now being mobilized to recognize and treat drug dependence is industry. It is estimated that between 6% and 10% of the nation's work force suffers from alcoholism. The total cost to the nation has been estimated to be as high as $43 billion a year because of absenteeism, health and welfare services, property damage, accidents, and medical expenses. Lost production alone may cost industry about $19 billion a year. The United Auto Workers, the AFL-CIO, and other unions have developed drug and alcohol abuse programs to aid in recovery of workers. Well over 300 major industries have now adopted similar programs, usually in cooperation with unions. In most cases the industry will sponsor the treat-

ment, pay for it, and place the recovered employee back on the job.

For many years the female alcoholic or drug-addiction problem was ignored. It is still considered more shameful in many parts of our society for a woman to have a drinking or a drug problem than a man. According to various estimates, anywhere from 24% to 50% of problem drinkers are women. When you consider that the National Institute on Alcohol Abuse and Alcoholism (NIAAA) estimates that 10% of the total population has a drinking problem, then you are talking about a large number of people in the United States. Prescription sedative use combined with alcohol is probably more common among women than men. Sixty percent of psychoactive drugs and 71% of antidepressant drugs are prescribed for women in response to complaints of anxiety. It seems that physicians are more likely to prescribe psychoactive drugs (Valium is number one) for women than for men. Because of the wide availability of these drugs and of alcohol, many women develop polydrug addictions. After ex-President Ford's wife, Betty Ford, admitted she had developed a drug addiction because of overuse of tranquilizers and pain medication, and entered a hospital voluntarily for treatment, many women were helped to admit comparable dependence.

Another area of drug addiction involves the elderly. As many as 90% of those over age 65 (about 25 million people) have suffered drug side effects. About 20% have been hospitalized for these effects. At one time people believed that there were no elderly narcotics addicts. We now know that there are hidden pockets of drug abusers and addicts to alcohol, tranquilizers, and other drugs in all levels of the population—young, old, blue-collar workers, professionals, male, and female.

CHAPTER 2

THE BODY AND DRUGS: STRUCTURE AND CONTROLS

CHAPTER OBJECTIVES

1. Define *homeostasis*, and give two examples of the process.
2. Compare how the endocrine and nervous systems control cellular and systemic processes.
3. List the parts of a typical neuron, and describe the function and relationship of each part to the others.
4. Trace the path of a nerve impulse through a chain of neurons, explaining how the impulse moves from one neuron across to the next neuron.
5. Define *neurotransmitter*, and list four types with their functions.
6. Name the two types of synapse classified according to their function, and explain how the function might be important in turning on or turning off a body function.
7. Define *receptor site*, and explain how drugs may affect receptor sites.
8. Describe natural and drug factors affecting dopamine, norepinephrine, and serotonin concentrations.
9. List the parts of the nervous system, and describe the function of each.
10. Define *blood-brain barrier*, and explain why a drug may act faster on some parts of the nervous system than on other parts.

HOMEOSTASIS AND CONTROLS

Drugs may have many effects on the body. Whatever the effect of a drug, it is due to an action on the body's control and information-processing systems. The following discussion will give you an idea of where drugs act, how they affect us, and why they may change moods or feelings.

The living organism is continuously coping with internal as well as external changes in environment. The way in which humans cope is dependent on the mechanisms they have developed during their evolution. It is necessary to maintain the various body systems within certain limits. For this purpose, the body systems have elaborate self-adjusting mechanisms that maintain limits of tolerance to variation. The name given to the self-adjusting action is *homeostasis*, which means the maintenance of internal stability or equilibrium. Examples of homeostasis are the regulation of body temperature, of glucose (sugar) levels in the blood, and of the amount of water inside and outside the cells. Two major systems help human beings maintain homeostasis: the *nervous system* and the *endocrine system*. These two systems are often referred to respectively as the *coordinating* and *regulating systems*. They greatly influence each other in turn and work closely together.

The endocrine system consists of endocrine glands that produce biochemical agents that are used by other cells within the body. The biochemical agents, called *hormones*, are information-transferring substances. A hormone is secreted into the bloodstream, usually, and is carried by the blood to all the organs and tissues of the body. Hormones affect selected tissues that are designed to receive the information. They may stimulate new tissue growth, assist in storage of nutrients, depress the activity of the tissue, or act in many other ways necessary to maintain a homeostatic balance. Hormones are often called *primary chemical messengers*. Within the target cell, there are other, secondary, chemical messengers that pick up the message from the hormone. Cyclic adenosine monophosphate (cAMP) is one of these secondary messengers. Hormones and secondary chemical messengers may be highly selective with regard to the cells or organs they influence, or they may influence the whole organism. The endocrine system more or less sets the limits for proper functioning of the nervous system. Because hormones are carried in the blood, the action of the endocrine system is much slower than that of the nervous system. The interpretation of the chemical messages in the various parts of the body is quite complex and is only now being deciphered.

The nervous system functions by means of biochemical substances and transfer of an electrical impulse, and it produces its effects more rapidly than the endocrine system. The nervous system receives and interprets stimuli, and it transmits impulses to organs that either become more active or more depressed in their activity in response to stimulation. Because we are more interested in the effects of psychoactive drugs and because the nervous system is the major system affected by such drugs, we will concentrate on this system and homeostasis.

STRUCTURE OF THE NERVOUS SYSTEM

The nervous system is a highly complex system composed of the brain, the spinal cord, and all the connecting neurons (nerve cells) to the other organs and tissues of the body. It enables the person to receive information about his or her internal and external environment and to make the appropriate responses essential to survival.

Some scientists have said that we know more about the surface of the moon than we do about our nervous system. This is an overstatement, but it indicates the magnitude of the problem. How billions of neurons can function in an integrated fashion with various homeostatic controls is being explored, with much known but more to be discovered and explained.

The Neuron—Basic Structural Unit of the Nervous System*

The functional unit of the nervous system is the nerve cell, or *neuron*. Each neuron is in close contact with other neurons, forming a complex network. There are over 10 billion neurons in the human brain alone. Each neuron is composed of specific parts (see Figure 2-1) that are similar, although they may differ in some structural aspects. The neurons do not form a continuous network. They always remain separate, never actually touching, although they are very close. The contact point between one neuron and another is a tiny gap called a *synapse*. This gap may be only 0.00002 millimeter, but it is essential for proper functioning of the nervous system (see Figure 2-2).

The neuron has a cell body with a *nucleus* and *dendrites*—short, treelike branches that pick up information from the environment. Dendrites have receptors where they pick up information. A *receptor* is a special protein on the membrane of the receiving neuron's synapse into which the neurotransmitter chemical molecule fits. The interaction between the transmitter molecule and the protein receptor triggers a response in the receiving neuron. Dendrites have the ability to change one type of information, such as light, sound, or scent, into electrical activity that is

then carried along the neurons. *Transduction* is the term used for the conversion of one type of input into a different form of signal. The other branch of the neuron is the *axon*, a threadlike extension of the neuron that picks up information from the dendrites in the form of an electrical impulse, then transmits the impulse to the termination point. Some axons may be quite long—for example, from the spinal cord to the toes. Thus an electrical impulse is transmitted from dendrite to axon to the terminals. The electrical information is usually a series of pulses, each with an amplitude of about one-tenth volt and each lasting one- to two-thousandths of a second. The electrical impulses are normally little affected by drugs directly, because they are generated by the neuron cell membrane. Some drugs, nevertheless, do influence information processing by acting on and changing the cell membrane.

At the synapse, information is transmitted chemically, not electrically, to the next neuron. The following list shows the series of steps involved in information transmission in the nervous system (see Figure 2-3):

1. Dendrites receive the neurotransmitter, convert it to an electrical impulse, and relay it to the axon.

2. Axon picks up the impulse and conducts it to terminals.

3. Chemicals called *neurotransmitters* are released from terminals.

4. Neurotransmitters diffuse across the synapse to receptor sites, where chemicals in receptor sites generate an electrical impulse.

5. Dendrites transmit electrical impulse to the axon, in which it initiates an impulse.

6. The electrical impulse reaches the spinal cord, in most cases, and will be switched to the proper circuit to carry the impulse to the brain

*This section is taken largely from Stevens, 1979.

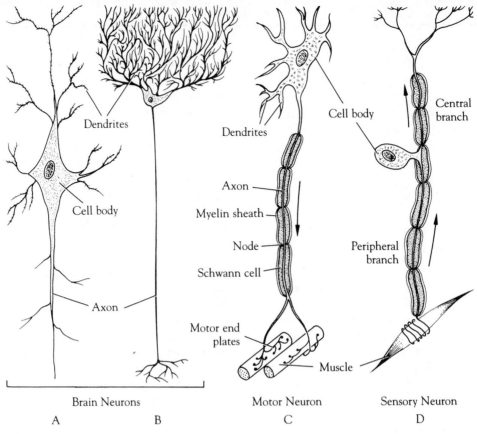

FIGURE 2-1

Neurons. (A) and (B) are brain neurons; (C) is a motor neuron; (D) is a sensory neuron.

for interpretation and further action. It is possible for some responses to be made without impulses moving through the brain. These are usually called *reflexes*. In the case of visual and auditory stimuli, however, the initial stimuli are detected by neurons in the head and do not pass through the spinal cord route. Because we are interested in the major concepts behind the functioning of the nervous system we will not spend any time on their many exceptions and variations.

There are two types of synapse: one is an *excitatory synapse*, which excites an impulse when stimulated; the other is the *inhibitory synapse*, which seems to inhibit the dendrite so it is less likely to initiate an impulse in the axon. A neuron may have over 10,000 synapses connecting it to other neurons and their potential information (Figure 2-2).

Neurotransmitters*

The impulse from one neuron is transferred to the next by means of biochemical messengers called *neurotransmitters*. Many drugs affect the

---

*This section is taken largely from Iversen, 1979.

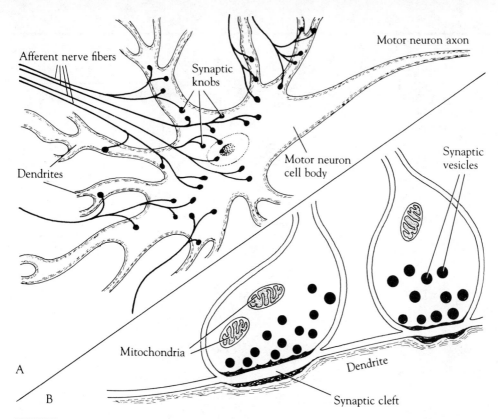

FIGURE 2-2

(A) Each neuron may have many synaptic knobs. These are designed to deliver short bursts of a chemical transmitter substance into the synaptic cleft, where it can act on the surface of the nerve cell membrane. Before release, molecules of the chemical transmitter are stored in numerous vesicles or sacs. (B) A close-up of the synaptic knobs showing the synaptic vesicles and mitochondria. The mitochondria are specialized structures that help to supply the cell with energy. The gap between the synaptic knob and the membrane is the synaptic cleft.

nervous system at this point of transmittal, so it is important to develop some understanding of what these biochemical substances are, how they are produced by the body, how they affect information transfer, and how the body disposes of them.

Many drugs affect the production, storage, or deactivation of neurotransmitters. By acting at any production, storage, or deactivation step, a drug may modify or block information transmission. Many drugs mimic, and some block, the receptor sites where the neurotransmitters

work. Thus some receptors might become very sensitive to the smallest impulse or, conversely, insensitive after they have been treated with drugs.

There is experimental evidence that there may be two dozen or more neurotransmitters, although the function of only about half a dozen is understood to any extent. These biochemical messengers are released from specific neurons. The chemicals considered to be neurotransmitters are: *dopamine, serotonin, acetylcholine, norepinephrine, epinephrine, gamma-aminobutyric acid, gly-*

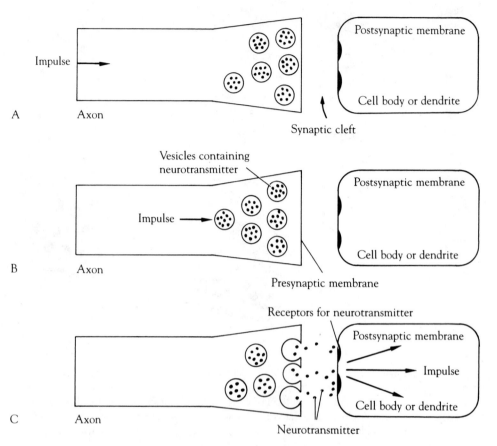

FIGURE 2-3
Movement of a nerve impulse across the synapse.

cine, *glutamate,* *histamine,* and *substance P* (see Appendix A-1). There are a number of other biochemical substances that are considered to be possible neurotransmitters, for which the proof of their action as biochemical messengers across the synapse is not as strong. Each neurotransmitter affects only its specific receptors, because other neurotransmitters differ in shape and are not released into the same synapse. Drugs affect receptors if they are sufficiently similar in shape

to the neurotransmitter. Table 2-1 summarizes what is known about the most common actions of the neurotransmitters.

Acetylcholine (Ach), first identified as a neurotransmitter in the peripheral nervous system, is present in large amounts in the brain. It is synthesized in the neuron from a molecule of choline (provided by diet and also by manufacture in the body) plus acetyl CoA (from glucose metabolism), which when combined give ace-

TABLE 2-1   Probable neurotransmitters and their actions

Neurotransmitters	Actions
Acetylcholine (Ach)	Usually stimulates muscle but can inhibit
Norepinephrine (NE)	Usually stimulates neurons and organs but can inhibit
Epinephrine (E)	Hormone from the adrenal gland; can stimulate neurons and organs
Dopamine (DA)	Can stimulate or inhibit various neurons in the brain; found primarily in brain
Serotonin (5-HT)	Mostly an inhibitor; may stimulate some areas
Gamma-aminobutyric acid (GABA)	Considered primarily an inhibitor
Glycine	Considered primarily an inhibitor
Glutamate	May be neurotransmitter
Substance P	Transmission of pain stimuli
Histamine	May be neurotransmitter

tylcholine. The presence of the enzyme acetylcholinesterase, which breaks acetylcholine down at the synapse, has been demonstrated. This biochemical is one of the major neurotransmitters in the autonomic portion of the nervous system.

Neurons that respond to Ach are distributed throughout the brain. Depending on the region, Ach can have excitatory or inhibitory effects. However, in order for any neurotransmitter to work, it must interact with receptors on the neuron receiving the transmitter molecule at what is called a *postjunctional receptor site*. The *cholinoceptive sites* (for those that respond to acetylcholine) have been divided into two subtypes based on the response to two drugs derived from plants, muscarine and nicotine. Muscarine (the substance in mushrooms that causes mushroom poisoning) and related drugs mimic the effect of natural acetylcholine. The effect of nicotine,

whether experimentally administered or from smoking tobacco, is more complex: it first stimulates the neuron like acetylcholine and then produces a blocking action. Cholinoceptive sites in the nervous system are either *nicotinic* or *muscarinic*.

Neurotransmitters must be removed after they have done their job. This removal, deactivation, or reabsorption of neurotransmitters is usually accomplished by enzymes. If a deactivating enzyme is blocked, the effect may be a prolongation or an intensification of the action of the neurotransmitter. For example, acetylcholine is released causing neurons to become stimulated, which in turn causes strong contraction of muscles. The acetylcholine is metabolized by the deactivating enzyme, acetylcholinesterase, into the choline and acetate molecules, and the muscles relax. Some of the nerve gases, developed for chemical warfare purposes, block the acetylcholinesterase enzyme. The neurons thus continue to be stimulated and continue firing their electrical impulses, causing a paralysis of the muscles because the muscles are contracting strongly. Some of the phosphate pesticides act like these nerve gases and were developed as a by-product of nerve gas research. Thus they can be dangerous if they are misused.

The *catecholamines* comprise the biochemical compounds norepinephrine, dopamine, and epinephrine, which are grouped according to their chemical structure. Neurons that synthesize catecholamines convert phenylalanine or tyrosine, which are amino acids obtained from protein digestion, to a compound called *L-dopa*. Then the L-dopa is converted to dopamine, followed by conversion to norepinephrine, and finally to epinephrine. Hence, phenylalanine, tyrosine, and L-dopa are called *precursors* for the catecholamines.

Unlike acetylcholine, the catecholamines are mainly reabsorbed by the neuron that released them, to be used over again. This is called *re-uptake*. There is also an enzymatic breakdown system involving the two enzymes catechol-O-methyltransferase (COMT) and monoamine oxidase (MAO). The re-uptake process and the activity of these enzymes, especially monoamine oxidase, can be greatly affected by some of the drugs to be discussed. If these deactivating enzymes are blocked, it is easy to see how the concentration of norepinephrine and dopamine may build up, causing a significant stimulatory effect. Amphetamine, for example, will prevent the reabsorption of norepinephrine, causing additional stimulation of neuron receptors until it is used up. Depletion of norepinephrine may be one of the reasons for the depression or "crash" that occurs after high doses of amphetamines are used.

Although norepinephrine and epinephrine are structurally very similar, their receptors can distinguish between them and do not respond with the same intensity to either or to sympathomimetic drugs (drugs that act similarly to norepinephrine and epinephrine). Just as the receptors to acetylcholine can be separated into muscarinic and nicotinic types, the catecholamine receptors are separated into the categories of alpha, beta-1, and beta-2. Receiving cells may have alpha or beta receptors, or both. When both types are activated, the response to one usually is stronger and predominates over the response to the other. Epinephrine and norepinephrine differ mainly in the ratio of their effectiveness in stimulating alpha and beta receptors. Norepinephrine acts predominantly on alpha receptors and has little action on beta receptors. The antagonistic (blocking) action of many drugs is selective for alpha, whereas others block only beta receptors.

Analogous to the effects of acetylcholine, the effects of the catecholamines on their targets may be excitatory or inhibitory. The effect is not generally related to whether the receptors are alpha or beta—it depends on the function of the target cell.

Serotonin (5-hydroxytryptamine, or 5-HT) is found in the upper brainstem, which is the enlarged extension of the spinal cord (Figure 2-4). Axons from tryptaminergic (serotonergic) neurons are distributed throughout the entire central nervous system. Serotonin has an inhibitory action on its target neurons, insofar as these are known. One important role of the tryptaminergic neurons may be to prevent overreaction to various stimuli, involving such behaviors as aggressiveness, motor activity, mood, and sexual behavior. Tryptaminergic neurons are also involved in the regulation of the release of hypothalamic hormones, which in turn regulate the anterior pituitary's release of its hormones, including prolactin, and the gonadotropins LH and FSH. Drugs interacting with these neurons affect some aspect of sexuality (Chapter 15).

There are several drugs chemically related to

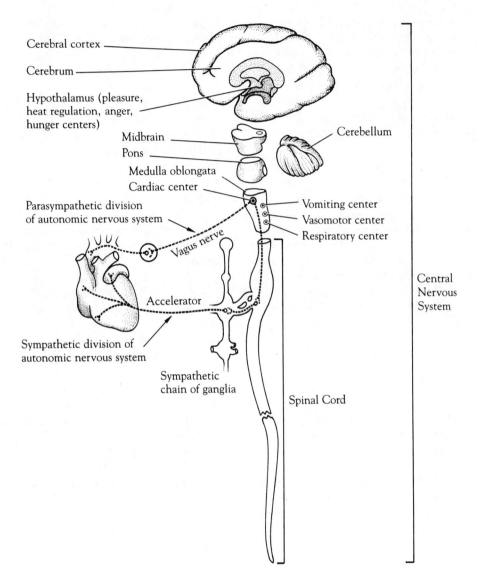

Cerebral cortex

Cerebrum

Hypothalamus (pleasure, heat regulation, anger, hunger centers)

Midbrain

Pons

Medulla oblongata

Cardiac center

Parasympathetic division of autonomic nervous system

Vagus nerve

Cerebellum

Vomiting center

Vasomotor center

Respiratory center

Central Nervous System

Accelerator

Sympathetic division of autonomic nervous system

Sympathetic chain of ganglia

Spinal Cord

FIGURE 2-4
Functional components of the central and autonomic nervous systems.

serotonin, such as psilocybin, N,N-dimethyl-tryptamine, and the synthetic LSD, which have potent effects on the brain and behavior; however, their use has not been as helpful as originally hoped in figuring out the role of serotonin. Abnormal functioning of tryptaminergic neurons and of serotonin synthesis and degradation has been proposed as a cause or factor in mental illness.

Serotonin is synthesized in tryptaminergic neurons and elsewhere in the body from the dietary source of tryptophan. Tryptophan is one of the essential amino acids, meaning that humans do not have the ability to synthesize it and must obtain it in the diet. Tryptophan seems to have little function other than as a precursor for the neurotransmitter serotonin in the brain. Normally, about 2% of the tryptophan in the diet is converted to serotonin. (Dietary tryptophan is also used to form serotonin in intestinal tissue, as an amino acid in proteins, as a precursor of melatonin in the pineal gland, and as a source, by conversion, of a small amount of vitamin B_4, niacin.) In brain tissue, serotonin synthesis depends on the concentration of tryptophan available; it is possible to deplete the brain of serotonin by about 50% in as little as 6 hours by providing a diet deficient in tryptophan during one 24-hour period (Fratta, Biggio, & Gessa, 1977). A drug, parachlorophenylalanine (PCPA), has also been used to block serotonin synthesis and produce deficiency. Serotonin is degraded by the enzyme, monoamine oxidase.

Drug Effects at the Neuron Level

To review nerve activity briefly: A stimulus is received by parts of the neuron where it is transformed into an electrical nerve impulse. The nerve impulse is transmitted to the axon, which in turn transmits the impulses to terminals where neurotransmitters are released. These biochemical messengers migrate across the synapse to receptor sites on the next neuron. In the meantime, the first neuron loses its electrical charge, and the membrane is said to be depolarized; in other words, for a short period of time, it has no electrical potential. The same process as described for neuron one continues in neuron two, and so on.

Much of our knowledge about the neurotransmitters has come from the study of drug effects. Agitated persons have inappropriate nervous activity and respond to tranquilizers by becoming calm. One of these tranquilizers, chlorpromazine, blocks the dopamine receptors. As a result, the dopamine is used up by the two degrading enzymes, MAO and COMT. Lithium salts inhibit the release of dopamine and norepinephrine, thus causing a calming effect. More will be said later about the use of these drugs in treating psychic disturbances. Nicotine mimics Ach and thus causes a stimulatory effect at first (as anyone addicted to tobacco will verify) and later causes a depressant effect. It is not understood what causes the depressant effect and whether the effect encourages further use of the drug. Nicotine is quite toxic in small doses, although an experienced user can build a tolerance to a dose that would be lethal to a beginning user.

Amphetamines stimulate the release of norepinephrine, causing neurons to fire with the slightest stimulus. This situation may induce an extreme sensitivity to stimulation, and thus certain sensations such as those experienced during sexual intercourse may become overwhelming. One antidepressant drug, tranylcypromine, inhibits the monoamine oxidase enzyme that normally destroys excess norepinephrine, causing a buildup of this neurotransmitter. Another antidepressant agent, imipramine, blocks the loss of NE from its receptors, causing rapid firing of nerve impulses. The drug parachlorophenylalanine blocks the formation of serotonin, thus preventing the cell membranes from becoming relaxed or inhibited and allowing the cells to be easily stimulated.

The preceding discussion linking drugs to neuron activity may make drug effects seem quite simple and straightforward. Actually some of the drug effects may vary in different parts of the nervous system. LSD, for example, blocks the action of serotonin in the peripheral nervous system, but in the brain its action is just the opposite. In other examples, the effects may differ if the internal environment is altered. The effect of many drugs at the molecular level is still in the investigative stage.

MAJOR DIVISIONS OF THE NERVOUS SYSTEM*

We can divide the nervous system into three functional components: the *central* (CNS), the *autonomic* (ANS) and the *peripheral* (PNS). The CNS and ANS exercise most of the body's integrative or homeostatic control; therefore, our brief description of the nervous system will cover these two parts. The PNS consists of the nerves outside the skull and spinal cord that connect the brain and spinal cord to the extremities of the body. As such, the PNS plays an indirect role in integrative processes and in psychoactive drug effects. Some parts of the ANS may be part of the CNS, and some of the outputs of the CNS travel via the ANS to muscles and glands, so these two functional components are not truly

---

* This section is taken largely from Nauta and Feirtag, 1979.

separate. Nevertheless, for ease in explaining the functions of these two major integrative systems, and because each has distinctive characteristics, each will be taken up in turn.

The Central Nervous System

The brain and spinal cord make up the CNS (see Figure 2-4). The human brain is an integrating and storage device unequaled by the most complex computers. Not only can it handle a great deal of simultaneous input from the senses, but it can evaluate and modify the output rapidly. Although the brain weighs only three pounds, with its 10 billion neurons it has a fantastic potential for performing a multitude of functions. The parts of the brain discussed here are those possibly involved in drug actions and effects. These are the (1) reticular activating system, (2) hypothalamus, (3) medial forebrain bundle, (4) periventricular system, (5) basal ganglia, and (6) cerebral cortex.

The Reticular Activating System

The reticular activating system (RAS) evolved long ago and is sometimes called the reptilian part of the CNS (Figure 2-5). The RAS is an area that receives input from all the sensory systems as well as from the cerebral cortex. The RAS is at the junction of the spinal cord and the brain, and it has a vast network of multiple synaptic neurons fanning out throughout the brain. Because of this complexity the RAS is quite susceptible to drugs. LSD has much of its effect on the RAS, as does amphetamine.

One of the major functions of the RAS is to control the arousal level of the brain. Arousal is especially linked to activity in the cerebral cortex. If the cortex is not aroused, it cannot handle input from the sensory system. The RAS

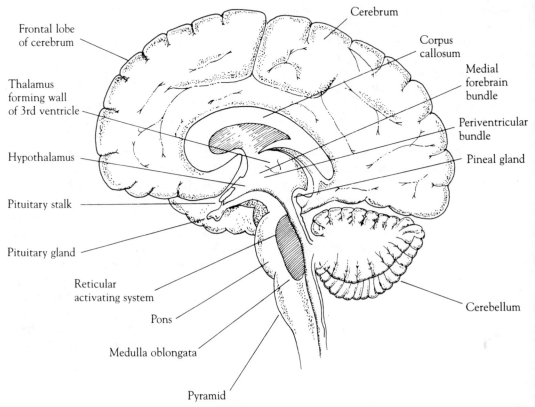

FIGURE 2-5
Sagittal section of the brain showing the major parts.

is stimulated by sensory input and will initiate its own impulses to the cerebral cortex, which becomes aroused if the impulses are of sufficient intensity or if they cause alarm. After the cortex is activated the organism is aroused, and the nervous system is active and alert to further stimuli from the environment, whether it is a baby's cry, a stomachache, or a mysterious sound on the stairs. The RAS also functions to filter out unimportant stimuli, allowing the person to concentrate intently, even to the point of being unaware of severe injury until the immediate, pressing situation is over.

The RAS probably uses norepinephrine as a neurotransmitter. High levels of epinephrine or norepinephrine activate both the RAS and the cerebral cortex. Compounds like amphetamines increase the sensitivity level of the RAS until it may be flooded with sensations.

The Hypothalamus

The hypothalamus (see Figures 2-4 and 2-5) is located near the base of the brain. It is an integrator of information from many sources as well as the control center for the autonomic nervous system. It is also the primary point of contact between the nervous and the endocrine systems. Because the hypothalamus is the control center for the ANS, it is also relevant to the maintenance of homeostasis in the organism.

The hypothalamus contains centers of neurons, called *nuclei*, which are clusters of the cell bodies of neurons located in this region. Some of these densely packed nuclei monitor blood levels of various biochemical substances essential to homeostasis. If the level of a particular substance in the blood goes outside the normal range, the hypothalamic neurons send impulses to appropriate control centers to restore normal levels. The continuous monitoring of such substances as glucose (blood sugar) and of sodium ion is of vital importance in maintaining a homeostatic environment in the organism. It is now known that many of the hormones of the body are regulated in part by the hypothalamus. If a hormone level drops below a certain point, a signal is sent from the hypothalamus to the appropriate gland, which will release the needed hormone.

The hypothalamus has a rich blood supply, and, shortly after they are taken, most drugs are found in high concentration in this region of the brain. The first symptoms induced by many drugs are due to effects on the autonomic nervous system, with changes in consciousness and mood developing more slowly as drug levels increase in the areas of the brain controlling these experiences. The rate at which drugs reach various areas of the central nervous system is affected by the filtering system between the blood and the neurons. It has been found that oxygen, glucose, amino acids, and other nutrients pass readily from the blood to the neurons, but that proteins, ionized molecules, and nonfat soluble substances are excluded or pass slowly. This selective filtering system is called the *blood-brain barrier*. The anatomic basis for the blood-brain barrier is believed to be the structure of the walls of the blood vessels supplying the brain. In addition, neurons in the central nervous system are densely surrounded by specialized cells called *glial cells* (*glial* comes from the Greek word for *glue*). Extensions from the glial cells cover most of the surface of blood capillaries in the brain. These extensions may be part of the selective filtration system.

The Medial Forebrain Bundle

The medial forebrain bundle (MFB) is a collection of axons of neurons along both sides of the hypothalamus. It is the location of the pleasure and reward center of the brain, and it probably uses norepinephrine as a neurotransmitter. When this center was located in laboratory rats, it was found that the animals would respond when the neurons in this area were activated through implanted electrodes. The rats were willing to cross an electrified wire grid in order to obtain more stimulation to this center, even when the shock was so severe that they would not cross the grid to obtain food when they were starved. Given the opportunity for self-stimulation by pressing a lever, they would stimulate this brain center until they collapsed in exhaustion.

Comparable stimulation of the MFB in human patients being operated on for brain tumors or other brain disorders shows that humans also experience pleasure as a response. Stimulation of the MFB seems to overcome feelings of depression as well. This area is very likely one of the regions associated with intense highs or euphoria reported after taking intravenous amphetamines or doses of cocaine. This region may also be where the sensations of orgasm are interpreted. The evidence that humans have a pleasure center is fascinating and may open up new possibilities for the treatment of depression and addiction. It is possible that the endorphins and the enkephalins (brain opiates; Chapter 3) may affect the functioning of this region.

The Periventricular System

The periventricular system is a collection of nerve fibers in the hypothalamus and thalamus (see Figure 2-5). This system of nerve fibers seems to be the substrate for punishment or avoidance behavior. In humans, stimulation of this region is followed by strong feelings of discomfort; in animals, stimulation seems to cause a slowing down or stopping of behavior. It is possible that the MFB and the periventricular system are linked, so that stimulation of one causes inhibition of the other. The periventricular system uses acetylcholine as its neurotransmitter.

The Basal Ganglia

The basal ganglia are the primary centers for involuntary motor control involving, for example, posture and muscle tone. The neurotransmitter in the basal ganglia is dopamine. Damage to neurons in this area may cause muscular dystrophy (weakening or degeneration of certain muscle groups). In Parkinson's disease, there is progressive degeneration of dopaminergic neurons that feed into the basal ganglia as an inhibitory control system, without deterioration of the cholinergic neurons, which are excitatory. This process results in an imbalance between dopamine and acetylcholine, which causes the person to be incapacitated by postural rigidity, tremors, and a decrease in facial expressiveness. Parkinson's disease may be treated with the drug L-dopa, which is the precursor of dopamine. Dopamine itself is not used, partly because it will not cross the blood-brain barrier and reach the area where it is needed.

Heavy use of the phenothiazine tranquilizers (major tranquilizers like Thorazine®, Stelazine®, and so on) in the treatment of psychotic patients causes Parkinson-like symptoms (see Chapter 10). If such drugs are given daily over several years, these symptoms may occur, and the damage is irreparable.

The Cerebral Cortex

The cerebral cortex, the brain's most complex structure, gives human beings their special place among the animals. The cortex is a layer of gray matter made up of nerve cells and supporting cells that almost completely surrounds the rest of the brain and lies immediately under the skull (see Figure 2-4). It is responsible for the interpretation of incoming information and for the initiation of voluntary motor behavior. The center for speech, and areas for perception of sensation from all parts of the body, are located in the cortex.

The cerebral cortex can be divided into *receiving areas*, *output areas*, and *association areas*. The receiving areas receive input from the various senses, and they are clearly affected by a number of psychoactive drugs. The sensory areas and their sense organs are connected in specific ways so that receptors responding to a particular stimulus always terminate in the same general area of the cortex. Any drugs that affect the electrical activity in the receptors, the connecting neurons, or the synapses in the pathway from receptor to cortex will thus affect that specific stimulus and perhaps the circuit the stimulus moves into.

The part of the cortex that has changed most in the evolutionary process is called the *association cortex*. In large part, the ratio of association cortex to cerebral cortex is a good index of the extent to which an animal is not under the direct influence of the environment; that is, the larger the association cortex, the more independent the animal is. The association areas do not directly receive inputs from the environment, nor do they directly initiate outputs to the muscles or the glands. The association areas may function to store memories or control complex behaviors. Some of the psychoactive drugs disrupt the normal functioning of these areas.

The Autonomic Nervous System

The ANS is one of the best understood integrative or regulatory systems. It is usually considered primarily a motor or output system, and most of its synapses are outside the CNS. A number of drugs cannot enter the CNS because of the presence of the blood-brain barrier, and thus they affect the ANS only. The ANS is divided into two functional components, the *sympathetic* (also called the *thoracolumbar*) and the *parasympathetic* (also called the *craniosacral*) nervous systems. Both systems send neurons to most visceral organs and to smooth muscles, glands, and blood vessels (see Figure 2-6).

Each system generally has the opposite effect on a particular organ or function. The workings of the heart give a good example of sympathetic and parasympathetic control (see Figure 2-4). The parasympathetic vagus nerve slows the heart rate, whereas the sympathetic innervation accelerates it. These actions constitute a constant biological check-and-balance, or regulatory, system. Because the two parts of the ANS work in opposite ways much of the time, they are viewed as physiological antagonists. These two systems control most of the internal organs, the circulatory system, and the glandular system. The sympathetic system is normally active at all times, the degree of activity varying from moment to moment and from organ to organ. The parasympathetic nervous system is organized mainly for discrete, localized discharge. It is concerned with conservation and restoration of energy rather than the expenditure of energy. For example, it slows the heart rate, lowers blood pressure, aids in absorption of nutrients, and is involved in emptying of the urinary bladder and in penile erection. Table 2-2 lists the structures and/or functions of the sympathetic and parasympathetic nervous systems and their effects on each other. Figure 2-6 shows where these structures are found.

The two branches of the autonomic nervous system generally use two different neurotransmitters. The parasympathetic branch releases acetylcholine at its synapses, whereas the sympathetic neurons release norepinephrine. An increase in epinephrine in the blood, or the

Table 2-2 Sympathetic and parasympathetic control

Structure or function	Sympathetic	Parasympathetic
Heart rate	speeds up	slows
Breathing rate	speeds up	slows
Stomach wall	slows motility	increases
Skin blood vessels (vasomotor function)	constricts	dilates
Iris of eye	constricts (pupil enlarges)	dilates
Vomiting center	stimulates	

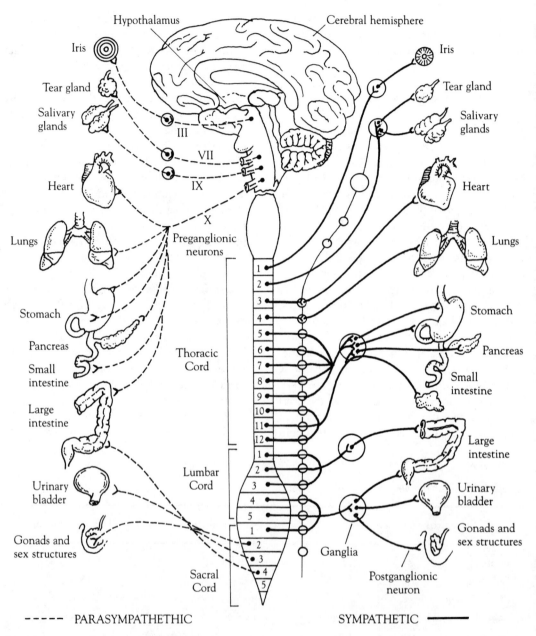

----- PARASYMPATHETHIC   SYMPATHETIC ———

FIGURE 2-6
Pathways of the (a) parasympathetic and (b) sympathetic nervous systems, and the organs affected.

administration of drugs that mimic norepineph-rine, causes the body to respond as if the sympathetic nervous system had been activated. Thus, taking amphetamines raises blood pressure, speeds up the heart rate, slows down motility of the stomach walls, and may cause the pupil of the eye to enlarge. Drugs like LSD are sympathetic stimulants. Other so-called "uppers" may have similar effects, although this depends on how the particular drug acts at various steps of its metabolism.

The ANS is essential to normal sexual function. In males, erection is primarily controlled by the parasympathetic innervation; ejaculation is a rather complex, sympathetically controlled function. The corresponding part of the female sexual response, vaginal lubrication, is probably also controlled by the parasympathetic system. Orgasm in males and females is believed to be predominantly controlled by the sympathetic system.

HOW AND WHERE DO DRUGS WORK?

HOW DO DRUGS WORK?

By this point you should have some understanding of how the integrative systems of the body work. You have also been given a brief explanation of how drugs influence some of the body's systems. This chapter discusses in more detail the ways drugs affect the body and how they may be taken, and it also gives a general background on drug types.

A drug must form a contact with a cell or a component of a cell in order to interact with it. Several common points of many drugs' interaction with a cell are at the membrane, at a receptor area on the membrane itself, or on transport mechanisms that are closely related to the cell membrane. Other drugs affect the interior components of the cell, inside the membrane. In the latter case, the drug most likely affects the action of enzymes in the cell's internal machinery. A drug can exert varied effects, depending on the function of the affected enzyme in the metabolic pathways (Fingl & Woodbury, 1975).

Drugs can mimic, facilitate, or antagonize a natural process that is already going on within the cell. By influencing a natural process, a drug can increase or decrease normal activity or sensitivity of a cell. This effect was explained in Chapter 2 in the section on the effects of drugs on neuron function, in which it was noted that adding amphetamines made some nerve cells extremely sensitive to stimulation because the normal neurotransmitters are released and not reabsorbed, thus causing an unusually high level of neurotransmitter concentration at the receptor sites. A drug's effect also usually depends on the drug concentration at the site of action. However, one does not necessarily have to take large amounts of a drug before the drug concentration will reach an effective level; some drugs or chemicals, such as epinephrine, are effective in small quantities.

When drugs enter the blood, they usually become attached to proteins in the blood. The *drug-protein binding* is called a *complex*. It is usually inactive and cannot leave the blood while the drugs and proteins are bound together. Usually inactivating enzymes will not attack the drug in this state. Many naturally occurring compounds, such as hormones, circulate in a protein-bound form, both for transport and for protection from inactivating enzymes. A drug like acetylsalicylate (aspirin) has a low protein-binding affinity, whereas the related salicylates have a higher protein-binding affinity. This means that acetylsalicylate has a more rapid action but one of shorter duration than salicylates. A simple chemical change greatly modifies protein binding.

The brain is a unique compartment in the body because many molecules are prevented from entering the brain's neurons and glial cells. The barrier to the passage of substances, called the *blood-brain barrier*, exists in part because brain capillaries have almost no free pores. Even small, water-soluble molecules cannot always leave the brain capillaries readily, but fat-soluble molecules (called *lipids*) can. Most of the capillaries are covered with glial cells (about 85% of the surface) with little free space. Active transport is needed to move chemicals into and out of the brain. The glial cells may play an active role in the entry of some chemicals. Sometimes a concussion (blow to the head) will cause a disruption of this barrier, and substances that are normally blocked will pass through. Chemicals like the barbiturates and LSD (only about 1%–2% of the LSD taken) will enter the brain.

Many drugs affect neurons at the cell membrane. Such drugs as anesthetics, including barbiturates and alcohol, influence the cell membrane. Stimulants usually do not have this effect.

A number of other drugs influence neurons by acting at the synapses, either mimicking or blocking one of the neurotransmitters, as described in Chapter 2.

The rate of removal, or deactivation, of a drug influences its effect. Some volatile gases such as ether may be eliminated unchanged, although they are the exceptions. Many drugs are made water-soluble and excreted in the urine. The liver has a large number of enzymes that break down, or metabolize, drugs. This activity is part of the important detoxification function of the liver. It has been found that such drugs or chemicals as meprobamate, phenobarbital, DDT, alcohol, and even tetrahydrocannabinol (THC) cause an increase in the activity of some enzymes in the liver. This fact may very likely be the rule rather than the exception, meaning that regular use of a drug over a period of time may speed up its metabolism and may alter the metabolism of other substances, such as hormones, normally metabolized by the liver enzymes (Chapter 4).

What other factors influence drug effects on the body? Some drugs, like alcohol and phenobarbital, increase each other's effects when taken together. This is called *potentiation*, or *synergism*, because the effect of the combination is greater than the sum of both drugs taken separately. This reaction can be caused, for example, either by interference with the typical metabolism of the drugs or by a greater inhibition of receptor sites. Liver or kidney damage can greatly influence a drug's effect. Old age can also influence a drug's effect because the overall metabolic rate decreases and because older persons have a higher fat-to-lean ratio than younger persons. In a fat person, a drug like a barbiturate tends to remain in the body longer than in a thin person, causing an effect of greater duration. A fat person of any age will react differently to a given dose of drug than a thin person.

There are also differences between the sexes: a woman may react differently to lipid-soluble drugs than a man will, because women have a higher percentage of body fat than men.

DRUG EFFECTS: PSYCHOLOGICAL CONSIDERATIONS

The general effect of most drugs is greatly influenced by a variety of psychological and environmental factors. Unique qualities of an individual's personality, his or her past history of drug experience, attitudes toward the drug, expectations of its effects, and motivation for taking it are extremely influential. These factors, which may completely obscure the typical pharmacological response to a drug, are often referred to collectively as the person's mental *set*. The *setting*, or total environment, in which a drug is taken may also modify its effect.

A few drinks of an alcoholic beverage may make a person feel drowsy and fatigued in some situations, whereas under different circumstances the same amount of alcohol may psychologically stimulate and arouse that person. The set and setting may be of greater significance with respect to the effects of psychedelic-hallucinogenic substances than to other drugs, and it has been suggested that psychological factors may often be the primary determinant of the quality or character of the psychedelic drug experience.

The Placebo

The word *placebo* derives from Latin and means "I shall please." The so-called *placebo effect* is a striking example of the importance of set and setting in determining the response to drugs. A placebo drug is a pharmacologically inactive substance that elicits a significant reaction because of what the person expects or desires to happen. In certain persons in particular settings, a placebo substance may have surprisingly powerful consequences. The placebo effect is specific to the person and the setting and not to any chemical properties of the substance involved. Therefore, in spite of the apparent drug effect, the placebo is not considered a pharmacological agent because it does not alter any bodily functions by its chemical nature.

The early Greek physician and anatomist Galen was describing the placebo principle in the second century A.D. when he stated "He cures most in whom most are confident." In therapeutic situations placebos have been reported to relieve to a significant extent such symptoms as headache and a variety of gastrointestinal complaints. The bulk of medical history may actually be a history of confidence in the cure—a history of placebo medicine—because many "effective cures" of the past have been shown to be without relevant pharmacological action. Medical researchers are further investigating the basis of psychological cures.

Many patients have no identifiable disease symptoms, yet they feel sick or have aches and pains. In many cases, these patients will respond to a few placebo pills and a generous supply of attention. Studies have shown that as many as 35%–45% of all prescriptions are for substances that are incapable of having an effect on the condition for which they are prescribed—for example, penicillin or sulfonamides for the common cold and vitamin B12 shots for a patient who does not have pernicious anemia (Bok, 1977). Some physicians have been known to give a potentially effective drug in ineffective doses to a patient in whom no cause for complaint was located. This is just another example of the use of a placebo. Perhaps it is easier for the physician to use a proven drug rather than an inactive substance as a placebo.

It would be foolish to dismiss the importance of the placebo effect simply because we are oriented toward chemicals that can be shown to have a specific effect at the molecular level. In many instances, the body simply needs time and opportunity to heal itself. In doing so, the body needs as little interference from stressful reactions as possible. If a person believes he or she has been given medicine to speed the healing process, and this "medicine" reduces his or her stress from the injury or illness, recovery will be faster. Clinicians are finding a significant difference in recovery time, and even in whether the person recovers or dies, based on their attitudes at the beginning of treatment. Along with effective drug treatment, a positive attitude is necessary to fight a disease—cancer, for example. Clinicians are just beginning to realize the importance of the mind's role in controlling disease.

Placebos are often effective against pain. This effect was difficult to understand until the *endorphins* and *enkephalins* were discovered. Both are peptides produced by the body, with action similar to morphine, and are believed to provide analgesia from different types of pain. Enkephalins were first isolated from the brain (*enkephalin* from the Greek word meaning *in the head*) and endorphins from the pituitary gland (*endorphin* from *endogenous morphinelike compound*). Some of these substances may act as inhibitory neurotransmitters (Chapter 2).

Research with endorphins shows that injection of these naturally occurring brain opiates will alleviate pain (Hughes, 1975). Furthermore, when a drug called *naloxone* (Chapter 12) is given, the placebo becomes ineffective against pain. What has happened is that naloxone binds to opiate receptors, blocking the action of opiates, including endorphins, and thus endorphins cannot relieve the symptoms. The placebo caused the release of a pharmacologically effective natural drug (endorphin) against pain. Other placebo effects may be shown to be due to similar release of biochemical substances already present in the body.

What makes a placebo effective? First, the physician's positive attitude. Second, two capsules are better than one. Third, injections are more effective than taking the drug orally. Fourth, color—a large brown, purple, or red pill is more effective than a white one. Fifth, taste—a bad-tasting substance is more effective than a neutral-tasting one (Evans, 1977). Effectiveness may also be related to the physician-patient relationship; for example, it has been shown that treatment involving appropriate physical contact is more beneficial than treatment without physical contact or by phone.

To control experiments on the influence of psychological factors in drug research, testing is usually done under at least two conditions. First, the drug under consideration is tested, and then a separate study is made of a placebo given under identical conditions. Often a drug is tested under what we call *double-blind, placebo-controlled* circumstances in a further attempt to isolate the placebo effect. This means that both the real drug and the placebo are coded and made to look identical. The physician administering both the drug and the placebo does not know the code, and the people who have agreed to participate in the study do not know whether they are getting the pharmacological agent or the placebo. Results are not decoded until after the study is over. By comparing double-blind, placebo-controlled conditions the effects of set and setting can be controlled, and the actual drug

effect (if any) can be identified. This type of controlled study is very important in testing for the drug potency and also for the possible side effects.

OTHER FACTORS THAT INFLUENCE DRUG EFFECTS

In determining how drugs affect the body, pharmacologists generally must answer five questions:

1. How does the drug enter the body? (administration)
2. How does the drug move from the site of administration into the body's systems? (absorption)
3. How is the drug distributed to various areas in the body? (distribution)
4. How and where does the drug produce what effects? (action)
5. How is the drug inactivated, metabolized, and/or eliminated from the body? (physiological fate)

DOSAGE FORMS OF DRUGS

Drugs may be taken in many forms. This section lists ways that drugs may be compounded and presents the terminology that pharmacists and physicians use to describe the drug's form.

Solutions are liquids containing a drug dissolved to a known concentration. The liquid may be a mixture of two or more liquids used to increase the drug's solubility and improve the taste. The various types of solution are:

1. Waters: volatile oils dissolved in water
2. Syrups: sugar and water, usually with additional flavoring

3. Elixirs: alcohol, sugar, and water, with additional flavoring
4. Spirits: volatile substances dissolved in alcohol
5. Tinctures: solutions of drugs in alcohol, or an alcohol-and-water mixture.

Suspensions are mixtures of a drug and a liquid, but in this case the drug is not dissolved. A suspension is used when the drug is insoluble in any liquid suitable for the purpose. These are always shaken to mix them before using. The two types of suspension are called:
1. Emulsions: fat globules in water
2. Magmas: finely ground particles of solid in water (milk of magnesia is an example).

Topical drugs are drugs that are for external use only. These include:
1. Liniments: mixtures of drugs with oil, soap, water, or alcohol
2. Lotions: mild liquid preparations to be applied to the skin, without rubbing
3. Ointments and creams: fatty or oily preparations using such typical bases as lard, wax, paraffin, or lanolin.

Solid forms of drugs are common. Some of these include:
1. Powders: for external, and sometimes internal, use
2. Tablets: powders that have been mechanically compressed into a convenient form (They usually have a binding agent, such as corn starch, with the drug uniformly mixed in it.)
3. Pills: powders held together with honey or candy, to be swallowed; often "pill" is used interchangeably with "tablet"
4. Capsules: the drug is packaged in a gelatin capsule, which is tasteless and may be easier to swallow than a tablet. Gelatin capsules come in a range of sizes and types:
   a. Enteric coated capsules: These have coatings over the drug that protect it from being acted on by stomach acids; the drug is released once the capsule has reached the intestine.
   b. Sustained release capsules: These are coated capsules that are designed to dissolve at specific rates to meter out the drug, so a relatively constant level of drug can be maintained for a specific period of time. There are also sustained release combination capsules that release several drugs at different times.
   c. Suppositories: These are inserted into a body opening, such as the vagina or the anus, to produce a local effect.

METHODS OF TAKING DRUGS

Oral Ingestion

One of the most common ways of taking a drug is orally. (This is also called *enteral;* all the other means of drug adminstration are called *parenteral.*) It is difficult to control drug dosage for three reasons: First, if taken orally, the drug must enter the bloodstream after passing through the stomach without being destroyed or changed to an inactive form. Once the drug is in the bloodstream it must diffuse to the target area and remain there in sufficient concentration in order to perform its function.

Second, in order to have an effect or get across cell membranes a drug must be in solution—it must be lipid(fat)-soluble because cell membranes are mostly lipid—and it must remain in the cells long enough to work. If a drug is water-soluble and if it ionizes readily, it will be excreted rapidly by the kidneys, which causes problems in providing effective dosages. The brain has a high lipid content, so drugs with a high lipid solubility are more likely to affect the brain. These drugs tend to be retained by the body and to show cumulative effects—that is, effects that increase following repeated doses because the drugs are not eliminated rapidly. Barbiturates are highly fat soluble; thus a person can build up a sizeable concentration of them in the fatty tissues. Tetrahydrocannabinol has been found to be retained in the body for up to 8–10 days because of its lipid solubility. If a lipid-soluble drug is taken with a fatty meal, it is absorbed slowly and the drug concentration may be ineffective. This is why a person taking barbiturates or methaqualone (sopors) responds differently to the drugs, depending on when he or she takes them—with a meal or on an empty stomach.

Third, the liver should not break down the drugs too rapidly, before the drugs are able to perform their function. The liver is the major detoxification organ in the body, which means it removes chemicals and toxins from the blood and changes them into a form that is easy for the body to excrete. This function is essential to survival, but it creates a problem for the pharmacologist developing effective drugs. It is especially problematic in the case of oral adminstration, because the substances absorbed from the digestive tract go to the liver before being distributed to the general circulation.

Suppositories

Another way of taking drugs is by suppository. This form of drug, depending on its purpose, is placed either in the rectum or the vagina, from which the drug is gradually released. Suppositories usually have a specific purpose, such as to treat a vaginal infection, but can be used to adminster a drug to the whole body.

Inhalation

A third way of taking a drug is by inhalation. The lungs have large beds of capillaries, so chemicals capable of crossing membranes can enter the blood quite readily. Ether, chloroform, and nitrous-oxide anesthetics, as well as aerosols, gasoline, and solvents such as in airplane glue, cleaning fluids, nicotine from tobacco smoke, and even alcohol can be effectively taken by inhalation. One serious problem with inhalation therapy is the potential of irritation of the mucous membrane lining of the lungs, and another is that the drug may have to be taken frequently to maintain the desired concentration. (The frequency of administration depends on the rate at which the drug is cleared from the body.)

Injection

A fourth way of taking drugs is by injection. Drugs can be administered intravenously (IV), intramuscularly (IM), or subcutaneously (SC). A major advantage of administering drugs by IV is the speed of action; the dosage is delivered rapidly and directly, and often less drug is needed because it reaches the site of action quickly. This method can be very dangerous, however, if the dosage is calculated incorrectly and is too high. Additionally, impurities in the injected materials may irritate the vein. The injection itself injures the vein—a tiny point of scar tissue forms where veins are punctured. If repeated injections are necessary, the elasticity of the veins is gradually reduced, and they may even collapse.

Subcutaneous injections may kill the skin at the point of injection if the drug irritates it. Intramuscular injection can damage the muscle directly, if the drug preparation irritates the tissue, or indirectly, if the nerve controlling the muscle is damaged. If the nerve is destroyed, the muscle will atrophy.

Implantable Drug-Delivery Systems

Administration of drugs by mouth, suppository, inhalation, or injection does the job, but, because the concentration of the drug increases rapidly and then declines in the blood, the concentration of drug swings widely between too much and too little (not effective). Implantable drug-delivery devices are being tested to provide a more constant, steady release of a variety of drugs. Using these devices, the person is exposed to lower total doses of drug and does not have to worry about remembering to take the medication.

One type is the subcutaneous implant, whereby a pellet is placed under the skin and the drug gradually dissolves. This device has been tested in Swedish women: one subcutaneous pellet provided a constant, low level of contraceptive hormone for six months. The drug "container" can be made of substances that are biodegradable, such as cholesterol or polymers of naturally occurring amino acids, so that it also is absorbed by the body when the drug is gone. These are not available in the United States at present. However, an antimotion sickness medication that is taped to the skin so the drug can be absorbed through the skin is being used. In addition, a hormone-releasing intrauterine device has been marketed since 1976 (see Chapter 14).

Another type of implantable device, the Ommaya reservoir, is a small container that is inserted under the skin of the scalp to deliver drugs to the cerebrospinal fluid. This is useful in the treatment of certain types of brain cancer and infection. The drug reservoir can be refilled with a hypodermic syringe. A different type of pump has been implanted in the chest wall to deliver heparin, an antiblood-clotting drug, to the bloodstream of patients with severe clotting problems. Prior to the development of this pump, such persons had to be hospitalized, but with the pump they need to return to the hospital only at four- to eight-week intervals to replenish the pump's supply of heparin (Blackshear, 1979).

DOSE, TIME, AND DRUG EFFECTS

The Dose-Reponse (Dose-Effect) Relationship

Two factors that must be considered in evaluating drug activity are dose and time. One's responses to all drugs differ both in the intensity and the character of the reactions, according to the amount of drug administered. This relationship is called the *dose-response*, or *dose-effect*, relationship. Most drugs show no effect until a certain amount of the drug is administered. The least amount of the drug needed to show an effect is referred to as the *threshold* of the drug. In using a drug to treat a certain condition or cause a certain effect, a known amount of the drug is given. The amount of the drug needed to cause the desired effect or response is called the *effective dose* (ED) and is usually stated as the ED-50, ED-95, and so on. The number refers to the percentage of animals or people responding in the expected way to a particular drug. This subject is discussed further in Chapter 4.

Some drugs cause an effect that may be calculated in a *linear* (straight-line) fashion, which means the more drug taken, the greater the effect. Other drugs cause a *biphasic* (two-part) response and actually may produce behaviorally opposite effects. For example, low doses of alcohol may be behaviorally stimulating, whereas higher doses generally have a strong sedating effect. Scopolamine (a belladonna alkaloid) may produce sedation at low doses and excitation, delirium, and hallucination at high doses. Toxic doses of this drug also produce sedation, but to the point of coma and even death.

The Time-Response Factor

The *time-response factor* is the relation between the time that has elapsed since administration of a drug and the effect produced. This factor, or response, is often classified as *immediate, short-term,* or *acute*—often referring to the response to a single dose. The response can also be *chronic,* or *long-term*—usually referring to a repeated dose. The intensity and quality of the overall effect may change considerably within a short period of time. For example, the main intoxicating effects of a large dose of alcohol generally reach a peak in less than one hour and then gradually taper off. An initial stimulating effect may later change to one of sedation. With some drugs, an initial state of tension or anxiety may later change to one of relaxation and a sense of well-being as a function of drug metabolism over time.

Chronic Use of Drugs

The long-term or chronic use of some drugs is one of the more difficult areas of drug investigation. The taking of small doses may not produce any apparent immediate detrimental effect, but the chronic use of a drug—frequent use over a long time—may show its effects years later. For example, although there is little evidence to show any immediate damage or detrimental

effect from short-term use of small doses of tobacco, there is evidence that its chronic use has a detrimental effect on heart and lung function. Often the type of research such as that done with tobacco extends over years and requires highly sophisticated statistics to demonstrate the effects. Thus the results are often open to argument and dispute by manufacturers' lobbies with vested financial interests in the substance being researched.

MAIN EFFECTS AND SIDE EFFECTS OF DRUGS

Most drugs have a number of effects on behavioral and physiological functions and produce a wide range of effects that are dependent on the relative strength of the drug and on the way it is taken. Thus a particular effect that is common at one dosage level may be rare at another. In the clinical setting, the physician is usually interested in a single effect, or perhaps in a small number of the many possible effects, of a drug. The desired effects are generally called *main* effects, whereas those that are unwanted are called *side* effects. The distinction between main and side effects is a relative one and depends on the purpose of the drug usage—that is, what effect is expected. A response that is considered unnecessary or undesirable in one situation may, in fact, be the main effect in another. The combination oral contraceptive may be prescribed for one woman because she needs the effective contraceptive, but prescribed for another (who may not need protection against pregnancy) to stop the abnormal growth of the uterine lining that is causing her pain. In general, most drugs have undesirable and toxic side effects if the dosage is increased sufficiently. Drug interaction will be discussed in Chapter 5.

TOLERANCE TO DRUGS

Tolerance is said to develop when the response to the same dose of a drug decreases with repeated use. In other words, one must increase the dose in order to elicit the same response. The extent of tolerance and the rate at which it is acquired depend on the drug, the person using the drug, and the dosage and frequency of administration. Some of the effects of a certain drug may be reduced more rapidly than others, when the drugs are used repeatedly. Tolerance to effects that are rewarding or reinforcing is usually reflected by a tendency for users to increase the dosage. Abstinence from a drug will usually reduce one's tolerance to it. However, the body does not lose sensitivity to all aspects of the reaction to a particular drug with equal rapidity or to the same extent.

For example, with repeated use, a moderate degree of tolerance develops to most effects of alcohol and barbiturates. A heavy drinker may be able to consume two to three times the alcohol tolerated by an occasional drinker. Little tolerance develops, however, to the lethal toxicity of these drugs. A heavy user of sedatives is just as susceptible to death by overdose as is a nontolerant person. Opiate narcotics, such as morphine, have the potential for inducing profound tolerance. Heavy users have been known to take up to ten times the amount that would kill a nonuser. By contrast, no noticeable tolerance to cocaine develops; a person may continue taking a set dose for a long period of time and apparently have the same response.

The exact mechanisms by which the body adapts, or becomes tolerant, to different drug effects are not completely understood, but several processes have been suggested. Drugs like barbiturates stimulate the body's production of metabolic enzymes, primarily in the liver, that deactivate the drugs. This is called *drug disposition tolerance,* referring to the rate at which the body disposes of the drug.

In addition, there is evidence that a considerable degree of central nervous system tolerance to certain drugs may develop independent of changes in the rate of absorption, metabolism, or excretion. This is called *pharmacodynamic tolerance,* whereby the nervous tissue or other target tissue adapts to the drug, so that the effect of the same concentration of drug decreases. A person tolerant to alcohol, for example, can be relatively unaffected by a large dose resulting in a high level of alcohol in the blood. It is uncertain whether this situation represents some general molecular adaptation to the drug at the level of the individual nerve cell, or whether it is perhaps a specific response by the central nervous system to counteract the sedating effects and maintain normal function.

Learning often appears to affect a person's response to a drug, resulting in *behavioral tolerance.* Effects that initially are strange or frightening may later be accepted without reaction or concern, or they may even be desired. There is evidence that people can learn to control some drug effects or otherwise learn to function normally in the presence of certain responses that might originally have been distracting or disruptive.

The Rebound Effect

Once tolerance occurs, physical dependence may or may not develop, depending on the type of drug used. Drugs like amphetamine and LSD cause tolerance but not physical dependence. Many other drugs, like barbiturates, opiates, alcohol, and other depressants, cause tolerance and also physical dependence. The latter drugs also cause a condition called the *rebound effect* if the user is physically dependent when he or she starts withdrawing from one of them. (The rebound effect is sometimes called the *paradoxical effect*, because its symptoms at this stage are nearly opposite to the effects of the drug.) For example, a person taking barbiturates or opiates will be greatly depressed physically, but when withdrawing he or she will be extremely irritable, hyperexcited, and nervous, and generally will show symptoms of extreme stimulation of the nervous system—all of which constitute the rebound effect.

There are several hypotheses about the causes of the rebound effect, but there is no completely adequate proof for any of them. One hypothesis is called the *redundancy*, or *alternate pathways*, *model* (Martin, 1978). This theory proposes that each drug has alternate or multiple pathways through which it works, and thus its effects are redundant. The drug suppresses some of the alternate pathways that are more vulnerable than others, and the pathway(s) not suppressed takes over the function(s) of the suppressed one(s) and becomes more active. When the drug that has caused the physical dependence is stopped, the suppressed pathways are activated, and the body reacts in an exaggerated, or "rebound," manner.

The *disuse hypothesis* concerning the rebound effect has been accepted by some experts. This states that the rebound effect from depressant drugs is related to disuse of nerve pathways resulting from repeated use of these drugs. Through disuse, these pathways and receptor sites become more sensitive to the neurotransmitter normally involved. Then, when the drug is stopped, the oversensitive pathways are reactivated by the liberated transmitter, and the symptoms of withdrawal occur (Way, 1978).

It is possible that addicts may develop tolerance to and dependence on a drug such as morphine because of a buildup of enkephalins within the neurons of the brain. If this is so, then a person would have to take more and more morphine to maintain the high level of enkephalins. If the person stopped taking the morphine, the receptors in the brain's neurons would be deprived of morphine and enkephalins (morphine triggers the release of enkephalins). In this case the neurons and the nervous system would no longer be inhibited and would become hyperexcitable. This process may explain both tolerance and withdrawal.

Reverse Tolerance

In the case of *reverse tolerance*, a drug user will have the same response to a lower dose of a drug as he or she did to the initial, higher drug dose. This seems to be most likely in users of marijuana and of some of the hallucinogens. Reverse tolerance is believed to be primarily a learning process, not a physiological one. It is possible, nevertheless, for a drug like marijuana to be stored in fatty tissues and released later as the fat is broken down. The fact that some of the drug products may remain in the body for extended periods of time may explain the reverse-tolerance effect.

Cross-Tolerance

A phenomenon known as *cross-tolerance* is often seen with certain types of drug. In this case, if a person develops a tolerance to one drug, he or she will also show tolerance to other drugs. This effect is due to altered metabolism resulting from chronic drug use. For example, a heavy drinker will usually exhibit tolerance to barbiturates, tranquilizers, and anesthetics, because the alcohol has caused changes in his or her liver and central nervous system enzymes. Cross-tolerance has been shown to develop with some of the hallucinogens, such as LSD, mescaline, and psilocybin.

DEPENDENCE ON DRUGS

Physical Dependence

Physical dependence is a physiological state of adaptation to a drug. This condition usually follows the development of tolerance and results in a characteristic set of withdrawal symptoms, or abstinence syndrome, when administration of the drug is stopped. As with tolerance, the reason for physical dependence and withdrawal is not understood. Their causes are probably related to the cause for the development of tolerance. Physical dependence on particular drugs will be discussed in more detail later.

Cross-Dependence

Withdrawal symptoms can be prevented or promptly relieved by the administration of a sufficient quantity of the original drug or of one with similar pharmacological activity. The latter case, in which different drugs can be used interchangeably to prevent withdrawal symptoms, is called *cross-dependence*. For example, barbiturates and tranquilizers can be used in treating the abstinence syndrome of the chronic alcoholic. Or, methadone can be used to treat withdrawal from heroin.

The person withdrawing from drugs that cause physical dependence may show the rebound effect. As described earlier, this phenomenon is manifested by physical activity opposite to that

of the drug the user is dependent on. For instance, withdrawal from the sedatives generally results in symptoms of acute and toxic hyperactivity and arousal, whereas the pattern following intense stimulant use (for example, of methamphetamine, or "speed") usually involves sedation, depression, hunger, and sleep.

Physical dependence can develop with the use of such common drugs as alcohol, tranquilizers, and barbiturates, but the majority of people using these drugs do not develop this condition. In the few persons who become physically dependent on these particular drugs, serious social, personal, and physiological consequences of drug use usually precede physical dependence. By contrast, the potent opiate narcotics tend to induce pronounced tolerance and physical dependence early in the history of regular use. These features soon become an integral part of the particular drug problem experienced by the users of opiate narcotics. Nevertheless, with these and other drugs, psychological factors of dependence are often more significant than physiological ones in the long run.

Psychological Dependence (Habituation)

Certain drugs cause a condition that is called *psychological dependence*, or *habituation*. These are difficult terms to define. A number of agencies have tried to define psychological dependence. The World Health Organization's (WHO) definition is as follows: "In this situation there is a feeling of satisfaction and a psychic drive that require periodic or continuous administration of the drug to produce a desired effect or to avoid discomfort." A major problem with the WHO definition is the difficulty in defining operationally and objectively what the characteristics of dependence are in a particular situation. By contrast, some scientists have defined psychological dependence as the repeated self-administration of a drug. This definition is too broad—it only indicates that the drug is in some way reinforcing or rewarding to the user, and merely states that the person is taking the drug.

Extreme cases of psychological dependence are easier to identify than subtle ones; they may be characterized by an intense craving for a drug or a compulsion to continue its use, with obvious behavioral manifestations. In many instances, psychological aspects may be considerably more significant than physical dependence in maintaining chronic drug use. The major problem with opiate dependence is not the physical aspects—because withdrawal can be successfully achieved in a few weeks—but the strong possibility that the person will later return to chronic use because of psychological dependence.

In discussing dependency—whether on drugs or not—one needs to specify what it is that is being depended on and for what reasons, and one must identify the consequences of its presence or absence. The significance of dependency changes according to whether a drug is relied on for the maintenance of life—as the diabetic relies on insulin—or whether the drug is used for escape from an unpleasant and seemingly intolerable situation, which all people face at some time in their lives. In one sense, psychological dependence may be said to exist with respect to anything that is part of one's preferred way of life, whether this be living in a communal situation or in isolation. In our society, this kind of dependency occurs frequently with respect to such things as television, music, religion, sex, money, foods, drugs, hobbies, and sports. Some degree of psychological dependency is, in this sense, a general and normal psychological condition.

THE MEANING OF ADDICTION

The term *addiction* has a variety of meanings. Often it is used interchangeably with *dependence*, either physiological or psychological; at other times it appears to be synonymous with the term *drug abuse*. The classical model of the addiction-producing drug is based on the opiate narcotics and has traditionally required the development of tolerance and physical and psychological dependence. Nevertheless, this approach has not been satisfactory, because only a few commonly used drugs—such as alcohol, barbiturates, methaqualone, and a few others—seem to fit the model. It is clearly inadequate for many other drugs that can cause serious dependency problems. For example, amphetamines can produce considerable tolerance and strong psychological dependence with little or no physical dependence, and cocaine can produce psychological dependence without tolerance or physical dependence. Furthermore, in some medical applications, morphine has been reported to produce tolerance and physical dependence without a significant psychological component.

Recognizing the problems regarding addiction, the World Health Organization proposed the following:

> It has become impossible in practice, and is scientifically unsound, to maintain a single definition for all forms of drug addiction and/or habituation. A feature common to these conditions as well as to drug abuse in general is dependence, psychic or physical or both, of the individual on a chemical agent. Therefore, better understanding should be attained by substitution of the term drug dependence of this or that type, according to the agent or class of agents involved. . . . It must be emphasized that drug

dependence is a general term that has been selected for its applicability to all types of drug abuse and thus carries no connotation of the degree of risk to public health or need for any or particular type of drug control. [World Health Organization, 1964]

The WHO committee presented short descriptions of various different types of drug dependence that may occur in some persons and situations. The list identifies drug dependence of the following types: morphine, barbiturate-alcohol, cocaine, cannabis (marijuana), amphetamine, khat, and hallucinogen (LSD). For example, the WHO defined drug dependence of the morphine type as having the characteristics of (1) strong psychic dependence that manifests itself as an overpowering drive to continue taking the drug and obtain it by any means; (2) early development of physical dependence that increases in intensity, paralleling increase in dosage; and (3) development of tolerance that requires an increase in dosage to obtain the initial pharmacodynamic effects.

In contrast, they defined drug dependence of the amphetamine type as being characterized by: (1) variable psychic dependence perpetuated by the psychic drive to attain maximum euphoria; (2) absence of a physical dependence, as measured by the criterion of a characteristic and reproducible abstinence syndrome; and (3) slow development of tolerance to many of these drug effects.

For reasons analogous to those just presented, the WHO further suggests that the term *dependent* rather than the ambiguous term *addict* be used to refer to a person who has developed drug dependence of either the physical or psychological type.

CHAPTER 4

PHARMACODYNAMICS:
THE MECHANISMS OF DRUG ACTION

CHAPTER OBJECTIVES

1. List two special biological barriers to drugs, and explain their functions and limitations.
2. What is a drug receptor? What are two effects a drug may have on a receptor?
3. List five ways drugs are excreted from the body, and explain which two are the most important.
4. What affects the way a given individual responds to a particular dose of drug?
5. Describe the allergenic reaction.
6. List steps taken prior to marketing a new drug.
7. Define the following terms: agonist, antagonist, liver induction, LD-50, ED-50, moderately toxic, margin of safety, therapeutic index, biotransformation, and hapten.

DISTRIBUTION OF DRUGS IN THE BODY

In order for a drug to act on a particular organ or system it must reach the target area. There are problems in getting the drug to the correct target in an amount that is effective. Most drugs are taken orally or are injected to be transported in the blood. Drug targets are rarely blood cells but are tissues or organs, such as the heart, liver, kidney, gall bladder, and so on. The circulatory system comprises many miles of arteries, veins, and capillaries. The blood volume of the average person is about 5 to 6 liters, not counting all the other related fluids bathing all the cells of the body. Substances in this extracellular fluid actively enter and leave the blood across the thin capillary walls. An average 150-pound lean person has about 41 liters of liquid, including the blood. This is about 58% of the person's total weight. Drugs introduced into the body are thus diluted immediately, which is one of the first problems encountered in getting a drug to its target location in the amount needed to correct a problem. The blood circulates completely, carrying a drug to all parts of the body, in about one minute.

Chapter 3 briefly discussed protein binding. Protein binding hinders the distribution of many drugs, because when a drug is bound to blood proteins it usually becomes inactive and can act only when freed from the protein. The drug-protein complex is usually a large molecule that cannot leave the blood to reach the cell membranes and thus cannot reach the tissue targets for the drug.

Fat solubility also affects drug distribution in the body. If a drug is fat-soluble, it can readily move through membranes, because membranes are partially composed of fats (lipids). Drugs like Pentothal®, tetrahydrocannabinol (THC) from marijuana, barbiturates, and others are fat-soluble and work rapidly. Pentothal®, a fat-soluble drug, is useful in anesthesia because, when injected intravenously, it acts within seconds. However, it is so fat-soluble a person eliminates it rapidly, and thus it is a short-acting drug.

Membranes influence drug distribution in several ways. Each cell membrane is made up of a double layer of *phospholipid*. These lipid molecules are arranged so that the water-soluble parts point outward toward the exterior and the interior of the cell, and the fat-soluble parts point toward each other. Clusters of protein molecules of various sizes float in the lipid part of the cell membrane. The proteins include *receptors* (see page 52) and *pores*. The pores, or transport channels, in the membrane control the entry and exit of molecules, thus regulating their concentration inside the cell. Most pores are rather selective and allow only water and some small molecules or ions through. If molecules are lipid-soluble, they pass into the cell readily. Others, with ionic charges, may or may not pass readily, depending on their chemical structure and the type of cell. It will suffice to say that membranes have active and passive mechanisms to control entry of drugs and other substances.

The capillaries play a vital role in the movement of drugs through the body. All drugs ultimately will be circulated in the bloodstream and pass through capillaries. It is from the capillaries that most drugs migrate to come in contact with the tissue membranes. Again, the lipid-solubility, protein binding, and ionic state of the drug influence the rate of migration and the ultimate concentration of the drug at the site where it will act. Figure 4-1 shows the sequence of steps most drugs will go through to reach their target areas.

Biological Barriers to Drugs

The brain constitutes only about 2% of a person's body weight, but it needs about 20% of

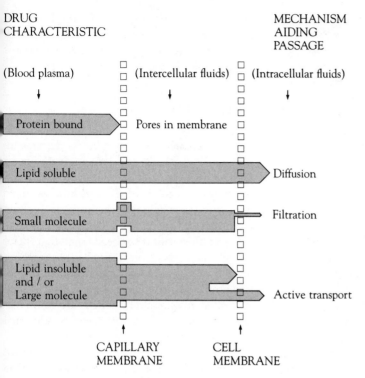

DRUG
CHARACTERISTIC

MECHANISM
AIDING
PASSAGE

(Blood plasma)   (Intercellular fluids)   (Intracellular fluids)

Protein bound   Pores in membrane

Lipid soluble   Diffusion

Small molecule   Filtration

Lipid insoluble
and / or
Large molecule   Active transport

CAPILLARY
MEMBRANE

CELL
MEMBRANE

FIGURE 4-1
Movement of drugs across membranes. Drug movement is influenced by protein binding, lipid solubility, size and charge of molecule, presence of active transport systems, diffusion, and other factors. Almost all drugs, with the exception of those that are protein-bound, can pass through the capillary wall into the interstitial fluids. Diffusion, filtration, or active transport will help other drug types move through the cell membrane into the intracellular fluid.

the blood, glucose, and oxygen consumed by the person at rest. The brain must have a continual flow of blood, with its nutrients and oxygen, as well as the opportunity to get rid of waste products continuously. The blood is carried to the nerve cells in a vast network of thin-walled capillaries. Water-soluble and fat-soluble molecules can move through the capillaries to some extent, with fat-soluble materials moving through readily. Many molecules, such as glucose, cannot pass through the capillary wall even though they are water-soluble; these molecules require special active transport systems. As described in Chapters 2 and 3, the blood-brain barrier apparently provides the brain with a protective mechanism to exclude many substances, but it creates special problems when it is desirable to treat the brain with certain drugs. It is possible to bypass

the blood-brain barrier by injecting the drug directly into the cerebrospinal fluid, but this procedure is difficult and dangerous. Penicillin, for example, is lipid-insoluble, so it cannot be used to treat infections of brain tissue unless large doses are given. This dosage level usually causes sufficient side effects such that other antibiotics are used for infections in the brain.

A second biological barrier, the *placenta*, prevents the transfer of certain molecules from the mother to the fetus. The capillary beds of the placenta and of the mother are in close apposition but do not connect directly, so that the blood supplies do not mingle. The fetus, not being genetically identical to the mother, has many different proteins that the mother's immune system would not recognize as compatible. If the fetal and maternal blood were to mix, the mother would form antibodies against these foreign proteins and destroy them.

There are many drugs that readily cross the placenta: all the fat-soluble and most water-soluble substances will pass into the fetal circulation. Drugs such as barbiturates, THC in marijuana, narcotics, and nicotine are examples of drugs that readily move across the placenta. This fact becomes very important when it is estimated that pregnant women each take an average of four prescription drugs plus numerous over-the-counter drugs. The medical profession has become sensitive to the possible teratogenic damage done to the developing fetus by these substances. There is evidence that a fetus may be damaged by many chemicals, including ingredients in cosmetics and household cleaning products, and by environmental pollutants. Some particularly dangerous substances that can cause fetal damage are chloroform (more commonly found in medicines and foods in the past than now), carbon tetrachloride (formerly a common cleaning fluid), and benzene (in cements and as a solvent). It is estimated that nearly 95% of pregnant women in the United States take or are given pain-relieving drugs during labor and delivery. Some of these analgesics are believed to cause long-term behavioral effects in children. One reason why children may sustain long-term effects from prenatal drug administration is because the fetal nervous system is immature, and thus its blood-brain barrier is not as effective as an adult's. Systematic studies are now being done on drugs as behavioral teratogens (Vorhees, Brunner, & Butcher, 1979).

The blood-placental interface provides a protective barrier against many substances that could harm the fetus, because the fetus is not able to efficiently remove many of the substances should they be introduced into its system. However, many of the synthetic drugs that are lipid-soluble can be quite toxic to the fetus

because they are not excluded—the barrier is not perfect. The fetus can also become addicted prenatally to such drugs as alcohol, the barbiturates, and narcotics.

DRUG RECEPTORS

It is not enough for a drug to be distributed throughout the body; it must have a means to interact with the cell. In drug research many of the findings about how drugs work and how they react with target cells is based on studies of drug receptors. Only parts of a cell are responsive to a drug or chemical. It has been found that there are specific parts of specific cells that react to drugs, just as they do to neurotransmitters and hormones. The parts of the cell that respond are called *receptors*. Thus there are hormone receptors, neurotransmitter receptors, and drug receptors, and many others to process the complex information each cell receives as it maintains metabolic constancy, or homeostasis. The discovery of specific drug receptors led to some surprising results: for example, there are opiate receptors naturally present in the animal brain (Snyder, 1977). Why would the brain have receptors for opiates, which are plant products? This led to the finding that the body produces its own opiates, the endorphins (see Chapter 3). Specific receptors have also been found for the minor tranquilizers, such as Valium®.

It is not known precisely how receptors respond or interact with drugs. Receptors that have been isolated and identified are protein molecules, and it is believed that the shape of the protein is essential in regulating a drug's interaction with a cell. If the drug is the proper shape and size and has a compatible electrical charge, it may activate the receptor protein by causing it to change its shape, or conformation. This process is similar to the "lock-and-key" hypothesis developed to explain how enzymes work.

There are two different effects that a drug may have on a receptor when they interact: *agonistic* or *antagonistic.* An agonistic drug interacts with the receptor and produces a response, whereas an antagonistic drug interacts with the receptor but prevents it from responding. By analogy, a key can be used to open a lock (agonistic effect), whereas another key that will fit in the lock, but not work, can jam the lock (antagonistic effect). An agonistic drug mimics the effect of a natural substance and causes the cell to do something, such as initiating a sequence of metabolic events, by its effects on the receptor.

An antagonist has the opposite effect. It inhibits the sequence of metabolic events that a natural substance or an agonist drug can stimulate, without initiating an effect itself. Antagonistic drugs can act either reversibly or irreversibly. The reversible (competitive) type of antagonist blocks a reaction from occurring by occupying a specific receptor. The antagonist prevents the stimulatory chemical from reaching the receptor, just as a key that is jamming a lock prevents the use of the correct key. The blocking effect can be reversed, if it is caused by a competitive antagonist, by increasing the concentration of the agonist or by diluting the competitive antagonist.

The effect of the irreversible (noncompetitive) type of antagonist cannot be reversed because of a permanent change that occurs when the antagonist binds to the receptors. The cell will eventually make more receptor molecules, which may be compared to replacing an entire jammed lock.

INACTIVATION AND REMOVAL OF DRUGS FROM THE BODY

Drugs are eliminated from the body in various ways. The body will either eliminate the drug directly with no change in the drug, or (in most instances) after the drug has been metabolized or modified. The body has means to metabolize all its naturally occurring information-transferring substances, the neurotransmitters and hormones, and attempts to treat drugs in the same manner—as something to be removed as efficiently as possible. It is important for homeostatic balance to have stimulating signals on for as short a time as necessary. Rapid clearance of neurotransmitters and hormones is part of the body's fine-tuning process, so that overstimulation or oversuppression does not become a problem. Pharmacologists must consider how a drug will be eliminated and what the resulting breakdown products will be.

The liver is the major organ that removes drugs (as well as hormones) from the body. It is a complex biochemical laboratory with hundreds of enzymes at work in many cells, continuously synthesizing, modifying, and deactivating biochemical substances. The healthy liver is capable of metabolizing all of the endogenous substances and many of the foreign chemicals introduced into the body. After the liver metabolizes a drug, the products usually pass into the bile, and then into the intestines, where they are eliminated in the feces. Many antibiotics and other drugs are removed this way.

The liver uses various enzymes to metabolize naturally occurring and foreign substances. These enzymes are associated with the cellular membranes and are often referred to as *microsomal enzymes.* The rate at which liver cells metabolize some substances can be increased if the demand is present. The increased rate is called *liver enzyme induction,* and it occurs if a particular drug is taken repeatedly over a period of time. Barbiturates, opiates, minor tranquilizers, and other drugs cause the liver enzyme activity to increase, which in turn increases the body's capacity to remove the drug and thus clear it from the body more rapidly. (However, enzymes are seldom totally specific, and whatever other substances those enzymes affect will also be metabolized more rapidly as well.) Increased liver enzyme activity lowers the effective concentration of a drug, which creates *drug disposition tolerance.* This means that the same dose of a drug becomes less effective when it has been taken repeatedly over a period of time. Tolerance may lead to dependence on some drugs but not others, as we discussed in Chapter 3. As an example, continual use of marijuana causes increased enzymatic activity (induction) but does not cause dependence, even though tolerance has built up to the drug. The amount of time it takes to remove half of the original amount of a drug from the body is called the *biological half-life* of the drug. In chronic users, marijuana has a biological half-life of nearly 30 hours, whereas in occasional users, it has a half-life of nearly 60 hours (Lemberger, Tamarkin, Axelrod, & Kopin, 1971). This example shows how the liver adapts to the need to remove a substance it treats as foreign and toxic by increasing its capacity to remove the substance.

The kidneys are probably the next most important protective organ that removes metabolites and foreign substances from the body. The kidneys are made up of several million complex filtration units, called *nephrons,* that constantly filter substances in the blood. The nephron conserves and returns to the blood valuable substances that should be saved, and concentrates and excretes metabolic wastes and toxic substances in the urine. It is estimated that the kidneys filter nearly 200 liters of fluid from the blood each day, with over 99% of the fluid returned to the blood along with bicarbonate, glucose, and other substances. The kidneys not only remove water-soluble substances but also regulate blood pressure and control sodium, potassium, and chloride levels in the body. The kidneys' rate of excretion of some drugs can be altered by making the urine more acidic or more alkaline. For example, nicotine and the amphetamines can be cleared faster by acidifying the urine slightly, and the salicylates and the barbiturates by making it more alkaline. These actions might be taken as part of the treatment for a toxic dose of drug.

The body may eliminate small portions of drugs through perspiration and by exhalation. About 1% of consumed alcohol is excreted in the breath, and thus may be measured using a breathalyzer. Most people are aware that consumption of garlic will change body odor because garlic is excreted by perspiration. Drugs are handled in the same way. The mammary glands are modified sweat glands, so it is not surprising that many drugs are concentrated and excreted in milk. These include antibiotics, nicotine, barbiturates, caffeine, and others.

DOSE-RESPONSE RELATIONSHIPS: POTENCY AND EFFECTIVE DOSE

A drug's concentration will influence its effect. A small concentration of drug may have one effect, whereas a larger dose may be expected to have different effects. Because there is some correlation of the response to a drug and the concentration of the drug dose, it is possible to calculate drug-response curves.

Each organism responds to a drug differently. Nevertheless, there is usually less variation among the individuals of a single species than between different species. This is because there is less genetic variability within a species than between different species. Once a drug-response curve for a particular drug is plotted, it can be used to predict the probable response of an organism to a particular dose of that drug in the future.

DOSE-RESPONSE RELATIONSHIPS: POTENCY AND EFFECTIVE DOSE

Like many variables, the drug-response curve follows certain distributive patterns. The drug-response curve of a truly random sample of the population tends to follow the Gaussian, or normal, distribution curve seen in statistics texts. Figure 4-2 shows a normal distribution curve one might expect when calculating a drug response influenced by the size of the dose.

The drug-response curve in Figure 4-2 is based on test results from a large population. If smaller samples are used, the data may not show an even, symmetrical curve because of individual variability in the population and the way they respond to a drug. The following illustration may help the preceding information: if a drug were given to a population, you would expect a particular dose of the drug to cause varied responses in that population. For example, the same dose of barbiturate might be very effective in some persons but have hardly any effect on others. It is this variation that makes it difficult to administer drug dosages accurately. This means that the physician will sometimes say, "Let's try this dose to see if it helps you. If you have any reaction, or if it is not working, I may change the dosage." The physician in effect is saying that he or she does not know for certain how you as an individual might respond, but the

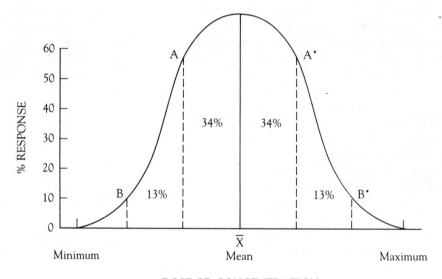

DOSE OR CONCENTRATION

FIGURE 4-2
Theoretical dose-response curve. Gaussian distribution, where X is the mean, or statistical average dose. The area between A and A* is plus-or-minus one standard deviation around the mean and totals about 68%. The area between B and B* is plus-or-minus two standard deviations around the mean, and totals about 94%. The curve represents the variability of responses in a representative population. (Loomis, T. A. 1978. *Essentials of Toxicology*. 3rd ed. Philadelphia: Lea & Febiger, p. 14. Used with permission of the author and publisher.)

probability is that you will respond to a certain dose in a predictable way. Predictability of response to a drug is critical during administration of anesthesia. However, anesthesiologists monitor patients closely, because one person may be more sensitive to sedation than the average person, and another person may be more resistant than expected and require more anesthesia than average.

There are many factors that can modify a response to a drug. Some of these are biological differences, such as tolerance, different levels of enzymatic activity in the liver, the acidity of the urine, ambient temperature, the time of day, and the state of health of the person. It is difficult to calculate the effect of some of these factors, and it is possible there are other variables we do not know about. The time-of-day factor is one example of a difficult variable to predict. The body has definite rhythmic changes it undergoes, some of which are understood and some of which are not. Most people cannot metabolize barbiturates and alcohol as rapidly in the early morning as they can in the late afternoon. If you ask someone whether a drink would have more effect in the morning or evening, he or she may intuitively understand that there is a difference but not know the reason why. The "one for the road" taken late at night will produce a longer lasting rise in blood alcohol level, because of a decreased rate of metabolism, than an identical drink taken earlier at the cocktail hour.

Cumulative Response or Dose-Response Curves

A new drug will be tested extensively on three species of animal before it is tested in humans. One of the first things a pharmacologist needs to know is the toxicity of the drug being tested.

In order to determine this, various dosages of the drug are given to test animals, and the lethal dose is determined. By careful calculations the lethal dose for 50% of the test animals is determined. This dose, also called the LD-50, is found by plotting the dose against the percentage of lethality.

Figure 4-3 is a typical graph of the lethality of two drugs given to test populations of animals. All such curves are based on the probability that a lethal result will occur. Usually one could conclude that the lethal dose would kill the expected percentage of the population from 90% to 95% of the time. When drugs are being tested further, the pharmacologist will then lower the dose until it approaches a level where the drug will be effective in doing what it is hoped the drug will do. In doing this, he or she will determine the *effective dose–50%* (ED-50), which refers to how effective the drug is on 50% of the test population, 90% to 95% of the time.

The LD and the ED of any drug may range from 1% (LD-1 or ED-1) to 100%. For alcohol, it is estimated that the LD-1 would be at 0.35%–0.38% alcohol in the blood, and the LD-50 would be about 0.50% blood alcohol. These figures mean that in a test population of 100 persons consuming alcohol until the level in their blood reaches about 0.35%, one of them would die from the effects of the alcohol, and at 0.50% about 50 of them would die. In most states, 0.10% is the legal intoxication level.

Potency versus Toxicity

In Figure 4-3 compound 2 is less potent than compound 1. In other words, it takes more of compound 2 to get the same response as from compound 1; some drugs are much more powerful than others so they must be taken in smaller doses. From the figure it can be seen that com-

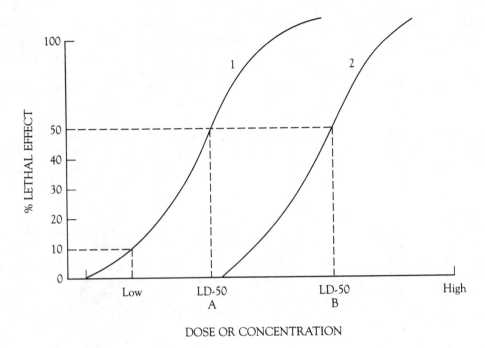

FIGURE 4-3

Dose-response calculations to find the lethal dosages. Note that the lethal dose for 50% (LD-50) is found by extending lines from the 50% lethal point to the dose of the drug. This graph makes it possible to compare the lethality of drugs. In this example, note that drug 1 has an overall lethality greater than drug 2, and the LD-50 of drug 2 is at a much higher dose range. (Loomis, T. A. 1978. *Essentials of Toxicology*. 3rd ed. Philadelphia: Lea & Febiger, p. 16. Used with permission of the author and publisher.)

pound 1 reaches the LD-50 with smaller amounts of drug than compound 2; therefore it must be more potent.

A drug with high potency often reaches toxic levels at low doses, so the amount given must be carefully measured and monitored. *Toxicity* refers to a drug's capacity to upset or even destroy the normal homeostatic balance. Toxic compounds are often called *poisons*, although almost any compound—such as sugar, table salt, aspirin, vitamin A, and so forth—can be toxic at a

sufficiently high dose. The body is in a finely tuned balance with biochemical substances interacting in a highly specific manner. If a new chemical is introduced into this environment, it may disrupt the balance. In many instances the body is able to compensate for this disruption, perhaps by induction of liver enzymes, and little effect is noted. In other cases the delicate balance is altered and the person becomes sick or even dies. If the homeostatic balance is already under stress from one cause, the introduction of a new chemical may have a much more serious effect than in a healthy person.

Doses of drugs may be given at one time or over a short interval of time; this is called an *acute dose*. If the drug is taken over a long period of time, it is called a *chronic dose* (refer to the section in Chapter 3 on acute and chronic use of drugs). In some treatments the best results are obtained with a large dose for a short interval whereas in others better results are obtained by spreading the dose over a long period of time. It may be necessary to start with small doses and gradually work up to effective levels. Table 4-1 shows a comparison of LD-50s for acute doses of a number of drugs and chemicals. (Most drugs are measured in metric units now, instead of apothecary units. Appendix B-1 gives a list of common units of weight that are used.)

TABLE 4-1 Comparison of the LD-50s in rats and mice for various substances[*]

Agent	LD-50 in mg/kg body weight
Ethanol	10,000
Sodium chloride	4,000
Ferrous sulfate	1,500
Morphine	900
Phenobarbital	150
DDT	100
Strychnine	2
Nicotine	1
Tubocurarine	0.5
Botulinus toxin	0.00001

[*]Loomis, T. A. 1978. *Essentials of Toxicology.* 3rd ed. Philadelphia: Lea & Febiger, p. 18. Used with permission of the author and publisher.

Potency depends on absorption of the drug, its distribution in the body, metabolism, the excretion method, and the rate of elimination. If a drug, such as a volatile gas like ether, is absorbed rapidly, it has a rapid action but may not stay in the body long. Injected sodium pentothal (a barbiturate) acts very rapidly and is very potent, but its action is short because it is metabolized quickly. A drug such as sodium pentothal is very effective, within a minute or two, when injected into the blood because it is distributed throughout the body rapidly. Some drugs stay bound to lipids or to proteins for long periods of time, so they are slow acting but long lasting. When water-soluble drugs go through the kidney-filtration system, they are removed rapidly. Other drugs break down very slowly so that the dosage given must be low and monitored carefully. A simple classification system is sometimes used to compare the potency of a drug to its toxicity. A drug is:

1. extremely toxic if the LD-50 is less than one milligram per kilogram of body weight (1mg/kg);
2. highly toxic if the LD-50 is between 1 and 50 mg/kg;
3. moderately toxic if the LD-50 is between 50 and 100 mg/kg;
4. slightly toxic if the LD-50 is between 0.5 and 5 grams/kg (g/kg).

Toxicity is not always related to dosage in a simple linear relationship (refer to drugs 1 and 2 in Figure 4-4). A small dose might be potent and show lethality while the potency increases at a slow rate (see drug 2 in Figure 4-4); another drug may be less potent but increase in toxicity or potency at a rapid rate with the dose given (see drug 1 in Figure 4-4). Note that, although the LD-50 of drug 2 is greater than that of drug 1, the reverse is true of their LD-5s.

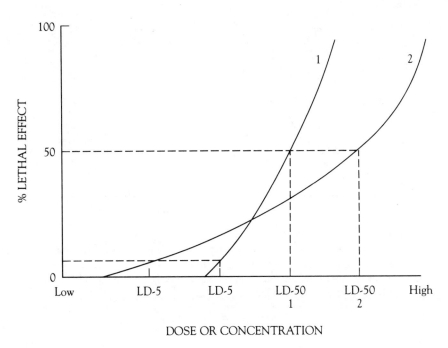

FIGURE 4-4

Dose-response curves for drugs 1 and 2. Note that drug 2 is more potent at a lower dose than drug 1, but less potent at higher doses. (Loomis, T. A. 1978. *Essentials of Toxicology.* 3rd ed. Philadelphia: Lea & Febiger, p. 19. Used with permission of the author and publisher.)

Margin of Safety

When developing new therapeutic drugs it is useful to plot how safe a drug is at various doses. It is important to know how much drug can be given without markedly increasing the lethality or the toxicity. The comparison of dosage and lethality is called the *margin of safety*. The margin of safety is determined by plotting the magnitude of range of doses from ineffective to lethal. Figure 4-5 shows a typical plot of drug toxicities. From such a plot it is easy to compare the margin of safety for each drug. Notice that drug 3 has a greater margin of safety than the others, and that drug 1 has a low margin of safety. It would

be more difficult to manage treatment with drug 1, because it has a narrow dose range in which it is effective without being toxic. Lithium carbonate is an example of this type of drug: a dose that is slightly too low is ineffective in the treatment of manic depression, but the effective dose is close to being toxic.

The dose of a drug may be very important when evaluating side effects. A side effect of a drug is usually an undesirable effect on the body. For example, anticholinergic drugs (atropine, scopolamine) cause dryness of the mouth, pupil enlargement, and influence the heart when they are used to control intestinal activity. Morphine is a good analgesic drug, but it depresses breath-

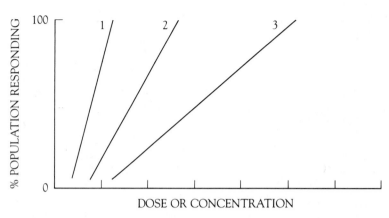

FIGURE 4-5

Dose-response curves for three drugs comparing margin of safety. Note that drug 3 has a greater margin of safety than drug 2 or 1. (Loomis, T. A. 1978. *Essentials of Toxicology.* 3rd ed. Philadelphia: Lea & Febiger, p. 20. Used with permission of the author and publisher.)

ing and slows down the intestines. Antihistamines and antibiotics may trigger sensitization in some people. Amphetamines are used to control hyperkinesis but will raise blood pressure and increase the heart rate. The known side effects must always be considered in drug selection in order to maximize the drug's therapeutic effect and minimize the unwanted side effects.

Therapeutic Index

Pharmacologists have developed the *therapeutic index* as a means to calculate the safety of a drug. To find the index, one divides the LD-50 dose by the ED-50 dose. Thus the therapeutic index is

$$\frac{\text{LD-50 dose}}{\text{ED-50 dose}}$$

Figure 4-6 shows how to calculate a therapeutic index and how to interpret the safety of a drug from such calculations. First the drug is tested for LD-50 and ED-50. In this particular situation, the values for LD-50 and ED-50 are 100 and 10, respectively. 100/10 = a therapeutic index of 10. Notice that there is still a lethal effect at the higher ED range. ED-100 may have an LD-5 effect. Normally one would not use a drug with this level of toxicity or lethality. In order to guarantee drug safety some pharmacologists have recommended using a therapeutic index of LD-1/ED-99. The use of this index would provide a greater margin of safety in drug use, but it might restrict the use of some drugs of value for people who are sensitive to higher doses.

There is no such thing as the perfect drug that goes right to the target, has no toxicity, produces few side effects, and that can be removed or neutralized when not needed. Unfortunately, most effective drugs are potentially dangerous. Pharmacologists refer to a perfect drug as a "magic bullet"—so far we have no magic bullets.

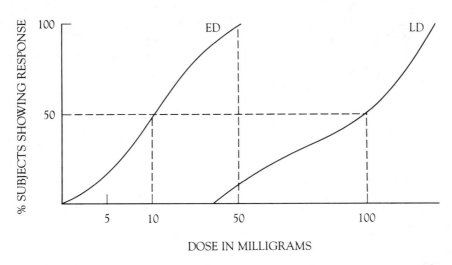

ED = Dose to cause given response   LD = Lethal dose, same compound

FIGURE 4-6
Calculating the therapeutic index (LD-50/ED-50). Note that the ED is the effective dose and LD is the lethal dose for 50% of the subjects. The therapeutic index is 10 (100/10 = 10). (Loomis, T. A. 1978. *Essentials of Toxicology.* 3rd ed. Philadelphia: Lea & Febiger, p. 22. Used with permission of the author and publisher.)

Biotransformation

The process of metabolism of drugs in the body is called *biotransformation.* During biotransformation a large variety of enzymes constantly transform drugs and other products to substances that can be eliminated from the body. Any interference or modification in the enzymes involved in metabolism of the drugs can influence the effects of the drug and the drug products on the body. If a drug is transformed rapidly before it can cause toxic effects, there usually is no problem. However, if there is a delay in transformation of potentially toxic substances, there may be serious consequences for the homeostatic balance systems. Genetic diseases in which metabolites accumulate illustrate this

problem. Phenylketonuria (PKU), in which the normal metabolic rate of the amino acid phenylalanine is greatly reduced, is one example. The person with this disease has a defective gene that fails to code for the enzyme that metabolizes phenylalanine. The resulting increased level of phenylalanine can damage the developing brain during the first two years of life, causing severe mental retardation.

There are a number of examples in which a drug's breakdown products, or *metabolites,* are more toxic than the drug. The drug prontosil, used to treat some infections, is rapidly changed to a more active substance called *sulfanilamide.* Some people retain sulfanilamide longer than others; so they are more likely to suffer toxic effects. This active metabolic compound may cause an increase in methemoglobin, thus decreasing the oxygen-carrying capacity of the blood, and can cause skin rashes, fever, and hemolysis (breakdown of the red blood cells). This is one example of a commonly used drug that can have toxic side effects. Other compounds that show increasing toxicity as a result of metabolism are listed in Table 4-2.

In general, biotransformation reactions convert lipid-soluble drugs into less lipid-soluble, more water-soluble metabolites that are more easily eliminated by the kidneys. There are few drugs that are sufficiently water-soluble to be eliminated in their original form by the kidneys.

Allergenic Mechanisms

Almost everyone has had a reaction to some chemical in the environment or to some type of drug. This is called an *allergenic reaction*. The flow chart shown in Figure 4-7 describes the development of the allergenic reaction.

TABLE 4-2 Compounds that increase their toxicity following biotransformation[*]

Compound	Product
Ethylene glycol	Oxalic acid
Methanol	Formaldehyde
Parathion	Paraoxon
Pyridine	N-Methylpyridinium chloride
Chloral hydrate	Trichloroethanol chloride
Selenate	Selenite
Codeine	Morphine

[*]Loomis, T. A. 1978. *Essentials of Toxicology.* 3rd ed. Philadelphia: Lea & Febiger, p. 60. Used with permission of the author and publisher.

FIGURE 4-7
The allergenic mechanism, showing how a person becomes sensitized to a foreign substance and how a subsequent immune response occurs if that person is exposed to the same hapten. (Loomis, T. A. 1978. *Essentials of Toxicology.* 3rd ed. Philadelphia: Lea & Febiger, p. 114. Used with permission of the author and publisher.)

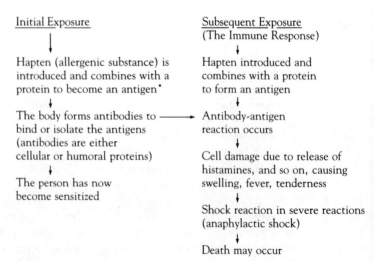

Initial Exposure

↓

Hapten (allergenic substance) is introduced and combines with a protein to become an antigen[*]

↓

The body forms antibodies to ──────► bind or isolate the antigens (antibodies are either cellular or humoral proteins)

↓

The person has now become sensitized

Subsequent Exposure
(The Immune Response)

↓

Hapten introduced and combines with a protein to form an antigen

↓

Antibody-antigen reaction occurs

↓

Cell damage due to release of histamines, and so on, causing swelling, fever, tenderness

↓

Shock reaction in severe reactions (anaphylactic shock)

↓

Death may occur

[*]Some drugs may be antigenic in nature rather than haptens.

The steps involved in formation of antibodies are referred to as the *immune reaction*. The allergenic reaction is a type of unwanted immune response. Initial exposure to a chemical does not result in cellular damage but causes the person to become sensitized to subsequent exposure to the chemical. If antibodies are formed and if there is subsequent exposure to the chemical, an antigen-antibody reaction may occur that could cause cell damage. Such drugs as penicillin and many other drugs are known to induce sensitization. This is one reason people should not use drugs when it is not necessary. The antibodies in the blood may vary in concentration, so that the number may be high at times and later decline to low levels or disappear. Because of this variability it is difficult to predict exactly how intense an immune or allergenic reaction will be, or if it will occur at all.

There are different types of allergenic reaction, but we are concerned only with one of the most common types, the *anaphylactic*. The anaphylactic reaction may be general or may occur in one part of the body only (local). It may result in a skin reaction called *urticaria* (hives), a respiratory reaction causing difficulty in breathing (asthma), or in a gastrointestinal reaction (diarrhea). Table 4-3 lists some of the

TABLE 4-3 Common types of sensitivity reaction[*]

Skin manifestations	Drugs involved
Contact dermatitis (skin is itchy, reddened, blistered, and sometimes necrotic)	Arsenicals, mercurials, penicillin, streptomycin, sulfonamides
Urticaria (hives with reddening, swelling)	Penicillin, pollens, salicylates, some foods
Exfoliation (loss of skin with swelling)	Barbiturates, sulfonamides, arsenicals, iodides

Systemic manifestations	Drugs involved
Blood abnormalities:	
1. Granulocytopenia (depression of granulocyte white cell count)	Arsenicals, gold salts, hydantoins, thiouracils, phenylbutazone
2. Thrombocytopenia (depression of the platelet number)	Arsenicals, quinine, sulfonamides
3. Aplastic anemia (depression of all blood cells)	Chloramphenicol, hydantoins, quinacrine, phenylbutazone, sulfonamides
Anaphylactic shock (flushing, lightheadedness, decrease in blood pressure, airway obstruction)	Iodides, local anesthetics, mercurials, penicillin, pollen extracts, serums, vaccines
Asthma (bronchiolar obstruction)	Pollen extracts, salicylates, serums

[*]Loomis, T. A. 1978. *Essentials of Toxicology.* 3rd ed. Philadelphia: Lea & Febiger, p. 123. Used with permission of the author and publisher.

common sensitivity reactions of humans, and the drugs involved.

Table 4-3 shows only a small number of the substances known to cause allergenic reactions. An allergist can treat many troublesome reactions to unavoidable substances, such as house dust and various pollens (like giant ragweed), by giving small amounts of the purified antigen to the allergic person. Although it is not understood why this treatment works, and it does not work uniformly well for all people, injection of small amounts of the antigen or *hapten* under the skin (subcutaneously) can make the person less sensitive to the antigen. (The hapten is the part of the antigen that determines its specificity. It does not itself cause the allergenic reaction.)

DRUG TESTING: DEVELOPMENT OF NEW DRUGS

All new drugs must be registered with the federal Food and Drug Administration (FDA). This body has regulatory control over all the substances used in the United States that are classified as drugs. (Drug regulations and their history in the United States are described in Chapter 19.) There are particular rules and regulations that all pharmaceutical companies must follow in seeking permission to market a new drug. The following are some of the required steps.

Animal Tests

First, a chemical is identified as having potential value in the treatment of a particular condition or disease. The company interested in marketing the chemical as a drug must run a series of tests on at least three species of animal. Usually

the LD-50 is determined as a start, followed by the ED-50 after further investigation, provided the drug is not too toxic. Careful records must be kept of side effects, absorption, distribution, metabolism, excretion, and the dosages of the chemical necessary to produce the various effects. Carcinogenic, mutagenic, and teratogenic variables are tested. The dose-response curve will be determined along with potency, and then the risk-benefit of the substance will be calculated. If the company still believes there is a market for the substance, it will forward the data to the FDA to obtain an Investigational New Drug (IND) number for further tests.

Human Tests

Animal tests provide a certain amount of information, but ultimately tests must be made on the species for which the potential drug is intended, the human. These tests are usually classified into three phases. The phase 1 test is called the *initial clinical stage*. Small numbers of volunteers, both healthy people and patients in free clinics, are used to establish drug safety, dose range for effective treatment, and to examine any side effects. Formerly much of this research was done on prison inmates, but, because of bad publicity and the possibility of coercion, fewer prisoners are used today. There has been a switch to medical students, paid college student volunteers, and volunteers being treated at free clinics. All the data are collected, analyzed, and sent to the FDA for approval before beginning the next phase of human subject testing.

Phase 2 testing is called the *clinical pharmacological evaluation stage*. The effects of the drug are tested in double-blind, placebo-controlled studies to eliminate investigator bias and to determine side effects and the effectiveness of

DRUG TESTING: DEVELOPMENT OF NEW DRUGS

the treatment. Statistical evaluation of all this information is done before proceeding with phase 3 testing.

Phase 3 is the *extended clinical evaluation.* By this time the pharmaceutical company has a good idea of drug effectiveness as well as dangers, so the drug can be offered to a wider group of participating clinics and physicians, who cooperate in administration of the potential drug—when medically appropriate—to thousands of volunteer patients. This stage makes the drug available on a wide experimental basis. Sometimes,

by this point, there has been publicity about the new drug, and people with the particular disease the drug was developed for may actively seek out physicians licensed to experiment with it. People not familiar with the sad consequences of taking inadequately tested drugs may protest at how long the drug-testing process takes.

During phase 3 testing, safety checks are observed along with any side effects that might show up now that more people are being exposed to the drug. After the testing program is over, careful analysis is made of the effectiveness, side

"THE CODEINE IS O.K. AND THE PHENOBARBITAL IS O.K., BUT THE FOOD AND DRUG ADMINISTRATION SAYS NO TO THE POWDERED BAT'S TOOTH."

effects, and recommended dosage. The information is sent to the FDA for final evaluation. The amount of information at this point usually comprises many thousands of pages of data and analysis, and the FDA must sift through it and decide whether the risks of using the drug justify its potential benefits. The FDA may call for further tests before deciding the drug is safe and effective and giving permission to the company to market it.

Permission to Market

At this point, the FDA grants permission to market the drug under its patented name. It may cost $7 to $10 million and take 5 to 8 years to develop a new drug in the United States. The situation is similar in other countries. In some European countries, the clinical evaluations are less stringent, but once the drug is marketed closer watch is kept over adverse effects than is kept in the United States. This activity makes it easier for a European country to recall permission to market the drug, if unexpected effects develop, than it is for the FDA. In some cases, adverse effects may not show up for a long time. For example, it was recently determined that diethylstilbestrol (DES), when given to pregnant women, caused developmental abnormalities in their sons and an increased risk of a rare type of vaginal cancer in their daughters when these children entered their teens and young-adult years. The FDA subsequently removed DES, in the form in which it had been used to treat pregnant women, from the market. The thalidomide tragedy, which stimulated passage of the law allowing the FDA to do this, is described in Chapter 19.

CHAPTER 5

THE CLASSIFICATION OF DRUGS AND DRUG INTERACTIONS

CHAPTER OBJECTIVES

1. List eight categories of psychoactive drugs, and give examples of drugs in each category.
2. List the functions and effects of sedatives, stimulants, and psychedelics on the body and brain.
3. Defend the following statement: Marijuana could be classified as a psychedelic or a sedative drug.
4. Compare antidepressants and major tranquilizers with respect to their use and their effects on the body.
5. Define drug interaction, name the three categories of drug interaction, and give an example of each.
6. List a potentially dangerous interaction between a tranquilizer, a phenothiazine drug, an antibiotic, an analgesic, an antihistamine, alcohol, food, and MAO inhibitors by naming the drugs of interaction and the reaction or response of their interaction.

DRUG CLASSIFICATION

Drugs have been categorized according to a variety of considerations. However, there appears to be little general agreement on the optimal scheme for ordering the universe of biologically active substances. For example, drugs might be organized according to chemical structure, clinical therapeutic use, potential health hazards, liability to nonmedical use (abuse), public availability and legality, effects on specific neural or other physiological systems, or influence on certain psychological and behavioral processes. Classification systems may overlap, although there often are striking incongruities among

TABLE 5-1 Classification of major psychoactive drugs

1. SEDATIVES AND HYPNOTICS[1]
   Barbiturates: for example, Nembutal® (pentobarbital), Seconal® (secobarbital), and Veronal® (barbital)
   Minor tranquilizers (also called *ataraxics*): for example, Librium® (chlordiazepoxide), Miltown® (meprobamate), Valium® (diazepam)
   Doriden® (glutethimide)
   Placidyl® (ethchlorvynol)
   Methaqualone (Quaalude®, Mequin®, Parest®)
   Others: bromides, ethanol, paraldehyde, chloral hydrate, antihistamines (Gravol®, methapyriline), anticholinergics (atropine, scopolamine, hyoscyamine)

2. STIMULANTS[1]
   Amphetamines: for example, Benzedrine® (amphetamine), Dexedrine® (dextroamphetamine), Stimdex® (methamphetamine)
   Ritalin® (methylphenidate)
   Preludin® (phenmetrazine)
   Cocaine
   Ephedrine, pseudoephedrine
   Others: for example, caffeine (in coffee, tea, cocoa, APCs, colas), theophylline (tea), theobromine (cocoa), khat, betel, kava

3. PSYCHEDLICS AND HALLUCINOGENS[2]
   LSD (lysergic acid diethylamide)
   Cannabis sativa (marijuana, hashish); tetrahydrocannabinol
   Mescaline (peyote)
   Psilocybin
   DMT (dimethyltryptamine)—found in cohoba snuff
   DET (diethyltryptamine)
   DOM, STP (2,5-dimethoxy-4-methylamphetamine)
   MDA (methylenedioxyamphetamine)
   MMDA (3-methoxy-4,5-methylenedioxyamphetamine)
   LBJ (methylpiperidylbenzilate)
   PCP (Sernylan®, phencyclidine)

them. For example, some drugs that appear closely similar in chemical structure may be quite different in pharmacological activity, and vice versa. Thus the intended use of the classification system determines its value.

The drug-classification system developed by the German toxicologist Louis Lewin (1931) has been used by pharmacologists for many years.

In many ways Lewin's system is outdated, but, because it is of historical interest and is still referred to, we will describe this system briefly before examining a more modern, complete system. Lewin classified drugs into five groups:

1. *Euphorica.* These drugs sedate mental activity and induce a state of physical and mental

---

TABLE 5-1   *(continued)*

---

4. OPIATE NARCOTICS[1]
   Opium
   Morphine
   Codeine
   Synthetic opiates: for example, heroin (diacetylmorphine), Demerol® (meperidine), Percodan® (oxycodone), Dolophine® (methadone), Dilaudid® (hydromorphone)

5. VOLATILE SOLVENTS[2]
   Examples—glues, gasoline, paint thinner, nail polish remover, lighter and cleaning fluids, spray cans and aerosols
   Active agents in these examples: toluene, benzene, naphtha, trichloroethylene, ether, chloroform, amyl nitrite, nitrous oxide (laughing gas), acetone, Freon, butyl nitrite (locker room)

6. NONNARCOTIC ANALGESICS[1]
   Aspirin (acetylsalicylic acid)
   Phenacetin (acetophenetidin)
   Tylenol® (acetaminophen)

7. CLINICAL ANTIDEPRESSANTS[3]
   Monoamine oxidase (MAO) inhibitors (Nardil®)
   Ritalin® (methylphenidate)
   Tricyclics—Tofranil® (imipramine)

8. MAJOR TRANQUILIZERS[3]
   Phenothiazines: for example, Thorazine® and Largactil® (chlorpromazine), Stelazine® (trifluoperazine), Compazine® (prochlorperazine)
   Rauwolfia alkaloids (snakeroot): for example, Serpasil® (reserpine)
   Butyrophenones: for example, Haldol® (haloperidol)
   Thioxanthenes: for example, Taractan® (chlorprothixene)

---

[1]Used medically and nonmedically
[2]Little or no medical use
[3]Wide medical use, with little or no nonmedical use

comfort. They include opium, its derivatives, and cocaine (today cocaine might be included in another group).

2. *Phantastica.* This category includes hallucinogens. It comprises a number of plant-derived drugs varying greatly in chemical structure. They may bring on visions, illusions, and hallucinations and may be accompanied or followed by unconsciousness or other symptoms of altered brain functioning. As examples Lewin listed mescal buttons and marijuana products. We would greatly expand this category today.

3. *Inebriantia.* These are drugs of drunkenness. Lewin included alcohol, chloroform, ether, and benzene.

4. *Hypnotica.* This group includes sleep-producing agents, or sedatives. Lewin listed chloral, veronal, and sulphonal. This group is now very large.

5. *Excitantia.* These are the mental stimulants, now more commonly called *analeptics,* meaning that they stimulate the central nervous system. Included in this group are caffeine, nicotine, betel, coffee, tea, and cocoa. This group would also be much larger now.

Today Lewin would probably add a sixth category called the *ataraxics,* or tranquilizers, and perhaps others. Because our major concern here is with the effects of psychoactive substances, the drug-classification system we will use is based primarily on general pharmacological and psychological considerations. Table 5-1 presents eight major classes along with some examples of drugs from each group. Although the categories are not exhaustive, the general system is applicable to the majority of drugs for their psychological and physiological effects. These categories are to some extent based on a typical reaction by an average subject to a common dose. Large variations in any of various factors can greatly alter a drug's effects and may reduce the reliability of the descriptions. After studying the classification system we will examine the topic of drug interaction.

EFFECTS OF MAJOR PSYCHOACTIVE DRUGS

The following is a brief summary of the major effects of each of the preceding categories of drug. Figure 5-1 compares drug effects on the central nervous system over the range of depression and stimulation. (Note that either extreme results in death.) Stimulation may distort perceptions of space and time, cause a sensation of euphoria, or perhaps cause nervousness. Convulsions result from intense stimulation. The depressants likewise vary in their effects, from simple relief of anxiety to anesthesia and also to convulsions.

Using the same drug categories as Figure 5-1, Figure 5-2 shows the range of drug effects and how they overlap. Note that there is little overlap between the stimulant effects of strychnine and amphetamine, but considerable overlap between the psychic energizers and the antidepressants. The hypnotic sedatives and the narcotics overlap almost completely in their depressant effects, and each can cause drowsiness, induce sleep, block perception of pain, and be addictive. The type of drug effect and the overlapping of effects are dependent on dose, time, individual physiology, drug interaction, and other variables. Nevertheless, Figure 5-2 gives an excellent comparison of the most commonly noted actions and effects.

Sedatives and Hypnotics

The group of drugs comprising sedatives and hypnotics generally decreases central-nervous-system (CNS) arousal, although there may be

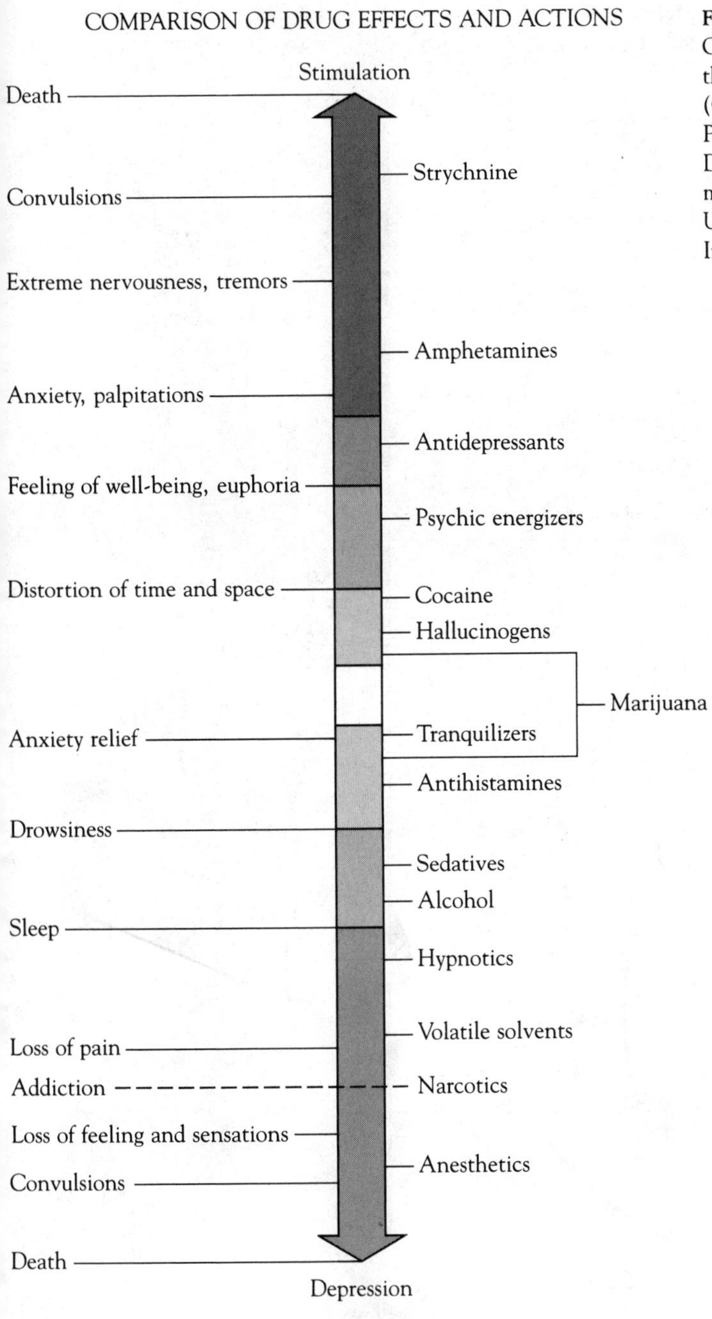

COMPARISON OF DRUG EFFECTS AND ACTIONS

FIGURE 5-1

Comparison of drug effects on the central nervous system (Courtesy of R. W. Earle, Ph.D., Senior Lecturer, Department of Medical Pharmacology and Therapeutics, University of California, Irvine)

Stimulation

Death ——————————

———— Strychnine

Convulsions ——————

Extreme nervousness, tremors ——

———— Amphetamines

Anxiety, palpitations ——————

———— Antidepressants

Feeling of well-being, euphoria ——

———— Psychic energizers

Distortion of time and space ——— Cocaine
———— Hallucinogens

———— Marijuana

Anxiety relief ——————— Tranquilizers

———— Antihistamines

Drowsiness ——————

———— Sedatives
———— Alcohol

Sleep ——————

———— Hypnotics

———— Volatile solvents

Loss of pain ——————

Addiction – – – – – – – – – – – – – – Narcotics

Loss of feeling and sensations ——

———— Anesthetics

Convulsions ——————

Death ——————

Depression

71

FIGURE 5-2

Range and overlapping of drug effects (Courtesy of R. W. Earle, Ph.D., Senior Lecturer, Department of Medical Pharmacology and Therapeutics, University of California, Irvine)

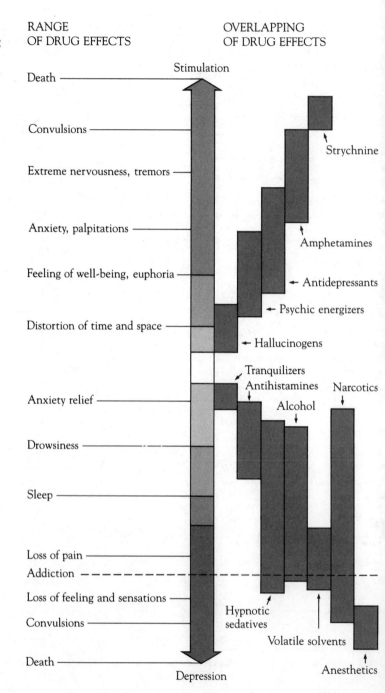

RANGE OF DRUG EFFECTS

OVERLAPPING OF DRUG EFFECTS

Stimulation

Death

Convulsions

Extreme nervousness, tremors

Anxiety, palpitations

Feeling of well-being, euphoria

Distortion of time and space

Anxiety relief

Drowsiness

Sleep

Loss of pain

Addiction

Loss of feeling and sensations

Convulsions

Death

Depression

Strychnine

Amphetamines

← Antidepressants

← Psychic energizers

← Hallucinogens

Tranquilizers
Antihistamines

Narcotics

Alcohol

Hypnotic sedatives

Volatile solvents

Anesthetics

psychological stimulation at low doses. Most of the drugs in this category are used medically to reduce anxiety and tension, to induce sedation (which usually includes muscle relaxation), and, at higher doses, to induce sleep. The difference between a sedative and a hypnotic often lies in the size of the dose, the hypnotic being a larger dose. A number of these drugs have the potential to produce physical dependence (physiological addiction). These include the barbiturates, the methaqualone preparations (for example, Quaalude®), and the minor tranquilizers (for example, Valium®). Each of these can cause dependence, although often under widely varying circumstances. For instance, a tranquilizer like Librium® might cause dependence if taken for over six months at a dose of 300–400 milligrams per day (mg/day), whereas another tranquilizer, Valium®, might cause dependence if over 80 mg/day were taken over a similar time. Data on dependence are very difficult to obtain because of the large number of variables, such as differences in body physiology, mental predisposition, the length of time the dose is taken, and so forth.

Drugs like the anticholinergics (for example, belladonna alkaloids such as atropine and scopolamine) are often used as sedatives at low doses. Larger amounts may cause excitation, delirium, and even death. The antihistamines usually have sedation as a side effect, but large doses may produce pronounced sedation. (Most of these drugs will be discussed in more detail later.)

Stimulants

This group includes drugs that suppress appetite (anorexiants) and increase alertness, increase tension, and cause general CNS arousal. As mentioned earlier, these drugs are sometimes called *analeptic drugs*, which means that they stimulate the CNS. At higher doses they can block sleep. Many of them are used as "pep" pills because they cause a sense of peppiness and well-being, although this effect varies among individuals.

Tobacco—with its nicotine—and coffee, tea, and cocoa—with their caffeine and other stimulants—are probably the most widely used stimulants in the world. In some countries, betel, khat, and kava are widely used as heavily as tobacco and coffee in the United States. Betel is a mild intoxicant and an expectorant, which makes the user spit or swallow excessively. The leaves of this climbing pepper plant are mixed with pieces of betel nut and powdered lime, and are sold in small packets by street vendors in India and southeastern Asia. When used over a long period of time betel will stain the teeth a dark color.

Kava, a widely used drink in Fiji, is made from a plant related to the pepper family. The roots are traditionally chewed communally and spit out into a large bowl to ferment (Lewin, 1931). It can also be made with water (for tourists). It has a mildly bitter flavor and numbs the mouth. Other natural plant stimulants that have been used for thousands of years include cocaine and ephedrine.

Psychedelics and Hallucinogens

This group of drugs is characterized in many ways—as psychedelic (mind manifesting), hallucinogenic (hallucination producing), psychotomimetic (psychosis mimicking), illusinogenic (illusion producing), and psychodysleptic (mind disrupting). All of these descriptive terms have been used at various times to describe the drugs in this category, and, because many are still found in the literature, they are listed here. *Hallucinogenic* is the term currently used; *psychotomi-*

metic is a term still used in medical circles, although many of these drugs do not truly mimic psychosis as we understand psychosis. One can see from this list of terms that the classification of drugs in this group is confusing and controversial.

Hallucinogenic drugs may produce profound alteration in sensation, mood, and consciousness at doses that result in comparatively small physiological changes. LSD, mescaline, psilocybin, DMT, MDA, and hundreds of synthetic drugs belong in this group. Marijuana is often placed in this group because in high doses it can cause hallucinations, but this rarely happens. A number of authorities place marijuana in a category by itself, because of its unique characteristics as a euphoriant, a mild sedative, and even as an antidepressant under certain circumstances. Chapters 6 and 7 give more information about the hallucinogens and marijuana.

Opiates

The opiate narcotics group includes those drugs that are derivatives of, or are pharmacologically related to, products from the opium poppy. The best known examples are heroin, morphine, and codeine. There are also many synthetic opiates, such as heroin, methadone, and propoxyphene (Darvon®). This large group of drugs is used medically primarily for their analgesic qualities (pain relief), but some are used to suppress coughing and to stop diarrhea. Most of these can be strongly addictive.

Volatile Solvents

This is a chemically diverse group and includes such common materials as glue solvent, gasoline, lacquer thinner, and nitrous oxide. These chemicals are often inhaled because of their volatile nature. Some of them are called *deliriants*, although delirium is only one of the effects of this diverse group. Many are quite similar in effect to the sedative group and might be placed in a subclass of that category. Others have slight hallucinogenic properties. Most have no known medical uses, although several, such as nitrous oxide, have been used as anesthetics.

Nonnarcotic Analgesics

The nonnarcotic analgesic group includes drugs used primarily to reduce aching pain and fever. In some instances they may act as mild sedatives or as anti-inflammatory agents. Aspirin and phenacetin are the most common drugs in this group, but acetaminophen is being used more and more because it has fewer irritating effects on the gastrointestinal tract than aspirin.

Antidepressants

The seventh group of drugs, antidepressants, is used almost exclusively to elevate mood in severely depressed persons. They have little effect on normal moods, so they are seldom abused. Tofranil® and Nardil® are examples in this category, but Ritalin® and even amphetamines have been used as antidepressants and may alleviate depression in some cases.

Major Tranquilizers

The major tranquilizers (as opposed to the minor tranquilizers) are primarily used to reduce the symptoms of psychosis. They have been especially valuable in treating schizophrenic patients, and their use has been largely responsible for the increasingly rapid release of mental patients from hospitals and an actual drop in mental-hospital population since 1955 (see Chapter 10). These drugs range from traditionally used reserpine to the more recently developed, potent synthetic phenothiazines (Thorazine®, Stelazine®, and Compazine®). They have not been involved much in nonmedical abuse, although haloperidol is an exception, because of its sedative effect.

Oral Contraceptives

These drugs, although not psychoactive, are so widely used we are including them for discussion of their effects and interaction. "The Pill," including all types of oral contraceptive, has been used in the United States since 1960. These drugs are used by perhaps 10 million women in the United States and by an estimated 25 million women worldwide. They have had an enormous effect on the control of fertility in large segments of our population. Today, two major types of oral contraceptive are used: the combination pill, formulated with an estrogen and a progestin, and the progestin pill (see Chapter 14). When used properly, they are extremely effective in preventing unwanted pregnancy. The original oral contraceptive pills had a high level of estrogen, which has since been shown to be responsible for many of the unwanted side effects, such as blood clots and nausea. The oral contraceptives recommended for routine use today contain much lower levels of estrogen and about one-fifth or less the level of progestin than was used in the original formulations, without sacrificing their effectiveness, and the incidence of side effects has been greatly reduced. The all-progestin pill has virtually no estrogenic side effects (there is some overlap in bioactivity in the synthetic estrogens and progestins).

DRUG INTERACTION

Many drugs are readily available to the average person, and, as discussed in Chapter 1, the typical person takes a large number and variety of drugs. These facts have created a serious medical problem, because many drugs influence the action or effects of other drugs. One of the difficult problems medical personnel have to face today, let alone the person responsible for a "care line" or drug-emergency service, is that of drug interaction. Even the fully qualified physician is often taken by surprise by drug effects and runs into complications that may be totally unexpected. Some of these complications can be dangerous, even fatal. Drug interaction is an area where much more research, and dissemination of the information obtained, is greatly needed. The following material describes some of the known drug interactions and possible modifications of drug effects by commonly consumed foods and chemicals.

By definition, drug interaction occurs whenever a drug action is modified by another substance. The interacting substance may be another drug, or it may be some substance in the diet or in the environment, such as a pesticide. Depending on the effect on the body, drug interaction may be categorized into three groups: *additive, inhibitory,* and *synergistic* (potentiation).

Additive Effects

An additive effect occurs when two drugs are given and the total effect is the sum of the effects of the two drugs. An example of a simple additive effect results from mixing three sulfonamide drugs, often called *trisulfapyrimidines.* If any one of the drugs is taken alone in an effective dose, there may be kidney damage; but, if one combines the three drugs—each drug at one-third of the total—there is usually no kidney damage, and the therapeutic effect is at the maximum.

Drug Inhibition Effects

The drug inhibition effect may be shown by drugs like barbiturates and antihistamines. For example, if a person is taking barbiturates for a mild sedative effect and decides to take antihistamines to reduce nasal congestion, he or she would have to take a massive dose of antihistamines to produce the desired effect. Otherwise the person will not become calm and will still have the nasal congestion, because these two drugs nullify each other by interfering with the common enzyme systems they work through.

Drug inhibition is not necessarily dangerous, although it could be. For example, a man was hospitalized for a heart attack. He was immediately given barbiturates to calm him down and to induce sleep. He was given an anticoagulant to prevent further blood clots, and his blood-clotting time was carefully measured as the dosage of anticoagulant was built up to an effective level. The dose of anticoagulant was larger than usual, because the barbiturate caused the enzymes that remove the anticoagulant to work more effectively. When the man returned home, he decided he did not need the barbiturates, and he stopped taking them. Without the inhibiting effect, the dosage of anticoagulant now was too high, and the man suffered severe internal bleeding.

Another example of a drug inhibition effect is that of taking tetracycline, an antibiotic, along with such things as milk, antacids, or even in combination with another antibiotic, penicillin. Each of these substances inhibits the action of tetracycline so that the infection being treated with tetracycline is not controlled. A person

taking penicillin should not be given other antibiotics, such as chloramphenicol or tetracycline, or antacids or milk, because of the same inhibiting effects of these materials. The effectiveness of oral contraceptives may also be decreased by enzyme induction (see Chapter 4). Liver enzyme induction occurs from taking barbiturates, diphenylhydantoin (Dilantin®), ampicillin, sedatives, and tranquilizers, and from exposure to halogenated insecticides (Martin, 1971). A final example is that of taking antihistamines and hydrocortisone at the same time. Hydrocortisone is taken for arthritis, and antihistamines cancel its therapeutic effect.

Potentiation Effects

The third type of drug interaction is often called *potentiation* (enhancement). In this case, the combination of the drugs results in a greater effect for each drug than it would have by itself. This interaction can be quite complex. The effect of one drug may be enhanced because of stimulation of specific enzymes, or formation of more potent metabolites, or unknown reasons. A well-known example is that of alcohol and barbiturates. It has been estimated that as many as 3000 people die each year from mixing barbiturates and alcohol. Alcohol is a CNS depressant, and when a barbiturate, also a depressant, is taken, the person becomes groggy. A person in this state may forget he or she has taken the pills and repeat the dose. The combination of these two depressants can depress the CNS to the point where vital functions such as breathing and heartbeat will cease. An alcoholic becomes tolerant to barbiturates, but it has been found that a single large dose of alcohol will temporarily block metabolism of barbiturates, producing a potentially dangerous situation (Rubin & Lieber, 1971).

In one example of potentiation, a housewife living in suburbia awoke with a cold, so she took aspirin and an antihistamine. In order to face coping with young children and the new day she took a "nerve pill" (tranquilizer). She also took her oral contraceptive and a diet pill to help her lose weight. Then she drove her husband to the railroad station, and on the way home she wrapped her car around a tree. She had taken a combination of drugs that depressed her central nervous system, and blacked out.

Another potentiation effect for which the cause was only recently discovered is triggered by the mixing of certain antidepressant drugs with particular foods. Cases of stroke and of hemorrhaging were reported when this group of drugs was first released. Then it was found that if the antidepressant, a monoamine oxidase inhibitor (Chapter 2) such as Nardil®, Parnate®, or Marplan®, is taken along with ripe cheese, beer, red wine, or even pineapple, the controls of blood pressure are inhibited to a point that allows the blood pressure to rise to an extremely high level. These foods contain tyramine, which is a "pressor" (a substance that elevates blood pressure). The elevated levels of tyramine potentiate with MAO inhibitors to increase blood pressure markedly.

Aspirin decreases the coagulating time of the blood—that is, the blood clots more slowly. If a person is taking an anticoagulant drug to prevent heart attacks or blood clotting and takes aspirin too, there may be severe bleeding. Oral contraceptives also affect anticoagulants. In some cases, if a woman were to take both, the dosage of the anticoagulant might have to be increased because the estrogen content of the oral contraceptive caused increased levels of clotting factors and thereby decreased the anticoagulant action. Other women may experience the opposite effect—that is, increased anticoagulant action. One interaction with serious consequences involves the combined use of oral contraceptives: women who smoke and take oral contraceptives greatly increase the probability of thromboembolism (obstruction of a blood vessel by a clot).

Although drug effects and interactions are not very well understood, we hope it is clear how important it is for us to know more about them. There is more and more evidence that many of the chemicals we deliberately take, whether prescribed or not, will act on one another and produce unexpected effects. It is frightening to know that many of the foods we eat and some chemical pollutants interfere with and modify drug actions. Pesticides, traces of hormones in meat and poultry, traces of metals in fish, nitrites and nitrates from fertilizers, and the wide range of chemicals used as food additives all have been shown to interact with some drugs. This interaction remains one of the important problems concerning pharmacologists as well as each and every one of us. (See Table 5-2, on the following four pages, for some of the more common interactions.)

TABLE 5-2 A guide to common drug interactions (Graedon, 1976; Martin, 1971)

Tranquilizers	Combined with	Interaction
Librium®, Valium®, Serax®, Miltown®	Alcohol	Increases effects of both
	Barbiturates	Increases effects of both
	MAO-inhibiting antidepressants (Nardil®, Parnate®, Marplan®, Eutonyl®)	Oversedation
	Oral contraceptives	May decrease effectiveness of contraceptive
	Phenothiazine tranquilizers (Thorazine®, Compazine®)	Increases effects of both
	Tricyclic antidepressants (Elavil®, Aventyl®, Tofranil®, Pertofrane®)	Increases effects of both
Phenothiazines (Thorazine®, Mellaril®, Compazine®)	Alcohol	Oversedation
	Antihistamines	Increases effects of both
	Antihypertensive drugs	Increases blood pressure-lowering action
	Barbiturates	Increases sedation
	MAO-inhibiting antidepressants (Nardil®, Parnate®, Marplan®, Eutonyl®)	Makes antidepressant less effective
	Demerol®	Increases sedation
	Tranquilizers (Valium®, Librium®)	Increases action of both
	Thiazide diuretics (Diuril®, Hydrodiuril®)	Increases blood pressure-lowering of both, could cause shock
	Tricyclic antidepressants (Elavil®, Aventyl®, Tofranil®, Pertofrane®)	Increases action of both

Antibiotics	Combined with	Interaction
Tetracycline (Aureomycin®, Panmycin®, Terramycin®)	Penicillin, antacid, or milk products (milk, cheese, ice cream, custard), almonds	Makes tetracycline less effective
Penicillin G	Chloramphenicol (Chloromycetin®), antacids, or tetracycline	Makes penicillin less effective

TABLE 5-2   *(continued)*

Antibiotics	Combined with	Interaction
Erythromycin (E-Mycin®, Erythrocin®)	Fruit juice, vitamin C	Makes antibiotic less effective
Griseofulvin (Fulvicin®, Grisactin®)	Anticoagulant	May make anticoagulant less effective
	Phenobarbital	Makes griseofulvin less effective
Sulfonamide	Antacid	Makes sulfa less effective
	Anticoagulant	Makes anticoagulant more potent
	Antidiabetics (Dymelor®, Orinase®, Diabinese®)	Makes antidiabetics too powerful

Analgesics	Combined with	Interaction
Aspirin	Anticoagulants (Coumadin®, Dicoumarol®, Miradon®)	Increases blood-thinning effect and could cause uncontrolled bleeding
	Arthritis medication (Butazolidin®)	Antagonizes, irritates stomach
	Oral antidiabetics (Diabinese®, Dymelor®, Orinase®, Tolinase®)	Hypoglycemia (blood sugar lowered too much)
	P-aminosalicylic acid (PAS)	Makes PAS toxic
Meperidine (Demerol®)	MAO-inhibitor antidepressants (Nardil®, Parnate®, Marplan®, Eutonyl®)	Increases action of Demerol®
	Phenothiazine tranquilizers (Thorazine®, Stelazine®)	Increases sedation
Phenylbutazone	Anticoagulant	Increases the blood-thinning effect and could cause bleeding
	Oral antidiabetics (Orinase®, Diabinese®)	May make the blood sugar too low

TABLE 5-2   *(continued)*

Antihistamines	Combined with	Interaction
Diphenhydramine (Benadryl®), chlorpheniramine (Chlor-Trimetron®), dimenhydrinate (Dramamine®), promethazine (Phenergan®)	Alcohol	Increases sedation
	Barbiturates	Nullifies both
	Hydrocortisone	Lessens effect of hydrocortisone
	Phenothiazine tranquilizers (Thorazine®, Compazine®)	Increases effects of both
	Reserpine	Depresses central nervous system
	Anticholinergics (slows intestinal movement)	Makes anticholinergic more potent

Oral Contraceptives	Combined with	Interaction
Estrogen-containing	Arthritis medication (Butazolidin®)	May increase metabolism of contraceptive
	Barbiturates (phenobarbital, Seconal®)	Lessens hormone activity by enzyme induction
	Chlordane, DDT	Lessens hormone activity by enzyme induction
	Tranquilizers (Librium®, Valium®)	Lessens hormone activity by enzyme induction

Alcohol	Combined with	Interaction
	Antidepressants, tricyclic (Aventyl®, Tofranil®)	Depresses CNS further; lethal combination
	Antidiabetics, including insulin	May lower blood sugar to a dangerous level
	Antihypertensives	Potentiates blood pressure lowering
	Barbiturates (Seconal®)	Potentiates sedative effect and CNS depression; potentially lethal
	Methaqualone (Quaalude®, Parest®)	Potentiates CNS depressant effect
	Tranquilizers (Librium®, Valium®, chlorpromazine, Compazine®)	Potentiates CNS depressant effect

TABLE 5-2   *(continued)*

Foods	Combined with	Interaction
Milk and dairy products	Some antibiotics like tetracycline	Inhibits absorption of drug
Aged cheese, chocolate, bananas, pineapple, tomatoes, beer, wine	MAO inhibitors (Nardil®, Marplan®, Parnate®) Parnate®)	Causes high blood pressure when taken with tyramine-containing foods
Soybean preparations, brussel sprouts, cabbage, turnip, carrots, pears	Thyroid extracts	Will block action (if any of these foods is eaten in large amounts, it may enlarge thyroid gland and interfere with basal metabolic tests)
Licorice (large amounts)	Diuretics (Esidrix®, Diuril®, Lasix®) Cortisone	Causes excretion of potassium. Can cause heartbeat changes and even heart attacks; especially dangerous if digitalis or other heart stimulants are used

Antidepressants	Combined with	Interaction
MAO inhibitors	Amphetamines	Increases amphetamine effect
	Barbiturates	Barbiturates are more potent
	Diuretics (Diuril®, Hydrodiuril®)	Lowers blood pressure
	Oral antidiabetics (Diabinese®, Dymelor®, Orinase®, Tolinase®)	Enhances hypoglycemic effect
Tricyclic antidepressants (Elavil®, Tofranil®)	Anticonvulsant medication (for epilepsy)—Dilantin®, Ekko®	Increases rate of seizures
	Alcohol	Profound sedation

Diuretics	Combined with	Interaction
Aldoril®, Diuril®, Esidrix®, Hydrodiuril,®, Buthiazide®	Cortisone (Aristocort®, Decadron®, Prednisone®)	Increased loss of potassium so heart muscle is influenced
	Oral antidiabetics (Diabinese®, Dymelor®, Orinase®, Tolinase®)	May interfere with medication so blood sugar could remain high or be depressed too much

CHAPTER 6

THE HALLUCINOGENS

CHAPTER OBJECTIVES

1. Compare and contrast the effects of hallucinatory doses of mescaline, MDA, and DOM as examples of compounds that probably influence norepinephrine neurotransmission.
2. List the anticholinergic alkaloid drugs found in the potato family, and describe the general effects on the body of low and high doses.
3. Compare and contrast the effects of hallucinatory doses of psilocybin, DMT, *Amanita muscaria*, morning glories, and nutmeg as examples of compounds that probably influence serotonin neurotransmission; list the active ingredients in each.
4. Discuss the use of hallucinogens such as MDA and LSD as aids in psychotherapy.
5. Describe the effect of LSD on creativity.
6. List the range of observed LSD experiences.
7. Discuss the occurrence of psychoses and flashbacks following LSD use.
8. Describe the physiological effects of LSD on the brain and on the body, including the possibility of genetic damage and birth defects.
9. Defend the following statement: street drugs are often not what they are sold as. Give examples.
10. Define the following terms: hallucinogen, psychotomimetic, psychedelic, peyote, mescaline, mescal, synesthesia, mayapple, soma, and ergotism.

We have drunk the Soma and become immortal!
We have attained the light, we have found
the Gods!
What can the malice of mortal man
or his spite, O Immortal, do to us now?
Rig Veda, book VIII, 48
(Sanskrit hymns, 1500 B.C.; Trans.
R. Panikkar, 1977) *

The preceding poem, or chant, provides evidence of the early use of drugs and gives some insight into the feelings the people had about the drugs. Some researchers believe *soma* may have been the mushroom *Amanita muscaria,* which causes hallucinations. Others believe soma was hashish or even nutmeg preparations. People have known and written about hallucinations for centuries. Many people throughout the ages perceived a person who saw visions or experienced hallucinations as a holy or sacred individual, or possibly bewitched. There are many indications that some of the medicine men, shamans, witches, oracles, and perhaps mystics and priests of various groups knew how to induce hallucinogenic experiences.

Through the years, peoples of the Americas have used over 130 plants that are psychoactive, but strangely enough the rest of the world has used only about 20 additional plants. Because there is no reason to believe that the Americas are richer in plants with psychoactive properties that the Old World, the reason for their extensive use of such plants may be cultural (Schultes & Hofmann, 1973). Probably the oldest record we have of hallucinogens in the western hemisphere is from a 4500-year-old grave of a South American Indian. In the grave were found his snuff tube (the *tabaco* that gave tobacco its name; see Figure 6-1) and some snuff. This type of

snuff is still being used today by some native tribes in that region and is called *cohoba snuff.* We know that cohoba snuff has the active ingredient dimethyltryptamine (DMT), which is a fairly potent hallucinogen.

In the 1940s through the 1960s, after LSD became available, people thought that this and similar drugs induced a model psychosis, and the term *psychotomimetic* was coined. Psychotomimetic means *psychosis-mimicking,* a term that is still used in medicine today, even though LSD and similar drugs do not precisely mimic psychoses. From the late 1940s through the 1950s psychiatrists in Europe took LSD in training sessions to better understand their psychotic patients and the nature of the disease. Technically LSD and other similar powerful drugs do not induce true hallucinations but rather induce illusions, although the difference between the two phenomena is slight. (A few people use the term *illusinogenic* for these drugs.) In 1957 a Canadian physician coined the term *psychedelic* (mind manifesting), which is a fairly descriptive term for these drugs. The psychedelic drugs have the capacity to induce or compel states of altered perception, thought, or feeling not otherwise experienced except in dreams or mystical exaltation (Jaffe, 1980).

We have organized the discussion of the hallucinogens into three sections according to the neurotransmitter they are thought to affect most: *norepinephrine, acetylcholine,* or *serotonin. Dopamine,* a neurotransmitter related to norepinephrine, may be influenced by some of these hallucinogens. Some of the psychoactive agents probably influence more than one neurotransmitter, but this method of organization can help keep in mind the more important mechanisms through which they work. The first type of hallucinogen has psychoactive chemicals that are similar in structure to norepinephrine; mescaline and the synthetic compound DOM, or STP,

---

* Copyright 1977 by Raimundo Panikkar; reprinted by permission of the University of California Press and Darton, Longman, and Todd, Ltd.

FIGURE 6-1
Indian using a *tabaco,* or snuff
tube.

are examples (Appendix A-2). The second type of drug is structurally similar to acetylcholine and may influence acetylcholine neurotransmission. This group of drugs includes such hallucinogens as henbane, nightshade, *Datura,* and a few others. These drugs are sometimes called the *anticholinergics,* because neurons that release acetylcholine are called *cholinergic neurons* (see Chapter 2). The third type of hallucinogenic drug may structurally mimic serotonin's indole structure and cause the body to react as if more, or in some cases less, serotonin were released from its neurons. The effects of hallucinogens on neurotransmitters are summarized in Table 6-1.

HALLUCINOGENS THAT MAY INFLUENCE ADRENERGIC NEUROTRANSMITTERS

Mescaline (Peyote)

Mescaline, from the peyote cactus (Figure 6-2), has been used for centuries in the Americas. One of the first reports on the peyote plant was made by Dr. Francisco Hernandez of the court of King Philip II of Spain. King Philip was interested in reports from the earlier Cortez expedition about strange medicines the natives used, and sent Hernandez to collect information about herbs and medicines. Hernandez worked on this from 1570–1575. He finally reported the use of more than 1200 plant remedies and of many hallucinogenic plants. He was one of the first to record the eating of parts of the peyote cactus and the resulting visions and mental changes.

La Barre (1970) describes the importance of this cactus to the Aztecs and to other Mexican Indians today. The cactus is usually harvested in November in a ritual ceremony. Arrows are shot into the cactus from at least three sides and sometimes from five sides. The cactus symbolizes the sacred deer, which is not killed but immobilized when hit with the three to five arrows. Women as well as men may participate in the ceremony, although the group usually has more men because of the arduous pilgrimage that is made to collect the plants. The top of the cactus is sliced into sections, called *buttons,* but the root is left intact so that the plant can regenerate. The root also represents the symbolic new life of the deer.

Peyote has been confused with mescal shrub, which produces dark red beans that contain an extremely toxic alkaloid called *cytisine.* This alkaloid may cause hallucinations, convulsions, and even death. There is also a mescal liquor, made from the agave cactus, which further adds to the confusion. Partly because of misidentification with the toxic mescal beans, the U.S. government outlawed the use of peyote and mescaline. This was not the first time authorities placed restrictions on the use of peyote. The Spanish missionary Padre de Leon directed priests to ask their Indian converts to confess to the use of peyote, which he believed they used to conjure up demons. De Leon was the priest who boastfully informed the Pope that he had burned all the Mayan codex manuscripts, which were records of their culture and history for a thousand years—because, he claimed, they were records of pagan rites.

However, nothing stopped the use of peyote, and there is evidence that it had spread by 1760 into what is now the United States. At present, there are an estimated quarter of a million Native Americans who follow a religion that is a com-

TABLE 6-1   Effects of the hallucinogens on neurotransmitters

Neurotransmitter	Hallucinogen
Norepinephrine (NE)	Mescaline, LSD decrease brain NE
Dopamine (DA)	MDA depletes NE, DA
	LSD, DOM mimic DA (psilocin, DMT, and 5-methoxyDMT do not)
Acetylcholine (Ach)	Scopolamine (hyoscine), hyoscyamine, atropine block Ach receptor sites
Serotonin (5-hydroxytryptamine, or 5-HT)	LSD, psilocin, DMT, 5-methoxyDMT, DOM, myristicin, and mescaline block 5-HT release
GABA (gamma aminobutyric acid)	Muscimol mimics GABA

FIGURE 6-2
The peyote cactus. The plant contains a number of drugs; the best known is mescaline.

bination of Christian doctrine and Native American religious rituals. They are located as far north as Canada. Peyote plays a central role in their ceremonies because they believe God made a special gift of this sacramental plant to the natives of this continent, so they might commune more directly with him. The first organized peyote church was the First-Born Church of Christ, incorporated in 1914 in Oklahoma. The Native American Church of the United States—a group that combines Christianity and the traditional beliefs and practices of Native Americans—was chartered in 1918 and is the largest such group at present. The articles of incorporation proclaim its function as follows:

The purpose for which this corporation is formed is to foster and promote religious believers in Almighty God and the customs of the several Tribes of Indians throughout the United States in the worship of a Heavenly Father and to promote morality, sobriety, industry, charity, and right living and cultivate a spirit of self-respect and brotherly love and union among members of the several Tribes of Indians throughout the United States . . . with and through the sacramental use of peyote. [La Barre, McAllester, Slotkin, Stewart, & Tax, 1951]

In 1918 bills were submitted to Congress to prohibit the use of peyote by Native Americans, but they were not passed. Federal and state legal battles over this issue ensued for half a century, until the Supreme Court finally heard the case of a Native American convicted of using the plant and ruled that Native Americans could use it within the confines of their religion.

More than 30 psychoactive chemicals have been isolated from peyote cactus. It appears that mescaline is the most active and is the one that induces intensified perception of colors and euphoria in the user (Appendix A-2). However, as Aldous Huxley said in *The Doors of Perception* (1954), his book about his experimentation with mescaline: "Along with the happily transfigured majority of mescaline takers there is a minority that finds in the drug only hell and purgatory." After Huxley related his experiences with mescaline, it was used by an increasing number of people.

Effects of Mescaline

The average dose of mescaline that will cause hallucinations and other physiological effects is from 300 to 600 milligrams (an aspirin is about 325 milligrams). It may take up to 20 peyote buttons to get 600 milligrams of mescaline (which is quite an amount!). Effects include dilation of the pupils (mydriasis), increase in body temperature, anxiety, visual hallucinations, and alteration of body image. The last effect is a type of hallucination in which parts of the body may seem to disappear or to become grossly distorted. Mescaline induces vomiting in many people, and some muscular relaxation (sedation). Apparently there are no aftereffects or drug hangover at low doses.

High doses induce cardiac depression, headaches, slowing of respiratory rhythm, contraction of the intestines and the uterus, difficulty in coordination, dry skin with itching, and hypertension (high blood pressure). It is estimated from animal studies that from 10 to 30 times the lowest dose that will cause behavioral effects in humans may be lethal (about 200 milligrams is the lowest mind-altering dose). Death in animals results from convulsions and respiratory arrest. Mescaline is perhaps 1000 to 3000 times less potent than LSD, and 30 times less potent than psilocybin.

It is typically reported that the mescaline user loses all awareness of time. As with LSD, the setting for the "trip" influences the user's reactions. Most mescaline users prefer nature settings. The visual hallucinations depend on the individual. Colors are at first intensified and may be followed by hallucinations of shades, movements, forms, and events. The senses of smell and taste are enhanced. Some persons claim (as with LSD) that they could "hear" pretty colors or "see" sounds, such as the wind. "Cross-sensing" is called *synesthesia*. This phenomenon occurs naturally in a small percentage of people.

At low to medium doses an ecstatic state of euphoria is reported. This feeling of elation is often followed by a feeling of anxiety, and less frequently by depression. The user often observes him- or herself as two people and experiences the sensation that the mind and body are two separate entities. A number of people have had cosmic experiences that are profound, almost religious, in which they discover a sense of unity with all creation. People who have had this experience believe they have discovered the value and meaning of existence. Almost every drug capable of altering the state of consciousness has occasionally produced this reaction in people—even philosophers (William James) and Supreme Court justices (Oliver Wendell Holmes)—but, unfortunately, relatively few have this beneficial experience using mescaline or other drugs.

Mescaline's Mode of Action

Within 30 to 120 minutes after ingestion mescaline reaches a maximum concentration in the brain, and the drug may remain in the brain up to 9 or 10 hours. Hallucinations may last up to two hours and are dependent to some extent on the dose level. About half the dose is excreted unchanged in about 6 hours and can be recovered for reuse. A slow tolerance builds up after repeated use, and there is cross-tolerance to LSD. As with LSD, mescaline intoxication can be alleviated or stopped by a dose of chlorpromazine (Thorazine®, a major tranquilizer) and to a lesser extent with diazepam (Valium®, a minor tranquilizer).

Mescaline acts at least partly by decreasing brain levels of norepinephrine, although its effects are not as strong or consistent in this regard as those of LSD. In addition, mescaline alters the turnover of serotonin, thus increasing the amount in brain tissue. LSD also increases serotonin, probably by depressing the release of the neurotransmitter. Mescaline does not appear to affect all the tryptaminergic neurons, unlike LSD and DMT (Bridger, Barr, Gibbons, & Gorelick, 1978). Serotonin, believed to function as a neurotransmitter, is found almost exclusively within neurons of the raphe nuclei. These nuclei are clusters of neurons on the midline of the brainstem that send some of their axons to portions of the visual cortex and to portions of the limbic system. The visual and the limbic systems are known to be important in emotional experience and expression. Thus altering the activity of these neurons is thought to be the basis for the effects of hallucinogens like mescaline and LSD.

Analysis of street samples of "mescaline" in a number of cities in the United States over the past decade shows that the chemical sold rarely is mescaline. Regardless of the color or appearance it usually is a form of LSD, DOM, or PCP. Occasionally someone will submit an authentic sample of the plant material for analysis, but this is rare. Real psilocybin is even less frequently found, and there is no such thing as "street" THC—analysis shows no active cannabinol, just LSD, PCP, or some similar drug. Table 6-2 lists some typical street drugs, includ-

ing what they were sold as and what they actually were.

If a person has already made a decision to take hallucinogenic or other street drugs, "let the buyer beware." Not only is the actual content often different and potentially much more toxic than the person bargained for, but the dosage is often not known even if the drug is genuine. Impurities are a serious problem with drugs made in illegal laboratories. These include unwanted by-products from faulty procedures and deliberate contamination with potentially dangerous materials (for example *Datura* in marijuana, strychnine in LSD), as well as dirt from handling and manufacture. Methamphetamine may be the street drug most contaminated with toxic materials: benzene, ether, and chloroform used in manufacture, as well as mercury, methylamine, and other chemicals. "Liquid" methamphetamine has been shown to contain human urine and a toxic floor cleaner (Dishotsky, Loughman, Mogar, & Lipscomb, 1971). Most street labs don't have very high standards of quality control or inspection.

MDA (3,4-methylenedioxy-amphetamine)—The Love Drug

MDA was first synthesized in 1910 and is structurally related to both mescaline and amphetamine (Appendix A-2). The drug is usually classified as a hallucinogen, but it also has some stimulatory characteristics. In early research it was found that MDA is an anorexiant (causing loss of appetite) and is a mood elevator in some persons.

On the street the drug has often been called the "love drug" because of its effects on the sense of touch and the attitudes of the people taking it. People who take this drug usually report experiencing a sense of well-being and heightened tactile (touch) sensations and thus increased

TABLE 6-2 Street drugs sold in Chicago in summer 1980*

Alleged content	Actual content	Description	Origin	Street price
LSD (25–500 mcg)	LSD (10 samples)	Clear (windowpane), chocolate windowpane, blue microdots, blotter acid	Chicago	$1–$2
THC	LSD (8 samples)	Small pink or red pill	Unknown	$1–$5
Mescaline	LSD (4 samples)	Brown to tan powder	Unknown	$1–$2
Cannabinol	PCP (4 samples)	White powder	Canada	$1–$2
Psilocybe mushroom	LSD (2 samples)	LSD dropped on it	California	$1–$2
Methaqualone and antihistamine	Sopor® (4 samples)	Blue pills	Detroit or Canada	$1–$2
Superpot	Marijuana and PCP (2 samples)	Marijuana with a spray giving a green color	California	$1–$2
Methamphetamine	Speed (2 samples)	White cross pill (homemade)	Unknown	$1
Biphetamine or black widow	Speed (1 sample)	Black capsule, plain	Unknown	$1
Marijuana	Marijuana (25 samples)	Most was called Colombian or Jamaican	Unknown	$25–$35 per oz
Cocaine	Cocaine plus additives (6 samples)	White powder ranging from 5%–20% cocaine, plus additives (lidocaine, amphetamine, quinine, and so on)	Florida	$80–$150 a gram

*There were many other pharmaceutical drugs sold, for example, Valium®. Most of these samples were apparently taken from legitimate sources, although some were given other street names. Source: Drug Enforcement Administration, Department of Justice, Washington, D.C.

pleasure through sex and expression of affection. The MDA experience is usually devoid of the visual and auditory distortions that mark the LSD experience. Those under the influence of MDA often focus on interpersonal relationships and demonstrate an overwhelming desire or need to be with or to talk to people. The unpleasant side effects most often reported are nausea, periodic tensing of muscles in the neck, tightening of the jaw and grinding of the teeth, and dilation of the pupils (mydriasis). Some users said they had a very pleasant "body high"—more sensual than cerebral and more empathic than introverted. Research shows that the mode of action of MDA is similar to that of amphetamine in some respects. It may cause extra release of norepinephrine and block reabsorption of the norepinephrine for a period of time. It also depletes dopamine. Just how the drug modifies brain activity is not known.

MDA has been used as an adjunct to psychotherapy. All eight volunteers in one study had previously experienced the effects of LSD under clinical conditions. Four of the eight were given 150 milligrams of MDA individually; each partner of one married couple was given 150 mg; and each partner of another married couple was given an additional 40 mg after the first hour. Effects of the drug were noted between 40 and 60 minutes following ingestion by all eight subjects. The subjective effects following ingestion peaked at the end of 90 minutes and persisted for approximately eight hours. None of the subjects experienced hallucinations, perceptual distortions, or closed-eye imagery, but they reported that the feelings the drug induced had some relationship to those previously experienced with LSD. The subjects found that both drugs induced an intensification of feelings, increased perceptions of self-insight, and heightened empathy with others during the experience. Most of the subjects also felt an increased sense of esthetic enjoyment at some point during the intoxication. Seven of the eight subjects said they perceived music as "three dimensional." In an earlier study of patients taking this drug, the authors reported that nearly half of the subjects had spontaneous reminiscences of childhood experiences but experienced no hallucinations (Naranjo, Shulgin, & Sargent, 1967).

Street doses of MDA range from 100 to 150 milligrams per dose. Serious convulsions and death have resulted from larger doses, but these are cases of use of street MDA that was not accurately measured. Ingestion of 500 milligrams of pure MDA has been shown to cause death. The only adverse reaction to moderate doses seems to be marked physical exhaustion, lasting as long as two days. This is thought to be caused by a depletion of the central nervous system neurotransmitters norepinephrine and dopamine (Marquardt, DiStefano, & Ling, 1978). The unpleasant MDA experience, if it occurs, should be treated the same as a bad trip with any hallucinogen—this involves talking the person down in as friendly and supportive a situation as possible. It may also be necessary to have medical attention. Under the Comprehensive Drug Abuse Prevention and Control Act of 1970, MDA is classified legally as a dangerous substance, and illegal possession is a serious offense.

DOM or STP (Dimethoxymethylamphetamine)

Although the basic structure of DOM is amphetamine (Appendix A-2), we discuss it here because it is a fairly powerful hallucinogen that seems to work through mechanisms similar to those of mescaline and LSD. DOM probably mimics the effect of dopamine and depresses the activity of serotonin-containing neurons (Jacobs

& Trulson, 1979). Doses of less than 3 milligrams produce heartbeat increases, pupil dilation, and increased blood pressure and body temperature. It causes a mild euphoria that may last from 8 to 12 hours, with peak reactions around the third to fifth hours. Street doses—measured in cities such as Chicago and San Francisco—averaged 10 milligrams, which is considered a very large dose that would cause trips lasting from 16 to 24 hours. These long trips would be more likely to cause panic reactions.

DOM produces a higher incidence of acute and chronic reactions than any of the other commonly used hallucinogens, with the possible exception of PCP. The effects of DOM are like a combination of amphetamine and LSD, with the hallucinogenic effects of the drug very often putting the peripheral amphetaminelike physiological effects out of perspective. (Peripheral—outside the central nervous sytem—effects of amphetamine may include headache, sweating, irregular heartbeat, nausea, vomiting, diarrhea, increased breathing rate, and pain and difficulty in urination.) As with LSD and mescaline, chlorpromazine will ease the experience of the long trip very rapidly, but it can also interfere with breathing. Bourne (1976) recommends using Valium® because there are fewer shock reactions than with chlorpromazine (Thorazine®, for example).

HALLUCINOGENS THAT MAY INFLUENCE ACETYLCHOLINE: THE ANTICHOLINERGICS

This group includes some of the naturally occurring drugs that have been known for many centuries. These drugs are often mentioned in folklore and in early literature as being used in "potions." They were probably used to kill the Roman emperor Claudius and to poison Hamlet's father, because they were the favorites throughout the ages to poison inconvenient people. (However, one of the problems in using anticholinergic drugs to poison people is that the victim usually turns bright red—a dead giveaway, as it were.) Hallucinogens affecting the cholinergic neurons were probably used in witchcraft to give the illusion of flying, to prepare sacrificial victims for cutting out their hearts, and even to give some types of marijuana its kick. Some types of "superpot" have been found to have had *Datura* compounds added, which are anticholinergic.

Curiously enough, it is the potato family of plants (Solanaceae) that includes the large variety of plants that contain most of these mind-bending drugs. Three in particular are potent compounds: (1) scopolamine, or hyoscine, (2) hyoscyamine, and (3) atropine (Appendix A-3). Scopolamine may produce excitement, hallucinations, and delirium even at therapeutic doses, whereas with atropine, doses bordering on the toxic are usually required to obtain these effects. The drug atropine (see the following section) is actually a mixture of the two stereochemical forms of hyoscyamine and may not occur naturally in the plant (Schultes & Hofmann, 1973). All of these active alkaloid drugs are acetylcholine antagonists (see Chapter 4). They occupy the acetylcholine receptor site but do not activate it, which renders it unusable by blocking it.

These alkaloid drugs are used as ingredients in cold-symptom remedies because they block production of mucus in the nose and throat (see Chapter 16). They also prevent salivation, so that the mouth becomes uncommonly dry, and perspiration may stop. Atropine may increase the heart rate by 100% and may dilate the pupils markedly, causing inability to focus on nearby objects.

The anticholinergics depress the reticular

activating system (see Chapter 2) and slow the brain waves, as shown on an electroencephalogram (EEG), considerably. At larger doses, a condition occurs that is similar to a psychosis, in which there is delirium, loss of attention, mental confusion, and sleepiness. Hallucinations may also occur at higher doses. At very high doses, paralysis of the respiratory system may cause death.

The Deadly Nightshade:
Atropa belladonna

Knowledge of this plant is very old, and its use as a drug is reported in early folklore. The name of the genus, Atropa, indicates the reverence the Greeks had for the plant: Atropos was one of the three Fates in Greek mythology, whose duty it was to cut the thread of life when the time came. This plant was one used for thousands of year by poisoners. In the Tales of the Arabian Nights, unsuspecting potentates were poisoned with atropine, or a relative of it. Fourteen berries of the deadly nightshade contain enough of the drug to cause death.

The species name, belladonna, means "beautiful woman." This name derives from the practice of putting a few drops of an extract of this plant into the eyes, causing the pupils to dilate. The early Roman and Egyptian women knew that girls with large pupils were considered attractive and friendly. (This perception was proved in recent times by using identical photos of women, altered only by retouching the pupils of the eyes, and showing them to experimental subjects.) Belladonna has also had a reputation as a love potion.

According to legend, witches are supposed to be able to fly. One of the recipes reputed as having the potential to give a witch the power to fly was the following: Take fat of babe (or lamb), juice of water parsnip, aconite (monks-

hood), cinquefoil, deadly nightshade, and soot of fire, and apply to the skin with the proper incantation (Schleiffer, 1979). Just what are the active ingredients in this witches' brew (other than the power of suggestion, an important factor in inducing the trip)? The water-parsnip juice is hemlock, the poison the Greeks used to put Socrates to death. Aconite is a plant of the buttercup family, called monkshood, with bright blue flowers (it contains the poison that killed Romeo). In small doses, the poison aconitine will cause irregular heartbeat and mild delirium. The deadly nightshade contains hyoscyamine and scopolamine, which have many effects on the body and mind. The fat makes the active materials stick to the skin (Schleiffer, 1979).

Witches' potions were used in the Black Mass, or Sabbat. This ceremony was a fertility rite in which those who took active part wore a wooden phallus, or dildo, and smeared themselves and the phallus with the witches' potion. In a short time, because the active ingredients could be absorbed into the bloodstream through breaks in the skin and across the vaginal wall, participants felt themselves "carried in the aire, to feasting, singing, dansing, kissing, culling and other acts of venerie, with such youthes as they loue and desire most" (Briggs, 1962). The sensation of flying may have come from the irregular heartbeat, the feeling of drowsiness, and the power of suggestion combined with jumping over the fire. Some of the women who took part brought their brooms as anointed phallic symbols; perhaps this gave rise to the idea that witches ride broomsticks.

The Mandrake:
Mandragora officinarum

The mandrake contains several active alkaloids: hyoscyamine, scopolamine, atropine, and mandragorine. As mentioned in Chapter 1, the mandrake has been used as a love potion for centuries. The root of the mandrake is forked and, viewed with a little imagination, may resemble the human body. Because of this resemblance it has been credited with human attributes, which has given rise to many superstitions. Shakespeare used this in *Romeo and Juliet:* in her farewell speech, Juliet says, "and shrieks like mandrakes torn out of the earth, that living mortals hearing them run mad."

The mayapple, found in the central United States, is sometimes called a mandrake. The chemicals in the mayapple, however, are not related to those of the mandrake, nor is the plant hallucinogenic. Its extract is used as a caustic to remove skin growths and as a purgative (laxative) (Claus, Tyler, & Brady, 1970).

Henbane: *Hyoscyamus niger*

Henbane is a plant that contains both hyoscyamine and scopolamine. In 60 A.D. Pliny the Elder spoke of henbane: "For this is certainly known, that if one takes it in drink more than four leaves, it will put him beside himself" (Jones, 1956). De Ropp has written about the use of henbane in the orgies and Bacchanalias of the ancient world:

These plants were undoubtedly used in the ancient world in connection with orgiastic rites characterized by sexual excesses. Thus at the Bacchanalia, when the wild-eyed Bacchantes with their flowing locks flung themselves naked into the arms of the eager men, one can be reasonably certain that the wine which produced such sexual frenzy was not a plain fermented grape juice. Intoxication of this kind was almost certainly a result of doctoring the wine with leaves or berries of belladonna or henbane. The orgiastic rites were never totally suppressed by the Church and persisted in secret forms through the Middle Ages. Being under the shadow of the

Church's displeasure, they are inevitably associated with the devil, and those who took part in them were considered to be either witches or wizards. [1957]

Jimsonweed: *Datura stramonium*

The *Datura* group of the Solanaceae family includes a large number of related plants that are found worldwide. The principal active component in this group is scopolamine; there are also several less active alkaloids. These plants are mentioned in early Sanskrit and Chinese writings and were revered by the Buddhists. There is also some indication that the priestess (oracle) at the ancient Greek temple of Apollo at Delphi was under the influence of *Datura* when she made prophecies (Schultes, 1970). Prior to the supposed divine possession, she appeared to have chewed leaves of the sacred laurel. There was also reported to be a mystic vapor that arose from a fissure in the ground. The sacred laurel may have been one of the *Datura* species and the vapors may have come from burning these plants, although Lewin (1931) thought the sacred laurel might have been henbane. (He based this on the ancient names for the plant and his knowledge of its hallucinogenic ingredients.)

The plant shown in Figure 6-3, *Datura stramonium,* was used by the Algonquin Indians for a problem we seem to be greatly concerned with today—solving identity crises in teenagers. Their ceremony of entry into manhood has been described:

The youths are confined for long periods, given no other substance but the infusion or decoction of some poisonous, intoxicating roots . . . they became stark, staring mad, in which raving condition they were kept eighteen or twenty days. . . . Thus they unlive their former lives and commence manhood by forgetting that they

FIGURE 6-3
Datura stramonium, or jimsonweed. This common plant
contains the hallucinogenic
drug scopolamine.

ever have been boys. [Schultes & Hofmann,
1973]

The jimsonweed gets its name from an incident that took place in the 17th century at
Jamestown. The British soldiers were trying to
capture Nathaniel Bacon, who had made seditious remarks about the king. Beverly describes
what happened:

The James-Town Weed . . . is supposed to be
one of the greatest Coolers in the World. This
being an early Plant, was gather'd very young for

a boil'd Salad, by some of the Soldiers sent
thither, to pacifie the Troubles of Bacon; and
some of them eat plentifully of it, the Effect of
which was a very pleasant Comedy; for they
turn'd natural Fools upon it for several Days:
One would blow up a Feather in the air; another
wou'd dart Straws at it with much Fury; and
another stark naked was sitting up in a Corner,
like a Monkey, grinning and making Mows at
them; a Fourth would fondly kiss, and paw his
Companions, and snear in their Faces, with a
Countanance more antick, than any in a Dutch
Droll. In this frantick Condition they were confined, lest they should in their Folly destroy

themselves; though it was observed, that all their Actions were full of Innocence and good Nature. Indeed, they were not very cleanly; for they would have wallow'd in their own Excrements, if they had not been prevented. A thousand such simple Tricks they play'd, and after Eleven Days, return'd to themselves again, not remembering any thing that had pass'd. [1947]*

Some authorities now believe that the reason that the marijuana used in Vietnam was more potent than usual is that it was treated with *Datura*. Its effects were similar to those induced by *Datura*, although pot smoked in Vietnam often had opium and even heroin added to it. Because *Datura* grows wild, it is widely available. Until the late 1960s one could buy, without prescription, cigarettes made of a mixture of chopped *Datura* leaves for alleviating asthma. This mixture does shrink the mucosal membranes, but too large a dose can be dangerous. The preparation, called Asthmador, has been banned from the market.

THE SEROTONIN-INFLUENCING (INDOLE) HALLUCINOGENS†

Psilocybin

Psilocybin is a drug that has a long and rich history. It was first used by some of the early natives of Central America, more than 2000 years ago. In Guatemala statues of large mush-

---

*From *The History and Present State of Virginia*, by Robert Beverly and edited by Louis B. Wright. Copyright 1947 by the University of North Carolina Press. Published for the Institute of Early American History and Culture, Williamsburg, Virginia.

†See Chapter 10, The Depressants, for a discussion of phencyclidine (PCP).

rooms that date back to 1000 A.D. have been found. The Aztecs later used the mushroom for ceremonial rites. Hernandez was the first White man to note the hallucinogenic properties of the mushroom that we today call *psilocybin*. When the Spaniards came into Mexico in the 1500s, the natives were calling the *Psilocybe mexicana* mushroom "God's flesh." Because of this seeming sacrilege they were harshly treated by the Spanish priests.

Gordon Wasson identified the *Psilocybe mexicana* mushroom (Figure 6-4) in 1955. The active ingredient was extracted in 1958 by Dr. Albert Hofmann, a Swiss chemist, who is probably best known for his synthesis of LSD (Appendix A-4). Hofmann wanted to make certain he would detect the effects of the mushroom, so he ate 32 of them, weighing 2.4 grams—a medium dose by Indian standards—then recorded his reactions. His experience illustrates how the personality of the drug taker and the setting can influence a drug's effects.

Thirty minutes after taking the mushrooms the exterior world began to undergo a strange transformation. Everything assumed a Mexican character. As I was perfectly well aware that my knowledge of the Mexican origin of the mushroom would lead me to imagine only Mexican scenery, I tried deliberately to look on my environment as I knew it normally. But all voluntary efforts to look at things in their customary forms and colors proved ineffective. Whether my eyes were closed or open, I saw only Mexican motifs and colors. When the doctor supervising the experiment bent over to check my blood pressure, he was transformed into an Aztec priest, and I would not have been astonished if he had drawn an obsidian knife. In spite of the seriousness of the situation it amused me to see how the Germanic face of my colleague had acquired a purely Indian expression. At the peak of the intoxication, about 1½ hours after ingestion of the mushrooms, the rush of interior pictures,

FIGURE 6-4
The *Psilocybe* mushroom, source of psilocybin and psilocin.

mostly abstract motifs rapidly changing in shape and color, reached such an alarming degree that I feared that I would be torn into this whirlpool of form and color and would dissolve. After about six hours the dream came to an end. Subjectively, I had no idea how long this condition had lasted. I felt my return to everyday reality to be a happy return from a strange, fantastic but quite really experienced world into an old and familiar home. [Hofmann, 1968]*

---

*From "Psychotomimetic Agents," by A. Hofmann. In A. Burger (Ed.), *Drugs Affecting the Central Nervous System*, Vol. 2, pp. 169–235. New York: Marcel Dekker, Inc. This and all other quotations from this source are reprinted by permission.

The dried form of these mushrooms contains from 0.2% to 0.5% psilocybin. The hallucinogenic effects of psilocybin are quite similar to those of LSD, and there is a cross-tolerance between them as well as between psilocybin and mescaline. The drug was synthesized in 1958, but it is not very common on the street.

The effects vary with the dosage taken. Up to 4 milligrams will cause a pleasant experience, relaxation, and some body sensation. In some subjects, higher doses cause considerable perceptual and body-image changes, with hallucinations. It stimulates the autonomic nervous system, causing mydriasis, piloerection, and hyperthermia. There is some evidence that psilocybin is changed into psilocin, which is more potent and may be the active ingredient. Some psilocin is found in the mushroom but in rather small amounts. Psilocin acts to block the release of serotonin, but unlike LSD it is not a dopamine agonist (mimic) (Jacobs & Trulson, 1979). Like the other hallucinogens, psilocybin apparently causes no physical dependence.

Dimethyltryptamine (DMT)

DMT is a short-acting hallucinogen found in the seeds of certain leguminous trees native to the West Indies and parts of South America (Schultes, 1978). For centuries the powdered seeds have been used as a snuff, called *cohoba*, in pipes and snuffing tubes. The Haitian natives claim that under the influence of the drug they can communicate with their gods. Its effects may last under one hour, and, because of this, it has sometimes been called the businessman's lunch-break drug. It is also prepared synthetically in illicit laboratories (Appendix A-4).

Because the drug has no effect when taken orally, it is inhaled either as smoke from the burning plant or in vaporized form. DMT is sometimes added to parsley leaves or flakes, to tobacco, and to marijuana in order to induce its hallucinogenic effect. The usual dose is 60 to 150 milligrams. It does not cause physical dependence. In structure and in action it is similar to psilocybin, although it is not as powerful. It is also similar to its chemical relative DET (diethyltryptamine), except that the effects of DET may last two to three hours.

Bufotenin

Bufotenin was first discovered in the dried skin glands of certain toads (Appendix A-4). It is present in the *Amanita muscaria* mushroom as well as many higher plants and animals. It can be made synthetically. When injected, it causes sweating and a rapid increase in blood pressure. Intravenous bufotenin is not hallucinogenic, although it was originally reported to be. It was supposed to be the hallucinogenic ingredient in several types of snuff used by South American natives, but the active compound in these substances was later found to be dimethyltryptamine. Bufotenin probably also does not contribute to the psychotomimetic activity of cohoba snuff. One reason is that bufotenin does not cross the blood-brain barrier as DMT does. Although it was reported to be present in the urine from schizophrenic patients, later studies have found that it is not present in urine from schizophrenics in greater amounts or with greater frequency than from normal people (Barchas, Berger, Matthysse, & Wyatt, 1978; Schultes & Hofmann, 1973).

Amanita muscaria (The Fly Agaric)

An unusual type of mushroom with an ancient history (Figure 6-5) can be found in Scandinavian and Eurasian countries. It is sometimes called the *fly agaric* mushroom, because, in the Middle Ages and earlier, flies were associated with madness. People who were "possessed" were believed to be infested with flies. The mushroom also has weak insecticidal properties: flies will suck the juice and go into a drunken stupor for two to three hours.

Human consumption of five to ten amanita mushrooms will cause severe effects of intoxication, such as muscular twitching, leading to jerking and twitching of the limbs, raving drunkenness with agitation, and vivid hallucinations. Later, as the drug wears off, there will be partial paralysis with sleep and dreams for hours (Claus et al., 1970).

Native tribes in Siberia developed a conservative custom of using *Amanita muscaria*. Because most of the hallucinogen passes through the body and is excreted in the urine unchanged, it can be recovered and reused four to five times. (This may provide an explanation for the verse in the *Rig Veda* in which priests are described as urinating soma.) Thus even the lowliest servants could partake of the drug, although they had to get it second-, third-, or fourthhand (Schleiffer, 1979).

Because bufotenin is found in the *Amanita muscaria*, it was once thought that it might be the potent active chemical in the mushroom. However, the amount of bufotenin contained in the mushroom is small and it has since been shown that bufotenin is probably not hallucinogenic. Several other chemicals—muscimol, ibotenic acid, and muscarine—have been isolated from *Amanita muscaria*. The first two chemicals have effects similar to the effects of LSD on neurotransmitters in the brains of experimental rats and mice. Pure muscimol is more potent as a hallucinogen than ibotenic acid in human volunteers and is excreted unchanged in the urine. Muscimol is used experimentally as an agonist (mimicking agent) for GABA, which is an amino acid thought to

FIGURE 6-5

The *Amanita muscaria*, sometimes called the *fly agaric*,
mushroom yields hallucinogenic drugs. This mushroom
may be the *soma* described in
the *Rig Veda*.

function as an inhibitory neurotransmitter in
the brain. Muscarine is a cholinergic agonist
that causes mushroom poisoning. It is found in
higher concentrations in various species of *Ino-
cybe* and *Clitocybe* mushrooms than in *Amanita
muscaria*. Muscarine poisoning causes nausea,
vomiting, headaches, visual disturbances, slowed
heart rate, and shock, but not hallucinations.

The Morning Glories (Ololiuqui)

The ancient Aztecs and Mayan Indians apparently knew that some of the morning glories and
their relatives had hallucinogenic properties.
When the priests wanted to commune with their
gods and to receive messages, they ate the seeds
of *Rivea corymbosa* (ololiuqui), which is still used

today in divinatory and healing rituals in Oax-
aca. Hernandez reported in the 1500s that the
seeds were not reserved for the priests alone,
but were used medicinally to cure flatulence, to
remove venereal troubles, to deaden pain, and
to alleviate tremors.

Dr. Hofmann analyzed the seeds of various
varieties of morning glories and found they contained several relatives of LSD, including the
monoamine form. This form of lysergic acid, as
compared to the diethylamine of LSD, was a
curiosity because until 1960 no one believed
that lysergic acid was found in any plants other
than some types of fungus, such as the ergot
fungus from which LSD was originally made.
However, several common garden varieties of
morning glories, such as "Heavenly Blue" and
"Pearly Gates," contain ergoline alkaloids. These

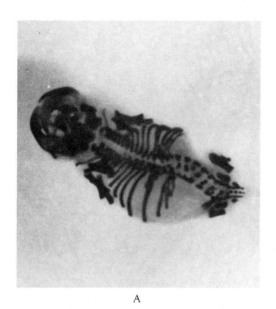
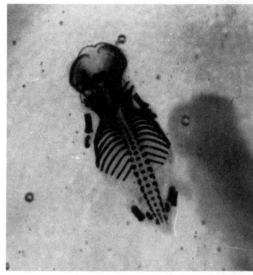

A   B

FIGURE 6-6
(A) Fetus from mouse given 1000 micrograms of elymoclavine, from morning glories, on day 9 of pregnancy. Note fused ribs and vertebrae. (B) Control mouse fetus, with normal ribs and vertebrae. Mother given control injection.

same alkaloids are also found in other members of the Convolvulacea plant family, such as the Hawaiian wood rose, sometimes in higher concentrations (Schultes, 1978).

Consumption of 100 to 300 morning glory seeds will produce hallucinatory effects, although this is variable. The dose needed to induce a trip depends on the age and variety of the seeds and the conditions under which they were stored. The visual hallucinations follow a stage of dizziness and one of a general feeling of well-being and drowsiness. The effects may last for several hours, often ending in stupor. Eating morning glory seeds can cause perceptual distortion, confusion, diarrhea, and severe anxiety. Cases of "morning glory psychosis" and an occasional related suicide have been recorded. Seeds sold in the United States may be coated with a fun-

gicide, such as Thiram, so that sprouts are more likely to survive, and so people will not eat the poisoned seeds. The ergoline alkaloids can act as teratogens, causing skeletal malformations (Figure 6-6).

Nutmeg and Mace

High doses of nutmeg can be quite intoxicating. Its symptoms are drowsiness, stupor, delirium, and sleep, which are the reasons for its abuse. Prison inmates have known about this drug for years, so in most prisons spices are prohibited beyond certain controlled areas. Two tablespoonsful of nutmeg (about 14 grams) are reported to cause a rather unpleasant trip with a dreamlike stage, rapid heartbeat, a dry mouth and thirst. Agitation, apprehension, and a sense of impending doom may last about 12 hours, with a sense of unreality persisting for several days (Claus et al., 1970).

Nutmeg contains 5% to 15% myristica oil, which is responsible for the physical effects. Myristicin (about 4%), which is structurally similar to mescaline, and elemicin are probably the most potent psychoactive ingredients in nutmeg. Myristicin blocks release of serotonin in raphe nucleus neurons. It is believed that myristicin can be converted in the body to MMDA (a close relative of MDA), which also affects the central nervous system. Mace, the exterior covering of the nutmeg seed, also contains myristicin.

Lysergic Acid Diethylamide (LSD)

History of LSD

LSD is a relatively new drug, but its chemical relatives have been known for a long time. In the Middle Ages accounts were written about a strange affliction that caused women to abort and people to develop strange burning sensations in their extremities. Today we call this condition *ergotism* and know that it is caused by eating grain contaminated by the ergot fungus.

The ergot fungus, *Claviceps purpurea*, grows on grain, especially rye, in damp weather and produces a group of compounds related to LSD (the ergot alkaloids) as well as a number of other compounds. The fungus forms a black mass on the grain which an Assyrian tablet dated 600 B.C. called a "noxious pustule in the ear of grain." The contaminated grain would not be eaten except by accident or in periods of famine.

Ingestion of a sufficient amount of ergot alkaloids induces specific symptoms, depending on the amount of chemical eaten. Lower dosages cause tingling, burning sensations under the skin of the extremities, along with muscle tremors and convulsions (convulsive ergotism). The person may hallucinate and hear imaginary sounds. Mental disturbances include mania, delirium, and psychosis. Higher dosages cause a more serious condition (gangrenous ergotism) in which the tissue in the feet, legs, hands, and arms becomes dry and black. The mummified limbs eventually fall off without loss of blood. The gangrene is the result of the action of the lysergic acid compounds on the smooth-muscle layers of blood vessels. These chemicals are known as *vasoconstrictors*: they cause a constriction or squeezing of the muscles of the blood vessels, which in turn shuts off circulation of the blood to the tissue. If the tissue is not supplied soon with nutrients and oxygen, it starts to die.

In the 12th century ergotism was called *St. Anthony's fire* because of the burning sensations it caused and also because people believed that the disease could be cured through the intercession of St. Anthony. It is not known how this belief originated, but by making a pilgrimage to the shrine of St. Anthony in Egypt the sufferers left the contaminated grain behind, thus eliminating the cause of their disease.

In Salem, Massachusetts, in 1692, several girls and women were tried as witches and condemned to death. This peculiar, isolated occurrence has never been adequately explained. Nonetheless, the hallucinations and physical symptoms of the so-called witches closely resemble those of convulsive ergotism. The farmers in Salem grew rye for breadmaking. Analysis of the records of weather conditions in 1691–1692 shows that the damp weather favored growth of the ergot fungus (Caporael, 1976).

Ergot is grown today by pharmaceutical companies. The vasoconstrictive alkaloids are used in treatment of migraine headaches and to help expel the placenta and control hemorrhage following childbirth.

In 1938, in the Sandoz Pharmaceutical Laboratories of Basel, Switzerland, Dr. Albert Hofmann was working on a series of ergot compounds in a search for active chemicals that might be of medical value. Lysergic acid was similar in structure to a compound called *nikethamide,* a stimulant, and Hofmann was trying to create slight chemical modifications that might be worth further testing. Following synthesis of the diethylamide derivative of lysergic acid, he noted nothing unusual about the product, so he stored it in a bottle on the laboratory shelf. In 1943 he was checking over some of the synthetic compounds he had worked on and started making further tests of LSD. Most organic chemists are remarkably careless about avoiding skin contact with and breathing the fine powder from crystalline compounds, and a small amount must have entered his blood. He noted that:

> Last Friday, April 16, 1943, I was forced to stop my work in the laboratory in the middle of the afternoon and to go home, as I was seized by a peculiar restlessness associated with a sensation of mild dizziness. Having reached home, I lay down and sank in a kind of drunkenness which was not unpleasant and which was characterized by extreme activity of imagination. As I lay in dazed condition with my eyes closed (I experienced daylight as disagreeably bright), there surged upon me an uninterrupted stream of fantastic images of extraordinary plasticity and vividness and accompanied by an intense, kaleidoscope-like play of colors. This condition gradually passed off after about two hours. [Hofmann, 1968]

Hofmann realized the experience was probably caused by the chemical he had been working with and decided to try a measured amount on himself. If the minute amount he had unwittingly taken caused the sensations he recorded, he thought 250 micrograms might be enough to prove the chemical's effects. Hofmann was to find out that LSD is one of the most potent drugs known. As low as 50 "mikes" can affect some people. This is the record of the first deliberate LSD trip:

> 4:20 P.M.: 0.5 cc (0.25 mg LSD) ingested orally. The solution is tasteless.
> 4:50 P.M.: no trace of any effect.
> 5:00 P.M.: slight dizziness, unrest, difficulty in concentration, visual disturbances, marked desire to laugh . . . [at this point the laboratory notes are discontinued]

The last words could only be written with great difficulty. I asked my laboratory assistant to accompany me home as I believed that my condition would be a repetition of the disturbance of the previous Friday. While we were still cycling home, however, it became clear that the symptoms were much stronger than the first time. I had great difficulty in speaking coherently, my field of vision swayed before me, and objects appeared distorted like images in curved mirrors. I had the impression of being unable to move from the spot, although my assistant told me afterwards that we had cycled at a good pace . . .

By the time the doctor arrived, the peak of the crisis had already passed. As far as I remember, the following were the most outstanding symptoms: vertigo; visual disturbances; the faces of those around me appeared as grotesque, colored masks; marked motor unrest, alternating with paresis; an intermittent heavy feeling in the head, limbs and the entire body, as if they were filled with metal; cramps in the legs, coldness and loss of feeling in the hands; a metallic taste on the tongue; dry constricted sensation in the throat; feeling of choking; confusion alternating between clear recognition of my condition, in which state I sometimes observed, in the manner of an independent, neutral observer, that I shouted half insanely or babbled incoherent words. Occasionally I felt as if I were out of my body.

Six more hours after ingestion of the LSD-25 my condition had already improved considerably. Only the visual disturbances were still pronounced. Everything seemed to sway and the proportions were distorted like the reflections in the surface of moving water. Moreover, all objects appeared in unpleasant, constantly changing colors, the predominant shades being sickly green and blue. When I closed my eyes, an unending series of colorful, very realistic and fantastic images surged in upon me. A remarkable feature was the manner in which all acoustic perceptions (for example, the noise of a passing car) were transformed into optical effects, every sound causing a corresponding colored hallucination constantly changing in shape and color like pictures in a kaleidoscope. At about 1 o'clock I fell asleep and awakened next morning somewhat tired but otherwise feeling perfectly well. [Hofmann, 1968]

Some researchers noted the similarity of LSD experiences to schizophrenic episodes and started active investigations into correlations between the two. They hoped to use LSD as a tool for producing an artificial psychosis, to aid in understanding the biochemistry of psychosis. However, interest in this use of LSD has declined because it is now generally accepted that LSD effects are different from natural psychoses. LSD has been used as an aid in psychotherapy and treatment of alcoholism. A few investigators find it very helpful in treating selected patients (Grof, 1976), whereas others do not believe the hallucinogen has any role in psychotherapy or treatment of alcoholism (Sellers & Kalant, 1978).

Nonmedical interest in LSD and related drugs began to grow during the 1950s, primarily among experimenters in the academic, professional, and artistic fields. The drug gained notoriety in the early 1960s as a result of experimentation by two Harvard University psychology professors, Drs. Richard Alpert and Timothy Leary, who invited others to "turn on, tune in, and drop out" of the existing social institutions. Their unorthodox religious orientation to the LSD experience is presented in a manual called *The Psychedelic Experience*, which is based on the *Tibetan Book of the Dead* (Leary, Metzner, & Alpert, 1964). This manual became the bible of the psychedelic drug movement. Another significant influence on this movement—one with considerably less religious orientation—was writer Ken Kesey's group, whose adventures are documented in a book called *The Electric Kool-Aid Acid Test* (Wolfe, 1968).

Leary had tried some psilocybin mushrooms in Mexico in 1960; apparently the experience influenced him greatly. On his return to Harvard he carried out a series of experiments using psilocybin with student groups. Leary was careless in experimental procedure and did some work in uncontrolled situations, which caused a major administrative upheaval ending in Leary's and Alpert's leaving Harvard.

One of the questionable studies was the Good Friday experiment in which 20 theological students were given either a placebo or psilocybin in a double-blind study; after which all attended the same two-and-one-half hour Good Friday service. The experimental group reported mystical experiences, whereas the control group did not (Pahnke & Richards, 1966). Leary believed that the experience was of value and that under proper control and guidance the hallucinatory experience could be beneficial.

In 1966 Leary started his religion, the League of Spiritual Discovery, with LSD as the sacrament. The movement grew, but most of the members used street LSD and did not follow the principles set up by Leary. In 1966 Leary addressed this problem:

> Turning on correctly means to understand the many levels that are brought into focus; it takes years of discipline, training and discipleship. To turn on on a street corner is a waste. To tune in means you must harness rigorously what you are learning . . . to drop out is the oldest message that spiritual teachers have passed on. You can get only by giving up.

Leary was convicted for possession of marijuana and LSD; he escaped to Algeria and spent several years wandering before he was extradited back to the United States. He served another few years before being released, when he claimed he was totally rehabilitated and would never again advocate the use of hallucinogens. Richard Alpert also went through a transition, described in his book, *Be Here Now,* while he was studying under the guidance of a guru in India. His guru renamed him Ram Dass (servant of God). He now has a following in the United States, where he is called Baba Ram Dass, and he spends time talking to many groups and holding meditative retreats. He now recommends the meditative "high" (see Chapter 20).

The Use of LSD in Psychotherapy

LSD has been tried in cases of alcoholism, autism, paranoia, schizophrenia, and various other mental and emotional disorders. Therapeutic use of LSD has not increased to any great extent over the years because of its limited success, legal aspects, difficulty in obtaining the pure drug, adverse reactions to the drug (bad trips can occur under controlled as well as uncontrolled conditions), and the problems of rapid tolerance buildup in the patient.

When LSD is used in therapy, it is used in one of two ways: as *psychedelic* therapy or as *psycholytic* therapy. Psychedelic therapy is a specialized form of intensive therapy on a one-time basis. A dose of 200 micrograms or more is used to create a typical LSD experience, in which it is hoped that the patient will be able to look at his or her problems from an altered perspective. This type of therapy is used with patients who have a basic loss of self-respect, self-esteem, and self-image, in the hope that the drug experience will enable them to realize there is no basis for their negativity. To be successful, this type of therapy must be preceded by extensive preparation for several weeks prior to therapy. In addition, the setting must be extremely supportive, including such things as special music, lighting, pictures, and so forth. A trained therapist must remain with the patient continuously during the treatment, which will take from 10 to 12 hours on the average. The therapist must shape, direct, and guide the direction of the session. He or she also provides reassurance, averts anxiety, and is responsible for the success of the experience. The session is followed with supportive therapy to help redirect the patient. Not all psychedelic therapy is effective, and bad trips have been known to happen under the most positive circumstances (Grof, 1976).

The second type of LSD therapy, psycholytic therapy, involves using a lower dose (50–70 micrograms) repeatedly over a number of sessions. This low, nonhallucinogenic dosage appears to facilitate recall, catharsis, and other reactions that may aid in psychoanalysis. In rationalizing the nonmedical use of LSD, one cannot cite the beneficial effects of either psychedelic or psycholytic therapy.

A little work has been done with administration of hallucinogenic doses of LSD to people in the final stages of terminal illness. When done with preparation by a trained therapist, this treatment seems to help these patients face their imminent death.

Effect of LSD on Creativity and Insight

The question usually raised by people interested in experimenting with LSD is: does it help expand the mind, and can it increase insight and creativity? This is an extremely difficult question to answer because no one has ever determined the origin of insight and creativity. Creativity is a mixture of mood, perception, and thought—and abilities that are inherent in the person–and is not easily judged.

Many subjects under the influence of LSD have expressed the feeling of being more creative, but the acts of drawing or painting, for example, are hindered by the motor effects of LSD. The products of creative artistic effort under the influence of the drug largely prove to be inferior to those produced by that artist prior to the drug experience. Paintings done in LSD-creativity studies have been described as reminiscent of schizophrenic art.

McGlothin, Cohen, and McGlothin (1967) tested 24 college students and found—through the use of creativity, attitude, and anxiety tests—that three LSD sessions, each of about 200 micrograms, had no objective effect of enhanced creativity six months later. However, many of the subjects said they *felt* they were more creative. This paradox is noted in several studies of LSD use: the subjects feel they have more insight and have better answers to life's problems, but they do not or cannot demonstrate this increase objectively. Overt behavior is not modified, and these new insights are short-lived unless they are reinforced by modified behavior (Cohen, 1978).

Psychological Effects of LSD

What is the nature of the "typical" LSD experience? There is no typical pattern. It varies for each user as a function of the person's set, or expectations, and setting, or environment, during the experience. The major responses are described as follows (Pahnke, Kurland, Unger, Savage, & Grof, 1970):

1. The *psychotic adverse reaction*, or *freak-out*. This is an intense, nightmarish experience to the point where the subject may have complete loss of emotional control, paranoid delusions, hallucinations, and catatonic seizures—in some instances, these reactions are prolonged.

2. The *nonpsychotic adverse reaction*. In this case, there may be varying degrees of tension, anxiety, fear, depression, and despair. This is not as intense a response as the first-mentioned reaction. A person with buried psychological problems or a strong need to be in conscious control, or one who takes the drug in an unfavorable setting, is more likely to have an adverse reaction than a person with a well-integrated personality.

3. The *psychodynamic psychedelic experience*. This experience may show emergence of unconscious or submerged ideas or behavior. Strong emotional feelings can accompany what may be experienced subjectively as a reliving of incidents from the past or a symbolic portrayal of important conflicts, which are often sought in LSD psychotherapy.

4. The *cognitive psychedelic experience*. In this instance, there is an impression of astonishingly clear thought, and problems can be seen from novel perspectives. Most subjects at this stage claim to see the interrelationship of many levels of meaning and to understand it.

5. The *esthetic psychedelic experience*. This experience entails a change in sensory impressions, which are also usually intensified. Fascinating alterations in sensation and perception, and synesthesia, may occur. Inanimate objects, such as ripples on water, may come alive. Ordinary things may become highly unusual and beautiful. One may also see intricate geometric forms and patterns.

6. The *psychedelic peak*—a cosmic, or mystical experience. Experiences at this level include a sense of unity or cosmic oneness with the universe, a feeling of being able to transcend time and space, a deeply felt joy, blessedness and peace, sacredness, awe and wonder, religious awareness, and a belief that the experience is above words, nonverbal, and impossible to describe. The use of LSD to achieve this experience is well described by Pahnke and Richards (1966). The peak experience does not happen in many individuals; it is usually fast moving and its full intensity does not last long. People who have experienced it recall this experience in a positive fashion months later, and some have claimed it initiated a change in their approach to life.

Prolonged psychoses caused by LSD are considered quite rare, but the incidence increases with casual use by persons with poorly integrated personalities. Psychiatrists who have used LSD as an adjunct to therapy find the drug puts the user in a hypersuggestible state, and vast changes in the user's perception and mood occur when the atmosphere is changed from supportive and friendly to impersonal and remote. Thus it is not surprising that persons who were not stable to begin with may, after LSD ingestion, become psychotic and require hospitalization for some time. Chronic anxiety following LSD use is usually self-limited, so it is difficult to assess the true proportion of prolonged bad reactions. When medical treatment is sought for adverse effects of LSD, is usually consists of psycho-

therapy and tranquilizers. If the person does not respond to this, electroconvulsive treatments may be used (Cohen, 1978).

Perceptual Effects of LSD

A person on a hallucinogenic dose of LSD cannot process the sensory information coming into the brain, so he or she reports many kinds of unusual illusions, such as shifting geometrical patterns along with intense color perception. Some subjects report movement of stationary objects and misinterpret sights, so that a speck on the wall may be seen as a large eye or an unfolding flower. Sounds are also perceived differently in the hallucinogenic state. For example, a dropped ashtray may be perceived as a gun being fired at the subject. Subjects often experience a heightened sense of touch and modified senses of taste and smell, depending on the mood and setting. A particular sensation may be either the best or the most disgusting one ever experienced.

For many people the sense of time is distorted, and hours may be perceived as years or an eternity. Unfortunately LSD can alter perceptions to the extent that a few people may feel they can walk on water or fly. Attempts at suicide are not as common as thoughts about suicide. Frequently the person on LSD is convinced his or her ideas are unique, great insights, and brilliant or creative deductions. When analyzed by a person not on LSD, however, or explained after the trip is over, these ideas are almost always quite ordinary. One of the most commonly reported effects, especially for a novice to LSD, is the sensation that the body is distorted and even coming apart.

The Flashback

Sometimes LSD causes *flashbacks*, during which the subjective sensations caused by LSD return, although the subject is not currently using the drug. The visual distortions and the subjective sense of time distortion seem to be the most common flashback sensations. The flashback is disturbing because it is unexpected when it occurs, and it is probably most upsetting to the person who had an unpleasant experience with the drug. Flashbacks have been known to last from a few minutes to several hours and to occur up to 18 months after the use of LSD. Their cause is not known. Physical or psychological stresses and certain drugs like antihistamines may also trigger flashbacks. Treatment consists of reassurance that the condition will go away and use of a minor tranquilizer if necessary to control anxiety (Cohen, 1978).

Genetic Damage and Birth Defects

Some researchers have been concerned about possible chromosomal damage in the cells of LSD users. Damaged chromosomes in actively dividing somatic cells might cause an increased risk of cancer in those cells. If the chromosomes in the male's sperm-forming cells or the rapidly dividing cells in the embryo in a pregnant woman were affected, birth defects might result. The first study in this area was done on human white blood cells and is now considered a rather poorly controlled and analyzed study of in vitro (in glass, or test tube) chromosomes. This and subsequent studies showed chromosomal breaks, attributed to LSD, in animal and human white blood cells, in cells taken from a fetus conceived by LSD users, and in animal fetuses experimentally exposed to LSD during various stages of pregnancy. However, later, more carefully controlled studies have not found such changes (Dishotsky, Loughman, Mogar, & Lipscomb, 1971).

There are a large number of chemicals and conditions that will cause chromosomal break-age in white blood cells in vitro, such as changes in temperature, oxygen pressure, antibiotics, water (unless it is distilled twice), and so on. For example, aspirin and LSD cause equal rates of chromosomal breakage in vitro. Because the body detoxifies substances, and because the in vitro damage occurs with high concentrations and/or long exposure times, the results obtained in vitro probably do not predict the effects of pure LSD in the human. In studies on blood cells taken from the same person before and after treatment with pure LSD, there was no effect on the chromosomes. Chromosomal damage in users of street drugs is probably due to other factors, such as contaminants and the known high rates of hepatitis and other viral illnesses, not to LSD (Dishotsky et al., 1971).

Numerous studies report no carcinogenic or mutagenic effects in experimental animals or humans, with the exception of the fruit fly. LSD is a mutagen in fruit flies if given in doses that are equivalent to 100,000 times the hallucinogenic dose for humans. Teratogenic effects occur in mice if LSD is given early in pregnancy. LSD may be teratogenic in rhesus monkeys if it is injected at doses (based on body weight) exceeding by least 100-fold the usual hallucinogenic dose in humans. Women who took street LSD, but not those given pure LSD, had a higher rate of spontaneous abortions and births of malformed infants. Still, the frequency of birth defects in street-LSD users is not significantly higher than it is in the general population (Dishotsky et al., 1971).

Physiological Effects of LSD

In its purified form LSD is a colorless, odorless, tasteless compound. It is remarkably potent: one ounce contains about 300,000 adult human doses. However, it is rather low in toxicity. In monkeys, the lethal dose has been determined to be about 5 milligrams per kilogram of body weight. In the rat the lethal dose (expressed as LD-100, which means it kills 100% of the test animals) is about 20 milligrams per kilogram. Strangely enough, one of the most sensitive animals to LSD is the elephant, and the next is the rabbit. One man gave an elephant a dose equal to about ½ milligram per kilogram; it keeled over and died of respiratory shock. The LD-50 for humans is estimated at 150 to 200 times the hallucinogenic dose.

When taken orally, LSD is readily absorbed and diffuses into all tissues. It will pass through the placenta into the fetus and through the blood-brain barrier. The brain receives about 1% of the total dose. Within the brain, the hypothalamus, the limbic system, and the auditory and visual reflex areas take up high concentrations. Electrodes placed into the limbic system show an electrical storm, or a massive increase in neural activity, which might explain the overwhelming flood of sensations and the phenomenon of synesthesia reported by the user. LSD also activates the sympathetic nervous system: shortly after the drug is taken the body temperature and blood pressure rise, the person sweats, and the pupils of the eyes become dilated (mydriasis). Its effects on the parasympathetic nervous system cause the increase in salivation and nausea. Tolerance to the effects of LSD develops more rapidly and lasts longer than tolerance to other hallucinogens.

The mechanism by which LSD produces the visual, auditory, and other distorted perceptions is not known. The serotonergic neurons become inactive when an animal is given LSD or when LSD is applied directly to the neurons. There is evidence that LSD blocks serotonin release by neurons in the brain and probably competes for receptor sites with the neurotransmitter. Adjacent neurons, normally inhibited by the sero-

tonergic neurons, thus might become hyperactive. (Other hallucinogens that produce similar psychic effects, such as psilocin and DMT, have similar chemical structures and also depress serotonergic neurons; see Table 6-1.) This might set the stage for hallucinations because the normal processing of sensory input from internal and external sources is upset.

LSD may affect the normal balance of norepinephrine, dopamine, and serotonin in the reticular activating system of the brainstem. In addition to its effect on serotonin, LSD may also mimic the action of dopamine. DOM has similar effects on serotonin and dopamine. Thus the most potent hallucinogens may be those that both inactivate brain serotonin and mimic brain dopamine (Jacobs & Trulson, 1979). As described in Chapter 2, the reticular formation is an arousal center that monitors and regulates the sensory input both from inside and outside the body. There may be as much as ten times the sensory input from our internal environment as from outside the body (the sounds of the heartbeat, of the blood pushing through capillaries, of the muscles in the rib cage and abdomen involved in breathing; tactile stimuli from all the points of contact of skin with clothing; from all the temperature sensory receptors, and so on). Most of this input never reaches the level of consciousness. If the filtering and integration of the reticular system is upset by LSD, the whole integration of information is upset and incorrect interpretation of impulses can occur. These distorted interpretations of sensory experience are called illusions or hallucinations.

Experiments with radioactive LSD show that about half of it is cleared from the body within 3 hours, and more than 90% is excreted within 24 hours. Tolerance develops quickly to repeated doses, probably because of a change in sensitiv-

THE SEROTONIN-INFLUENCING (INDOLE) HALLUCINOGENS

ity of the target cells in the brain rather than a change in liver enzymes. Tolerance wears off within a few days after the drug is discontinued. Because there are no withdrawal symptoms, a person does not become physically dependent but can become psychologically dependent on LSD (Cohen, 1978).

CHAPTER 7

MARIJUANA

CHAPTER OBJECTIVES

1. State the conclusions of the Indian Hemp Drug Commission, the Panama Canal Zone Report, and the LaGuardia Committee.
2. Describe changes in the frequency and extent of marijuana use in the United States.
3. Explain why it is difficult to relate blood levels of tetrahydrocannabinol to behavioral or physiological effects of the drug.
4. Discuss experimental factors affecting interpretation of psychological and intellectual damage following chronic, heavy use of marijuana.
5. List and discuss the immediate (short-term) and long-term effects of marijuana on the body.
6. Describe effects of marijuana on driving performance.
7. Discuss the occurrence of psychoses and flashbacks following cannabis use.
8. List potential therapeutic uses of marijuana and synthetic cannabinoids.

HISTORY OF MARIJUANA

No other drug today has been the object of so much controversy as has cannabis (marijuana, pot). Even the origin of the word *marijuana* (or *marihuana*) is debatable: it may come from either a Portuguese or a Spanish word meaning *intoxicating*. The resin from the plant has been used for thousands of years, but its pharmacological effects are still not completely clear. As you read about the history of marijuana, you will learn about the variety of cultures that have used it and abused it, and perhaps you will gain a better insight into drug use in general. Given careful research into the biological effects of this drug, perhaps we will finally be able to make intelligent decisions about its use and legalization.

Carolus Linnaeus, a Swedish botanist, classified marijuana as *Cannabis sativa* in 1753. *Cannabis sativa* is a plant that grows readily in many parts of the world. Most botanists agree that there is only one species (*sativa*) and that all the variants (*indica, americana,* and *africana*) belong in that species. Others, however, believe there are three distinct species: *C. sativa, C. indica,* and *C. ruderalis* (Schultes, 1978). *Indica* is considered to have the most potent resin, but climate, soil, and selective plant breeding all influence potency. Cannabis is *dioecious,* meaning that there are male and female plants (Figure 7-1). After the male plant releases its pollen, it usually dies. The world's record marijuana plant was 39 feet tall, and its woody stem was nearly 3 inches in diameter.

In many societies marijuana has been a valued crop. It is often called *hemp,* because the woody fibers of the stem yield a fiber that can be made into cloth and hemp rope. The term *cannabis* comes from the Greek word for hemp. For thousands of years the seeds have been pressed to extract a red oil that was used for medicinal and nonmedical uses. Cannabis was apparently brought into this hemisphere by the Spaniards as a source of fiber and seeds. The plant (both male and female) produces a resin with active ingredients that affect the central nervous system. There are a number of chemicals in the resin; the two or three with psychoactive properties are known as *tetrahydrocannabinols* (THC). In the United States, cannabis has been used for medical purposes for a fairly long time; however, nonmedical uses are relatively new.

The first known record of marijuana use is the book of drugs written about 2737 B.C. by the Chinese Emperor Shen Nung, who prescribed marijuana for the treatment of gout, malaria, gas pains, and absentmindedness. The Chinese apparently had a great deal of respect for the plant, and obtained fiber for clothes as well as medicine from it for thousands of years. They gave it a name that means "valuable" or "endearing"—*ma* (maw). In the 1930s marijuana was still called *ma.*

Around the year 500 B.C. another Chinese book of treatments referred to the medical use of marijuana. However, the plant got a bad name from the moralists of the day, who claimed that youngsters became wild and disrespectful from the recreational use of *ma.* They called it the "liberator of sin" because, under the influence, the youngsters would actually refuse to listen to their elders and do other such scandalous things. Marijuana was banned in China at that time but later was legalized.

India has had a long and varied history of marijuana use. There are indications that it was used thousands of years ago and was an essential part of early Indian religious ceremonies. The well-known *Rig Veda* and other chants describe the use of soma, which some believe was marijuana (as mentioned earlier, others believe it was the *Amanita* mushroom). Early writings describe a ritual of collection of the resin from the plants. After fasting and purification, cer-

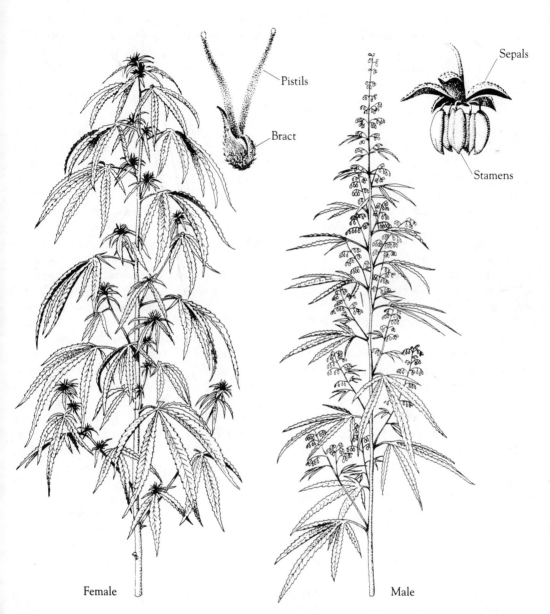

Pistils

Bract

Sepals

Stamens

Female

Male

FIGURE 7-1
Male and female marijuana plants.

tain men ran naked through the cannabis fields. The clinging resin was scraped off their bodies, and cakes were made from it and used in feasts. For centuries missionaries in India tried to ban the use of marijuana, but they were never successful because its use was heavily ingrained in the culture.

Records from Assyria in 650 B.C. referred to a drug called *azulla* that was used for making rope and cloth and also as a euphoric. The ancient Greeks knew about the drug: Galen described the general use of hemp in cakes, which when eaten to excess were narcotic. Herodotus described the Scythian custom of burning marijuana seeds and leaves to produce a narcotic smoke in steam baths; it was known that breathing the smoke from the burning plants would cause frenzied activity. Groups of people stood in the smoke and laughed and danced as it took effect (one of the early "pot roasts"). Pliny the Elder related that the sails and cordage of the Roman galleys were made of hemp. In the 19th century the explorer Burton mentioned African natives burning plants and inhaling the smoke, which seemed to intoxicate them.

One legend about cannabis is based on the travels of Marco Polo in the 12th century. Marco Polo told of the legendary Hasan Ibn-Sabbah, who terrorized a part of Arabia in the early 1100s. His men were some of the earliest political murderers and were supposed to kill under the influence of the drug hashish. The cult was called the *hashishiyya*, from which came the word hashish. The word *assassin* may derive from the name Sheik Hasan. A political leader by that name did live at that time, and so part of the tale may be true. However, it is hard to believe that using hashish would turn people into killers. Experience shows that people would tend to become sleepy and indolent rather than violent killers after eating some of the strong cannabis preparations available in Arabia. Hasan's

men were probably given the drug to relax after they had done their deeds. Authorities on Islamic history say there is no basis for the colorful stories about the use of hashish to drug young men into becoming killers (Abel, 1980).

Napoleon's troops brought hashish to France after their campaign in Egypt at the beginning of the 19th century, even though Napoleon had given strict orders that none was to be brought back. By the 1840s the use of hashish, as well as opium, was widespread in France, and efforts to curb its use were unsuccessful. One of the famous novels of that time, *The Count of Monte Cristo*, by Alexandre Dumas, mentions the use of hashish. In it Dumas, himself an experimenter with the drug, uses the story of the assassins and their use of hashish.

In the 1840s a group of popular literary people and artists in France formed the *Club des Hachichins* (club of hashish users), which had as its goal the search for new experiences and impressions of life. Such notable writers as Gautier, Baudelaire, and Dumas were regular members. Balzac was interested, although he was against the use of drugs. In fact, he warned against using tea, coffee, alcohol, and even sugar. Baudelaire became addicted to opium and later became violently opposed to the use of drugs, even to treat the painful symptoms of tertiary syphilis he was to die from a few years later.

Baudelaire wrote with finesse about his experience with hashish. Although his descriptions are exaggerated in light of what we know today, he did identify certain symptoms of intoxication.

At first, there is a certain absurd, irresistible hilarity that overcomes you. These unprovoked paroxysms of mirth, of which you are almost ashamed, recur frequently, interrupting periods of stupor during which you try in vain to collect yourself. The most ordinary words, the most trivial ideas, assume a new and bizarre aspect

. . . endless puns, and comic sketches keep gushing from your brain. The demon has invaded you; it is useless to resist this hilarity, which racks you like a good tickling. . . . The mirth, the uneasiness you feel even in your joy . . . generally last only a fairly short time. Soon, the relations between ideas become so vague . . . that only your fellows can understand you. . . . The frolics and bursts of laughter, not unlike explosions, seem to be true madness . . . to anyone who is not in the same condition as you. . . . A greater keenness becomes apparent in all the senses. The senses of smell, sight, hearing and touch alike participate. . . . It is then that the hallucinations begin. One by one, external objects slowly assume strange appearances . . . sounds are clad in color, and colors contain a certain music. This, you will say, is only quite natural, and any poetic mind, in its normal state will easily comprehend such analogies. But I have *already* informed the reader that there is nothing exactly supernatural in hashish intoxication: it is only that *now* the analogies assume an unaccustomed vividness . . . the mere contemplation of external objects will cause you soon to forget your own existence, and become inextricably fused with theirs. [Fox, 1971]

The club died out by the 1850s. At this time marijuana use was widespread enough for the psychiatrist Moreau de Tours to advocate it for his students to help them gain insight into mental conditions he believed marijuana intoxication mimicked (Moreau, 1845).

Hemp was planted near Jamestown in 1611 to be used for making rope, but there is no evidence it was used medicinally. By 1630 half of the winter clothing at Jamestown was made from hemp fibers. The hemp plant was also valuable as a source of fiber for clothing and rope for the Pilgrims. To meet the demand for fiber, a law was passed in Massachusetts in 1639 requiring every householder to plant hemp seed. However, it took a great deal of manual labor to get the hemp fiber into usable form, resulting in a chronic shortage of fiber for fish nets, and so on (Abel, 1980).

George Washington had a field of hemp at Mt. Vernon. There is some indication that it was used for medicine as well as for making rope, because Washington once mentioned that he forgot to separate the male and female plants. This separation was usually done because the female plant gave more resin if unpollinated. In the early 1800s U.S. physicians used marijuana extracts for a tonic and as a euphoriant. They did so until 1937, when the Marijuana Tax Act prohibited its use as an intoxicant and regulated its use as medicine.

Most of the abuse of marijuana in the United States during the early part of this century occurred near the Mexican border and in the ghetto areas of the cities. Cannabis was mistakenly considered to be a narcotic, like opium, and legal authorities treated it as such. In 1931 Harry Anslinger, who later would be largely responsible for the enforcement of marijuana laws, thought that the problem was slight, but by 1936 he had claimed that the increase in the use of marijuana was of great national concern (Anslinger & Cooper, 1937).

Some usually accurate magazines reported that marijuana was partly responsible for crimes of violence. In 1936 *Scientific American* reported:

Marijuana produces a wide variety of symptoms in the user, including hilarity, swooning, and sexual excitement. Combined with intoxicants, it often makes the smoker vicious, with a desire to fight and kill.

One of the famous posters of the day, called "The Assassination of Youth," was effective in molding attitudes against drug use (Figure 7-2). Largely as a result of the media's effect on public opinion, Congress passed the Marijuana Tax Act.

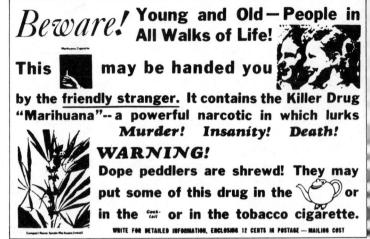

FIGURE 7-2
Antimarijuana poster distributed by the Federal Bureau of Narcotics in the late 1930s.

It was not until 1969 that the Tax Act was declared unconstitutional, and only since 1971 has marijuana not been classified as a narcotic.

Marijuana grows wild in a large number of American states today. Curiously, one of the reasons for this is that during World War II the fiber used to make rope (sisal) was hard to import, so the government subsidized farmers to grow hemp for rope fiber. Much of today's crop comes from these plantings. Another reason for the spread of the plants is that, until recently, the seeds were used in birdseed. Canaries sing better after eating a little THC. Leftover seed was discarded in the garbage and thus spread to landfill dumps, where they sprouted. Birdseed with marijuana seeds is still available, but the seeds are sterilized so they cannot germinate.

The Indian Hemp Drug Commission Report in the 1890s and the 1930s Panama Canal Zone Report on marijuana stressed that available evidence did not prove marijuana to be as dangerous as it was popularly thought, but these reports were given little publicity and were soon forgotten. In 1944, the LaGuardia Committee on Marijuana made its report. This committee consisted of 31 qualified physicians, psychiatrists, psychologists, pharmacologists, chemists, and sociologists appointed by the New York Academy of Medicine. One of the key summaries of the paper stated that marijuana was not the killer that many thought it to be:

> It was found that marijuana in an effective dose impairs intellectual functioning in general. . . . Marijuana does not change the basic personality structure of the individual. It lessens inhibition and this brings out what is latent in his thoughts and emotions but it does not evoke responses which would otherwise be totally alien to him. . . . Those who have been smoking marijuana for a period of years showed no mental or physical deterioration which may be attributed to the drug. [Solomon, 1966]

Much of the early research was done without analyzing the potency of the marijuana used, so the results from one study are difficult to compare with those of another. Because of the large variation in the quality of marijuana, it is impossible to know the amount of drug taken without analyzing the original material and the leftover stub, or roach. Conditions like soil moisture and fertility, amount of sunlight, and temperature have effects on the amount of active ingredients in marijuana plants. Cannabis grown in Ohio or Indiana, for example, often does not have more than 0.2% to 1.0% tetrahydrocannabinol, whereas some of the cannabis from Mexico, Jamaica, Morocco, and Hawaii may have 2%–5%. The U.S. Government now grows marijuana to supply licensed researchers with standardized material.

In addition to standardized marijuana cigarettes, pure synthetic THC is now available to researchers. It can even be made with radioactive carbon or hydrogen labels (for that extra glow) to trace its metabolism. This type of research is controlled by the National Institute of Mental Health (plus the Drug Enforcement Administration, and the Nuclear Regulatory Agency if the radioactive labelled versions are needed). If you have a license to do research in the area (it is extremely difficult to get one), NIMH supplies the capsules of THC free of charge, along with a thick stack of reporting forms.

Street "THC" is not THC. THC is a difficult compound to synthesize, and dealers who claim to have it would have to keep it under very cold, oxygen-free conditions, because the compound breaks down readily. It would thus be very expensive and probably not effective by the time it was used. Analysis of all samples of THC collected at Ohio University, the University of Michigan, the Haight-Ashbury Clinic, and the University of Chicago up to 1981 has shown that the "THC" on the market is usually LSD, PCP, or a mixture of both. A few samples contained DOM or MDA, and in some instances a bit of methamphetamine was mixed with the LSD or PCP. The same is true for a white powder sold as "cannabinol." Laboratories using THC for research prepare the THC in a solution, such as alcohol or sesame oil. Such solutions are relatively stable: although they keep better under refrigeration, there is no significant loss of THC activity after storage at room temperature for a week.

FREQUENCY AND EXTENT OF MARIJUANA USE

According to most recent surveys in the United States, marijuana use starts at an earlier age and is more likely to be frequent, rather than experimental, than use in the early and mid-1970s. National surveys of drug use completed in 1977 and in 1979 show that 35% of young adults were currently using marijuana by late 1979, a figure nearly a third larger than that of 1977. Among high school seniors, for example, daily use nearly doubled among the members of the classes of 1978 and 1979 compared with the class of 1975 (from 5.8% to 10.7% and 10.3%). Moreover, the percentage of each of these senior classes that began use in the ninth grade or earlier also nearly doubled (from 16.9% of the class in 1975 to 30.4% of the 1979 class) (Petersen, 1980).

Young adults show the greatest use of marijuana according to the 1979 National Survey (see Table 7-1). In the age group of 18–25, two-thirds reported having ever used marijuana. Females use less marijuana than males in all age groups. It is estimated that in the 12–17 age group, 23% of females and 33% of males had used marijuana. For those over 18, nearly twice as many males are current users as females, whereas in the 12–17 age group about half again as many males as females are users (Petersen, 1980).

TABLE 7-1 Percentages of people who have used marijuana*

Age group	Have ever used marijuana
12–13	8%
14–15	32%
16–17	51% (10.3% daily use)
18–25	68%
26–34	44%
34 and over	7%

* Petersen, 1980.

Although the use of alcohol continues to exceed that of marijuana, daily use of marijuana among high school seniors in the class of 1978 (10.7%) was nearly double that of alcohol (5.7% daily use) and was exceeded only by daily cigarette smoking (27.5%). Considering marijuana is an illegal drug, it is startling to discover that nearly one out of every ten high school seniors is using marijuana daily.

In national surveys prior to 1977, people with college training were far more likely to have used marijuana than those with no college education, but in recent surveys this gap has narrowed to a 28% versus 26% use rate, respectively. According to the national surveys in 1977 and 1980, if one extrapolates to the general population, as many as 43 million and 46 million persons, respectively, have tried marijuana at some time. In addition, one can estimate that 16 to 17 million people had used marijuana in the month preceding each survey.

CHEMISTRY AND METABOLISM OF MARIJUANA

There are over 400 known chemical constituents in marijuana. More than 60, known as *cannabinoids*, are found only in cannabis. One of these is *delta-9-tetrahydrocannabinol*, or *delta-9-THC*, referring to the chemical structure of a specific cannabinol that accounts for the major psychoactive effects of the plant (Appendix A-4). THC is found most abundantly in the upper leaves, bracts, and flowers of the resin-producing variety of the plant. Some variants, raised primarily for the hemp fiber, do not have as high concentrations of the active ingredients. The dried leaves may contain up to 4% to 5% THC; hashish, which is the dried and pressed flowers and resin, up to 12%; and hashish oil, a crude extract of hashish, up to 60%. (The concentration of THC in hashish oil is limited only by the skill and equipment available to extract it—a level of 93% has been recorded.) Only a few years ago, most of the potent marijuana being imported had only 2% to 3% THC, but plant breeders are now producing a plant that yields a greater amount of THC.

THC is rapidly changed in the liver to a compound called *11-hydroxyTHC*, which is also psychoactive, and to more than 20 other products that are inactive. Until recently, there were no reliable methods for estimating the concentration of THC and its breakdown products in body fluids, other than the measurement of radioactivity in blood and tissues after the administration of a dose of radioactive THC. Measurement of THC and "total cannabinoids" is now possible by either radioimmunoassay or gas liquid chromatography coupled with mass spectroscopy, but these methods are only available in a few research laboratories. The problem of THC measurement has made it difficult to study the metabolism of THC in humans and to develop practical assays for law-enforcement and medical-diagnostic purposes (Jones, 1980).

THC leaves the blood rapidly through metabolism and through efficient uptake into the tissues. There is a tendency for THC and its metabolites to bind to proteins in the blood and to remain stored for long periods in body fat. Because of the difficulty of THC measurement, it may never be practical to measure THC or total cannabinol levels in the blood and relate these levels to behavior or to physiological effects (as opposed to alcohol blood levels, which are easily measured and are closely related to brain levels). Five days after a single injection of THC, 20% remains stored, whereas 20% of its metabolites remain in the blood. Complete elimination of a single dose can take up to 30 days. Measurable levels of THC in blood from chronic users can be detected for up to six days after their last marijuana cigarette. The biological half-life (the time it takes for the body to eliminate half of the drug) of THC was reported to be 56 hours in subjects who had never before had cannabis, and 28 hours in those who had used it repeatedly (Lemberger, Tamarkin, Axelrod, & Kopin, 1971). In recent work with more sensitive measurement methods, the biological half-life for THC in chronic users was found to be 19 hours, whereas metabolite half-life was 50 hours (Jones, 1980). In smokers, lung absorption and transport of THC to the brain are quite rapid, with the THC reaching the brain within as little as 14 seconds after inhalation. Smoking is even more efficient than intravenous injection, and it is three to five times more potent, and works hours faster, than oral ingestion (Jones, 1980).

A previous section mentioned the failure of early research to analyze the large variation in the quality of marijuana. Calculating cannabis dosage runs into other problems that were also not considered in most earlier research. For example, researchers did not examine the difference in the length of time smokers held their breath. They also did not consider how much THC was burned up as the joint was smoked, and how much was left in the end of the joint (roach). It has been estimated that about 50% of the THC is destroyed as a joint burns and hence it should not have been counted in the dosage; at least 25% of the THC might be found in the roach. Smokers knew the roach was potent, but researchers did not seem to consider it in early studies.

Some of the effects of cannabis described in the following sections are unquestionably toxic in that they can either directly or indirectly produce adverse effects on one's health. Others may be beneficial in certain situations. The use of marijuana, THC, and synthetic cannabinoids, either alone or in combination with other drugs, is currently being investigated for use in treatment of epilepsy, wide-angle glaucoma, anorexia nervosa, asthma, and for the relief of nausea and vomiting produced during chemotherapy for cancer. These applications are discussed in a later section.

BEHAVIORAL AND MENTAL EFFECTS

In most individuals, the casual use of low to moderate doses of cannabis produces euphoria and a pleasant state of relaxation. This state is usually mild and short-lived; a typical "high" from one joint may last from two to three hours. The user experiences an altered perception of space and time, an impaired memory of recent events, and impaired physical coordination. An occasional high is not usually hazardous unless the person attempts to drive a car, operate heavy machinery, fly a plane, or function in similar ways requiring coordination. Even low doses of marijuana adversely affect one's perception of relationships, such as the speed of an approaching vehicle or how much to slow down on an exit-ramp turn. This effect has been demonstrated in driving simulators, on test tracks, and in actual city driving situations. States such as California are setting up testing procedures for the presence of THC in urine or blood samples from apparently intoxicated drivers.

An acute dose of cannabis can produce adverse reactions ranging from mild anxiety through panic and paranoia in some users. A few rare cases exhibit psychoses characterized by detachment from reality, delusional and bizarre behavior, and hallucinations. These reactions occur most frequently in individuals who are under stress, anxious, depressed, or borderline schizophrenic, and in normal users who accidentally take much more than their usual dose. They can also occur as a result of ingesting marijuana treated with such things as LSD, PCP, or other additives, like *Datura* (jimsonweed) leaves. Based on limited evidence from survey studies, it is estimated that mild adverse reactions are experienced on one or more occasions by more than one-half of regular users; they are mainly self-treated and usually go unreported. The small number of users who experience severe adverse reactions usually respond well to psychiatric treatment and recover in one or two days (Jones, 1980).

There is evidence that chronic heavy use of cannabis can lead to lasting behavioral changes in some users. Apathy, lack of concern for the future, and loss of motivation have been described in some heavy users, and psychotic and paranoid symptoms have been observed in others. These symptoms usually disappear when regular drug use is discontinued, and they recur when use is resumed. Such reactions are relatively rare, although case studies suggest that certain cannabis users may be more susceptible than others (NAS[*] 1982; Petersen, 1980). Many psychiatrists are concerned about such reactions in youthful drug users (11 to 15 years of age), because of the possibility that regular use may produce adverse effects on psychological, as well as physical, maturation. (This concern involves all psychoactive drugs, including alcohol.)

A few cannabis users experience spontaneous recurrences of the symptoms of acute intoxication days or weeks later, similar to the LSD flashback. These recurrences are not common and require little or no treatment. Because THC is stored in fat, it is possible that the flashback might be triggered by something that mobilizes the THC from the fat cells, but this is not known.

Are there other changes in brain function that persist after the high? Limited clinical evidence suggests that some users do not recover completely when they discontinue drug use. Psychological functioning, which includes perception, coordination, intelligence, and other factors, has been tested in heavy users in Jamaica, Costa Rica, Greece, Egypt, and India. The conclusions from these studies conflict and in some cases are difficult to interpret accurately, because of poor experimental methods and possibly biased investigators. Studies with the largest groups of subjects, done in Egypt and India, showed significant differences between users and matched nonusers, whereas the studies using much smaller samples in Jamaica and Costa Rica did not show any significant differences between users and nonusers (Jones, 1980).

---

[*] Institute of Medicine, National Academy of Sciences, 1982. *Marijuana and Health.* Washington, D.C.: National Academy Press.

Can marijuana cause a lack of motivation and reduced productivity—the *amotivational syndrome?* The term is deceptively simple, but difficult to define in a way it can be measured. In laboratory studies, subjects seem in some respects to be unmotivated during the acute phase of intoxication, but in others they work very hard at the assigned experimental tasks. In studies of chronic use done with subjects living in research wards, some types of productivity decreased as the level of intoxication increased. It is oversimplified, however, to claim that these changes are in motivation alone, because the drug effects are quite complex. In studies of chronic users in Greece, Jamaica, and Costa Rica, productivity of marijuana users did not appear to be lower than that of nonusers. However, the types of work (animal herding, nonmechanized farm labor) done in these countries are much less complex than in an industrial country such as the United States. Uncontrolled clinical reports from areas of the world where cannabis is readily available continue to report decreased productivity and initiative in chronic cannabis users. Uncontrolled reports from observation of chronic users in this country suggest the same thing, but few controlled experiments have been done to prove this one way or the other (Jones, 1980).

Schaeffer, Andrysiak, and Ungerleider (1981) studied seven men and three women who smoked large quantities of marijuana daily as part of their religion. Their ages ranged from 25 to 36; the mean number of years of education was 13.5 (all were born, raised, and educated in the United States) and all were Caucasian. They furnished samples of urine for analysis of THC content immediately before taking a series of neurophysiological tests designed to assess a broad range of cognitive functions. No impairment of cognitive function was found. All the subjects were actively engaged in some form of daily work, largely agricultural and business. Their mean IQ scores were all in the superior to very superior range; there was nothing to suggest impaired mental functioning due to brain dysfunction resulting from prolonged and heavy use of marijuana.

Experimental studies on rats and monkeys show that long-term exposure to doses of cannabis equivalent to those taken by humans who are heavy users produce significant effects. For example, learning impairment and changes in brain waves persist months after the end of chronic intoxication. These disturbances are accompanied by subtle changes in synaptic connections (Chapter 2) that can be seen under the electron microscope. This experimental evidence of brain damage is consistent with clinical observations in humans. There were earlier reports of brain atrophy (shrinking) in chronic users, but the most recent work using computer axial tomography (the three-dimensional CAT scanner) has not shown this (NAS, 1982). At present, discrepancies among studies cannot be reconciled.

PHYSIOLOGICAL EFFECTS

The Respiratory System

Marijuana is often smoked like tobacco, and it would be unusual if there were not some effects from its repeated inhalation, just as there are from the inhalation of any combustion products. When tobacco is smoked, for example, nearly 70% of the total suspended particles in the smoke are retained in the lungs. There is reason to believe that, because marijuana smoke is inhaled more deeply than tobacco smoke, a greater percentage of products is retained. Smoke is a mixture of tiny particles suspended in gas, mostly carbon monoxide. These solid particles combine to form a residue called tar. Cannabis produces more tar (up to 50% more) than an equivalent weight of tobacco and is smoked in a way that would facilitate tar deposition in the lungs (Jones, 1980).

Over 150 chemicals have been identified in marijuana tar. A few of these are proven carcinogens; however, many of them have not yet been tested for carcinogenicity. Benzo(a)pyrene, for example, is 70% more abundant in marijuana smoke than tobacco smoke. If cannabis tar is applied to the skin of experimental mice in a standard test for carcinogenicity, it causes precancerous lesions similar to those caused by tobacco tar. If isolated lung tissue is exposed to these same tars, it also undergoes precancerous changes (Jones, 1980; Turner, 1980).

There are special white blood cells in living lung tissue, called *alveolar macrophages*, that play a role in removing debris from the lungs. When these cells are exposed to smoke from cannabis, they become less able to remove bacteria and other foreign debris from the lungs. Smoking only a few marijuana cigarettes a day for only six to eight weeks can significantly impair pulmonary function. Laboratory and clinical evidence tends to show that heavy use of marijuana causes cellular changes, and the users have a higher incidence of laryngitis, pharyngitis, bronchitis, asthma-like conditions, cough, hoarseness, and dry throat (Jones, 1980).

Most marijuana users in the United States are not exposed to as high a level of tar as tobacco smokers are because the amount of cannabis smoked is much less. Thus there will likely be a longer interval of time before any pathology becomes obvious. However, the increase in usage by teenagers might increase the incidence of pathology. There are some indications now that more and more 20-year-old smokers of hashish and tobacco have lung damage comparable to that found in heavy tobacco smokers over 40

years of age. It is believed that the tar from tobacco and from marijuana each have damaging effects, but it is not known whether smokers who use both products suffer synergistic or additive effects (Jones, 1980).

The Cardiovascular System

In humans, cannabis causes both an increase in heart rate related to the amount of THC consumed and a reddening of the eyes. In physically healthy users, these effects, as well as slight changes in heart rhythms, are transitory and do not appear to be significant. In patients with angina pectoris, however, the increased oxygen requirement due to the increased heart rate can cause anginal pain more readily in response to exercise. The effect of cannabis on people with heart rhythm irregularities is not known.

Marijuana usage may cause changes in blood pressure. Abnormally low pressure in a standing position is most frequently observed. Users sometimes mention that they feel lightheaded when they stand up after smoking. Chronic administration of large doses of THC to healthy volunteers shows that they do adapt to the increase in heart rate, and the decrease in blood pressure, as well as an increase in blood volume. How this affects patients with cardiovascular disease is not known. The National Academy of Sciences' Institute of Medicine recommends that persons with cardiovascular disease avoid the drug. There are still many unanswered questions about the effects of chronic cannabis use on the cardiovascular system.

The Reproductive System

There are a number of ways that drugs may interfere with reproduction. They may alter sexual behavior, affect fertility, damage the chromosomes of germ cells in the male or the female, or adversely affect fetal growth and development. The Indian Hemp Commission, which wrote the first scientific report on cannabis, commented that cannabis had a sexually stimulating effect like alcohol. However, the report also said cannabis was used by Indian ascetics to destroy the sexual appetite. This apparent discrepancy may be a dose-related effect. Short-term, occasional use may act as an aphrodisiac by releasing central-nervous-system inhibitions on behavior. In addition, the altered perception of time under the influence of the drug could make the pleasurable sensations appear to last longer than they actually do. Marijuana affects the sympathetic nervous system to increase vasodilatation in the genitals and to delay ejaculation (Harclerode, 1980). High doses over a period of time lead to depression of libido and impotence, possibly due to the decreased amount of testosterone, the male sex hormone (see Chapter 15).

Cannabis has several effects on semen. The total number of sperm per ejaculate is decreased, as is the concentration of sperm per unit volume of ejaculate fluid. There is an increase in the proportion of sperm with an abnormal appearance and reduced motility. Abnormal appearance and reduced motility are usually associated with lowered fertility and a higher probability of abnormal embryos if fertilization does take place. As of 1982, there were no documented reports of children with birth defects in which the abnormality was definitely linked to the father's smoking marijuana. It is possible that the damaged sperm simply are incapable of fertilization, so that only the normal sperm reach the egg, or that the abnormal appearance is meaningless in terms of birth defects. When marijuana use is discontinued, the quality of the semen gradually returns to normal over several months (Harclerode, 1980; NAS, 1982).

There is less reliable data available on the effects of cannabis on female libido, sexual response (ability to respond to sexual stimulation with vaginal lubrication and orgasm), and fertile reproductive (menstrual) cycles. Preliminary data from Bauman, at the Reproductive Biology Research Foundation, show that chronic smoking of cannabis (at least three times per week for the preceding six months) adversely affects the reproductive cycle. Her results with women are correlated with work in rhesus monkeys: THC blocks ovulation.

Data on effects during pregnancy and lactation are inconclusive. Pregnant rhesus monkeys treated with THC equivalent to moderately heavy marijuana use (according to U.S. standards) had an abortion and fetal-death rate about four times higher than the drug-free control monkeys. THC and other cannabinoids pass through the blood-placental barrier and concentrate in the fetus's fatty tissue, including its brain. Ethical considerations prevent duplication of the experiment in humans. Women who smoke marijuana during pregnancy often also use other drugs, such as alcohol and tobacco, that are known to have adverse effects on the developing fetus. Like many other substances, THC is taken up by the mammary glands in lactating females and is excreted in the milk. Effects on human infants have not been determined (Petersen, 1980).

The Immune System

In animal experiments it is possible to show that THC, cannabis extracts, and marijuana smoke in doses comparable to typical use by humans suppress the immune system reactions. In humans, some studies, but not all, indicate that heavy use of marijuana may interfere with the T-lymphocyte part of the immune system. This component is known to play a role in resistance to viral infection and to cancer. The combination of inhaled carcinogens and depressed T-lymphocyte function could mean a greater risk of cancer. An increased frequency of cancer has not been apparent in countries where cannabis use is traditional and extensive (for example, Jamaica, India). However, in many of these countries the people have relatively short life spans, and the persons who might have developed cancer may not have lived to the ages when the cancers more commonly develop. The question of decreased immunity in chronic users must be determined in countries where the life span is longer. Cancer often takes 20 to 30 years to develop from the time of beginning exposure to carcinogens.

In *in vitro* experiments cannabis inhibits the intracellular synthesis of complex biological molecules, including proteins, DNA, and RNA, and it inhibits cell division. Alcohol and opiates have similar effects. However, this inhibition has not been shown to occur in the human body. Some investigators have suggested that it may be responsible for the impaired immune response.

Tolerance and Dependence

It has been known for many years that tolerance to some effects of cannabis builds rapidly in animals (the drug effect becomes less intense with repeated administration). Frequent use of high doses of marijuana or THC in humans produces tolerance similar to that observed in animals. For example, increasingly higher doses must be given to obtain the same intensity of subjective effects and increased heart rate that occur initially with small doses. Frequent high doses of THC can also produce mild physical dependence. Healthy subjects who smoke several joints a day or who are given comparable amounts of THC orally experience irritability, sleep distur-

bances, weight loss, loss of appetite, sweating, and gastrointestinal upsets when the drug is stopped abruptly. This mild form of withdrawal is not experienced by all subjects. It is much easier to show psychological dependence in heavy users of marijuana (Jones, 1980).

Driving and Driver Performance

There is good evidence that marijuana use at typical social levels definitely impairs driving ability and related skills. This effect is shown in laboratory assessment of driving-related skills, such as eye-hand coordination and reaction time, and in driver simulator studies, test course performance, and actual street driving performance. As use of marijuana becomes more common and socially acceptable, and as the penalty for simple possession decreases, more users are likely to risk driving while high. In limited surveys, from 60% to 80% of marijuana users indicated that they sometimes drive while high. A study of drivers involved in fatal accidents in the Greater Boston area showed that marijuana smokers were overrepresented in fatal highway accidents as compared to a control group of nonusers of similar age and sex. A 1979 study found that of nearly 1800 blood samples taken from drivers arrested for driving while intoxicated, 16% were positive for marijuana. When no detectable alcohol was present in the blood sample (about 10% of the drivers) the incidence of marijuana detected rose to 24% (Petersen, 1980). Because some of the perceptual or other performance deficits resulting from marijuana use may persist for some time after the "high," users who attempt to drive, fly, operate heavy machinery, and so on may unwittingly expose themselves and others to danger: they may not recognize their impairment, because they no longer feel high (NAS, 1982).

Possible Therapeutic Uses of Marijuana

Marijuana has been used in folk and formal medicine to treat a variety of human ills for thousands of years. As recently as 1937, tinctures of cannabis were still listed in the U.S. Pharmacopeia, which is the list of currently used therapeutic drugs. Physicians had difficulty with cannabis dosage because the plant material's effectiveness decreases with repeated use; also, the inhalation route requires experience with smoking. Then, after marijuana was legally classified as a narcotic and the Marijuana Tax Act of 1937 required its use be reported, medical use effectively ceased. In the past decade there has been renewed interest in possible medical uses for cannabis. A few potentially valuable uses are now known, and others are being investigated to a limited extent.

The use of marijuana, THC, or related drugs for the treatment of the extreme nausea and vomiting that often accompany cancer chemotherapy is perhaps the single most promising application. They are not always effective but can sometimes help when other antinauseant drugs have failed. THC-treated cancer chemotherapy patients show improved appetite and diminshed weight loss. THC has been found to have an antiemetic effect (prevents vomiting) and stimulates the appetite; as casual users put it, it gives them the "munchies." The dose level and timing are important in such treatment. When the THC-like synthetic drug nabilone was compared to prochlorperazine (a standard antinauseant drug), 80% of the patients responded to nabilone and 32% to prochlorperazine. Sleepiness was the most common side effect (Petersen, 1980). Nabilone has now been discontinued by the pharmaceutical manufacturer, Lilly, because of toxic effects on test animals.

One widely publicized use of marijuana is to reduce the vision-destroying intraocular pressure that occurs in a type of glaucoma. Early studies of this treatment showed mixed results, with the most effective use as a supplement to other drugs. In a recent study in which 16 glaucoma patients smoked marijuana, 8 of whom had hypertension and 8 had normal blood pressure, the hypertensive patients showed a significantly greater drop in intraocular pressure (Petersen, 1980). However, the long-term safety and effectiveness of marijuana and other cannabinoids used to treat glaucoma have not been established. There are no data from long-term controlled studies to show whether these preparations can actually preserve sight in people with glaucoma. Some state laws now permit a patient with medically certified wide-angle glaucoma to get government-grown marijuana of known potency for medical use. Further research is necessary before this drug will be released for widespread use (Petersen, 1980; NAS, 1982).

A number of other potential uses of marijuana and THC have been suggested. For example, marijuana has the effect of dilating the lung's air passages (bronchodilation) and was thought to have promise in treating asthmatics. It was found, however, that the lung-irritating properties of marijuana smoke seem to offset its benefits. It still may prove to be useful when other drugs are not effective because of a different mode of action in causing bronchodilation.

Marijuana has also been found to have both convulsant and anticonvulsant properties and thus has been considered for prevention of epileptic seizures. In animal experimentation, the cannabinoids reduced or increased seizure activity, depending on how the experiment was done. One or more of the marijuana components may possibly be useful in combination with other standard antiseizure medication, although at present their value seems to be limited. A survey of young epileptics who smoked marijuana did not show a change in seizure patterns, but caution is advised (Cohen, 1980).

Additional proposed uses include reduction of muscular spasticity in paraplegics and patients with multiple sclerosis, and treatment of depression, pain, alcoholism, and drug dependence. Cannabis and the synthetic cannabinoid synhexyl have been used successfully in Great Britain as specific euphoriants for the treatment of depression. In South Africa, native women smoke cannabis to dull the pain of childbirth. As an analgesic, cannabis has the advantage of not depressing the respiratory center, unlike the morphine group (Solomon, 1966). Whether or not cannabis, one of its synthetic constituents, or a chemically related compound once again finds a place in medicine depends on several considerations. For example, it must be determined whether the pharmaceutically desirable effects are useful for treating chronic conditions. Tolerance is known to develop rapidly for a number of the effects of naturally occurring THC; this may also be true for new, chemically related compounds. Like any other medication, marijuana and related products must be carefully tested for toxicity and for therapeutic effectiveness. This process is time consuming as well as expensive, and, unless a new chemical promises dramatic improvement in treatment, it is unlikely to reach the market.

CHAPTER 8

THE STIMULANTS

CHAPTER OBJECTIVES

1. State the amounts of coffee, tea, and cocoa consumed per person in the United States in 1980.

2. Rank the three stimulants found in coffee, tea, mate, and cocoa from most to least potent in their physiological effects.

3. Give reasons why many employers schedule coffee breaks for workers.

4. Explain what tests on military personnel and on athletes showed about effects of small doses of amphetamines on performance.

5. Discuss some of the reasons for the epidemic of amphetamine abuse in the United States.

6. Describe the use of amphetamines or related stimulants in narcolepsy, hyperkinesis, and weight reduction.

7. List behavioral effects, physiological effects, and dangers of high doses of intravenous amphetamines.

8. Discuss whether caffeine, amphetamine, and cocaine will cause physical dependence.

9. Describe the effect of amphetamines and cocaine on the neurotransmitters norepinephrine and dopamine.

10. Describe the behavioral and the physiological effects of cocaine, following acute and chronic administration.

11. List two medical uses of cocaine.

12. Define the following terms: speedball, formication, behavioral stereotypy, anorexiant, narcolepsy, hyperkinesis, tinnitus, mydriasis, hyperpyrexia, free basing, and Brompton's cocktail.

Stimulants are substances that act on the central nervous system, causing the person who takes the drug to feel more lively. He or she may become restless, talkative, and may be unable to sleep. Among the stimulants are the amphetamines, cocaine, strychnine, coffee, tea, chocolate, and nicotine. Because nicotine has a unique combination of stimulant and depressant properties, it is covered in the next chapter.

MINOR STIMULANTS: COFFEE, TEA, AND CHOCOLATE

Coffee

No one knows for certain when coffee was first used, but one interesting legend about the origin of coffee consumption concerns a goat herder, Kaldi of Arabia. It seems Kaldi noticed that his goats became lively and danced around after eating the berries of certain plants on the hillside. He followed the goats to the plants and ate some of the berries. He too danced, and stayed up most of the night. A holy man saw the scene and tried the berries himself. They had the same effect on him. Later Mohammed instructed the holy man how to make a brew from the dried berries that would keep holy men awake to continue with their prayers.

Coffee drinking was popular in Arabia and is mentioned in writings dating back to 900 A.D. In fact, in Mecca coffee drinking was so popular that people spent too much time in coffeehouses, and the use of coffee was outlawed for a short period of time. However, illicit coffeehouses sprang up immediately, and the coffee prohibition was repealed.

Coffee probably reached Europe through Tur-

key, and it most likely was used initially as a medicine. By the middle of the 17th century there were coffeehouses in England and in France. They were places to relax and talk, to learn the news, to make business deals, and perhaps to hatch plots. In England, King Charles II was so disturbed by the rumors of seditious and slanderous talk in the coffeehouses that he ordered them closed. The prohibition lasted for 11 days, until threats of rioting caused him to change his mind. These coffeehouses turned into the famous "penny universities" of the early 18th century, where for a penny a cup you could listen to some of the great literary and political figures of the day. Lloyds of London, the insurance firm, started in Edward Lloyd's coffeehouse about 1700. One of the interesting exchanges of opinion about coffee was made between the "coffee widows" of the 1670s and their husbands who frequented these houses. Here is an excerpt from the Women's Petition Against Coffee (1674):

> Certainly our Countrymens pallets are become as Fanatical as their Brains; how else is't possible they should Apostatize from the good old primitive way of Ale-drinking, to run a Whoreing after such variety of destructive Foreign Liquors, to trifle away their time, scald their Chops, and spend their Money, all for a little base, black, thick, nasty bitter stinking, nauseous Puddle water: Yet (as all Witches have their Charms) so this ugly Turkish Enchantress by certain Invisible Wyres attracts both Rich & Poor. . . . [Meyer, 1954]

Coffee is America's national nonalcoholic drink. In 1980, Americans spent an estimated $4.2 billion on coffee imports, $130 million on tea, and about $1 billion on chocolate. They each consumed an estimated 9.7 pounds of coffee, 0.9 pounds of tea, and 3.3 pounds of cocoa beans, all of which contain caffeine.

Tea

Tea contains two stimulant drugs, caffeine and theophylline. As with coffee, the earliest use of tea is not known. One of the quaint legends about tea attributes its discovery to the founder of Zen Buddhism, Daruma. One day Daruma fell asleep while meditating. He vowed he would never allow this to happen again, and to make sure, he cut off both eyelids and threw them to the ground. As they touched the earth, plants sprang up, and from their leaves a brew could be made that would help one to stay awake.

The first reliable account of the use of tea is from an early Chinese manuscript written around 350 A.D. This record describes tea as a medicinal plant (supposedly good for tumors, abscesses, bladder trouble, and many other ailments), but its recreational use slowly grew. The nonmedical use of tea is mentioned in a book written about 780 A.D. on the cultivation of tea. Buddhist monks had already carried their information on tea to Japan. The Dutch brought the first tea to Europe in 1610, where it was accepted rather slowly. The first European record of tea mentions its use for the alleviation of fever, headache, stomachache, and arthritis. After a series of disputes with England over trade, the Dutch finally gave England the trade rights to India and other countries of the continent. The British East India Company rapidly and energetically expanded its spice trade and encouraged sales of tea from China. From about 1760 the British pushed the sale of tea through a strong advertising program, and sales grew. Tea revenues made it possible to colonize India and also helped to bring on the Opium Wars in the 1800s, which benefited British colonialism (see Chapter 12). Gradually tea replaced coffee as Britain's national drink.

Because so many people in England were drinking tea, coffee, and chocolate, the tax revenues from alcoholic beverages dropped, so a tax was charged on tea and chocolate. The British also established a tea monopoly by banning Dutch tea. Almost 100 years later the British levied high taxes on the tea being shipped to the American colonies. This was a factor in the beginning of the American Revolution and the birth of the United States.

Chocolate

Chocolate contains the alkaloid theobromine, named after the cocoa tree *Theobroma cacao*. *Theobroma* is an Aztec word meaning fruit of the gods. The Aztecs thought very highly of the fruit and seed pods from the tree, and they used cacao beans as a medium of exchange in bartering. The Mayan Indians adopted the food and made a warm drink from the beans that they called *chocolatl* (warm drink). The original chocolate drink was a very thick concoction that had to be eaten with a spoon. It was unsweetened because the Mayans apparently did not know about sugar cane.

Cortez took some chocolate cakes back to Spain with him in 1528, but the method of preparing them was kept a secret for nearly a hundred years. It was not until 1828 that the Dutch worked out a process to remove much of the fat from the kernels to make a chocolate powder. This was the forerunner of the cocoa we know today. The cocoa fat, or cocoa butter as it is called, was later mixed with sugar and pressed into bars. In 1847 the first chocolate bars appeared on the market. By 1876 the Swiss developed milk chocolate. Today milk chocolate must contain at least 12% milk solids; the better grades contain up to 20%.

Physiological Effects of the Active Substances in Coffee, Tea, and Cocoa

Caffeine is classified as a *xanthine*, which is one of the oldest stimulants known to man. This chemical is one of three found in such beverages as coffee, tea, mate (the national drink in many South American countries), and cocoa. It is added to many carbonated soft drinks as well. Caffeine was so named because the chemical was first isolated from coffee, in 1820. The other xanthine chemicals are *theophylline* (means divine leaf), which is found in tea, and *theobromine* (divine food), which is found in chocolate (Appendix A-5). The cured coffee bean contains about 1% caffeine. Dried tea leaves have about 5% caffeine plus theophylline. Cocoa has little caffeine, but about 2% theobromine. Of the three, caffeine and theophylline have potent effects on the central nervous system, whereas theobromine has relatively little effect. Theo-phylline has its greatest effect on the cardiovascular system. The caffeine contents of beverages and chocolate candy are shown in Table 8-1.

These minor stimulants, especially caffeine and theophylline, have proven medicinal value. They stimulate the central nervous sytem, act on the kidneys as a diuretic (as any heavy tea drinker undoubtedly knows), stimulate cardiac muscle, and relax smooth muscle. Persons who have bronchial spasms or asthma probably have noticed that they can breathe a bit easier after drinking a cup of tea. Table 8-2 summarizes the relative potencies of caffeine, theophylline, and theobromine for their common biological effects.

At a dose level of 150 to 250 milligrams (one to two cups of coffee or tea), caffeine activates the cortex and the EEG shows an arousal pattern. Caffeine's main effect is to increase the rapidity and clarity of thought. In noncaffeine users, the 150 to 250 milligram dose may cause a significant reduction in heart rate, by about four beats a minute. This reduction does not

TABLE 8-1 Caffeine content of beverages and chocolate

Beverage	Milligrams of caffeine	Amount
Brewed coffee	90–125	5 oz
Instant coffee	14–93*	5 oz
Decaffeinated coffee	1–6*	5 oz
Tea	30–70	5 oz
Cocoa	5 (but 100 of theobromine)	5 oz
Coca-Cola®	45	12 oz
Pepsi-Cola®	30	12 oz
Chocolate bar	22	1 oz

*The caffeine content of more than three dozen brands of instant coffee is given in the October 1979 issue of *Consumer Reports*.

occur in habitual users. Higher dose levels (over 500 milligrams) affect the autonomic centers of the brain, and heart rate and respiration may increase. Caffeine may increase the blood levels of lipids and of glucose. In the dose range of about eight cups a day, there is an induction of liver enzymes that metabolize the drug. Caffeine is not very toxic, but high doses (from 1 to 10 grams) can cause convulsions and respiratory failure.

Caffeine has a mild accelerating effect on metabolic rate. Approximately half a gram of caffeine, the equivalent of three or four cups of coffee, can increase the basal metabolic rate from 10 to 25% for up to four hours. The temperature in the extremities may increase a degree or more, which reflects the change in metabolic rate.

A dose of 200 to 300 milligrams of caffeine will partially offset a fatigue-induced drop in performance of motor tasks. For example, a typist often will be able to work faster and make fewer errors after a coffee break. However, there is evidence that caffeine, unlike amphetamines, may not improve motor skills involving muscular coordination. Caffeine prolongs the amount of time an individual can perform physically exhausting work; it slows the onset of boredom and increases the attention span (Weiss & Laties, 1962). The popularity of the coffee break has a practical basis: people do work better afterwards.

Heavy use of caffeine leads to various symptoms, such as irregular heartbeat, tinnitus (ringing in the ears), restlessness, extreme nervousness, and inability to sleep. People vary widely in their development of "coffee nerves." Tolerance and psychological dependence can occur in some people drinking five or more cups of coffee a day. At this level, the caffeine is a central nervous system stimulant. If the person abruptly discontinues coffee and all other sources of caffeine, a depression will follow similar to that caused by withdrawal of other central nervous system stimulants.

The essential oils found in coffee may cause gastrointestinal problems, such as diarrhea, at high levels of consumption. However, the tannin in tea works just the opposite, and causes constipation.

TABLE 8-2   Comparison of potencies of the active ingredients (xanthines) in coffee, tea, and cocoa[*]

Physiological effects of xanthines	Order of potency (most to least)
Central nervous system stimulant	Caffeine = theophylline > theobromine
Stimulant effect on respiratory center	Caffeine > theophylline > theobromine
Increases capacity for muscular work	Caffeine > theophylline > theobromine
Stimulation of cardiac muscle	Theophylline > theobromine > caffeine
Diuretic action	Theophylline > theobromine > caffeine
Relax smooth muscle of bronchi	Theophylline most potent
Increases basal metabolic rate	Caffeine most potent

[*] Based on data from Rall (1980). = means equivalent in this particular physiological effect; > means greater than.

Caffeine has been shown to be mutagenic and teratogenic in experimental animals, but only at concentrations much in excess of those used therapeutically or those resulting from drinking coffee or tea. It is not considered a significant toxic hazard in humans. Nevertheless, pregnant women should be cautious about consumption of large amounts of caffeine, such as in over-the-counter stimulant preparations and carbonated beverages. Coffee consumption has also been tentatively linked with cancer of the pancreas.

STRYCHNINE

Strychnine, a drug that has been used as a poison for a long time, is a powerful nervous system stimulant. It is the primary alkaloid from the plant *Strychnos nux-vomica*. Legend has it that the Creator made a thumbprint on the seed, so a taxonomist named the plant *vomica*, or *depression*, because of the imprint. (Indeed, taking more than 30 to 40 milligrams will usually put the drug taker in a position to meet the Creator!) Strychnine was a drug used by athletes in the early Olympics (1920s) to stimulate and to override the feelings of fatigue. Although it has long been popular as a "tonic" to stimulate the appetite and the gastrointestinal tract, it is neither safe nor effective (Franz, 1980).

Strychnine is briefly discussed here because it is found as an adulterant in street drugs. It is probably more often combined with LSD than with any other street drug. We have, however, found it added to illegal methaqualone in small amounts, usually about 1 to 5 milligrams. Stimulants seem to sensitize the central nervous system for the effects of drugs like LSD. In fact, sometimes a fairly large dose of strychnine is added to LSD; this combination is called "white acid."

Strychnine works by blocking inhibitory neurons, thus causing a direct and concentrated stimulatory effect on the entire nervous system, especially the spinal cord. This excitation affects all voluntary muscles and in adequate doses causes death by convulsions and asphyxiation (refer to Figures 5-1 and 5-2 on pp. 71 and 72).

AMPHETAMINES

Other than coffee and nicotine (see Chapter 9 for a discussion of tobacco), the most widely used stimulants in the United States are amphetamine and chemically related compounds. Legally these are taken under the supervision of a doctor; however, many users of amphetamine do so on their own. It has become clear that many people are dependent on the amphetamine group of drugs. One amphetamine, methamphetamine (speed, or crystal), has a particularly powerful effect on the brain. It has recently been associated with a wide range of medical and personal problems. The term *speed* refers to the intravenous use of amphetamine, methamphetamine, or amphetamine-related drugs.

Amphetamines are synthetic amines that are similar to the body's own neurotransmitter, norepinephrine, and the hormone for emergencies, epinephrine (adrenalin) (Appendix A-6). The amphetamines generally cause an arousal or activating response not unlike one's normal reaction to emergency situations or to stress. The central nervous system–stimulating properties of amphetamines were discovered in 1927, and these drugs were used medically in the 1930s. Although a variety of related drugs and mixtures currently exist, the most common amphetamine substances are amphetamine (Benzedrine® by trade name), dextroamphetamine (Dexedrine®), and methamphetamine (Methedrine®, or Desoxyn®). Generally, if doses are adjusted, the psychological effects of these various drugs are similar, so they will be discussed as a group. Other drugs with similar pharmacological properties are phenmetrazine (Preludin®), and methylphenidate (Ritalin®). Common slang terms for amphetamines include *speed, crystal, meth, bennies, dexies, A, uppers, pep pills, diet pills, jolly beans, copilots, hearts, footballs,* and so on.

The stimulating effects of the amphetamines made them suitable for wide use in World War II to counteract fatigue. The Germans, Japanese, and British made extensive use of these drugs in the early 1940s. The U.S. Armed Forces issued amphetamines on a regular basis during the Korean War. The American military tested amphetamines in a series of studies mimicking field conditions as closely as possible. In one, for example, two officers and 14 enlisted men marched 18 to 20 miles with 26-pound packs and were then assigned to guard duty most of the night. At 6 P.M. and at midnight, experimental and control subjects received one of the following: 7.5 grams of caffeine, 10 milligrams amphetamine, 5 milligrams methamphetamine, or a placebo of 5 grams milk sugar. When they came off guard duty, the subjects were then tested for 90 minutes. Amphetamine produced the fewest negative symptoms (sleepiness, nervousness, tension, dizziness, difficulty in concentrating, exhaustion and tremor) and the most positive symptoms (lack of sleepiness, talkativeness, excitement, and exhilaration) (Seashore & Ivy, 1953). These and other studies indicate that relatively small doses of amphetamine can reduce the effects of fatigue, help maintain a high level of efficiency during boring, tedious tasks, and improve mood in a majority of test subjects.

History of Amphetamine Abuse*

Amphetamine abuse is typically thought of as a purely American phenomenon. It has been abused in many other industrial nations, but only Japan and Sweden have had large-scale epidemics of amphetamine abuse comparable to the experience in the United States in the 1960s.

Japan had a major problem with amphetamines after 1945. These drugs were widely used there to maintain the war effort. After the war, to reduce large stockpiles of methamphetamine, the drug was sold without prescription. The drug companies advertised them for "elimination of drowsiness and repletion of the spirit." As a result, drug abuse grew rapidly so that by 1948 there were an estimated one million Japanese with a serious amphetamine addiction. Controls were placed on the drugs in 1948, but abuse continued to grow until 1954, when the government passed strong laws that instituted severe penalties for illegal use, established treatment centers, and initiated education on the dangers of the drug. By 1958 there was no detectable amphetamine problem. Japan still maintains very tight control on production of these drugs.

Despite legal restrictions, by 1942 to 1943 about 3% of the Swedish population were using amphetamines. An amphetamine-centered subculture developed around intravenous use of amphetamine, methamphetamine, dextroamphetamine, phenmetrazine, and related compounds, depending on availability. Analysts cri-

---

* This section is largely from Spotts and Spotts, 1980.

ticize both the medical community for being slow to respond to the problem and the pharmaceutical firms for being irresponsible in distributing the drugs. Ultimately the Swedish government banned prescription of amphetamine and related chemicals for all but a few special medical conditions.

Amphetamine was introduced into American medical practice in the late 1930s as a drug that produced wakefulness, self-confidence, elation, and euphoria without adverse side effects. Careless medical prescription and illicit use began almost immediately, and widespread use of this drug was already established in the general population prior to the American amphetamine epidemic. Korean veterans going back to college used amphetamine tablets to help cram for examinations, and other students quickly picked up on this. There was widespread use of amphetamines among truck drivers making long hauls—it is believed that one of the earliest distribution systems for illicit amphetamines were the truck stops along major U.S. highways. High-achieving people under continuous pressure in the entertainment fields, business, and industry relied on amphetamines to counteract fatigue. Housewives used them for weight control and to combat boredom from unfulfilling lives.

The Benzedrine® inhaler, marketed for nasal congestion, was widely abused. The inhalers contained 250 milligrams of amphetamine base, which is a volatile liquid form of the drug, impregnated in a piece of folded paper. Each fold of the paper (called a *strip* by users) would thus have contained about 31 milligrams. The usual dose among prisoners and other abusers was one-half to two strips taken orally every two to four hours (Monroe & Drell, 1947). These inhalers were available over the counter until 1949, when Smith, Kline, and French Laboratories substituted Benzedrex® for the Benzedrine®. This new preparation had the same nasal

decongestant characteristics but not the stimulatory effects of amphetamine. Because of a loophole in a law that was passed later, one brand of nasal decongestant containing 150 milligrams methamphetamine was on the open market until 1965. It was not until 1971 that other amphetamine-like compounds in nasal inhalers were withdrawn from the market.

At the height of the American epidemic in 1967, some 31 million prescriptions were written for anorexiants (diet pills) alone. This means that 6% to 8% of all adults could have used legal, prescription amphetamine. This figure does not include unknown illegal amphetamine use (Ellinwood, 1974).

In the late 1950s some West Coast narcotics addicts were using a combination of amphetamine and heroin to get an effect similar to that of heroin and cocaine (cocaine was almost unavailable). These addicts would also use amphetamine alone when heroin was unavailable. By the early 1960s intravenous amphetamine was the drug of first choice for a majority of users in western coastal cities in the United States. Individuals would get prescriptions for large amounts of methamphetamine for treatment of heroin addiction. The abuse of legally obtained methamphetamine became so prevalent that a number of physicians and pharmacists were prosecuted and convicted for such abuse, and injectable amphetamine was withdrawn from the market.

However, amphetamine and methamphetamine are not difficult to synthesize, and illegal products became available all over the country. And illegal manufacture was not the only source. In 1966 the FDA estimated that more than 25 *tons* of legitimately manufactured amphetamine were diverted to illegal sales; at times, about 90% of the legal supply went into the illegal market.

Ellinwood (1974) noted striking similarities

among amphetamine abuse epidemics in Japan, Sweden, and the United States. In all three cases, amphetamine abuse started with avant-garde artists, musicians, entertainers, and trend-setting people, progressed through the middle class, and became established in people with marginal social adaptation. All three countries placed cultural emphasis on personal productivity and achievement, and were in the midst of changing social values and patterns of living. Within this setting, the role of the pharmaceutical companies and the medical profession was crucial: there had to be an initial oversupply of legal amphetamine that found its way into legal and illegal markets. In all three countries large segments of the population were exposed to amphetamine through medical, antifatigue, and ultimately casual use. This exposure led to widespread knowledge of the amphetamine experience, development of a subculture of chronic amphetamine abusers who established and maintained a market for illegal amphetamine, increasing use of intravenous administration, and development of illegal laboratories to compensate for government curbs on the legal supply.

Legal Uses of Amphetamines

Until 1970 amphetamines had been prescribed for a large number of conditions including depression, fatigue, and long-term weight reduction. In 1970 the Food and Drug Administration, acting on the recommendation of the National Academy of Sciences, restricted the legal use of amphetamines to three types of condition: *narcolepsy, hyperkinetic behavior,* and *short-term weight reduction programs.*

Narcolepsy, or Sleep Epilepsy

The use of amphetamine for the treatment of narcolepsy is of minor importance because it is not a widespread ailment. *Narcolepsy* comes from the Greek words for *numbness* and *seizure.* A person who has narcolepsy goes to sleep as frequently as 50 times a day if he or she stays in one position very long. Taking amphetamine will keep this person alert to normal daily existence. The usual total dose of dextroamphetamine is 30 to 50 milligrams per day, in divided portions.

Hyperkinesis

This common behavioral problem in children and adolescents involves an abnormally high level of physical activity. About four out of every 100 grade school children and 40% of school-children referred to mental health clinics because of behavioral disturbances are hyperactive. Boys are much more likely to be diagnosed as hyperactive than girls. Such children have short attention and concentration spans. Their behavior is aggressive, irrelevant, without clear direction, and hard to predict. Their aggressiveness, talkativeness, and restless, impulsive behavior disrupt the classroom and often their home life as well.

Hyperkinetic children have frequently been described as having "minimal brain damage," but the evidence for this is inconclusive. Some of these children have medical histories of having had a difficult birth or a viral encephalitis infection in infancy. There are studies reporting a higher incidence of abnormal encephalograms (EEGs) in hyperkinetic children compared to normal children. However, many hyperkinetic children do not show abnormal EEGs or medical histories, so the significance of these factors is not clear. There is no evidence that all or even most of these children are mentally retarded, but their scholastic achievement is usually quite poor.

The drug commonly used to treat the hyperkinetic child is methylphenidate (Ritalin®). Ritalin® is a mild stimulant of the central nervous system that counteracts physical and mental fatigue while having only slight effects on blood pressure and respiration. Its potency is intermediate between that of amphetamine and caffeine. Methylphenidate and amphetamine are about equally effective in treating hyperkinesis, but methylphenidate is thought to stunt growth less than amphetamine (Weiner, 1980a). Stimulants are believed to work on hyperactive children by stimulating inhibitory areas of the brain, thus facilitating better control of motor activity and concentration.

Nonstimulant drugs such as the tranquilizer chlorpromazine have also been used to treat hyperkinesis with about 60% of the patients showing a reduction in symptoms. Many other drugs have been tried with varying degrees of success in treating these children. Imipramine (Tofranil®), a psychic stimulant or mood elevator, has produced good results. Some seriously disturbed hyperkinetic children who are not helped by Ritalin® respond to Tofranil® (Sleator & Sprague, 1978).

The management of a hyperkinetic child has many aspects; drug treatment is only one. Family counseling and psychotherapy may be necessary to keep a family from breaking up under the stress. The child may also require remedial education or special tutoring. He or she should not be kept on drug treatment indefinitely, because one of the side effects is a stunting of growth.

Alternatives to drug treatment are worth trying. For example, a few hyperkinetic children improve dramatically when food dyes and additives are excluded from their diet. These children may have been misdiagnosed originally, or the treatment may have a placebo effect. (The special diet requires close supervision of the child and "works" better if the child's cooperation can be elicited, which helps to make him or her responsible for the cure.) A small number improve following diagnosis and treatment of allergies.

Weight Reduction

One of the legal uses of amphetamines is for the treatment of obesity. According to accepted medical and health standards, over 35% of Americans are overweight. This is a major health problem, because statistics show that being overweight is an important factor in heart disease, coronary artery disease, and cerebrovascular disease. Excess poundage must be a matter of concern to many people, because millions of dollars are spent annually for over-the-counter diet aids and appetite suppressants.

Unfortunately the only ways to control weight still are: eat less or work more! With the possible exceptions of caffeine, thyroid hormone, and several highly toxic substances, no drugs are available that appreciably increase the rate at which we burn calories. Thyroid hormone, by increasing the metabolic rate, will increase the rate at which our bodies use food energy, but it has serious cardiovascular side effects when taken in amounts greater than needed. It is ethically used only to treat cases of thyroid inadequacy. Thyroid hormone has the drawback, too, of having an appetite-stimulating action at doses effective for weight loss.

Amphetamine and chemically similar compounds are used for appetite control because they decrease hunger. A drug that suppresses appetite is called an *anorectic drug*, or an *anorexiant*. Amphetamines are thought to act by affecting the appetite center in the hypothalamus. They do not affect blood sugar levels, but they do decrease food intake. This is the reason that the FDA approved short-term use of amphetamines for weight loss programs. Unless the dose s continuously increased, the appetite-suppressing action of this drug, together with the pleasant stimulating effects, usually wears off after about two weeks. At high doses the anorexic effect returns, but an even higher tolerance will then develop. Because of this buildup of tolerance, the FDA issued a warning about the danger of long-term use of amphetamines.

Many authorities feel that the euphoric effect of the amphetamines is the real basis for their continued use in weight reduction programs. Although the drugs are effective in short-term treatment of obesity, their effectiveness is not related to their depression of the appetite center; it is due to their stimulating action. In other words, fat people may be taking amphetamines for the same reason speed freaks take them. Long-term weight reduction and weight maintenance at the desired level require modification of the person's behavior. They cannot be obtained with drugs.

Amphetamines in Athletics

Amphetamines are also abused to improve athletic performance. Many studies report that amphetamine does not enhance optimal rested performance, although there is some evidence that at low doses (5 milligrams) it may improve the attitude of individuals toward their work. One experiment studied the effects of amphetamine (at a dosage of 14 milligrams per 70 kilograms of body weight) on the performance of swimmers, runners, and weight throwers. In this case it was found that the performance of highly trained athletes, of the classes studied, can be significantly improved in the majority of cases (about 75%) by the administration of amphetamine (Smith & Beecher, 1959). This study is the mainstay of those who believe that amphetamine does improve performance above that

reached in the rested, nondrug state. A review of this area of research concluded:

> It is true that for a number of simple tasks there seemed to be little effect of amphetamine except in subjects whose performance had deteriorated as the result of prolonged work or sleep deprivation. On the other hand, data indicating a true enhancement are most convincing. Those on athletic performance obtained by Smith and Beecher . . . found that the effects of amphetamine were more apparent in rested than in fatigued subjects. [Weiss, 1969]

Amateur athletic organizations have begun to take steps to control drug use by competing athletes. The Medical Commission of the International Olympic Organization conducted their first "doping" tests on a few athletes participating in the Winter Games at Grenoble in 1968. All tests proved negative. The Medical Commission has defined *doping* as the use of any drug with the aim of attaining an artificial and unfair increase of performance capacity in competition. Forbidden substances include: psychomotor stimulant drugs, sympathomimetic amines (amphetamine and others), central nervous system stimulants such as strychnine, narcotic analgesics (morphine, cocaine, procaine, and so on), and the anabolic steroids. In the 1968 games in Mexico the Medical Commission broadened the list to include the use of any and all medication. As a result of this ruling, one of the American athletes in the 1972 Summer Olympics forfeited his gold medal because ephedrine (an alkaloid similar in action to epinephrine), which he had been taking for his asthma, was detected in his urine. Forty million dollars were budgeted for doping control at the 1980 Olympics in Moscow. The abuse of stimulants continues to be a widespread problem in professional athletics.

Distribution of Amphetamines and Misuse

At the 1970 hearings on amphetamines before the Select Committee on Crime, it was estimated that over 5 billion amphetamine doses had been manufactured legally the year before. The Department of Justice reported in 1970 that it was unable to account for 38% of the total amount of amphetamines manufactured in the United States—nearly 2 billion doses. About 8% of all prescriptions in the United States that year were for amphetamines. The amounts manufactured far exceeded the needs for medical purposes. Nearly 99% of amphetamines sold were for weight control. In 1972 a new law took effect setting a quota for amphetamine production: 235 million units—a sizeable drop in volume. Accurate figures on the amount of illegal amphetamine manufactured and sold are not available, but estimates run from 10% to 25% of the amount on the legal market.

Since the late 1970s the medical associations have asked all physicians to be more careful in the use of prescribed amphetamines. In fact, their use is recommended only for narcolepsy and some cases of hyperkinesis. Amphetamines are not recommended for weight loss. Probably less than 1% of all prescriptions now written are for amphetamines.

Truck drivers are usually the group most people think of when talking about misusing amphetamines to combat fatigue. The term often heard in this connection is the *Los Angeles turnaround*, which means taking enough amphetamine to enable a truck driver to make a round trip between New York and Los Angeles without resting.

One obvious misuse of amphetamines is taking them just for the fun of it. A dose of 10 to 30 milligrams of Dexedrine® will make a person feel quite good—alert, talkative, and "turned on." Unfortunately this dosage is likely to cause hyperactive and nervous or jittery feelings that can encourage the use of another drug, like methaqualone (sopors) or a barbiturate to relieve the discomfort of those feelings.

Speed is methamphetamine in liquid form for injection, subcutaneously or intravenously. Speed can also be synthesized as a white crystalline powder. The profit for the manufacturer is big enough to make its illegal production worthwhile: one estimate is that a pound of methamphetamine crystal can be made for about $100 and sold in quarter- or half-ounce amounts on the street for about $2500 a pound. Methamphetamine is relatively easy to synthesize if the chemicals are available. In 1969 it was reported that a nine-year-old child synthesized speed in her home. Another 15-year-old "speed cook" admitted synthesizing methamphetamine with only a vacuum, a big glass, a cooking pan, a heater, and a hair dryer.

Effects of High Doses of Amphetamines

The speed freak uses chronic, high doses of amphetamines intravenously. The cycle or pattern of use usually starts with several days of repeated injections, usually of methamphetamine, gradually increasing in amount and frequency. Some users may inject up to several thousand milligrams in a single day. Initially the user may feel energetic, talkative, enthusiastic, happy, confident, and powerful, and may initiate and complete highly ambitious tasks. He or she does not sleep and usually eats very little. The pupils of the eyes are dilated, the mouth is dry, and the body temperature is elevated (hyperpyrexia).

After the first day or so, toxic unpleasant symptoms become prominent as the dosage is increased. The toxic effects are similar to those found in people who use lower doses less frequently, but they are intensified. Symptoms commonly reported at this stage are teeth-grinding, confused and disorganized patterns of thought and behavior, compulsive repetition of meaningless acts, irritability, self-consciousness, suspiciousness, and fear. Hallucinations and delusions similar to a paranoid psychosis occur. The person is likely to show aggressive and antisocial behavior for no apparent reason. Severe chest pains, abdominal pain that mimics appendicitis, and fainting from overdosage are sometimes reported. The range of physical and mental symptoms from low to high doses is summarized in Table 8-3.

"Cocaine bugs" is one bizarre effect of high doses of amphetamine: the individual feels something, like insects, crawling under his or her skin. Amphetamine and cocaine probably stimulate nerve endings in the skin, thus causing this sensation. A similar effect appears to occur in experimental animals given large doses of methamphetamine chronically.

Towards the end of the "run," which usually lasts less than a week, the toxic symptoms dominate. When the drug is discontinued, because the person has no more of it or because the symptoms have become too unpleasant, prolonged sleep follows, sometimes lasting several days. On awakening, the person is lethargic, quite hungry, and often severely emotionally depressed. He or she may overcome these effects with another injection, initiating a new cycle.

TABLE 8-3 Summary of the effects of amphetamine on the body and the mind

	The body	The mind
Low dose	Increased heartbeat	Decreased fatigue
	Increased blood pressure	Increased confidence
	Decreased appetite	Increased feeling of alertness
	Increased breathing rate	Restlessness, talkativeness
	Inability to sleep	Increased irritability
	Sweating	Fearfulness, apprehension
	Dry mouth	Distrust of people
	Muscle twitching	Behavioral stereotypy
	Convulsions	Hallucinations
	Fever	Psychosis
	Chest pain	
	Irregular heartbeat	
High dose	Death due to overdose	

Barbiturates, tranquilizers, or opiate narcotics are sometimes used to ease the "crash" or to terminate an unpleasant run.

Continued use of massive doses of amphetamine often leads to considerable weight loss, sores and nonhealing ulcers, liver disease, hypertensive disorders, cerebral hemorrhage (stroke), and kidney damage. It is often impossible to tell whether these effects are a result of the drug, poor eating habits, or other factors associated with the life-style of people who inject methamphetamine. Experiments in which rhesus monkeys were injected intravenously with methamphetamine every other day for one week, or twice a week for a month, or twice a week for a year, have shown that methamphetamine is capable of producing direct injury to arteries and veins, which causes severe brain damage. Oral methamphetamine given to monkeys and rats results in cerebral vascular changes and kidney damage as serious as that caused by intravenous methamphetamine (Rumbaugh, 1977).

Heavy use of amphetamines or cocaine may induce a psychosis that is indistinguishable from paranoid schizophrenia. In addition, several investigators contend that schizophrenics and others with borderline psychotic conditions are more likely to use the drug intravenously than are other individuals. In one study, 41% of those requiring hospital treatment for amphetamine use were thought to have been schizophrenic before taking the drug (Hekimian & Gershon, 1968).

The proportion of amphetamine users who develop psychosis and the predisposing factors are still unknown. Psychotic reactions occur occasionally in persons taking amphetamines for narcolepsy or for hyperkinesis. The majority of acute psychotic reactions occur toward the end of a run, and such symptoms usually dissipate after a few days' rest. In fact, psychiatrists used this to distinguish between amphetamine psychosis and paranoid schizophrenia before there

was a reliable chemical assay for amphetamine in the urine. Patients were kept under close supervision for several weeks, and, if the symptoms disappeared, they were probably suffering from amphetamine-induced psychosis.

Speed freaks are generally unpopular with the rest of the drug-taking community, especially the "acid heads," because of the aggressive, unpredictable behavior associated with intravenous methamphetamine use. Consequently, these individuals may live together in "flash houses" totally occupied by amphetamine users. Heavy users are generally unable to hold a steady job because of the drug habit and often have a parasitic relationship with the rest of the illicit drug-using community.

Although amphetamines do not cause physical dependence, they cause so many physical problems after a binge that one can compare them with the depressant drugs and their effects during withdrawal. The tendency of tolerance-producing drugs to manifest a rebound effect upon withdrawal has been thoroughly studied. After the amphetamine binge, the chronic user is generally lethargic and depressed both in mood and physiological function. This type of rebound effect is opposite to that of the depressant drugs, in which the user shows severe and toxic overstimulation, even to the point of convulsions. Many observers believe that the chronic use of intravenous amphetamines represents a thinly disguised suicidal tendency as well as an attention- and sympathy-getting device.

Other Drugs Used with Amphetamines

Amphetamines are frequently used in conjunction with, or alternately with, a variety of other drugs such as barbiturates, alcohol, and heroin. About one-half of all regular users of amphetmine diet pills are also heavy users of alcohol Chambers & Griffey, 1975).

Amphetamines intensify, prolong, or otherwise alter the effects of LSD, and the two drugs are sometimes used together. The majority of peed users have also had experience with a variety of psychedelic and other drugs. Persons dependent on the opiate narcotics also frequently use amphetamine or cocaine, called speedballs, either mixed with the narcotics or separately.

DOM (STP), MDA, and MMDA are structurally related to the amphetamines, yet they are potent hallucinogens (see Chapter 6). DOM n doses of less than 3 milligrams causes pupil dilatation and increases heart rate, blood pressure, and body temperature. It causes a mild euphoria that may last from 8 to 12 hours, with the peak reaction around the third to fifth hour after it is taken. Most street doses tested in San Francisco in the Haight-Ashbury area contained about 10 milligrams. The higher dosages last 16–24 hours, and acute panic reactions have been reported at this or slightly higher doses. In addition, an LSD-like trip occurs simultaneously. Often the mind is flooded with a variety of irrelevant and incoherent thoughts, then becomes absolutely blank.

How and Where Does Amphetamine Work in the Body?

Amphetamines stimulate the reticular activating system (see Chapter 2). The activation is transmitted to all parts of the brain, and the individual becomes aroused, alert, hypersensitive to stimuli, and feels "turned on." These effects occur even without external sensory input. This activation may be a very pleasant experience in itself, but a continual high level of activation may produce anxiety.

Amphetamines have potent effects on the reward (pleasure) center in the medial forebrain bundle (see Chapter 2). Increases in activity in this system are experienced as pleasurable; thus the user is encouraged to continue the experience. The "flash" or sudden feeling of intense pleasure that is experienced when amphetamine is taken intravenously probably results from the delivery of a high dose of the drug to the reward center. Some users describe the sensation as a "whole body orgasm," and many associate intravenous methamphetamine use with sexual feelings. Some report that sexual activity under its influence is prolonged and may continue for hours. When orgasm finally is reached it may be more pleasurable than usual. Other users find that they cannot reach orgasm under any circumstances. Although the number of users reporting increased sexual activity is in the minority, they may give this as their reason for taking amphetamine.

Amphetamine has three actions on neurotransmission. First, amphetamine causes the neurotransmitter norepinephrine to leak spontaneously from the presynaptic sites. This leakage cause stimulation of the next neuron across the synapse, as if a normal impulse were being transmitted. Second, when electrical impulses occur in the presynaptic fiber, the presence of amphetamine increases the amount of neurotransmitter released with each impulse. Third, amphetamine enhances its own effects as well as those resulting from electrical stimulation by blocking the reuptake of dopamine and norepinephrine, so that the stimulus is continuous across the synapse to the next neuron. (Remember that normally at least a third of these neurotransmitters are reabsorbed and used again.)

A curious condition that has been reported many times in heavy amphetamine users is behavioral stereotypy, or getting "hung up." This means that a simple activity is repeated over and over again. An individual who is hung up will get caught in a repetitious thought or act for hours. For example, he or she may take objects, like radios or clocks, apart and carefully categorize all the parts. Or this person may sit in a tub of water and bathe all day, hold a note or repeat a phrase of music, or repeatedly clean the same object. This phenomenon seems to be peculiar to the amphetamines, although it may occur to a lesser extent in the course of a psychedelic trip.

Behavioral stereotypy may occur because amphetamines inhibit the uptake of dopamine in the brain. Dopamine is the neurotransmitter associated with the complex controls for some of the motor functions of the body. When the reuptake of dopamine or norepinephrine is blocked, the neurons become more sensitized (Sulser & Sanders-Bush, 1971). This change is not rapidly reversed. Chronic use of high doses of amphetamines causes dramatic decreases in the neurotransmitter dopamine that persist for months after the drug is stopped (Jaffe, 1980). The accumulation of dopamine might also explain the hallucinogenic effects of large doses of amphetamines. People with paranoid schizophrenia show the same pattern of repetitive acts as heavy amphetamine users; the correlation, if any, may be clear when the various control systems of neurotransmitters and neural pathways are better understood.

PHENMETRAZINE (PRELUDIN®) AND METHYLPHENIDATE (RITALIN®)

Both phenmetrazine and methylphenidate are central nervous system stimulants (Appendix A-6). Both have been used in place of amphetamine. Phenmetrazine, for example, is used in diet pills and has had an interesting history a an abused drug. The best-known example of abuse was in Sweden in the 1950s and 1960s Preludin® was marketed in Sweden in 1955, and it was soon noted that it induced euphoria. The drug reached the street almost immediately. (Part of the reason for the increase in use of phenmetrazine was the earlier outlawing of amphetamines.) In 1959, Sweden placed strong legal sanctions on Predludin®, but this only seemed to increase its use through black marketing. The controls increased the price and seemingly the demand for the drug. It was reported that there was an increase in the illegal manufacture of the drug as well as other amphetamines. The use of these drugs finally declined because of lack of easy availability, strict laws, and an extensive educational program warning of the problems of using illegally manufactured drugs.

Methylphenidate is a relatively mild central nervous system stimulant that has been used to alleviate depression. Research now casts doubt on its effectiveness for treating depression, but it is effective in treatment of narcolepsy. As mentioned previously, it has been proven to aid in calming down hyperkinetic children, and it seems to be the drug of choice for this use now. The strength of the drug lies between that of caffeine and amphetamine. It is not used much on the street because amphetamines have always been plentiful.

COCAINE

History of Cocaine

Cocaine has been used as a stimulant for thousands of years. The most accurate record of its use dates back to about 500 A.D., from a gravesite found in Peru in which there was a supply of coca leaves. Pottery showing people with the characteristic cheek bulge of the coca chewer has also been found in Peru. Natives of Peru, Bolivia, and Colombia have long used the leaves of the *Erythroxylon coca* shrub for stimulation and to combat fatigue. Leaves of the coca plant contain up to 1% of the alkaloid cocaine; very little is known about the effects of the more than one dozen other alkaloids present in the coca leaves. The natives prefer leaves with low cocaine content, because cocaine has a bitter taste. Approximately 2 oz of coca leaves (an average daily amount) contain almost the minimum daily vitamin requirement and some essential minerals, which could be significant in the monotonous and limited diet available to these people (Carroll, 1977a).

When Pizarro invaded Peru in the 16th century, he found that the Incas had built a flourishing, complex civilization. Coca leaves were an important part of their culture. They were used in religious ceremonies and in bartering. The Spanish adopted this custom of barter and paid the native laborers in coca leaves for mining and transporting silver and gold.

In the last half of the 19th century a Corsican chemist, Angelo Mariani, made an extract of the active ingredients (one of which is cocaine) in the coca leaf. This extract was made into cough drops and into a special wine called Mariani's Coca Wine. The pope gave Mariani a medal in appreciation for the fine work he had done. The coca extract was publicized as a magical drug that would free the body from fatigue, lift the spirits, and cause a sense of well-being.

Sigmund Freud was a staunch advocate of the use of cocaine. In 1884 he said, "I have been working with a magical drug. I have had dazzling success in treatment of a case of gastric catarrh. If it goes well, I will write an essay on it and I expect it will win its place in therapeutics by the side of morphium, and superior to

it. . . . I take very small doses of it regularly against depression and against indigestion, and with the most brilliant success." Freud was so convinced of the value of the drug that he tried to get his fiancee, his sisters, and all his friends to try it. The dangers of this drug became evident to Freud when he tried using cocaine to cure his friend Fleischl of morphine addiction. Following administration of large doses of the powerful stimulant, Freud spent one frightful night nursing Fleischl through an episode of cocaine psychosis, and thereafter he was bitterly against all drug use (Holmstedt, 1967).

Sherlock Holmes was a user of cocaine. In the 1890s this must have been a reasonably common occurrence among prominent Englishmen.

> Sherlock Holmes took his bottle from the corner of the mantelpiece, and his hypodermic syringe from its neat morocco case. With his long, white, nervous fingers he adjusted the delicate needle and rolled back his left shirtcuff. For some little time, his eyes rested thoughtfully upon the sinewy forearm and wrist, all dotted and scarred with innumerable puncture marks. Finally, he thrust the sharp point home, pressed down the tiny piston, and sank back into the velvet-lined armchair with a long sigh of satisfaction. [Doyle, 1938; published with the permission of the copyright owner of the Sir Arthur Conan Doyle literary estate]

Robert Louis Stevenson may have written his famous book, *Dr. Jekyll and Mr. Hyde*, while he was under the influence of cocaine. He wrote the book, with several revisions, in six days. The characterizations show the swings of personality that occur when one is under the influence of this drug.

Cocaine was first used in America as a local anesthetic for eye surgery and then as a nerve tonic. The famous Birney's Bitters of the 1890s contained 4% cocaine—a dose that would really jolt your nervous system. In 1886 Dr. J. C. Pemberton formulated a new nerve tonic from extracts of the coca plant and the nuts of the cola plant. This tonic was named *Coca-Cola.* An early advertisement for the nerve tonic extolled its valuable properties thus:

> This "Intellectual Beverage" and Temperance Drink contains the valuable Tonic and Nerve Stimulant properties of the Coca plant and Cola (or Kola) nuts, and makes not only a delicious, exhilarating, refreshing and invigorating Beverage . . . but a valuable Brain Tonic, and a cure for all nervous affections—Sick Headache, Neuralgia, Hysteria, Melancholy, etc. [Huisking, 1968]

Business was not too good for several years, so Coca-Cola® was then publicized as a stimulating soda fountain drink. Until 1903, the cocaine-containing extract of coca leaves was used together with other ingredients for flavoring. Then the manufacturer discontinued the use of cocaine-containing syrup. After cocaine is extracted from the leaves for medical purposes, the plant products are sent to the Coca-Cola® manufacturer, where they are used as flavoring. The only stimulant now in Coca-Cola® is the added caffeine: there are about 45 milligrams of caffeine in a 12-ounce bottle, equivalent to about half a cup of coffee.

Effects of Cocaine

Cocaine is still legally classified as a narcotic (Schedule II) drug, although its action is just the opposite to that of a narcotic. Cocaine induces intense euphoric and hallucinatory effects for a short period of time. The drug is often sniffed or "snorted," hence the common name, "nose candy." However, cocaine's strong vasoconstrictive effect will cause the nasal membranes to deteriorate. Some chronic snorters have even lost the nasal septum, the cartilaginous part that divides the nasal passages, but a runny, inflamed nose is more commonly suffered by users.

Cocaine, introduced either intravenously or absorbed from the nasal epithelium, produces an increase in heart rate and blood pressure, but the extent of the effect varies. In one study using human subjects, 25 mg of snorted cocaine produced minimal changes in the systolic blood pressure, whereas 100 mg produced significant changes. When administered intravenously, 10 or 25 mg cocaine produced a significant increase in heart rate and systolic blood pressure. The onset of these effects occurred in two minutes, but peaked earlier (five to ten minutes compared to 15–20 minutes) when taken intravenously. The precise time values vary from one study to another and depend, in part, on the subject's expectations. The rate of absorption varies with the route of administration. Within a few minutes following I.V. injection, the total dose is present in the blood, whereas after snorting, the concentration of cocaine in the blood rapidly increases for 20 minutes, peaks at one hour, and then gradually declines for at least three hours after application (Byck & Van Dyke, 1977).

Cocaine probably works initially on the cerebral cortex. Motor activity increases at low doses. At higher doses convulsions may occur. At still higher dosages the respiration centers of the brain are affected, and the breathing rate increases. Cocaine increases heart rate and blood pressure; high levels of the drug delivered intravenously may stop the heart. Cocaine prevents reuptake of released dopamine and norepinephrine, so the neurotransmitter's effect is enhanced. The average street dose is 20 to 50 milligrams intranasally. A lethal dose is about 1200 milligrams if taken in one dose. At this dosage, respiratory failure occurs. However, users have taken up to 10 grams in one day with repeated injections.

A common side effect of cocaine is the increase in body temperature. This is partly due to the vasoconstrictive effect on blood vessels. The pupils of the eyes become dilated (mydriasis), because muscles controlling the iris constrict.

Cocaine's effects are similar to those of amphetamine in that both drugs reduce fatigue and induce euphoria and mood elevation; however, cocaine's effects do not last as long as the effects of amphetamine. Many experimental subjects are unable to tell initially whether they have been given amphetamine or cocaine. Whether the euphoria from cocaine is due to the local anesthetic or the sympathomimetic effect is not known (Wesson & Smith, 1977). In order to maintain cocaine's extreme high or "flash" it may be necessary to inject every 15 minutes. As with amphetamine, the flash is often described as a "total body orgasm." (Some users take a depressant drug like heroin at the same time to keep from reaching the extreme high.) When this feeling begins to fade, depression sets in, and another dose of cocaine is strongly desired. Continued use results in loss of appetite, loss of weight, malnutrition, insomnia, digestive disorders, paranoia, and hallucinations. The unusual tactile hallucination, *formication* ("cocaine bugs"), may occur just as it does with intravenous methamphetamine use.

Use of cocaine does not cause physical dependence, even when taken in huge doses over a period of time. There are no obvious withdrawal effects, although states of depression may occur immediately after the euphoria following cocaine injection has faded. The possibility of psychological dependence, however, is real and has been demonstrated to be very strong in some people—from Freud, to entertainers under pressure to perform, to trendsetters in the higher socioeconomic classes, such as stockbrokers, financiers, and executives.

Chronic Use of Cocaine

Cocaine has varying effects on the body, depending on whether the amount is taken over a short period of time or a long period of time. Short-term administration is called *acute dosage*, whereas long-term repeated use is called *chronic dosage*. Acute dosage usually causes euphoria, a sense of confidence, increased energy, increased heart rate and blood pressure, dilated pupils, constriction of blood vessels, a rise in body temperature, and an increase in metabolic rate (Byck & Van Dyke, 1977).

Apparently only a small number of people use cocaine chronically, because of its high cost and the difficulty of obtaining it, and because the drug is not physically addicting. If cocaine is taken daily in fairly large amounts, it can disrupt eating and sleeping habits, produce minor psychological disturbances including irritability and difficulty in concentration, and create a serious psychological dependence. Cocaine is only psychologically addicting, but some persons show mild withdrawal symptoms like anxiety and depression. Some types of hallucination, paranoid thinking, and (rarely) psychoses can occur in heavy users. Chronic users sometimes suffer from runny, inflamed, swollen, and even ulcerated noses. However, a perforated nasal septum is rare today (Grinspoon & Bakalar, 1979). If a user develops anxiety on the drug, the short-term treatment is usually diazepam (Valium®). Psychotherapy is often recommended for long-term treatment of cocaine-induced anxiety or paranoia.

In experiments in which unlimited access to intravenous cocaine is provided, animals will kill themselves by voluntary injections. This type of experimental result is similar to that obtained with methamphetamine and dextroamphetamine. Although humans usually do not use cocaine this way, craving can become a serious problem in persons who have constant access to the drug. Users sometimes find it necessary to deny themselves access to cocaine for a few days or weeks, and some have been known to try to lock up their bank accounts so that they will not spend all their money on the drug.

The U.S. federal government has developed a computer system that analyzes the data from all drug-related medical problems. In 1975–1976 only 3.6% of the cases reported at drug crisis centers and only 1.2% at federally funded medical clinics were caused by or related to cocaine. These figures added up to 650 patients all across the country. Some problems probably are not reported, but how many is not known. It is likely that some of the most serious cocaine-related problems, such as paranoia, and problems caused by taking depressants like heroin, barbiturates, or alcohol with cocaine are not reported or are taken care of in nonmedical settings. Because cocaine and amphetamines mimic functional psychoses more closely than any other drugs, they are being used in experimental medicine to investigate mental disorders.

Cutting and Selling Cocaine

In over a decade of analyzing street drugs, we have never found street cocaine with more than 20% of the drug. Usually, 10% or less of cocaine is mixed with a variety of fillers. Laboratories in the Los Angeles area, however, report an average purity of about 58%. "The rich man's drug" has several cutting materials that are used more frequently than others. The white powder *mannitol*, or *mannite*, is commonly used. This material resembles cocaine in appearance but is actually a type of sugar, and is a mild laxative. If a person had diarrhea after using cocaine, it is likely that mannitol was the filler. Other sugars are often used: lactose, dextrose (glucose), and sometimes powdered sucrose (cane sugar) are found in analyzed samples of street cocaine. Inositol, a vitamin in the B complex, is another filler. This compound is harmless, as are mannitol and the other sugars, but they may cause the user's nose to run. Procaine, amphetamine, and quinine are other additives that are used as stretching agents or fillers. Quinine and amphetamine can both cause harm to the nasal membranes.

There are many synthetic drugs similar to cocaine. Most of these have the ability to numb the tissue but will not produce a high if snorted. If someone bought what he or she thought was cocaine and ended up with a numbed nose and no rush, it is likely that the product was actually procaine, tetracaine, or some other synthetic instead of cocaine. Lidocaine, however, is a euphoriant like cocaine when snorted (Jaffe, 1980).

Cocaine often is sold in the form of little pellets, called *rocks*, or sometimes as flakes or powder. If it is in pellet form, it must be crushed before using. Such exotic names as *Peruvian rock* or *Bolivian flake* are bandied about to convince the buyer that the "stash" is high grade. Some users have become quite proficient in testing cocaine for impurities. Common and rapid tests used are the chlorox, the melting-point, and the combustion tests. If a small sample of cocaine is dropped into chlorox, various patterns and colors are produced according to the cutting materials and adulterants. In addition, each impurity has its own melting point. And, if the sample is burned, pure cocaine leaves very little residue (Lee, 1976). The information gained from these tests can give clues about the purity of the drug, but only a thorough analysis with professional laboratory methods is accurate.

In the past few years, a method called *free basing* has been used to purify and concentrate cocaine so that, when snorted, it gives a more potent rush. In this process, the cocaine, which is usually in the form of the hydrochloride salt, is treated with a liquid base to remove the hydrochloric acid. The free cocaine is then dissolved in a solvent such as petroleum ether or diethyl ether, from which the purified cocaine is crystallized. These crystals are then crushed and used in a special heated glass smoking pipe. This preparation is supposed to give a much more powerful high than regular cocaine.

When snorting cocaine, users often will scratch lines on a mirror and place the powder in the lines. Then they will form a cone from paper money, or use a straw, and inhale the powder from the line. One dose is sometimes called a line, in fact. Some people use special snorting spoons that fit in the nostril. A few users eat the drug. However, oral use is not common in the United States, even though the subjective highs are equal to or greater than after intranasal administration (Van Dyke, Jatlow, Ungerer, Barash, & Byck, 1978). Still others inject the drug. Injection can be dangerous, however, due to the effect of high doses on the heart.

Medical Uses of Cocaine

The only recognized medical uses for cocaine in the United States are as a local anesthetic in eye, ear, nose, and throat surgery, and as an anesthetic when examining the digestive and respiratory tracts with instruments. Cocaine combines vasconstriction (valuable in nasal surgery), long duration of anesthesia (over an hour), and low toxicity in a way no presently available synthetic can match. Cocaine is used in England and Canada as an ingredient in Brompton's cocktail, a preparation for treating the severe chronic pain in terminal cancer. The mixture contains 10 milligrams cocaine, 5 to 20 milligrams morphine, and 2.5 milliliters of alcohol in a 20-milliliter solution of sugar syrup. The cocaine seems to work by preventing too much sedation and clouding of the senses, while enhancing pain relief. In the United States, a similar use has been found for amphetamine in combination with morphine to enhance alertness in the terminally ill (Grinspoon & Bakalar, 1979).

CHAPTER 9

TOBACCO

CHAPTER OBJECTIVES

1. Discuss the reasons why the first major drug controversy of global dimensions arose around the use of tobacco.
2. List three ways the nicotine content of cigarettes can be reduced.
3. Describe the actions of nicotine and carbon monoxide on the body.
4. List reasons why nicotine is believed to be the active substance in tobacco that causes dependence.
5. Explain why the risk of premature death for female smokers is expected soon to equal that of men.
6. Defend the following statement: there is a dose-response relationship between the number of cigarettes smoked per day and particular tobacco-related illnesses. Give five examples.
7. List factors that have synergistic relationships to tobacco smoking in increasing the risk of cardiovascular disease, lung and laryngeal cancers, and bronchopulmonary disease.
8. Describe the effects on the fetus and infant if the mother smokes; if the father smokes.
9. List the risks associated with involuntary smoking.
10. Describe ways a person who cannot manage to quit smoking can reduce his or her health risks.
11. Explain why it is difficult for most smokers to quit.
12. List biological and behavioral approaches used in helping smokers quit. Why is the "nonsmokers' rights" movement important?
13. Define the following terms: mortality ratio, aneurysm, alpha-1-antitrypsin deficiency, sidestream and mainstream smoke, and the rapid smoking and stimulus control methods.

HISTORY AND TECHNOLOGY OF TOBACCO USE

Tobacco is one of the New World's contributions to the rest of the world. The word *tobacco* may have come from the *tabaco*, which was a two-pronged tube used by the natives of Central America to take snuff. Columbus reported receiving tobacco leaves from the natives of San Salvador in 1492. However, the natives had been smoking the leaves for many centuries before Columbus arrived. Practically all the natives from Paraguay to Quebec used tobacco. The Maya regarded tobacco smoke as divine incense to bring rain in the dry season. The oldest known representation of a smoker is a stone carving from a Mayan temple, showing a priest puffing on a ceremonial pipe. The Aztecs used tobacco in folk medicine and in religious ritual. Indeed, the Native Americans used tobacco in every manner known: smoked as cigars, cigarettes (wrapped in corn husks), and in pipes; as a syrup to be swallowed or applied to the gums; chewed; snuffed; and administered rectally as a ceremonial enema (Schultes, 1978)!

Tobacco reached Europe and was at first merely a curiosity, but its use spread rapidly. Europeans had no name for the process of inhaling smoke, so they called this "drinking" the smoke. Perhaps the first European to inhale tobacco smoke was Rodrig de Jerez, a member of Columbus's crew. He had seen people smoking in Cuba and brought the habit to Portugal. When he smoked in Portugal, his friends, seeing the smoke coming from his mouth, believed him to be possessed by the devil! He was placed in jail for several years (Heimann, 1960).

In 1559 the French ambassador to Portugal, Jean Nicot, grew interested in this novel plant and sent it as a gift to Catherine de Médicis, queen mother of France. In fact, the plant was named *Nicotiana tabacum* after him. It is a solanaceous plant, related to potatoes, belladonna, henbane, mandrake, and other plants described in Chapter 6. (It was originally called *Peruvian henbane.*) The next several hundred years saw a remarkable increase in the use of tobacco. Portuguese sailors smoked tobacco and left tobacco seeds scattered around the world. Over the next 150 years they introduced tobacco to and set up tobacco trade with India, Brazil, Japan, China, Arabia, and Africa. Many of the large tobacco plantations around the world got their start from the Portuguese.

One of the early Christian religious leaders, Bishop Bartolome de las Casas (1474–1566) reported that the Spanish settlers in Hispaniola (Haiti), like the natives, smoked rolled tobacco leaves in cigar form. When the bishop asked them about this disgusting habit, they replied that they found it impossible to give the habit up. The addictive qualities of tobacco were recognized even then (Corti, 1931).

As the use of tobacco spread, so did the controversy about whether it was bad or good. It was the first major drug controversy of global dimensions. Tobacco as a medicine was at first almost universally accepted, whereas smoking for pleasure was controversial. Nicholas Monardes, in his description of New World plants (1574), recommended tobacco as an infallible cure for 36 different maladies. It was described as a holy, healing herb, a special remedy sent by God to man. Opponents of tobacco use disputed the medical value. They pointed out that tobacco was used in the magic and religion of Native Americans (Monardes had also described ritual use by native priests). Tobacco was attacked as an evil plant, an invention of the devil. King James I of England was fanatically opposed to smoking. In an attempt to limit tobacco use, he raised the import tax on tobacco and also sold the right to collect the tax (Austin, 1978). (This may be the first example of indirect prohibition; see Chapter 7 and the Marijuana Tax Act.)

Nevertheless, tobacco use increased. By 1614, the number of tobacco shops in London had mushroomed to over 7000, and demand for tobacco usually outstripped supply. It was literally worth its weight in silver, so it was smoked in pipes with very small bowls (Figure 9-1). Use of tobacco grew in other areas of the world as well. Africans on the west coast of that continent were capturing and selling inland natives to the Portuguese for the equivalent of about 450 pounds of Brazilian tobacco per slave (Brooks, 1952).

From sailor to pope, the use of tobacco increased. In 1642 Pope Urban VIII issued a formal decree forbidding the use of tobacco in church under penalty of immediate excommunication. The priests as well as the worshippers were staining the floors with tobacco juice. One priest in Naples sneezed so hard after taking snuff that he vomited on the altar in full sight of the congregation. Pope Innocent X issued another edict against tobacco use in 1650, but the clergy as well as the laity continued to take snuff and smoke. Finally in 1725 Pope Benedict XIII, himself a smoker and snufftaker, annulled all previous edicts against tobacco (Austin, 1978).

In the 1600s, Turkey, Russia, and China all imposed the death penalty for smoking. Sultan Murad the Cruel executed many of his subjects caught smoking. The Romanov tsars publicly tortured smokers and exiled them to Siberia. The Chinese decapitated anyone caught dealing in tobacco with the "outer barbarians." Yet smoking continued to grow to epidemic proportions. Despite their opposition to anything foreign, the Chinese became the heaviest smokers in Asia, thus facilitating the later spread of opium smoking (see Chapter 12) (Austin, 1978).

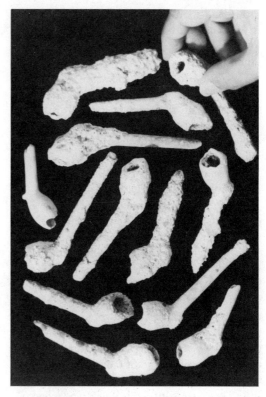

FIGURE 9-1
Clay pipes, part of the cargo for the American Colonies. Recovered from the wreck of the *Virginia Merchant*, 1661, off the coast of Bermuda, by Patricia Jones-Witters.

Thus far no nation whose population has learned to use tobacco products has been successful in outlawing their use or in getting people to stop.

Snuffing first became fashionable in France during the reign of Louis XIII and spread throughout European aristocracy. Snuffing was regarded as daintier and more elegant than constantly exhaling smoke. King Louis XIV, however, detested all forms of tobacco and would not permit its use in his presence. (He would have banned it, but he needed the tax revenue tobacco brought in.) His sister-in-law, Charlotte of Orleans, was one of the few at court who agreed with him. As she wrote to her sister: "It is better to take no snuff at all than a little; for it is certain that he who takes a little will soon take much, and that is why they call it 'the enchanted herb,' for those who take it are so taken by it that they cannot go without it." Napoleon is said to have used 7 pounds of snuff per month (Corti, 1931).

Tobacco played a significant role in the successful colonization of the United States. In 1610 John Rolfe was sent to Virginia to set up a tobacco industry. At first the tobacco planted in Virginia was a native species, *Nicotiana rustica*, that was harsh and did not sell well. But in 1612 Rolfe managed to obtain some seeds of the Spanish tobacco species, *Nicotiana tabacum*, and by 1613 the success of the tobacco industry and the Virginia colony was ensured. The importance of tobacco as a substitute for money was noted by George Washington during the Revolutionary War: "I say, if you can't send money, send tobacco." (In World War I, General Pershing said "You asked me what we need to win this war. I answer tobacco as much as bullets." General Douglas MacArthur said about the same thing in World War II, because he believed tobacco was essential for good morale.) Tobacco played a strategic role in the Revolutionary War because of its value to the French, who loaned the colonists money in exchange for tobacco. The British realized this, so General Cornwallis made the destruction of the Virginia tobacco plantations one of his major campaign objectives (Heimann, 1960).

The history of tobacco smoking in the United States is rich in the tremendous number of laws, rules, regulations, and customs that rose out of the habit of smoking. Many states had laws prohibiting the use of tobacco by young people and also by women. In the 1860s, for instance, it was illegal in Florida for anyone under 21 to smoke cigarettes. A 20-year-old caught smoking could be taken to court and compelled to reveal his source (the cigarette pusher). In Pennsylvania, as in South Carolina, any child not informing on his cigarette supplier was a criminal.

Chewing and snuffing were the most common ways of using tobacco in the United States until fairly recently. In 1897 half of all tobacco was prepared for chewing. (Spittoons were required by law to be placed in all public buildings until 1945.) Cigars started to become popular in the United States in the early 1800s. The cigar manufacturers fought introduction of cigarettes for many years. They spread rumors that cigarettes contained opium, were made with tobacco from discarded cigar butts and with paper made by Chinese lepers, and so on (Heimann, 1960). But by about 1920 cigarette consumption started to exceed that of cigars. The introduction of the cigarette rolling machine in 1883 spurred cigarette consumption, because they became cheaper than cigars. By 1885 a billion cigarettes a year were being produced. Over 615 billion cigarettes a year were consumed in 1978, or about 4000 per person aged 18 or older.

An important chapter in the history of tobacco was written in the early 1960s. After years of study of hundreds of research reports about the effects of smoking, the Advisory Committee to the United States Surgeon General reported in 1964 "Cigarette smoking is causally related to lung cancer in men; the magnitude of the effects of cigarette smoking far outweighs all other factors." Congress passed legislation in 1965 setting up the National Clearinghouse for Smoking and Health. This organization has the responsibility for the monitoring, compilation, and review of the world's medical literature that bears on the health consequences of smoking. Reports were published in 1967, 1968, and 1969. The statistical evidence presented in 1969 made it difficult for Congress to avoid warning the public that smoking was dangerous to health. Since 1 November 1970, all cigarette packages and cartons have had to carry the label: "Warning: The Surgeon General Has Determined That Cigarette Smoking Is Dangerous to Your Health." Further pressure on Congress encouraged laws that prohibited advertising tobacco on radio and television after 2 January 1971. These media were making the habit of smoking seem glamorous and sophisticated.

In 1970 Public Law 91-222 set up the funds and direction for a comprehensive study of the medical literature to be published as the studies continued. Reports are published periodically bringing research findings to public attention. The 1979 publication, *Smoking and Health: A Report of the Surgeon General,* gives up-to-date information on research about the effects of tobacco on cardiovascular disease, bronchopulmonary disease, cancer, peptic ulcer, and pregnancy, and it emphasizes the increase in smoking by women and girls in the past 15 years. The 1981 report, *The Changing Cigarette,* gives further information.

Tobacco farming, the fifth largest legal cash crop in the United States, is done largely with hand labor. The mature leaves are 1 to $2\frac{1}{2}$ feet long. The nicotine content is from 0.3% to 7%, depending on the variety, leaf position on the stalk (the higher the position, the more nicotine), and the growing conditions. The flavor of tobacco comes from *nicotianin,* also called tobacco camphor (U.S. Surgeon General, 1979).

After harvesting and drying, the tobacco leaves are shredded, blown clean of foreign matter and stems, remoisturized with glycerine or other chemical agents, and packed in huge wooden barrels called hogsheads. These barrels are placed in storehouses for one to two years to age, during which time the tobacco gets darker and loses moisture, as well as nicotine and other volatile substances. When aging has been completed, moisture is again added and the tobacco blended with other varieties. There are many types of tobacco with varying characteristics of harshness, mildness, and flavor. *Bright,* also called *flue-cured* or *Virginia,* is the most common tobacco type used in cigarettes. (Flue-cured tobacco is heated in curing sheds to speed the drying process.) This type, developed just before the Civil War, made tobacco smoke more readily inhalable. The blend proportion is a close trade secret, but most cigarettes contain up to half of flue-cured bright, about a third of burley, a small amount of Maryland type, and up to a fifth of Turkish or Greek blends (Heimann, 1960).

Interestingly, the amount of leaf tobacco in a cigarette has gone down about 25% since 1956. There are two reasons for this, not considering the introduction of filtertip cigarettes. (If a filtertip is the same size as a plain one, it has about one-third less tobacco.) The first reason is the use of reconstituted sheets of tobacco. Parts of the tobacco leaves and stems that were discarded in earlier years are now ground up, combined with many added ingredients to control factors such as moisture, flavor, and color, and then rolled out as a flat, homogenized sheet of reconstituted tobacco. This sheet is shredded and mixed with regular leaf tobacco, thus reducing production costs. Nearly a quarter of the tobacco in a cigarette comes from tobacco scraps made into reconstituted sheets. A second technological advance further reduces the amount of tobacco needed. This process, called puffing, is based on freeze-drying the tobacco and then blowing air or an inert gas, such as carbon dioxide, into the tobacco. The gas expands, or puffs up, the plant cells so they take up more space, are lighter, and can take up additives better. Thus the use of reconstituted sheets and puffing have reduced the tar and nicotine in cigarettes simply by reducing the amount of leaf tobacco (U.S. Surgeon General, 1979).

Tobacco additives are not controlled by the Food and Drug Administration or any other government agency. Additives may include extracts of tobacco as well as nontobacco flavors such as licorice, cocoa, fruit, spices, and floral compositions. (Licorice was first used in tobacco as a preservative around 1830 and came to be appreciated as a sweetener.) Synthetic flavoring compounds may also be used. The selection of tobacco-flavor additives from the GRAS (Generally Regarded As Safe) List, or from natural extracts, and the testing of their smoke decomposition products for toxicity or other biological activity are not required by law, but are done voluntarily by manufacturers (U.S. Surgeon General, 1981).

In the 1870s a cigarette girl could roll about four cigarettes per minute by hand. When James Duke leased and improved the first cigarette rolling machine in 1883, he could make about 200 cigarettes per minute. This was the last link in the chain of development leading to the modern American blended cigarette. Today's machines make over 3600 uniform cigarettes per minute. Filter cigarettes are made by a machine that attaches a double-size filter between two cigarettes and then cuts them apart (Heimann, 1960).

The majority of cigarettes today are low-tar and some are low-nicotine types (Figure 9-2). The filtertip, in which the filter is made of cellulose or charcoal, has also become common (Figure 9-3); over 90% of all cigarettes sold currently in the United States are filtertips. The filter does help remove some of the substances in smoke, but most, such as carbon monoxide, pass through into the mouth and lungs. Over 2000 substances have been identified in tobacco smoke. Many of these are known carcinogens, whereas many more have not been adequately analyzed as to their health consequences.

The cost of making cigarettes (not counting the tobacco) is about three cents a pack. Total cost varies with the company but usually is not more than five to seven cents a pack. Total cost to the American consumer is about $25 billion a year for all tobacco products, with over 90% of that for cigarettes. In 1980 the tax revenue on cigarettes to the U.S. government was about $3 billion, with over $1 billion more in state taxes.

NICOTINE: PRIMARY DRUG OF DEPENDENCE IN TOBACCO

The alkaloid nicotine was isolated from tobacco in 1828 (Appendix A-3). About 60 milligrams is a lethal dose for an adult, although tolerance does build up rapidly. A cigar contains about 120 milligrams of nicotine, enough to kill the person who inhales the smoke like cigarette smoke. The average cigarette delivers 0.05 to 2.5 milligrams of nicotine (1980 average, less than 1 mg) (Jaffe, 1980; U.S. Surgeon General, 1981). The smoker who inhales gets about 90% of the nicotine in his or her bloodstream, compared to 20% to 50% from smoke taken into the mouth and then exhaled (Volle & Koelle, 1975). The blood carries the nicotine to the heart first, which distributes it rapidly throughout the body. Nicotine from inhaled tobacco smoke reaches the brain in seven seconds—twice as fast as from intravenous administration in the arm!

Nicotine is believed to be the substance in tobacco that causes dependence. This conclusion is based on nicotine's metabolism and effects. Regular smokers commonly use about 20 to 30

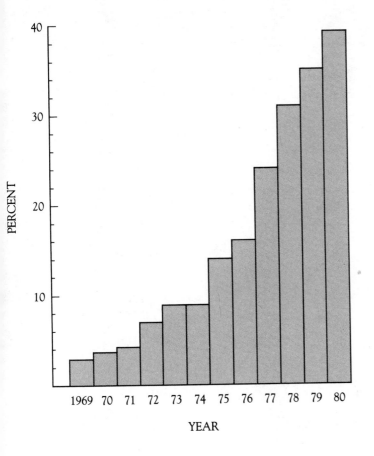

FIGURE 9-2
Market share of cigarettes with "tar" 15 mg or less, 1967–1978 (1979 projected) (U.S. Surgeon General, 1979, p. A-21).

cigarettes per day, or one every 30 to 40 minutes. The biological half-life of nicotine in humans is approximately 20 to 30 minutes. Most of it is metabolized in the liver to inactive compounds that are removed through the kidneys. The rate of urinary excretion is faster when the urine is acidic.

Nicotine is a curious drug, because it first stimulates and then depresses the nervous system. The stimulatory effect is due to release of norepinephrine and to the fact that nicotine mimics the action of acetylcholine. Nicotine thus stimulates cholinergic nerves first, but is not removed from the receptors very rapidly, so the next effect is depression, caused by blocking nerve activity. Nicotine will actually increase the respiration rate at low dose levels because it stimulates the receptors in the carotid artery (in the neck) that monitor the brain's need for oxygen. At the same time, nicotine stimulates the cardiovascular system by release of epinephrine, causing increases in coronary blood flow, heart rate, and blood pressure. The effect is to increase the oxygen requirements of the heart muscle, but not the oxygen supply. This may trigger heart attacks in susceptible persons.

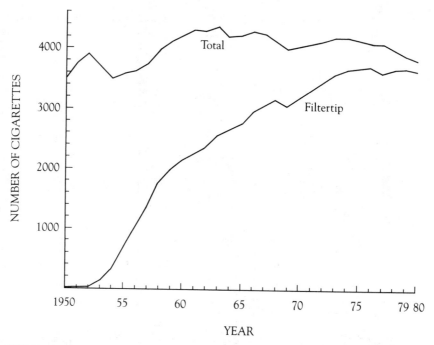

FIGURE 9-3

Annual consumption of cigarettes and filtertip cigarettes per person aged 18 years and over, 1950–1978 (U.S. Surgeon General, 1979, p. A-5).

Nicotine causes an initial stimulation of salivary and bronchial secretions followed by inhibition. The excess saliva associated with smoking is caused by the irritating smoke, not the nicotine (Taylor, 1980).

Nicotine, and perhaps other substances in tobacco smoke, tends to inhibit hunger contractions in the stomach for up to one hour. At the same time there is a slight increase in blood sugar and a deadening of the taste buds. It may be these characteristics that decrease hunger in many smokers. Smokers have often reported that they gain weight after they stop smoking and that their appetite increases. In addition, when a one-plus pack-a-day smoker quits, there may

be a decrease in heart rate (2–3 beats per minute) and up to a 10% decrease in basal metabolic rate (Jarvik, 1979). The body is being stressed less, so it converts more food into fat.

Nicotine and other products in smoke, such as carbon monoxide, produce still other effects. Carbon monoxide is picked up by the red blood cells where it binds to the hemoglobin molecules and forms carboxyhemoglobin. Up to 10% of all the hemoglobin in smokers may be in the carboxyhemoglobin form. This form of hemoglobin cannot carry oxygen, so up to 10% of their blood is effectively out of circulation as far as normal oxygen-carbon dioxide exchange is concerned. This situation could easily cause a smoker to become out of breath from exertion. It is a factor in heart attacks and in the lower birth weight and survival rate of infants born to women who smoke during pregnancy.

SMOKING AND HEALTH: RESEARCH FINDINGS*

Morbidity, Mortality, and Life Span

The risk of premature death is significantly higher (about 70%) for men who smoke cigarettes than for men who do not. The risk of premature death for female smokers compared to nonsmokers is lower than 70% at present, because women as a group began smoking later, and they generally use filtertip cigarettes. However, with the increase in smoking by teenage girls, the risk of premature death for women will soon be the same as for men. Women are not in a lower risk group! Estimates of premature deaths associated with cigarette smoking have ranged up to 300,000 per year. A 30-year-old male who smokes two packs a day has a life expectancy that is 8.1 years shorter than his nonsmoking counterpart. The death rate increases with the amount smoked: a two-pack-a-day smoker has a mortality rate two times higher than nonsmokers (Table 9-1; Figure 9-4). Overall mortality rates are greater for those smoking longer, and the death rate is directly proportional. Thus the longer one smokes, the higher the mortality rate (Table 9-1).

The tar and nicotine contents of cigarettes affect the mortality rate. Smokers of low tar and

---

*This section is largely from the U.S. Surgeon General, 1979; 1981.

nicotine cigarettes have a mortality ratio 50% greater than nonsmokers, but 15% to 20% less than for cigarette smokers as a group (Table 9-2). The mortality ratio is the number obtained by dividing the death rate of smokers by the death rate of nonsmokers.

Exsmokers have overall mortality ratios that decline as the number of years off cigarettes increases. After 15 years, the overall mortality of exsmokers from all smoking-related diseases is similar to persons who have never smoked. The mortality rate for exsmokers is related to the number of cigarettes they used to smoke per day and to the age at which they started to smoke. The mortality rate for cigar smokers is somewhat higher than for nonsmokers and is related to the number of cigars used. The mortality rate for pipe smokers is only slightly greater than for nonsmokers.

Not only do cigarette smokers tend to die at an earlier age than nonsmokers, but they also have a higher probability of certain diseases. These include cancer of the lung, larynx, lip, esophagus, and urinary bladder; chronic bronchitis and emphysema; diseases of the cardiovascular system, including coronary artery disease and atherosclerosis; and peptic ulcer.

Following the U.S. Surgeon General's report in 1964, the National Center for Health Statistics began collecting information on smoking. These findings are helpful in assessing the relationships between tobacco use and illnesses, disability, and other health indicators. Among other things, the Center found that men and women currently smoking cigarettes tend to have more chronic health problems, such as chronic bronchitis, emphysema, chronic sinusitis, peptic ulcers, and arteriosclerotic disease (hardening of the arteries), than persons who never smoked. There is a dose-response relationship between the number of cigarettes smoked per day and the particular illness. Men smoking two

TABLE 9-1   Estimated years of life expectancy (LE) for males at various ages by amount smoked (25-state study)*

Cigarettes smoked per day	Age of males							
	30		40		50		60	
	LE	Years lost	LE	Years lost	LE	Years lost	LE	Years lost
Nonsmokers	43.9	0	34.5	0	25.6	0	17.6	0
1 to 9	39.3	4.6	30.2	4.3	21.8	3.8	14.5	3.1
10 to 19	38.4	5.5	29.3	5.2	21.0	4.6	14.1	3.5
20 to 39	37.8	6.1	28.7	5.8	20.5	5.1	13.7	3.9
40 plus	35.8	8.1	26.9	7.6	19.3	6.3	13.2	4.4

*U.S. Surgeon General, 1979, p. 2-12.

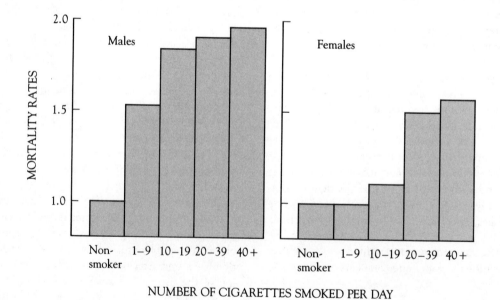

NUMBER OF CIGARETTES SMOKED PER DAY

Figure 9-4
Mortality ratios for male and female cigarette smokers across all ages by amount smoked (based on data from the U.S. Surgeon General, 1979, pp. 2-18, 2-26).

TABLE 9-2 Overall mortality ratios of cigarette smokers compared to nonsmokers by sex and by tar (T) and nicotine (N) content of cigarettes usually smoked*

Sex	Nonsmokers	Low T, N	Medium T, N	High T, N
Males	1.00	1.66	1.85	1.96
Females	1.00	1.37	1.45	1.65
Total	1.00	1.52	1.64	1.80

*Mortality ratio = death rate of smokers divided by death rate of nonsmokers. For example, male smokers of high-tar- and high-nicotine-content cigarettes have nearly double the death rate (1.96) of nonsmoking men, matched for age and occupation. U.S. Surgeon General, 1979, p. 2-25.

packs a day have a four times higher rate of chronic bronchitis and/or emphysema compared to nonsmokers. Women smoking two or more packs a day have a rate of these diseases nearly ten times higher than nonsmokers.

Other indicators of sickness studied were workdays lost, days spent in bed because of illness, and days of limitation of activity resulting from chronic diseases. Male smokers had a 33% excess, and female smokers a 45% excess, of workdays lost compared to nonsmokers. Male former smokers had an excess of 41%, and female former smokers an excess of 43%, of workdays lost. The 1974 survey calculated that more than 81 million workdays were lost in the United States every year by smokers compared to nonsmokers (Table 9-3). This is a tremendous financial and productivity loss for the nation.

Data on disability and illness show continued high risk among former smokers. The most likely reason is that smokers quit because of a smoking-related illness that had already severely damaged the cardiovascular system or lungs. The data on workdays missed by former smokers needs further analysis to determine how they are affected by the length of time these people smoked and how many cigarettes they used per day.

Cardiovascular Disease

There is now overwhelming proof that cigarette smoking increases the risk of cardiovascular disease. Data collected from the United States, the United Kingdom, Canada, and other countries show that smoking is a major risk factor for heart attack. The probability of heart attack is related to the amount smoked, and this factor has a synergistic relationship to other risk factors, like obesity. Smoking cigarettes is a major risk factor for arteriosclerotic disease and for death from arteriosclerotic aneurysm of the aorta (an aneurysm is a weakened area in a blood vessel that forms a blood-filled sac). Smokers have a higher incidence of atherosclerosis of the coronary arteries that supply blood to the heart, which blocks these arteries with fat deposits. The effect is dose-related. Both the carbon monoxide and the nicotine in cigarette smoke can precipitate angina attacks (painful spasms in the chest when the heart muscle does not get the blood supply it needs). Smokers of low tar and nicotine cigarettes have less risk of coronary artery disease, but their risk is greater than that of nonsmokers. The risk goes down if the person quits: after about ten years, the risk of coronary disease in exsmokers approaches that of nonsmokers. As described in Chapter 14, women who smoke and use oral contraceptives have a significantly higher risk of death or disability from stroke, heart attack, and other cardiovascular diseases than nonsmokers both on and off the "pill."

Cancer

Collectively, the many types of cancer have been the second leading cause of death in the United States since 1937. There were an estimated 390,000 deaths from all types of cancer in 1978, of which 92,400 were from lung cancer. Lung cancer is the most common type in men and the second most common type in women. There has been a dramatic increase in lung cancer in women: four-fold in 25 years. The lung cancer mortality rates in women are increasing more rapidly than in men. If present trends continue, it will be the leading cause of cancer death in women by 1990. Women who smoke die just as male smokers do; there is a direct relationship

TABLE 9-3   Days lost from work per year because of illness and injury per currently employed person age 17 and older by smoking status, age, and sex: United States, 1974[*]

| Sex and age | Days per person per year | | |
	Present smoker	Former smoker	Never smoked
Male			
17 plus	5.1	5.0	3.4
17 to 44	5.5	4.2	3.0
45 to 64	4.5	5.5	4.4
65 plus	0.3	7.9	?
Female			
17 plus	5.6	?	4.5
17 to 44	5.3	?	4.3
45 to 64	6.5	?	5.4
65 plus	?	?	?

? Means data are incomplete.
Note: Actual number of workdays lost plus expected if compared to nonsmokers is 81,368,000.
[*] Adapted from U.S. Surgeon General, 1979, p. 3-13.

between smoking and lung cancer in both genders (Figures 9-5 and 9-6). The risk of lung cancer increases with increasing amounts of smoking as measured by the number of cigarettes
smoked per day, the duration of smoking, the
age at which the person started smoking, the
degree of inhalation, and the tar and nicotine
content of the cigarettes. Use of filter cigarettes
and of lower tar and nicotine cigarettes decreases
the lung cancer mortality rate, but the rate is

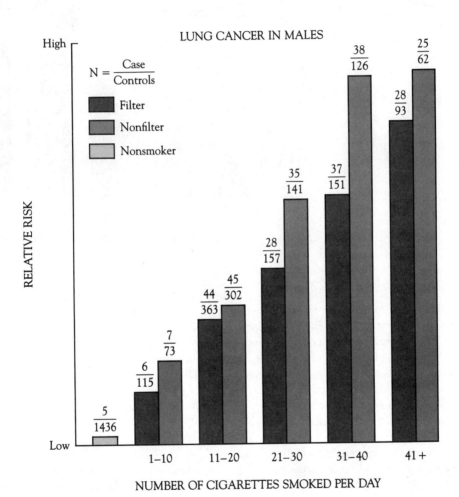

FIGURE 9-5
Relative risk of lung cancer for males by number of cigarettes smoked per day and
long-term use of filter (F) or nonfilter (NF) cigarettes (U.S. Surgeon General, 1979,
p. 5-18).

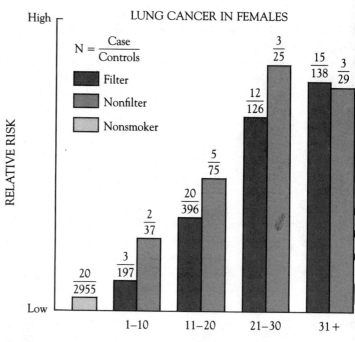

FIGURE 9-6
Relative risk of lung cancer for females by number of cigarettes smoked per day and long-term use of filter (F) or nonfilter (NF) cigarettes (U.S. Surgeon General, 1979, p. 5-19).

still significantly higher than for nonsmokers. If a smoker quits, the lung cancer mortality rate goes down but will not approach the nonsmoker rate until 10 to 15 years of abstinence. Pipe and cigar smokers have lung cancer mortality rates above nonsmokers but lower than those of cigarette smokers. Exposure to certain air pollutants in the environment or in industry—especially the asbestos, uranium, nickel, and chemical industries—acts synergistically with cigarette smoking to increase lung cancer mortality rates far above what each would cause separately.

Cancer of the larynx is significantly higher in smokers compared to nonsmokers and is related to the amount smoked. Pipe and cigar smokers have about the same rate of laryngeal cancer as cigarette smokers. There is a synergistic effect between smoking and alcohol consumption and between exposure to asbestos and smoking, for this type of cancer. The risk of laryngeal cancer goes down if the person stops smoking, but it is higher than the nonsmoker for nearly ten years.

There is also a causal relationship between smoking and cancers of the oral cavity, esophagus, urinary bladder, pancreas, and kidney.

Bronchopulmonary Disease

It is now well established that cigarette smoking is the most important cause of bronchopulmonary disease. Cigarette smokers have higher death rates from pulmonary emphysema and chronic bronchitis and more frequently have impaired pulmonary function and other symptoms of pul-

SMOKING AND HEALTH: RESEARCH FINDINGS

monary disease than nonsmokers (Table 9-4). Respiratory infections are more prevalent and more severe among cigarette smokers, particularly heavy smokers, than among nonsmokers. The risk of developing or dying from bronchopulmonary disease among pipe or cigar smokers is higher than for nonsmokers, but lower than for cigarette smokers. Exsmokers have lower death rates from bronchopulmonary disease than do continuing smokers.

The reason for lung damage may be due to impaired immune system activity in lung tissue, genetic factors, and deficiencies in certain substances in the tissues. It is known that persons with a low amount of an enzyme called *alpha-1-antitrypsin* are more likely to develop emphysema. Severe alpha-1-antitrypsin deficiency is a genetic trait occurring in approximately 1 per 2000 people. In Sweden, people are screened for this enzyme deficiency so they can avoid

TABLE 9-4   Means of the numerical values given to lung sections at autopsy of male and female smokers and nonsmokers, standardized for age[1,2]

	Subjects who never smoked regularly	Current pipe or cigar smokers	Current cigarette smokers (pk/day)			
Males			<.5	.5–1.0	1–2	>2
Number of subjects	175	141	66	115	440	216
Emphysema	0.09	0.90	1.43	1.92	2.17	2.27
Fibrosis	0.40	1.88	2.78	3.73	4.06	4.28
Thickened arterioles	0.10	1.11	1.35	1.66	1.82	1.89
Thickened arteries	0.02	0.23	0.42	0.68	0.83	0.90
Females			<1		>1	
Number of subjects	252	—	33		64	
Emphysema	0.05	—	1.37		1.70	
Fibrosis	0.37	—	2.89		3.46	
Thickened arterioles	0.06	—	1.26		1.57	
Thickened arteries	0.01	—	0.40		0.64	

[1]Numerical values were determined by rating each lung section on scales of 0 to 4 for emphysema and thickening of arterioles, 0 to 7 for fibrosis, and 0 to 3 for thickening of arteries.
[2]U.S. Surgeon General, 1979, p. 6-26, 6-27.

exposure to certain pollutants and occupations. This is not done in the United States, but the American Cancer Society is very much interested in this program. Less severe deficiencies are found in 2% to 10% of the population. Smoking is especially dangerous for such people.

Smokers are more prone to develop bronchopulmonary disease in the presence of air pollutants, such as sulfur oxides and asbestos, than are nonsmokers. Coal dust, cotton dust, and chlorine have an additive effect with cigarette smoking on the development of bronchopulmonary disease. Exposure to fumes and dust, especially talc and carbon black in the rubber industry and uranium and gold dust in the mining industry, acts synergistically with cigarette smoking in the development of bronchopulmonary disease (a synergistic effect is stronger than an additive one).

Effects of Smoking on the Fetus

Cigarette smoking during pregnancy has a significantly harmful effect on the development of the fetus, the survival of the newborn infant, and the continued development of the child. Adverse effects on pregnancy range from increased risk for spontaneous abortion, impaired fetal growth, stillbirth, premature birth, and neonatal death. Babies born to mothers who smoke have a lower average body weight, are shorter, and have a smaller head circumference. The more the woman smokes, the greater the effect on the infant's size. If she gives up smoking during the entire pregnancy, her infant will probably be of normal weight and strength.

The below-average weight of babies born to smokers is caused by carbon monoxide and nicotine. The carbon monoxide reduces the oxygen-carrying capacity of the fetus's blood just as it does the mother's. Fetal growth is retarded because the tissue is starved for oxygen. The inhaled nicotine enters the mother's blood from her lungs and rapidly constricts blood flow to the placenta, reducing available oxygen and nutrients until the effect of the nicotine has worn off. In addition, nicotine crosses the blood-placental barrier to the fetal bloodstream. It has the same effects on the fetus's nervous system and blood circulation as on the mother's. However, the fetus cannot metabolize nicotine efficiently, so the effects last longer than in the mother.

One known carcinogen in tobacco smoke, benzo(a)pyrene, crosses the placenta and enters the fetal blood. Experiments with pregnant mice exposed to benzo(a)pyrene showed that their offspring had a markedly higher incidence of cancer. The impact of smoking during pregnancy on the incidence of human cancer is not known.

Infants born to mothers who smoke have a reduced probability of survival. They are more likely to die from sudden infant death syndrome (SID) and other causes related to their retarded growth. There may be long-term effects on physical growth, mental development, and behavioral characteristics of those babies who survive the first four weeks of life. It appears that children of mothers who smoke do not catch up with children of nonsmoking mothers in various stages of development, at least up to the age of 11. Smoking during pregnancy may also be a cause of hyperkinesis in children (see Chapter 8).

The father's smoking, even when the mother does not smoke, may affect the fetus through secondhand smoke (see the following section) or through an effect on the sperm. There is a much higher mortality rate for newborn infants whose fathers smoked more than ten cigarettes per day. Babies fathered by heavy smokers had twice the expected incidence of severe birth defects.

Involuntary Smoking (Secondhand Smoke)

Smoke that comes from the lighted tip of the cigarette between puffs is called *sidestream smoke*. This smoke has much higher concentrations of some irritating and hazardous substances, such as carbon monoxide, nicotine, and ammonia, than inhaled (*mainstream*) smoke. If a number of people smoke in an enclosed area, the carbon monoxide (CO) may reach a level that is higher than the safe limit recommended by the Environmental Protection Agency. Nine parts CO per million parts air is the regulatory limit, but this can easily be exceeded. Under conditions of heavy smoking and poor ventilation, concentrations of CO as high as 50 ppm can occur from sidestream smoke. CO is a gas and is not removed by most standard air-filtration systems. It can only be diluted by increasing ventilation with low CO-containing fresh air. Formation of CO can be reduced by increasing the amount of oxygen available during the burning of the tobacco. This can be done by using perforated cigarette paper and perforated filtertips. Regular and small cigars produce more CO than cigarettes, because the tobacco-leaf wrapper reduces the amount of oxygen available at the burning zone. The levels of CO created by smokers may cause nonsmokers with coronary heart disease to have angina attacks.

Nicotine from sidestream smoke tends to settle out of the air. The body absorbs small amounts from heavily polluted air; however, these amounts of nicotine are probably not hazardous. Several carcinogens, such as benzo(a)pyrene and dimethylnitrosamine, are also absorbed in small amounts from sidestream smoke. The extent of the carcinogenic hazard is not known.

The irritation of the eyes, nose, and respiratory tract from sidestream smoke is probably caused by. *acrolein*. Although acrolein is a toxic gas, levels from sidestream smoke are probably not hazardous to healthy nonsmokers—just irritating. However, the carbon monoxide and irritating substances are hazardous to nonsmokers with cardiovascular disease or bronchopulmonary disease and to young children. Children of parents who smoke are more likely to have bronchitis and pneumonia during the first year of life than children of nonsmokers.

WHO SMOKES AND WHY?

The percentage of the total population that smokes is decreasing, although some age groups show an increase. Teenagers are the largest group to show an increase. At present, nearly a million teenagers a year are starting to smoke. It appears that peer pressure, role modeling, and nicotine addiction are three of the most important reasons why there are about one million new smokers a year. Most teenagers who smoke come from homes where the parents smoke. The U.S. Surgeon General reported in 1979 that the percentage of adults who regularly smoke cigarettes fell from an estimated 41.7% in 1965 to an estimated 33.2% in 1978. During the same time period, because of the increase in population, the total number of smokers (age 17 and older) increased from about 53 million to 54 million.

About one-third of the American public continue to smoke even though they are aware of the many potentially detrimental effects of smoking. Nearly 25% smoke over a pack a day. If one asks tobacco users why they smoke, the answers are similar to those given by cannabis users. These include: (1) for relaxation and to enhance social interactions; (2) to decrease the unpleasant effects of tension, anxiety, and anger; (3) because it is addictive, and smoking decreases craving; (4) it's a habit; (5) its stimulating action increases energy and arousal; and (6) manipulating objects is pleasing (the cigarette, pipe, and so on). Not all tobacco smokers give all these reasons for smoking. Pleasurable relaxation and reduction of tension and craving were rated as the most important. Habit, stimulation, and manipulation were of substantial, but lesser, significance (Jones, Farrell, & Herning, 1978).

There are a number of reasons why a high level of dependence on tobacco should be expected. These include:

1. The habit can be rapidly and frequently reinforced by the inhalation of tobacco smoke (about 10 reinforcements per cigarette or 200 with one pack).

2. The rapid metabolism and clearance of nicotine allows frequent and repeated use, which is encouraged by the rapid onset of withdrawal symptoms.

3. Smoking has complex pharmacological effects, both central and peripheral, that may satisfy a variety of the smoker's needs.

4. Some groups offer psychological and social rewards for use, especially the peer groups of young people.

5. Smoking patterns can be generalized; that is, the smoker becomes conditioned to combine smoking with other activities. For example, some smokers feel the need to smoke after a meal, when driving, and so on.

6. Smoking is reinforced by both pharmacological effects and ritual.

7. There is no marked performance impairment; in fact, smoking enhances performance in some cases. (Nicotine produces a state of alertness, prevents deterioration of reaction time, and improves learning.)

8. In general, smoking is socially accepted.

9. Cigarettes cost less and are more readily available than other psychoactive drugs (Jones et al., 1978).

The preceding reasons may explain not only why smoking is continued, but also why it seems hard to stop. Nicotine is probably the reinforcing substance in tobacco. This likelihood is apparent for several reasons: First, experimental animals can discriminate between nicotine and other stimulant drugs. This implies that the drug affects the central nervous system. It can alter the emotional state, which might help maintain dependency. Second, rats and monkeys will self-administer nicotine intravenously. This means that nicotine is a reinforcer; that is, it strengthens and maintains behaviors that lead to its availability and ingestion (Goldberg, Spealman, & Goldberg, 1981). Third, smokers appear to regulate their intake of nicotine. If a low-nicotine cigarette is used, the smoker smokes more and inhales more deeply. Fourth, there appear to be specific receptors in the brain that respond to nicotine. Fifth, the average one-pack-a-day smoker is estimated to self-administer 70,000 pulses (one pulse per inhalation) of nicotine in a year. This surpasses by far the rate of any other known form of substance abuse. A habit that is reinforced as frequently and easily as smoking is very hard to break (Krasnegor, 1979).

An incident that happened at Synanon illustrates how strong the smoking habit is. Synanon treats heroin addicts and has a philosophy of allowing an addict to use no drugs at all while he or she is being rehabilitated. In 1970 Synanon decided to ban cigarettes because of cost and because they seemed to serve as a crutch for people getting off other drugs. About 100 people left and chose possible readdiction to hard drugs rather than stay at Synanon without cigarettes. Residents of Synanon noted that the withdrawal symptoms for tobacco lasted much longer than for other drugs, and they believed it was easier to quit heroin than cigarettes.

LOWERING THE RISKS, IF YOU MUST SMOKE

It is clear that exposure to cigarette tars, carbon monoxide, nicotine, and other smoke ingredients leads to increased health risks among smokers. Elimination or reduction of smoking obviously is the best and quickest way to reduce the health hazards. The longer a person remains an exsmoker, the more likely it is that his or her health status will approach that of nonsmokers. This may take up to 15 years for a person who has been a heavy smoker for a long period of time; also, some damage to lung and heart function is irreversible. However, many pleasant changes take place within a few weeks after one stops smoking. There is a reduction in smoker's cough, nasal discharge, and saliva production. Shortness of breath usually improves rapidly. Food tastes better, sleep is sounder, fatigue diminishes, breath odor improves, and tobacco stains on the teeth and fingers disappear. The following are offered as suggestions to smokers who wish to reduce their personal risk. Because none of these suggestions would eliminate the hazards to others from sidestream smoke, they are one-sided but may be worthwhile to smokers.

1. Inhale less. Concentrate on inhaling at a slower pace, and make it shallow. This will keep a higher percentage of smoke and tars out of *your* lungs.

2. Smoke fewer cigarettes. Because the amount of tobacco consumed is significant, stretch out the smoking by postponing the next cigarette. Place the cigarettes in an inconvenient place.

Change your time of smoking so you start to break the behavioral reinforcement pattern.

3. Take fewer puffs per cigarette. It may seem expensive to watch your cigarette burn up in the ashtray, but in the long run it is more economical to regain your health.

4. Smoke one-third of the cigarette. Regardless of the brand, most of the tars are concentrated into the butt during the burning. The first one-third may deliver only 2% of the tar and nicotine, because the tobacco itself acts as a filter, whereas the last third may yield 50% of the tar and nicotine.

5. Choose a low-tar and low-nicotine cigarette, but be careful not to increase your total consumption. Reducing the nicotine content of tobacco may not reduce the amount of nicotine the smoker gets. Smokers using low-nicotine cigarettes tend to smoke more cigarettes than when they use high-nicotine cigarettes. They also smoke the cigarette to a shorter butt, thus getting more tar and nicotine, and tend to inhale more deeply and hold the smoke longer, enhancing absorption of smoke products into the bloodstream.

6. Note that low-tar and low-nicotine cigarette use will not reduce the amount of carbon monoxide. For this, select a brand with perforated paper and/or a perforated filter. Selection of a low-tar, low-carbon-monoxide, *high*-nicotine cigarette may help the truly nicotine-dependent smoker reduce the number of cigarettes. The carbon monoxide appears to be a more important risk factor in cardiovascular disease, and the tar in cancer, than nicotine.

7. Nicotine is metabolized more slowly when the urine is alkaline. Taking bicarbonate (up to 4 grams per day) has been tried (under medical supervision) in smokers who wished to reduce their smoking. Note that bicarbonate of soda can be dangerous for people who have peptic

ulcers, who are on low-sodium diets, or who have difficulty maintaining the correct blood pH. Get clearance from a physician before trying this method.

METHODS OF STOPPING SMOKING

Since the U.S. Surgeon General's report in 1964, an estimated 30 million men and women have stopped smoking. However, the current 54 million smokers in the United States consume over 615 billion cigarettes per year. The health damage has been estimated to cost this nation over $27 billion in medical care, absenteeism, decreased work productivity, and accidents. Cigarette smoking is the single most important preventable environmental factor contributing to illness, disability, and death in the United States.

When habitual smokers stop smoking, they may experience a variety of unpleasant withdrawal effects. These can include craving for tobacco, irritability, restlessness, dullness, sleep disturbances, gastrointestinal disturbances, anxiety, and impairment of concentration, judgment, and psychomotor performance. The intensity of the withdrawal effects may be mild, moderate, or severe and are not necessarily correlated with the amount the person smoked. The onset of these symptoms may occur within hours or days after quitting and may persist from a few days to several months. They are a major factor in the person's taking up smoking again (Pomerleau, 1979).

After the exsmoker successfully overcomes withdrawal symptoms during the first few weeks, he or she is still at risk. Various internal and external stimuli may serve as triggers for craving or withdrawal symptoms. Stressful situations, such as an argument with a spouse, being with friends who smoke, or various types of social events, may cause a response similar to withdrawal. This sets the stage for readdiction. Once the behavioral modification approach was understood, new methods for helping people to quit smoking were developed. In most nonbehavioral clinics, fewer than half the smokers quit, and, of those who did, only 25% to 30% were still nonsmokers 9 to 18 months later. The long-term abstinence rate is about 13% (Pomerleau, 1979).

The three main types of behavioral treatment involve *punishment* and *aversive therapy*, *stimulus control*, and *controlled smoking procedures*. Aversive conditioning techniques use cigarettes themselves to break the behavior pattern of smoking by making it so intense it becomes unpleasant. A method called *rapid smoking* illustrates one successful use of aversive conditioning. The procedure is to smoke cigarettes at a rapid rate, inhaling smoke about six seconds after each exhalation, until the smoker cannot bear any more. Sessions are repeated on a daily basis until the person no longer desires a smoke. Follow-up sessions are held if the desire returns. In a review of several studies using rapid smoking, the abstinence rate was 54% in short-term follow-up and 36% in long-term follow-up (two to six years after treatment) (Pomerleau, 1979). The rapid smoking method essentially involves acute self-poisoning at a rate the person finds physiologically uncomfortable, compared to maintenance self-poisoning at the usual rate of smoking. It can be dangerously stressful for a person who has cardiovascular problems or reduced bronchopulmonary function.

Use of stimulus control is another approach to modification of smoking behavior. This is based on the assumption that smoking is associated with, or controlled by, environmental cues and that these cues contribute to the persistence of the habit. Programmed restriction of the stimuli hat trigger smoking theoretically leads to a gradual elimination of smoking behavior. The person might be asked to keep a daily record of the circumstances in which he or she smoked each cigarette, which increases his or her awareness of smoking, and be given designated daily quotas as targets for reduction. In general, stimulus control by itself is not very effective. Better results are obtained when stimulus control procedures are combined with methods that reimburse deposited money for reaching a goal, and with other techniques. Multiple method approaches give results about equal to the rapid smoking method, with 61% of the participants quitting smoking after eight sessions of treatment and 32% remaining nonsmokers after a year. There is about a 50% return to addiction over longer periods of time after treatment (Pomerleau, 1979).

The American Cancer Society has developed a list of alternative activities the new exsmoker might try as aids to get through the withdrawal period. These include: Sip a glass of water when the craving for a cigarette arises. Nibble on fruit, celery, or carrots; chew gum or spices such as ginger, cinnamon bark, or a clove. Use nicotine replacements if necessary, such as lobeline sulphate tablets (unless you have an ulcer) or nicotine-containing chewing gum. Moderately strenuous physical activity, such as bicycling, jogging, or swimming, is good (if the person's heart and lungs are not too damaged). Spend as much time as possible in places where smoking is prohibited, such as movie theaters, libraries, and so on. Use mouthwash after each meal.

To these might be added: get rid of the drug paraphernalia, such as ashtrays and lighters. How serious the person is about quitting can often be gauged by how willing he or she is to give up an expensive coffeetable style ashtray, cigarette box, or engraved lighter. If these are kept on the rationalization that guests will expect such accessories, the person is setting him- or herself up for readdiction.

Although behavioral modification treatments are more effective than earlier methods, rates of 50% recidivism and 33% long-term abstinence leave considerable room for improvement. When relapse rates for heroin users, cigarette smokers, and alcoholics were plotted on graph paper, the curves for the percentage of relapse over a one-year period were virtually identical. However, these data were taken from persons who sought treatment. Heroin users and alcoholics who quit on their own have a much higher success rate. We know very little about the success rate for the estimated 30 million American smokers who have quit on their own. It could be that those who seek treatment have a more severe form of dependence (Jaffe & Kanzler, 1979). As Mark Twain said, he could give up smoking with ease and had in fact done so "hundreds of times."

More effective methods of motivating smokers to quit, and of discouraging teenagers from starting, are clearly needed. Changing social attitudes toward smoking may help reduce smoking. The harmful effects of tobacco are well established; what is needed is for smokers to start taking them personally! The willingness of nonsmokers to speak up as firmly as necessary against being exposed to secondhand smoke is having an effect on smoking habits (Warner, 1981).

Some of the restrictions on smoking in the United States have been due to the assertiveness of nonsmokers who have become more vocal about wanting unpolluted air. There are several organized groups of nonsmokers, such as Action on Smoking and Health (ASH), the Group Against Smoker's Pollution (GASP), the American Lung Association, the American Cancer Society, and professional medical and dental associations. These groups have been instru-

mental in passing legislation restricting or banning smoking in public places; banning cigarette commercials on television; requiring
separate nonsmoking sections on commercial
aircraft, interstate buses, and some restaurants;

and prohibiting smoking in some elevators,
indoor theaters, libraries, art galleries, museums,
and dining cars of passenger trains. Table 9-5
summarizes legislative actions concerning the
rights of nonsmokers.

TABLE 9-5 Key events, regulations, and laws in the United States concerning smoking

1945 Mayo Clinic cautions against use of cigarettes by patients with cardiovascular disease. American
      Cancer Society announces parallelism between cigarette sales and lung cancer.

1957 American Cancer Society, National Cancer Institute, American Heart Association, and
      National Heart Institute issue report calling for government action regarding smoking and
      public health.

1958 Tobacco Institute formed by major cigarette manufacturers to counteract possible political effects
      of health studies.

1964 Surgeon General's report on smoking and health.

1965 National Clearinghouse for Smoking and Health (NCSH) established within the Public Health
      Service.

1966 Federal Cigarette Labeling and Advertising Act requires each package to have the statement:
      Caution: Cigarette Smoking May Be Hazardous To Your Health.

1967 Federal Communications Commission rules that the Fairness Doctrine applies to cigarette
      advertising: television and radio must carry antismoking messages. Federal Trade Commission
      issues first report on tar and nicotine content.

1970 Cigarette package statement changed by law to: Warning: the Surgeon General has determined
      that cigarette smoking is dangerous to your health.

1971 Radio and TV smoking commercials banned, and the Interstate Commerce Commission restricts
      smoking to the rear five rows of interstate buses.

1973 Arizona is the first state to prohibit smoking in all elevators, indoor theaters, libraries, art
      galleries, museums, concert halls, and buses. All airlines required to designate smoking and
      non-smoking areas in planes.

1975 Minnesota passes Indoor Clean Air Act, which makes smoking illegal in all public places and
      public meetings except where otherwise designated.

1976 Superior Court of New Jersey decision in case of *Shimp vs. New Jersey Bell Telephone Co.* Worker
      must be allowed to have a nonpolluted work environment.

1978 Civil Aeronautics Board bans cigar and pipe smoking on all American commercial airlines.

DEPRESSANT DRUGS

CHAPTER OBJECTIVES

1. Differentiate among "sedative," "hypnotic," and "anesthetic" in terms of depressant activity.
2. Debate the following statement: alcohol potentiates with all central nervous system depressant drugs.
3. List symptoms of bromide, paraldehyde, methaqualone, barbiturate, phencyclidine, and volatile substance intoxication.
4. Describe the factors that determine how rapidly barbiturates, benzodiazepine tranquilizers, phencyclidine, and volatile substances are cleared from the body.
5. Compare withdrawal symptoms from methaqualone, the barbiturates, the minor tranquilizers, phencyclidine, and the volatile substances, and state which symptom and which drug is the most dangerous.
6. List medical uses for barbiturates and compare these to the minor tranquilizers.
7. Describe approaches to detoxifying a person addicted to a sedative-hypnotic, and give the reasons for using each.
8. Phencyclidine has depressant, stimulant, hallucinogenic, and analgesic properties: give an example of each.
9. Describe a PCP-induced psychosis and its medical treatment.
10. List long-term effects from benzene, chloroform, methylene chloride, n-hexane, and gasoline inhalation.
11. Define the following terms: Mickey Finn, barbiturate, insomnia, REM sleep, benzodiazepine, detoxification, catalepsy, antipsychotic, neuroleptic, nystagmus, minor and major tranquilizer, tardive dyskinesia, anesthesia, and organic brain syndrome.

The depressants are a diverse group of drugs. Basically they reduce the activity of the central nervous system, probably by decreasing the activity of the reticular activating system in the brain stem (see figure 2-5 on p. 28). This in turn reduces the level of awareness. We often classify certain groups of depressants according to their medical effects on the body. The sedatives, for example, cause a mild depression of the central nervous system (CNS) and decrease excitability and anxiety. These effects are not necessarily the same as drowsy or sleepy feelings. Usually sedatives have a muscle-relaxing property that is sought after by many abusers of drugs. A hypnotic (from Hypnos, the Greek god of sleep) is a drug that induces sleep. A larger dose of a sedative may have a hypnotic effect. Often the difference between a sedative and a hypnotic is the dosage. By increasing the dose still further an anesthetic state can be reached. Anesthesia is deep depression of the CNS. If the dose is increased much more, coma or death may ensue, because the CNS may become so depressed that vital centers controlling breathing or heartbeat may simply cease to function. In this chapter we discuss some of the nonbarbiturates—such as chloral hydrate and methaqualone—the barbiturates, tranquilizers, phencyclidine, antidepressant drugs, and volatile solvents (see Appendix A-7 for structures). Alcohol and the opiates are classified as depressants but are covered in Chapters 11 and 12, respectively.

THE NONBARBITURATES

In this group of depressants, glutethimide and methyprylon are Schedule III drugs; chloral hydrate, paraldehyde, and ethchlorvynol are Schedule IV drugs; and bromides are over-the-counter drugs. The basis for the classification is the relative potential for physical and psychological dependence. Abuse of Schedule III drugs may lead to moderate or low physical dependence, or high psychological dependence. Schedule IV drugs are considered relatively less likely to cause either type of dependence.

Bromides

The bromides were used in the late 1800s as anticonvulsants and as sedatives. They are used very little now because of their slow onset of action and their toxicity. Bromides are still available in a few over-the-counter preparations. The rate of excretion is slow. Daily use results in accumulation in the central nervous system, causing bromide poisoning, with symptoms of a rash similar to acne, confusion, irritability, tremor, stupor, and coma. The old slang phrase, "take a powder," meaning "go away!" came from the use of bromide powder.

Chloral Hydrate

Chloral hydrate, or knock-out drops, has the unsavory reputation of being a drug that is slipped into a person's drink to make him or her unconscious. The combination of chloral hydrate and alcohol got the name Mickey Finn on the waterfront of the Barbary Coast of San Francisco when sailors were in short supply. As legend has it, the name of one of the bars dispensing unwanted knock-out drops was Mickey Finn's. An unsuspecting man would have a friendly drink and wake up with a headache and an upset stomach as a crew member on an outbound freighter to China.

It takes about 30 minutes for chloral hydrate (Noctec®) to take effect. Chloral hydrate is rapidly metabolized to trichloroethanol, which is the active hypnotic agent. Alcohol accelerates the rate of conversion and potentiates with the CNS depressant effect. Chloral hydrate does not depress the CNS as much as a comparable dose of barbiturates. It is an excellent hypnotic, but it has a narrow margin of safety. Chloral hydrate is a stomach irritant, especially if given repeatedly and in fairly large doses. Chloral addicts may take enormous doses of the drug; they develop tolerance and physical dependence (Harvey, 1980).

Paraldehyde

Paraldehyde is a sedative-hypnotic drug that has been used clinically since 1882. It is effective as a CNS depressant with little respiratory depression and a large safety margin (see Chapter 4). However, it has a bad taste and a strong odor that saturates the breath. It is irritating to the throat and stomach. Its use is essentially limited to hospitalized or institutionalized patients, most often in treatment of delirium tremens in alcoholics. It is administered as a retention enema. The paraldehyde addict usually gets started on the drug during treatment for alcoholism and comes to prefer it to alcohol. It causes tolerance and dependence (Harvey, 1980).

Ethchlorvynol

Ethchlorvynol (Placidyl®) is a short-acting sedative-hypnotic drug. Placidyl® causes side effects in some people, such as facial numbness, blurred vision, nausea, dizziness, gastric upset, and skin rashes. It is usually taken in 100- to 200-mg doses from two to four times a day as a sedative; as a hypnotic (sleep-inducing drug), in a 500-mg to 1-g dose. Abusers may take up to 4 g a day. They develop tolerance, and physical as well as psychological dependence. A dose of 10 to 25 g can cause death. It is potentially lethal if taken with alcohol. Placidyl® is sometimes found as a street drug.

Glutethimide

Glutethimide (Doriden®) is another example of a nonbarbiturate that has been abused. Doriden® causes side effects similar to those of Placidyl® in some persons. In addition, it induces blood abnormalities in sensitive individuals, such as a type of anemia and abnormally low white cell counts. In children, the drug may cause paradoxical excitement (unusual agitation and stimulation). Nausea, fever, tachycardia (rapid heartbeat), and convulsions occasionally occur in patients who have been taking this sedative regularly in moderate doses. The sedative dose for adults is 125 to 250 mg taken one to three times a day. As a hypnotic the dose is usually 250 to 500 mg at bedtime. Doriden® seems to have less margin of safety than barbiturates, and it potentiates with alcohol. It builds up tolerance and causes physical dependence. It was used more commonly as a street drug before it was definitely proved to be addictive and tighter controls were put on it.

Methyprylon

Methyprylon (Noludar®), a nonbarbiturate whose effects do not last long, is used as a sedative and hypnotic. The effects are similar to those of Doriden®, and it is capable of causing tolerance, physical dependence, and addiction. Death has occurred during untreated withdrawal. Dosage for sedation is 50 to 100 mg three or four times a day. For inducing sleep the dosage is usually 200 to 300 mg.

METHAQUALONE

Few drugs have become so popular so fast as has methaqualone. It is a nonbarbiturate sedative-hypnotic that was introduced into India in the 1950s as an antimalarial agent. The sedative properties, however, were soon discovered. After several years of street abuse, methaqualone was classified as a Schedule II drug. This category includes drugs with dangerous potential for psychological or physical dependence. It is available in the United States as Quaalude®, Mequin®, and Parest® (Lemmon). It is also imported illegally in large quantities from countries such as Colombia.

In humans, the drug accumulates in fatty tissue and readily enters the brain, just as barbiturates do. It causes increased microsomal enzyme activity in the liver and may therefore induce tolerance. Methaqualone has less effect on REM sleep (see p. 177) than do the barbiturates. Common side effects are fatigue, dizziness, anorexia, nausea, vomiting, diarrhea, sweating, dryness of the mouth, depersonalization, headache, and paresthesia of the extremities (a pins-and-needles feeling in the fingers and toes). Hangover is frequently reported.

The standard hypnotic dose of methaqualone is 150 to 300 mg, whereas the average dose for daytime sedation is 75 mg three to four times daily. Coma may occur if a dose of 2 g is taken; doses between 8 and 20 g can be fatal. Lower doses can be fatal if methaqualone is taken with

alcohol or other CNS depressants, because of potentiation of the sedative effect. Mild overdosage causes an excessive CNS depression much like that from barbiturates. During coma, it does not cause as marked a depression of heartbeat and respiration as do barbiturates. Severe overdose can cause delirium, restlessness, muscle spasms, and even convulsions (Harvey, 1980).

High doses of methaqualone can cause psychological and physical dependence, and dangerous withdrawal symptoms when the drug is stopped. People who had taken 600 to 3000 mg of methaqualone daily had insomnia, abdominal cramps, headaches, anorexia, and nightmares. Severe grand mal (major motor) convulsions may occur after withdrawal from high doses. The symptoms are similar to the delirium tremens during withdrawal from alcohol. Treatment for withdrawal from methaqualone and other sedative-hypnotics is described in a following section.

THE BARBITURATES

Barbiturates are defined as any of a group of barbituric acid derivatives used in medicine as sedatives and hypnotics. Barbituric acid was synthesized by Dr. A. Bayer (of aspirin fame) in Germany in 1864. The reason for the name *barbituric acid* is not known. Some have speculated that the compound was named after a girl named Barbara whom Bayer knew. Others think that Bayer celebrated his discovery on the Day of St. Barbara in a tavern that artillery officers frequented (St. Barbara is the patron saint of artillery men).

The first compound, barbituric acid, is not a depressant, but with slight modification it becomes a barbiturate, which is a CNS depressant. The first barbiturate, barbital (Veronal®), was used medically in 1903. Barbiturates' names end in "al," indicating a chemical relationship to barbital, the first one made.

The barbiturates have considerable medical value. However, uncontrolled use may cause a state of acute or chronic intoxication. Initially there may be some loss of inhibition, euphoria, and behavioral stimulation. When taken in the presence of extreme pain or mental stress, they may cause delirium and other side effects that can include nausea, nervousness, rash, and diarrhea. The person intoxicated on barbiturates may have difficulty in thinking, defective judgment, increased emotional instability, inability to coordinate, unsteadiness in walking, and slurring of speech.

Continued misuse of barbiturate drugs has a cumulative toxic effect on the CNS that is more life threatening than the opiates. In large doses or in combination with other CNS depressants,

barbiturates may cause death. Barbiturates are probably involved in three-fourths of all deaths (accidental or suicide) from drugs, currently estimated at nearly 5000 per year. Repeated misuse induces tolerance and physical dependence for the drug. Discontinuance of a short-acting barbiturate (one whose effects don't last long), after the dosage exceeds 400 to 600 mg a day for more than a month, causes dangerous withdrawal symptoms. (Table 10-1 summarizes the range of effects of barbiturates on the mind and body.)

Mechanism of Action and Metabolism

Barbiturates depress the reticular activating system (RAS) by interfering with oxygen consumption and energy-producing mechanisms in

TABLE 10-1   How the body and mind can react to barbiturates and other depressants

	Body	Mind
Low dose	Drowsiness	Decreased anxiety, relaxation
	Trouble with coordination	Decreased ability to reason and solve problems
	Slurred speech	
	Dizziness	Difficulty in judging distance and time
	Staggering	
	Double vision	Amnesia
	Sleep	
	Depressed breathing	Damage to brain
	Coma (unconscious and cannot be awakened)	
	Depressed blood pressure	
High dose	Death	

the neurons. Like other cells, neurons take up oxygen and glucose from the blood and convert the glucose into a usable form of energy, the ATP molecule. Barbiturates inhibit the breakdown of glucose and the formation of ATP. Thus the neurons are deprived of their usable form of energy and become less active. The depression of the RAS greatly reduces the number of impulses reaching the cerebral cortex, thus promoting calmness, drowsiness, and sleep, depending on the dosage.

Barbiturates can be classified in terms of duration of action (Table 10-2). In general, the more lipid-soluble the barbiturate is, the faster it will act and be metabolized and the more potent it will be as a hypnotic. Barbiturates are eliminated through the kidneys at varying rates, depending on the proportion of the drug that is bound to albumin. A higher percentage of the more lipid-soluble barbiturates are bound to this blood protein (see Chapter 3). Thus the rate of clearance primarily depends on how quickly the drug is metabolized in the liver. Excretion of free (unbound) barbiturate is faster when the urine is alkaline. Because barbiturates are not completely removed from the body overnight, even the short-acting ones used for insomnia

can cause subtle distortions of mood, and impairment of judgment and of motor skills the following day. The user may have mild withdrawal symptoms such as hyperexcitability, nausea, and vomiting (Harvey, 1980). The long-acting barbiturates, like phenobarbital, will cause a drug hangover because they are metabolized more slowly. Another factor in the duration of barbiturates' effects is their fat solubility: they are fat-soluble and may be stored. The fat content of the body can influence dosage effects. Because women have a higher body fat ratio than men, their reaction to barbiturates may be slightly different.

Effects and Clinical Uses of Barbiturates

Barbiturates have many actions: they will depress the activity of nerves, skeletal muscle, smooth muscle, and cardiac muscle and have effects on the CNS ranging from mild sedation to coma, depending on the dose. At sedative or hypnotic dosage levels, only the CNS is significantly affected. Anesthetic doses cause slight decreases in blood pressure, heart rate, and flow of urine.

TABLE 10-2   Classification of common barbiturates

Classification	Duration of pharma- cological effect	Drug
Ultrashort-acting	$\frac{1}{4}$ to 3 hours	Thiopental (Pentothal®)
Short-acting	3 to 6 hours	Amobarbital (Amytal®)
		Pentobarbital (Nembutal®)
		Secobarbital (Seconal®)
Intermediate-acting	6 to 12 hours	Butabarbital (Butisol®)
Long-acting	12 to 24 hours	Phenobarbital (Luminal®)

The enzyme systems in the liver are also affected. Barbiturates may cause liver damage if the person is hypersensitive to them or if he or she takes high doses over a long time. The barbiturates combine with one enzyme in the liver, cytochrome P-450, and interfere with the metabolism normally handled by this enzyme. This interference can cause adverse drug interactions and hormone imbalance. Barbiturates induce increased microsomal enzyme activity, which can cause a host of adverse drug interactions (Harvey, 1980).

Barbiturates have varied medical uses. For example, they are used as anticonvulsants: phenobarbital is used for its CNS depressant activity to alleviate or prevent convulsions in epileptic persons and convulsions from strychnine, cocaine, and other drugs. Thiopental (Pentothal®) and others are used as anesthesia for minor surgery and as preoperative anesthetics in preparation for major surgery.

Small doses will relieve tension and anxiety. Because of their antianxiety and antitension properties, a number of barbiturates began to be abused, at which time their dangers became apparent. The tranquilizers were developed in part because of the search for safer depressant drugs, ones without the potential for long-term addiction. The tranquilizers and mood modifiers have taken over much of the treatment of reducing anxiety and tension for which the barbiturates were used for many years.

Barbiturates have been used extensively to alleviate insomnia (inability to sleep) but are no longer the drugs of choice for this. Insomnia may be caused by stress and anxiety, pain, depression, and some endocrine abnormalities.

Barbiturates reduce rapid eye movement (REM) sleep. This phase of sleep appears to be essential to well-being. If a person is deprived of REM sleep and the dreams that occur during it, he or she grows irritable and anxious. REM sleep accounts for one-fifth to one-fourth of a person's total sleep time if he or she is not taking any sleep medication. Barbiturate sleeping pills cause a reduction in REM sleep during the first week of use. Using the drugs for as short a time as two weeks induces some tolerance, so that it takes longer to fall asleep; at this point, total sleep time is shorter, although REM sleep time rises to nearly normal levels again. After the drugs are discontinued, there is a large increase in REM sleep. It takes several weeks to catch up on REM sleep, during which the person has nightmares, is restless, and has difficulty sleeping. As a result, the person feels he or she is not getting enough sleep and may become anxious about it. Many return to taking barbiturates to "cure" the problem. A number of other drugs, such as CNS stimulants, alcohol, narcotics, and scopolamine, also cause sleep disturbances by affecting the REM phase or other phases of sleep.

The benzodiazepines (see Minor Tranquilizers, p. 178) are now used instead of barbiturates in cases of insomnia and other neurotic symptoms, because they are believed to have fewer side effects. Flurazepam (Dalmane®) accounted for over 50% of total sleeping pill prescriptions in the late 1970s. About 7% of male and 13% of female adults in the United States use sleeping pills—about half more than once per week—according to the National Center for Health Statistics.

Drug Dependence on Barbiturates

The American Medical Association (1965) has developed a list of the different types of people who abuse the sedative drugs:

1.   Those who seek sedative effects to deal with emotional stress. These people are trying to escape from problems.

CHAPTER 10 • DEPRESSANT DRUGS

2. Those seeking the excitation that occurs especially after some tolerance has been developed; instead of depression they will feel exhilaration and euphoria.

3. Those that try to counteract other drugs, such as some stimulants, LSD, and other hallucinogens.

4. Those that use sedatives in combination with other depressant drugs, such as alcohol and heroin. Alcohol plus the sedative gives a faster "high" but can be dangerous because of the multiple depressant effects. Heroin users often resort to barbiturates if their heroin supply is cut off.

The development of tolerance and physical dependence are usually necessary for true physiological dependence to occur. Two types of tolerance develop when barbiturates are taken repeatedly at short intervals. *Drug-disposition tolerance* results from enzyme induction in the liver. This causes more rapid metabolism of the drug, a decrease in sleeping time, and an increase in the average dose required. *Pharmacodynamic tolerance* involves adaptation of nervous tissue to the drug. This means that barbiturate addicts are often resistant to the hypnotic effects of barbiturates and other general depressants, including alcohol. Drug-disposition tolerance reaches its peak in a few days, whereas pharmacodynamic tolerance develops over a period of weeks to months with chronic administration of gradually increasing dosages (Harvey, 1980).

Development of physical dependence on barbiturates is a relatively slow process, requiring weeks or months before withdrawal symptoms would occur if the drug were abruptly stopped. Doses of 200 mg to 400 mg of pentobarbital or secobarbital can be taken daily for a year with little or no physical dependence. It would take daily doses of between 400 to 600 mg for more than one month to induce withdrawal symptoms (as described in a following section) when

the drug is stopped (Smith, Wesson, & Seymour, 1979). Withdrawal of the depressant causes rebound hyperexcitability because of restoration of depressed neural pathways. The symptoms are the same for withdrawal from all the sedative-hypnotics (see Treatment for Sedative-Hypnotic Drug Withdrawal, p. 182). Table 10-3 gives details on the barbiturates that are abused most frequently.

THE MINOR TRANQUILIZERS

The term *minor tranquilizer* was introduced into the medical literature in the 1950s to distinguish the medicine prescribed to reduce anxiety and tension from the *major tranquilizers*, like chlorpromazine, which are used as antipsychotic drugs in the treatment of severe mental illness, such as schizophrenia. The minor tranquilizers reduce anxiety, tension, and agitation without other significant side effects on mental processes.

The first of the modern *antianxiety agents*, as the minor tranquilizers are often called, was a muscle relaxant called *mephenesin*. However, because mephenesin had a short duration of action, research was done to find an agent of longer duration. In 1952 a new compound, meprobamate, was developed that seemed to be what was needed. It was marketed as Miltown® in 1955 and met with immediate and phenomenal acceptance. Sales went from $7500 in May of 1955 to $500,000 in December. Librium® was developed for medical use and marketed about 1960; Valium® came on the market about the same time. (These later drugs, the benzodiazepines, have a different structure.) the public now had its "happy pills." Abuse of meprobamate was reported within a year of introduction and has continued despite a substantial decrease in clinical use. In 1970 the U.S. Bureau of Narcotics

TABLE 10-3 Details on the most frequently abused barbiturates

Drug	Nickname	Description and dose
Amobarbital (Amytal®)	Blues, Blue Heavens, Blue Devils	65- or 200-mg blue capsule
Pentobarbital (Nembutal®)	Nembies, Yellow Jackets, Yellows	30- or 100-mg yellow, 50-mg orange-and-white capsule
Phenobarbital (Luminal®)	Purple Hearts	Purple tablet
Secobarbital (Seconal®)	Reds, Red Devils, Red Birds, Seccy	50-, 100-mg red capsule
Tuinal® (50% amobarbital and 50% secobarbital)	Tooeys, Double Trouble, Rainbows	50-, 100-, 200-mg capsule, blue body with red-orange cap

Nembutal®. Pentobarbital is short-acting. A dose of 30 to 50 mg is usually sufficient to induce sleep, but for true hypnosis as little as 100 mg is sufficient for a six- to eight-hour period of fretful sleep without much hangover. Will cause euphoria and excitation at first, so it is abused.

Seconal®. Secobarbital is short-acting with a prompt onset of action. It usually lasts under three hours and is commonly abused to produce intoxication and euphoria by blocking inhibitions.

Amytal®. Amobarbital has moderately rapid action and a duration of three to six hours. It takes 15 to 30 minutes to take effect.

Tuinal®. The "Rainbow" is a mixture of amobarbital and secobarbital. This combination results in a rapidly effective, moderately long-acting sedative. A sedative dose is around 50 mg; a hypnotic dose is 100 to 200 mg.

A fatal overdose of all these commonly used barbiturates is usually about ten times the hypnotic dose. Death is from respiratory failure.

and Dangerous Drugs acted to restrict the number of times a prescription for meprobamate could be refilled. It and the benzodiazepine tranquilizers are now classified as Schedule IV drugs.

The minor tranquilizers are often overlooked as drugs of abuse or addiction. However, in the past several years medical groups have become sensitive to the fact that a number of patients have developed seizures and other side effects that are part of a withdrawal syndrome. At present, more tranquilizers are sold in the United States than barbiturate sleeping pills, amphetamines, and opiate narcotics combined. An estimated 5 billion doses of minor tranquilizers were sold in 1979, Valium® accounting for about one-third of the total. The largest manufacturer of tranquilizers, Roche, sold $1.4 billion worth of these drugs. Since the late 1970s, 44 million prescriptions for Valium® have been written each year in the United States. The Roche company claims there are nearly 700 Valium® imitations or substitutes on the market. Minor tranquilizers are so widely prescribed that the American Medical Association warned doctors about overprescription, and prolonged and unsupervised administration. Chronic tranquilizer dependence is becoming quite frequent.

Medical Uses of Minor Tranquilizers

Minor tranquilizers are considered mildly sedative. With increasing dosage they have a definite sedative and hypnotic action. They are an exception to the rule that any sedative-hypnotic in sufficient dosage can induce anesthesia. The minor tranquilizers fall into several chemical classes. Some of these are diazepam (Valium®), chlordiazepoxide (Librium®), flurazepam (Dalmane®), and meprobamate (Miltown®, Equanil®, and others).

The minor tranquilizers are widely used today for patients suffering from anxiety, tension, behavioral excitement, and insomnia. They are also used in the treatment of lower back pain, convulsive disorders, and withdrawal symptoms from opiate-narcotic and alcoholic dependence. They are not a great improvement over the barbiturates, but they are used more frequently now because of the potential addictive nature of the barbiturates. Also, barbiturate overdose is often lethal, barbiturates interact more with other drugs, and withdrawal from them is more dangerous.

Effects of Minor Tranquilizers on the Body

The minor tranquilizers seem to have their primary action on the limbic system. The limbic system is considered to be the intermediary between the hypothalamus and the cerebral cortex, and it appears to control emotion. The antianxiety drugs may depress information transfer between these regions of the brain and blunt emotion. Like barbiturates (but to a lesser extent), they decrease both the spontaneous activity of the reticular activating system and its response to incoming sensory input.

The exact mechanism by which these drugs work is not known. Valium® and other benzodiazepines potentiate the effects of the neurotransmitter GABA (gamma aminobutyric acid; see Table 2-1 on p. 23). This neurotransmitter is believed to act as an inhibitor for certain parts of the brain. An increase in GABA may lower the amount of norepinephrine and serotonin in the brain. These latter two neurotransmitters are believed to be responsible for some of the symptoms of anxiety. If they are reduced it could possibly explain the reduction of anxiety effected by the minor tranquilizers. Surprisingly, the brain has specific receptor sites for Valium®, Librium®, and the other benzodiazepines, even though no similar chemicals have been discovered to be secreted by the body. None of the known neurotransmitters combines with these receptors (Tallman, Paul, Skolnick, & Gallagher, 1980). It is possible that we generate our own minor tranquilizers; anxious, nervous people may be deficient in a natural substance.

Reported side effects of minor tranquilizers are drowsiness, lethargy, skin rashes, nausea, diminished libido, irregularities in the menstrual cycle, blood cell abnormalities, and increased sensitivity to alcohol. High doses may depress respiration, induce coma, and even cause death. There is no clear evidence of permanent, irreversible damage to neurological or other physiological processes, even with long-term use. The benzodiazepines have less effect on REM sleep than the barbiturates. However, prolonged use of hypnotic doses may cause rebound increases in REM sleep and insomnia when the drug is stopped.

Drug Dependence on Minor Tranquilizers

After repeated use, tolerance usually develops to most of the effects of the minor tranquilizers, and the dose must be increased to obtain the desired results. However, no tolerance develops to the lethal dose. Both psychological and physiological dependence on these drugs resemble dependence on alcohol and the barbiturates. The benzodiazepines used for anxiety (like Valium® and Librium®) are converted to active metabolites. This conversion markedly extends the effective biological half-life. High doses must be given for long periods of time and then abruptly withdrawn before marked withdrawal symptoms appear. Because of the formation of active metabolites, withdrawal symptoms may not appear for a week (Baldessarini, 1980).

Withdrawal symptoms are nearly identical to those of barbiturate addiction. Death has resulted from poorly controlled or untreated withdrawal.

Cross-tolerance and cross-dependence (Chapter 3) exist among the minor tranquilizers and with other sedative drugs. Cross-tolerance does not appear to affect the lethal dose. If alcohol or barbiturates are taken simultaneously with minor tranquilizers, there may be an additive and dangerous reaction. Heavy abusers of these drugs may switch sedatives if necessary or convenient. Alcoholics often use barbiturates and tranquilizers to sustain inebriation. Persons dependent on opiate narcotics often also use large quantities of minor tranquilizers to prevent withdrawal symptoms or to withstand them. Table 10-4 summarizes the most frequently abused minor tranquilizers.

TABLE 10-4   Most abused minor tranquilizers

Valium® (diazepam): In addition to use as a tranquilizer, this drug is used to treat convulsions and as a muscle relaxant. It is more potent than Librium®. Diazepam reaches peak concentration in the blood about an hour after taking a tablet, in contrast to chlordiazepoxide and others in which the peak concentration may not be attained for several hours. This may largely account for the greater popularity of diazepam as a street drug (Baldessarini, 1980). Physical dependence and subsequent withdrawal are dangers with this drug also. Over 120 mg a day for over two months is known to produce physical dependence.

Miltown® and *Equanil® (meprobamate)* are used to treat anxiety; insomnia, especially in elderly patients; and mild epilepsy. Because meprobamate alleviates deep-seated anxieties, it can cause a psychological dependence. If large doses are taken (daily doses above 2.4 g for several weeks), physical dependence can occur. Once physical dependence has developed, untreated withdrawal can be quite dangerous. Common withdrawal symptoms are anxiety, insomnia, tremors, gastrointestinal upset, and hallucinations. Grand-mal-like convulsions occur in about 10% of cases. Meprobamate may potentiate with alcohol (Harvey, 1980).

Librium® and *Librax® (chlordiazepoxide)* are more potent than Miltown®. They too alleviate tension, anxiety, and apprehension. Large doses are used to treat alcohol withdrawal symptoms. If doses over 300 mg per day are taken for over two months, physical dependence develops, with resulting severe withdrawal symptoms when the drug is stopped.

TREATMENT FOR SEDATIVE-HYPNOTIC DRUG WITHDRAWAL

All sedative-hypnotics, including the nonbarbiturates and alcohol, can produce physical dependence and a barbiturate-like withdrawal syndrome, with convulsions, if the drug is taken in sufficient dosage over a long enough period. Symptoms include anxiety, tremors, nightmares, insomnia, anorexia, nausea, vomiting, seizures, delirium, and maniacal activity. The time course depends on the particular drug: with pentobarbital, secobarbital, meprobamate, and methaqualone, withdrawal symptoms may begin 12 to 24 hours after the last dose and peak in intensity between 24 and 72 hours. The withdrawal reactions to phenobarbital, diazepam, and chlordiazepoxide develop more slowly and peak on the fifth to eighth day (Smith et al., 1979).

There are two approaches to detoxifying a person addicted to a sedative-hypnotic. These are: (1) gradual withdrawal of the addicting agent using a short-acting barbiturate, and (2) the substitution of long-acting phenobarbital for the addicting agent, then gradual withdrawal of the phenobarbital. Use of a substitute is necessary because abrupt withdrawal in a person who is physically dependent is dangerous. This treatment represents the same rationale as the treatment of heroin withdrawal by methadone use. It is usually combined with supportive measures such as vitamins, restoration of electrolyte balance, and prevention of dehydration. The patient must be watched closely during this time, because he or she will be apprehensive, mentally confused, and unable to make logical decisions (Smith et al., 1979).

If the person is addicted to both alcohol and barbiturates, the phenobarbital dosage must be increased to compensate for the "double" withdrawal. Many barbiturate addicts who go to a hospital for withdrawal are also hooked on heroin. In this case, the first thing to be treated should be the barbiturate withdrawal, because of the life-threatening danger involved. The phenobarbital is combined with methadone; the phenobarbital is withdrawn first. Detoxification from any sedative-hypnotic should be done in a hospital (Smith et al., 1979).

Detoxification is only the first step; nothing has been done yet to keep the person from becoming readdicted. The process of psychological and social rehabilitation after sedative-hypnotic drug withdrawal is similar to that for the heroin addict (see Chapter 20).

PHENCYCLIDINE (PHENYLCYCLOHEXYLPIPERIDINE OR PCP)

PCP was developed in the late 1950s as an intravenous anesthetic. Although it was found to be an effective anesthetic, it had side effects that led to its being discontinued as a drug for human use. Sometimes persons coming out of the anesthetic had delirium and near manic states of excitation lasting 3 to 18 hours. PCP is a Schedule II drug now, legitimately available only as an animal anesthetic under the brand name Sernylan®. It is useful for anesthetizing monkeys. The street source is mainly synthesized from readily available chemical precursors in illicit laboratories.

PCP first appeared on the street drug scene in 1967 as the *PeaCe Pill.* In 1968 PCP reappeared in New York as *Hog.* By 1969 PCP was found under a variety of guises. It was sold as *Angel Dust* and sprinkled on parsley for smoking. The use of parsley caused confusion in law enforcement agencies that had obtained strange-looking marijuana through arrests, only to have their crime labs report that no marijuana or THC was found. It was at this time that PCP began to find its way into a variety of street drugs sold as psychedelic chemicals. By 1970 drug laboratories noticed that phencyclidine was used widely as a main ingredient in psychedelic preparations. It is frequently substituted for, and sold as, LSD and mescaline. Analysis of street drugs since 1970 shows that most "mescaline" and "THC" sold on the street is PCP in part or entirely. The drug called *cannabinol* is also usually PCP. It is also often found in other preparations called *superpot, monkey weed, horse tranquilizer, superweed, crystal T,* and others in amounts ranging from 2 to 110 mcg in a single dose.

One difficulty in estimating the effects of PCP is caused by the variance in purity of the drug. Also, there are about 30 analogs (drugs almost identical in structure) of PCP, and some of these have appeared on the street. Another difficulty is determining the extent of use. PCP has so many other street names people may not know they are using PCP, or they may have been deceived when buying what they thought was LSD, mescaline, and so on. Users may not question the identity of the substance unless they have a bad reaction. In the 1977 national drug survey taken by the National Institute on Drug Abuse, about 6% of 12- to 17-year olds and 14% of 18- to 25-year olds had tried or were using PCP (Petersen & Stillman, 1978). The 1979 national survey did not break down the PCP abuse separately from hallucinogens, so the extent of PCP use is still not clear.

In the late 1960s through the early 1970s, PCP was mostly taken orally, but it is now commonly smoked or snorted. By smoking the experienced user is better able to limit his or her dosage to a desired level. After smoking, the subjective effects appear within 1 to 5 minutes and peak over the next 5 to 30 minutes. The high lasts about 4 to 6 hours, followed by a 6- to 24-hour comedown. There is a 30-second to a 1-minute lag to onset of effects if the drug is snorted; the rest of the sequence of events is the same. When the drug is taken orally a longer period elapses before it takes effect, thus users may take too much, causing more overdoses and adverse effects than if the drug is smoked or snorted (Petersen & Stillman, 1978).

Physiological Effects of PCP

Phencyclidine has depressant, stimulant, hallucinogenic, and analgesic properties. Quite a combination! The effects of PCP on the central nervous system vary greatly. At low doses the most prominent effect is similar to that of alcohol intoxication, with generalized numbness; the person becomes less sensitive to pain. As the dose of PCP is increased, the person becomes even more insensitive and may become fully anesthetized. Large doses can cause coma, convulsions, and death.

The majority of peripheral signs of PCP effects are apparently related to activation of the sympathetic nervous system (Chapter 2). Flushing, excess sweating, and a blank stare are common, although the size of the pupils is unaffected. The cardiovascular system reacts by increasing blood pressure and rapidity of heart action. Analgesia, side-to-side eye movements (nystagmus), muscular incoordination, double vision, dizziness, nausea, and vomiting occur in many people taking medium to higher doses.

Psychological Effects of PCP

The drug has negative effects most of the time it is used. Why, then, do people use it repeatedly as their drug of choice, instead of another street drug? This is difficult for nonusers to understand. The fact that PCP has the ability to markedly alter the person's subjective feelings may be reinforcing, even though that alteration is not always positive. There is an element of risk, not knowing how the trip will turn out. PCP may give the user feelings of strength, power, and invulnerability. Other positive effects include heightened sensitivity to outside stimuli, a sense of stimulation and mood elevation, and dissociation from the surroundings. PCP is a social drug: virtually all users report taking it in groups rather than as a solitary experience (Petersen & Stillman, 1978).

People who have taken PCP have had accidents because of serious perceptual distortions. Users cannot accurately interpret the environment and may walk in front of moving cars or jump off buildings because they feel indestructible or weightless. A major PCP-related cause of death in California (a state with a large number of PCP experimenters) was by drowning. In a study of the causes of death in 19 cases in which PCP was the only drug found at autopsy, 11 were due to drowning (one in the shower). Apparently some PCP users lose their orientation while swimming or immersed in water and drown, sometimes in small amounts of water (Petersen & Stillman, 1978). High oral doses have been used to commit suicide, with respiratory depression the specific cause of death.

Chronic users may take PCP in runs extending over two to three days, during which they do not sleep or eat much. In later stages of chronic use, users may develop outright paranoid and violent behavior, with auditory hallucinations. PCP's role in precipitating long-term psychosis is poorly understood. Many of those who become psychotic with PCP appear to resemble those who become psychotic using LSD (Petersen & Stillman, 1978).

Evidence shows clearly that PCP can cause a psychosis in some subjects similar to that seen in schizophrenics. It may last for days or weeks and characteristically becomes more severe during the first few days of its course. During initial clinical trials of PCP as an anesthetic, one-sixth of the volunteers became severely psychotic for several hours after they woke up. Because of these postanesthetic reactions, the focus of investigation shifted from using PCP as an anesthetic to using it to produce model psychoses, until the drug was withdrawn from experimental use in humans. PCP has no equal in its ability to produce brief psychoses nearly indistinguishable from schizophrenia. The psychoses, induced with moderate doses given to normal, healthy volunteers, lasted about two hours and were characterized by changes in body image, thought disorders, estrangement, autism, and occasionally rigid inability to move (catalepsy). Subjects reported feeling numb, had great difficulty differentiating between themselves and their surroundings, and complained afterward of feeling extremely isolated and apathetic. They were often violently paranoid during the psychosis. When PCP was given experimentally to hospitalized chronic schizophrenics, it made them much worse, not for several hours, but for six weeks. "PCP is not just another hallucinogen, to be warned about in the same breath as LSD . . . PCP is far more dangerous to some individuals than the other abused drugs" (Luisada, 1978).

Medical Management of PCP Intoxication

The diagnosis of PCP overdosage is frequently missed because the symptoms often closely resemble those of an acute schizophrenic episode. Table 10-5 compares the symptoms commonly seen at low, moderate, and high doses of PCP. Simple, uncomplicated PCP intoxication

PHENCYCLIDINE (PHENYLCYCLOHEXYLPIPERIDINE, OR PCP)

can be managed with the same techniques of handling other psychedelic drug cases. It is important to have a quiet environment, limited contact with an empathic person capable of determining any deterioration in the patient's physical state, protection from self-harm, and the availability of hospital facilities. Talking down is not helpful; the patient is better off isolated from external stimuli as much as possible.

There is no specific antagonist to reduce the toxic effects of PCP. A drug, verapamil, has been tried in dogs and may prove useful in humans (Altura & Altura, 1981). Because PCP tends to stay in the body, removal should be speeded up by acidification of the urine with substances like citric acid, ammonium chloride, and others.

Valium® is often used for its tranquilizing effect to prevent injury to self and to staff, and also to reduce the chance for severe convulsions. Haldol® is also used to make the patient manageable, but phenothiazines (Thorazine® and others; see the following section, Major Tranquilizers) should not be used, since they potentiate the anticholinergic actions of PCP.

The medical management of comatose or convulsing patients is more difficult. The patient may need external respiratory assistance and external cooling to reduce the fever. Blood pressure may have to be reduced to safe levels and convulsions controlled. Restraints and four to five strong aides are often needed to prevent the patient from injuring him- or herself or the med-

TABLE 10-5 Comparison of symptoms commonly seen in emergency room patients having taken low, moderate, and high doses of PCP*

Low dose (under 5 mg)	Moderate dose (5 to 10 mg)	High dose (over 10 mg)
Agitation	Coma or stupor	Long coma (12 hr to days)
Serious incoordination	Eyes remain open	Eyes closed
Blank stare	Pupils in middle and reactive	High blood pressure
Catatonic rigidity	Vomiting	Muscular rigidity
Unable to speak	Extreme salivation	Convulsions
Lessened response to pinprick	Repetitive motor movements	No peripheral sensation
Flushed	Profuse sweating	Profuse sweating
Profuse sweating	Shivering	Decreased corneal and gag reflexes
Sensitive to sound	Nystagmus	Hypersalivation
Nystagmus	Flushing	Fever
	Fever	Repetitive motor movements
	Insensitive to pain, touch	Posture may be bowed (abdomen out)

*Oral sedative dose 1–5 mg; subanesthetic dose 7.5 mg (Petersen & Stillman, 1978).

ical staff. After the coma lightens, the patient typically becomes delirious, paranoid, and violently assaultive (Petersen & Stillman, 1978).

THE MAJOR TRANQUILIZERS

The group of drugs known as the *major tranquilizers* are not abused to any great extent. They have been extremely valuable in treating the mentally disturbed. These drugs are often called *antipsychotics,* or *neuroleptics,* because of their effect on the mind. They are used to control psychotic states. They do not cure mental problems, but alleviate the symptoms and facilitate therapy.

Of all the patients in mental hospitals, the largest group, about 50%, are diagnosed as schizophrenic. It is estimated that 2% of the population shows signs of schizophrenia at some point in their lives. The phenothiazines are one important class of major tranquilizers used in the treatment of schizophrenia and other psychotic states. Chlorpromazine, the first phenothiazine, was synthesized in 1950 in a search for anesthetic drugs. It was discovered that chlorpromazine by itself did not induce anesthesia but potentiated anesthetic properties of other drugs and decreased the patient's interest in what was going on around him or her. As a result of the finding that it induces loss of interest, chlorpromazine was tried in the treatment of the mentally ill, in whom not only did it reduce anxiety but it also acted on the psychotic process itself. Chlorpromazine was first used in the United States in 1954 for the treatment of psychomotor excitement and manic states. Another antipsychotic, haloperidol (Haldol®) became available for clinical use in psychiatry in 1958. (It is a butyrophenone, a different

chemical structure from the phenothiazine class of antipsychotic drugs.) Since then, other antipsychotics have been developed (Baldessarini, 1980). Common major tranquilizers used today are Thorazine® (chlorpromazine), Stelazine®, Prolixin®, Mellaril®, and Haldol®.

Major tranquilizers have revolutionized the treatment of psychotic patients and dramatically reduced the residential patient population in mental hospitals, as the following statistics make clear. From 1945 to 1955, there was an average increase each year of about 13,000 patients residing in state mental hospitals. Because of these increases, the population of state mental hospitals quadrupled from 133,000 to over 500,000 from 1903 to 1952. The year 1955, when the phenothiazines were introduced, was the turning point. If the 1945 to 1955 rate of increase had continued to the present, there would now be nearly 900,000 hospitalized patients. Instead, the number has decreased each year since 1955, so that in 1980 there were an estimated 450,000 fewer patients in those hospitals than in 1955 (see Figure 10-1). This decline has occurred in spite of an increase in the number of admissions to state hospitals, because the drugs have changed the whole method of treatment of the mentally ill. First, the length of hospitalization has decreased remarkably. In 1955 the average stay in a mental hospital was about six months; in 1966, two months; and in 1980, about 21 days. More and more patients are being treated as outpatients rather than being hospitalized. The increase in the number of aftercare facilities has also been significant in the continuing treatment of persons with psychiatric problems.

How effective are the antipsychotics, or major tranquilizers? It may take three or more weeks to show a positive effect and may require six weeks to six months of treatment to reach full effectiveness in hospitalized patients. After six

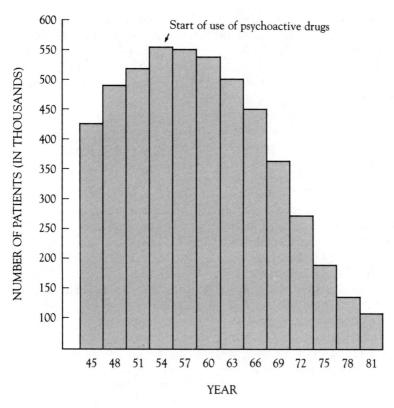

FIGURE 10-1
The impact of major tranquilizers on the number of institutionalized patients in the United States.

weeks, most acute schizophrenics receiving phenothiazines show either moderate or marked improvement, whereas comparatively few of those receiving placebos show improvement. Another test of effectiveness of these drugs is whether they prevent relapse to the original condition. Use of any of the antipsychotic drugs prevents relapse in about 85% of the patients. If patients are withdrawn from antipsychotics and put on a placebo, about 56% relapse (Baldessarini, 1980).

Side Effects and Medical Problems of the Antipsychotics

The phenothiazines are not addictive. They are extremely difficult to use to commit suicide, although a few such cases have been reported. Some of the problems that do occur are a type of low blood pressure, photosensitivity of the skin, skin rashes, and a serious (but rare) type of low white blood cell count. Persons given antipsychotic dosages of many of these drugs

develop involuntary *(extrapyramidal)* movement of muscle groups. In *Parkinsonism* caused
by phenothiazines and haloperidol, the person
has nervous tremors, rigidity of limbs, and a
shuffling walk due to inability to control some
of the muscle groups. In *akathesia,* the patient
may feel he or she has to get up and walk or
move about continuously. *Tardive dyskinesia*
occurs following months or years of antipsychotic drug treatment. The symptoms are involuntary facial movements, such as slow, rhythm-
ical movements in the region of the mouth, with
protrusion of the tongue and smacking of the
lips. About 40% to 50% of patients in state
mental hospitals have this disfiguring side effect.
It may be partially reversible if the drug is discontinued for a while, until psychotic symptoms
reappear. Adding choline to the diet (in the
form of lecithin) increases formation of acetylcholine in the brain and alleviates symptoms in
some patients. The dosage of antipsychotic drug
should be reduced to the lowest effective level
that controls the psychotic symptoms (Baldessarini, 1980).

Mechanisms of Action and Metabolism

The phenothiazines and the other antipsychotic
agents antagonize the actions of the neurotransmitter dopamine in key areas of the forebrain.
The more effective the antipsychotic drug, the
more tightly it binds to a particular type of dopamine receptor. This finding, which is revolu-
tionizing antipsychotic drug development, led
to the formulation of the dopamine theory of
psychotic behavior. The dopamine deficiency
produced by chlorpromazine and other nonspecific antipsychotic drugs causes the involuntary
motor movements (extrapyramidal symptoms)
as a side effect (Kolata, 1979).

Chlorpromazine is extensively degraded in the
body: there are probably 10 to 12 metabolites
in man (Garattini & Morselli, 1978). The
removal of these products is very slow and in
some cases may take up to three months.

MOOD MODIFIERS: SMOOTHING OUT DEPRESSION AND MANIA

The Antidepressants

Mood variations are more common than disorganized thinking in the general population and
are tolerated to a greater degree. Mental depression is common. States of depression are grouped
in many ways: those precipitated by a severe
mental shock or stress, those with a physiological basis, and so on. One of the most effective
treatments for depressed patients is electroconvulsive therapy. It may be equivalent in value
to the antidepressant drugs. Because it looks
brutal (the patient is given an electric shock to
the brain with electrodes), clinicians have tried
to find other ways to treat the depressed patient.
However, results are obtained more rapidly with
electroconvulsive therapy than with drug treatment. It is the technique of choice for a suicidal
patient, for whom antidepressant drugs may not
bring relief quickly enough (Baldessarini, 1980).

The story of the antidepressant drugs began
with clinical reports on treatment of tuberculosis. Until about 1955, tuberculosis was a major
disease in the United States. Starting in 1952
certain drugs were found that were effective in
treating TB. Two of these were *isoniazid* and
iproniazid. Iproniazid was chosen for widespread
use because of the two drugs it proved to be less
toxic. Clinical reports soon mentioned that
patients receiving the drug had unusually high

spirits and an extremely elevated mood. In 1955 iproniazid was first used extensively as an antidepressant drug.

Iproniazid is a monoamine oxidase (MAO) inhibitor. MAO is the only enzyme involved in the deactivation of serotonin, and it also deactivates norepinephrine. Blocking MAO results in high levels of serotonin in the brain, as well as norepinephrine. Unfortunately, MAO inhibitors cause a serious side effect in combination with the pressor substance, tyramine: high blood pressure. Tyramine is found in sufficiently high amounts in foods such as aged cheese (cheddar and others), chocolate, raisins, chianti wine, and beer to cause problems. Iproniazid was removed from the market in 1961 after 54 deaths. In view of this and their other toxic effects, MAO inhibitors are not used much any more as antidepressants (Weiner, 1980b).

A second group of antidepressant drugs, the tricyclics, came into use about this time. Unlike the MAO inhibitors, these do not cause mood elevation in normal subjects. They will relieve depression (elevate mood) in depressed people after two to three weeks of drug treatment. The reason for this slow onset of action is not known. Tricyclic antidepressants block histamine receptors and may affect levels of serotonin, dopamine, and norepinephrine secondarily (Kolata, 1979). However, it is not proven that this is the basis for their antidepressant activity.

Tricyclics have a number of serious side effects. They cause rapid heart rate, decreased blood pressure, and an increased risk of heart attack and congestive heart failure. They cause some patients to switch abruptly from depression to manic excitement with delirium. They also cause blurred vision, dry mouth, constipation, and urinary retention. Delayed orgasm and inability to achieve orgasm have been reported for both men and women. The tricyclics, like the MAO inhibitors and lithium (see the following section), are potentially lethal in doses that are readily available to patients who have a high risk anyway of committing suicide (Baldessarini, 1980).

Lithium Salts

Lithium salts are effective in the treatment of the manic phase of manic-depressive illness, as mood stabilizing drugs when used chronically in manic depressives, and as antidepressants. Lithium is unique in that it has no psychoactivity in normal subjects—it is neither sedative nor euphoriant. The lithium ion has no known biological role. It mimics some of the biological properties of both extracellular sodium and intracellular potassium. In a biological system, it acts more like sodium than any other ion. Passage through the blood-brain barrier is slow, but lithium does enter the brain's neurons. It inhibits the release of norepinephrine and dopamine, but not serotonin. Lithium salts presently available for use have a low therapeutic index (Chapter 4): they are toxic at a dosage very close to the therapeutic dose, and blood levels must be monitored closely (Baldessarini, 1980).

ABUSED VOLATILE SUBSTANCES

Substances inhaled to alter subjective states can be divided into three basic classes: the commercial and related *volatile solvents*, the *aerosols*, and the *anesthetics*. Of the *volatile solvents*, the most important is plastic (model) cement, which in its varying commercial formulations may contain toluene, acetone, naphtha, aliphatic acetates, hexane, and cyclohexane. Household cements contain toluene, acetone, isopropyl alcohol, methyl and ethyl ketone, and methyl isobutyl ketone. Fingernail polish removers contain acetone, aliphatic acetates, benzene, or alcohol. Lacquer thinners contain mixtures of toluene and higher alcohols. Gasoline, kerosene, and lighter fluid are also in this class.

Aerosols are products that are discharged by the propellant force of compressed gas. Chemicals in the aerosol product and the propellant used can be toxic. Many abused aerosols contain gasses of chlorinated or fluorinated hydrocarbons, nitrous oxide, and vinyl chloride. *Anesthetics* include ether, chloroform, nitrous oxide, enflurane, halothane, methoxyflurane, and related gases. Nitrous oxide ("laughing gas") is the most widely employed: it is available as an anesthetic and commercially as a tracer gas to detect pipe leaks, as a whipped-cream propellant, and as a pressurized product designed to reduce preignition in racing cars.

Younger children, the poor, and prison inmates are the most common groups who abuse the volatile solvents and the aerosols. There are two major types of inhalant abuser: experimenters, or transitional users, who move on to other drugs, and chronic abusers. Chronic abuse is limited to the young and the very poor, who have limited access to more popular mind-altering substances. Inhalant experimentation is extremely widespread among the young—nearly everyone tries some form of inhalant. Within their own neighborhoods, chronic inhalant abusers come from the most unstable, disorganized, and problem-ridden families. Abuse is related to parental alcoholism and neglect/abuse. Inhalant abusers do not develop ritual or jargon—they are not part of a drug subculture (Carroll, 1977b).

The abused volatile substances are classified as depressants because they depress the activity of the central nervous system. These substances are often called *deliriants*, but this classification is a misleading one because delirium may or may not occur. Some have psychedelic characteristics. Most are lipid-soluble. (Remember that lipids make up a sizable proportion of all cell membranes and body organs such as the brain; see Chapter 3.) Many of these volatile solvents are either gases at room temperature, or they rapidly evaporate from a liquid state to a gaseous state. This property is desired for many substances used in industrial and household processes in which fast drying, coating, or cleaning is wanted. Volatile solvents are usually highly inflammable.

People have known about intoxicating chemical fumes for more than 150 years, but it has only been in the past 30 years that they have become aware of the real dangers of inhaling these fumes. Many of the volatile substances have not been investigated for their physiological effects, because they were never intended to be inhaled except in very small amounts under industrial circumstances.

Nitrous oxide, diethyl ether, and chloroform—three of the best-known volatile anesthetics until recently—had considerable recreational use, which preceded their medical use. Here is an advertisement displayed in Hartford, Connecticut in 1844:

A Grand Exhibition of the effects produced by inhaling Nitrous Oxid, Exhilarating or Laughing Gas! will be given at Union Hall this (Tuesday) Evening, Dec. 10th, 1844.

Forty gallons of Gas will be prepared and administered to all in the audience who desire to inhale it.

Twelve Young Men have volunteered to inhale the Gas, to commence the entertainment.

Eight Strong Men are engaged to occupy the front seats to protect those under the influence of the Gas from injuring themselves or others. This course is adopted that no apprehension of danger may be entertained. Probably no one will attempt to fight.

The effect of the Gas is to make those who inhale it either Laugh, Sing, Dance, Speak or Fight, and so forth, according to the leading trait of their character. They seem to retain consciousness enough not to say or do that which they would have occasion to regret.

N.B.—The Gas will be administered only to gentlemen of the first respectability. The object is to make the entertainment a genteel affair.

The promoter of this entertainment, a former medical student who dropped out when he realized he could make more money this way, showed an appreciation of the variety of potential effects of the drug and the importance of the individual personalities of those taking it.

Nitrous oxide is currently used by older teenagers and young adults of both genders. It is available in small containers for whipping cream ("Whippets" and other brands) and is widely sold in head shops. It is used as a general anesthetic in hospitals and dental offices. Reports in the medical literature suggest that anesthesiologists, doctors, nurses, dentists, and inhalation specialists abuse nitrous oxide as well as other inhalation anesthetics, such as enflurane (Chenoweth, 1977).

Prior to its introduction into medical practice, diethyl ether was widely used as an intoxicant. It is a highly volatile liquid at room temperature, so it can be either inhaled or drunk. It served as a substitute for alcohol when liquor was expensive in Ireland in the 19th century. Americans used ether during Prohibition, and the Germans used it in World War II, when alcohol was scarce. Before the turn of this century in the United States, upper-class sophisticates used ether and chloroform as experimental drinks. Medical students had ether parties, or *jags* as they were called. It was the observation of the effects of ether that led Dr. Long to recommend using ether during surgery. (Prior to

the use of ether, surgeons used strong men to hold the patient down and just worked as fast as possible.) Oliver Wendell Holmes suggested the word *anesthesia* to describe the state of insensibility that accompanies the unconsciousness induced by sufficient doses of these substances (Cohen, 1975).

Diethyl ether is available in an anesthetic grade and several chemical grades, for laboratory and industrial use. Although it is still abused to some extent, how much is difficult to assess. Those who have access to chemical supplies are also likely to have access to 190-proof ethanol (the beverage type), which is supplied in 5-gallon drums and easily diverted to graduate student or medical student (and faculty!) parties.

Methods of Abuse of Volatile Substances

Many of the active volatile substances are absorbed if taken orally. Inhalation, however, is a rapid means of taking the chemical. The desired alteration in consciousness may be achieved within one or two minutes of inhaling a high concentration and in up to five to ten minutes with a lower concentration. Absorption from the lungs puts lipid-soluble substances into the brain about as fast as intravenous injection. The concentration in the central nervous system reflects the concentration of substances in inhaled air delayed only by the circulation time from the lungs to the brain.

Inhalation techniques are designed to maximize the gas concentration. Frequently the substance is emptied into a plastic or paper bag, which is held tightly over the nose and mouth, and the fumes are inhaled. A cloth may be dipped in a liquid, or the active substance may be applied to the cloth, which is then rolled up and held against the nose and/or mouth. In a few cases the chemical, such as amyl nitrite, is available in an ampule that can be broken, and the vapor is breathed directly. Amyl nitrite is a short-acting vasodilator occasionally used to treat angina pectoris. Butyl nitrite is a chemical relative of amyl nitrite and is sold under *Lockerroom, Rush,* and other names. The chemical is used in industry and is readily available because it is not a licensed drug like amyl nitrite. People sniff it and become intoxicated from its effect of dilating the blood vessels in the brain. Their faces become flushed; they become very light-headed and may faint. The drug got its reputation by its apparent effect if used during sexual relations near orgasm. Street users called it an aphrodisiac, and this stimulated interest. However, users afterward may have a tremendous headache and feel nauseous for a while. Most people who try it do not continue to use it.

Physiological Effects of Volatile Substances

The commonly abused volatiles do not cause significant tolerance or physical dependence but can cause a wide variety of adverse effects and physical abnormalities. These include changes and damage to the kidney, the liver, bone marrow, and the brain. Gastroenteritis, hepatitis, jaundice, and blood abnormalities are among the complications that occur following use of these substances. Alteration of consciousness and cardiac arhythmias are immediate; whereas persistent organic brain syndrome, peripheral nerve injury, reduction in blood cell formation, and liver and kidney damage are delayed. Long-term effects may not appear for 10 to 30 years and consist primarily of an increased rate of cancer.

Chronic exposure to benzene (in some solvents and gasoline) can cause leukemia and severe anemia. Glue and contact cement contain n-hexane, which can damage the nervous system and cause numbness, loss of touch sensation in the feet, and limb weakness. Ketones in rubber cements, printing ink, and paint can cause similar nerve damage. Methylene chloride, used as a solvent in spray paints and thinners, is converted to carbon monoxide (see Chapter 9) in the body. Freon® aerosol propellants in such products as frying-pan spray have caused sudden death by cardiac arhythmias when sniffing was followed by vigorous exercise. Freon® has been removed from most consumer aerosol products. Gasoline additives such as TCP cause degeneration of motor nerves, and the lead additives cause lead poisoning (Comstock & Comstock, 1977; Hecht, 1980). Heavy users of volatile substances commonly have slow-healing ulcers around the mouth and the nose. Loss of appetite and poor eating habits may cause nutritional deficiencies as they do in the chronic alcoholic.

Nitrous oxide seems to be the least toxic of the abused volatile substances. Repeated exposures for 24 hours or more may depress the bone marrow and cause death from impaired ability to form blood cells. Anesthesiologists and surgical personnel exposed to anesthetics over long periods of time have an increased risk of miscarriage, birth defects, and kidney and liver disease. Diethyl ether is explosive: it is heavier than air and can be touched off by electrical sparks from outlets or electrical equipment some distance away from where it is being used. Chloroform is no longer used as an anesthetic because it has toxic effects on the liver and kidney, and its use sometimes has caused cardiac arrest. Chloroform, trichloroethylene, and halothane all have the potential to cause cancer.

Overdose treatment, if the abuser survives long enough to be taken to the hospital, consists of using supportive measures until he or she excretes the toxic substance. The person taken to the emergency room may have *acute organic brain syndrome* entailing a loss of muscular coordination, lethargy, irritability, confusion, and possible disorientation and impaired short-term memory. The condition clears up gradually as the lipid-soluble inhalant comes out of fat stores and is excreted. Most of the volatile hydrocarbons (toluene, hexane, and so on) and nitrous oxide are eliminated unchanged through the lungs.

A number of deaths have been attributed to volatile-solvent abuse. These fatalities have usually occurred when the user was alone. Death may be caused by respiratory failure or suffocation from the plastic bag used to contain the inhalant. Some types of aerosol propellant, such as Freon®, may cause cardiac arrest and kill the user that way. Other inhalants, such as hair spray, kill by coating the lungs and preventing the exchange of oxygen and carbon dioxide. An estimated 700 people died in the 1970s from inhaling all types of aerosols.

ALCOHOL

CHAPTER OBJECTIVES

1. List two examples of the economic role of alcoholic beverages in the United States.
2. Give examples of medicinal uses for alcohol.
3. Describe factors that influence blood alcohol levels.
4. Describe differences between the metabolism of alcohol and that of other caloric substances, and of alcohol and that of other depressant drugs.
5. Explain what types of tolerance develop to alcohol.
6. List short-term effects of increasing blood alcohol levels.
7. Name the two metabolites of alcohol that contribute to hangover.
8. Describe the effects of long-term, heavy drinking on the heart, brain, and liver.
9. Describe the effect of heavy drinking during pregnancy on the child's development.
10. Formulate a working definition of alcoholism.
11. Discuss the physiological, psychological, and sociological bases for alcoholism.
12. Name the most important factors in successful rehabilitation of an alcoholic.
13. Define the following terms: distilled spirits, denatured alcohol, grain alcohol, proof, congener, alcohol dehydrogenase, acetaldehyde, polyneuritis, salsolinol, DTs, AA, and Al-Anon.

HISTORY OF ALCOHOL

People have known about the effects of alcohol since the beginning of recorded history. There are several basic ingredients or conditions that must be present in order for alcohol to be made: sugar, water, yeast, and warm temperatures. This process, called *fermentation,* is a natural one. Fermentation occurs in ripe fruit and berries and even in honey that wild bees leave in trees. All of these substances have sugar and water, and are found in warm climates where there are yeast spores transported through the air. Animals will seek out and eat fermented fruit: elephants, baboons, birds, wild pigs, and even bees. It is a comical sight to see elephants bumping into one another and stumbling around or bees flying a rather unsteady beeline toward their hives. Birds eating fermented fruit become so uncoordinated they cannot fly, or, if they do, they crash into windows or branches.

Fermented honey, called *mead,* may have been the first alcoholic beverage. The Egyptians had breweries 6000 years ago; they credited their god Osiris with introducing wine to man. The ancient Greeks used a great deal of wine and credited the god Bacchus (or Dionysus) with introducing the drink. Today we use the words *bacchanalia* and *Dionysian rites* to refer to revelry and drunken events. The Romans were heavy users of wine, as were the ancient Hebrews. The Bible contains at least five different words for alcoholic beverages: *yayin,* meaning wine; *homer,* meaning fresh, young, unmixed wine; *tiros,* meaning strong wine; *meseg,* meaning mixed wines; and *sekhor,* meaning strong drink (implying the presence of stronger beverages than wine—perhaps with opium dissolved in it). The Bible mentions that Noah, just nine generations after Adam, made wine and became drunk.

Alcohol is produced by a single-celled microscopic organism, one of the yeasts, which by a metabolic form of combustion breaks down sugar, releasing carbon dioxide and forming water and ethyl alcohol as a waste product. Carbon dioxide creates the foam on a glass of beer and the fizz in champagne. Fermentation continues until the sugar supply is exhausted or until the concentration of alcohol reaches the point at which it kills the yeast (12% to 14%). Thus 12% to 14% is the natural limit of fermented wines or beers. The distillation device, or *still,* was developed by the Arabs around 800 A.D. and was introduced into medieval Europe around 1250 A.D. (Figure 11-1). The word *alcohol* derives from the Arabic *alkuhl,* which means something subtle, or the essential spirit of wine. Arnauld de Villeneuve, a professor of medicine at the University of Montpellier toward the end of the 13th century, thought it was the universal panacea and called the distillate *aqua vitae,* or *water of life.* Later the Irish used the distillation technique on fermented grain and called the drink *usquebaugh,* the Irish-Gaelic equivalent of aqua vitae. The word gradually became *whiskey.* The Scots used fermented ("malted") barley; they dried it in kilns fired with burning peat, which gives Scotch whisky its distinctive flavor. The Dutch distilled a strong drink from fermented fruit juice, which they called *brandewijn,* or *burnt* (distilled) *wine* (Roueché, 1960).

Distillation increases the potency of alcoholic beverages 400% to 500% (from 14% to 50% concentration of alcohol or more), and, because distillation made it easier for people to get drunk, it greatly intensified the problem of alcohol abuse. However, even before the advent of the still, alcoholic beverages had been known to cause problems in heavy users. It had been noticed that some individuals were sensitive to alcoholic beverages and became dependent on

FIGURE 11-1
Medieval still.

them. One of the oldest records noting the dangers of excess drinking was written in Egypt about 3000 years ago, under the title of *Wisdom of Ani:*

> Don't drink yourself helpless in the beer garden. You speak, and you don't know what you are saying. If you fall down and break your limbs, no one will help you. And your drinking companions will get up and say, "Away with this drunkard!" [National Institute on Alcohol Abuse and Alcoholism, 1980]

From the Middle Ages on, wines that had a higher concentration of alcohol added to them were called *fortified.* These had a concentration of about 20% alcohol. They were given names according to the types of grape used or the region where they were made. The most famous and perhaps most enduring of these wines are sherry, port, Madeira, muscatel, and champagne. Medieval physicians used alcohol in medicinal preparations, and it was a natural step from this to make a liqueur—a fortified spirit containing various herbs. Many liqueurs, or cordials, also contained sugar and even minerals. Drambuie®, Chartreuse, and Benedictine are examples of old liqueurs that are still made today. Benedictine is made by the Benedictine monks, who keep the recipe a secret.

Like most drug use, alcohol consumption has good and bad aspects. Shakespeare observed in Act II of *Othello:* "Good wine is a good familiar creature if it be well used." In excess, however,

"Some of the most dreadful mischiefs that afflict mankind proceed from wine; it is the cause of disease, quarrels, sedition, idleness, aversion to labor, and every species of domestic disorder." Similar sentiments concerning excessive drinking are found in Greek, Roman, Indian, Japanese, Chinese, and Hebrew literature (NIAAA, 1980).

The so-called hard liquors were also developed in the Middle Ages. These were made from grain, potatoes, or starchy plant parts. The grain was "malted," or allowed to sprout slightly. The sprouting process activates digestive enzymes in the grain that break down starch to sugars. The yeast can then more readily form alcohol as a by-product of the fermentation process. After the fermentation process, the "mash" is distilled and the alcoholic contents are filtered, mixed, or processed in whatever way is needed.

In the 1600s the Dutch distilled alcohol from grain with juniper berries added for flavor and called the concoction *junever,* the origin of the word *gin.* Gin had a rather unsavory reputation in Europe in the 18th century and later, as a drug used to pacify crying babies and also as an agent to use for infanticide, sometimes mixed with laudanum (an opium preparation). About the same time gin was made, the Russians were fermenting a strong drink from potatoes or grain that had to be diluted with water. This was named *vodka,* for *little water;* it was and still is used heavily in Russia.

Alcoholic beverages have played an important role in the history of the United States. The Pilgrims stopped at Plymouth Rock (present-day Massachusetts) instead of going farther south, because "our victuals were much spent, especially our beer." A decade later, the Puritans stocked their ship, the Arabella, with 10,000 gallons of wine, 42 tons of beer, and 14 tons of water (Lee, 1963).

Although the early settlers were rather straightlaced, they did not frown on drinking in moderation. Nevertheless, by 1619, 12 years after the start of the Virginia Colony, excessive drinking resulted in a law decreeing that any person found drunk for the first time was to be reproved privately by the minister; the second time, publicly; the third time to "lye in halter" for 12 hours and pay a fine. Yet in that same year the Virginia assembly passed other legislation encouraging the production of wines and distilled spirits in the colony. In the Massachusetts Bay Colony, as in Virginia, occasional drunkenness was punished by whipping, fines, and confinement in the stocks.

Homemade beers and wines were an important source of fluid and nutrition to early American farmers. Sanitation was unknown, and the family well was often contaminated by human and animal wastes. Cows' milk was known to transmit "milk sickness" (tuberculosis). Although the alcoholic content of home brew must have helped to make the rugged nature of pioneer life more endurable, the alcohol was primarily a preservative for the beverage. Homemade beers and wines were not purified as our commercial products are today. The nutritional and medicinal value of the yeast left over from the brewing process had been recognized by people around the world for centuries. Because American colonial beers and wines were not clarified, but were left with the spent yeast, they supplied many of the vitamins and minerals needed for good nutrition (Brown, 1978).

The caloric content may also have been a significant part of the diet. The most similar situation nowadays exists in the hills of Tibet, where the climate is not unlike that of New England: between one-third and one-half of the daily caloric intake of a hardworking Tibetan farmer comes from the beer he drinks. The early

HISTORY OF ALCOHOL

American settlers used the available sugar sources: honey, maple and birch sap, boiled cornstalks, and malted barley. Hops were commonly used as a preservative for beer, but where the hops plant did not grow, people used ground ivy (for the similar flavor), spruce, ginger, sweet mary, tansy, sage, wormwood, and sweet gale. Even greater variety is found in the family, or folk, wines. Almost anything in the kitchen garden or back fields or woods was used. There are published recipes for wines made from apple, apricot, balm, carrot, celery, cherry, chokecherry, clove, clover, coconut, cornstalk, cowslip, cranberry, cypress, dandelion, date, elderberry, elder flower, ginger, goldenrod, gooseberry, grape, grape leaf, grape tendril, hawthorn, hop, Jerusalem artichoke, juniper, lemon, lettuce, loganberry, marigold, may blossom, mint, mulberry, nettle, oakleaf, orange, pansy, parsnip, peach, peapod, pineapple, plum, potato, potato stalk, primrose, pumpkin, quince, raisin, raspberry, rhubarb, rice, rose, rose hip, rowenberry, sage, spinach, spruce, squash, strawberry, sycamore, tomato, turnip, walnut, wheat, whortleberry, and yarrow (Brown, 1978).

Rum, the alcoholic essence of fermented molasses, was probably invented by the first European settlers in the West Indies. Manufacture of rum became New England's largest and most profitable industry, in the so-called triangular trade. Yankee traders would sail with a cargo of rum to the west coast of Africa, where they bartered the "demon rum" for slaves. From there they sailed to the West Indies, where they bartered the slaves for molasses, which they took back to New England where it was converted into rum, thus completing the triangle. For many years the New England distilleries flourished and the slave trade proved highly lucrative. This continued until 1807, when an act of Congress prohibited the importation of slaves. About this time, too, agricultural production of corn and rye made domestic whiskey cheaper (Roueché, 1960).

Whiskey production in America was introduced by a post–Revolutionary War wave of Scottish and Irish settlers to whom the making of pot-still whiskey was a natural phase of farming. Almost every home had a still or fermentation crocks to make beers, wines, or whiskeys. Whiskey first came into prominence as a backwoods substitute for rum in western Maryland and Virginia, southwestern Pennsylvania, and eastern Kentucky. Because it cost more to transport a barrel of flour made from the grain than the flour would have sold for on the eastern markets, the farmer converted the grain into whiskey. A packhorse, which could carry only 4 bushels of grain, could carry the equivalent of 24 bushels in liquid form. Whiskey became a medium of exchange. In Bourbon County, Kentucky, the Rev. Elijah Craig aged his whiskey in charred-oak barrels. This process made the whiskey, called *bourbon*, more smooth. Kentucky bourbon was the highest rated of the "whiskey currencies" (Roueché, 1960).

In 1791 the federal government placed an excise tax on liquor. This triggered the so-called Whiskey Rebellion in 1794 in southwestern Pennsylvania. The farmers were incensed because they considered whiskey an economic necessity and used it as a medium of exchange. They refused to pay the tax, and tarred and feathered the revenue officers. President Washington, alarmed, summoned the militia of several states and put down the rebellion. The consequences of this insurrection were significant: the federal government was substantially strengthened, and its authority regarding the right to make and enforce federal laws was established.

The period of heaviest drinking in America began during Jefferson's terms of office (1800–

1808). The stability of society had been weakened: there was an increase in the transient population, especially in the seaport cities, and the migration westward had begun. The temperance movement began with the goal of temperance in its literal sense: moderation. In the 1830s, at the peak of this early campaign, temperance leaders (many of whom drank beer and wine) recommended abstinence only from distilled spirits. Over the next decades, the meaning of temperance was gradually altered from moderation to total abstinence. All alcoholic beverages were attacked as unnecessary, harmful to health, and inherently poisonous. The demand gradually arose for total prohibition (Austin, 1978).

Almost every civilized country has passed prohibition laws, but few such laws have worked for long. Attempts to control, restrict, or abolish alcohol have been made in the United States, but they all met with abysmal failure. From 1907 to 1919, 34 states passed prohibition laws. Finally in 1919 the 18th Amendment to the Constitution was ratified in an attempt to stop the rapid growth of alcoholic addiction. During this time crime flourished. Speakeasies (illegal places where one could buy alcoholic beverages), bootlegging (named after the custom of placing illegal materials in the top of a boot), prescription whiskey from doctors and druggists, and alcoholic patent medicines filled the vacuum for many drinkers. By 1928, doctors made an estimated $40 million per year writing prescriptions for whiskey (Austin, 1978). The history of the patent medicines is an interesting and important part of the history of this country, and it provides the background for the Pure Food and Drug Act and other consumer protection laws. Some patent medicines had alcoholic contents as high as 50%, but most had less, such as Whisko, a "nonintoxicating stimulant" that actually was 55 proof ($27\frac{1}{2}$% alcohol). Another example is Kaufman's

Sulfur Bitters, which "contains no alcohol," but actually was 40 proof (20% alcohol) and did not contain sulfur. There were dozens of others, many of which contained other types of drugs, such as opium.

Both Prohibitionists and critics of Prohibition were shocked by the violent gang wars that broke out between rivals seeking to control the lucrative black market in liquor. More important, a general disregard for the law developed. Corruption among law enforcement agents was widespread. Organized crime was spawned and grew to be one of the nation's most gigantic "businesses." Prohibition was officially repealed in 1933 by the 21st Amendment.

How did Prohibition affect the consumption of alcohol? The figures in Table 11-1 show that there was little long-term effect on gallons consumed per capita. Deaths that could be attributed to alcoholism declined at first: the alcoholic death rate in 1920 was only 20% of the pre-Prohibition rate. In 1930 the alcoholic death rate was up again, to 70% of the 1917 rate. Alcohol-related diseases, such as cirrhosis of the liver and pneumonia, followed the same pattern: the rate dropped after the start of Prohibition and then rose again near the end of Prohibition. Prohibition worked at first, but then fell apart. In 1980, an estimated 93% of high school seniors had used alcohol. Nearly 7% used alcohol on a daily basis; about 41% said they had had five drinks on one occasion in the preceeding two weeks. Clearly, alcohol use starts early and is heavily ingrained in our culture.

NATURE OF THE BEAST

An alcohol is a chemical structure that has a hydroxyl group (OH, for an oxygen and a hydrogen atom) attached to a carbon atom. There are many types of alcohol, of which two are important in this context. The first is *methyl alcohol* (*methanol*, or *wood alcohol*, so called because it is made from wood products). Its metabolites are poisonous. Small amounts (4 ml) cause blindness by their side effects on the retina; larger amounts (80–150 ml) are usually fatal (Ritchie, 1980). It is added to *ethyl alcohol* (*ethanol*, or *grain alcohol*, the drinking type) intended for industrial uses so people will not drink it. The mixture is called *denatured alcohol*. Methyl alcohol is sometimes found added to bootleg liquor.

Pure ethyl alcohol is recognized as an official drug in the *U.S. Pharmacopeia*, although the various alcoholic beverages as such are no longer listed for medical use. Alcohol is used as a solvent for other drugs, or as a preservative, and thus is found in tinctures and elixirs. It is used to cleanse, disinfect, and harden the skin, and to reduce sweating. Seventy-percent alcohol is an effective bactericide. However, it should not be used on open wounds because it will dehydrate the injured tissue and make the damage worse. It cools the skin by evaporation, so alcohol sponges are commonly used to reduce fever. It is a solvent for the irritating oil in poison ivy and can prevent the formation of rash if used quickly enough after contact. Alcohol may be deliberately injected in or near nerves to treat severe pain; it causes local anesthesia and deterioration of the nerve. For the elderly or convalescent patient who enjoys it, a drink before meals will improve appetite and digestion (Ritchie, 1980). Alcohol is used in small amounts by many physicians as a tranquilizer or sedative for convalescent and geriatric patients.

In all alcoholic beverages—beer, wines, liqueurs or cordials, and distilled spirits—the psychoactive ingredient is the same: ethyl alcohol. The concentration of alcohol is usually about 4% by volume in American beers, 10% to 12% in table wines, between 17% and 20% in cocktail or dessert wines, such as sherries, 22% to 50% in liqueurs, and 40% to 50% (80 to 100 proof) in distilled spirits. The amount of alcohol is expressed either as a percentage by volume or in the older "proof" system, based on the military assay method. In order to make certain that they were getting a high alcohol content in the liquor, the British military would place a sample on gunpowder and touch a spark to it. If the alcohol content was over 50%, it would burn and ignite the gunpowder. This was "proof" that there was at least 50% alcohol. If the distilled spirits were "under proof," the water content would prevent the gunpowder from igniting. The percentage of alcohol by volume

TABLE 11-1 Per capita consumption in gallons of beer, wine, and distilled spirits in the United States

Year	Beer	Wine	Distilled spirits
1917	32.0	2.0	2.16
1920	2.0	0.8	0.5
1930	11.5	1.4	2.2
1980	22.0	4.0	2.0

is one-half the proof number. For example, 100-proof whiskey has a 50% alcohol content.

In addition, alcoholic beverages contain a variety of other chemical constituents that come from the original grains, grapes, and other fruits and from added flavorings or colorings. Other constituents are produced during fermentation, distillation, or storage. These nonalcoholic constituents, called *congeners*, contribute to the effects of certain beverages, either directly affecting the body or affecting the rate at which the alcohol content is absorbed into the blood. Beers and wines contain many organic compounds, minerals, and salts, none of which is toxic. The higher molecular-weight alcohols, or *fusel oils*, are toxic, but usually are found in such low concentrations that there is no appreciable hazard. Vodka and gin tend to have lower concentrations of congeners than the whiskeys and rum.

BLOOD ALCOHOL LEVELS, METABOLISM, AND TOLERANCE

Alcohol enters the bloodstream quickly and directly from the stomach and even more rapidly across the walls of the small intestine. Once the alcohol is in the small intestine, its absorption is largely independent of the presence of food, unlike in the stomach, where food retards absorption. The rate at which alcohol enters the blood is a key factor in the blood alcohol concentrations to which the brain is exposed. This rate largely determines the behavioral and physical responses to alcoholic beverages. On the behavioral side, the drinking situation, the drinker's mood, and his or her attitudes and previous experience with alcohol will all contribute to the reactions to drinking. Each person has an individual pattern of psychological functioning that may affect his or her reactions to alcohol. Emptying time of the stomach may be either slowed or speeded by anger, fear, stress, nausea, and the condition of the stomach tissues.

The blood alcohol levels produced depend on the presence of food in the stomach, the rate of consumption of the alcohol, the concentration of the alcohol, and the drinker's body composition. Fatty foods, meat, and milk slow the absorption of alcohol, allowing more time for its metabolism and reducing the peak concentration in the blood. When alcoholic beverages are taken with a substantial meal, peak blood alcohol concentrations may be as much as 50% lower than would have occurred if the alcohol was consumed by itself. If large amounts of alcohol are consumed in a short period of time, the brain is exposed to higher peak concentrations than if the same amount is drunk more slowly. In general, the more alcohol in the stomach, the greater the absorption rate. There is, however, a modifying effect of strong drinks on the absorption rate. Drinks stronger than 100 proof actually inhibit absorption. This may be due to a blocking of passage into the small intestine or irritation of the lining of the stomach, causing mucus secretion, or both.

The presence of congeners also modifies the rate of absorption. The higher the concentration of the congeners, the slower the absorption of the alcohol content. The net result is that beer and wine have slower effects than when the same amount of alcohol is consumed in the form of distilled spirits. Diluting an alcoholic beverage with water also helps to slow down absorption, but mixing with carbonated beverages increases the absorption rate. The carbonation causes the stomach to empty its contents into the small intestine more rapidly. The carbonation in champagne has the same effect.

Once in the blood, alcohol is fairly uniformly distributed throughout all tissues and fluids,

BLOOD ALCOHOL LEVELS, METABOLISM, AND TOLERANCE

ncluding the fetal circulation in a pregnant woman. Because the brain has a large blood sup-ply, its alcohol concentration quickly approaches that of the blood. Body composition—the amount of water available for the alcohol to dissolve in—is a key factor in blood alcohol concentration. The greater the muscle mass, but not fat, the lower will be the blood alcohol concentration from a given amount of alcohol. This is because fat has less fluid volume than muscle. For example, the blood alcohol level produced in a 180-pound man drinking 4 oz of whiskey will be substantially lower than that of a 130-pound man drinking the same amount over the same time period. The larger man will show fewer effects. A woman of equivalent weight to a given man will have a higher blood alcohol level, because women on the average have a higher proportion of fat and will be affected more by identical drinks. Table 11-2 shows the relationship of body weight and degree of intoxication.

TABLE 11-2 Relationship between body weight and blood alcohol levels

Body weight (lb)	Blood alcohol levels (percent alcohol in blood) Drinks*											
	1	2	3	4	5	6	7	8	9	10	11	12
100	.038	.075	.113	.150	.188	.225	.263	.300	.338	.375	.413	.450
120	.031	.063	.094	.125	.156	.188	.219	.250	.281	.313	.344	.375
140	.027	.054	.080	.107	.134	.161	.188	.214	.241	.268	.295	.321
160	.023	.047	.070	.094	.117	.141	.164	.188	.211	.234	.258	.281
180	.021	.042	.063	.083	.104	.125	.146	.167	.188	.208	.229	.250
200	.019	.038	.056	.075	.094	.113	.131	.150	.169	.188	.206	.225
220	.017	.034	.051	.068	.085	.102	.119	.136	.153	.170	.188	.205
240	.016	.031	.047	.063	.078	.094	.109	.125	.141	.156	.172	.188

Under .05: driving is not seriously impaired	.05 to .10: driving becomes increasingly dangerous; legally drunk in some states	.10 to .15: driving is dangerous; legally drunk in most states	Over .15: driving is very dangerous; legally drunk in any state

*One drink equals 1 ounce of 100-proof liquor or 12 ounces of beer.

CHAPTER 11 · ALCOHOL

Alcoholic beverages have virtually no vitamins, minerals, protein, or fat—just rather large amounts of a carbohydrate that is unlike any other carbohydrate. It cannot be used by most cells; it must be metabolized by an enzyme (alcohol dehydrogenase) that is found almost exclusively in the liver. Alcohol provides more calories per gram than carbohydrate or protein and only slightly less than pure fat. Because alcohol does provide calories, the drinker's appetite may be satisfied, and he or she may not eat properly. The caloric value of various alcoholic beverages is given in Table 11-3.

Ethyl alcohol is converted to acetaldehyde and hydrogen ions by the liver enzyme, alcohol dehydrogenase. The acetaldehyde is further metabolized to acetate, which then enters the energy-producing pathways and ultimately is excreted as carbon dioxide and water. Between 90% and 98% of the alcohol is completely oxidized, unlike many other drugs that may be excreted unchanged in the urine. About 2% to 5% may be removed by exhalation and excretion in urine, tears, or sweat, but the rest must be oxidized. The metabolism of alcohol differs from that of most other substances in that the rate of oxidation is nearly constant with time. The average rate at which it can be oxidized is about 10 ml of 100% alcohol per hour; thus 4 ounces of whiskey or 1.2 liters of beer would require five to six hours to be oxidized by a person of average size. The maximum daily metabolism in the human is about 450 ml. Alcohol can also be metabolized to a small extent by the

TABLE 11-3   Caloric value of various alcoholic beverages

Beverage	Approximate calories
Dinner wine (12%, 4 oz)	100
80-proof distilled spirits (gin, rum, scotch; 1 shot*)	110
Highball (1 oz whiskey, 4 oz ginger ale)	140
Manhattan (1 shot whiskey, $\frac{3}{4}$ oz sweet vermouth)	145
Beer (12 oz, 4%)	150
"dry" Martini (1 shot gin, $\frac{1}{2}$ oz 12% dry vermouth)	150
100-proof distilled spirits (1 shot)	150
Tom Collins (1 shot gin, lemon, sugar)	154
Dessert wine (22%, 4 oz)	160
Sweet sherry or ruby port (fortified wines; 4 oz)	200
Sweet liqueurs (2 oz)	200
Grasshopper or Brandy Alexander	300

* One shot glass is $1\frac{1}{2}$ ounces.

microsomal mixed-function oxidase enzymes in the liver. This explains the known interaction between alcohol and the many other drugs oxidized by this enzyme system, such as the barbiturates (Ritchie, 1980).

Alcohol induces a number of deleterious metabolic changes in the liver. It causes increased production of lactate, which is an organic product of metabolism that can cause an upset in the blood acid-base balance. Alcohol causes an increased production of fatty acids in the liver, excess uric acid (a toxic nitrogen waste product) in the blood, and increased urinary loss of several essential ions (magnesium, calcium, and zinc) (Ritchie, 1980).

Tolerance develops to alcohol, comparable to the barbiturates (see Chapter 10). *Drug-disposition tolerance* results from enzyme induction in the liver, which causes more rapid metabolism of alcohol. (The drug is being disposed of faster.) *Pharmacodynamic tolerance* causes the nervous system to adapt to the continual presence of alcohol. (Thus more and more of the drug is needed to produce the same effects.) *Behavioral tolerance* allows the person to adjust to the effects of alcohol on speech, vision, and motor control (Jaffe, 1980). Some persons can learn to cover up the typical signs of intoxication.

PHYSIOLOGICAL EFFECTS OF ALCOHOL

Short-Term Effects

The short-term effects of alcohol are primarily on the central nervous system. In moderate quantities, it slightly increases the heart rate, slightly dilates blood vessels in the arms, legs, and skin, and moderately lowers blood pressure. It stimulates appetite and increases production of gastric secretions, and it markedly stimulates urine output. The overall effects of alcohol depend on the concentration in the specific cells affected (NIAAA, 1980).

Alcohol depresses functions of the central nervous system. The reticular activating system is affected first, which decreases inhibition of the higher cortical centers. The effects are not necessarily related to the total amount of alcohol consumed, but to the concentration in the blood. When blood alcohol levels are low, the effect is usually mild sedation, release of inhibitions, and relaxation. Slightly higher levels may produce behavioral changes which suggest stimulation of the brain. The person becomes talkative, aggressive, and active. This is a result of release of higher cortical centers from inhibition, not a direct stimulatory effect. The first mental processes lost are those that depend on training and previous experience. The person becomes more confident that he or she can perform well, but actually his or her motor skills and ability to solve complicated mental problems are reduced. As drinking continues, the depressant effect shows up in the areas controlling muscular coordination, speech, breathing, and vision. At levels above 0.03% to 0.04%, reflex responses, reaction time responses, and performance in such activities as automobile driving and many kinds of athletics generally change for the worse. Unfortunately, as drinking drivers' performance deteriorates, their confidence increases, and they become more aggressive and believe they are driving better (NIAAA, 1980).

The effects of alcohol on skilled performance are not necessarily related directly to alcohol concentrations in the blood. Alcohol influences skilled performance, and the CNS in general, more markedly when the concentration is rising than when it is falling. A person may thus have impaired performance at a given blood alcohol level when the concentration is rising, but not at the same level when the concentration is going down. Further, identical blood alcohol levels in the same individual can be associated with remarkably different psychomotor performance, depending on whether the individual consumed the alcoholic beverage with or without food.

At still higher levels of alcohol, severe depression of the motor control areas of the brain occurs, producing incoordination, confusion, disorientation, stupor, anesthesia, coma, and death. The lethal level of alcohol is between 0.4% and 0.6% by volume in the blood. Death is caused by severe depression of the respiration center in the brainstem, although the person usually passes out before drinking this much. Even though an alcoholic person may metabolize more rapidly, the alcoholic toxicity level stays the same. In other words, it takes the same amount of alcohol to kill a nondrinker as a drunk. The amount of alcohol required for anesthesia is very close to the toxic level, which is why it is not used as an anesthetic. The depressant effects are enhanced if alcohol is taken with a sedative-hypnotic drug (Chapter 10) or analgesics like propoxyphene (Darvon®) and opioids (Chapter 12). Such combinations can markedly reduce the lethal dose of alcohol. (See Table 11-4 for a summary of the psychological and physical effects of various blood alcohol concentration levels.)

The rate of alcohol metabolism controls the rate at which one becomes sober again. Heavy drinkers have increased alcohol dehydrogenase enzymatic activity in their livers and may metabolize alcohol more rapidly than light drinkers. This is the basis for alcohol tolerance, which means that a heavy drinker will be able to handle more alcohol than an occasional drinker. There are no significant differences in ability to oxidize alcohol that differentiate the alcoholic person from the nonalcoholic who drinks regularly, although the alcoholic may have a different circadian rhythm of alcohol metabolism than the nonalcoholic (Jones & Paredes, 1974).

As a general rule, it will take as many hours as the number of drinks consumed to sober up completely. Drinking black coffee, taking a cold shower, breathing pure oxygen, and so forth will not hasten the process. Stimulants like coffee may help keep the drunk person awake, but will not improve judgment or reflexes to any significant extent. Drinking coffee only produces a wide-awake drunk. There has been some research on use of fructose, the form of plant sugar found in grapes, to speed up the sobering process. Fructose increases the rate of alcohol oxidation by about 25%. However, the dosage required causes gastrointestinal upset, diarrhea, lactate acidosis, and excess uric acid in the blood (see Hangover, in the following section). If the person has dangerously high levels of blood alcohol or possibly has taken other drugs as well, the alcohol may be safely and quickly removed from the blood by dialysis (Sellers & Kalant, 1978). Usually, however, the best course is to wait and let the liver do its work.

The Hangover

A familiar aftereffect of overindulgence is fatigue combined with nausea, upset stomach, headache, sensitivity to sounds, and ill temper—the hangover. The symptoms are usually most severe many hours after drinking, when little or no alcohol can be detected in the body. There is no simple explanation for what causes hangover (other than having had too much to drink), how to prevent it (other than moderation), or how to alleviate it effectively. There are many theories about what causes hangovers: accumulation of acetaldehyde, dehydration of the

PHYSIOLOGICAL EFFECTS OF ALCOHOL

issues, poisoning due to tissue deterioration, depletion of important enzyme systems that are needed to maintain routine functioning, metabolism of the congeners in alcoholic beverages, and others.

The body loses fluid in two ways through alcohol's diuretic action: First, the water content, such as in beer, will increase the volume of urine. Second, the alcohol depresses the center in the hypothalamus of the brain that controls release of a water conservation hormone (antidiuretic hormone). With less of this hormone, urine volume is further increased. Thus, after drinking heavily, especially the highly concentrated forms of alcohol, the person is thirsty. However, this does not explain many of the symptoms of hangover.

As alcohol is metabolized to acetaldehyde and hydrogen ions, the excess hydrogen unbalances the liver cell's chemistry. This causes hypoglycemia (unless the person is careful to eat properly) and accumulation of fat and of metabolites

TABLE 11-4 Psychological and physical effects of various blood alcohol concentration levels*

Number of drinks**	Blood alcohol concentration	Psychological and physical effects
1	0.02%–0.03%	No overt effects, slight mood elevation
2	0.05%–0.06%	Feeling of relaxation, warmth; slight decrease in reaction time and in fine-muscle coordination
3	0.08%–0.09%	Balance, speech, vision, hearing slightly impaired; feelings of euphoria, increased confidence; loss of motor coordination
	0.10%	Legal intoxication in most states; some have lower limits
4	0.11%–0.12%	Coordination and balance becoming difficult; distinct impairment of mental faculties, judgment
5	0.14%–0.15%	Major impairment of mental and physical control: slurred speech, blurred vision, lack of motor skills
7	0.20%	Loss of motor control—must have assistance in moving about; mental confusion
10	0.30%	Severe intoxication; minimum conscious control of mind and body
14	0.40%	Unconsciousness, threshold of coma
17	0.50%	Deep coma
20	0.60%	Death from respiratory failure

* For each hour elapsed since the last drink, subtract 0.015% blood alcohol concentration, or approximately one drink.
** One drink = one beer (4% alcohol, 12 oz) or one highball (1 oz whiskey).
Source: modified from data given in Ohio State Police Driver Information Seminars and the National Clearinghouse for Alcohol and Alcoholism Information, 5600 Fishers Lane, Rockville MD 85206.

such as lactate in the liver cells. The lactate buildup has other effects. As it is transferred to the blood, it alters the blood's acid-base balance. Large amounts of lactate diminish the alkali reserves of the blood, causing impaired respiratory exchange of carbon dioxide and oxygen in the lungs. (This is why scuba divers should not drink the night before diving.) Lactate buildup also interferes with excretion of uric acid in the kidneys. The toxic metabolite of alcohol, acetaldehyde, accumulates and spills over into the blood when there is more alcohol than the enzyme systems in the liver can manage (Lieber, 1976). This altered body chemistry contributes to the various symptoms of the classical hangover.

The type of alcoholic beverage one drinks may influence the hangover that results. Some people are more sensitive to particular congeners than others. For example, they have no problem with white wine, but an equal amount of some red wines gives them a hangover. Whiskeys, scotch, and rum may cause worse hangovers than vodka or gin, given equal amounts of alcohol. Vodka and gin have fewer congeners. There is little evidence that mixing types of drinks causes a worse hangover; the person probably consumed more than usual by trying the different drinks.

A common technique to alleviate hangover is taking a drink of the same alcoholic beverage that caused the hangover. This is called "taking the hair of the dog that bit you" (from the old notion that the burnt hair of a dog is an antidote to its bite). It is possible it might help the person who is physically dependent, the same way giving heroin to a heroin addict will ease the withdrawal symptoms. The "hair of the dog" method might work by depressing the centers of the brain that interpret pain. There are psychological factors involved in hangover; distraction or focusing attention on something else may ease the effects.

Another folk remedy is to take an analgesic compound like APCs before drinking. The aspirin and phenacetin are analgesics and would help control headache; the caffeine may help counteract some of the depressant effect the alcohol has. But these ingredients would have no effect on the actual sobering up process. Products like aspirin, phenacetin, and Alka-Seltzer® can irritate the stomach lining to the point where the person actually feels worse. (Besides, those bubbles from Alka-Seltzer® are so noisy!)

Long-Term Effects

Drinking in moderation apparently does little permanent harm. (The exception is moderate drinking during pregnancy, in which case alcohol has little effect on the mother, but can cause irreversible mental retardation in her child.) However, when taken in large doses over long periods of time, alcohol can cause structural damage to several major organs, such as the heart, the brain, and the liver.

Prolonged heavy drinking causes various types of muscle disease and tremor. One essential muscle affected by alcohol is the heart: the myocardium. Laboratory investigations have shown that alcohol is directly toxic to the heart and to other muscles as well. It causes irregular heartbeat, which can be fatal. A common example of this is "holiday heart," so called because people drinking heavily over a weekend turn up in the emergency room with a dangerously irregular heartbeat. Chronic excessive use causes congestive heart failure. Malnutrition and vitamin deficiencies associated with prolonged heavy drinking contribute to cardiac abnormalities (Ritchie, 1980).

Liver damage commonly results from heavy drinking. Liver disease occurs because metabolizing alcohol has priority over the liver's normal functions. Its final stage, *cirrhosis* (scarring) of

PHYSIOLOGICAL EFFECTS OF ALCOHOL

the liver occurs about six times more frequently in alcoholics than in nondrinkers. Cirrhosis is the general name for many types of liver damage that are similar in appearance. The heavy drinker develops a fatty liver first, which is reversible if he stops drinking. When alcohol is present, the liver uses it, and the liver's regular fuel (fatty acids), as well as proteins, accumulate. The engorged liver cells die, triggering the next stage, an inflammatory process called *alcoholic hepatitis*. Cellular death and inflammation cause the last stage: cirrhosis. Scar tissue forms barriers that interfere with blood flow to liver cells that are still alive, further decreasing liver function. The fibrous scar tissue cannot carry out any of the normal functions of the liver for detoxification or metabolism. Accumulation of fat, cellular death and inflammation, and finally cirrhosis, when the liver is irreversibly damaged with nonfunctional fibrous tissue, have been produced in experimental animals by giving them large amounts of alcohol. Vitamin deficiency and malnutrition (especially protein deficiency, which is fairly common in alcoholics) are important factors in the development of cirrhosis. Nevertheless, alcohol in the proportion of daily calories routinely consumed by alcoholics (35% to 50% of daily calories) will cause development of cirrhosis even with an adequate diet (Lieber, 1976).

Heavy drinking over many years may result in serious mental disorders and permanent, irreversible damage to the brain and peripheral nervous system. Memory, judgment, and learning ability can deteriorate severely. Korsakoff's syndrome is a characteristic psychotic condition caused by alcohol use and the associated nutritional and vitamin deficiencies. Patients cannot remember recent events and compensate for their memory loss with confabulation (making up fictitious events that the patient accepts as fact). Polyneuritis—an inflammation of the nerves that causes burning and prickly sensations in the hands and feet—has the same origin. B-complex vitamins are often used to treat the polyneuritis and memory deficit, but the damage is not always reversible (Seixas, 1980).

Heavy drinkers have lowered resistance to pneumonia and other infectious diseases. Malnutrition is a factor, but lowered resistance may also occur in well-nourished heavy drinkers. Heavy drinking appears to directly interfere with the bone marrow, where various blood cells are formed. The suppression of the bone marrow contributes to alcoholic anemia, in which red blood cell production cannot keep pace with the need. Heavy drinkers are also likely to develop alcoholic bleeding disorders, because they have too few platelets to form clots (Seixas, 1980).

Alcohol, especially undiluted, irritates the gastrointestinal tract. Nausea, vomiting, and diarrhea are mild indications of trouble. The more frequently heavy consumption takes place, the greater the irritation: one out of three heavy drinkers suffers from chronic gastritis. The heavy drinker has double the probability of developing cancer of the mouth and other tissues on the way to the stomach. If he or she smokes, the risk goes up to 15 times higher for oral cancers.

Women who are alcoholics or who drink heavily during pregnancy have a higher rate of spontaneous abortion, suggesting that alcohol is toxic to developing embryos. Infants born to drinking mothers have a high probability of having fetal alcohol syndrome (FAS). These children have a characteristic pattern of facial deformities (Figure 11-2), growth deficiency, and mental retardation. The growth deficiency occurs in embryonic development, and the child usually does not catch up after birth. There is mild to moderate mental retardation that does not appear to improve with time, apparently because the growth impairment affects growth of the brain as well. The severity of the FAS appears to be dose-response related: the more the mother drinks, the worse off the infant is. A safe lower

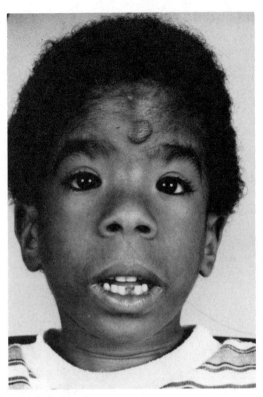

FIGURE 11-2
The effects of fetal alcohol syndrome (FAS) on a child's face. (Courtesy of Dr. Marilyn T. Miller. From "Fetal Alcohol Syndrome," by M. Miller, J. Israel, and J. Cuttone, *Journal of Pediatric Ophthalmology and Strabismus*, 1980, 18(4), 6–15. Reprinted by permission of the author and publisher.)

level for alcohol has not been established for pregnant women. Birth weight decrements in humans have been found at levels corresponding to about two drinks per day on the average. Clinical studies have established that alcohol causes the syndrome, not the effects of smoking, maternal age, parity (number of children a woman has borne), social class, or poor nutrition (Streissguth, Landesman-Dwyer, Martin, & Smith, 1980). Studies in experimental animals show that ethyl alcohol by itself can cause all of the damage associated with FAS. The animals were retarded mentally and physically (Brown, Goulding, & Fabro, 1979; Diaz & Samson, 1980).

ALCOHOLISM AND PROBLEM DRINKING: EXTENT OF THE PROBLEM

According to most estimates, there are between 9 and 10 million adults in the United States with drinking problems. Society as a whole pays a high price through the loss of productive members and also through the harm done to others with whom the alcoholic comes in contact. Problem drinking and alcoholism cost the nation over $43 billion dollars in 1979. This figure includes about 46% of the total to loss of production, 29% in health and medical costs, 13% in motor vehicle accidents, 7% in violent crimes, 4% in social responses (public education on highway safety, role of alcohol abuse in decreased production, and so on), and about 1% in fire losses. The personal and societal costs are summarized in Table 11-5. The cost in human suffering is incalculable.

Alcohol is involved in one-third to one-half of all highway fatalities. Serious problem drinking has been implicated in almost half of the alcohol-related deaths; the other half involved young drinkers and social drinkers with a high blood alcohol level at the time of the accident. One-third of all traffic injuries are related to alcohol. There are several volunteer groups of the relatives of victims of drunken drivers who are lobbying for mandatory jail sentences and revocation of driving licenses for drivers convicted of driving while intoxicated. This seems to be a deterrent to drunken driving in several European countries. The National Highway Traffic Safety Administration (NHTSA) has

TABLE 11-5 Costs of problem drinking and alcoholism in the United States*

Life expectancy	Reduced 10–12 years compared to nonalcoholic
Mortality rate	Increased at least 2.3 times over expected rate
Family members affected (spouses, children)	At least 36 million people
Alcohol-related traffic deaths	70 per day; 26,000 per year
Industrial deaths and injuries	Estimated 12,600 deaths; 2,200,000 injuries in 1975 were alcohol related
Civilian aviation accidents	44% of all accidents in which pilot died were alcohol related
Drownings: boating accidents, swimmers	Up to 69% were alcohol related
Fire fatalities	Up to 83% were alcohol related; 53% of victims were alcoholics
Fire burns	Up to 62% were alcohol related; 23% of victims were alcoholics
Injuries from falling	Up to 70% of all deaths, 63% of all injuries were alcohol related
Homicides	50% were alcohol related
Suicides	More than one-third were alcohol related
Rape	50% of rapists, 31% of victims had been drinking immediately before the assault
Assault	72% of attackers, 79% of victims had been drinking immediately before the assault
Child abuse	Up to 77% of child abusers had been drinking immediately before the offense; 40% of child-abusing parents have history of drinking problem
Robbery	Up to 72% of robbers were drinking immediately before committing a robbery
Arrests	One-third of the 10.2 million arrests in 1977 were for drunkenness, driving under the influence, and so on; costs for arrests, trials, and jail: $100 million per year
Absenteeism from work	Three times the rate for employees without a drinking problem
Cost of lost production and services	About $20 billion in 1975 (total for industry, government, and the military)

*Based on data from *Facts about Alcohol and Alcoholism*. 1980. Washington, D.C.: National Institute on Alcohol Abuse and Alcoholism.

devised a test that gauges the attitude of teenagers toward drinking and driving. Nearly 8000 young Americans aged 16 to 24 are killed each year, and 40,000 are disfigured in accidents involving alcohol. The NHTSA wants to encourage teenagers to consider social and psychological factors associated with their urge to drink and drive or to ride with drinking friends. The two-part test lets people evaluate themselves and then compare their own knowledge, values, and beliefs about alcohol with an average profile compiled from responses of other students. The following section includes this test.

Attitudinal Test for Drinking and Driving*

Part 1: Alcohol knowledge test

In response to each statement, circle either T (true) or F (false).

T   F   1. Mixing different kinds of drinks can increase the effect of alcohol.

T   F   2. The average 4-oz drink of wine is less intoxicating than the average 1-oz drink of hard liquor.

T   F   3. A can of beer is less intoxicating than an average drink of hard liquor.

T   F   4. A cold shower can help sober up a person.

T   F   5. A person can be drunk and not stagger or slur his or her speech.

T   F   6. It is easy to tell if people are drunk even if you don't know them well.

T   F   7. A person drinking on an empty stomach will get drunk faster.

T   F   8. People's moods help determine how they are affected by alcohol.

T   F   9. A person who is used to drinking can drink more.

T   F   10. A person who weighs less can get drunk faster than a heavier person.

T   F   11. Of every ten traffic deaths, up to five are caused by drinking drivers.

T   F   12. The surest way to tell if the person is legally drunk is by the percent of alcohol in the blood.

T   F   13. People who are drunk cannot compensate for it when they drive.

T   F   14. In a fatal drunk-driving accident, the drunk is usually not the one killed.

T   F   15. Drinking black coffee can help sober up a person.

T   F   16. Alcoholic beverages are a stimulant.

Answers: (1) F, (2) F, (3) F, (4) F, (5) T, (6) F, (7) T, (8) T, (9) F, (10) T, (11) T, (12) T, (13) T, (14) F, (15) F, (16) F

Part 2: Alcohol attitude test

Directions: If you strongly agree with the following statements, write in 1. If you agree, but not strongly, write in 2. If you neither agree nor disagree, write in 3. If you disagree, but not strongly, write in 4. If you strongly disagree, write in 5.

Set 1

____ 1. If a person concentrates hard enough, he or she can overcome any effect that drinking may have on driving.

____ 2. If you drive home from a party late at night when most roads are deserted,

---

*Courtesy of the National Highway Traffic Safety Administration.

there is not much danger in driving after drinking.

___ 3. It's all right for a person who has been drinking to drive, as long as he or she shows no signs of being drunk.

___ 4. If you're going to have an accident, you'll have one anyhow, regardless of drinking.

___ 5. A drink or two helps people drive better because it relaxes them.

___ Total score for questions 1 through 5

Set 2

___ 6. If I tried to stop someone from driving after drinking, the person would probably think I was butting in where I shouldn't.

___ 7. Even if I wanted to, I would probably not be able to stop someone from driving after drinking.

___ 8. If people want to kill themselves, that's their business.

___ 9. I wouldn't like someone to try to stop me from driving after drinking.

___ 10. Usually, if you try to help someone else out of a dangerous situation, you risk getting yourself into one.

___ Total score for questions 6 through 10

Set 3

___ 11. My friends would not disapprove of me for driving after drinking.

___ 12. Getting into trouble with my parents would not keep me from driving after drinking.

___ 13. The thought that I might get into trouble with the police would not keep me from driving after drinking.

___ 14. I am not scared by the thought that I might seriously injure myself or someone else by driving after drinking.

___ 15. The fear of damaging the car would not keep me from driving after drinking.

___ Total score for questions 11 through 15

Set 4

___ 16. The 55 mph speed limit on the open roads spoils the pleasure of driving for most teenagers.

___ 17. Many teenagers use driving to let off steam.

___ 18. Being able to drive a car makes teenagers feel more confident in their relations with others their age.

___ 19. An evening with friends is not much fun unless one of them has a car.

___ 20. There is something about being behind the wheel of a car that makes one feel more adult.

___ Total score for questions 16 through 20

Set 5

___ 21. I usually do things that everybody else is doing.

___ 22. What my friends think of me is the most important thing in my life.

___ 23. I would ride in a friend's car even if that person had been drinking a lot.

___ 24. Often I do things just so I won't feel left out of the group I'm with.

___ 25. I often worry about what other people think about things I do.

___ Total score for questions 21 through 25

Set 6

___ 26. Adults try to stop teenagers from driving just to show their power.

___ 27. I don't think it would help me to go to my parents for advice.

___ 28. I feel I should have the right to drink if my parents do.

___ 29. My parents have no real understanding of what I want out of life.

___ 30. I wouldn't dare call my parents to come and take me home if either I or a friend I was with got drunk.

___ Total score for questions 26 through 30

Scoring the self-test

Set 1   13–25 points: realistic in avoiding drinking-driving situations; 5–6 points: tends to make up excuses to combine drinking and driving.

Set 2   15–25 points: takes responsibility to keep others from driving when drunk; 5–9 points: wouldn't take steps to stop a drunk friend from driving.

Set 3   12–25 points: hesitates to drive after drinking; 5–7 points: is not deterred by the consequences of drinking and driving.

Set 4   19–25 points: perceives auto as means of transportation; 5–14 points: uses car to satisfy psychological needs, not just transportation.

Set 5   16–25 points: cares about what others think, but acts according to own beliefs and values; 5–10 points: goes along with the crowd.

Set 6   18–25 points: accepts adult and parental responsibility and concern for one's safety; 5–10 points: rejects parental concern or control.

TOTAL POINTS PER SET

Set 1. You are more likely than others to make excuses for your actions.

Set 2. You feel less responsibility to protect others.

Set 3. You don't take seriously the consequences of drinking and driving.

Set 4. Cars are very important to your personal life.

Set 5. Going along with the group is very important, even if you don't think you should.

Set 6. You very often reject adult authority.

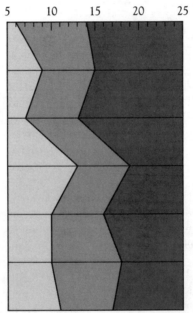

Set 1. You are less likely than others to make excuses for your actions.

Set 2. You feel more responsibility to protect others.

Set 3. You take consequences of drinking and driving seriously.

Set 4. Cars are less important to your personal life.

Set 5. You are less likely to go along with the group if you don't want to.

Set 6. You less often reject adult authority.

Lowest 25%   Average scores   Upper 25%

FIGURE 11-3
Assessment of attitudes about drinking and driving (courtesy of the National Highway Traffic Safety Administration).

Plot your drinking-driving profile against that of Pennsylvania teens who took the test by placing a dot on each horizontal line in Figure 11-3 to represent your score in each set. Connect the dots. The unshaded area represents the average scores.

Alcoholism is a chronic behavioral disorder manifested by repeated drinking of alcoholic beverages in excess of the dietary and social uses of the community and to an extent that interferes with the drinker's health or his social or economic functioning. [Keller, 1958]

DEFINITION OF ALCOHOLISM

To many people, the concept of an alcoholic is the skid-row derelict (those who have skidded off the path of virtue). Nevertheless, the stereotypic skid-row bum makes up less than 5% of problem drinkers and alcoholics. Most problem drinkers are employed, family-centered people. Estimates vary, but it appears that about three-fourths of problem drinkers are men and one-fourth are women. The proportion of women has been rising in recent years, perhaps because they are increasingly willing to acknowledge the problem and seek treatment. Female problem drinkers may therefore now be more visible rather than more numerous.

Alcoholism is addiction to alcohol. However, if one tries to expand this definition to include symptoms of the condition and psychological and sociological factors, one will find that no one definition satisfies everyone. The World Health Organization defines the Alcohol Dependence Syndrome as: a state, psychic and usually also physical, resulting from taking alcohol and characterized by behavioral and other responses that always include a compulsion to take alcohol on a continuous or periodic basis in order to experience its psychic effects and sometimes to avoid the discomfort of its absence; tolerance may or may not be present (NIAAA, 1980).

The following is another widely accepted definition of alcoholism:

CAUSES OF ALCOHOLISM

For many years, people with drinking problems were lumped together under the label *alcoholic*, and all were assumed to be suffering from the same illness. It has become evident that there are many kinds of drinking problem, many diverse types of person who have them, and many reasons why they begin and continue to drink to a harmful extent. The search for a single cause of alcoholism has shifted to interdisciplinary exploration of factors that might, singly or in combination, account for the development of problem drinking in various types of individual. There is no generally agreed-on model of how alcoholism starts; a number of circumstances are probably required to make a person become a problem drinker. A report by the Cooperative Commission on the Study of Alcoholism suggests that an individual who (1) responds to beverage alcohol in a certain way, perhaps physiologically determined, by experiencing intense relief and relaxation; who (2) has certain personality characteristics, such as difficulty in dealing with and overcoming depression, frustration, and anxiety; and who (3) is a member of a culture in which there is both pressure to drink and culturally induced guilt and confusion regarding what kinds of drinking behavior are appropriate, is more likely to develop trouble than most other persons. The importance of the different causal factors of alcoholism no doubt varies from one individual to another. Research into physiological, psychological, and sociological dimensions of this problem and integration of the findings in these and other areas has resulted in greater understanding of the conditions that precede, underlie, and maintain problem drinking (NIAAA, 1980).

Physiological Factors

Much research has been devoted to finding reasons, either in the alcoholic beverage itself or in the biological makeup of alcoholics, that could account for alcoholic addiction. Vitamin deficiencies and hormone imbalances have been suggested as causes of alcoholism. However, investigations show that the nutritional deficiencies and hormonal imbalances found in individuals with advanced alcoholism are results, rather than causes, of excessive drinking. Allergy has been blamed for some cases of alcoholism, but there is no proof that alcoholic individuals are generally allergic to alcohol itself or to other components of alcoholic beverages. Another theory suggested that alcoholism was caused by some nonalcoholic component of beer, wine, whiskey, rum, or brandy. There is also no proof of this.

A major difficulty with research into causes of alcoholism is that, although laboratory animals can be made dependent on alcohol and this process can be studied, there is no good model to study spontaneous development of alcoholism as it occurs in humans. For example, if rats have minute quantities of an alcohol solution injected directly into their brains through an implanted tube (cannula) every two or three hours for several days, they will drink alcohol whenever it is offered to them. However, the drug must be forced on them in this or some other manner in the beginning in order to make them dependent. Strains of mice have been bred that demonstrate a selective preference for alco-

hol, which they drink in large amounts. This preference is genetically determined: it is not affected even when the young mice are raised by females of a different strain or are exposed to various conditions of stress or isolation. However, the mice of these heavy-drinking strains also happen to be able to metabolize alcohol much more rapidly than mice of other strains. Thus it is difficult to determine whether their increased alcohol intake is related to a particular taste for alcohol or to their ability to consume more alcohol without becoming intoxicated. As described earlier, under controlled conditions, both alcoholic and normal subjects have an increased rate of alcohol metabolism while consuming relatively large amounts. Hence the mouse data are probably irrelevant to the study of alcoholism (Goodwin, 1979).

Alcoholism occurs more frequently in children of alcoholics and probably has some hereditary basis. This is based on studies showing (1) a 25% to 50% lifetime risk for alcoholism in the sons and brothers of severely alcoholic men; and (2) a 55% or higher concordance rate for alcoholism in identical twins, compared to a 28% rate for same-sex fraternal twins. In addition, studies using either the half-sibling method or adoption samples demonstrate a four times or higher increase in alcoholism for the children of alcoholics over those of nonalcoholics, even when the children had been separated from their natural parents shortly after birth, and raised without knowledge of their parents' drinking problem. Children adopted through the same adoption agencies, but without alcoholic biological parents, showed relatively low rates of alcoholism, even if they were raised by an alcoholic parent figure or experienced a subsequent severe psychological trauma, such as parental death or divorce (Schuckit & Rayses, 1979).

A number of genetic diseases are transmitted in a sex-linked manner, such as through the female parent on the X sex chromosome. Other genetic diseases are caused by defects in the somatic, or nonsex, chromosomes and can be transmitted through either parent. The genetic mode of transmission of alcoholism, if there is one, is not certain. One study looked at the rate of alcoholism in the grandsons of known alcoholic men to see if there was a difference in genetic transmission through the mother or the father, and it found no substantial difference between the two groups of grandsons. The rate of alcoholism by the time the grandsons were 50 or older was 43%, approximately three times that of the general male population and even higher than that of the brothers of alcoholic persons. The results do not support either a sex-linked or a recessive gene but are compatible with the assumption of a dominant gene (Kaij & Dock, 1975). However, alcoholism also occurs in children of teetotalers.

The extent to which genetic factors might contribute to alcoholism in the population is unknown. It is not as clearcut as the genetic contribution to the development of diabetes, for example, although there are parallelisms. Perhaps future studies will clarify the role of genetics in the development of alcoholism.

Alcoholic addiction may also be caused by a defect or modification in the metabolism of acetaldehyde. As described earlier, acetaldehyde spills over into the blood when the liver's enzymatic capacity is exceeded. Alcoholics may suffer from this problem to a greater extent than nonalcoholics. When a moderate dose of pure ethyl alcohol was given to 20 healthy young men with alcoholic parents or siblings, their blood acetaldehyde levels were significantly higher than those of matched controls with no history of alcoholism in their families (Schuckit & Rayses, 1979). Acetaldehyde can combine with the neurotransmitter dopamine to form a compound called *salsolinol.* This is an opioid-like compound that is comparable in action to morphine (Ross, Medina, & Cardenas, 1974). Concentrations of salsolinol were significantly higher in urine samples from alcoholics than nonalcoholics (Collins, Nijm, Borge, Teas, & Goldfarb, 1979). Thus the alcoholic's body might be generating its own addictive substances to a greater extent than nonalcoholics.

Psychological Factors

Although the terms *prealcoholic personality* and *alcoholic personality* have been used, there is little agreement on the identity of alcoholic personality traits, or on whether they may be the cause or the result of excessive drinking. Psychologists and psychiatrists have described alcoholic drinkers as neurotic, maladjusted, unable to relate effectively to others, sexually and emotionally immature, isolated, dependent, unable to withstand frustration or tension, poorly integrated, and marked by deep feelings of sinfulness and unworthiness. Some have suggested that alcoholism is a disastrous attempt at the self-cure of an inner conflict and might well be called "suicide by ounces." Nevertheless, these observations are based on clinical impressions of alcoholics who are in treatment—because they have been arrested, were sick enough to be committed, or were rich enough to enter one clinic or poor enough to enter another. There have been no long-term prospective studies to answer the question: what was the person like *before* he or she drank? (Aronow, 1980). Several are in progress and may provide an answer in the next few years.

Sociological Factors

Drinking practices and alcohol problems within and among various cultures and societies have been compared to find out why alcoholism is widespread in some national, religious, and cultural groups, but rare in others. Groups with the highest rates of alcoholism include the northern French, the Americans (especially the Irish-Americans), Native Americans (including the Alaskans), the Swedes, the Swiss, the Poles, and the northern Russians. Relatively low incidence groups include some Chinese, Orthodox Jews, Greeks, Portuguese, Spaniards, and the southern French (Aronow, 1980; NIAAA, 1980).

The rate of alcoholism is low in those groups in which the drinking customs, values, and sanctions are well established, known to all, and consistent with the rest of the culture. In contrast, groups with marked ambivalence toward alcohol (such as the Anglo-Saxon Protestant group in America), with no agreed-on ground rules, tend to have a high alcoholism rate. When such conflict exists, with its pressures, guilt feelings, and uncertainties, the alcoholism rate may be relatively high. This has been noted among Mormons who drink, among moderate drinkers who feel forced to overindulge to maintain status in their group, and especially among children exposed to conflicting attitudes, such as those of a father who sees drinking as masculine and a mother who is opposed to drinking.

The full significance of ambivalent feelings as a cause of alcoholism is yet to be determined. For groups that use alcohol to a significant degree, the lowest incidence of alcoholism is associated with certain habits and attitudes:

1. The children are exposed to alcohol early in life, within a strong family or religious group.

2. The beverage is served in very dilute and small quantities. It is considered mainly as a food and usually consumed with meals. Abstinence is socially acceptable. It is no more rude or ungracious to decline a drink than to decline a piece of bread.

3. Parents present a constant example of moderate drinking. Excessive drinking or intoxication is not socially acceptable. It is not considered stylish, comic, or tolerable.

4. No moral importance is attached to drinking, nor is it viewed as proof of adulthood or virility.

5. Finally, and perhaps most important, there is wide and usually complete agreement among members of the group on what might be called the "ground rules" of drinking (Aronow, 1980; NIAAA, 1980; Ullman, 1958).

In interpreting sociological data, it must be noted that small amounts of alcohol cause a skin flush and unpleasant, Antabuse®-like* reactions in about three-fourths of Orientals. Their rate of alcoholism may be low because they are physiologically intolerant of alcohol (Goodwin, 1979). Systematic studies of the metabolic disposition of alcohol and its metabolic products have not been done in other racial and cultural groups (Aronow, 1980). Thus it is impossible at present to decide whether a physiological reaction, experienced by a large proportion of the population, *led to* the social customs described, or not. But the possibility should be investigated.

TREATMENT OF ALCOHOLISM†

Alcoholism is a treatable illness from which about two-thirds of those affected can recover—that is, stop the compulsion to consume alcohol.

---

*Antabuse® is a drug used to treat alcoholism; it produces a sensitivity to alcohol that results in a highly unpleasant reaction.
†This section is largely from the National Institute on Alcohol Abuse and Alcoholism, 1980.

There are many misunderstandings about alcoholism that make it difficult for alcoholics to seek and get the help they need. Many think of alcoholism as a form of moral weakness rather than an illness. This stigma causes problem drinkers and their families to hide their problem, rather than face it and seek treatment. There is a widespread belief, even among physicians, that alcoholism is not treatable and that the alcoholic is unmanageable and unwilling to be helped. None of these assumptions is true.

About 70% of alcoholics are men and women who are married and living with their families, who hold a job, and are accepted and reasonably respected members of their communities. For those of this group who seek treatment, the outlook is optimistic. One problem is that many individuals deny their alcoholism even to themselves. This type of person is not inclined to seek treatment until the pain, severity, and duration of the symptoms or a personal crisis becomes overwhelming. As the circumstances in such a person's life fluctuate and become less painful, the motivation for recovery lessens, and the alcoholic may discontinue treatment and relapse into a serious alcoholic condition. Nevertheless, it is quite possible for a person with a drinking problem to recover completely. This does not mean the person is cured; it means he or she can stop or control compulsive or uncontrolled drinking.

Rehabilitation Methods

Rehabilitation, in this instance, means a return to successful living without the need to have alcohol. The patient is rehabilitated when he or she maintains or reestablishes a good family life, work record, and a respectable position in the community. Relapses may occur, but they do not mean that the problem drinker or the

treatment effort has failed. Satisfactory rehabilitation can be expected in at least 60% of cases, according to the National Institute on Alcohol Abuse and Alcoholism (NIAAA). Some therapists have reported success in 70% to 80% of their cases. The recovery rate depends on the personal characteristics of the patient, the competence of the therapist, the availability of treatment facilities, and the support of the family, employer, and community. Unfortunately, the prognosis is less optimistic for the skid-row alcoholics and patients with alcoholic psychoses, usually in state mental hospitals. Less than 10% to 12% of this segment of the alcoholic population achieve full recovery.

The type of therapy provided is less important than the patient's personal characteristics and environmental experiences. Motivation is the most important characteristic, followed by high socioeconomic status and social stability. Similar results seem to be obtained regardless of whether treatment is provided in the more expensive inpatient settings or in the less expensive outpatient and intermediate care settings. In outpatient therapy, the length of time the patient stays in treatment seems to have a positive effect on the outcome; this is a function of the patient's motivation. As in any other illness, the earlier treatment is begun, the better the prospects for improvement, although many alcoholics have been treated successfully after many years of excessive drinking.

Diagnosing Alcoholism

Many professionals who could diagnose alcohol problems are often slow to recognize them. Thus the diagnosis of alcoholism is often made only when the illness is in its advanced stages—when the victim is unable to control the drinking, when he or she may no longer have an established family life or be able to hold a job, or when malnutrition or organic damage is already present. Because alcoholics rarely volunteer the information, family physicians must make special efforts to discover the illness in its early stages. Unfortunately, there is no simple diagnostic procedure for detecting alcoholism. Block (1980) has found the following clusters of questions useful to recognize the early stages of alcoholism:

1. Does the patient desire a drink frequently?

2. Is there a need for a drink at a certain time of day—for example, does he or she anticipate drinking in the evening? Does he or she use alcohol to get to sleep?

3. Does the frequency of drinking go beyond ritual socializing? Is the person more interested in getting high and maintaining that state? Is he or she disappointed if there are no drinks served at a restaurant or party?

4. Is the patient's drinking criticized by his or her spouse or friends? Does he or she resent these remarks?

5. Does the patient drink to relieve discomfort or tension of any kind?

6. Does he or she take care to keep a good stock of liquor "just in case"?

7. Does the patient prefer the company of those who drink as he or she does and avoid people who do not drink?

Diagnostic services and information can usually be obtained from one or more of the following: the family physician; clergy; public health nurse; social worker; Alcoholics Anonymous; Al-Anon Family Group; alcoholism clinic or information and referral center; community mental health center; Veterans Administration; health, welfare, or family service agency; some employers and labor unions; and local affiliates of the National Council on Alcoholism.

Aspects of Treatment Methods

The treatment of alcoholism consists of getting the alcoholic safely through the withdrawal period, correcting the chronic health problems associated with alcoholism, and helping him or her to change long-term behavior so that destructive drinking patterns are not continued. The individual may begin treatment during a spell of temporary sobriety, during a severe hangover, or during acute intoxication. For many it will be during the drying out, or withdrawal, stage.

Getting Past the DTs

An alcoholic who is well nourished and in good physical condition can be withdrawn with reasonable safety as an outpatient. However, an acutely ill alcoholic needs medically supervised care. A general hospital ward is best for preliminary treatment. The alcohol withdrawal syndrome is quite similar to that described in Chapter 10 for the barbiturates and other sedative-hypnotics. Symptoms appear within 12 to 72 hours after total cessation of drinking, but can appear whenever the blood alcohol level drops below a certain point. The alcoholic has severe muscle tremors, nausea, weakness, and anxiety. Grand mal seizures can occur, but are less common than in barbiturate withdrawal. There may be terrifying hallucinations. The syndrome reaches peak intensity within 24 to 48 hours. About 5% of alcoholics in hospitals, and perhaps 20% to 25% who suffer the DTs without treatment, die as a result. Phenobarbital, chlordiazepoxide (Librium®), and diazepam (Valium®) are commonly used to prevent withdrawal symptoms. Controlled withdrawal may take from 10 to 21 days and cannot safely be hurried. At the same time, the alcoholic may need treatment for malnutrition and vitamin deficiencies (especially the B vitamins). Pneumonia is also a frequent complication (Jaffe, 1980).

Once the alcoholic patient is over the acute stages of intoxication and withdrawal, tranquilizers may be continued for a few weeks, with care taken not to transfer dependence on alcohol to tranquilizers. Long-term treatment with tranquilizers (Librium®, Valium®) does not prevent relapse to drinking or assist with behavioral adaptation. A prescription of disulfiram (Antabuse®) may be offered to encourage patients to abstain from alcohol. Antabuse® blocks metabolism of acetaldehyde, and drinking any alcohol will result in a pounding headache, flushing, nausea, and other unpleasant symptoms. The patient must decide about two days in advance to stop taking Antabuse® before he or she can drink. Antabuse® is an aid to other forms of supportive treatment, not the sole method of therapy.

Psychological and Behavioral Therapies

After the withdrawal symptoms are over, the person usually goes right back to drinking unless he or she can be persuaded to start other therapies that attempt to get at the factors underlying the drinking problem. Most successful therapists say that pleading, exhortation, telling the patient how to live his or her life, and urging him or her to use more willpower are useless and may be destructive. They emphasize the need to create a warm, concerned relationship with the patient. Psychotherapy is quite effective for some patients. Psychotherapy for alcoholics tends to be directed more to action, focusing on the patient's immediate life situation and drinking problem. Many therapists bring members of the patient's family into the therapy program. Family support and understanding are often crucial to success. Sometimes a member of the family, perhaps more emotionally disturbed than the patient, may be partly responsible for the alcoholic's drinking behavior. A psychotherapeutic approach begins by getting the patient (and perhaps his or her family) to accept alcoholism as an illness and not as a moral problem or weakness. The patient must genuinely accept the idea that he or she needs help. Once these attitudes are established, the therapist and patient try to solve those problems that can be readily handled and to find an approach that will enable the patient to live with those problems that cannot be solved.

Behavioral psychologists believe drinking is a learned behavior pattern. Behavioral therapies try to reverse the reinforcement pattern so that abstinence or moderate drinking brings reward or avoids punishment. Techniques used include aversion therapies; assertiveness, coping, and relaxation; biofeedback; blood alcohol discrimination training; and controlled drinking. The current trend is to observe drinking patterns and to develop techniques that will change them. Analysis of drinking behavior focuses on cues and stimuli, attitudes and thoughts, specific drinking behavior, and consequences of drinking. Because these variables are complex and highly individualized, they require careful assessment to change in each patient the attitudes and behaviors that lead to excessive drinking. No one treatment plan is suitable for everyone.

Sobering up means the alcoholic must face a backlog of personal, family, financial, and social problems. Without help to work out these problems that are closely related to alcoholism, he or she will probably return to the same escape method as before. Effective treatment cannot be conducted on a hit-or-miss, intermittent basis restricted to straightening out occasional drinking episodes, and it should be tailored to the individual's needs and rate of progress.

The Helping Agencies for Rehabilitation

It is important to remember that the alcoholic commonly has a number of social problems that must be successfully handled in order to be productive in society. There are many organizations and agencies, staffed largely by nonmedical personnel, that aid countless thousands of alcoholics and help them reestablish better relations with their families, employers or employees, and communities.

Alcoholics Anonymous (AA) is a loosely knit, voluntary fellowship of alcoholics whose sole purpose is to help themselves and one another to get sober and stay sober. AA has been characterized first as a way back to life and then as a way of living. In the AA approach, the alcoholic must admit that he or she lacks control over drinking behavior and that his or her life is unmanageable and intolerable. For some, this realization may not come until they have lost everything and everyone. For a few, it may occur when they are first arrested by police or are warned by their employers. At this point, "the individual must decide to turn over his life and his will to a power greater than his own." Much of the program has a nonsectarian, spiritual basis. It has over 356,000 members in about 19,000 groups in the United States and more than 200,000 members participating in 11,500 groups in Canada and other countries. Despite its scope, AA reaches only a small percentage of the

approximately 10 million alcoholics and problem drinkers in the United States.

During the early years of AA, some members insisted that "only an alcoholic can understand an alcoholic," and there was little cooperation between AA workers and physicians, the clergy, and the social workers. As they have come to know one another better, most AA members no longer hold this view, and cooperation with professional therapists has been increasing. Conversely, professionals strongly encourage membership in AA as part of the treatment programs in detoxification centers, general and psychiatric hospitals, clinics, and prisons. Many professionals emphasize that, valuable and widely accessible as it is, AA should not be considered as a complete form of treatment for all alcoholics; rather, it should be viewed as a support to, and not a substitute for, other forms of therapy. Some alcoholics simply do not mesh well with the AA approach but can be helped by other treatment modalities. The AA model has been used for treatment of other drug addictions, such as heroin.

Al-Anon and *Alateen* were formed to help families cope with an alcoholic member. Al-Anon is for spouses and other relatives of alcoholics whether or not the alcoholic is in AA or some other rehabilitation program. Members learn that they are not alone in this predicament and benefit from the experiences of others. Alateen is a parallel organization for teenage children of alcoholic parents. These organizations are listed in most phone directories.

The National Council on Alcoholism (NCA) provides leadership in public education, advocacy of enlarged government involvement in prevention and treatment, and consultation services, particularly to industry. There are more than 200 member councils across the country. At the community level, information and referral services and short-term pretreatment counseling are offered to problem drinkers and their families.

Salvation Army, Volunteers of America, and *clergy:* The Salvation Army and the Volunteers of America provide food, shelter, and rehabilitation services, often through halfway houses. Many religious groups have developed programs and therapy groups to aid alcoholics and their families. Most clergy have training in counseling, some in psychotherapy, so they provide a valuable service.

Department of Transportation (DOT): There are thousands of deaths and hundreds of thousands of serious accidents on the highways each year because of alcohol consumption. The DOT has developed an information program to persuade people to prevent their friends from driving while drunk and a technical assistance program to help state and local governments develop systems for apprehending drunk drivers and bringing them for treatment.

The National Institute on Alcohol Abuse and Alcoholism (NIAAA) provides policy guidance for federal action on alcohol-related problems and channels funds for research, training, prevention, and development of community-based services for treatment of alcoholics, a national information and education program, and other special projects.

The Veterans' Administration (VA) hospitals conduct the largest alcoholism treatment and research program in the country. Over 100,000 alcoholic patients are treated yearly. Eligible veterans receive alcoholism treatment at no charge. Treatment for acute intoxication is available at any VA hospital in the country; many now offer comprehensive follow-up treatment and rehabilitation services.

Industrial programs: It is estimated that business, industry, and government employ about 5.8 million problem drinkers—up to 6% of the nation's labor force and perhaps 10% of the executives. Because the problem is substantial, the federal government and industries now commonly have programs to help employees whose job performances suffer through their use of alcohol. Organized labor has also become involved. Programs for alcoholic employees have been included in contract agreements. The unions also have developed their own training programs and provide services for their members in trouble with alcohol. Trice presents a good evaluation of job-based alcohol abuse treatment programs in the *Handbook on Drug Abuse* (1979).

Job-based treatment programs have an average 70% success rate. Because the drinking problem is identified much earlier in alcoholic employees than in unemployed persons, treatment is begun before physical health has entirely deteriorated, before financial resources are totally gone, and while emotional support still exists in the family and community. Also, the threat of job loss motivates the employee to accept treatment.

A SELF-QUIZ ON FACT AND FANCY ABOUT ALCOHOL

Indicate whether the following statements are true or false by circling either T or F.

T F 1. Alcohol is a drug; it can cause tolerance and physical dependence.

T F 2. Alcohol may be a stimulant in small doses, because the person drinking a few drinks is often stimulated.

T F   3. Alcohol can cause death by overstimulating the nervous system.

T F   4. Alcohol has no nutritional value.

T F   5. Alcohol is absorbed into the bloodstream and digested the same way foods are.

T F   6. It is possible to prevent symptoms of a hangover by eating fats or carbohydrates or by taking massive doses of vitamins before doing some heavy drinking.

T F   7. Drinking large quantities of black coffee or taking spiced juices will help in sobering up.

T F   8. One can become intoxicated more rapidly on vodka or gin than on scotch or whiskey.

T F   9. Champagne often affects a person more rapidly than whiskey.

T F   10. A blood alcohol level above 0.15% is considered legal intoxication in all states.

T F   11. A tall obese person should be able to drink more without getting drunk than a shorter obese person or a tall muscular person.

T F   12. If a person is chilled in cold weather, taking a few drinks will increase the body temperature and warm him up.

T F   13. If a pregnant woman drinks, it will not harm the fetus.

T F   14. Alcohol is an aphrodisiac.

T F   15. Cirrhosis of the liver is not the most common effect of alcohol in heavy drinkers.

T F   16. Alcohol can be used to treat snakebite.

T F   17. Alcohol can cure a cold.

T F   18. Social drinking is the first step toward alcoholism.

T F   19. Alcoholics tend to follow a predictable pattern of behavior as they become alcoholics.

T F   20. Most alcoholics are found on skid row or in squalid surroundings.

T F   21. All alcoholics have psychological problems that are the reasons for becoming alcoholic.

T F   22. There is no cure for alcoholism.

T F   23. The son of an alcoholic has a higher probability of becoming alcoholic whether he is raised with his natural family or adopted by nondrinking foster parents.

Answers: (1) T, (2) F, (3) F, (4) T, (5) F, (6) F, (7) F, (8) F, (9) T, (10) T, (11) F, (12) F, (13) F, (14) F, (15) T, (16) F, (17) F, (18) T, (19) F, (20) F, (21) F, (22) T, (23) T

Explanations for the answers

1. True. Ethyl alcohol is a central nervous system depressant drug. Prolonged, heavy use causes tolerance to its effects. In addition, the user may become physically dependent. Once the person becomes physically dependent, he or she will undergo withdrawal if he or she reduces or stops drinking.

2. False. Alcohol first affects the higher cortical centers of the brain. When this region is depressed, persons exhibit behaviors that are usually kept submerged. This has been described as "removing the veneer of civilization." Thus any stimulation that may occur is due to the release of inhibitions acquired over a lifetime. Alcohol is correctly classified as a depressant.

3. False. The neural centers become more and more depressed as the dose of alcohol is increased. Death from an overdose of alcohol is rare but can occur from depression of respiration (Table 11-4). Very rapid drinking, such as trying to consume a bottle of liquor without stopping

to breathe, can block the gag reflex, and the person may choke to death. The drinker may also become unconscious and suffocate in his or her vomit. In contrast, the brain is stimulated when an alcoholic is undergoing withdrawal. The brain may become so stimulated ("rebound stimulation") that the person may go into convulsions and even die.

4.   True. Alcohol has no nutritional value in the sense that it provides nothing that is needed by the body to grow or to maintain tissues. Alcohol provides more calories per gram than carbohydrate or protein and is only slightly less caloric than pure fat. Although alcoholics commonly are found to be suffering from malnutrition caused by poor eating habits, even a perfect diet will not prevent the damage to the liver and brain caused by excess alcohol consumed over a period of time.

5.   False. Alcohol follows the same pathways for absorption into the bloodstream as food, but does not need to be broken down by digestive enzymes first as most foods do. Unlike food, alcohol is broken down into a toxic substance (acetaldehyde). Another difference: alcohol can be absorbed directly through the walls of the stomach, although most of it is absorbed from the first part of the small intestine. Alcohol has a low molecular weight and is completely soluble in water, so that it moves rapidly through the entire system.

6.   False. There is no evidence that special diets have any effect on the rate of metabolism of alcohol. Almost any kind of food (especially milk, fatty foods, and meat) in the stomach before the person starts drinking will slow the absorption of alcohol. Food will reduce the peak concentration of blood alcohol the person would have had after drinking on an empty stomach. The alcohol must still be metabolized at its constant rate, about one-half ounce per hour. Massive doses of vitamins have not been shown to

have any effect on the severity of hangovers. Little harm would be done by taking large quantities of the water-soluble B complex vitamins, but the lipid-soluble vitamins (A, D, and E) can be toxic.

7.   False. Coffee has been given to more drunks than any other remedy to help sober them up. Coffee does contain the mild stimulant caffeine, but caffeine does not increase the rate at which alcohol is metabolized. Black coffee will simply produce a slightly more alert drunk, not significantly improve his or her judgment or driving skills. Coffee has some diuretic effect, but the amount of alcohol excreted unchanged in the urine is very small. Drinking spiced tomato juice or other juice will reduce the rate of absorption of alcohol from the gastrointestinal tract, as will most foods. Coffee and spiced juice would help if taken *instead of* a final drink.

8.   False. The amount of alcohol taken, and not the type of liquor, is the problem. It does not matter what the drink is, unless it is over 100 proof or has a carbonated mixer (see question 9). If a drink is 80-proof alcohol rather than 60 proof, it has more alcohol per unit volume and thus is more potent. An alcoholic drink containing around 40% alcohol enters the blood faster than drinks with a higher concentration (over 100 proof).

9.   True. The carbonation in champagne, mixers, and carbonated wines makes the stomach contents pass through more quickly into the small intestine, from which the alcohol is efficiently absorbed. Thus a person feels an effect from a carbonated alcoholic beverage first, then from a drink around 40% (80 proof) alcohol content, and then from a highly concentrated drink (over 100 proof).

10.   True. Because alcohol plays a significant role in traffic accidents, most states have set legal intoxication at a blood alcohol level of 0.10% or lower. The average person with a blood

alcohol level of 0.10% or 0.15% is 7 to 25 times, respectively, more likely to have a fatal accident than the driver with no alcohol in his or her blood (Ritchie, 1980). About 4 to 5 oz of whiskey, gin, or vodka drunk by an average man (160–170 pounds) over a period of one hour would give a blood alcohol concentration of about 0.10%.

11. False. The drinker's size and body composition are factors in blood alcohol concentration. Fatty tissue has a lower percentage of water than muscle, so there is less water for the alcohol to dissolve in. The obese person therefore is affected to a greater extent, because more alcohol dissolves in the blood and reaches the central nervous system than in a lean muscular person of the same height. A short fat person is affected more than a tall fat person.

12. False. In cold weather, the peripheral blood vessels automatically constrict to prevent loss of heat. However, alcohol dilates these vessels and overrides the body's attempt to regulate heat loss, thus making the person susceptible to frostbite and hypothermia (a life-threatening loss of body heat). Alcohol tends to cause a drop in blood pressure, which causes a further susceptibility to chilling and frostbite. Drinking in cold weather is a dangerous way to warm up.

13. False. Alcohol readily crosses the placenta from the woman's blood to the fetus. It is probably the most common agent causing mental retardation known to the Western world (Ritchie, 1980). The amount of alcohol necessary to produce the fetal alcohol syndrome is not known, and a safe limit has not been established. Women are being cautioned to keep daily consumption much lower than they otherwise would for the duration of the pregnancy and to avoid drinking heavily on any single occasion, such as a special party.

14. False. Alcohol has been linked with sexuality throughout history; however, its func-

tion is not to stimulate desire but to suppress inhibitions, including sexual inhibitions. As Ogden Nash put it: "Candy is dandy, but liquor is quicker." Sexuality is greatly influenced by psychological factors, and alcohol can make a person more susceptible to suggestion. As a person continues to drink, his or her sexual ability tends to diminish because of loss of neural control and coordination. Shakespeare refers to this in *Macbeth*: "Lechery, sir, it provokes, and unprovokes; it provokes the desire, but it takes away the performance."

15. True. About 8% of alcoholics develop cirrhosis. Nearly three-fourths of all alcoholics have abnormal liver function, but not cirrhosis. More alcoholics have significant nutritional and vitamin deficiencies, damage to the heart and skeletal muscle, an inflamed stomach lining, and brain damage than have true cirrhosis.

16. False. The idea that taking alcohol is useful in treating snakebite goes back over 2000 years to the Greeks. Alcohol was thought to be a specific antidote that neutralized the venom (Roueché, 1960). It has no basis in fact.

17. False. Alcohol cannot cure a cold or alleviate its symptoms. Its only benefit would be to make the person relaxed and sleepy enough to go to bed and keep him or her from spreading the virus. It could potentiate with antihistamine drugs in producing sedation.

18. True. Alcoholism today is considered a disease. The term *alcoholism* refers to complex set of conditions that involve physiological, psychological, and sociological factors. Social drinking is usually the first step for most alcoholics, but the majority of social drinkers do not become alcoholics.

19. False. Until the early 1950s, it was believed that alcoholics progressed along a sequence of controlled social drinking, occasional escape from tension, escape drinking, blackouts, loss of ability to stop at one drink,

and finally physical dependence (Jellinek, 1952). This is no longer generally accepted (Aronow, 1980; Cahn, 1970).

20.   False. Most alcoholics are found in the middle class of society. They are found in every type of occupation. It is surprising how many housewives are found to be in the later stages of alcoholism and yet have been able to keep this fact hidden for years.

21.   False. There are three major hypotheses about the cause of alcoholism. One concerns personality: Alcoholics are thought to be insecure, anxious, oversensitive, and in general, dissatisfied with themselves. Alcohol gives such people a temporary escape and a way to cope. The second hypothesis involves biochemical defects: The alcoholic might have an abnormal physiological constitution. This hypothesis is closely related to genetic causes for alcoholism. As yet, a purely biochemical or genetic hypothesis has not been proven. Social causes, which constitute the basis for the third hypothesis, are associated with religion and culture, escape mechanisms in society, attitudes toward drinking, and age. Some societies have such ambivalent or complex goals that an individual may become so pressured he or she must find escape, and alcohol provides that escape. Drinking might tend to run in families because the family members never learn how to cope, and they all select the same escape route.

22.   True. After the alcoholic is safely through the detoxification phase, there are many treatment programs available that have a high rate of success in helping the person live a normal life. However, the alcoholic is not cured in the sense that few can ever resume social drinking in a controlled manner.

23.   True. Male offspring of alcoholics do have a higher than average chance of becoming alcoholics. The probability is estimated as four times higher than offspring of nonalcoholics. The probability for daughters of alcoholics is less clear.

CHAPTER 12

OPIUM AND ITS DERIVATIVES

CHAPTER OBJECTIVES

1. Describe the early medical uses of opium and morphine.
2. Discuss the history of the opium poppy in China and its impact on the United States.
3. List three factors in the history of the opiates that contributed to narcotics addiction in the late 1800s and early 1900s.
4. Describe the physiological effects and side effects of morphine on the body.
5. Name two common adulterants in street heroin and explain their effects.
6. Compare primary and secondary psychological dependence on heroin.
7. Describe symptoms of withdrawal from opiates.
8. Cite evidence to show that the typical young heroin addict is antisocial and has a criminal record before starting heroin use. ˒
9. Describe how some people can use heroin, become addicted, and then stop (Vietvets) and how others may be nonaddicted, controlled users indefinitely.
10. Explain how methadone, LAAM, and naltrexone work in an addict maintained on these drugs.
11. List characteristics and uses of Dilaudid®, Demerol®, codeine, Talwin®, Darvon®, paregoric, and dextromethorphan.
12. Define the following terms: narcotic, laudanum, army disease, opioid, naloxone, miosis, skin popping, mainlining, chippers, acetylmethadol, LAAM, and endorphin.

HISTORY OF
THE NARCOTICS

The meaning of the word *narcotic* varies. It has been used many ways for many substances, from opium to marijuana and cocaine. The translation of the Greek word *narkoticos* is *benumbing;* or *deadening,* which gives some idea of the original meaning of the word. The term *narcotic* is sometimes used to refer to a central nervous system depressant, producing insensibility or stupor, and at other times to refer to an addicting drug. Most people would not include marijuana among the narcotics today, although for many years it legally was in this category. Although cocaine, a stimulant, is not a narcotic either, it is still legally classified as one. Perhaps part of this confusion is due to the fact that cocaine is used as a local anesthetic.

The opium poppy, *Papaver somniferum,* from which opium is obtained, has been cultivated for a long time (Figure 12-1). A 6000-year-old Sumerian tablet has an ideograph for the poppy shown as "joy" plus "plant." The Egyptians listed

FIGURE 12-1
The opium poppy.

opium along with approximately 700 other medicinal compounds in the famous Ebers papyrus (about 1500 B.C.). The ancient Greeks knew that opium was produced after the petals drop, but before the seed pods mature. In the third century B.C. the Greek writer Theophrastus referred to a method for extracting poppy juice, *opion*, by grinding up the entire plant.

Homer's *Odyssey*, about 1000 B.C., mentions the use of a potion that sounds like an opiate. The spirits of the people, who had gathered in sad commemoration of Ulysses and his trying ordeals, were given a lift when:

> Helen, daughter of Zeus, poured into the wine they were drinking a drug, nepenthes, which gave forgetfulness of evil. Those who had drunk of this mixture did not shed a tear the whole day long, even though their mother or father were dead, even though a brother or beloved son had been killed before their eyes. [Scott, 1969]

The Greek god of sleep, Hypnos, and the Roman god of sleep, Somnus, were portrayed as carrying a container of opium pods, and the Minoan goddess of sleep wore a crown of opium pods (Figure 12-2). The opium pod can also be seen on Greek gold coins (Figure 12-3). According to Greek mythology, the poppy was sacred to Demeter, the goddess of sowing and reaping, and to her daughter Persephone.

By the first century A.D. the use of opium had spread, and the technique to extract opium from the pod was developed. Today opium is harvested as it has been for thousands of years. In the early morning the workers make shallow gashes in the green pods. The next day the white sap, which has now become a reddish-brown color, is scraped off into a bowl and shaped into balls of gum opium.

The Greek physician Galen (2nd century A.D.) used opium in his treatments for many ailments.

FIGURE 12-2
A Minoan goddess of sleep, with a headband of opium poppies.

FIGURE 12-3
A Greek gold coin dated 700 to 500 **B.C.** Note the opium poppy pod.

Here is what he said in one of his writings about opium:

> It resists poison and venomous bites, cures chronic headache, vertigo, deafness, epilepsy, apoplexy, dimness of sight, loss of voice, asthma, coughs of all kinds, spitting of blood, jaundice, hardness of the spleen, urinary complaints, fevers, dropsies, leprosies, the troubles to which women are subject, melancholy, and all pestilences. [Terry & Pellens, 1928]

Galen mentioned the use of opium in sweets, but he did not mention addiction. Alcoholism was a significant problem in classical Greece and in Rome, but opium was used primarily in medicine. However, Galen's descriptions of his patient, Roman Emperor Marcus Aurelius, fit the symptoms of addiction to opiates (Africa, 1961). The opium poppy was valued by the Romans. The poppy is represented in the ornate carvings on Emperor Augustus's tomb.

During the so-called Dark Ages that followed the collapse of the Roman Empire, Arab traders were actively engaged in traveling the overland caravan routes to China and to India, where they introduced opium. Eventually those two countries grew their own opium poppies. Sometime around 900 A.D. the Arabian physician Al Rhazi wrote a vast encyclopedia that included all Greek, Arabic, and Indian medical knowledge. A century later another Arabian physician, Avicenna (980–1037 A.D.), wrote his five-part *Canon of Medicine,* perhaps the most influential textbook ever written. It established a complete system of medical science. Both used opium preparations in their medical practices. (Avicenna died from drinking an accidental overdose of opium in wine.) During their occupation of Spain, the Moors made an invaluable contribution to Western medicine by gathering in libraries important works written by Greek and Arabian physicians. Later, European scholars translated these works back into Latin. This knowledge spread throughout Europe and formed the basis of the science of modern medicine.

After the 16th century, opium was widely used in European medicine. One of the early opiate preparations, laudanum, was compounded by the English physician Sydenham (1624–1689 A.D.): 2 ounces of strained opium, 1 ounce of saffron, and a dram each of cinnamon and cloves dissolved in 1 pint of Canary wine. Dr. Sydenham devoutly expressed his gratitude for the medicinal value of opium in 1680: "Among the remedies which it has pleased Almighty God to give to man to relieve his sufferings, none is so universal and so efficacious as opium" (Austin, 1978; Scott, 1969).

In the early 1800s a number of writers experimented with opium and recorded their experiences. The most eloquent of these opium users was Thomas De Quincey, who, in his famous book *Confessions of an English Opium Eater,* praised opium: "Thou hast the keys of Paradise, O just, subtle, and mighty opium." De Quincey described many of the sensations experienced by the addict. He believed that opium enhanced his creativity, just as many people believe today. De Quincey used opium all his life. Despite his high praise for the drug, he was unable to write for periods of time because of the lassitude that resulted from his addiction. One of the major problems caused by a narcotic drug like opium is that it takes the edge off any ambition and drive that the user has, which makes it very difficult to sustain a literary effort or piece of artistic work. Elizabeth Barrett Browning, Baudelaire, Gautier, Dumas, Edgar Allan Poe, and Samuel Taylor Coleridge were all addicted to laudanum. As in De Quincey's case, the common pattern was to start laudanum for pain relief and then get hooked. Coleridge's splendid dream picture, "Kubla Khan," was conceived while he was in an opium reverie. As in the case of De Quincey, his bondage to the narcotic drug habit inhibited his periods of creativity (Scott, 1969).

The opium poppy was a factor in a drastic change that took place in China: widespread drug addiction among its population. The poppy was introduced into China about 800 A.D. by Arab traders. At first the seeds, and later opium, were used medically. Recreational use was not a problem until the introduction of opium smoking in the late 1690s. Just like a communicable disease, drug addiction starts from a point of initial infection and spreads. This is what happened with opium smoking in China, which is similar to the history of tobacco smoking there. The Chinese government, fearful of the weakening of national vitality by these two drugs, especially the potent opiate, forbade their use by the people. In the 17th century the use of tobacco was forbidden under threat of death by strangulation. In 1729 China outlawed the sale of opium; the penalty was death by strangula-

tion. At one point decapitation was decreed, a much more serious penalty than strangulation because the Chinese believed the body must be intact in order to reach paradise. Despite these strong rules the habit of opium smoking became so widespread that the Chinese government forbade its importation from India, where most of the opium poppy was grown. The British East India Company (and later the British government in India) encouraged cultivation of opium. British companies were the principal shippers to the Chinese port of Canton, which was the only port open to Western merchants. During the next 120 years, a complex network of opium smuggling into China developed with the help of local merchants, who got substantial profits, and local officials, who pocketed bribes to ignore the smugglers. The amount of opium entering China rose from 200 chests in 1729, to 30,000 to 40,000 chests (about 130 lb each) in 1838 (Austin, 1978; Scott, 1969).

Everyone involved in the opium trade was making money until the Chinese government ordered the strict enforcement of the edict against importation and sent an honest, vigorous official, Imperial Commissioner Lin Tse-Hsu, to Canton to handle the problem. Lin commanded the foreign importers to surrender their stores and cargoes of opium. When the British traders refused, he threatened the Chinese merchants who were illegally trading in opium. The British then turned over their supplies of opium to Lin, who had the drug destroyed. However, pressures grew and helped trigger the Opium War of 1839–1842 (the war was really caused by Britain's commercial expansion). Britain sent in an army, and, by 1842, 10,000 British soldiers won a victory over 350 million Chinese (see Figure 12-4).

Britain protested that it was not an opium war, that it was a war over impediments—high import tariffs and corrupt courts—to the entire

FIGURE 12-4
A famous cartoon showing a
British sailor shoving opium
down the throat of a Chinese
man. This drawing dates back
to the 1839 Opium War.

import trade. The British wanted to force China
to open its ports to trade. By the Treaty of
Nanking in 1842, five ports were opened to the
British, the island of Hong Kong was ceded to
them, and an indemnity of $6 million was
imposed on China to cover the value of the
destroyed opium and the cost of the war. In 1856
a second Opium War broke out. Peking was
occupied by British and French troops, and China
was compelled to make further concessions to
Britain. The importation of opium continued
to increase until 1908, when Britain and China
made an agreement to limit the importation of
opium from India (Austin, 1978).

The rapid spread of opium use in the United
States and the first opium control laws can be
traced to the flourishing use of opium in China
in the 1800s and the importation of Chinese
laborers to build the railroads. The Chinese
laborers brought opium with them, which they
smoked for recreation and relaxation. Because
the opium was heated, not burned, the Chinese

opium "smoker" was actually inhaling the vol-
atilized morphine. Smoking was much less potent
than morphine injection, because the opium used
for this was a special weak type, and less than
10% of the morphine content enters the bloodstream by the inhalation route (Brecher, 1972).

In 1803 the addictive potential of opium was
significantly increased when a young German
named Frederick Serturner extracted the active
ingredient in opium. The ingredient was ten
times more potent than opium and was named
morphine after Morpheus, the Greek god of dreams
(Appendix A–8). This discovery stimulated work
with opium, and by 1832 a number of different
alkaloids had been isolated from the raw material. In 1832 the second compound was purified:
this was *codeine*, named after the Greek word
for *poppy capsule*.

The next major step in facilitating the use of
opiates and addiction to them came in 1853
when Dr. Alexander Wood perfected the hypodermic syringe. Sir Christopher Wren and others

had worked with the idea of injecting drugs directly into the body by means of hollow quills and straws, but the idea never was successful or well received. Wood had hoped to prevent addiction to morphine by injection directly into the veins rather than by oral administration. Unfortunately, injection of the drug increases the potency and the chances of addiction. The hypodermic syringe was used during the Civil War to administer morphine for treating pain, dysentery, and fatigue. A fairly high percentage of the men coming home after the war were addicted to morphine. Opiate addiction was called "soldier's disease" or "army disease." Nevertheless, historical analysis shows it is questionable whether returning soldiers contributed to opiate addiction in the country to any significant extent.

Around the turn of the century, an estimated one million Americans were addicted to the opiates (Abel, 1980). This problem was caused by the Chinese laborers' bringing in opium to smoke (it was legal then to smoke opium in the United States), the availability of morphine and the hypodermic syringe, and the lack of controls on the large number of patent medicines that contained fairly large doses of opium derivatives. Opium smoking was not popular in the United States at the turn of the century, but the use of morphine was. The widespread use of opiate-containing patent medicines and morphine were probably the main reasons for the spread of, and increase in, addiction. (Interestingly, physicians at that time frequently gave morphine to treat alcoholism.)

Until about 1914, when the Harrison Narcotic Act (regulating opium, coca leaves, and their products) was passed, the average opiate addict was a middle-aged, Southern, White woman who functioned well and was adjusted to her role as a wife and mother. She bought opium or morphine legally by mail order from Sears, Roebuck or at the local store, used it orally, and caused very few problems. A number of physicians were addicted as well. One of the best known morphine addicts was Dr. William Halsted, one of the founders of Johns Hopkins Medical School. Dr. Halsted was a very productive surgeon and innovator, although secretly an addict for most of his career. He became addicted to morphine as a substitute for his cocaine addiction (Brecher, 1972).

Not content to leave well enough alone, chemists found that addition of two acetyl side groups to the morphine molecule results in a more potent compound. In 1898 diacetylmorphine was placed on the market as a cough suppressant by Bayer Laboratories. It was to be a heroic drug, without the addictive potential of morphine, so it was named *Heroin* (Figure 12-5).

PHYSIOLOGICAL ACTIVITY OF HEROIN AND MORPHINE

Morphine and other opiates (or *opioids* as they are often called) are narcotic sedatives that exert their major effects by depressing the central nervous system. The opiates work by interacting with specific receptor sites in the brain and peripheral nervous system to inhibit the release of dopamine, norepinephrine, and other neurotransmitters. These opioid receptors are present in highest concentration in the limbic system (frontal and temporal cortex, amygdala, and hippocampus), thalamus, hypothalamus, and spinal cord. There are believed to be at least two different types of receptor on which morphine acts. One type of receptor that morphine affects appears to control the analgesic action, respiratory depression, euphoria, and physical dependence; the second type of receptor appears

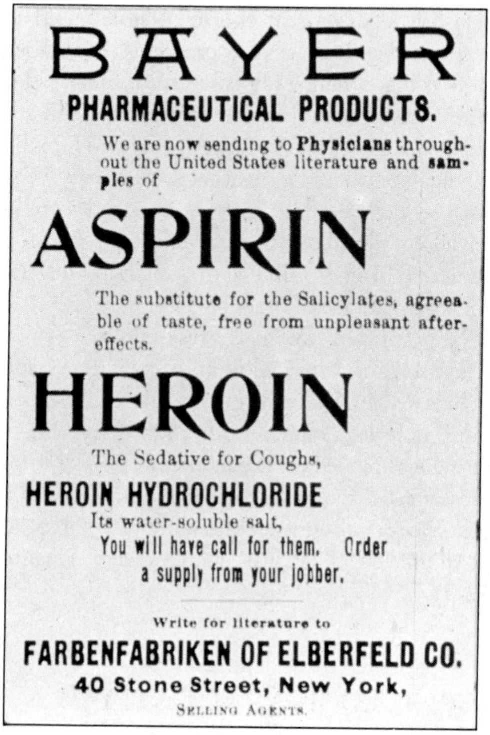

FIGURE 12-5
Early poster used by Bayer to sell their new product, Heroin.

and intestines. One problem that most opiate addicts experience is constipation, because of interference with the nervous system controls of the gastrointestinal tract. Heroin has an analgesic effect; it causes depression, blocks hunger, dulls aggression, and blocks the menstrual cycle in female addicts. The idea still persists that heroin addicts are sex fiends, but actually the drug diminishes libido in most addicts. Heroin also causes drowsiness: the user keeps nodding his or her head ("on the nod") as if he or she were about to fall asleep. Morphine, heroin, and other opioids cause constriction of the pupils (*miosis*) and the release of histamine, making the addict's skin feel itchy. Intermediate to large doses seem to affect the medial forebrain bundle, or pleasure center, and other mood control centers of the limbic system.

HEROIN ABUSE

In the United States, heroin was first used as a cough remedy and to combat addiction to other drugs. However, its inherent addictive properties were quickly discovered. When injected, heroin is more addictive than morphine because of the intense feeling of euphoria it induces. Heroin was banned from American medicine in 1924. It is now a Schedule I drug, with a high potential for abuse and no currently accepted medical use.

From 1970 through 1976 most of the heroin reaching the United States originated in the Golden Triangle region of Southeast Asia, which includes parts of Burma, Thailand, and Laos. During that period of time the United States and other nations purchased much of the legal opium crop from Turkey in order to stop the opium from being converted into heroin. From 1975 till 1980 the major heroin supply was from

to control the extent of sedation. These are the same receptor sites that the endorphins and enkephalins, the natural opiates of the body, interact with. Antagonists have been discovered that can block the effects of opiates by occupying the receptor sites. One of these, naloxone, is valuable in treatment of overdosage. An overdose of an opiate will cause death because of selective depressant action on the respiratory center in the medulla (Jaffe & Martin, 1980).

Like morphine, heroin produces its most marked effects on the central nervous system opium poppies grown in Mexico. The U.S. government furnished the Mexican government with helicopters, herbicide sprays, and some financial assistance to destroy the poppy crop. This somewhat reduced the 1980–1981 street supply of heroin in the United States. Changes in political climates may well shift the source of supply back to the Golden Triangle, Turkey, or elsewhere. The opium poppy can be cultivated commercially almost anywhere there is cheap labor available during the brief harvesting season.

Pure heroin is a white powder. Other colors, such as brown Mexican heroin, result from unsatisfactory processing of morphine or from adulterants. It is usually "cut" (diluted) with lactose (milk sugar) to give it bulk and to increase profits. Heroin has a bitter taste, so quite often it is cut with quinine, a bitter substance, to disguise the fact that the heroin has been diluted. To counteract the constipating effect of heroin, mannitol is often added for its laxative effect. When heroin first enters the country it may be up to 95% pure, but by the time it is diluted it may be anywhere from 3% to 5%.

Addicts are always talking about the *dynamite bag* (the really potent one), but if they do find an unusually potent one, there is a good chance they will get more than they bargained for. The National Institute on Drug Abuse (NIDA) reported that there were over 3626 drug-related deaths in 1979. It obtained this figure from reports from the Drug Abuse Warning Network (DAWN), which is a centralized reporting system of drugs mentioned in medical records of emergency-room patients and morgues. About 900 hospitals in 25 cities across the country are included in the system. This network covers approximately 30% of the U.S. population, although the regions sampled were metropolitan, where the most deaths occur. No one knows exactly how many people die from drug overdoses in the United States or even from which drugs, but NIDA estimates about one-third are narcotic-related deaths.

Addicts are sometimes found dead with the needle still in the vein after injecting heroin. Medical examiners and police have questioned whether the person died from an unusually concentrated dose of heroin because of (a) the swiftness of the fatal reaction; (b) the low dose of heroin in most street bags; (c) the frequency of pulmonary edema (accumulation of fluid in the lungs); and (d) the isolated nature of the phenomenon. When addicts shoot up in groups, it is rare for more than one to have an OD reaction. It is more likely that death associated with heroin injection is due to concurrent use of alcohol or barbiturates or to adulterants than it is to concentrated heroin. Quinine is thought to be one of the deadly adulterants. Part of the "flash" from direct injection of heroin might be caused by the quinine. It is an irritant, and it causes vascular damage, acute and potentially lethal disturbances in heartbeat, depressed respiration, coma, and death from respiratory arrest. Opiate poisoning causes acute pulmonary edema as well as respiratory depression. Heroin plus quinine has an unpredictable additive effect (Bourne, 1976).

In 1971, the Select Committee on Crime in the United States released a report on methods used to combat the heroin crisis that arose in the 1950s and 1960s. This report was one of the turning points in setting up treatment programs for narcotics addicts. The report stated that the drug arrests for heroin use had increased 700% since 1961, that there were as many as 4000 deaths per year from heroin, and that the cost of heroin-related crimes was estimated to be over $3 billion a year. There have been other studies since that time linking heroin addiction with criminality.

That heroin use is linked to crime is not surprising. Trafficking in narcotics is illegal to start with, and few addicts have the financial resources to maintain their habits without recourse to illegal activities. Between 40% and 80% of addicts had preaddiction conviction or arrest records; compared to nonaddicted persons, they also had a higher percentage of arrests and/or convictions during treatment and afterwards (Nurco, 1979).

In 1972 the U.S. Bureau of Narcotics and Dangerous Drugs estimated that there were 559,224 narcotic addicts in the United States (Figure 12-6). In 1973 the Special Action Office for Drug Abuse Prevention estimated there were closer to 300,000 narcotics addicts in the country. In 1980 the NIDA estimated there were about 400,000 narcotic addicts. It is fair to say

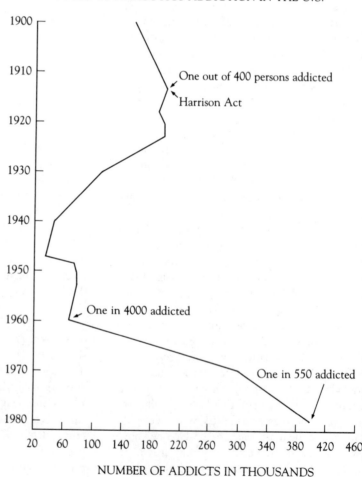

HISTORY OF NARCOTICS ADDICTION IN THE U.S.

One out of 400 persons addicted

Harrison Act

One in 4000 addicted

One in 550 addicted

NUMBER OF ADDICTS IN THOUSANDS

FIGURE 12-6
History of narcotic addiction in the United States with the estimated number of narcotic addicts. The earlier data is from the Bureau of Narcotics and Dangerous Drugs but the final 1980 estimate is from the National Institute on Drug Abuse. The actual number of narcotic addicts is not known but may be 400,000 (nearly 600,000 according to the Bureau of Narcotics and Dangerous Drugs).

hat we do not know the exact number, but the 980 figure is probably reasonable considering he role of the treatment programs and the work f the Drug Enforcement Administration (DEA) n breaking up some of the major narcotic traffic.

The attitude of the country toward narcotics hanged when it became obvious that the prob- m was no longer confined to the inner city. It as infiltrated the suburban areas and small towns. hese new drug populations have more finan- ial resources than people in the inner city, and hey are usually able to get confidential medical reatment and are not subject to constant police irveillance. For these reasons it is very difficult determine the level of heroin use in these eas.

A study from the Haight-Ashbury Free Med- al Clinic in San Francisco offers some insight to the ghetto-bred and the middle-class, White eroin user. There appear to be three distinct ypes of heroin user: (1) the "old-style junkie" ho fits the traditional picture of a ghetto res- lent with a long-term habit; (2) the "transition inkie" who was first a flower child and who en turned to mind-expanding drugs and finally heroin to escape the collapse of his or her ibculture; and (3) the "new junkie" who went irectly from alcohol to heroin as an escape from is or her problems and despair. Some members f the last group were introduced to the drug in 'ietnam. The present-day addict is nearly as ften female as male, is considerably older than sed to be the case when he or she first gets ivolved with opiates and also is older at the me of first running afoul of the law. This last ype may prove easier to rehabilitate than the ld-style (pre-1968) junkie. Many of them are ot truly addicted (Newmeyer, 1974).

Many heroin users start by sniffing the pow- er or injecting it into a muscle (intramuscular) r under the skin ("skin popping"). Sometimes is smoked, but most addicts consider this

wasteful. In Vietnam, many of those who became addicted to heroin started out by smoking it with tobacco or marijuana, or sniffing it. Heroin available in Vietnam was nearly 95% pure.

The effects of heroin are often not pleasura- ble, especially after the first injection. It is not uncommon to experience nausea and vomiting or otherwise feel sick after injection, but grad- ually the euphoric effects cover up all other effects. There are two major stages in develop- ment of psychological dependence on heroin. At first there is a rewarding stage, in which there is euphoria and feelings and sensations usually pleasurable to at least 50% of the users; these feelings and sensations increase with continued use. In the second stage, by which time he or she is heavily addicted, the heroin user must take the drug to avoid withdrawal symptoms that will start within about 12 hours after the last dose taken. At this stage it is said that "the monkey is on his back." These two stages are called *primary psychological dependence* and *sec- ondary psychological dependence,* respectively. If one grain of heroin (about 65 mg) is taken over a two-week period on a daily basis, the user becomes physically dependent on the drug.

Established heroin addicts usually mainline the drug (intravenous injection). The syringe needle is the indispensible part of the addict's equipment. The rest of the device can be made from an eyedropper, although disposable hypo- dermic syringes are sometimes used. Mainlining drugs causes the thin-walled veins to become scarred, and they collapse. Addicts become ex- pert in locating new veins to use: in the feet, the legs, and the temple. When they do not want scars, or needle tracks, to show, they inject under the tongue or in the groin.

It is quite common for addicts to have a place where they can stash supplies and equipment. These places are often called *shooting galleries.* Some addicts become fixated on the paraphernalia, especially the needle. They can get a psychological high from playing with the needle and syringe. The injection process and syringe plunger action appear to have sexual overtones for them.

After the effects of the heroin wear off, the addict usually has 4 to 6 hours in which to find his or her next dose before withdrawal symptoms begin. These start with a runny nose, tears, and minor stomach cramps. The addict may feel as if he or she is starting a bad cold. Between 12 and 48 hours after the last dose, the addict loses all appetite, vomits, has diarrhea and abdominal cramps, feels alternating chills and fever, and develops goose pimples all over ("going cold turkey"). Between two and four days later, the addict continues to experience some of the symptoms just described plus aching bones and muscles, and powerful muscle spasms that cause violent kicking motions ("kicking the habit"). After four to five days the worst is over,

and the person may clean up and start eating again. However, the compulsion to repeat use of the drug is unchanged. The severity of the withdrawal can vary according to the purity and strength of the drug used and the personality of the user. The symptoms of withdrawal from heroin, morphine, and methadone are summarized in Table 12-1. Withdrawal symptoms from codeine, Demerol®, and others are similar, although the time frame and intensity vary (Jaffe 1980).

WHAT CAUSES A PERSON TO BECOME AN ADDICT?

There is no single cause of addiction. However, many experts believe that addiction requires some persistent behavior on the part of the individ

TABLE 12-1. Symptoms of withdrawal from heroin, morphine, and methadone

Symptoms	Time in hours		
	Heroin	Morphine	Methadone
Craving for drugs, anxiety	4	6	24–48
Yawning, perspiration, runny nose, tears	8	14	34–48
Pupil dilatation, goose bumps, muscle twitches, aching bones and muscles, hot and cold flashes, loss of appetite	12	16	48–72
Increased intensity of above, insomnia, raised blood pressure, fever, faster pulse, nausea	18–24	24–36	72 plus
Increased intensity of above, curled-up position, vomiting, diarrhea, increased blood sugar, foot kicking ("kicking the habit")	26–36	36–48	

WHAT CAUSES A PERSON TO BECOME AN ADDICT?

ual. It seems clear that the behavior in the initial stage of addiction is maintained either by the induction of positive feelings or the reduction of unpleasant feelings. It is possible to predict to some extent whether a person will become an addict. Young addicts as a group share three characteristics: they become frustrated very easily, they have strong feelings of depression and see their lives as futile, and they have no optimism or hope for the future.

Nurco (1979) lists a series of predictors for future drug addicts:

1. Family influence is important. Young persons from single-parent families having less rigid convictions and more opportunistic life-styles than average have a higher incidence of addiction. Parents who use drugs and/or approve of drug use pass this behavior on to their children. This is especially true if the parent is an addict or an alcoholic.

2. Antisocial behavior is commonly seen in the young addiction-prone person long before he or she starts using drugs. This person usually was a poor or failing student, skipped school, broke rules and regulations, used marijuana or alcohol in school, dropped out, got into trouble with the law, had early experience with sex, and so on. The more deviant the behavior and the earlier it appeared, the stronger is the likelihood of future addiction. Having an antisocial father is a strong predictor for the youth's being antisocial. Three situations substantially contribute to the probability of adult antisocial behavior, including drug abuse: (a) as a child, being placed in a residence away from both parents, (b) growing up in extreme poverty, and (c) growing up in a family lacking parent figures of each gender.

3. There may be genetic factors that predispose a person to deviant behavior and addiction, although there is little concrete evidence

for this. The fact that only a small percentage of those who experiment with narcotics ever become full-fledged addicts in spite of unfavorable environmental pressures seems to support this hypothesis. If a specific biochemical abnormality were discovered, it could be valuable as a predictor.

Some addicts are not able to, or simply do not care to, carry out many normal functions, whereas others can keep a job and are able to function fairly normally. There are known cases of surgeons, lawyers, and persons in other professions carrying out their jobs while on opiates. Still other narcotics users apparently are able to limit their use and do not become truly addicted. We know very little about controlled users, or "chippers." They are extremely secretive, in contrast to the usual addict found in a treatment program. Between one-third and one-half of those applying to methadone maintenance programs are refused, because they use heroin infrequently and are not addicted, and they would become addicted to methadone during the course of treatment. It has been estimated that the heroin-using population in the United States is between 3 and 4 million people, of whom only 10% are addicted. There was no common personality type found in one study of "chippers." They were more afraid of being forced into abstinence than of losing control and becoming addicted. This type of user regulates the circumstances and frequency of heroin use to prevent detection, addiction, and side effects. Typical examples of self-imposed rules are using the drug only on Friday and Saturday evenings, so one could go to work Monday morning, budgeting the amount spent on heroin, and being careful to sterilize injection equipment (Zinsberg, 1979).

Even people who have become addicted apparently can control their addiction when circumstances change. A study on addicted Viet-vets showed that only 20% had used opiates occasionally after return. Only one-eighth of this group had had any period of stateside addiction (Zinsberg, 1979).

OTHER NARCOTICS

A large number of narcotics are found on the street or in medical use today. Some of these are methadone, codeine, hydromorphone (Dilau-did®), paregoric, meperidine (Demerol®), and many more synthetics. A few of the more commonly abused opioids will be discussed briefly. Except where noted, they are all Schedule II drugs.

Methadone

Methadone was first synthesized in Germany in 1943, when opiate analgesics were not available because of the war. It was first called *Dolophine®* after Adolph Hitler; one company still uses that trade name. Other trade names are Adanon®, Westadone®, Amidone®, and several others. It is an effective analgesic, equal to morphine if injected and more active if taken orally. The physiological effects of methadone are the same as those of morphine and heroin. It is a narcotic and produces both psychological and physical dependence. Tolerance to the drug and then physical dependence develop if repeated doses are taken. It is often considered as addictive as heroin if injected.

One of methadone's most useful properties is that of cross-tolerance with other narcotic drugs. If it reaches a sufficiently high level in the blood, methadone blocks heroin euphoria. Withdrawal symptoms of patients physically dependent on heroin or morphine, and the post-addiction craving, can be suppressed by oral administration of methadone. Up to 40 mg per day is the usual amount, but as much as 100 mg may be needed. There were an estimated 70,000 to 75,000 addicts being treated with methadone in 1980. Side effects from methadone are the same as those from morphine and heroin, including constipation. Properly used, it is a safe drug. The only documented death directly related to methadone in a person using it as prescribed was caused by untreated, severe constipation.

On the street the pills are often called *dollies*, after the original name, Dolophine®. When injecting methadone, some people get a euphoric feeling similar to that obtained from heroin; addicts on methadone maintenance sometimes get euphoric if the dose is increased too rapidly. Methadone is soluble in water but is formulated with insoluble excipients (inert ingredients) to deter abuse by injection. There are cases of persons who injected it like heroin and developed serious lung conditions from particles that lodged in the tissue, creating a condition somewhat like emphysema. Deaths from overdose of the drug have been higher than from heroin in some of the major cities like New York. Many of these deaths were in young children of parents in methadone programs permitted to take a few doses home, or teenagers trying to shoot up with street methadone or methadone in combination with other drugs. If the person is found in time, treatment with the antagonist, naloxone, will reverse the narcotic effects.

Methadone is only effective for about 24 to 36 hours, so the addict usually must take methadone every day. Experimental clinical use began in the mid-1970s with a longer-acting drug called *acetylmethadol* (levo-alpha-acetylmethadol, or LAAM). LAAM is effective for up to three days, so patients need only come in for their dose three times a week. This makes it easier for them to hold down jobs and gives them more freedom than with methadone maintenance. It also reduces or eliminates altogether the risk of giving an addict doses of methadone to take at home. LAAM is an addictive narcotic: its effects and side effects are the same as morphine, including a withdrawal syndrome after tolerance has developed (Ling & Blaine, 1979).

Hydromorphone

Hydromorphone (Dilaudid®) is prepared from morphine. It is used as an analgesic and cough suppressant. It is a stronger analgesic than heroin. On the street, it is taken in tablet form or injected.

Meperidine

Meperidine (Demerol®) is a synthetic drug that is used as an analgesic. It can be taken in tablet form or injected. It is about one-tenth as powerful as morphine, but it can be addictive. This drug has been given too freely by some physicians: tolerance is acquired rapidly, and over a period of time it causes physical dependence. Meperidine addicts may use large daily doses (3 to 4 g per day).

Codeine

Codeine is a naturally occurring constituent of opium. It is not very powerful, but it is a narcotic and can be addictive if enough is taken. It is not used much on the street now, because it would take a sizable amount to maintain a habit. At one time many cough syrups contained codeine, such as terpin hydrate and codeine elixir, and addicts would buy large quantities. There are tighter controls on codeine cough syrups now, but there are still over 40 codeine mixtures on the market to treat coughs and colds or to provide pain relief. Thirty milligrams of codeine taken orally is equivalent in analgesic action to one or two aspirin (325 to 600 mg aspirin).

Pentazocine

Pentazocine (Talwin®) was synthesized in an effort to develop an effective analgesic with low abuse potential. When taken orally, it is approximately equivalent to codeine in analgesic potency. Its effects on the central nervous system are similar to those of the opioids, but it will not prevent withdrawal symptoms in a narcotic addict. In fact, it will precipitate withdrawal symptoms if given to a person on methadone maintenance who needs an analgesic (Lowinson & Millman, 1979). Talwin® is not commonly abused orally, but the drug can be extracted from the tablet and injected with the antihistamine, tripelennamine (pyribenzamine). This combination is known as *Ts and Blues*. For this reason, Talwin® was placed in Schedule IV.

Propoxyphene

Propoxyphene (Darvon®, Dolene®, and so on) is structurally related to methadone but is a much weaker analgesic. Darvon® is about one-fifth to one-tenth as potent as codeine. It and codeine are frequently given in combination with aspirin. Darvon® is used for treatment of mild to moderate pain that is not adequately relieved by aspirin. Toxic doses cause delusions, hallucinations, and convulsions. Taken orally, it is weaker than codeine in its respiratory depressant effect. However, propoxyphene potentiates with alcohol and other CNS depressants in depression of respiration. This Schedule IV drug ranks second only to the barbiturates as the leading prescription drug associated with drug deaths.

Paregoric

Paregoric is a mixture of opium, camphor, benzoic acid, and anise oil in alcohol. The formulation was first used about 1715; the name *paregoric* means *soothing preparation*. This Schedule III preparation was used to control diarrhea and as a cough suppressant, but it has largely been replaced by synthetic opioids. Paregoric has been abused by mixing it with tripelennamine (the same antihistamine used with Talwin®): it is then called *Blue Velvet*.

Dextromethorphan and Levopropoxyphene

Dextromethorphan and levopropoxyphene (Novrad®) are synthetics used in cough remedies that can be purchased without prescription.

NARCOTIC ANTAGONISTS

There are several drugs, called *narcotic antagonists*, that are available for clinical or investigational use to (1) treat opioid overdose, (2) treat opiate addicts, and (3) diagnose physical dependence. First, opioid overdose treatment to reverse respiratory depression might be called for to treat a newborn infant whose mother was given meperidine during labor, to bring a person out of anesthesia more quickly, or to treat a

person who took an overdose of some street opiate and was brought in to an emergency room barely breathing and comatose. Second, some opiate addicts find the treatment programs that use an antagonist are better suited to their needs than the methadone or LAAM maintenance programs. They are not substituting one addicting drug for another, as the methadone programs do. (Various treatment programs are described in Chapter 20.)

The effects of the antagonists vary, depending on their structure and on whether the person who takes them is physically dependent on opioids. Naloxone and nalorphine reverse respiratory depression within one to two minutes after injection. The effects last from one to four hours, depending on the dose. If the person has taken an overdose of heroin or morphine, he or she will probably not need additional injections of the antagonist. However, methadone and especially LAAM have a much longer action than heroin or morphine, and the person who overdosed on one of these two drugs may relapse into a fatal respiratory depression if he or she leaves the medical facilities too soon.

Naloxone and nalorphine are not effective if taken orally. Cyclazocine and naltrexone are antagonists that are effective if taken orally, and they are used as investigational drugs in the treatment of addicts. For example, a 100-mg oral dose of naltrexone will block the euphoric effects of 25 mg of heroin, injected intravenously, for 48 hours (Jaffe & Martin, 1980). (An average bag of street heroin contains about 10 mg.)

The third use of narcotic antagonists, diagnosis of addiction, uses the drugs to precipitate the withdrawal symptoms in a clinical setting when a person applies for admission to a methadone or a LAAM maintenance program. A significant number of applicants do not give convincing case histories: their reported amount of narcotic use seems low, they do not have extensive needle track scars, analysis of urine samples is negative, and they seem more addicted to the perceived glamor of heroin addiction than to the drug. Sometimes the applicant is a reporter looking to discredit a maintenance program by showing how easy it is to obtain free methadone. Small, subcutaneous doses of naloxone will precipitate a moderate to severe withdrawal syndrome in a person physically dependent on opioids. It occurs within minutes and lasts about two hours. The drug has no effect on a person who is not addicted.

ENDORPHINS: ENDOGENOUS OPIOID PEPTIDES

The products of the opium poppy are the most effective pain killers known to medicine. Why should this particular plant product, or indeed any plant product, have this effect in an animal? The effectiveness of morphine is an accident of molecular architecture. Morphine's chemical nature is such that enough survives the acid in the stomach and is absorbed across the intestines, enters the bloodstream, and crosses the blood-brain barrier into the brain; many natural products would not make it that far. Like curare, muscarine, and nicotine, morphine has an effect on the nervous system because the receptors that respond to these drugs are really receptors for endogenous compounds, which the plant products just happen to fit well enough to activate a response.

A great deal of research was done in the 1960s to characterize receptors on the surface of, and inside of, cells to understand how cells respond to hormones and neurotransmitters. The effects of many synthetic modifications of morphine were studied in animals. Scientists learned exactly what molecular architecture was required to produce the characteristic effects of morphine. It gradually became apparent that there must be highly specific receptors on nerve cells in particular locations in the brain, spinal cord, and nerves to the intestines that responded to morphine. By 1973 the opiate receptors had been located by using radioactively labeled opiates that bound tightly to the receptors. Then the search began for an endogenous morphine-like neurotransmitter.

In 1975, two substances were discovered in animal brain tissue that have the same pharmacological actions as morphine and heroin. These were small peptides, each consisting of a chain of five amino acids. They were named *enkephalins*, from the Greek word meaning *in the head.* Soon thereafter much larger peptides were isolated from the pituitary gland. The term *endorphin* is now used in a general way to mean any endogenous morphine-like peptide.

Since this discovery, endorphin-containing neurons and opiate receptors have been located in the pain pathways in the brain and spinal cord and in the nerves supplying the intestines. The endorphins are in the nerve terminals, like neurotransmitters. This means they can be released by nerve activity to act on the opiate receptors of adjacent neurons. Thus release of endorphin in the spinal cord can shut down pain messages and prevent their ascent to the brain by inhibiting other neurons. Suppose a nerve cell uses acetylcholine or dopamine as its neurotransmitter. If this acetylcholine- or dopamine-containing nerve cell has opiate receptors, and if endorphin is released nearby, the release of acetylcholine or dopamine will be decreased. Thus the function of the nerve cell on which the acetylcholine or dopamine would have acted will be depressed. However, we still know very little about what kinds of circumstances turn the release of endorphins on or off, and where this occurs in the brain or spinal cord (Goldstein, 1979).

Certain types of artificial stimulation that bring about pain relief may work through release of endorphins. A small electric current applied to specific areas of the central nervous system has been used to treat intractable pain. This, and acupuncture, seem to work by releasing endorphins (see Chapter 13). Naloxone blocks the effect of electrical stimulation and of acupuncture, just as it blocks the effect of morphine. A study of one patient with congenital insensitivity to pain further suggests a role of endorphin release in modulating pain. Injection of naloxone caused a dramatic but temporary ability to feel pain like normal subjects (Goldstein, 1979).

Although it is interesting to speculate on the possible role of endorphins in heroin addiction, there is at present no evidence showing endorphin abnormalities in addicts. It is possible that an inborn defect in endorphin production might predispose some individuals to become heroin addicts. It is also possible that the withdrawal syndrome is due to an endorphin deficiency caused when the heroin, morphine, or methadone is taken away. Research in this new area may solve these riddles.

DRUGS AND PAIN

Although we do not understand pain, it is one of the major reasons we take drugs. Pain is basically a warning device telling us something is wrong. However, we all have different pain thresholds that vary even in the same person from one situation and time of day to another. There are some people who feel no pain. These people must be very observant and careful, because, without the warning signal of pain that could prevent damage, they could break a bone, get a serious infection, or burn themselves. In this chapter we will first discuss the important psychological and physiological factors that influence pain perception, then how methods of treatment, including drugs, interact with these factors.

PSYCHOLOGICAL ASPECTS OF PAIN

People perceive and react to pain differently. Both perception of and reaction to pain are to a large extent learned. In most cultures certain individuals are taught that they must not show a reaction to pain or that only particular types of reaction are acceptable. In many societies reaction also varies with age and gender. For example, in most Western countries, if a girl falls off her bicycle and scrapes her knee or elbow in gravel, it is more acceptable for her to cry a bit than if a boy of the same age is injured in exactly the same manner. One expects the boy to grimace, cover his pain with the best laugh he can manage, and get back on the bicycle. The older the child, the less sympathy one is likely to show, even though the injury is identical. There is evidence that women have a lower maximum tolerance to pain but are not more sensitive (threshold level) than men (Notermans & Tophoff, 1975). It is likely that societal

programming is involved in sensitivity to some extent.

Under the influence of hypnosis or in a self-induced trance some people feel no pain. For example, there are religious groups called *flagellants* who beat themselves with whips, as part of a ritual of penitence, until the blood flows down their backs. Yet they are apparently in a trance, even smiling, as they make their way in the procession. In experiments with experienced meditators or yogis it has been shown that their pain threshold is much higher when they are in an altered state of consciousness and that it took a strong stimulus to get a painful response.

Some physiologists believe there is a relationship between hair color or skin pigmentation and tolerance to pain. Redheads have been shown to be the most sensitive to pain, blonds were next, and brunettes were least sensitive. No reasonable physiological hypothesis has been found to explain this observation, and other studies have not found the relationship. There is, however, evidence that the time of day is important in sensitivity to pain. The daily (circadian) rhythm for males and females shows that they both are likely to be more sensitive in the mornings and less sensitive in the evenings (Procacci, Della Corte, Zoppi, Romano, Maresca, & Voegelin, 1974).

Some studies indicate that introverted persons tend to be more sensitive to pain than extroverts. The introverted person is quite often more self-aware and more conscious of his or her inner feelings and bodily sensations. The U.S. Army Research Institute of Environmental Medicine made a series of psychological studies relating to the way pain was sensed and the person's level of sensitivity to pain. It was found that analytical, introverted people were more sensitive to pain than the opposite psychological type—the impulsive, easygoing, extroverted type. The latter was more impulsive, more apt to try things without studying them through first, and was more tolerant of pain. The research team pointed out that the analytical, more introverted type of person tends to focus more sharply and acutely on details of his or her environment, which includes aches and pains.

Another surprising fact was that right-handed persons report that they are more sensitive to pain in their right hand than in the left. In studies at the New York University Medical Center it was shown that the right hand had a lower pain threshold than the left. The dominant side of the body, which is usually the right, is either more sensitive or more closely integrated with a person's affective behavior than is the subordinate side.

Studies have also shown that pain is felt less by older people than by younger. Whether older persons simply ignore pain or whether they have a higher pain threshold because of aging nervous systems is not clear. Shock, stress, and anger also affect pain perception. Reports on injured soldiers have shown that a high level of arousal or intense concentration on a vital task can completely block the perception of pain until the situation is over. Even severe wounds and blood loss can be blocked out when it is sufficiently important to the person. Athletes often report similar experiences with less severe injuries. For example, a marathon runner received a slight skull fracture from a rifle bullet; when he completed the race and was being treated, he said he thought it was something like an insect bumping into him. Anger can make a person block out pain temporarily; however, this mechanism is also not clearly understood. Research must be done to show whether it is caused by pain blockade, pain interpretation, controlled release of endorphins, suppressed release of pain-interpreting neurotransmitters, or something else. Understanding natural pain-blocking mechanisms could lead to much more effective treatment of severe pain, such as that caused by terminal cancer or extensive burns.

Studies of the effects of placebo drugs have been done to help researchers understand the psychological aspects of pain perception. For example, in studies made by Henry Beecher of Harvard Medical School of postoperative treatment in hospitals, it was found that an astounding 35% of the patients had their pain satisfactorily relieved by placebos. This percentage is very high when one considers that morphine alleviates pain in only about 75% of the cases, not 100%. Furthermore, the effectiveness of a placebo is much greater when the patient is under severe psychological stress than when he or she is not. A placebo is effective in only 3.2% of persons voluntarily participating in pain research projects. In other words, a placebo is ten times more effective in relieving pain of pathological origin (for example, following surgery) than experimentally produced pain (Beecher, 1975)!

Another curious, unexplained phenomenon in pain perception is *phantom pain*. This may occur following amputation of a limb. Some amputees actually suffer pain "in" a missing arm or leg. How or why this occurs is not understood.

There are complex psychological ramifications of pain perception. One of these is *sadism*, named after the Marquis de Sade. He wrote many of his accounts while he was in prison after being convicted of whipping and torturing prostitutes. A sadist obtains sexual satisfaction from inflicting pain on others and may require this to reach orgasm. The opposite extreme—the enjoyment of having pain inflicted on oneself—is called *masochism*, after von Sacher Masoch, who wrote about his enjoyment of pain. An old joke says that the perfect relationship would be between a sadist and a masochist, in which the masochist begs "Beat me!" and the sadist sneers and says "No—you enjoy it too much." Masochism is sometimes linked to religious penance, although it is discouraged as self-indulgence by religious authorities. Civil authorities may intervene to prevent devotees from maiming or killing themselves, such as in crucifixion or flagellation rites. In early Christian orders, some people wore hair shirts next to the skin. This caused intense itching, both from the irritating hair and from the population of body lice that thrived in this environment. This use of discomfort or pain for penance was a factor in the slowness of the acceptance of pain-relieving drugs in the Western world. St. Augustine, the early Catholic theologian (354–430 A.D.), frowned on the use of analgesics such as salicylic acid (the natural compound from the willow family used to make aspirin), because he believed that pain was punishment for sins. The use of anesthetics for relief of pain during childbirth was withheld for years because people believed the birth process should be painful. This belief was partially due to the Biblical statement, "in labor you shall bear children," and partially to the opinion that anesthetics would harm the child (as was often the case with the early types of anesthesia).

PHYSIOLOGICAL ASPECTS OF PAIN

What Is Pain?

The entire surface of the body, except the eyes, the nails, and the natural orifices, is covered with skin in which there are pain receptors as well as receptors for temperature and pressure. Some parts of the skin have more nerve receptors for pain, called *nociceptors*, than others. Thus a sharp needleprick on the fingertip will cause pain, but one on the back may cause no pain. Fingertips have a large number of pain receptors, whereas the skin on the back has only scat-

tered receptors. This insensitivity was known to witch hunters in the Middle Ages and in the 1600s in Salem, Massachusetts. They called the insensitive areas on the back *witches' spots*, where demons were supposed to be hiding.

Organs such as the liver, kidneys, spleen, and pancreas are insensitive to mechanical or chemical stimulation. Pain that arises in these organs is caused by interference with their blood supply or with adjacent organs. The brain itself can feel no pain, because it lacks pain receptors, but the meninges (membranes that cover the brain and spinal cord) and the blood vessels in the brain send pain impulses in response to stimuli. Infection of the meninges causes one of the most severe forms of pain known. The uterus is another pain-insensitive organ, because it has few pain receptors, and it can be surgically cut or electrocauterized (burned to stop bleeding) with very little sensation of pain. Some pain can occur during childbirth as the cervix of the uterus is dilated, or enlarged, to permit delivery. One of the most sensitive organs to pain is the testicle: the squeezing or striking of the testicle causes intense pain that may cause vomiting and even send the man into shock.

Headache is one type of pain experienced by almost everyone. On the basis of the cause, headaches have been classified into three categories and fifteen types. The first category includes headaches that arise from the blood vessels supplying the head; they are known as *vascular headaches*. Migraine is the most common of the chronic vascular headache types and is by far the most incapacitating. Migraine has been recognized since early times. Our first description of this type of headache comes from Arateus of Cappadocia, who wrote about it in the first century. Galen later called this type of headache *hemicrania*, from the words *hemi* and *kranion*, because the pain is often limited to one side of the head. Migraines are believed to occur when the blood vessels in the head have been enlarged (dilated) longer than necessary to supply nutrients to the brain. As the blood vessel walls expand, they exert pressure and thus activate pain receptors. The vascular headache may be brought on by anxiety-provoking situations and even physical stress.

The second category of headache arises from muscles and muscular contractions. The *tension headache*, as it is called, occurs when there is sustained contraction of the skeletal muscles supporting the head and neck. The result of prolonged contraction is pain: a dull, steady pain, as opposed to the throbbing pain typical of vascular headaches. People suffering from migraine headache may compound their problems with prolonged tension, resulting in a headache that has both vascular and muscular components.

In both categories of headache described so far there are no structural changes evident between attacks, and there is a close relationship between the occurrence of headache and anxiety-provoking situations. Psychological factors may be involved in several ways. First, the factors may precipitate changes in specific physiological functions, such as cranial vascular changes, sustained muscle contraction, and the increased or decreased activity of the various endocrine glands. Second, these changes may come about as a "hysterical" response—that is, the conversion of an emotional conflict into a hysterical dysfunction.

The third category of headache is caused by direct irritation of the nerves of the head. These headaches can be caused by neuritis, Meniere's disease (a disease of the inner ear), and injury to a nerve. This class is less common than the others.

The American Medical Association has classified headaches into 15 different types, with most of them fitting into one of the three major categories just discussed. As one studies the "common" headache it becomes apparent that each type may be highly specific to the individual, the situation, and a particular part of the brain.

The nociceptors are very much like other receptors in the body that perceive warmth, cold, and touch. All of these sensations apparently can produce pain if they are intense enough. The pain from these receptors seems to be caused by increased activation—the steady firing of nerve impulses that stimulates the pain receptors. The nociceptors are on neurons leading to the spinal cord and brain. The chain of neurons carrying pain messages is often called a *fiber*, or *pain tract*. Some of these pain fibers carry pain messages at varying rates to the spinal cord and brain and cause perception of different types of pain. The A-delta fibers carry pain quickly and give the feeling of pricking or sharp pain. The C-fibers are slow carriers and give a sensation of dull, diffuse, or burning pain. Interpretation of pain is carried out in specific areas of the cerebral cortex after the pain message travels through the pain tracts to and through the thalamus. The thalamus (see Figure 2–5 on p. 28) is believed to be a pain-signal terminal, or switchboard (Bond, 1979). The thalamus is linked to the emotional centers of the brain through the limbic system and hypothalamus. It is thought that their close connections may help explain how stress and emotional states can modify the way we feel pain.

There are other ways to classify pain besides sharp and dull. One classification divides it into two types, depending on its location: *visceral* or *somatic*. Visceral pain, such as intestinal or stomach cramps, arises from the nonskeletal portions of the body. Narcotics are quite effective in reducing pain of this type. Somatic pain arises in the skeletal muscle or bone. It is usually caused by muscle strains, sprains, arthritis, and even some types of headache caused by muscle stress in the neck muscles. Somatic pain is usually relieved by aspirin or similar drugs.

Another way of classifying pain relates the type of neuron or fiber that carries the pain signal and the pain type. Bright pain is associated with the large, fast neurons (A-delta) and lasts a relatively short period of time. Dull, aching pain and diffuse or burning pain are associated with small, slow-acting neurons, or C-fibers. This pain lasts for a longer period of time. An example of each type: bright pain results from hitting your finger with a hammer, and dull pain is the long-term ache afterwards. The A-delta fibers are low-threshold, meaning that the stimulus does not have to be powerful, and the C-fibers are high-threshold.

Some biological substances are thought to be related to pain signals. First it was found that, if some of the fluid in the tissue surrounding a severe wound was injected under uninjured skin, intense pain resulted in the site of injection. Later it was found that the substances *histamine* and *bradykinin* were probably responsible for this pain. A peptide called *substance P* may also be involved in neurotransmission of painful stimuli. This biochemical compound is found in nerves known to transmit pain impulses, and, when its concentration is depleted following repeated stimulation, the pain goes away. The chemical in red peppers, capsaicin, is used in pain experiments because it causes instant, intense pain. The amount of substance P in nerve tracts increases following administration of capsaicin. After repeated administration of capsaicin, the painful effect wears off, and the amount of substance P is depleted (Marx, 1979). This might mean that, if substance P release could be blocked in burn victims or terminal cancer patients, their pain could be alleviated.

It is believed by some researchers that the enkephalins or endorphins, the endogenous morphine-like compounds, may produce pain-relieving effects by blocking substance P release. It has been hypothesized that there is a "pain gate" that opens to allow pain messages to go through the spinal cord to the brain. If the pain gate were closed, then there would be no perception of pain (although the cause of the pain would still be there). It is possible that the endorphins may close the pain gate and thus block the effect of substance P (Marx, 1979).

The cutting off of blood (*ischemia*) to an area of tissue causes intense pain. This may be due to lack of oxygen, because rapid oxygenation alleviates the pain. There is also evidence that when tissue is injured, a substance called *neurokinin* is formed that will stimulate sensory nerves. Neurokinin seems to stimulate the pain pathways either through substance P or some other mechanism. Histamine, mentioned earlier, is a breakdown product of damaged tissue, and it causes swelling and reddening of tissue along with increased sensitivity. Pain may be partly caused by pressure from the swollen tissue as well as the biochemical irritants (histamine and bradykinin).

How Is Pain Measured?

Pain threshold is that level at which a stimulus is first recognized as unpleasant (the "ouch!" point), whereas pain tolerance is that greater level of stimulation at which the subject says he or she can't stand any more. Pain threshold is more dependent on physiological factors, and pain tolerance on psychological factors.

The increase in stimulus intensity that will cause a barely detectable difference in degree of pain is called a *just noticeable difference* (JND). By applying all different stimulus intensities between the level of no pain at all and the most intense pain that the subject can tolerate, it has been found that the average person can discern approximately 22 JNDs. By contrast, vision brightness detection has about 100 steps, and hearing about 120 JNDs. For measurement of pain, two JNDs are equal to one measure of pain intensity. This unit is often called a *Dol*.

One common method of producing a standard pain stimulus is to plunge the arm into ice water. After a few minutes the pain will become intense. Another method is to apply pressure around the arm, thus cutting off the flow of blood (just like leaving a blood pressure cuff on too long). This will result in pain in a short period of time. A third method is to shine a light of known intensity onto a spot of lampblack on the forehead or skin for a set length of time. Standards have been determined for this method. Other methods are subjecting the skin to a set pressure (a pain machine was made for this purpose), pressing a solid object against a protruding bone, such as the elbow, with a measured force, heating the skin with measured amounts of heat, and applying a controlled electrical stimulus to the teeth. All these have the advantage of being nondestructive to tissue and are used to test the effectiveness of new pain-relieving (analgesic) drugs.

Almost all pain-relieving drug tests start with experimental animals, such as laboratory rats. The rats are lined up in test cages with their tails hanging down into a tank. Some rats are given various dosages of the drug to be tested, whereas control rats are given something inert, to control for the effect of handling the animal and administration of the drug. Hot water is poured into the tank over the rats' tails, and the length of time it takes each rat to elevate its tail out of the water is recorded. Another test is to place the animals, some of which have been given the test drug, on a laboratory hot plate and record the time it takes them to lick their paws.

A harmless way to measure your own pain resistance is to measure the time in seconds you can comfortably refrain from blinking your eyes (not looking at a light). The cornea is sensitive to drying out, and stimulates a blink reflex. Most people will want to blink within 30 to 45 seconds.

METHODS USED TO RELIEVE PAIN

This section will describe some techniques used to alleviate pain. Although there are still mysteries about the nature and causes of pain, a number of techniques will lessen it. However, the means by which these methods work are also not always known. The methods currently being used include *physiotherapy, manipulation, counterirritation, chemical agents, nerve blocking* and *surgery, electrical stimulation,* and *behavioral modification.*

Physiotherapy

Physiotherapy usually entails treatment by natural means, such as massage and the application of heat or cold, which relieve some types of pain. One of the major reasons that these techniques seem to work is that they help to overcome muscle spasm. Muscle spasms cause constriction of the muscular walls of arterioles, which causes pain. Diathermy and use of radiant heat are techniques that have developed from heat and massage treatment. Cold may be effective in some cases for the relief of pain by raising the threshold of pain in the nociceptors. Cooling the area of a burn, for example, or applying a cooling evaporating lotion may relieve the discomfort in a painful area. Application of an icebag to the neck or forehead used to be frequently recommended for headaches as well as for pain in joints, and it sometimes helped.

Manipulation

Manipulation is one of the more controversial methods used to relieve pain, partly because of the damage that can be done by unqualified or inept practitioners and partly because of our orientation toward use of drug, or chemical, cures. This method involves correction of a problem, such as a pinched nerve, by manipulation of the structures to relieve the pressure on the nerve. It would also include correction of a dislocated limb by careful positioning so that the joint slips back into place. A qualified osteopathic physician is trained to use both manipulative and drug therapy and uses the approach he or she thinks best suited to the situation. A chiropractor (from the Greek words for *hand* and *practical*) is trained that disease is caused by interference with nerve function and that this can be corrected by adjusting the appropriate segments of the spinal column. Clearly, an unqualified person can paralyze a patient by forceful manipulation of the spine, whereas a good chiropractor can give more relief to some patients than drugs can.

Counterirritation

Counterirritants are substances that substitute one type of pain for another. The presence of pain in one area of the body seems to raise the threshold of pain elsewhere. Hippocrates recommended biting the lips when pain was severe. People have long used something to bite down on, such as a stick or wad of cloth, to help them endure pain (hence the saying "bite the bullet"). The old method of applying hot mustard plasters if a person had internal pain seemed to work because their irritating effect canceled out the original pain that he or she was very much aware of. When muscle spasms or circulatory problems were the cause of the pain, the mustard plasters improved blood flow and helped to

ease discomfort. Some types of muscle liniment do the same thing, and, although they may not be able to cure or stop pain, they make the person less aware of it and indirectly may aid in relieving muscle spasms, circulatory problems, and so forth.

Acupuncture, in which needles are inserted at specific points and depths on the surface of the body, seems to be related to the technique of counterirritation, but there are still many unanswered questions about how it works. Why would insertion of needles produce analgesia in distant parts of the body? Why does analgesia take about 20 minutes to develop and persist for some time after the needles have been withdrawn? The mild stimulation of the acupuncture needles may activate the A-delta pain fibers; when these impulses reach the spinal cord and brain they interfere with transmission from the C-fibers, so that severe pain is kept from conscious awareness. There also is some evidence that acupuncture may work by releasing endorphins. As previously discussed, these natural opiates are potent pain relievers. Experiments on monkeys and humans have shown that acupuncture does not work if the endorphin receptors in the brain are blocked with the drug naloxone.

Enough data are now available to show that acupuncture does truly enable the patient to stand what would usually be a painful type of surgery. Not all patients respond to acupuncture, and facilities that use this type of analgesia for surgery usually also have alternative methods available that are more familiar to Western physicians.

Chemical Agents

There are two classes of drug that reduce pain or the awareness of pain. *Anesthetics* (meaning *non-sensing*) reduce awareness or block consciousness completely. The barbiturates and the volatile anesthetics, such as ether, are the primary examples of this kind of substance. The second group are the *analgesics* (meaning *without pain*). These drugs reduce pain without causing loss of consciousness. The narcotics fit in this class, as do aspirin and phenacetin.

Chemical agents are the pain relievers most frequently used today. There are hundreds of chemicals that can give local or general pain relief. The science of anesthesia is now quite complex, but until about 150 years ago there were only a few important drugs used to relieve pain—opium, belladonna, marijuana, and alcohol. The first reference to the possibility of surgical anesthesia by inhalation was made in 1799 by Davy, who experimented with nitrous oxide (laughing gas). It was used in dentistry first; in fact, a dentist gave the first surgical demonstration of inhalation anesthesia to a group of physicians at Massachusetts General Hospital in 1846. William Morton administered ether during removal of a neck tumor. Unlike an earlier demonstration with nitrous oxide, in which the patient woke up during the surgery screaming in pain, the surgery was completed with the patient unconscious, and the skeptical physicians were greatly impressed. Since that time, many other anesthetics and analgesics have been developed (Cohen, 1975).

Most chemical pain relievers act by interrupting pain pathways, canceling the perception of pain, or by modifying the person's feeling toward pain. Some induce forgetfulness, so that when the person recovers he does not remember the painful experience. Others, such as LSD, alter perception, so that while the pain continues (as in terminal cancer) the patient can be calm about it and observe the state he or she is in, instead of being totally involved in the pain.

The psychotropic drugs are frequently used to relieve pain, not because they have analgesic properties, but for their calming and tension-relieving effect. These drugs include the minor tranquilizers (Valium®, Librium®), the major tranquilizers (Thorazine® and others), antidepressants, and even stimulants in some cases (amphetamine, caffeine, and others). Valium®, for example, both reduces tension and can relax muscles as well. This is why it is used to relieve tension headaches.

The treatment of extremely severe, long-lasting pain is still difficult. The most effective drugs, such as heroin and morphine, are strongly addicting. The victim of severe burns may have to undergo withdrawal from the narcotics used to control his or her pain after recovery from the burns. The terminal cancer patient, however, is not likely to recover and then face an addiction problem. Some countries, such as Great Britain, recognize this and use heroin legally with the aim of making dying patients' final weeks as comfortable as possible, so they can interact with their families and come to terms with imminent death. The heroin is given orally with cocaine, both of which are dissolved in a mixture of sugar water, alcohol, and chloroform (Brompton's cocktail—see Chapter 8). Morphine may be substituted with approximately equal effectiveness. "Brompton's mixture" is now used in a general sense to designate an alcoholic solution of an opioid (usually heroin or morphine) and either cocaine and/or a phenothiazine tranquilizer. Development of tolerance is not rapid—analgesia can be maintained for months (Jaffe & Martin, 1980).

Nerve Blocking and Surgery

Nerve blocking with an anesthetic or with a nerve-destroying agent is useful if the person is in too weak condition for surgery. The injection must place the drug as close to the nerve as possible. Nerve blocks are not permanent, but can give relief for up to one to two years.

Surgery is a radical way to stop pain, but some types of severe pain can be stopped only by cutting the nerves that carry pain messages. This is done on peripheral nerves, parts of the spinal cord, and in the brainstem (see Figure 2-4 on p. 25). The tradeoff for pain relief is that the person loses function in that part of the body.

Electrical Stimulation

It has been found that electrical stimulation of certain neural pathways can give relief from pain for hours. Electrodes are implanted into the major nerve trunks near the spinal cord and are powered by a battery pack about the size of a pack of cigarettes. The patient turns on the battery stimulator for short periods of time when he or she feels pain, and relief is obtained. This method works best for relief of pain from damaged peripheral nerves and has the advantage of reducing the person's dependence on drugs. Whether the electrical stimulation triggers the release of endorphins, prevents the release of substance P, or blocks the pain pathway in some other way is not known.

Electrical stimulation of the brain has also been tried. Stimulation of a particular region of the brainstem is as effective as opiates for controlling chronic pain. Both stimulation and opiates appear to work by inhibiting the neurotransmission of pain nerves ascending into the brainstem.

Behavioral Modification

Nearly eight of ten persons with chronic pain have no physical basis for their symptoms. Treatment of chronic pain patients requires evaluation of whether there is still a physical cause for the pain behavior (*respondent pain*) or whether the person is expressing learned pain behavior (*operant pain*). Respondent pain often cannot be helped with surgery, and indeed may be made worse. The operant pain patient, however, is not consciously faking his or her pain behavior. Both types genuinely feel pain and need help. Using pain-relieving drugs and tranquilizers may make treatment easier for the physician, but it only masks the problem. A behavioral analysis of a chronic pain patient begins with the attitude that it is irrelevant whether the pain has a "real" or an "imaginary" basis. The relevant question is: what are the factors that influence or control the pain?

The behavioral modification approach withdraws reinforcers, such as bed rest and drugs, and encourages "well behavior" along with a carefully designed exercise program. The medical staff is not unsympathetic to pain and does not try to convince patients it is "all in their head." Instead, nurses will stop to chat with patients as long as they are not discussing pain. The physician asks such things as "How far did you walk yesterday?" instead of "How do you feel?" The physiotherapist will not encourage patients to exercise more than they say they can tolerate, but will only praise them when they complete their current exercise quotas. A high percentage of patients have thus avoided further surgery, hospitalization, and medication. Many have been able to return to work. One pain specialist commented, "People who have something better to do don't hurt as much" (Fordyce, 1976; Greenberg, 1979).

Psychotherapy has been used to a certain extent for relief of pain. It does not have a high rate of success and may be largely replaced by behavioral modification treatment techniques. Hypnosis is another closely related technique. Because its success is so variable and dependent on the individual hypnotist, this potentially valuable method is not widely accepted. The discovery of the endorphins and their role in endogenous pain relief suggests that it is possible that the success of psychotherapy and hypnosis lies in the patient's subconscious ability to release endorphins.

Pain is a complex subject and is not well understood. However, research in this field is progressing rapidly. It is estimated that there are 75 million persons with chronic pain in the United States, 50 million of whom are partially or completely disabled. There are over 295 pain clinics in the United States at present, which indicates how many people are afflicted with chronic pain. Because the need is so pressing, it is probable that better ways of treating pain will be available in the near future.

CHAPTER 14

THE CONTRACEPTIVE DRUGS

CHAPTER OBJECTIVES

1. Describe the types of active hormone found in the three types of oral contraceptive, the injectable contraceptive, and the medicated intrauterine devices.
2. Compare the product (clinical) failure rates of oral contraceptives, intrauterine devices, and spermicidal products. Explain why the actual failure rates are higher.
3. List some drugs that may reduce the effectiveness of oral contraceptives.
4. Name the important life-threatening risks associated with use of oral contraceptives, intrauterine devices, and spermicides.
5. Discuss the connection, if any, between cancer and use of oral contraceptives, intrauterine devices, and spermicides.
6. Discuss the factors involved in the return of fertility following use of oral contraceptives, intrauterine devices, and spermicides.
7. List one beneficial side effect of each of the following: oral contraceptives, a medicated intrauterine device, and a spermicide.
8. Define these terms: progestin, estrogen, androgen, cardiovascular disease, ectopic pregnancy, and pelvic inflammatory disease.

The connection between sexual intercourse and pregnancy is something that human societies learn at an early stage in cultural development. Cultures having this knowledge are very interested in regulating fertility in order to decrease or to increase childbearing or to affect the sex of the offspring. Anthropologists have recorded a rich variety of plant and animal products used to regulate fertility. Some of these, such as crocodile dung paste described in the Petri Papyrus, dated 1850 B.C., were to be placed in the vagina to prevent conception. Others were supposed to be effective if taken orally, such as the water extract prepared by the Paraguayan Matto Grosso Indian women (Himes, 1963; Planas & Kuć, 1968). The latter practice implies an interesting conceptual shift to the idea that taking a plant product by mouth regularly every day—not associated with the time of sexual intercourse—will prevent pregnancy.

Despite continued attempts over the centuries to regulate fertility, it has only been the past generation that has had highly effective, relatively safe contraceptive drugs available. These include the products used intravaginally, such as spermicidal foam tablets; intrauterine devices, with a hormone or an active metal agent; injections that gradually release a hormone for a month or so, and the several types of oral contraceptive.

ORAL CONTRACEPTIVES

Development of effective oral contraceptives (OCs) as we know them depended on the isolation of the natural hormones involved in reproduction. The chemical structures of the important male and female hormones from the gonads (testes and ovaries) were determined in the 1930s. However, the pure hormones isolated from blood and gonads were extremely expensive. It was not until the early 1950s, when chemists found a way to extract similar compounds from a plant (the Mexican yam) and chemically modify them, that synthetic hormones became generally available for contraceptive experiments.

There was no general consensus to concentrate on oral contraceptives for women, although that is what happened. Women are born with all of the germ cells (eggs, or ova) they will ever have. Their reproductive cycle is designed to bring one of these eggs to maturity and release it during each cycle (ovulation). If the egg is not fertilized, another cycle begins. Men are born with germ cell precursors—that is, cells that can form sperm. From puberty through old age they produce millions of sperm daily. Reproductive biologists and physicians involved in the development of oral contraceptives believed it would be easier to prevent the maturation of one germ cell every 28 days (female) than millions of germ cells per day (male). Thus research into a male oral contraceptive has lagged much further behind.

Types of Oral Contraceptive

There are several types of contraceptive pill used by women: the combination, the low-dose progestin ("minipill"), the postcoital ("morning after"), and the sequential. (Sequentials have been almost entirely removed from the market.) The activity of the synthetic hormones depends on their similarity of action to the natural hormones from the ovary, *progesterone* and *estradiol*. Progestins are those synthetically modified compounds that mimic progesterone, estrogens are those that are similar in action to estradiol, and androgens are those that are similar to the male sex hormone, testosterone. The activity of a synthetic progestin is not purely like progesterone, however. It may have some androgenic activity, some estrogenic activity, or even antiestrogenic activity, depending on the progestin's chemical structure. There are about 20 different synthetic progestins and two synthetic estrogens in use in oral contraceptives.

The combination pill contains a fixed ratio of a progestin and an estrogen. The amount of progestin is 10 to 20 times greater than the amount of estrogen, depending on the brand of pill. The woman takes the same composition pill at the same time each day, beginning on the 5th day after the start of menstruation through the 25th or 26th day, again depending on the brand. Then she stops taking pills for that cycle. (Some combination-pill packs include seven placebo tablets to be taken at the end of the cycle, so the woman will not get out of the habit of taking a pill each day.) About two to three days after the last hormone-containing pill is taken, menstruation starts and is counted as day one of the next cycle. If the woman does not menstruate, she should still start taking pills again on the 7th or 8th day after the last pill, or check with her physician about a pregnancy test. The exact schedule should be carefully explained to the woman when she first gets the prescription. When oral contraceptives are taken as directed, the accidental pregnancy rate is less than four per 1000 woman-years of use.

The sequential pill was developed with the idea that it would resemble the pattern of estrogen production followed by progestin in the natural reproductive cycle. The first 15–16 tablets of the sequence were estrogenic, and the final 5–6 tablets were a combination progestin-estrogen. This formula has not been shown to have any advantage over the combination pill, and it exposes women to higher concentrations of synthetic estrogen over a longer period of time. It has a significantly higher risk of pregnancy than the combination pill—about eight per 1000

woman-years of use when taken as directed, with much higher failure rates if the woman forgets to take it daily.

The low-dose progestin pill ("minipill") is taken daily, even during menstruation. It contains no estrogen and has a dosage of progestin that is lower than many combination pills. It has a product failure rate of about eight per 1000 woman-years of use.

The postcoital ("morning after") drug may be either a pill or an injection. Several types of estrogen and progestin have been used for this, including the synthetic diethylstilbestrol (DES), the estrogens used in combination oral contraceptives, and conjugated (natural) estrogens more typically thought of for treatment of postclimacteric problems. An injectable form of hormone may be used instead of an oral form because high doses of estrogen cause nausea and vomiting. When given within 24–72 hours after coitus, DES is almost 100% effective in preventing pregnancy. The effectiveness of postcoitally administered estrogen is less if too much time has elapsed before the treatment is started. The effectiveness of the postcoital progestins is probably comparable but has not been established (Hatcher et al., 1978).

The effectiveness rates for the combination, low-dose progestin, and postcoital contraceptive drugs can be expressed in two ways: The *product effectiveness* rate is the rate obtained in clinical studies; it shows the maximum effectiveness obtained when the woman takes her pill *exactly* as directed. The *user effectiveness* rate indicates a pill's effectiveness when it is taken under everyday, varying circumstances. The user effectiveness rate of a contraceptive will be lower than the product effectiveness rate. For example, if a woman forgets her pill one evening and takes it the following morning, the effective levels of the synthetic hormones in her blood will fluctuate more than they would if she took her pill on time in the evening. If she forgets to take two or more pills, especially in the middle of her cycle, she should use an additional method of contraception for the remainder of that cycle, because the concentration of the pill's hormones in the blood may have declined to ineffective amounts.

In Chapter 5 we discussed drug interactions—mutual effects that can either increase or decrease the action of drugs. There are several drugs that can decrease the effectiveness of oral contraceptives by altering the rate at which the hormones are metabolized and removed from the body. These mostly affect the estrogenic part of the combination oral contraceptive by accelerating its metabolism and thus reducing the effective concentration. For example, diphenylhydantoin (Dilantin®), when used regularly as an anticonvulsant, is known to reduce the effectiveness of oral contraceptives. Phenobarbital, rifampin (used to treat tuberculosis), and the antibiotic ampicillin have the same effect, caused by enzyme induction in the liver. Other drugs, such as antihistamines and tranquilizers that induce liver enzymes, may also reduce the effectiveness of oral contraceptives (Hatcher et al., 1978).

How Estrogens and Progestins Work as Contraceptives

It may seem peculiar to use synthetic hormones that mimic the action of natural hormones to prevent pregnancy. The reproductive cycle is a preparation for pregnancy. It is the result of a complex pattern of hormonal signals between two endocrine glands, directed by the hypothalamus, by which hormones are secreted in particular amounts at specified points. Estradiol and progesterone play an especially important role in this cycle. The estrogen and progestin

in the oral contraceptives disrupt this delicate balance and time sequence.

Maturation of the egg and ovulation, for example, require a particular sequence of two hormones, including estradiol, in specified amounts over a two-week interval. The estrogen in the combination pill is the wrong amount at the wrong time, so ovulation does not occur. The progestin in the combination pill and the progestin pill changes the biochemistry of the reproductive tract in several ways to reduce fertility. For instance, progestin changes cervical mucus secretion so that the mucus becomes increasingly thick and hostile to sperm; the sperm have a difficult time penetrating the mucus barrier. The progestin-produced environment in the vagina, cervix, and uterus is also hostile to sperm metabolism, so fewer sperm are likely to be capable of fertilization. The fertilized egg must implant in the nutrient-rich lining of the uterus (endometrium) or it will not survive. The high doses of estrogen used in the postcoital pill, as well as the progestin in the progestin-only and the combination pill, alter the uterine lining so that implantation does not take place (Hatcher et al., 1978).

Risks Involved in Taking Estrogens and Progestins

The oral contraceptive is the most effective reversible means of preventing unwanted pregnancy, but its use brings various risks with it, depending on the health, habits, and medical history of the user. Women considering taking contraceptive pills may wish to answer the following seven questions before making their decision.

1. *What risks are being compared?* It is important to clarify whether one is talking about risk of unwanted pregnancy, risk of serious danger

to the life and health of the user, or risk of having annoying but minor side effects.

The probability of a young, healthy, sexually active woman becoming pregnant, if she uses no means of protection, is about 20%–30% per reproductive cycle. The statistical risk of dying during pregnancy and childbirth is about 25 per 100,000 women in the United States. Women with access to excellent medical care in the United States have a death rate of about 12 per 100,000; with poor care, the rate is higher than the average. Death rates for pregnancy and childbirth for women under age 20 are about 30% higher than for those aged 20–24, and they increase again markedly over age 40. Pregnant women in a country such as Bangladesh have a death rate of about 200 per 100,000. The point is, pregnancy is by no means risk free. In general, oral contraceptives are much safer than childbirth at all ages below age 40 in both technologically advanced and undeveloped countries (Rinehart & Piotrow, 1979); however, the risks for users are influenced by several variables that will be discussed next.

2. *What is the most important risk for women taking the pill?* The occurrence of circulatory system diseases increases in women using oral contraceptives and is strongly associated with the estrogenic component rather than the progestin. Circulatory system diseases include pulmonary embolism (blood clots, usually from the legs, getting caught in the lungs), myocardial infarction (heart attack), hypertension (high blood pressure), and cerebral hemorrhage (a type of stroke in which the brain is damaged from the uncontrolled bleeding). A study of 46,000 British women showed that pill users had about five times higher death rates from circulatory system diseases than women who had never used oral contraceptives (25.8 per 100,000 versus 5.5 per 100,000 woman-years). The risk increases with the length of time the woman takes the pill, so that women who used pills for five years or more faced a ten times higher risk of death from circulatory system disease than women who never used the pill.

There are two important modifying factors to consider: age and tobacco use. Smoking by itself increases the risk of many circulatory system diseases for all women, regardless of their contraceptive method, and the risk increases with the number of cigarettes smoked daily. Death rates for pill users are high for both smokers and women over 35—about 40 per 100,000 woman-years—and much lower for nonsmokers and women under 35—under 15 per 100,000. So far no study has determined the extent of risk for pill users under 35 who do not smoke and who are not predisposed to develop a circulatory system disease. Although an increased risk probably exists, it is very small (Rinehart & Piotrow, 1979).

Smoking acts synergistically with oral contraceptive use to increase dramatically the risk of stroke. Unlike the risks associated with other types of cardiovascular disease, the risk of stroke appears to persist after the woman stops taking the pill. British and U.S. data also reveal a powerful synergism between smoking and oral contraceptive use for risk of heart attack. Nonsmokers who take oral contraceptives have a slightly higher probability of heart attack than those who neither smoke nor take birth control pills. The risk of blood clots forming in the deep veins of the legs is about four times higher for OC users than nonusers. The blood clot mortality rate associated with pill usage is about two to three per 100,000 women annually. The probability does not appear to increase with duration of pill use but has been associated with the dosage of hormone in the pill. Development of hypertension (high blood pressure) while on oral contraceptives is very rare. Most women can expect to have very small increases in blood pressure when they start to take OCs (about 4 mm Hg in systolic pressure and about 1 mm Hg in diastolic pressure), which is not considered clinically important. The blood pressure usually returns to previous readings when the woman discontinues taking the pill (Rinehart & Piotrow, 1979).

The statistical recommendations are clear. Women who smoke, especially those over 35, should select a means of contraception other than an estrogen-containing pill, or give up tobacco. Older women who are certain they want no more children might give serious consideration to having their fallopian tubes tied, so they can stop taking the pill.

3. *Does the pill cause cancer?* One of the original arguments against oral contraceptive use was the possibility that it causes cancer. The observation that cancers have long latent periods in humans has been used to argue against reaching any conclusions prematurely. Because combination pills have now been in general use since the early 1960s, that line of reasoning is losing some of its force.

In any given year in the United States about one-quarter of female deaths are caused by cancer, and one-quarter of those die of breast cancer. Fortunately, there does not appear to be any relationship between these cancer deaths and the use of oral contraceptives, including number of years of use, age at first use, and length of time since first use. Pill users have a slightly lower rate of ovarian cancer than women who have never used oral contraceptives. A slightly higher rate of cervical cancer is found in pill users, but the increase may not be due to the oral contraceptive. Cervical cancer is caused by a virus, and the earlier the woman starts having intercourse and the greater the number of different sexual contacts she has, the greater is her chance of contracting the disease. Sexually active young women seem more likely to start taking pills to prevent pregnancy than teenagers who have sex occasionally (Rinehart & Piotrow, 1979); thus the pill is implicated in the occurrence of cervical cancer.

A rare type of nonmalignant liver cancer has been found in some OC users—mostly in older women who have used them for a long time. Skin cancer may occur slightly more often in pill users than in nonusers, but the number of cases is small, and the differences between the two groups is not significant.

At the hormone levels used in the combination pills and the progestin pills, oral contraceptives will probably not cause any increase in cancer. The levels of estrogen in the postcoital pill may carry a higher risk, although these are used for short periods of time. There is evidence to show that large doses of estrogens, such as DES and others, taken by postclimacteric women for a number of years increase the incidence of uterine cancer and may increase the incidence of breast cancer. In 1979 the FDA asked manufacturers of estrogen for oral administration to print warning labels so that women would be informed of the danger.

The physician treating a woman needing postcoital contraception must balance the benefits and the risks associated with the estrogens: if she has been raped and is physically and psychologically battered, she may not be able to cope with a possible pregnancy, and estrogens may be the best solution. If another woman needing postcoital contraception simply lost or forgot her diaphragm, the better choice may be insertion of a copper-containing intrauterine device. Both are highly effective.

4. *How long after discontinuing the pill does it take before the woman is fertile?* The risk of infertility after pill discontinuance depends partly on whether the woman has ever been pregnant and why oral contraceptives were prescribed. If the woman has borne one healthy child and is tak-

ing pills to "space" her fertility, the first cycle off the pill probably will not be fertile, but by the third or fourth month she will have returned to normal. Use of another means of contraception, like a diaphragm with spermicidal jelly, for the first three cycles before attempting to get pregnant is often recommended so the pill-associated reproductive changes will have disappeared. Women in their 20s have little suppression of fertility, regardless of how long they have used the pill.

Oral contraceptives are also prescribed for their side effects—for example, to regulate an irregular menstrual cycle, to reduce the volume of the menstrual flow, and to reduce pain associated with menstruation (dysmenorrhea). Women who take the pill for these reasons have a higher probability of reduced fertility both before they start taking the pill, because of the abnormalities in their reproductive pattern, and afterwards, when they wish to become pregnant. An estimated 1% of all women will develop amenorrhea (no menstrual cycle) persisting for a year or more after they discontinue OCs. A few women will even go into a premature climacteric. In some studies, over 50% of the women developing amenorrhea had irregular or dysfunctional menstrual cycles before starting on the pill (Odell & Molitch, 1974). Young women considering the pill only to control the reproductive cycle should probably have a thorough medical evaluation first: perhaps the cycle is irregular because of obesity or a thyroid problem. Regular, strenuous exercise, such as running or ballet, can greatly reduce the volume of menstrual flow. The prostaglandin inhibitors, taken for one or two days per cycle, are effective in controlling dysmenorrhea.

5. *Does the pill cause birth defects?* Several studies involving large numbers of women have found no correlation between oral contraceptive use *prior to* pregnancy and congenital malformations (birth defects). In one U.S. study, 1370 infants with birth defects were compared with 2968 normal infants. The mothers of the babies with birth defects were slightly less likely to have used oral contraceptives in the year before the babies were conceived than were the controls. In another study involving 3000 pill users and over 13,500 nonusers, congenital malformations were also less frequent among infants born to women who had used the pill (Rinehart & Piotrow, 1979).

However, continuing to take oral contraceptives *during* early, undiagnosed pregnancy has been associated with a small increased risk of birth defects such as limb reduction (absence of arms and legs) and heart defects. Heavy smoking (more than 20 cigarettes a day) and use of oral contraceptives before pregnancy is diagnosed appear to act synergistically to produce birth defects. If the woman does not menstruate on schedule for two pill cycles, she should check with her physician and get a pregnancy test as soon as possible.

6. *How important are the other side effects?* Oral contraceptive pills are different from other prescribed drugs in that they are intended to prevent a normal physiological process from occurring, not to treat a disease. This creates ambivalence about taking the pill, as do the widely publicized scare stories about its side effects. However, the psychological and physiological side effects of any drug are difficult to measure. Oral contraceptives have been blamed, with and without justification, for causing migraine headaches, asthma, allergies, increases and decreases in libido, changes in weight and facial pigmentation, mental depression, dizziness, nausea, vomiting, abdominal cramps, fluid retention, and so on, as well as for increasing the risk of the serious conditions previously described, like blood clots.

Oral contraceptives change many aspects of

metabolism and affect the results of laboratory tests in areas not related directly to reproduction. For example, OC use increases blood levels of vitamin A, copper, and iron, whereas it reduces vitamin B2 (riboflavin), vitamin B6 (pyridoxine), vitamin B12, vitamin C, and folic acid levels. Supplemental folic acid is recommended to pill users, and a tenfold increase in the recommended dietary allowance of vitamin B6 may be needed to normalize the metabolic processes that result in low levels of this vitamin. Not all women will need supplements, because their diets vary in natural sources of vitamins. Mental depression associated with oral contraceptives may be relieved by additional vitamin B6 or by changing to the low-dose progestin pill. Treating depression as a symptom is complicated; it can be caused by excessively high estrogen levels, by high progestin levels, and even by inadequate estrogen levels, as well as psychological factors associated with taking oral contraceptives. Of course, many causes of depression are not related to the pill (Hatcher et al., 1978).

Migraine headaches appear to have multiple causes, including dietary and psychological ones, and the pill may make them worse. Another side effect, an increase in libido, is attributed to reduced worry about unwanted pregnancy. Decreases in libido may be due to depression and fatigue or to complex psychological factors related to the reduced potential for pregnancy. Most women report an increase in libido, but some have a significant reduction. Nausea, vomiting, and fluid retention are not as common today as they once were, because the pills have lower levels of estrogen. If morning sickness is a problem, the woman might try taking the pill at dinner instead of at bedtime. Some women may have a problem with acne when they take Ovral®, which has a high androgenic activity, and no problem with acne when the prescription is changed to Demulen® or Ovulen®, which have low androgenic activity. Susceptibility to moniliasis, a vaginal fungus infection, may be decreased by a more estrogenic pill.

Increased weight and nervousness are likely to be psychological side effects. One double-blind, placebo-controlled study compared the incidence of nervousness, depression, and weight gain in five groups of women. Four groups received effective oral contraceptives and one received a placebo; all were instructed to continue using a vaginal diaphragm during the study. The oral contraceptives used included one sequential type, two combination types, and one low-dose progestin type. There was no significant difference among the five groups for depression and nervousness. In a fascinating verification of the placebo effect, the women in the placebo group gained more weight than the women in three of the four oral contraceptive groups, which they blamed on the "pill" (Goldzieher, Moses, Averkin, Scheel, & Taber, 1971).

7. *What effects do oral contraceptives have on the nursing infant?* Small amounts of the synthetic progestins and estrogens have been detected in nursing mothers' milk. Nevertheless, since the pills began to be used in the mid-1950s, very few side effects in breast-fed infants have been reported. A few cases of gynecomastia (abnormal breast enlargement) have been found. Studies in which lactating rhesus monkeys were given large doses of the synthetic estrogens used in the pill showed no effect on the infant monkeys. However, combination oral contraceptives may reduce the amount of milk the mother produces. Thus a low-dose combination or a progestin pill may be the best choice during lactation (Nilsson & Nygren, 1979). The use of oral contraceptives during lactation should also be considered in light of the deleterious effects on the woman, her child, and the developing fetus if she becomes pregnant again too soon.

PROGESTIN INJECTIONS

Long-acting synthetic progestins, in the form of a shot given once every 90 days, are used in about 65 countries by about one million women. The effectiveness of this form of contraception ranks between the combination oral and the progestin oral contraceptive pill. Its mechanism of action is the same as the oral progestin-only pill. Injectable progestin has a very low risk of producing the serious side effects associated with the synthetic estrogens, such as cardiovascular diseases, and it does not reduce milk volume in a lactating mother. However, it may cause irregular menstruation, and it takes an average of 6–12 months after the last shot has ceased effectiveness to return to fertility. Injectable progestins have also been associated with mammary tumors in one test animal. This form of contraception has not been licensed in the United States because beagles given large doses of Depo-Provera®, one of the injectable progestins, developed breast cancers. It has been argued that women metabolize this hormone differently than dogs and that women in countries where Depo-Provera® has been used for many years have not developed breast cancer. Female rhesus monkeys have been given large doses of this hormone without adverse effects.

MEDICATED INTRAUTERINE DEVICES

The intrauterine device, or IUD, is a foreign object placed within the central cavity of the uterus through its opening, the cervix. The original device used in humans in the late 1800s was actually not an IUD, because it had a stem that extended through the cervix into the vagina. The discovery of the effectiveness of the IUD to prevent pregnancy may have been made when the stem broke off, leaving the uterine part in place. Several physicians at this time used intrauterine devices successfully in their practices, but the method did not gain general acceptance. Other physicians were afraid of introducing infection into the woman's reproductive organs, and at that time there were no antibiotics to treat serious infections. It was not until inexpensive plastic IUDs could be produced and there was general availability of effective antibiotics to treat infections that IUDs began to be used.

During the 1960s plastic IUDs in various shapes and sizes were tested and used worldwide. The shape of the IUD does not appear to be important in the contraceptive action, but it is the chief determinant of retention in the uterus. The second generation of intrauterine devices were the medicated devices, in which the plastic became a carrier for other substances such as metals, hormones, and antibleeding agents. The first medicated IUDs were the copper 7 (Cu-7®) and copper T (Tatum-T®), which had fine copper wire wound around the vertical part of the plain plastic devices shaped like a "7" and a "T." Copper was used to improve the IUDs' effectiveness as contraceptives. Researchers in this area believe development of unmedicated devices has gone as far as it can and that breakthroughs in effectiveness will come with the medicated devices.

Types of Medicated Intrauterine Device

In developing medicated IUDs, several considerations need to be studied, such as: What pharmacologic agents should one use? Where should they be placed on the IUD? How much is needed, with what release rate per day? How long will they be effective? Most research with metals is focusing on the optimal amount and placement of copper. The copper 7 and copper T have been available in the United States since the mid-1970s. The copper in these IUDs may be either in the form of a fine wire, with or without a silver core (to prevent the delicate wire from fragmenting), or in the form of bead-like sleeves over the plastic. The amount of surface area of copper exposed to the uterine environment affects its contraceptive action. The copper IUDs are effective for about three years, after which the available copper is sufficiently low that protection is based on the presence of the IUD alone. It should then be replaced with a new copper device. The pregnancy rate for the copper devices is about 15 per 1000 woman-years of use, which is somewhat better than the unmedicated devices (20 per 1000), although there is considerable variability across the range of published studies (Piotrow, Rinehart, & Schmidt, 1979).

The Progestasert®, which releases the hormone progesterone gradually into the uterine cavity, has been available for use since 1976. It maintains effective levels of the hormone for about a year, after which it must be replaced if the woman wishes to continue using this method, although the remaining plastic IUD is almost as effective as the medicated one. Other devices that release progesterone or a synthetic progestin for three or more years are being tested. Pregnancy rates for the Progestasert® are 19 per 1000 woman-years when inserted in women who have had at least one child (Piotrow et al., 1979).

How Intrauterine Devices Work

The precise mechanism by which IUDs prevent pregnancy in humans is not known, partly because research done in animals shows that different mechanisms work in different species.

For example, in sheep, the IUD blocks sperm transport; in guinea pigs, cows, and pigs, the IUD inhibits implantation. The most important effect in humans is believed to be the inflammatory, or foreign-body, reaction in the uterine environment, plus the effect of the metal or hormone in the medicated IUD.

The IUD is a foreign object, and the uterus reacts to it in the same way the body reacts to anything foreign. The insertion of an IUD produces what is called an *inflammatory reaction*: there is a great increase in the number of phagocytes (white blood cells that engulf bacteria, sperm, and other foreign objects) in the central cavity of the uterus. The phagocytes normally attack and engulf slow-moving or dead sperm found in the uterus, and the increased number and activity of phagocytes present in an IUD-containing uterus probably means there are many fewer sperm available for fertilization. The phagocytes may also attack and engulf a fertilized egg that enters the uterus and tries to implant. Other changes that are part of the inflammatory reaction may make the uterine environment unfavorable for implantation.

The metallic copper on the copper IUD slowly dissolves in the uterine fluid. It does not enter the bloodstream in appreciable amounts, but is excreted with the menstrual flow. The copper increases the inflammatory reaction over the effect of a plain plastic device. In addition, the copper interferes with several enzyme systems present in the uterine lining that are required for a favorable environment for implantation; it also interferes with the cellular metabolism of the uterine lining and with the action of estrogen on the cells in the uterus. The progestin-releasing IUD interferes with the normal hormone-stimulated growth cycle of the uterine lining. By maintaining a high progestin level it keeps the uterus in a state unreceptive for implantation. Like the amount of copper on copper-releasing devices, the amount of progestin is small and does not enter the bloodstream in significant quantities (Piotrow et al., 1979).

Risks Involved in Using Intrauterine Devices

Next to the oral contraceptives and the progestin shot (if available), IUDs are the most effective reversible means of preventing unwanted pregnancy. The types of risk associated with IUD use are different from those associated with the pill. Again, when referring to risks, it is important to clarify whether one is talking about risk of method failure, risk of serious danger to the life or health of the user, or annoying side effects. In terms of method failure, IUDs are not as reliable as oral contraceptives, provided each method is used correctly. But, for the woman who has difficulty remembering to take her pill at the same time each day, the IUD provides protection as long as it is in place and may thus be a better method. Like the oral contraceptives, the intrauterine devices are much safer than childbirth at all ages below 40 in both technologically advanced and underdeveloped countries.

1. *What are the important, life-threatening risks associated with IUD use?* A 1978 report by the U.S. Food and Drug Administration estimated the current mortality rate at between one and ten deaths per one million woman-years of use. This is about half the mortality rate associated with oral contraceptive use in developed countries like the United States. Unlike the risk of cardiovascular diseases associated with the pill, the significant dangers associated with the IUD are due to method failure: ectopic pregnancy and uterine pregnancy with the IUD in place, leading to complications such as septic second-trimester abortion.

An ectopic pregnancy occurs when the fertilized egg implants and grows outside the uterus. The most common ectopic site is the fallopian tube, followed by the abdominal cavity and the ovaries. It is a life-threatening condition that requires immediate surgical removal of the embryo and the placenta, because the ectopic placenta may rupture with little warning. The woman may have severe loss of blood and go into shock or even hemorrhage to death. In the United States and Britain, ectopic pregnancy accounts for about 10% of maternal deaths. When a woman using an IUD becomes pregnant, the chances that the pregnancy will be ectopic are estimated to be seven to ten times greater than for a non-IUD user. A complicating problem for the IUD user is that the symptoms of ectopic pregnancy—abdominal pain and heavy bleeding—are often attributed simply to the presence of the IUD. In one U.S. study of 70 ectopic pregnancies in IUD users, a shockingly high 85% were misdiagnosed on the first visit to the physician (Piotrow et al., 1979).

The risk of ectopic pregnancy increases with age and is higher for women with a history of previous ectopic pregnancy or of pelvic infection. In developed countries, including the United States, the rate of ectopic pregnancies has doubled in the past two decades. Because less than 10% of American women of reproductive age use IUDs, the IUD is not a major factor in this increase. The increase in ectopic pregnancies is probably due to the great increase in pelvic infection. IUD users do run a higher risk of pelvic inflammatory disease (PID, pelvic inflammation) than nonusers (Piotrow et al., 1979).

Normal pregnancy can occur in the uterus with the IUD in place. The usual recommendation if the woman wishes to continue the pregnancy is for the physician to remove the IUD as carefully as possible. If the IUD is left in place, about half of these pregnancies will end in spontaneous abortion, usually in the first trimester. This figure is about 3–8 times higher than the rate of miscarriage without an IUD in place. If the pregnancy continues, there is an increased probability of premature delivery and stillbirth, but there is no evidence of an increased probability of birth defects. The total number of maternal deaths associated with IUDs is very small: 15 per 100,000 pregnancies with an IUD remaining in place. Most of these are caused by septic abortion, which can occur if the contents of the uterus become infected in the second trimester of pregnancy. This risk can be avoided by removing the IUD, and minimized by special prenatal care if the physician realizes the additional danger of septic abortion.

2. *Does the intrauterine device cause cancer?* Cancer of the uterus is the second most common type of cancer in women, with cancer of the cervix making up about half of these cases. Nearly 2% of all women ultimately develop this type of cancer. The U.S. Food and Drug Administration's 1978 report on the IUD states that there is no evidence of any kind that IUDs cause or promote cervical or uterine cancer.

3. *How long does it take for fertility to return after the IUD is removed?* Unlike the oral contraceptives or the progestin shot, the IUD does not change hormone balance or metabolism the way the synthetic hormones in the pill or the shot do. It does not prevent ovulation. When the IUD is removed, the risk of associated uterine inflammatory reaction and pelvic inflammatory disease is also removed, and the uterus will probably return to its previous state within one or two menstrual cycles. The woman might use a diaphragm with spermicidal jelly for 2–3 cycles before attempting to get pregnant.

Pelvic inflammatory disease (PID) is about four times more common in IUD users than in nonusers. The risk of getting PID is higher not only immediately after insertion, but also for as long as the device remains in place. Pelvic inflammatory disease among IUD users can be caused by a number of microorganisms, such as gonorrhea, many of which can spread throughout the reproductive system and even into the abdominal cavity. There is a long-term danger of fallopian tube infection, scar tissue formation, and subsequent higher probability of ectopic pregnancy or complete sterility. In many cases the infection may be low-grade and without sufficient symptoms to suspect an infection. Women deciding to use an IUD who may want to become pregnant in the future should realize that they are risking a higher probability of infertility resulting from infection and ectopic pregnancy than with other methods of birth control. If a woman develops pelvic inflammatory disease while she has her IUD, many physicians recommend that it be removed and another method selected if she wishes to become pregnant in the future. If a woman has a history of PID or has had one ectopic pregnancy and wishes to become pregnant in the future, she should not start using an intrauterine device (Hatcher et al., 1978).

4. *Can the IUD "get lost in there"?* The IUD can be expelled from the uterus without the woman's realizing it. It can also perforate the uterine wall and migrate into the abdominal cavity. Both occurrences are related to the insertion process and can lead to anxious moments for both the patient and the physician.

IUD expulsion rates range from about 5 to 20 per 100 women within the first year of use. About 20% of IUD expulsions, when the device moves through the uterine cervix into the vagina and is lost, go unnoticed, and approximately one-third of pregnancies among IUD users occur after unnoticed expulsion. An IUD can also be forced partway out of the uterus and get stuck in the cervix. Expulsion takes place most frequently during the first menstruation after the device is inserted. Other factors that influence the likelihood of expulsion are the correct size of the device to fit the particular uterus, the amount of experience the insertor has with fitting IUDs, and whether the woman has borne a child. Women who have never given birth have a higher expulsion rate. The woman must be taught how to check the threads of the IUD to make sure it is still in place.

Fundal perforation (perforation through the top of the uterus) is believed to occur almost exclusively during insertion of the IUD. Fundal perforation is suspected if pregnancy occurs, if the tail of the IUD is not visible coming through the cervix, or if the patient has a sharp pain at the time of IUD insertion. When the nylon thread (tail) of the IUD cannot be seen coming out through the cervix where it should be, the clinician cannot tell whether the IUD is in the uterus or not. In this case, the simplest approach is to try to retrieve the nylon thread from the uterus. If this does not work, other methods are used to see if the IUD is in the uterus or abdominal cavity. Most IUDs have a radioopaque substance incorporated into the plastic so they can be located by X rays of the abdomen if necessary. Copper IUDs that are in the abdominal cavity must be removed because the copper causes an intense tissue reaction. There is insufficient experience with the progestin-containing IUDs to know if it is safer to leave them in the abdominal cavity or remove them surgically. The rate of fundal perforations is estimated at about one per 1000 IUD insertions, but this rate can be considerably higher if the insertor has limited experience (Piotrow et al., 1979).

5. *Do intrauterine devices affect menstruation?* The most frequent problem for IUD users is increased bleeding, often with cramp-like pain or lower back pain. About 5–15% of all IUD users have an unmedicated device removed within the first year because of this side effect. The copper-containing IUDs cause a smaller increase of bleeding than the unmedicated ones. One advantage of using the progestin-releasing IUDs is that the volume of menstrual bleeding is reduced below preinsertion levels by about 40%. Also, dysmenorrhea (painful menstruation) is significantly reduced. Aside from its inconvenience, the most serious effect of increased bleeding is the probability of anemia. About 5%–25% of well-nourished women in the United States and as many as 50% of women in developing countries are anemic. Insertion of a progestin IUD has been shown to reduce anemia (Piotrow et al., 1979).

6. *Does the IUD affect lactation?* Because neither the copper nor the progesterone from medicated devices gets into the blood, it cannot be incorporated into the milk to affect the infant. These devices do not reduce the amount of milk as oral contraceptives can. An IUD with absorbable chromic sutures (to prevent expulsion for several weeks) can be inserted after delivery if the woman is unlikely to come back to the hospital or clinic, or it can be inserted at the six-week postpartum checkup; it will provide excellent protection against pregnancy while she is nursing the infant. The IUD may even have a beneficial effect on lactation. One study of about 800 women who delivered in a hospital found that the average duration of breast-feeding was three months if they selected oral contraceptives, seven months if they used conventional contraceptives like a vaginal diaphragm, and nine months if they were fitted with an IUD. Biologically, there is no apparent basis for a cause-and-effect relationship between IUD use and breast-feeding duration (Piotrow et al., 1979).

Both medicated and plain intrauterine devices are effective means of preventing unwanted pregnancy. Serious side effects are less frequent than the side effects associated with oral contraceptives, but the higher-than-average incidence of associated pelvic infection indicates that an IUD may not be a good choice of contraceptive for a young woman who has not completed her family.

SPERMICIDAL PRODUCTS

Vaginal contraceptive preparations are among the oldest and simplest of all techniques to prevent pregnancy. A wide variety of gummy substances, such as honey, cocoa butter, and elephant dung, have been mixed with ingredients thought to kill sperm. Some ingredients, such as lemon juice, vinegar and lactic acid, may have reduced fertility, whereas others, such as quinine sulfate, were ineffective.

Spermicidal products are available today in several different forms: creams, jellies, foams in pressurized containers, foaming tablets, and vaginal suppositories. Each consists of a relatively inert base material that physically blocks the passage of sperm and serves as a carrier for a spermicide. A spermicide is a biochemically active agent that makes the sperm incapable of fertilization. Only two spermicides are used: nonoxynol-9 and TS-88 (menfegol). All of the varieties of spermicidal products are generally available worldwide as over-the-counter drugs.

1. *Are spermicides effective?* It is difficult to make an accurate comparison between the product effectiveness of spermicidal preparations and that of contraceptives like the pill or the IUD. In fact, the major drawback of spermicides is the high failure rate often found in actual use, despite the fact that laboratory tests show spermicides to be highly effective. Clinical studies yield failure rates as low as three pregnancies per 1000 woman-years (equivalent to the combination oral contraceptive) and as high

as 400 per 1000 woman-years of use. The most important variable is not the product, but the user. In the study with the failure rate of three pregnancies per 1000 woman-years, the subjects were all the patients of one doctor who instructed them individually, had each of them insert a vaginal suppository while she was in the clinic, and then did a vaginal exam to make sure the suppository was placed correctly. The highest failure rates were found in women who had to figure out the often confusing package-insert directions for use by themselves (Coleman & Piotrow, 1979). Literacy, even a college education, does not guarantee correct usage. We know one nurse who inserted a contraceptive suppository in her rectum instead of her vagina. Another woman inserted a foaming contraceptive tablet in her vagina without removing it from its aluminum foil wrapper, and her boyfriend had to be treated at the emergency room for lacerations of the penis.

Another important factor in comparing spermicide effectiveness to oral contraceptives and the IUD is coitus-related. The spermicide must be placed correctly in the vagina and allowed to disperse uniformly, which may take 5–10 minutes, depending on the product. The suppository will be less effective if the man ejaculates before it has melted or finished foaming. Although most spermicides are effective for two hours, and some for up to six hours after insertion, a new one must be used after that time or if the couple has intercourse a second time. In practical terms, women who select spermicide should realize that, although it is possible to achieve 95% protection or better by using the product each time correctly, in actual practice failure rates are about 150 per 1000 woman-years of use.

2. *What are the risks and side effects of spermicides?* The safety of spermicides is one of their strongest assets. There are no reports of sper-

micide-related mortality. The only side effect is occasional local irritation of the vagina or of the penis from a reaction to the ingredients. This irritation may not be caused by the active spermicide but by the perfuming agents. One of the foaming tablets, a Japanese product, generates a noticeable sensation of heat as it takes up moisture from the vagina and spreads the spermicide. Most users enjoy this characteristic: there is even a T-shirt available that reads "Neo Sampoon—for that warm sensation."

There have been no reports of a systemic effect on the woman resulting from absorption of the spermicide through the vagina. There may be an increased risk of spontaneous abortion, of damage to a developing embryo through accidental use during early pregnancy, and of genetic damage to embryos involving sperm affected by spermicides (Jick et al., 1981).

The spermicidal products are useful for women who have intercourse infrequently enough that they do not want to take oral contraceptives or have an intrauterine device fitted. Spermicides greatly increase the effectiveness of other methods, such as a vaginal diaphragm or a condom, when they are used together. Spermicides are useful as a back-up method if the woman has run out of pills, and they require no prescription. They may decrease the chances of infection with trichomoniasis (a sexually transmitted organism that causes vaginal irritation and itching) and of gonorrhea (Hatcher et al., 1978).

CHAPTER 15

DRUGS AND
HUMAN SEXUALITY

CHAPTER OBJECTIVES

1. List unwanted side effects that may result from treatment of hypertension and of peptic ulcer. Describe the neurotransmitters and the parts of the nervous system that are involved.
2. Explain the effects of tranquilizers on male and female sexual responses and reproductive cycles.
3. Define aphrodisiac. Cite variables encountered in animal studies of purported aphrodisiac substances. Name the neurotransmitters involved.
4. Describe the effects of chronic, intensive use of cannabinoid products on testosterone, LH, FSH, sperm count, and libido in healthy young human males. Explain how narcotics and alcohol interact with marijuana with respect to testosterone.
5. Name the effects of yohimbine, cocaine, and amyl nitrite that might be interpreted as being aphrodisiac.
6. State the effects of alcohol consumption on LH, FSH, testosterone, and spermatogenesis.
7. Discuss whether narcotics adversely affect male and female sexual function.
8. Explain why narcotics and barbiturates are more dangerous to the fetus than to an adult.
9. Describe the unusual ability of the breast to concentrate tobacco products.
10. Explain how smoking tobacco affects fertility, pregnancy, and lactation.
11. List side effects that may occur in women and men taking anabolic steroids over a period of time.

This chapter discusses how drugs can influence sexual functioning and the endocrine system through their effects on the central and peripheral nervous systems. The discussion includes both appropriately used and abused drugs and those used specifically for their supposed sexually enhancing properties. As we discussed in Chapter 2, the central nervous system consists of all the neurons (nerve cells) that make up the brain and spinal cord. The peripheral nervous system consists of all the neurons outside the central system. A few of the drugs to be discussed affect only the peripheral, a few only the central nervous system; most affect both. "Effects" of the drug implies that the drug alters the usual process of information transfer, perhaps by accelerating or inhibiting the usual processes that neurons regulate. Examples of the processes regulated include sexual drive, penile erection, and orgasm. Discussion of specific drugs is divided into (a) *therapeutic* drugs, which are prescribed for a particular medical or psychiatric condition and which incidentally have been found to have effects on hormone systems or sexual functioning, and (b) *recreational* drugs, which may have valid medical uses but are of interest because of their supposed aphrodisiac or other desired effects.

There are important gender differences in drug response. The effects of drugs on male sexuality are better documented, in part because the male responses of erection and ejaculation are more visible and quantifiable. The effects of drugs that impair erection and emission are well understood, but there have been no comparable studies of the effects on female sexual response. It is assumed by analogy that, like erection, lubrication is controlled by cholinergic nerves and that the anticholinergic drugs that adversely affect erection may also impair the corresponding component of the female sexual response. Because there is no phase in the female orgasm that corresponds directly to ejaculation in the male, adrenergic blocking drugs that impair emission in the male may be expected to have no particular effect on orgasm in women. The substances that affect libido by action on the brain, either as stimulants or as depressants, probably have similar sexual effects on both men and women (Kaplan, 1974).

THERAPEUTIC DRUGS

Antihypertensive Drugs

Hypertension, or high blood pressure, affects a substantial portion of the human population. Depending on the extent of blood pressure elevation over normal values, the hypertension is arbitrarily classified as mild, moderate, or severe, and treatment is selected accordingly. Mild hypertension is frequently treated with a diuretic drug to enhance the kidneys' ability to excrete sodium and thus reduce the plasma volume. This prescription plus reduction of weight, if the person is fat, and of sodium intake reduces the high blood pressure to safer levels.

Depending on the diuretic, there may be adverse effects on sexual functioning. Spironolactone, to be effective as an antihypertensive, is taken at dosages of 100 to 200 mg per day. Impotence, decrease in sperm count and motility, gynecomastia (development of the breasts), and decreased libido are recognized side effects in men at daily doses exceeding 100 mg. The mechanism by which spironolactone causes these effects is not known, but it probably interferes with tissue receptors for testosterone (Caminos-Torres, Ma, & Snyder, 1977). In other words, even though testosterone (the male sex hormone) levels remain normal, the tissues cannot respond as well. In women, irregular menses have been reported. Adverse reactions usually disappear when the drug is stopped, although gynecomastia may persist. The thiazide diuretics have not been reported to have these particular side effects.

Reserpine is sometimes used to treat mild hypertension, and, in combination with other drugs—usually a thiazide diuretic—it is used in many prescriptions for moderate hypertension. Reserpine's most serious side effect is mental depression, which in itself may impair sexual drive; it can also decrease libido without general mental depression. In women, it inhibits the reproductive cycle, apparently by blocking release of pituitary gonadotropins, FSH and LH, and may induce prolactin secretion and galactorrhea (excessive milk flow) (Daughaday, 1974). In males, reserpine has been reported to weaken erection and delay ejaculation, and, like spironolactone, cause gynecomastia. It probably produces these effects by action on central nervous system neurotransmission. Reserpine is known to deplete serotonin, norepinephrine, and dopamine (Weiner, 1980b; Whalen, Gorzalka, & DeBold, 1975). In addition to causing depletion of catecholamines, reserpine acts on the autonomic control of the genitals and can also impair sexual response at this level (Kaplan, 1974).

Moderate hypertension may be treated with a compound called *methyldopa,* which is closely related to the neurotransmitter L-dopa (see Chapter 2). At low doses (200 mg per day), methyldopa is not likely to cause problems, but at the usual dose of one gram per day, impotence is a fairly common side effect. The major antihypertensive effect of methyldopa is believed to be on the central nervous system. It decreases the concentrations of serotonin, dopamine, and norepinephrine both in the central and most parts of the peripheral nervous system. It has not been shown to have a specific effect on the parasympathetic nerves responsible for erection or on the sympathetic nerves responsible for ejaculation. The impotence might be related to the sedative effect of the drug. In some patients, methyldopa, like reserpine, may produce a psychomotor depression, resulting in decreased libido. Another side effect, involving the endocrine system, is the release of prolactin, causing lactation. Both the impotence and the inappropriate lactation are reversible when the drug is withdrawn, which is not true for all drugs causing impotence (Blaschke & Melmon, 1980). The man may have developed "fears of performance," or mental blocks requiring psychological therapy to regain function.

Guanethidine has been used since the early 1960s to treat severe hypertension. It blocks adrenergic activity, inhibiting responses to sympathetic nerve activity by reducing the amount of norepinephrine and then restricting the release of what little there is; it also blocks alpha and beta adrenergic receptors equally. It does not affect the brain's adrenergic functions, because it does not cross the blood-brain barrier. Reserpine and guanethidine also stimulate release of serotonin (5-HT) from central and peripheral sites; many of their major effects may be caused by this action (Koelle, 1975).

A commonly reported unfortunate side effect of chronic guanethidine treatment in men is the inability to ejaculate. Antiadrenergic drugs may cause difficulties with ejaculation, because the reflex muscular contractions of the internal male reproductive organs involved in emission are controlled by adrenergic nerves. Although erection is a parasympathetic and ejaculation a sympathetic nervous system function, some men become impotent during guanethidine treatment presumably because of psychological factors associated with their ejaculatory problem. In contrast to the ganglionic blocking drugs, which are not used much for hypertension any more, guanethidine by itself does not produce impotence (Nickerson & Collier, 1975).

There is some concern that guanethidine may, at high doses over considerable time, permanently damage the nerves involved in ejaculation, so that even if the drug dosage is reduced or stopped altogether, the ejaculatory function may not return. In laboratory rats, guanethidine specifically damages the adrenergic neurons supplying the male's reproductive organs, causing among other things retention of sperm. The drug does not seem to have this destructive effect on the sympathetic nervous system in other laboratory animals such as rabbits and hamsters (Johnson, Macia, & Yellin, 1977). Whether it affects humans similarly to rats or to rabbits is not known. To our knowledge, no information has been reported on deleterious effects of guanethidine on female orgasm.

Parasympathetic Blocking Drugs

Neurons employing acetylcholine may have two types of receptor, *nicotinic* or *muscarinic*, classified by their response to these two plant products. The antimuscarinic drugs inhibit the actions of Ach on postganglionic parasympathetic nerve endings with little effect on the actions of Ach at nicotinic receptor sites. Furthermore, all parasympathetically innervated organs are not equally sensitive. Unfortunately, doses of antimuscarinic drugs that are large enough to depress gastric secretion, such as those used to treat peptic ulcer, invariably affect the more sensitive receptors and may cause impotence as one of the side effects (Figure 2-6, p. 32).

The antimuscarinic drugs include the alkaloids of the belladonna plants: atropine, scopolamine, and others from the deadly nightshade, jimsonweed, and henbane group (see Chapter 6). Chemically modified forms of the naturally occurring compounds are available along with synthetic antimuscarinic drugs. Although the naturally occurring compounds are found in over-the-counter cold remedies and allergy medications, the amounts are small. Belladonna and synthetic antimuscarinic drugs are used in the treatment of peptic ulcer in amounts that may cause impotence. This effect is rarely produced by antimuscarinic drugs alone, and it is the result of a ganglionic block. Ganglionic blocking agents may impair both the adrenergic and the cholinergically controlled phases of the sexual response, because they block transmission in the intermediate ganglia of both components of the autonomic nervous system (Kaplan, 1974).

Antipsychotics, Lithium, and Minor Tranquilizers

The major tranquilizers (used to treat severe mental illness), the minor tranquilizers (used to reduce anxiety, tension, and agitation), and lithium carbonate (used to treat manic depressive illness) all may adversely affect sexual function. As discussed in Chapter 10, chlorpromazine is considered typical of the phenothiazine antipsychotic or *neuroleptic* drugs. These produce an effect of emotional quieting and relative indifference to one's surroundings.

Chlorpromazine and the other phenothiazines frequently inhibit ejaculation and may weaken erection (Byck, 1975). Thioridazine, one of the phenothiazines, may cause "dry orgasm"— that is, orgasm without ejaculation. It is believed that this is due to the peripheral autonomic action on a sphincter muscle essential for normal routing of the ejaculate, causing the semen to empty into the urinary bladder instead of into the urethra. The major tranquilizers facilitate social adjustment by reducing symptoms and behav-oral deviations, but they also inhibit sexual drive. The resulting frigidity, impotence, and loss of libido may themselves cause depression or otherwise disrupt treatment.

Chlorpromazine depresses the hypothalamic regulatory mechanism and affects the pituitary gland because of its action on the hypothalamus. It reduces the levels of gonadotropins FSH and LH, and through them blocks the reproductive cycle in women and spermatogenesis in men (Chapter 14). If given to a prepubertal patient, it causes delay of the onset of puberty. When LH is suppressed by action of a drug such as chlorpromazine, production of the hormone prolactin is increased. This is how the major tranquilizers induce inappropriate secretion of prolactin, with resulting lactation. The mechanism is probably by catecholamine receptor blockade.

Haloperidol, another major tranquilizer, is structurally different from the phenothiazines but similar in action. It blocks aggressive and violent activity in animals and people and also greatly reduces sexual activity. These drugs have been used to reduce or block undesirable, compulsive sexual behavior. Haloperidol and chlorpromazine are powerful blockers of dopamine receptors. It is thought that serotonin is a major inhibitor of both aggressive behavior and of sexual activity, whereas dopamine appears to be the primary neurotransmitter for these behaviors (Byck, 1975; Everett, 1975). The thioxanthenes, also considered major tranquilizers, likewise may adversely affect libido and cause lactation in women and gynecomastia in men taking large doses.

The popular minor tranquilizers, primarily diazepam and chlordiazepoxide, also have side effects. Valium® was the most commonly prescribed drug, and Librium® was third or fourth, of all prescribed drugs in the United States in the late 1970s. Both are reported to cause delayed, impaired ejaculation. Menstrual irregularities, failure to ovulate, gynecomastia, and galactorrhea may result from treatment (Byck, 1975).

Lithium carbonate is effective in treatment of the manic phase of manic depressive illness and as a mood-stabilizing drug when used chronically in manic depressives. Male patients being treated with lithium carbonate for manic depression have reported difficulties achieving erection. That this problem is caused by the lithium treatment was shown by first substituting a placebo drug and later putting the men back on the lithium, without their knowledge (Hollister, 1975).

Neurotransmitter Precursors

Levodopa (L-dopa) has benefited many thousands of patients with Parkinson's disease since its introduction as a drug in the United States in 1970. Progressive degeneration of dopaminergic neurons that feed into the basal ganglia (a motor control area) as an inhibitory control system, without deterioration of the cholinergic neurons, which are excitatory, results in an imbalance between dopamine and acetylcholine (see Chapter 10). Because dopamine does not cross the blood-brain barrier, its precursor L-dopa is used. The L-dopa is believed to act by supplying an increased amount of the precursor for the missing neurotransmitter, dopamine.

In addition to alleviating the tremor, rigidity, and inability to move, which are characteristic of Parkinson's disease, L-dopa at least partially relieves the apathy and depression associated with the disease. Some patients resume sexual activity because they feel better and because their muscular coordination is improved. However, about 15% of patients develop serious psychiatric disturbances, including inappropriate or excessive sexual behavior. This correlates with animal data, which show that sexual behavior is inhibited by brain serotonin and stimulated by dopamine. Of all therapeutic drugs, other than replacement sex steroids used to treat inadequate levels of sex hormones, L-dopa has been best documented as increasing sexual function (Bianchine, 1980; Gessa & Tagliamonte, 1975; Hollister, 1975).

To reduce nausea and other side effects such as hypotension, the daily dosage of L-dopa is divided into three equal amounts, usually taken with food. It takes two to three months to work up to an effective dosage for control of Parkinson's disease symptoms. L-dopa does not seem to have been tested in the treatment of low libido in otherwise healthy human subjects, male or female. Treatment with L-dopa, or L-dopa plus a serotonin inhibitor, markedly enhances the level of copulatory behavior in male rats with low libido (Gessa & Tagliamonte, 1975).

Antihistamines

In therapeutic doses, all antihistamines have side effects, the most common of which is sedation. Digestive tract side effects, such as loss of appetite and nausea, are the next most common. Other side effects, such as dryness of the mouth and, more rarely, difficulty in urination and impotence, are related to the anticholinergic activity of the antihistamines.

RECREATIONAL DRUGS

Aphrodisiacs

Many licit and illicit drugs, such as opium, alcohol, the psychedelics, marijuana, hashish, yohimbine, amphetamines, and numerous herbal preparations, have reputations as enhancers of sexual pleasure. Some are toxic and dangerous at all dosages—for example, the cantharides ("Spanish fly"). Others have lower toxicity but produce damage with long-term use. There is not as yet a true aphrodisiac—a drug that will produce a sexually enhancing effect in a person who does not expect this result. It is theoretically possible, if the neural centers responsible for libido are located, that a specific agonist (mimic) or neurotransmitter could be synthesized that would cross the blood-brain barrier like L-dopa, and stimulate the libido center. Alternatively, such an aphrodisiac drug might work by blocking inhibitory input to the libido center. After thousands of years of experimentation with plant and animal products, and more recently with synthetics, no such direct-acting substance has been found.

Drugs that do work as aphrodisiacs do so indirectly by removing inhibitions imposed by higher brain functions, such as alcohol, or by action on the peripheral portion of the autonomic nervous system, such as yohimbine. Spanish fly is exceptional because it is not a placebo, meaning its action does not depend on the person's expectations, but it is also not an aphrodisiac. It works by irritating the urinary bladder and the urethra in both male and female, and thus it may stimulate a sense of sexual excitement. In men, it may cause priapism (prolonged erection). Permanent penile damage resulting in impotence has occurred as a result of priapism. The urethral irritation may be sexually stimulating for the woman but is more likely to be extremely uncomfortable until the effect of the drug wears off.

It is difficult to extrapolate from animal studies of so-called aphrodisiacs to human beings. Test results vary even among animals, depending on the species studied, because different species of animal have different patterns of mating, under different degrees of hormonal and environmental control, and because different species may react differently to the same drug (Whalen et al., 1975).

Initial sexual responsiveness of animals varies—many laboratory species can be arbitrarily separated into "high, medium, and low" sex drives. Usually, males are studied by placing them in a test arena, giving them an opportunity to explore and become accustomed to it, and then presenting them with a sexually receptive female. For example, an average male guinea pig, when placed with an estrous female, will (1) nibble her fur, (2) nuzzle around the anogenital region, (3) mount her, (4) place his penis in the vagina and make pelvic thrusting motions (if he mounted correctly), and (5) ejaculate. Then he grooms himself and is quiet. Males were scored on a factor of 1 for nibbling, 2 for nuzzling, and so on. An animal that mated within the first 15 seconds was rated 20.0, and an animal that did nothing for the entire 10-minute test period was rated 0.0 (Grunt & Young, 1952).

When evaluating an "aphrodisiac" drug, some investigators (but not all) do a prior separation to enable them to report whether there was a differential effect on low-, medium-, and high-sex-drive animals. Parachlorophenylalanine (PCPA), a serotonin depleter, seems to increase sexual activity in male rats that have low to moderate drive but not in those with high drive prior to drug treatment (Whalen et al., 1975). Other investigators using PCPA have not found an aphrodisiac effect in animals. There is no clear-cut evidence of an increase in sexual interest in patients or healthy volunteers treated with PCPA (Hyyppä, Falck, Aukia, & Rinne, 1975).

The amount of prior sexual experience may influence how rapidly an animal responds. There are dose-response relationships that are not well understood, in which one dose level may enhance and a different dose may inhibit sexual response. How are such results to be interpreted? Does a drug like PCPA that increases male-to-male mounting activity in fact increase "sex drive," cause general arousal and activity, or simply reduce "fear"? If a drug inhibits sexual performance, does it make the animal hypoaroused, disoriented, or insensitive to important sexual stimuli, such as olfactory cues (Whalen et al., 1975)?

Perhaps instead of a specific neurotransmitter, a specific neural blocker to block inhibitory input to a "libido center" would act as an aphrodisiac. PCPA, which inhibits an enzyme in the biosynthetic pathway for serotonin, seems to stimulate sexual behavior. However, it is not completely specific for this effect. In one study, laboratory rats and rabbits were fed a diet deficient in tryptophan, the amino acid that is the precursor in the brain for serotonin. Because tryptophan is used elsewhere in the body, feeding a diet deficient in tryptophan results in a rapid removal of tryptophan available to the brain for serotonin synthesis. This should mimic, by a nonpharmacological means, the action of PCPA. At the time of maximal serotonin depletion, about six hours after feeding, a marked increase in male-to-male mounting behavior in both rats and rabbits was found. This behavior could be blocked by injection, ten minutes before the behavioral test, of the immediate biochemical precursor to serotonin (Fratta, Biggio, & Gessa, 1977).

We have defined an aphrodisiac as a substance that enhances sexual response in a healthy person who does not know the substance is supposed to have any such effect. There are therapeutic drugs that, when used to correct a physiological problem, would have an aphrodisiac effect while restoring health. The drugs most likely to do this are the ones used to treat nutritional deficiencies and/or sex hormone (gonadal) deficiencies. Because of the connection between aphrodisiac effects and treatment of nutritional deficiency, indiscriminant dietary supplementation is an occasional problem.

However, supplementation has at best a psychological benefit and at worst is toxic. Dietary and gonadal deficiencies require professional diagnosis and correction (Spark, White, & Connolly, 1980).

Marijuana and the Hallucinogens

Of the several active ingredients in marijuana and hashish, delta-9-tetrahydrocannabinol (THC) is responsible for the euphoric effect and is the most important psychoactive ingredient (see Chapter 7). Hash oil is a concentrate that is approximately ten times stronger than hashish. The cannabinoid products are usually smoked, because this is an efficient means of absorbing the active ingredients, and it is easier to regulate the amount desired. There is a biphasic effect after marijuana ingestion that is highly dosage dependent: initial stimulation and euphoria are followed by sleepiness and dreamlike states. Although marijuana is used by a much higher proportion of people to enhance sexual relations compared to cocaine, this is due to greater availability and lower price. It probably influences sexual response by acting on higher brain centers to relax inhibitions and reduce the usual restraints on behavior, rather than having a specific enhancing effect on libido in the central nervous system or peripheral nervous system activation (Hollister, 1973).

Some problems with marijuana-hashish studies with humans and animals make it difficult to say what the exact effects are. For example, it is difficult to define "moderate" and "heavy" use, partly because the percentage of active cannabinoid varies greatly among samples. In addition, in retrospective studies, the experimenters rely on their subjects' honesty and accuracy of recall of other drug use, and on their accuracy

in reporting nutritional and health status. Another problem is created by the fact that cannabinoids are highly lipophilic, so that they accumulate in fatty tissue. Thus, although they are important, it is difficult to obtain baseline metabolic characteristics even if the subjects stop smoking for a few days at the start of a study.

One study on marijuana found that chronic, intensive use may produce alterations in male reproductive physiology through action on either the hypothalamus or the pituitary. Twenty heterosexual men aged 18–28 who used marijuana at least four days a week for a minimum of six months, without the use of other drugs (with the exception of tobacco and alcohol), were compared to matched nonmarijuana-smoking controls. The levels of testosterone, the male sex hormone, were significantly lower (416 nanogram per 100 ml of blood) in marijuana smokers than in nonsmokers (742 ng/100 ml), and they were related to the amount of marijuana smoked. When the subjects were divided into those who smoked five–nine joints/week and those who smoked ten or more/week, the testosterone levels were, respectively, 503 ng/100 ml and 309 ng/100 ml. Similarly, the sperm count of the heavier smokers was less than half the value for the moderate smokers, and FSH levels were depressed. Two of the heavy smokers were impotent; one recovered sexual function following abstention from marijuana, the other decided he liked marijuana better than sex. Measurements of liver function, LH, prolactin, and thyroid were within normal limits (Kolodny, Masters, Kolodner, & Toro, 1974).

Unfortunately, the results of the study just described were controversial, because the marijuana used was supplied by the subjects and was neither standardized nor analyzed for cannabinoid content. In addition, the use of other drugs known to depress testosterone levels was not excluded. A subsequent study investigated the effect of marijuana smoking on plasma testosterone in a group of 27 men, aged 21–26, who were housed in a tightly controlled hospital metabolic ward for the duration of the study. Thus the researchers were quite certain that other drugs were not used. Their subjects' nutritional status was known, and the amount of marijuana used was determined by supplying the men with standardized U.S. Government marijuana cigarettes that could only be smoked in the presence of an attendant, to whom the roach was given for analysis of remaining cannabinoid. Subjects were requested to abstain from all marijuana use for two weeks prior to starting the study. There was a baseline period of 5 days, then a 21-day period during which the subjects could smoke as much as desired, and a final period of 5 days with no marijuana. Testosterone was measured daily before, during, and after marijuana use. When the testosterone levels of both the moderate and heavy users were compared to the baseline values, no differences were found (Mendelson, Kuehnle, Ellingboe, & Babor, 1974).

The discrepancy between the two studies just described was resolved by several follow-up studies, one of which used 20 cannabis smokers who lived in a hospital ward for nearly three months. The men used no drugs for the first 11 days, then were given an average of five joints per day of standardized marijuana cigarettes for nine weeks. There was no change in testosterone during the first four weeks of cannabis use. However, after four weeks there were substantial decreases in LH. During the fifth week, the subjects' testosterone levels began dropping and continued to drop throughout the rest of the study. After the subjects had smoked for eight weeks, there were significant decreases in FSH. At the end of nine weeks, the average testosterone level had fallen by 33%. Although the averages were still within the normal range for

men of that age, concentrations for several men were down to the point at which impotence and/or infertility could result (Cohen, 1976).

Thus chronic use of marijuana by young, healthy men will decrease testosterone levels and sperm counts, but, in the absence of other factors such as heavy alcohol use or narcotics, impotence is not a problem for most men. The effect of marijuana on testosterone has been reversible in the subjects studied so far. The deleterious effects of combining marijuana with other drugs is significant, especially as marijuana usage gradually increases in middle-aged men. Reduced fertility in young men could be a problem as well, because sperm count reductions of about 60% were found after a four-week study period. A variety of abnormalities, such as changes in lipid concentration, protrusion of chromatids from the sperm nucleus, and marked changes in the balance of acidic and basic amino acids in the histone proteins that encapsulate the sperm DNA have been found in the sperm of men who have smoked cannabis for many years (Harclerode, 1980).

The mechanism by which marijuana or its major active ingredient, THC, reduces the levels of the pituitary hormones FSH and LH is not known (Smith, Besch, Besch, & Smith, 1979). THC is a beta-adrenergic agonist, or mimic of the adrenergic neurotransmitter, and its peripheral effects (increased heart rate especially) are blocked by propranolol, a beta-adrenergic blocker; however, its psychic effects are not blocked (Byck, 1975). That propranolol crosses the blood-brain barrier may be irrelevant, because the neurons believed to control FSH and LH are probably located in the portion of the hypothalamus that is outside the blood-brain barrier.

The psychedelic drugs, such as LSD, mescaline, and marijuana, produce alterations in consciousness, mood, and perception by mechanisms that are also not well understood. They do not seem to have specific effects on the sexual centers of the brain, but they may affect sexuality as part of their general action on the central nervous system. When comparing marijuana, hashish, and LSD—as used specifically for sexual enhancement—"pot" and hashish were rated approximately equal to LSD, with LSD being more conducive to fantasizing and marijuana and hashish being more effective in maintaining erection. Peripheral effects, such as increasing the chances of multiple orgasm, were reported in the instances of the cannabinoids, the psychedelics, and cocaine (Gay, Newmeyer, Elion, & Wieder, 1975).

MDA (3,4-methylenedioxyamphetamine) is chemically related to both mescaline and amphetamine, and is classified as a hallucinogen. MDA has been reported to have some truly sexually stimulating effects, not as an isolated phenomenon, but as closely related components of the personality and current psychic state of the person. Sometimes called the *Mellow Drug of America,* it is reputed to make one more sensitive and receptive to tactile stimuli.

DOM or STP (2,5-dimethoxy-4-methylamphetamine) and MMDA (3-methoxy-4,5-methylenedioxyamphetamine) are like MDA in that they are amphetamines with hallucinogenic activity. They are structurally related to both mescaline and amphetamine. As with the other hallucinogens, DOM and MMDA's effects depend on the user's personality, expectations, and environment. The physiological effects of MDA, DOM, and MMDA are similar to those of LSD—increased pupil size, blood pressure, and pulse rate. At high doses, small increases of body temperature may occur in some users.

At low doses, DOM and its chemical relative DOE (2,5-dimethoxy-4-ethylamphetamine) produce mild euphoria and enhanced self-awareness without perceptual distortion or hallucinogenic effects. At high doses DOM exhibits psychedelic activity typical of LSD and mescaline, but DOE appears to have a rather wide dose range before producing psychedelic effects.

Stimulants: Yohimbine, Strychnine, Amphetamines, and Cocaine

Two physiological functions are intimately associated with sexual stimulation: increased vasocongestion and muscular tension. Both functions are dependent on the autonomic nervous system's activity. Some of the older so-called aphrodisiac drugs, such as yohimbine, act on the autonomic nervous system. The active ingredient, yohimbine, is an alkaloid obtained from the bark of a West African tree. The alkaloid is closely related chemically to the *Rauwolfia* alkaloids, the source of the antihypertensive tranquilizer, reserpine. The shredded bark may be purchased by mail order or from health food stores, although its authenticity is questionable without chemical analysis. The bark is soaked in boiling water, the same as brewing tea. One folk source recommends adding vitamin C to enhance absorption of the alkaloid.

Purified yohimbine is available by prescription as a mixture of the pure alkaloid plus methyltestosterone, or with strychnine and thyroid hormone (Billups & Billups, 1981). The literature supplied by one pharmaceutical company in the 1978 *Physicians' Desk Reference* says the latter drug mixture is "indicated for sexual feebleness of psychogenic origin for symptomatic treatment of male impotence." The dosage levels in this combination probably would not be pharmacologically effective, but let us describe the effects of its components.

Strychnine is thought to excite the whole nervous system, especially the spinal cord, where the reflex arcs for erection and ejaculation are

(Hollister, 1975). This powerful convulsant drug acts by blocking the normal inhibitory impulses at neuronal synapses, affecting all voluntary muscles; in adequate doses it causes death by asphyxiation. Although it has long been popular as a "tonic" to stimulate the appetite and the gastrointestinal tract, it is neither safe nor effective (Franz, 1980). It is difficult to justify the use of thyroid hormone as a sexual stimulant, although short-term thyroid hormone administration to a person in good thyroid balance would not permanently affect thyroid function. Hypothyroidism is known to be one endocrine cause of sexual dysfunction (Spark et al., 1980), but this disease is better treated by correct diagnosis and thyroid hormone replacement, without the strychnine and yohimbine. Thyroid hormone levels must be adjusted rather carefully to individual requirements and require continuing medical supervision.

Yohimbine acts by producing a state of parasympathetic predominance and vasodilatation, which might aid in achieving penile erection. Two closely related compounds, corynanthine and a synthetic derivative called *ethyl yohimbine,* have pharmacological properties very similar to yohimbine but are less toxic. These three compounds produce an alpha-adrenergic blockade for a limited time. Yohimbine also blocks peripheral serotonin (5-HT) receptors. It penetrates the blood-brain barrier and causes a number of effects on the brain, including elevation of blood pressure, increased heart rate, irritability, tremor, sweating, nausea, and vomiting (Weiner, 1980b). Experiments using yohimbine in animals have not indicated that yohimbine has an aphrodisiac effect (Johnson & Diamond, 1969). Believers in this substance point out that most animal studies use injection—subcutaneous, intramuscular, intraperitoneal, and so on—rather than the oral route and claim that, in order to be effective, the alkaloid must be acted on by the hydrochloric acid in the stomach.

Cocaine and amphetamine, although chemically different, are also central-nervous-system stimulants. Cocaine is highly regarded in practically all aspects of sexuality enhancement. It increases libido, enhances enjoyment, and lowers inhibitions without causing loss of ability to maintain erection and control when orgasm occurs, unlike some other drugs used as aphrodisiacs. The amphetamines in small doses are considered to have similar properties, but they are not as effective as cocaine. Cocaine at low dose levels may have a truly stimulating effect both on erotic interest and sexual performance, but at chronic and higher doses cocaine users (like amphetamine users) become more interested in the drug than in sex.

Systemic effects of cocaine are obtained by application to a mucous membrane, such as the nose, the gums, the back of the throat, or the vagina, or by intravenous injection. Oral use is not common in the United States, although the subjective highs after oral ingestion are equal to or greater than after intranasal administration (Van Dyke, Jatlow, Ungerer, Barash, & Byck, 1978). Some women, applying cocaine to the vaginal mucosa, report that intercourse is prolonged and that their orgasms are more intense. Others report being unable to achieve orgasm but have a high, prolonged level of sexual excitement. Occasionally male users have difficulty achieving erection, but once erection occurs they are able to have intercourse for an extended period. For heavy users (few, because the drug is so expensive) the orgasmic effects of cocaine injection become a substitute for sexual intercourse (Wesson & Smith, 1977).

Like cocaine, amphetamines stimulate the central nervous system, resulting in decreased fatigue, mood elevation, stimulation of the medullary respiratory center, and stimulation of the peripheral sympathetic nervous system. Methamphetamine in low doses has a more prominent effect on the central nervous system and a smaller effect on the peripheral system than amphetamine (Weiner, 1980a). The amphetamines have a longer action on the body than cocaine. Many users claim that amphetamines delay orgasm in both male and female, so that sexual activity may be prolonged and orgasms are more intense and pleasurable (Jaffe, 1980).

Unlike popular beliefs about yohimbine and strychnine, the anecdotal reports of the effects of cocaine, LSD, and amphetamines have some animal studies to back them up. A dose of amphetamine, injected intraperitoneally (IP, through the muscle layer covering the abdomen, so that the drug is absorbed from the blood supplying the intestines) produced a generalized hyperactivity in male rats. This was followed by an increase in sexual behavior, including a significant increase in the number of ejaculations, a large decrease in the time between ejaculations, and persistence of erection after ejaculation. However, when the same dose of amphetamine was continued daily, by the fourth to fifth day intense general excitement continued but sexual behavior decreased markedly, sometimes disappearing entirely. The male rat no longer seemed able to focus its attention on a receptive female rat. Again supporting anecdotal reports, low doses of LSD given to rats in the same manner produced similar effects as low doses of amphetamines (Soulairac & Soulairac, 1975). There do not seem to be any reports of controlled studies in laboratory primates, such as the squirrel or the rhesus monkey.

Poppers and Saltpeter

The nitrites and organic nitrates, especially nitroglycerine, are used therapeutically to relieve anginal pain (when the blood supply to the heart muscle is inadequate). Amyl nitrite is a faster-acting vasodilator than nitroglycerine, but it has worse side effects, such as a painful, throbbing headache, so most anginal patients prefer nitroglycerine. Amyl nitrite (Vaporole®) is formulated as a *pearl*—that is, a small crushable capsule—in street jargon, a "popper."

When the volatile fumes of amyl nitrite are inhaled shortly before orgasm, it is said to trigger a greater, more sensual orgasm, which may also be prolonged. The pharmacological action that causes this sensation is difficult to explain. The only action of the drug is smooth-muscle relaxation, resulting in vasodilation, a drop in blood pressure, an increase in pulse rate, and cutaneous flushing similar to the sexual flush shortly before a normal orgasm. The abruptly lowered blood pressure produces a feeling of dizziness and faintness that might account for the supposed increase in orgasmic intensity. Amyl nitrite users also might be associating the drug-induced cutaneous flush with the sexual flush and subconsciously getting a psychological boost to orgasm in this manner. The vasodilating effect may lessen the intensity of erection, which might delay orgasm and ejaculation. It may also relax the internal anal sphincter muscle, facilitating anal intercourse, as heroin is reported to do. The drug could be dangerous for people with cardiovascular problems.

Butyl nitrite, sold as "locker room," a foul-smelling liquid reminiscent of sweaty gym clothes, is reputed to have an aphrodisiac effect analogous to amyl nitrite. It also causes a skin flush and headaches (the odor alone seems sufficient to cause a headache). It does not have medical uses, because of side effects.

Potassium nitrate, better known as saltpeter, supposedly has an anaphrodisiac effect (reducing sex drive). The name *saltpeter* comes from its mining origin: *sal* refers to salt and *petrae* to rock, the two together meaning *salt of rock*. There is also Chilean saltpeter, which is sodium nitrate. Both were mined for use in dynamite manufacture and as fertilizer to add nitrogen to soil. Inorganic nitrites and nitrates are poisonous at high doses and act to reduce the oxygen-carrying capacity of red blood cells. It is difficult to pinpoint the reason for the anaphrodisiac reputation of potassium nitrate. It may come from the association of the chemical's common name with the slang term for penis. Although it is generally believed that saltpeter is added to food in prisons to reduce the male prisoners' sex drives, there is no good evidence to support this. It would take a lot of saltpeter to produce chronic anemia sufficient to reduce libido in a healthy adult. Furthermore, the phenothiazine tranquilizers work better to reduce aggression among inmates, and they are used for this.

Alcohol

The favorite mood-altering drug in the United States, as in most societies, is ethanol (ethyl alcohol, or grain alcohol). It has multiple effects on the endocrine and nervous systems, which, like those of other drugs, are related to the amount consumed, the length of time the body has been exposed to it, and individual susceptibilities. In different quantities for different people, alcohol is a toxic drug. Very little alcohol can be disposed of through the lungs or kidneys. Most alcohol must be oxidized in the liver, the organ that contains the enzymes necessary for degradation of alcohol. This is why so many deleterious effects of alcohol involve the liver (Lieber, 1976). The testis is susceptible to alcoholic damage because it also has the enzyme alcohol dehydrogenase to metabolize alcohol (Van Thiel, Gavaler, & Lester, 1974).

The effects of alcohol on the nervous system are the same as those of most other anesthetic agents. Alcohol has both short-term and long-term effects on neural function. Small doses of alcohol depress the parasympathetic control of penile erection in the dog. At higher doses the sympathetic components controlling ejaculation reflexes are depressed (Marks & Chakraborty, 1973). These short-term effects are probably due to alcohol's anesthetic action. However, impotence resulting from prolonged high alcohol intake in men may persist even after years of sobriety. The problem does not seem to be either psychological (fear of performance) or hormonal, but results from the destructive effect of alcohol on the parasympathetic neural reflex arc (Lemere & Smith, 1973).

Alcohol has significant effects on testosterone metabolism that are independent of cirrhosis, the pathological changes found in the liver after long-term alcohol abuse, and nutritional factors. The typical male alcoholic is feminized—with impotence, sterility, gynecomastia, and changes in body-hair distribution—but it had been thought that these changes were due to cirrhosis. Using 19 male medical students, aged 19–25, it was shown that a single dose of ethanol sufficient to trigger a severe hangover in some of them depressed the blood levels of testosterone significantly. Those who had the worst hangovers had the most depressed testosterone levels (Ylikahri & Huttunen, 1974). When alcohol is given as 42% of total calories, with plenty of protein and adequate fat and carbohydrate, to healthy young male subjects for time periods of up to four weeks, testosterone metabolism is markedly influenced. The daily morning increases were suppressed first, followed by decreases in both the blood concentration and the production rate of testosterone. The decreased blood concentration reflected the accelerated metabolic clearance rate; the altered metabolism in the liver made the liver remove the testosterone faster than in normal men. LH levels did not rise adequately or consistently in response to the decreased levels of testosterone (as LH does in the normal male), indicating a possible effect of alcohol on the LH-control center in the hypothalamus. In contrast to findings in men with established liver disease, no changes were found in blood levels of estrogen or in the amount of testosterone converted to its metabolites (Gordon, Altman, Southren, Rubin, & Lieber, 1976).

In addition to alcohol's short-term effect on testosterone, there is a long-term effect on FSH and spermatogenesis. Because spermatogenesis in humans requires about ten weeks, FSH must be deficient at least this long in order for the sperm count to decline. The alcoholic with cirrhosis has altered liver metabolism resulting in decreased testosterone and increased estrogen. Demasculinization also occurs through alcohol's action on the testis, which, like the liver but unlike most body tissues, has the enzyme alcohol dehydrogenase. Testicular energy metabolism is probably as drastically altered by excess alcohol as liver energy metabolism (see Chapter 11). This is thought to be the mechanism by which short-term alcohol consumption decreases blood concentrations of testosterone (Van Thiel & Lester, 1976).

At various points in the complex pattern of spermatogenesis, the presence of hormones, including FSH and testosterone, and several vitamins are required. Vitamin A (retinol) is essential at one point, and alcohol dehydrogenase is required at another for the conversion of retinol to biologically active retinal in the testis. Ethanol inhibits the conversion of retinol by the testis. Testicular atrophy and aspermatogenesis (lack of sperm production) are found in 50%–75% of chronic alcoholics with cirrhosis. However, azoospermia (no sperm in the ejaculate) can occur in relatively mild liver disease. Incidentally, studies have demonstrated that alcohol dehydrogenase activity occurs in the retina of the eye and have shown that alcoholics experience night blindness because of the deficient formation of the active form of vitamin A (Van Thiel et al., 1974).

Disulfiram (Antabuse®)

Alcoholics who have decided to abstain from alcohol and who wish assistance in resisting temptation may take the drug disulfiram. Consumption of even small amounts of alcohol after disulfiram causes the "Antabuse® syndrome" because of accumulation of acetaldehyde: the face becomes flushed, intense throbbing is felt in the head and neck, and a pulsating headache may develop. Respiratory difficulties, nausea, copious vomiting, sweating, thirst, and chest pain may follow and may last between 30 minutes and several hours. By itself, disulfiram is relatively nontoxic, but it may cause lassitude, fatigue, restlessness, headaches, dizziness, and reduced sexual potency (Ritchie, 1980). It seems that the unfortunate male alcoholic can't win either way with his sex life!

Narcotics

The narcotics, including heroin, morphine, methadone, and others (see Chapter 12), apart from generally depressing the central nervous system, seem specifically to reduce sex drive and capacity. Their reputation as aphrodisiacs, like that of alcohol, comes from the use of low, infrequent doses and the accompanying release from inhibitions. It may be related to the orgastic sensation evoked by intravenous injection of these substances. Experienced users who enjoy the cannabinoids, cocaine, and the psychedelics as sexual potentiators do not use the barbiturates, methaqualone, heroin, and large doses of amphetamines or alcohol because these diminish libido and potency (Gay et al., 1975).

Several studies on humans and laboratory animals have shown deleterious effects of narcotics on sexual functioning and hormones. In one study, 29 participants in a methadone-maintenance program were compared to 16 heroin addicts and 43 narcotic-free control male subjects. Both the methadone and heroin users had problems, especially delayed ejaculation, impotence, and failure to ejaculate. Several reported painful ejaculation. All the heroin users and 97% of the methadone users had substantially lower libido when on either narcotic than when they were drug free (Cicero, Bell, Wiest, Allison, Polakoski, & Robins, 1975). Methadone maintenance appears to have a greater suppressing effect on testosterone levels in blood than heroin, which were reduced by 40%–50% in methadone users (Azizi, Vagenakis, Longcope, Ingbar, & Braverman, 1973; Cicero et al., 1975). The dosage of methadone makes a difference. Low-dose maintenance (10–60 mg/day) does not reduce testosterone significantly (Hollister, 1975). The motility of sperm in samples from methadone users was markedly lower than normal, and secretion from the seminal vesicles and prostate was reduced by over 50%. Heroin users appeared to fall between the methadone and control subjects on all measures of secondary sex organ and testicular function.

Methadone may directly block the ejaculatory response. The process of ejaculation is mediated by adrenergic neurons and can be blocked by alpha-adrenergic blocking drugs. Narcotics, including methadone, have a degree of alpha-adrenergic blocking activity, at least in the laboratory rat. For this reason, alpha-adrenergic blocking drugs produce low ejaculate volumes and a reduction in the amount contributed by the seminal vesicles and prostate to the ejaculate. In addition, testosterone levels in rats were reduced by 70% within 6 hours after morphine administration. Within 24 hours the weights of the secondary sex organs (seminal vesicles and prostate) were greatly reduced. Both morphine and methadone in the rat inhibit the secretion of LH without affecting FSH (Cicero, Meyer, Bell, & Koch, 1976).

Morphine is known to block ovulation in experimental animals. Menstrual cycle abnormalities are common among female heroin addicts while on heroin, or while on methadone maintenance, probably because of suppression of LH and perhaps FSH. However, long-term tolerance to methadone may develop, and normal reproductive cycles may return after a year or two, while the woman is still on the drug. Women on long-term methadone maintenance may also become pregnant (Santen, Sofsky, Bilic, & Lippert, 1975). No data on sexual functioning—libido, lubrication, achievement of orgasm—were reported.

Spontaneous abortions are common in addicted women. Infants born to addicts are addicted themselves and require careful withdrawal procedures. Also, the newborn infant that has been exposed to narcotics will have difficulty establishing normal breathing because of the suppressant effect of the narcotics on the respiratory center. The narcotics have a greater effect on the central nervous system of the fetus because the blood-brain barrier is not completely established until the period of brain growth that occurs after birth.

Gynecomastia in male heroin addicts may be due to chronic liver disease, although injection of morphine into healthy women stimulates secretion of prolactin (Tolis, Hickey, & Guyda, 1975). Prolactin is one of the hormones required for milk production.

Hypnotics and Sedatives: The Barbiturates and Methaqualone

The most popular nontherapeutically used sedatives are the short-acting barbiturates, especially secobarbital, but also the nonbarbiturate drugs methaqualone, glutethimide, and meprobamate. Methaqualone is prescribed as a sleeping pill (hypnosis) or for daytime sedation. There is a popular view among abusers that it has aphrodisiac activity and causes a dissociative high achieved without the drowsiness that barbiturates cause; its effects have been compared to the effects of heroin. As with the other sedatives and CNS depressants, any enhancing effect this drug has on sexual pleasure comes from the release of inhibitions. Users report they feel more relaxed, friendly, receptive, and uninhibited, but they have a reduced physical ability to perform. Although methaqualone has a shorter half-life than any barbiturate used for hypnotic sleep induction, hangover is frequent. Mild overdosage usually causes excessive central depression much like that from barbiturates, but restlessness and excitement sometimes result instead.

The subjective effects of the barbiturates are similar to those of alcohol, and their endocrine effects are similar to those of morphine. Barbiturates used during labor have a depressant effect on the infant's respiration, because the drug crosses the placenta and enters the neurons in the brain. Women breast-feeding their babies should limit intake of barbiturates, because small amounts appear in the milk.

Tobacco

Nicotine is readily absorbed, through smoking tobacco, from the oral mucosa and the respiratory tract (Chapter 9). Approximately 80%–90% of inhaled nicotine is metabolized to other compounds before being eliminated in the urine. Nicotine is also excreted in the milk of lactating women. In addition to the infant's being exposed to carbon monoxide and other noxious gases from cigarette smoke, the milk from heavy smokers may contain 0.5 mg of nicotine per liter (Volle & Koelle, 1975). It also contains more DDT than milk from a nonsmoking woman (Coleman, Piotrow, & Rinehart, 1979).

Even when she is not lactating, an adult woman's breasts secrete and reabsorb a small amount of fluid. Analysis for nicotine in samples of breast fluid from women smokers showed that nicotine is five to ten times more concentrated in breast fluid than the concentration in their blood plasma. Long-term effects of nicotine and its metabolites on breast tissue are not known, but the results indicate that the breast may concentrate other hazardous components from tobacco smoke as well, which are established carcinogens (Petrakis, Gruenke, Beelen, Castagnoli, & Craig, 1978).

Although it is difficult to train laboratory rats to smoke, it has been shown in rats that the ovulatory release of LH can be delayed by inhalation of tobacco smoke. The extent of the delay is dose-related to the nicotine content. Women who smoke are known to be less fertile; this might be caused by a comparable effect on their reproductive cycle. In addition, prolactin release in response to the suckling stimulus was blocked by tobacco smoke in rats with nursing pups. These results on LH and prolactin were not obtained in animals when the usual experimental means of administration of the drug, injection of a soluble nicotine salt, was used. It is possible that during the passage of tobacco smoke through the lungs, nicotine may be retained by the lung tissue and released slowly, thus having a more sustained effect than when injected. Further, the nicotine in smoke may be less easily dissolved in plasma when compared to the soluble salt used for injections. These results raise important questions about possible cumulative adverse effects on the neuroendocrine system as the result of habitual use of tobacco (McLean, Rubel, & Nikitovitch-Winer, 1977).

In addition to being less fertile, women who smoke have more spontaneous abortions, are at greater risk of losing the pregnancy in preeclampsia (a toxic, dangerous state in late pregnancy characterized by high blood pressure, protein in the urine, and accumulation of watery fluid in the tissues), and have a higher probability of delivering an underweight infant that has a poorer than average chance of living. Women smokers also enter the climacteric, or menopause, earlier than nonsmokers (Coleman et al., 1979).

Pumping Iron— The Anabolic Steroids

This category of therapeutically misused drug is different from all others. The taking of the drug is not an end in itself: although anabolic steroids may produce a feeling of well-being, even euphoria, they are not taken for that reason. The world-class or would-be world-class athlete taking large quantities of anabolic steroids has considered the side effects carefully and made a decision that the benefits are worth the risks. The drug is only one part of a program meticulously (to the outsider, fanatically) designed to bring muscular function to a peak of development precisely timed for major athletic events. In addition to physiological risks, the athlete must stop taking the drug in order to eliminate all traces of it from the body by the time of competition, because anabolic steroids are considered in the category of augmenting drugs. This athlete knows if he or she wins, a urine sample and perhaps blood will be analyzed for these illegal compounds.

The naturally secreted hormone from the testes, testosterone, is one of the most potent anabolic steroids. Testosterone has two types of action: androgenic, which promotes development of the male reproductive structures and sexual characteristics, such as distribution of hair, voice changes, and so forth; and the more general anabolic effect on the body as a whole and the muscles in particular. Many derivatives of testosterone have been synthesized and tested in the search for compounds with anabolic activity that promote general body growth without the masculinizing effects. The ratio of anabolic to androgenic effect is often referred to as the therapeutic index relative to that of testosterone, which is taken as equal to 1. The best of the synthetic anabolic steroids have an index of 2 to 3.

The intended clinical uses of the anabolic steroids are to treat the debilitated person who is physically run down because of certain diseases or starvation; for the treatment of diseases from a number of causes; to slow down or reverse osteoporosis (weakening of the bones) as seen in the aged of both sexes, but especially in the postmenopausal woman; during treatment with corticosteroids to counterbalance the negative nitrogen balance and calcium balance; and in the treatment of breast cancer. The use of androgens in breast cancer has its basis in the finding that some cancerous tissue is stimulated to grow by estrogens, other by progestins, other by both, and some by neither estrogen nor progestin (see Chapter 14). Androgens may suppress cancerous growth after the breast cancer has spread to other sites.

All of the androgens carry the risk of masculinization when used in women: acne, growth of facial hair, and voice changes are the earliest changes. With continued treatment, such as in mammary carcinoma or by an athlete, baldness, excessive body hair, prominent musculature and veins, and hypertrophy (increase in size) of the clitoris develop. These effects are generally irreversible (Murad & Haynes, 1980). Increased libido in women is sometimes noted, but this occurs at the high dose levels used in breast cancer and usually is not a welcome side effect for these generally very sick women.

Excess androgen in men may produce azoospermia (zero sperm count) because of inhibition of gonadotropin secretion and conversion of the androgen to estrogen in the liver. Anabolic steroids may also produce azoospermia, and, because they can also suppress natural production of testosterone, impotence can result after withdrawal of the anabolic steroid (Murad & Haynes, 1980). One athlete who took ten times the accepted dose of anabolic steroid was very strong, but his testosterone production was almost completely suppressed. (Sexual intercourse is supposed to be bad for athletes anyway!) In physically immature teenagers, anabolic steroids can stop growth of long bones, thus stunting growth, and cause *macrogenitosomia praecox*, which is excessive bodily development with a marked enlargement of the genital organs occurring at an unusually early age.

Water retention in association with sodium chloride accounts for a portion of the weight gain found in users of anabolic steroids. In dosages used to treat hypogonadism (inadequate secretion of testosterone), water retention usually does not lead to detectable edema (excessive retention of fluid), but it may become a problem at higher dosages, such as in treatment of malnutrition or as used by athletes.

Jaundice is a problem at higher dosages of orally active anabolic steroids that have a particular synthetic addition—a 17-alpha substituent, especially the 17-alpha methyl. This problem occurs with use of methyltestosterone,

fluoxymesterone, methandriol, methandrostenolone, oxandrolone, and norethandrolone. Jaundice is the main clinical sign of a type of liver damage called *cholestatic hepatitis*, which is caused by stasis and accumulation of bile in the biliary capillaries of the central portions of the lobules of the liver, without obstruction in the larger ducts. There are increases in bilirubin and in blood serum glutamic-oxaloacetic transaminase enzyme, often abbreviated SGOT. Even small doses of compounds such as methyltestosterone are metabolized with difficulty by the liver, so large doses may be expected to have cumulative effects. Clinical practice in the use of the 17-alpha substituted steroids is to give short courses of treatment of three to four weeks, interrupted by drug-free intervals of similar length (Murad & Haynes, 1980). Common practice among athletes is to take the drug for 21 days, followed by one week off, the same as oral contraceptive use among women. Most anabolic steriods given by injection do not have this methyl or ethyl side group at the 17-alpha position and do not cause cholestatic hepatitis.

Small numbers of patients receiving replacement androgens for hypogonadism, or anabolic steroids for prolonged periods (one to seven years), develop hepatic adenocarcinoma, a type of liver cancer (Murad & Haynes, 1980). It may be significant that there is an increased risk of the same type of cancer among women who have used oral contraceptives for a number of years, although the orally active steroids in contraceptives are somewhat different structurally from the orally ingested anabolic steroids. The increased risk associated with the estrogen in the oral contraceptives is thought to arise from the difficulty the liver cells have in removing a comparable synthetically added methyl group. It is also interesting that these drugs have been associated with cholestatic hepatitis (Edmonson, Henderson, & Benton, 1976). The risk of liver cancer to athletes taking large doses of anabolic steroids is not known.

Do anabolic steroids increase strength, anthropometry, and physical performance? These anabolic effects are most pronounced in eunuchoid men, in boys before puberty, and in women. Studies in healthy young males produce varying results for several reasons. First, the anabolic steroids differ from one compound to another. Second, the dosage levels used in the few double-blind, placebo-controlled studies (see Chapter 3) are usually much lower than athletes select for themselves. The intensity of physical training and the motivation of the subjects also vary widely, which influences the effects of anabolic steroids.

One study showed that statistically significant gains in strength were made by weight lifters who received a placebo drug when they believed they were being given Dianabol®, one of the most commonly used anabolic steroids (Ariel & Saville, 1972). Another study on weight lifters started the men on low dose, high dose, or placebo pills that were coded; neither the men nor the doctors knew the code until the study was over. After six weeks the men were changed over to either steroid or placebo, depending on what they had received during the first six weeks. All subjects correctly guessed what the code was from the effects on their performance, although they were probably getting clues from the drug's side effects. The men who started on steroid showed much greater improvement in measured weight lifting performance than those who were started on placebo. After the change to steroid, all but one of the men who had begun on placebo showed greatly improved performance. There was no difference between the low dose and the high dose groups. Side effects of the steroid included acne, high blood pressure, headache, nausea, and reduced sexual activity (Freed, Banks, Longson, & Burley, 1975).

Other studies in men and male rats have found no enhancement in physical performance not obtained by a training regimen including a good diet, and regular, strenuous workouts (Brown & Pilch, 1972). It seems that anabolic steroids in athletic competition are like aphrodisiacs and sexual performance—given a basically healthy person in good physical condition, the drug does nothing more than enhance the person's psychological set. If the athlete believes it will help, it probably will, but not from any biochemical property of the drug.

CHAPTER 16

OVER-THE-COUNTER DRUGS

CHAPTER OBJECTIVES

1. Briefly describe the Food and Drug Administration's regulatory power regarding OTC drugs.
2. Name some factors to consider when selecting internal analgesics, sleep aids, cold and cough remedies, antacids, laxatives, and antidiarrheal drugs.
3. Describe one problem resulting from overuse of nasal spray decongestants.
4. Define the following terms: analgesic, tinnitus, antipyretic, topical, rubefaction, vesicant, insomnia, sleep apnea, antitussive, gastritis, and iatrogenic.

Nearly $8 billion is spent each year on drug products that are purchased "over the counter" (*33rd Annual Report on Consumer Spending,* 1981). These are the nonprescription drugs that may be obtained and used without a physician's supervision. Some of these drugs can be dangerous at certain dosages or in combination with other drugs. A great number are of questionable effectiveness in alleviating the physical ailments for which they are taken.

The U.S. Food and Drug Administration (FDA) has the responsibility to regulate nonprescription drugs. In 1972 the FDA set up an ambitious program to screen and evaluate all over-the-counter (OTC) drugs (see Table 16-1 for a brief history of OTC drug regulation). At that time it was estimated that there were nearly 300,000 nonprescription drugs on the market. If each one had to be screened, it would have been an impossible task. However, these products contained only about 500 significant active ingredients. Thus, instead of examining the 8000 brand name antacid products, the FDA evaluated only the active ingredients, of which there were about 30.

The final reports on all the ingredients have

TABLE 16-1 History of OTC drug legislation and regulation in the United States*

Date	Event	Result
1906	Pure Food and Drug Act	Drugs must meet standards of purity and strength claimed by manufacturer. Must list opiate, cocaine, alcohol, and cannabis content.
1912	Sherley Amendment	Cannot make false or fraudulent therapeutic claims about a product. Difficult to enforce.
1938	Food, Drug, and Cosmetic Act	New products judged safe before marketing.
1951	Humphrey-Durham Amendment	Drugs divided into prescription and nonprescription types.
1962	Kefauver-Harris Amendments	Manufacturer must establish safety and effectiveness of all drugs manufactured after 1938.
1966	NAS/NRC–FDA Study of Drugs	National Academy of Sciences/National Research Council evaluates 3400 new drugs marketed between 1938 and 1962, including 512 OTC drugs. Only 15% of the OTC products judged effective.
1972	FDA OTC Drug Products Evaluation Program	17 panels of experts to review all OTC drugs (over 300,000 on market).

*Copyright 1979 by the American Pharmaceutical Association, *Handbook of Nonprescription Drugs,* 6th ed., p. xvii. Reprinted with permission of the American Pharmaceutical Association.

not been completed over a decade after the start of the program, but most of the data have been collected and recommendations have been made. This information is placed in the *Federal Register* as it is completed. Each drug is classified into one of three OTC categories: Category I—generally recognized as safe and effective for the claimed therapeutic indication; Category II—not recognized as safe and effective; and Category III—additional data needed to decide safety and/or effectiveness. Category II products must not be shipped to stores after six months following the final report on the product, unless it is considered dangerous. In such cases the product can be banned immediately. Several products have been so treated, such as hexachlorophene in antibacterial soaps.

It is extremely important that consumers be given accurate information concerning the OTC drugs they purchase. There are many examples of inaccurate or incorrect assumptions about OTC drugs. One is "the government wouldn't let the company claim that if it weren't true." The U.S. Federal Trade Commission (FTC) does prosecute manufacturers for fraudulent claims, but the process is excruciatingly slow. A company can tie up legal proceedings for years—it took the FTC 16 years to get the word "liver" removed from Carter's Little Liver Pills. Another incorrect assumption involves confusion between relief of symptoms and curing the condition. Drugs like the cold remedies are often used by people to "cure" a cold, but there is no cure for the common cold. One treats the symptoms until the body's defense mechanisms cure the cold. Sleep and tranquilizing compounds sold over the counter are often misrepresented. The dosages of these OTC drugs are usually ineffective for the purpose, or they work by drug interaction. In this chapter we discuss the major classes of OTC drugs that are of general interest and give a brief background on the composition of some of them and their effects on the body.

INTERNAL ANALGESICS (PAIN RELIEVERS)[*]

In 1980 the American public spent more than $1.3 billion on internal analgesics, the largest sales category of OTC drugs. Most of the money was for aspirin, acetaminophen, salicylamide, and phenacetin, respectively (the compositions of common OTC internal analgesics are given in Table 16-2). Selection of an analgesic depends on the condition being treated. Some of them have more than just an analgesic effect: they may also be antipyretic (reduces fever) or antiinflammatory (lessens inflammation). These products vary considerably in their toxicity and in their interaction with other drugs.

Aspirin and other nonnarcotic analgesics are effective in the treatment of mild to moderate musculoskeletal pain and headache, less effective in conditions such as toothache, sore throat, and menstrual pain, and ineffective in relieving discomfort from abrasions, cramps, and smooth muscular pain.

Aspirin

Aspirin is manufactured from a class of chemicals called the *salicylates* (the name comes from *salix*, the Latin word for *willow*). Over 2400 years ago the Greeks used extracts of willow bark and poplar bark for the treatment of pain and gout. These remedies were apparently lost during the

---

[*] This section is largely from Van Tyle, 1979.

TABLE 16-2. Internal analgesics[*]

Product	Aspirin	Phen-acetin	Salicyl-amide	Acetamino-phen	Caffeine	Other
Alka-Seltzer®	324 mg	——	——	——	——	sodium bicarbonate; citric acid
Anacin®	400 mg	——	——	——	32.5 mg	——
Arthritis Pain Formula®	486 mg	——	——	.	——	aluminum hydroxide; magnesium hydroxide
A.S.A. Compound®	227 mg	160 mg	——	——	32.5 mg	——
Aspergum®	228 mg	——	——	——	——	——
Aspirin Free Anacin-3®	——	——	——	500 mg	32 mg	——
Bayer Aspirin®	325 mg	——	——	——	——	——
Bromo-Seltzer®	——	130 mg	——	325 mg	32.5 mg	sodium bicarbonate; citric acid
Bufferin®	324 mg	——	——	——	——	magnesium carbonate; aluminum glycinate
Datril®	——	——	——	325 mg	——	——
Doan's Pills®	——	——	——	——	32 mg	magnesium salicylate
Duragesic®	325 mg	——	——	——	——	salicylsalicylic acid
Empirin®	227 mg	162 mg	——	——	32 mg	——
Excedrin®	194 mg	——	130 mg	97 mg	65 mg	——
Goody's Headache Powder®	455 mg	325 mg	——	——	32.5 mg	——
Liquiprin®	——	——	——	48 mg	——	——
PAC®	228 mg	163 mg	——	——	32 mg	——
Percogesic®	——	——	——	325 mg	——	phenyltoloxamine
Sine-Aid®	——	——	——	325 mg	——	phenylpropanola-mine
St. Joseph®	325 mg	——	——	——	——	——
Tylenol Extra Strength®	——	——	——	500 mg	——	——
Vanquish®	227 mg	——	——	194 mg	33 mg	magnesium hydrox-ide; aluminum hydroxide

[*]Copyright 1979 by the American Pharmaceutical Association, *Handbook of Nonprescription Drugs*, 6th ed., pp. 137–140. Reprinted with permission of the American Pharmaceutical Association.

early Christian era. St. Augustine believed that pain was caused by demons and was punishment from God, and therefore willow bark extracts should not be used to relieve pain. The early American Indians used willow preparations in their medicine. There is no indication that willow bark extract was used in Europe until around 1750, when Edward Stone, an English clergyman, tried it and found it worked. The active agent was later identified as salicylic acid.

One major problem with salicylic acid was that it irritated the stomach lining and caused nausea. The acetylated form of salicylic acid was synthesized in 1853 but not used medically until 1899. This chemical modification is less irritating to the stomach wall. Bayer Laboratories coined the name Aspirin for the compound and marketed it, along with another acetylated preparation (diacetylmorphine, or Heroin). In 1917 the patent on Aspirin expired, and several other companies began manufacturing and selling the drug under the same name, aspirin. Bayer sued, but during World War I the German company was seized as alien property, and the lawsuit was not resolved in their favor. Today a number of companies produce and sell aspirin. The consumption of aspirin is almost unbelievable: production and sales figures indicate that 10 to 20 thousand tons of aspirin are consumed annually in the United States. This is between about 27 and 55 tons of aspirin per day!

Aspirin works to reduce pain, inflammation, and fever by inhibiting synthesis of a substance called *prostaglandin E*. This substance is believed to increase the sensitivity of pain receptors, so if levels of prostaglandin E are reduced, pain receptors will become accordingly less sensitive to stimulation. Aspirin reduces fever by increasing heat loss from the body; it increases perspiration and blood flow to the skin. Despite the side effects, such as stomach irritation and internal bleeding, aspirin is still one of the most effective drugs used against inflammation caused by arthritis.

Aspirin slows the normal clotting time of the blood, so it causes some internal bleeding. It is estimated that the average person may lose up to 10 ml (2–3 tsp) of blood per two aspirin tablets. The bleeding is not noticed because it takes place in the intestines. The effect on clotting may last four to seven days, during which bruises occur more readily. An estimated 30,000 people per year are admitted to hospitals for serious internal bleeding linked to aspirin use. Anemia-prone persons may be seriously affected by large amounts of aspirin.

Aspirin can also trigger ulcers in the stomach. The tiny pieces of aspirin tablets in contact with the stomach wall are the probable cause. If the aspirin is taken in liquid or powder form or is dissolved in a glass of water first, the likelihood of stomach irritation is reduced. The combination of alcohol and aspirin will increase the irritation and greatly increase the probability of bleeding. Another side effect in heavy aspirin users, and in some sensitive people, is *tinnitus*, or a ringing sensation in the ears. Hearing will return to normal when aspirin consumption is reduced. An occasional person will develop an aspirin hypersensitivity reaction, which causes symptoms of a runny nose, hives, and asthma. A severe reaction may cause the person to go into shock and die. Acetaminophen (see the following section) is less likely to cause this reaction.

Phenacetin and Acetaminophen

These two compounds are effective mild pain relievers and antipyretics, but they are not effective as anti-inflammatory agents. Phenacetin is converted in the body to acetaminophen, which is probably responsible for its therapeutic action. Doses above 1 to 2 grams of phenacetin a day may cause some destruction of blood cells; some individuals who are sensitive to low doses may develop hemolytic anemia (a serious disease involving destruction of red blood cells). Some of these sensitive persons—about 13% of Amercan Blacks—lack an enzyme, glucose-6-phosphate dehydrogenase. Phenacetin does not cause bleeding but can cause kidney or liver damage in sensitive people or in heavy users, so it has been removed from most OTC preparations. It is still found in A.S.A. Compound®, Bromo-Seltzer®, Empirin®, PAC®, and other products.

Acetaminophen does not produce as much bleeding as aspirin and is not as irritating to the stomach, so it is becoming popular. Liver damage has been known to result from acetaminophen, but usually from doses above 6 or 7 grams over a short period of time. Some of the trade names for acetaminophen-containing products are Datril®, Febrinol®, Fendon®, Nilprin®, Sinarest®, Sine-Aid®, Tylenol®, and many others.

Salicylamide

Salicylamide is one of the four commonly used drugs in OTC pain relievers. It does not cause bleeding to any great extent at normal doses. Its disadvantages are that it is about one-half as potent as aspirin as an antipyretic, and it is inactivated during absorption and in the liver so effectively that little reaches the bloodstream unless the person takes more than the equivalent of two aspirin tablets. Thus currently recommended doses (300 to 600 mg) are probably ineffective.

Caffeine and Other Additives

A number of OTC analgesic products contain caffeine. There is no conclusive evidence to show that caffeine is an aid to pain relief. In most preparations the amount of caffeine is less than that found in one-fourth to one-half cup of coffee (see Chapter 8). Other ingredients, such as antacids, antihistamines, decongestants, and alcohol, have little or no analgesic action.

EXTERNAL ANALGESICS

There are a large number of OTC drugs that are used externally, in the form of liniments, gels, lotions, and ointments, to relieve pain in muscles, organs, and joints. This type of pain is often called *deep-seated pain*. The products are used topically (applied to the surface) and work by a counterirritant action rather than by a direct analgesic action (see Chapter 13). Most of these products have irritants that stimulate sensory receptors in the skin, causing increased blood flow to the painful area and in some cases apparently blocking pain pathways by interference or some other means. They work in part by taking one's mind off the original pain and focusing it on a different type of skin pain caused by the irritants. As rubefacients, they increase blood flow and cause the skin to redden without blistering.

Most of the drugs employed as counterirritants are volatile substances that have a "medicinal" odor. There is a placebo effect of pain relief for many people when they smell a "medicinal" odor and when they feel the warmth that is caused by irritation of the pain receptors in the skin. It is possible that the massage as the counterirritant is applied and the increased blood flow may help relieve muscle tension, but these drugs probably do not cure muscle damage, joint or ligament damage, and cellular damage in organs. Such treatment in fact may be harmful. It is only fair to say that the irritants can give pain relief to some persons with neuralgias, rheumatoid arthritis, bursitis, and some types of muscle cramp. However, relief should not be confused with cure.

Volatile substances employed as counterirritants include methyl salicylate, menthol, camphor, thymol, allyl isothiocyanate, capsicum oleoresin, turpentine oil, cinnamon oil, clove oil, chloroform, methacholin chloride, and histamine dihydrochloride. Methyl salicylate is the most commonly used. This external analgesic is quickly absorbed through the skin. Infants and small children are more sensitive to the toxic effects of the salicylates, and care must be taken to prevent accidental ingestion. One teaspoon of methyl salicylate is equivalent to about 12 aspirin tablets and could poison a young child. The wintergreen oil odor can be attractive to children, who mistake it for candy.

Menthol is rather interesting, because it has a mild anesthetic action as well as being an irritant. The drug also stimulates the nerve receptors that perceive cold, but depresses those that send out pain impulses. Clove oil is another strongly irritating substance. The chief constituent is eugenol. Most people are familiar with the use of clove oil or pure eugenol as a temporary pain reliever for toothache. Another compound familiar to many people is allyl isothiocyanate, or oil of mustard. This drug is a powerful rubefacient and will cause blisters on the skin if it is too concentrated (vesicant action). Oil of mustard is the active ingredient in the old-fashioned mustard plaster remedy.

The use of external analgesics is decreasing somewhat because of greater use of internal analgesics. Nevertheless, sales of external analgesics amounted to $160 million in 1980.

SLEEP AIDS AND OTHER SEDATIVES

It is estimated that about 50% of the population experiences insomnia (the inability to get to sleep or to stay asleep) at some time, and 33% complain of sleep difficulties on a continuing basis. The millions of people having sleep difficulties spent about $31 million in 1980 on the over 100 different OTC products advertised as inducing a "safe and restful sleep" or that relieve "nervous tension." The products are described as nonbarbiturate and non-habit-forming. They are low potency products that have a minimal action on the sleep and wakefulness centers of the brain, controlled through the reticular activating system (RAS) (see Chapter 10).

The drugs commonly used in OTC sleep and sedative preparations are antihistamines, salicylates, salicylamide, scopolamine, and other belladonna derivatives. None has proven satisfactorily safe and effective. The antihistamines used included methapyrilene until 1979, when products containing methapyrilene were recalled. Antihistamines have been shown to be teratogenic in animals, and methapyrilene is carcinogenic. Many products that contained methapyrilene have been reformulated with pyrilamine, which is also suspected of being carcinogenic.

Bromides were used as sedatives starting in the late 1800s and are still available in a few OTC preparations, such as Lanabrom®, Neurosine®, and Peacock's Bromides® (Billups & Billups, 1981). They accumulate in the body and cause toxic effects in long-term users. Scopolamine (hyoscine) was found by the FDA Select Committee to be ineffective at the recommended doses in OTC sleep aids and to be potentially toxic at higher doses (Chapter 6). Some of the liquid OTC sleep aids contain alcohol, which potentiates when combined with antihistamines and scopolamine to make the person drowsy. Salicylates are added to some products for the dubious reason that a minor pain may be keeping the person from getting to sleep. Salicylamide, another internal analgesic, has sedative properties, but the dose recommended in OTC sleep preparations is probably too low to be effective. It is rapidly inactivated in the digestive tract and liver.

COLD, ALLERGY, AND COUGH REMEDIES*

The common cold is the most expensive single illness in the United States. More time is lost from work and school because of the common cold than from all other diseases combined. About one-half of all absences and approximately one-fourth of the total work time lost each year in industry are due to cold symptoms. Americans spent over $1 billion in 1980 for cough, cold, allergy, hayfever, and sinus products—the second largest sales category of OTC drugs.

The incidence of the common cold varies with age. Children between the ages of 1 and 5 are most susceptible; each child averages 6 to 12 respiratory illnesses per year, most of which are common colds. Individuals 25 to 30 years old average about 6 respiratory illnesses a year, and older adults average 2 or 3.

There are usually three peak seasons of the common cold per year: one in the autumn, a few weeks after schools open; another in midwinter; and a third in the spring. The U.S. Public Health Service studies show that, during the winter, about 50% of the population experience a common cold. Each epidemic is associated with different viruses.

Perhaps 90% to 95% of colds are caused by viruses. More than 120 different viruses are known to produce cold symptoms in humans. Perhaps as much as 10% of all minor respiratory

*This section is taken largely from Cormier and Bryant, 1979.

diseases are caused by a *Streptococcus* bacterium. In fact, if a person has a prolonged cold with fever, it is probably caused by a bacterial infection. Getting chilled does not cause a cold, although it may precipitate one in a person who is already infected. Telling the difference between a viral cold and a bacterial cold is difficult, and it is not uncommon to find complicating factors like allergic responses. Allergies can cause symptoms similar to colds, such as a runny nose, red, itchy eyes and nose, and a sore throat. The most common allergies are to pollens, so the seasonal nature of the symptoms would aid diagnosis. However, many people are allergic to a wide range of year-round substances, such as house dust, animal danders, and so on. These allergies can be tested at an allergy clinic.

The mucous coating of the nasal passageways, the throat, and the lungs have several infection-fighting substances: lysozyme, glycoproteins, and immunoglobulins (antibodies). Lysozyme is an enzyme that is an important defense against bacteria and pollens. It readily digests the cell wall of some bacteria and of pollens, and the subsequent release of antigens from those pollens causes allergic reactions. The mucus glycoproteins may slow down or delay viral infections by combining with the virus. Immunoglobulins in the mucus may also decrease the infectivity of certain viruses. Use of oils, especially mineral oil, and nasal spray decongestants interferes with the action of the lysozymes, glycoproteins, and antibodies.

Cells that are invaded by viruses produce the substance *interferon*. Interferon is active not only against the virus that triggered its production, but against other, unrelated viruses. Interferon works better at the elevated temperatures (fever) that often accompany infections. It is possible that taking aspirin to lower the fever may make you feel better, but may prolong your cold by slowing interferon action.

Regardless of origin, colds have similar general symptoms: the first stage, in which the throat and nose are dry, and the second stage, in which secretions accumulate in the air passages, nose, throat, and bronchial tubes. The second stage is marked by continuous sneezing, nasal obstruction, sore throat, coughing, and nasal discharge. There may be watering and redness of the eyes and pain in the face and ears. One of the most bothersome symptoms of the common cold is the congestion of the mucous membranes of the nasal passages. This is probably caused by the release of free histamine from tissues in the upper respiratory area as a result of viral invasion. Histamine causes the capillaries to become more permeable, and this allows more fluids to escape, causing some of the drainage and also inflammation due to fluid-swollen tissues.

Cold, allergy, and cough products are formulated with such drugs as antihistamines, aspirin or acetaminophen, belladonna alkaloids, vitamin C, decongestants, vasoconstrictors (called *sympathomimetic amines*) such as ephedrine, phenylephrine, propanolamine, and pseudoephedrine. The antihistamines will reduce congestion caused by allergies but are relatively ineffective in the case of virus-initiated colds. Antihistamines will also decrease mucus secretion, relieving the runny nose, although this action is probably insignificant at recommended doses of OTC preparations. This drying action may be harmful because it may lead to a serious coughing stage. Antihistamines also may cause dizziness, drowsiness (thus their use in OTC sleep aids), and impaired judgment.

Belladonna alkaloids dry up the nasal secretions and may trigger uncontrolled coughing. However, the dosage in OTC and allergy preparations is too low to have this effect if taken as directed. Atropine may also slow the cilia of the respiratory tract, blocking an effective normal defense mechanism. Belladonna alkaloids may cause increased intraocular (in the chamber of the eye) pressure; this can be serious for someone with early symptoms of glaucoma.

Vitamin C is an ingredient in many OTC cold remedies, although there is little evidence that this has a beneficial or preventative effect. (Linus Pauling advocates using large doses of this vitamin.) It should be noted that doses of 4 to 12 grams daily can cause kidney stones and that high levels can cause unreliable glucose tests in diabetics. If the person is convinced it will help, it seems more reasonable to take supplemental doses of vitamin C separately than to buy it mixed with a cold remedy.

The sympathomimetic amines used as decongestants cause shrinking of the nasal membranes, which reduces the congestion found in colds and allergies. These can be used in the form of sprays or drops (topical decongestants), or orally (oral decongestants). Ephedrine is a natural product that is similar to the neurotransmitter norepinephrine. Other sympathomimetic amines include phenylephrine (probably the most effective topical), naphazoline, oxymetazoline, and xylometazoline. Nasal sprays have the potential to cause "congestion rebound" due to tissue addiction. After using a nasal spray regularly, for longer than the recommended period of time, the nasal membranes become dependent and get very congested between applications. Then the person uses the spray more and more, until the tissue will not respond and the sinus passages become almost totally obstructed. Allergists frequently get new patients who are "hooked" on nasal spray and are desperate for relief from congestion. This problem can be prevented by using the nasal sprays sparingly and for no longer than recommended on the package. Oral use of the sympathomimetic amines gives less relief, but does not cause congestion rebound.

The cough reflex is an essential means to clear

the lower respiratory tract of foreign matter. There are two types of cough: the productive and the nonproductive. A productive cough clears mucous secretions and foreign matter so that breathing is improved. A nonproductive cough causes throat irritation and is often self-perpetuating because of the irritation. Some type of cough suppressant (antitussive) medication is useful for the nonproductive cough.

Most cough mixtures, whether OTC or prescription, are shotgun remedies containing from one to nine different drugs aimed at controlling the cough in different ways. The ingredients will, it is hoped, reduce nasal congestion, thin the thickened secretions so they can be expelled more effectively, cause bronchodilation, depress the cough center, and/or tranquilize the patient. (If you take enough drugs, one of them should do the job!)

There are two types of antitussive agent available as OTC preparations: (1) cough suppressants, such as codeine and dextromethorphan, which act on the central nervous system to raise the threshold of the cough coordinating center, thus reducing the frequency and intensity of a cough; and (2) expectorants, such as glyceryl guaiacolate, ipecac, terpin hydrate, and ammonium chloride, which act to increase the production of respiratory tract fluids that have a soothing action on the irritated respiratory tract membranes and that decrease the thickness of the accumulated congestion. The tickling sensation in the throat that triggers a cough can be eased by sucking on a cough drop. This stimulates saliva flow to soothe the irritated membranes. Unless the cough is severe, sour hard candy works just as well as a more expensive cough lozenge.

Cough remedies, like other medications, have a psychological value. Many patients with a cough due to disease of the respiratory tract report reduced coughing after the use of cough remedies, even when it is objectively demonstrated that the remedies reduce neither the frequency nor the intensity of the cough. Cough remedies work in part by reducing the patient's anxiety about the cough and making him or her believe that objective improvement has resulted. If the person believes in the remedy, he or she can probably get as much relief from a simple, inexpensive product as from the most elaborate and costly one. If a cough does not ease in a few days, the person should seek a doctor's help.

Unfortunately, modern medicine and pharmacology have no cure for the common cold. The best treatment is rest, increased fluid intake to prevent dehydration, humidification of the air if it is dry, and gargling with dilute salt water (2 tsp per quart). Allergy symptoms, on the other hand, can often be greatly reduced by desensitization injections based on what the person is allergic to, and elimination of the allergens from the person's environment as much as possible. (See Tables 16-3, 16-4, and 16-5 for the ingredients in some antitussives, cold and allergy preparations, and decongestants available over the counter.)

ANTACIDS*

Over $500 million was spent in 1980 for antacid preparations. These are advertised as giving relief from indigestion caused by excessive eating or drinking, heartburn, and for long-term treatment of chronic peptic ulcer disease.

The stomach is a complex organ that has the function of receiving food, mixing it thoroughly

---

*This section is taken largely from Garnett, 1979.

with specific juices and secretions, and continuing the role of digestion that was started in the mouth. The stomach produces hydrochloric acid, pepsin (an enzyme to start protein digestion), and protective mucus (which prevents the acid and pepsin from damaging the stomach lining). The anticipation of eating, and the smell, taste, chewing, and swallowing of food cause the stomach to release hydrochloric acid, pepsin, and mucus secretions, so that digestion can proceed.

It is estimated that as much as 50% of the population have had one or more attacks of gastritis, or irritation of the stomach. This condition is often referred to as acid indigestion, heartburn, upset stomach, or sour or acid stomach. The most common reason is caused by the hydrochloric acid getting through the mucus and entering the gastric lining, causing blood vessel injury and erosion of tissue. Inflammation and bleeding can and often do occur to varying degrees. Antacids can help alleviate and control this condition, and healing takes place in two to five days. Most cases of gastritis do not become chronic peptic ulcer disease. Peptic ulcers most frequently affect the duodenum (first part of the intestine) and the stomach. This condition is serious, but can be treated effectively with antacids. A person developing acute, severe stomach pain or chronic gastritis should see a physician promptly and not attempt to treat him- or herself. The ulcer seems to be a disease of complex civilization; it is not found in primitive tribes or in nonhuman primates or other animals unless they are stressed. Pigs get peptic ulcers readily when they are stressed.

The primary action of antacids is to neutralize some of the gastric acid and thus raise gastric pH. The pH of stomach fluid is normally as low as 1.5 to 2.0, which is extremely acidic. The antacids do not neutralize all of the stomach acid, nor do they bring the pH up to a neutral

7.0 (or you would develop a terrible upset stomach and a massive case of indigestion!). It is estimated that, if the stomach is brought to a pH of 2.3, 90% of the acid has been neutralized; at a pH of 3.3, 99% has been neutralized.

The ingredients used in antacids are sodium bicarbonate (baking soda), calcium carbonate, and salts of aluminum and of magnesium. Sodium bicarbonate is an excellent acid neutralizer, and it is cheap. However, it has a high sodium content that can be harmful to those who should restrict their sodium intake. Products with sodium bicarbonate include Alka-Seltzer® and Soda Mint® (Table 16-6).

Calcium carbonate is another widely used antacid. This chemical neutralizes acid, but it seems to cause a rebound effect, so that the stomach later will secrete even more acid than before. Calcium carbonate may make kidney stones worse in people who have a tendency to form stones. OTC products containing this substance are Alkets®, Dicarbosil®, and Tums®.

Aluminum hydroxide and related compounds are used in Aludrox®, Amphogel®, and Rolaids®. Aluminum salts are frequently used in combination with magnesium salts. Both are efficient antacids, and the constipating effect of the aluminum salt is counterbalanced by the opposite effect of the magnesium salt. This combination is used in DiGel®, Gelusil®, Maalox®, Mylanta®, WinGel®, and others.

Some antacid formulations have ingredients to release gas from gastric contents. The most commonly used, simethicone, breaks up gas bubbles and thus relieves pressure by facilitating belching and passing gas. Alginic acid, bismuth salts, and other substances are used in some products. None of these ingredients is effective in neutralizing acid.

Generally speaking, antacid preparations with calcium carbonate and concentrated antacids are the most potent and are safe for occasional use

TABLE 16-3 Antitussives[*]

Product	Cough suppressant	Expectorant	Sympathomimetic	Antihistamine	Other
Actol Expectorant®	noscapine	guaifenesin	—	—	alcohol
Alamine Expectorant®	codeine	guaifenesin	phenylephrine	chlorpheniramine	menthol; alcohol
Atussin D.M. Expectorant®	dextromethorphan	guaifenesin	phenylephrine phenylpropanolamine	chlorpheniramine	sucrose
Cerose®	codeine	potassium guaiacolsulfonate; ipecac	phenylephrine	phenindamine	sodium citrate; citric acid; glycerin; alcohol
Cheracol®	codeine	guaifenesin	phenylephrine	—	alcohol
Chlor-Trimeton Expectorant®	codeine	ammonium chloride; guaifenesin	phenylephrine	chlorpheniramine	sodium citrate; alcohol
Codimal DM®	dextromethorphan	potassium guaiacolsulfonate	phenylephrine	pyrilamine	sodium citrate; citric acid; alcohol
Coricidin®	—	ammonium chloride; guaifenesin	phenylpropanolamine	chlorpheniramine	—
Creo-Terpin®	—	creosote; terpin hydrate	—	—	sodium glycerophosphate; alcohol
Formula 44®	dextromethorphan	—	—	doxylamine	sodium citrate; alcohol
Hold 4 Hour®	dextromethorphan	—	—	—	benzocaine

Hydriodic Acid®	—	hydrogen iodide	—	—	alcohol
Pertussin 8 Hour®	dextromethorphan	—	—	—	—
Quiet-Nite®	dextromethorphan	—	ephedrine	chlorpheniramine	acetaminophen; alcohol
Robitussin A-C®	codeine	guaifenesin	—	—	alcohol
Romex®	dextromethorphan	guaifenesin	phenylephrine	chlorpheniramine	—
Triaminicol®	dextromethorphan	ammonium chloride	phenylpropanolamine	pheniramine; pyrilamine	—
Trind®	—	guaifenesin	phenylephrine	—	acetaminophen; alcohol
Tussar-2®	codeine; carbetapentane	guaifenesin	—	chlorpheniramine	sodium citrate; citric acid; methyl-paraben; alcohol
Tussciden Expectorant®	—	guaifenesin	—	—	—
Vicks Cough Syrup®	dextromethorphan	guaifenesin	—	—	sodium citrate; alcohol

TABLE 16-4   Cold and allergy preparations[*]

Product	Sympathomimetic	Antihistamine	Analgesic	Other
Alka-Seltzer Plus®	phenyl-propanolamine	chlorpheniramine	aspirin	———
Bayer Decongestant®	phenyl-propanolamine	chlorpheniramine	aspirin	———
Chlor-Trimeton®	———	chlorpheniramine	———	———
Codimal®	pseudo-ephedrine	chlorpheniramine	salicylamide; acetaminophen	———
Contac®	phenyl-propanolamine	chlorpheniramine	———	belladonna alkaloids
Coricidin®	———	chlorpheniramine	aspirin	———
Co Tylenol®	pseudoephedrine	chlorpheniramine	acetaminophen	———
Dristan®	phenylephrine	chlorpheniramine	aspirin	caffeine; aluminum hydroxide; magnesium carbonate
Inhiston®	———	pheniramine	———	———
Neo-Synephrine®	phenylephrine	thenyldiamine	acetaminophen	caffeine
Novafed A®	pseudoephedrine	chlorpheniramine	———	alcohol
NyQuil®	ephedrine	doxylamine	acetaminophen	alcohol
Sinarest®	phenylephrine	chlorpheniramine	acetaminophen	———
Sine-Aid®	phenyl-propanolamine	———	acetaminophen	———
Sine-Off®	phenyl-propanolamine	chlorpheniramine	aspirin	———
Sudafed®	pseudoephedrine	———	———	———
Super Anahist®	phenyl-propanolamine	phenyltoloxamine; thonzylamine	acetaminophen; aspirin; phenacetin	caffeine
4-Way Cold Tablets®	phenylephrine	———	aspirin	magnesium hydroxide; white phenolphthalein

[*] Copyright 1979 by the American Pharmaceutical Association, *Handbook of Nonprescription Drugs*, 6th ed., pp. 107–112. Reprinted with permission of the American Pharmaceutical Association.

TABLE 16-5 Topical decongestants: nasal sprays, drops, and inhalers*

Product	Sympathomimetic	Other ingredients
Afrin®	oxymetazoline	sorbitol; aminoacetic acid; sodium hydroxide
Benzedrex®	propylhexedrine	aromatics
Coricidin®	phenylephrine	———
Dristan®	phenylephrine	pheniramine; menthol; eucalyptol; methyl salicylate
Neo-Synephrine®	phenylephrine	———
Privine®	naphazoline	———
Sinex®	phenylephrine	methapyrilene; menthol; eucalyptol; camphor; methyl salicylate
St. Joseph®	oxymetazoline	———
Super Anahist®	phenylephrine	alcohol
Vicks®	levodesoxyephedrine	menthol; camphor; methyl salicylate; bornyl acetate
4-Way®	phenylephrine; naphazoline; phenyl-propanolamine	pyrilamine

at low, recommended doses. Aluminum-magnesium hydroxide gels have low toxicity and an adequate neutralizing capacity. All antacids may interact with other drugs; they may interfere by altering other drugs' gastrointestinal absorption or their renal elimination. For example, antacids inhibit the absorption of tetracycline antibiotics; thus these antibiotics should not be taken at the same time as antacids. Antacids also can decrease both the absorption of iron from an iron supplement or the diet and the absorption of the major tranquilizer chlorpromazine, which is used to treat schizophrenia. On the other hand, it has been found that antacid users have a greater absorption of the following drugs into the blood:

levodopa (used in treating Parkinson's disease) and the anticoagulant dicumarol (increased in blood levels by 50%). Amphetamine excretion is slowed by antacids.

As you can see, even OTC drugs have the potential for dangerous interactions. The FDA Committee on Antacids recommended the following guidelines for their use:

1. Antacids for relief of indigestion should not be taken longer than two weeks. If relief is not obtained, a physician should be consulted.

2. The user should know that antacids may cause diarrhea (magnesium salts) or constipation (aluminum salts).

TABLE 16-6 Antacids[*]

Product	Dosage form	Calcium carbonate	Aluminum hydroxide	Magnesium oxide or hydroxide	Other ingredients
Albicon®	tablet	560 mg	150 mg	———	magnesium carbonate
Alka-2 Chewable®	tablet	500 mg	———	———	———
Alka-Seltzer Effervescent®	tablet	———	———	———	sodium bicarbonate; citric acid; potassium bicarbonate
Alkets®	tablet	780 mg	———	65 mg	magnesium carbonate
Aluminum Hydroxide Gel®	suspension	———	70 mg/ml	———	sorbitol; peppermint; sucrose
Amphojel®	tablet	———	300 mg	———	———
BiSoDol®	tablet	195 mg	———	180 mg	———
Di-Gel®	tablet	———	codried with magnesium carbonate, 282 mg	85 mg	simethicone
Gelusil®	tablet	———	200 mg	200 mg	simethicone
Maalox Plus®	tablet	———	dried gel, 200 mg	200 mg	simethicone
Mylanta®	tablet	———	200 mg	200 mg	simethicone
Nutrajel®	suspension	———	60 mg/ml	———	———
Phillip's Milk of Magnesia®	suspension; tablet	———	———	81 mg/ml 311 mg	———
Phosphajel®	suspension	———	———	———	aluminum phosphate
Rolaids®	tablet	———	———	———	dihydroxyaluminum-sodium carbonate
Soda Mint®	tablet	———	———	———	sodium bicarbonate; peppermint oil
Titralac®	tablet	420 mg	———	———	glycine
Tums®	tablet	500 mg	———	———	peppermint oil
WinGel®	tablet	———	180 mg	160 mg	mint flavor

[*]Copyright 1979 by the American Pharmaceutical Association, *Handbook of Nonprescription Drugs*, 6th ed., pp. 14–18. Reprinted with permission of the American Pharmaceutical Association.

3. Patients with restricted salt intake because of blood pressure problems and the like should be aware that many antacids contain sodium, and they should select a product that does not.

4. The tablet form of antacids is less effective than liquid preparations. If tablets are preferred, they should be chewed thoroughly and followed with a full glass of water to help dispersion in the stomach. Effervescent tablets are supposed to be dissolved in a glass of water first; most of the bubbles should be allowed to subside before swallowing the preparation.

5. The user should be aware there can be significant drug interactions and consult his or her pharmacist or physician for further information.

AIDS FOR INTESTINAL PROBLEMS

Many millions of people use OTC drugs to treat constipation and diarrhea. We are a bowel-conscious society, and spent over $337 million in 1980 for nearly 700 OTC drugs that are classified as laxatives or cathartics and about $112 million on drugs to alleviate diarrhea. It is apparent that, as we have become more industrialized and advanced technologically, we have had more problems with our digestive systems. Some of the reasons include stress, modified eating habits, and the types of food that we eat. We often face deadlines and pressures that can cause problems with our digestive systems, from indigestion and ulcers to constipation or diarrhea. The typical Western diet has many highly processed foods with little fiber. Instead of altering life-styles or eating habits, people take drugs. Many people suffer from abuse of laxatives or of antidiarrheal compounds. Such people have taken laxatives on a long-term basis and now must continue to do so because they have a

bowel "addiction." This is a type of iatrogenic illness, which means that you become ill from the treatment itself.

The frequency of defecation varies among people. For some people, two bowel movements a day are normal; for others, two or three a week are normal. The elimination of waste materials is a complex process, involving nervous and hormonal controls and coordination of several muscle types. Interference with any part of the process will cause a change that may lead either to constipation, the slowing down of the elimination process, or diarrhea, the speeding up of the process.

Laxatives*

The following are some of the causes of constipation:

1. Neglect in responding to the defecation urge, which can weaken the normal defecation reflexes, and failure to acquire a regular habit of defecation.
2. Faulty eating habits; for example, failure to include enough bulk in the diet, low fluid intake, and excessive ingestion of foods like processed cheese.
3. Mental stress and change of environment.
4. Prolonged use of drugs such as aluminum hydroxide and calcium carbonate (antacids), opiates, anticholinergic drugs, and laxatives.
5. Anatomic or physiological problems, such as growths, damage to intestinal sphincter valves, and so on.

Treatment of constipation is often possible without the use of drugs; switching to a higher

---

* This section is largely from Darlington and Curry, 1979.

fiber diet, drinking plenty of water, and getting regular exercise are all ways to treat this problem. Dietary fiber is that portion of vegetables, grains, fruit, and other plant products that the human gastrointestinal system cannot digest. It absorbs water and adds bulk to the intestinal contents. Adding fiber to the diet often works to correct chronic constipation, whereas laxatives are useful to alleviate the immediate problem. There are several classes of laxatives:

1. Bulk-forming laxatives provide the bulk necessary to stimulate the defecation reflex. These substances will create bulk by absorbing fluid and swelling. They require 12 to 72 hours for effect.

2. Contact laxatives act on the intestine to reduce absorption of electrolytes and water and to stimulate the propulsive activity of the intestine. These substances are not recommended if the person has abdominal pain, nausea, or vomiting, because these can be symptoms of appendicitis. The contact laxatives are effective, but are probably the most abused of all the laxatives. These drugs are not recommended for simple constipation, and they should never be used for more than one week of regular treatment. Most of the drugs in this category require six to eight hours for effect.

3. Emollients are surfactants (wetting agents) and emulsifiers (substances allowing the mixing of fats and water) that will soften the fecal mass. These laxatives should not be used any longer than a week without consulting a physician. These also require about 12 to 72 hours to act.

4. Glycerin suppositories: the glycerin absorbs fluid and the soap irritates the intestine. These act within 15 to 60 minutes.

5. Lubricants: mineral oil and olive oil are good examples. These oils penetrate and soften fecal matter. Repeated, prolonged use of mineral oil can cause problems because of absorption of the oil, which accumulates in the body.

Lubricants also impair absorption of fat-soluble vitamins like A and D. Children and the elderly tend to inhale some mineral oil when swallowing a laxative dose. As described previously, mineral oil droplets interfere with the action of the lysozymes, glycoproteins, and antibodies in the mucous coating of the nasal passageways, throat, and lungs. Lubricants require about 6 to 8 hours for effect.

6. Saline laxatives pull water from the body tissues, adding bulk and encouraging peristaltic action of the intestine. This type is used in preparation for examination of the bowel or to eliminate drugs in suspected cases of food or drug poisoning; the drugs are used in purging doses to empty the large intestine.

Regular use of most laxatives, particularly the contact preparations, can result in laxative abuse. In fact, excessive use of laxatives can cause diarrhea and vomiting, leading to fluid and electrolyte losses, and muscular weakness. (Electrolytes are ions such as sodium, potassium, calcium, bicarbonate, chloride, and others that are dissolved in body fluids.) Heavy use of laxatives over a long period of time can cause anatomic harm to the intestines (see Table 16-7 for a list of ingredients in laxative preparations).

Antidiarrheals*

Antidiarrheal compounds are used occasionally by millions of people in the United States, although there are some that take such preparations on a routine basis. Diarrhea has various causes. Drugs that can cause diarrhea include the broad-spectrum antibiotics, antacids based on magnesium salts, and antihypertensives. Usually diarrhea is a symptom of a minor, tran-

---

* This section is largely from Longe, 1979.

TABLE 16-7 Laxatives*

Product	Dosage form	Contact	Bulk	Emollient	Other laxatives
Agoral®	emulsion	phenolphthalein	agar gel	mineral oil	—
Alophen®	tablet	phenolphthalein	—	—	—
Bisacodyl®	tablet	bisacodyl	—	—	—
Black Draught®	tablet	senna	—	—	—
Carter's Little Pills®	tablet	aloe; podophyllum	—	—	—
Ex-Lax®	tablet	phenolphthalein	—	—	—
Feen-A-Mint®	chewing gum	phenolphthalein	—	—	—
Fletcher's Castoria®	liquid	senna	—	—	—
Haley's M-O®	emulsion	—	—	mineral oil	magnesium hydroxide
Metamucil®	powder	—	psyllium	—	—
Phillip's Milk of Magnesia®	suspension	—	—	—	magnesium hydroxide
Serutan®	powder	—	psyllium	—	—
Stimulax®	capsule	cascara	—	dioctyl sodium sulfosuccinate	—
Tonelax®	tablet	danthron	—	—	—

*Copyright 1979 by the American Pharmaceutical Association, *Handbook of Nonprescription Drugs*, 6th ed., pp. 48–54. Reprinted with permission of the American Pharmaceutical Association.

sient gastrointestinal disorder. The person has a sudden onset of frequent, liquid stools, gas, abdominal pain, and often weakness, fever, and vomiting. Chronic diarrhea is the persistent or recurrent passage of unformed stools. It is usually the result of multiple factors, including many serious diseases involving the kidneys, heart, liver, thyroid, and lungs. The FDA requires the following statement to be included on the label of all OTC antidiarrheal preparations: "Warning—do not use for more than two days, or in the presence of high fever, or in infants or children under three years of age unless directed by a physician."

Diarrhea in infants and children can be dangerous because of the loss of water and electrolytes. Water loss in an infant or young child with severe acute diarrhea might approach 10% of the total water content, which is near the limit at which serious dehydration and even death could occur. An adult could die of dehydration if he or she lost more than about 12% of body water.

It is not unusual for travelers to come down with diarrhea, typically caused by an alteration in the types of bacteria in the intestines. The intestines respond by producing large quantities of fluid and by increasing motility to flush out the infection, causing diarrhea. "Traveler's trot" is bothersome, but usually of short duration and treatable. Travelers in areas where sanitation is poor should eat only thoroughly cooked foods and drink only boiled or bottled water, bottled soft drinks, beer, or wine. They should avoid drinking beverages with ice cubes (probably made from tap water) and brushing their teeth with tap water. This will reduce the number of foreign microorganisms entering the system at one time, perhaps to the point at which the body's defense mechanisms can handle the situation.

There are more than 100 OTC antidiarrheal drugs on the market. Some of them work against

the symptoms of diarrhea, some against the cause, and others against the effect of the disease—that is, loss of nutrients or electrolytes. The categories of drugs used include opiates, adsorbents, astringents, electrolytes, nutrients, bulk laxatives (as absorbents), anti-infectives, digestive enzymes, sedatives, tranquilizers, smooth muscle relaxants, and anticholinergics. Many of these, such as the pure opiate preparations, anti-infectives, and sedatives are prescription drugs in the United States.

The opiates are safe and effective, but purchase is regulated. All derivatives of opium tend to cause constipation. The normal dose is 15 to 20 mg of opium or 1.5 to 2.0 mg of morphine. Paregoric alone is a Schedule III prescription drug; however, it is possible to buy OTC paregoric in combination with other antidiarrheal drugs. OTC paregoric cannot contain more than 100 mg of opium (about 25 ml of paregoric) per 100 ml of liquid. Some OTC preparations have ineffective dosages. OTC sales of some Schedule V drugs, such as Amogel®, Donnagel-PG®, Parelixir®, and Parepectolin®, are forbidden in some states.

Polycarbophil (Sorboquel®) is the only OTC preparation, other than opiates, that is both a safe and an effective antidiarrheal. It is an adsorbent and has a marked capacity to take up free water in the bowels, thus drying up the stool.

The adsorbents, such as aluminum hydroxide, attapulgite, bismuth subsalts, kaolin, magnesium trisilicate, and pectin, are the most frequently used type of drug in OTC antidiarrheal preparations. The FDA says the adsorbents are safe to use in the recommended doses, but it claims there is insufficient evidence to classify them as effective. The adsorbents probably adsorb toxins, bacteria, and various noxious materials that irritate the intestine and thus cause diarrhea. They will adsorb nutrients and some drugs, like the tetracyclines, as well. Bismuth subsalts, like Pepto-Bismol®, will turn the stools dark. Kaopectate®, Pargel®, and Quintess® are examples of adsorbent antidiarrheals with no other active ingredients.

The anticholinergics, such as the belladonna alkaloids, are prescription antidiarrheal drugs. One can buy combination OTC antidiarrheal preparations containing belladonna compounds, but the low dosage is ineffective. When combined with adsorbents, the anticholinergics may also be adsorbed, thus making them even less likely to be effective. Donnagel® is an example of an OTC adsorbent-anticholinergic combination.

A kaolin-pectin mixture can be safely used for a short period of time by an adult to treat acute diarrhea. Medical attention should be sought for an infant or young child, or for an adult if diarrhea persists. Travelers who will be exposed to poor sanitation should consult a physician about receiving a shot of immune globulin a few days before departure, or obtaining a prescription for paregoric, loperamide (Imodium®), or diphenoxylate plus atropine (Lomotil®). Lomotil® is a Schedule V narcotic; availability as an OTC preparation varies depending on the state.

CHAPTER 17

SPECIAL PROBLEMS
IN THE ELDERLY*

CHAPTER OBJECTIVES

1. Explain how the elderly differ from other age groups according to the type and number of drugs they take.
2. Describe the physiological and metabolic differences that affect the way an average elderly person's body responds to drugs, compared to a young adult.
3. Summarize how guidelines for medication for the elderly differ.
4. Explain which type of sedative-hypnotic drug is likely to be better for an older person, and why.
5. List side effects of the sedative-hypnotics, tricyclic antidepressants, antipsychotics, and over-the-counter drugs that are of particular significance to the older patient.
6. Describe special problems associated with alcohol abuse.
7. Define the following terms: Librium rage, dementia, control drugs, young-old, and old-old.

*We appreciate Gary Martin's library research and preparation of a paper on this topic as part of the course requirements for his Ph.D. in clinical psychology, as well as his insight from his experience with the elderly.

317

Although definition of the term *aged* is complex, most societies designate people over the age of 65 as aged. This is primarily a social definition related to retirement programs in technologically advanced countries. It is more difficult to define *aged* biologically or chronologically, because there can be great variation between biological age and chronological age. A person's biological age may be younger than expected for his or her chronological age if he or she has been in excellent health, or older than expected, if the person has not taken care of him- or herself or has developed genetically related diseases (diabetes, high blood pressure, and so on). Social gerontologists (those who study the aged) further subdivide the aged into the "young-old"—those between ages 65–75—and the "old-old"—those aged 76 and up.

The increase in the absolute numbers and in the proportion of those who are 65 and older is a relatively recent phenomenon. In the United States, the life expectancy at birth has increased from 47.3 years in 1900 to 72.5 years in 1975, averaging the figures for males and females. This trend is expected to continue in this country and elsewhere in the world. Currently, between 10% and 11% of the U.S. population is 65 and older.

A major reason why the proportion of elderly people is increasing is improved health care in their earlier years. But, because these people have lived longer, they are more likely to have developed the diseases of old age: cardiovascular problems, dementia (senility), and others. As a group, the elderly are not as healthy as younger adults, and they receive more medications than other age groups. The elderly account for a quarter of all drug prescriptions, more than twice what would be expected for their numerical proportion of the population. Two-thirds of all older adults use at least one prescription drug daily, with many using several prescriptions.

Four of the ten drugs most often prescribed for the elderly are psychoactive sedative-hypnotics (see Chapter 10): Doriden® (glutethimide), Valium®, Librium®, and phenobarbital. Older adults are given a disproportionate number of prescriptions for psychoactive drugs, with the greatest number being given to older women. Elderly women, who comprise 6% of the population, receive 17% of the prescriptions written for Thorazine® (a major tranquilizer), a similar percentage of those written for Elavil® (an antidepressant), and about 20% of those for the nonbarbiturate sedative-hypnotics. A quarter of the community-based elderly (those living by themselves or with others, instead of in a nursing home) take psychoactive drugs. Furthermore, many psychoactive drugs have a psychological addiction potential. One study demonstrated that 50% of a community's elderly citizens who used psychoactive drugs reported that they could not perform their regular daily activities without their medication (Prentice, 1979).

Half of those living in nursing homes and long-term care institutions are given psychoactive drugs. (Approximately 5% of the elderly are institutionalized.) In institutional settings such as nursing homes, 8 of the 10 most frequently prescribed drugs are psychoactives, and the average patient takes 4.1 drugs daily. More than 35% of patients had orders for sedative-hypnotics to take at the discretion of the nursing staff or the patient, although their medical histories did not indicate a need for such drugs. Far too many patients are given psychoactive medications without physical examinations or good nursing care, and the dosage is often excessive. Over 80% of all acute drug reactions (Chapter 18) in the elderly involved the misuse of such drugs, primarily Tuinal® and Luminal® (barbiturates), and Valium®. Nursing homes may contribute directly to misuse of drugs; many such institutions give "control" drugs simply to manage difficult patients. Some 80% of aged mental patients are receiving major and minor tranquilizers unnecessarily (Eisdorfer & Basen, 1979; Petersen & Whittington, 1977; Prentice, 1979).

AGING AND PHYSIOLOGICAL CHANGES

Drug treatment of elderly adults requires special considerations because of the physiological and metabolic changes that occur with aging. The absorption, excretion, and activity of psychoactive drugs are altered as a result of the aging process, causing many drugs to be retained in the body longer than in younger adults. Consequently, the clinical and toxic effects of such drugs may be more pronounced in older people. The physiological factors include the following:

1.   A decreased cardiac output, so the heart is less able to handle stress and supplies the brain and kidneys with less blood.

2.   Systolic blood pressure is typically higher than when the person was younger.

3.   The reduction in intestinal blood flow causes delayed drug absorption.

4.   Kidney function is typically seriously diminished, so drugs that are excreted by this route are not eliminated as efficiently as they once were (Gotz & Gotz, 1978).

5.   The average older person has less total body water and proportionately more fat to lean tissue than when he or she was younger, which means a given drug will be distributed differently. If it is a fat-soluble drug, there is proportionately more fat for it to dissolve in, leading to a longer retention time in the body. If it is a water-soluble drug, it will be present in higher concentrations (less water to dissolve in) than in a younger person, which may cause toxic effects.

Metabolic changes in the elderly include the following:

1.   There is a reduction in the concentration of neurotransmitters in the central nervous system and a decrease in functional neurons. The central nervous system is the most sensitive to age-related changes. In general, the action of stimulants is lessened, whereas the action of depressants is enhanced.

2.   The gastric juice is less acid, which affects the solubility of drugs, and the stomach empties more slowly.

3.   There is less serum albumin available to transport drugs that are bound to this protein, so there is a higher ratio of free to bound drug and a greater probability of toxicity. This enhances the effects of the benzodiazepine tranquilizers (Valium®, Librium®) and the tricyclic antidepressants (Chapter 10) (Piland, 1979).

4.   Some enzyme systems in the liver, such as the microsomal enzymes, are impaired in the elderly. This reduces the rate at which many drugs, such as the psychoactive agents, the anticonvulsants, and the oral anticoagulants, are metabolized. However, metabolism of other drugs, such as alcohol, is not significantly affected. In other words, aging does not affect the liver metabolism of drugs consistently (Earnest & MacGregor, 1982).

Because of these physiological and metabolic changes, the elderly are less able to deal with the stress of disease and are more sensitive to adverse effects of drugs. On top of this situation, psychoactive drugs may be used inappropriately because of diagnoses of psychiatric symptoms that fail to take into account the unique physiological, psychological, and sociological characteristics of the older person. Even when the diagnosis is appropriate, the prescription may not be appropriate for the altered metabolic capacity of the older person (Piland, 1979).

Neurotoxic effects, such as confusion, oversedation, paranoid delusions, perceptual problems, and paradoxical reactions (see "Librium rage," p. 322) from normal adult doses of antidepressant and antipsychotic drugs are not uncommon in the elderly. These symptoms are easily misinterpreted and are treated with *increased* dosages or with additional drugs! Side effects of such drugs that may be lethal to the elderly include impairment of the cardiovascular system, stress on the kidneys, and decreased respiratory efficiency. Parkinsonism is a common drug effect in older persons, as is tardive dyskinesia, which may occur sooner than it would have otherwise (Chapter 10) (Piland, 1979). These are iatrogenic conditions, which means the condition was caused by the treatment procedure, not by a disease.

Nonpsychoactive drugs may produce psychoactive effects in the elderly, including depression, pseudodementia, and anxiety. Many peripheral effects are also more pronounced in the aged. Older adults have seven times the rate of serious side effects that younger adults have. Those who have had a previous adverse reaction are more likely to have another, even to a completely unrelated drug (Davison, 1978; Piland, 1979).

THE GRANNY-PROOF CAP AND OTHER PROBLEMS

Medication guidelines that take into account the differences associated with aging include:

1. Psychoactive drugs should be given at lower dosages, 33% to 50% lower, than those dosages typically prescribed for younger adults. Increases in dosages, if needed, should be more gradual.

2. Dosages should generally be spread out during the day, rather than the entire dosage given at once, although there are exceptions. The elderly may be less able to tolerate the sudden absorption of a large drug dose into their circulation.

3. Polypharmacy, the giving of more than one drug, should be avoided to reduce the possibility of adverse reactions (Gulevich, 1977).

4. A complete medical examination should be given before starting psychoactive drug therapy. Although this seems so obvious it should not have to be specified, a study of 75 nursing homes showed that two-thirds of the patients had not been given physical examinations at admission, and, of those who had, the exam was often incomplete. Drug treatment may be complicated by any number of medical problems commonly found in the elderly. Similarly, medical problems often aggravate or precipitate psychiatric symptoms.

5. Dosage, progress, and possible side effects should be evaluated frequently. Pulse, blood pressure, and neurological status should be checked at regular intervals. Forty percent of the elderly patients in the study just mentioned had not been seen by a physician for over three months, and 35% of those receiving tranquilizers had not had so much as their blood pressure recorded in over a year (Prentice, 1979).

Cognitive changes associated with aging, particularly impaired memory, should also be taken into consideration when prescribing psychoactive drugs. It is important that older adults be given clear, complete verbal and written instructions about their medications to mini-mize difficulties associated with forgetfulness. Memory and visual aids can be used to assist the elderly to remember the timing and dosage of their medications. Pill bottles could include large, color-coded dots stuck to their caps that cor-respond to a color-coded chart with instructions and warnings written in large letters. Compart-mental pill containers help some persons mon-itor their dosages. These can be purchased or made out of household items like styrofoam egg cartons, if the drugs do not need special storage conditions. A simple medication check list is often useful. Family members or friends can be enlisted to assist in distributing and monitoring drug dosages.

Davison (1978) believes that three or four different preparations are about the maximum that most elderly persons can manage by them-selves. Senile or very frail old people with poor supervision are liable to skip taking their med-ications. Fitter old people are more likely to prescribe for themselves and are liable to save leftover drugs "just in case." Davison recom-mends that the old person's living quarters be periodically cleared of all medicines that are no longer being prescribed. (Sounds like a good idea for all ages!)

Of medication errors in the elderly, the most common is omission, and the second most com-mon is self-prescribing, of which about 7% lead to serious problems. Incorrect dosages (over or under) account for about 6% of errors. Errors in timing or sequence are made by about 3% of community-based patients and by a higher per-centage of people administering drugs to the institutionalized. Drugs are most often admin-istered just after meals, because that is the most convenient time for the nursing staff, despite the fact that 30%–50% of almost any medica-tion will not be absorbed when administered with food (Bozzetti & MacMurray, 1977).

SPECIFIC CLASSES OF MEDICATION AND THEIR USE IN THE ELDERLY POPULATION

Sedative-Hypnotics

Of the antianxiety agents (discussed in Chapter 10), the benzodiazepines are considered to be the safest and most effective for treating anxiety in the elderly. Librium®, Valium®, and Serax® are the benzodiazepines most frequently used. Librium®, Valium®, Verstran®, and others are metabolized into other compounds that also have sedative and antianxiety actions and conse-quently have effects for several days. Their bio-logical half-lives range from 80% to 175% longer for the aged compared to younger adults, and they will not come to a *steady state* for as long as three weeks. (Steady state means that, when the aged person starts taking the tranquilizer daily, as is routine practice, the concentration in his or her body keeps increasing for up to three weeks before the rate of elimination matches the rate of intake). Serax® and Ati-van®, however, have less complicated patterns of metabolism and excretion. They have shorter half-lives that are similar for older and younger adults and reach steady state after only a few days (Conrad, 1982). Serax® is considered to be the drug of choice for the elderly, particular-ly those on long-term treatment, because it is the shortest-acting drug of the benzodiazepines (Piland, 1979). Starting doses of the benzodi-azepines for elderly persons should be much lower than those given to younger persons and should be adjusted to the individual to prevent over-sedation.

Side effects of the benzodiazepines include drowsiness, unsteadiness of gait, and possible confusion, with susceptibility to side effects increasing with age. In particular, the elderly have a greater vulnerability to "Librium rage," a paradoxical reaction characterized by irritability and hostility occasionally found in persons taking Librium®. The drowsiness and unsteadiness of gait increase the probability of an already frail older person falling and breaking a bone, usually the hip. Hip fractures are a major cause of death in the elderly—not from the broken bone, but from the immobilization necessary to allow the bone to heal. When the person cannot move around, he or she is much more likely to develop pneumonia and die.

The use of antihistamines, sedative-hypnotics like meprobamate (Miltown®, Equanil®), and the barbiturates to treat anxiety and insomnia seems ill advised. The antihistamines have anticholinergic effects, whereas their sedative effects are only a secondary pharmacologic property. Sedatives like Miltown® and Equanil® are easily abused and are addictive, as discussed in Chapter 10, and are considered somewhat less effective than the benzodiazepines. Although the barbiturates are cheaper than the benzodiazepines, they commonly produce more sedation and even delirium in the elderly and should not be used. There are risks of habituation with the barbiturates, and they accelerate liver microsomal metabolism of other drugs, decreasing their clinical effects. Barbiturate overdose accounts for 14.5% of all drug deaths in the elderly. When the barbiturates are taken in nonfatal doses but combined with other depressants, the combination accounts for almost 20% of deaths (Eisdorfer & Basen, 1979; Piland, 1979).

Antidepressants

Because approximately 20% of the elderly suffer from some form of psychiatric disorder, the greater incidence of depression in this group is not surprising. Depression is the most common functional disorder, but it is often overlooked because its symptoms may be regarded as consistent with the aging process, and may also be confused with various disease conditions. Depression may be the first symptom of a serious disease, such as Parkinson's syndrome, a type of anemia, hypothyroidism, cardiovascular disease, and cancer. Depression can also be caused by, or aggravated by, many drugs commonly used in the elderly. As many as 50% to 70% of patients receiving antihypertensives (high blood pressure medications) may exhibit sadness, apathy, agitation, and insomnia. Endogenous depression, caused by reduced brain function, not by life events, disease, or drugs, may respond well to treatment with antidepressants or antipsychotics (Lamy, 1980).

The tricyclic antidepressants are the preferred antidepressant drugs for the elderly. However, like the benzodiazepine tranquilizers, the tricyclics have a longer biological half-life in the elderly (40 to 60 hours for those 65 and older, compared to 20 to 35 hours for younger adults). Steady state levels may not be reached for as long as two weeks. Recommended starting doses are typically one-third to one-half of those used for younger patients, with maintenance doses being one-half of that for younger patients. Also, dosage levels should be increased more gradually, because of the longer biological half-life (Bressler, 1982a).

Tricyclic antidepressants have anticholinergic effects that are particularly hazardous for the elderly, who are especially vulnerable to them because of decreased liver function. An anticholinergic effect that commonly occurs with older patients is a confusional state characterized by short-term memory impairment, disorientation, impaired attention span, anxiety, and hallucinations. Other common anticholinergic effects that are potentially problematic with the elderly are dry mouth, constipation, blurred vision, and urinary retention. A dry mouth may create difficulties with dentures; already present bowel and bladder problems may worsen; and blurred vision may exacerbate existing vision problems. The tricyclic antidepressants can cause excessive sedation and postural hypotension (low blood pressure causing dizziness when the person stands up), making falls and broken bones more likely (Piland, 1979).

Monoamine oxidase (MAO) inhibitors are rarely recommended for use in older persons, except when treatment with tricyclic antidepressants has failed. The elderly are more likely to have hypertension, to be taking other medications that interfere with the MAO inhibitors, and to have difficulty remembering all of the precautions and dietary restrictions necessary to avoid a hypertensive crisis. Stimulants are not appropriate for treating depression in the elderly (and are not often used in younger adults), because of their dangerous cardiovascular effects and their questionable overall effectiveness (Piland, 1979).

Antipsychotic Medications

In addition to treating schizophrenia, the antipsychotics are useful for mild to moderate dementia (senility). In treating dementia, the antipsychotic drugs cannot restore mental faculties, but they can improve the elderly patient's quality of life. Of the psychoactive medications, the antipsychotics are the most widely prescribed, with Mellaril® (thioridazine, one of the phenothiazines discussed in Chapter 10) topping the list. Clinically, the various antipsychotics are considered to be equally effective, both in younger and older populations. However, a wide range of potentially serious side effects, particularly for the elderly, are frequently associated with the use of these drugs. It is extremely important to tailor the use of antipsychotic medications to the needs of the individual, taking into account relative susceptibility to the expected potential side effects of the respective drugs (Lamy, 1980).

Exaggerated drug effects, both therapeutic and adverse, can be expected with the use of antipsychotics in older adults, because of their decreased ability to distribute, metabolize, and eliminate drugs. Consequently, it is recommended that starting doses for the elderly be one-half to two-thirds the typical adult dose, and that dosage increases be gradual. Side effects found more frequently in the elderly include oversedation, akathisia (inability to sit still), hypotension, and toxic effects on the cardiovascular system. Central nervous system side effects of delirium, dementia, assaultiveness, delusions, and hallucinations are common. A particular risk for the elderly is an increased susceptibility to the involuntary ("extrapyramidal") side effects (see Chapter 10). One-half of all persons over 60 years of age who take antipsychotic drugs experience extrapyramidal symptoms (Bressler, 1982b; Piland, 1979).

Thioridazine (Mellaril®) is generally considered to be the drug of choice among the antipsychotics. This is primarily because it has a relatively low incidence of extrapyramidal side effects and Parkinsonism. However, Mellaril® also tends to produce marked side effects of sedation and hypotension. Haloperidol (Haldol®) is considered to be as effective as Mellaril®. The risk of oversedation and hypotension with haloperidol is lower, but the risk of extrapyramidal symptoms is higher (Lamy, 1980). Perhaps the best-tolerated antipsychotic drug in the elderly is Tindal® (acetophenazine). It has relatively low sedative and hypotensive effects, with no extrapyramidal symptoms (Bressler, 1982b).

Over-the-Counter (OTC) Drugs

When compared with other age groups, the elderly do not use OTCs excessively. However, 70% do use OTC drugs regularly, and OTC preparations do pose potential hazards for the elderly. As they are to many other drugs, the elderly are more susceptible to the side effects of OTC drugs than are younger age groups. Aspirin, for example, alters blood-coagulation time and can irritate the stomach lining. In addition to costing money and having sometimes dubious benefits, OTCs such as aspirin, antacids, and laxatives can interfere with the action of many prescription drugs. Also, many OTC drugs contain high levels of sodium, which few older persons can handle (see Chapter 16).

Constipation is a problem for at least 25% of older patients. Laxatives, which are heavily used by the elderly, can impair nutrient absorption, alter body fluid levels, and create bowel dependency. Although aging *per se* does not cause bowel disturbances, the elderly tend to eat less, use highly processed foods with low fiber content, consume less liquids, be less physically active, and have poorer muscle tone than younger people, all of which contribute to digestive problems.

Antacids are also heavily used by the elderly, because of the increased incidence of gastritis. Antacids may increase antibiotic absorption; reduce digitalis, psychoactive drug, and nutrient absorption; and mask such conditions as stomach cancer. Chronic use of large amounts of aluminum-based antacids affects several aspects of bone-mineral metabolism (calcium, phosphorus, and fluoride) and thus can exacerbate the weakening of the bones that is already a problem for the elderly. Antacids also tend to cause bowel disturbances in older persons, with calcium- and aluminum-based antacids causing constipation, and magnesium-based antacids causing diarrhea. Furthermore, some antacids are high in sodium (see Table 16-6 on p. 310) (Earnest & MacGregor, 1982).

ALCOHOL AND THE ELDERLY

Alcohol abuse tends to be an underrecognized problem in the elderly. It is estimated that alcohol abuse or alcoholism occurs in up to 10% of the elderly, more in men than women. Older adults actually tend to reduce their alcohol consumption with age, but what alcohol they do drink tends to make up a higher percentage of total calories and fluid intake than when they were younger. One drink may account for 10% to 15% of an older adult's total calorie intake. Alcohol problems in the elderly are associated with greatly increased mortality (20% to 50% of all older adults' admissions to general hospitals are a result of serious alcohol involvement), social withdrawal, falls and accidents, malnutrition, depression, suicide, and central nervous system effects (not to mention the expenditure of limited income). Given proper treatment, the elderly are as likely, or more likely, to recover from alcoholism as younger people. However, they are systematically excluded from many treatment facilities on the assumption that they are poor risks in a situation with a limited number of treatment slots (Bozzetti & MacMurray, 1977; Mishara & Kastenbaum, 1980).

There appear to be two types of alcoholism associated with aging. The first comprises those who have been abusers of alcohol most of their lives and who have survived into old age. These persons are typically unhealthy in that they have developed one or more physical disorders associated with drinking, such as chronic brain damage, cardiovascular disease, and cirrhosis of the liver (see Chapter 11). The second type represents those older persons who began using alcohol as a means of coping with the life stresses associated with aging—illness, loneliness, retirement, loss of income, lower status, and bereavement. As many as one-third of all elderly alcoholics are of the second type (Petersen & Whittington, 1977).

The picture is not totally bleak—low to moderate use of alcohol may actually be beneficial. Numerous studies in nursing homes, geriatric wards of hospitals, and so on support the idea that small amounts of alcoholic beverages, such as a glass of beer, hard cider, or wine, especially in a social setting, have positive effects: patients need much less sedative medication and staff assistance. Even patients who were incontinent (unable to control bowel and bladder), totally confused, and completely unsociable prior to the institution of a "happy hour" became much better. The improvement in the ward conditions is also good for staff morale. Beer, cider, and various types of wine are safer than distilled liquor because they are more dilute, are absorbed more slowly, irritate the gastric and duodenal mucosa less, and have less potential for adverse interactions with other drugs (Lamy, 1980; Mishara & Kastenbaum, 1980).

CHAPTER 18

FIRST AID IN ABUSED DRUG
EMERGENCIES

CHAPTER OBJECTIVES

1. Describe why a panic reaction or aggressive behavior is not useful in identifying a particular type of drug overdose.
2. Identify the greatest danger from opiate, sedative-hypnotic, amphetamine and volatile substance overdoses.
3. Describe how the size and responsiveness of the pupils of the eyes can be valuable in diagnosing drug overdose.
4. List two substances valuable in a first aid treatment kit for drug emergencies.
5. Name the most dangerous type of drug withdrawal.
6. Define the following terms: miosis, mydriasis, tachycardia, and nystagmus.

Diagnosing the seriousness of a drug overdose or withdrawal and determining what treatment is appropriate are risky procedures for a person without medical training. A wrong decision can mean the difference between life and death, or worse still, life with impaired brain function. When in doubt, call a poison control center or the nearest emergency medical service. Hospitals that receive any form of federal funding are prevented by law from refusing to treat drug abuse cases; nor are such hospitals allowed to report the identity of adult drug abuse cases to legal authorities. Laws regarding treatment of minors without parental consent vary from state to state. Our recommendation is, it might be better to live with a record.

Diagnosis in a drug emergency is made difficult by several factors. The identity of the drug, the dosage, and the purity are often not known. The patient may have taken more than one drug, either deliberately (like Ts and Blues) or accidentally, without realizing the potentiation effect (like Darvon® and alcohol). The person may not be having difficulty with the abused drug itself, but from a concurrent injury (such as a concussion) or from a serious infection from nonsterile injection techniques (common with the "needle habits"). The person might not be suffering from a drug effect at all, but might be withdrawing from tranquilizers, alcohol, barbiturates, or narcotics. Or, he or she might have a medical condition, such as epilepsy, diabetic coma, or acute schizophrenia. Check for a Medic Alert necklace or bracelet. There may be medical information in the person's wallet or purse, as well as needed identification. The following signs and symptoms are intended only as a *guide* to first aid when a drug abuse problem is suspected, not as a substitute for professional diagnosis and treatment!

DIFFERENTIAL DIAGNOSIS*

General Appearance

Behavioral symptoms of drug intoxication are usually so nonspecific as not to be of much help. The hallucinogens, amphetamines, phencyclidine, cocaine, and marijuana all can cause acute panic or paranoid reactions. Amphetamines and cocaine can induce paranoid delusions and aggressive behavior. The person intoxicated on alcohol or barbiturates may be aggressive, but aggression is very rare in opiate intoxication. The person who is high on phencyclidine (PCP) has a characteristic blank stare and is catatonic; he or she does not usually become psychotic and aggressive until coming down from the PCP. Restlessness or agitation suggests amphetamines, LSD, or withdrawal from barbiturates or heroin. A quiet, withdrawn appearance suggests barbiturates, heroin, or hallucinogens, or "crashing" from amphetamines. The speech of the barbiturates user is often thick and slurred, somewhat like an alcoholic's; the heroin user's may be slowed, but his or her diction remains intact.

Convulsions

Convulsions are not useful for identifying the type of drug that might be involved. Convulsive seizures can occur (1) if the person has taken toxic doses of codeine, propoxyphene (Darvon®), methaqualone, amphetamines, cocaine, strychnine, or LSD; (2) after an overdose of depressant, because the brain has been deprived of oxygen; (3) during withdrawal from the sed-

---

* This section is largely from Bourne, 1976.

ative-hypnotics and alcohol; and (4) in drug users who already suffer from some other cause of seizures, such as epilepsy.

Breathing

Opiates, barbiturates, minor tranquilizers and other sedatives, and alcohol are respiratory depressants, and it is the depressant action that puts the patient in immediate danger. Knowing how to do mouth-to-mouth resuscitation or, if necessary, cardiopulmonary resuscitation until an ambulance arrives can mean the difference between the victim's incurring severe brain damage or death and surviving intact. Narcotics can cause pulmonary edema (fluid in the lungs). This might be detected by a wheezing or whistling sound as the person breathes. This is another indication that there is no time to be lost in taking the person to an emergency medical facility.

A reddened, ulcerated nose suggests cocaine, volatile substances, or relatively pure marijuana. A runny nose (rhinorrhea) is an early sign of heroin withdrawal.

The odor of some of the depressants may be detectable on the breath. Examples include alcohol, ether, paraldehyde, ethchlorvynol (Placidyl®), and volatile substances (see Chapter 10).

Eyes

The size of the pupils and how they respond to light may be valuable information, if modifying factors are considered. (For example, if the person has fallen and suffered a concussion, the size and response of the pupils will not tell anything about the drug that may be involved.) Pinpoint pupils (miosis) in dim light suggests heroin or another opioid. If both pupils are dilated (my-

driasis) and responsive to changes in light intensity, the patient could be in opioid withdrawal, or intoxicated with LSD, the tryptamines (like DMT), mescaline, or morning glory seeds. Dilated and sluggishly reactive pupils suggest glutethimide (Doriden®) or high doses of amphetamine. Both pupils dilated but nonresponsive to light changes suggests high doses of anticholinergic drugs. (Effects of commonly abused drugs on the pupils are illustrated in Figure 18-1.)

A reddened, irritated appearance of the whites of the eyes (conjunctival injection) is characteristic of marijuana. Side-to-side eye movements (lateral nystagmus) suggests PCP, barbiturates, or barbiturate withdrawal. An exaggerated blink reflex is commonly found in barbiturate withdrawal.

Skin

If a person has taken enough drug to be having a bad reaction, or is in a type of withdrawal, he or she will be perspiring. This nonspecific stress response is not really helpful, because it only indicates that the person's body is under stress. Dry, flushed skin suggests an anticholinergic drug, such as jimsonweed or a preparation containing atropine or scopolamine (see Chapter 6). Gooseflesh occurs with an LSD reaction or during withdrawal from narcotics. Needle tracks usually mean narcotics, but can be from amphetamines.

Pulse

A rapid heartbeat (tachycardia) is a nonspecific stress response found in most acute drug reactions. A fast, irregular pulse suggests amphetamine or volatile substance abuse. (Blood pres-

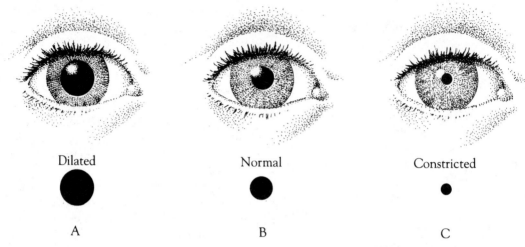

| Dilated | Normal | Constricted |

A   B   C

FIGURE 18-1

Pupil reactions to various drugs: (A) Dilation of pupils (mydriasis) may be caused by amphetamines, LSD, mescaline, psilocybin, DMT, MDA, and the anticholinergics, such as scopolamine and atropine. The anticholinergics cause the pupil to remain fixed even when light strikes it. Mydriasis also occurs during withdrawal from narcotics. (B) Normal pupil seen in average light. Marijuana, barbiturates, and PCP would usually leave the pupil like this. (C) Constricted pupils (miosis) that are not responsive to dim light are characteristic of the opiates, such as heroin.

sure may be dangerously elevated after taking amphetamines, but most people don't carry a sphygmomanometer around!) A fast pulse rate is not dangerous unless the person has a cardiac condition. Cardiac arhythmias occur with volatile substances and large doses of codeine, propoxyphene (Darvon®), methaqualone, amphetamines, methylphenidate (Ritalin®), and alcohol. The condition can be life-threatening and requires medical attention as soon as possible. If the heartbeat stops, cardiopulmonary resuscitation can save the person's life.

Temperature

Fever may be present after LSD ingestion or during withdrawal from narcotics or barbitu-

rates. It may also be caused by an infection if the person has one of the "needle habits."

FIRST AID FOR COMMONLY ABUSED DRUGS*

As most drug users know, not all overdoses are emergencies. A good rule of thumb for the person trying to assess whether an emergency exists or not is: if the dose was taken more than two hours before you appeared on the scene and the taker is still conscious and coherent, there is

---

*This section is largely from McConnell, Dupree, and Parcel, 1977.

probably no great cause for alarm. No action may be necessary other than emotional support and having someone reliable stay with the "tripper" until the effects of the drug have worn off. Some hallucinogens give fairly long trips (12 to 18 hours), depending on the dosage. Because the tripper's time sense is distorted, this may seem much longer to him or her. Reassurance and a supportive atmosphere are essential. The person having a bum trip is at real risk of committing suicide either intentionally or unintentionally because he or she cannot discriminate between illusions and reality. (We lost one student some years ago, because he was not prevented from jumping out a window under the influence of LSD.) Comforting physical contact, such as holding the patient's hand, is probably more useful than words.

Giving another drug to counteract the drug the person took should NEVER be done except by medical personnel. Do not force coffee, tea, milk, or other liquids on an unconscious or semiconscious patient; the person may choke on them and/or inhale them into the lungs. Do not make an unconscious, semiconscious, or convulsing person vomit, for the same reason. If it is appropriate to empty the stomach, have the person either stick a finger down the throat or drink syrup of ipecac (available in dose-size bottles for first aid kits). The ipecac may be used once more if vomiting has not occurred within 15 to 20 minutes. Use of a salt solution to cause vomiting can be more dangerous than not inducing vomiting at all, especially in children. If activated charcoal is available in a first aid kit, it can be given after vomiting ceases. It will adsorb many toxic substances and, if used in recommended amounts, will do no harm. The old home remedy mixture of burnt toast, strong tea, and milk of magnesia is useless.

Typical effects of commonly abused drugs and of withdrawal symptoms are summarized in Tables 18-1 and 18-2. Professional treatments for the more serious drug intoxications and withdrawals were described earlier in the appropriate chapters.

Alcohol

Alcohol overdose is not usually a medical emergency, unless the heartbeat is irregular or the person is in a coma (see Table 11-4 on p. 207). The two immediate causes of death are from cardiac arhythmia ("holiday heart") and respiratory depression. If the person is seriously uncoordinated and possibly has also taken a depressant like barbiturates or minor tranquilizers (like Valium®), or a medication for pain (like Darvon®) or the like, the risk of respiratory failure is serious enough that a physician should be consulted. Otherwise, keep the person warm and assist him or her to a bathroom to vomit as necessary. Do not let this person drive!

If methyl alcohol (wood alcohol) poisoning is suspected, induce vomiting and get medical attention as rapidly as possible. The most common sources of wood alcohol are canned heat and cooking fuels. If you are isolated and a long distance from medical help, have the victim drink regular alcohol after he or she finishes vomiting. The liver will preferentially oxidize the grain alcohol, and this may be enough to save the victim's vision or life. Isopropyl ("rubbing") alcohol is not as toxic as methyl alcohol. It will cause severe gastrointestinal symptoms, such as nausea, vomiting, and diarrhea.

Withdrawal from alcohol dependence has a mortality rate of up to 25% without treatment. The alcoholic needs medical treatment, usually in a hospital, for 10 to 21 days, to withdraw safely. The initial symptoms are severe muscle tremors, nausea, weakness, and anxiety. The alcoholic in withdrawal will be actively seeking

TABLE 18-1 Typical effects of acute drug intoxication

Drug	Psychological effects	Physical effects
Amphetamines	Confused; disoriented; agitated; irritable; aggressive; may hallucinate and be paranoid at high doses	Sweating; irregular pulse; hyperactivity; cardiac arhythmia
Anticholinergics	Disoriented; no distortion of space and time; visual hallucinations	Decreased salivation; mydriasis; dry, flushed skin
Barbiturates	May be disoriented; loss of inhibitions; euphoria	Nystagmus; coma at high dose; respiratory depression
LSD type	Disoriented; anxious; emotionally labile; hypersuggestible; delusions	Gooseflesh; mydriasis; stress reaction symptoms
Marijuana	Oriented; space, time distortion; mild anxiety to panic	Reddening of whites of eyes
Narcotics	Oriented; normal; quietly euphoric	Miosis; drowsy, nodding
Phencyclidine (PCP)	Disoriented; excited; confused; feelings of isolation, apathy; may become acutely psychotic	Blank stare; catatonic; nystagmus; impaired motor coordination; stress reaction symptoms
Volatile substances	Disoriented; confused; may be delirious	Impaired motor coordination; cardiac arhythmia

TABLE 18-2 Early "crashing" and withdrawal symptoms

Drug	Psychological effects	Physical effects
Amphetamines	Sleepy; lethargic; depressed	Hungry; muscles ache
Alcohol and barbiturates	Confused; disoriented; extreme restlessness; delirium	Tremors; insomnia; fever; nystagmus; exaggerated blink reflex with barbiturates; severe convulsions; cardiovascular collapse
Narcotics	Restless; agitated	Runny nose; teary eyes; mydriasis and pupils responsive to light; gooseflesh; low back pain

alcohol or, as a substitute, minor tranquilizers like Valium®.

Amphetamines

Amphetamine overdose can be fairly serious (see Table 8-3 on p. 139). If the person has *just* taken an oral dose, induce vomiting. If he or she is already showing signs of overstimulation, do not induce vomiting, because this can send the person into convulsions. If he or she is having chest pains, has an irregular pulse, or has a history of heart trouble, he or she should be taken to an emergency room immediately. Otherwise, this person should be kept as calm and quiet as possible. A bad amphetamine trip is not as receptive to "talking down" as a bad hallucinogen trip. Amphetamines induce paranoia, fear, and sometimes a temporary psychosis. Occasionally there is a long-term anxiety or even paranoia, which responds to psychotherapy.

The person "crashing" after amphetamines may be extremely depressed and perhaps suicidal. However, the physical symptoms are not usually cause for alarm, because there is no physical dependence.

Barbiturates

Barbiturate overdose can be very serious, depending on the dosage and whether or not it was combined with alcohol. Alcohol potentiates the depressant effect (see Table 10-1 on p. 175). If the drug was taken recently, induce vomiting. Try to keep the patient awake and moving. If the person is conscious, get him or her to drink strong coffee or tea. If he or she lapses into unconsciousness, call for medical help. Be ready to use mouth-to-mouth resuscitation (or cardiovascular resuscitation if no pulse can be detected) to prevent brain damage and death.

Withdrawal from a barbiturate or other sedative-hypnotic drug dependency is quite dangerous, because of the risk of convulsions and death. It definitely requires medical treatment. Symptoms are similar to withdrawal from alcohol.

Cocaine

Cocaine overdose probably is not serious. The drug causes increased heart rate, blood pressure, temperature, and respiratory rate, but these effects wear off quickly. Afterwards, the user may be depressed. Treatment is the same as for amphetamines.

Depressants

Depressant overdose may be very serious (see Barbiturates). People who overdose with depressants often are reaching out for help in a dangerous way.

Depressant withdrawal is more dangerous than withdrawal from heroin, and it requires specific medical treatment (see Chapter 10).

Hallucinogens

Hallucinogen overdose is rarely dangerous. The main problem is the suggestibility of the person, causing him or her to misinterpret the surroundings and become frightened. Quiet surroundings and reassurance are usually the best treatment; use the person's suggestible state to convince him or her everything will be all right. A bad trip can be aborted with a tranquilizer, like Valium®, but this usually just makes the medical personnel feel better, not the patient. An occasional LSD user, or user of other hallucinogens, will develop chronic anxiety or even a true psychosis that persists for months afterwards. These typically will respond to minor tranquilizers or psychotherapy, respectively.

Flashback reactions are a return of the subjective sensations in the absence of the drug. They most commonly result from LSD, but can occur from morning glory seeds, marijuana, and so on. Treatment consists of reassurance that the condition will go away. If anxiety persists, a physician may prescribe a minor tranquilizer.

Marijuana

Marijuana intoxication is rarely serious. An overdose of marijuana or hashish puts the user to sleep. Hashish or hash oil may trigger hallucinations and panic reactions, requiring reassurance and quiet surroundings to let the drug effects wear off. Do not let the user drive!

Narcotics

Narcotic overdose is usually serious. If the person has taken another depressant, like a barbiturate, tranquilizer, or alcohol, that is still in his or her system, he or she is in greater danger of respiratory failure and death from the combination than from a simple overdose of heroin. If the drug was taken orally and recently, a glass of milk may help, but narcotics are typically injected. If the person is unconscious, check his or her airway, breathing, and pulse. Arrange for medical assistance and be ready to do mouth-to-mouth resuscitation or, if necessary, cardiopulmonary resuscitation. Narcotic antagonists, such as naloxone, can be injected by a physician to reverse the respiratory depression. The patient should not leave the hospital until the staff is certain he or she is out of danger, because methadone and especially LAAM have a longer duration of action than heroin, and the patient may lapse into another coma as the naloxone wears off.

Withdrawal from heroin or other opioids can be quite unpleasant, but it does not require treatment with the urgency that withdrawal from the alcohol-barbiturate type of dependence does.

Phencyclidine (PCP)

Phencyclidine was originally developed as an anesthetic. Low doses make the drug abuser feel numb; increasing doses produce anesthesia; large doses can cause coma, respiratory depression, convulsions, and death. The physical signs are like a stress reaction: sweating, flushing, and a rapid pulse. The blank stare appearance and the tendency to remain in whatever position the person is placed (catatonia) appear to be effects unique to PCP abusers. The pupil size remains normal, and the presence of side-to-side eye movements (lateral nystagmus) plus poor muscular coordination help distinguish PCP intoxication from stimulant and LSD abuse (Lerner & Burns, 1978).

Simple, uncomplicated PCP trips are handled like other hallucinogen trips, except that it is not helpful to try to talk the person down. PCP is more likely to cause severe psychotic reactions than other hallucinogens. The person who goes into a coma should be taken to a hospital immediately. The medical management of PCP overdose is described in Chapter 10.

Stimulants

Stimulants are not usually life threatening except to those with weak hearts or other serious medical complications. Stimulant overdose may cause tremors, convulsions, hallucinations, paranoia, or simple hyperactivity (see Amphetamines). Large doses of amphetamines and methylphenidate (Ritalin®) can cause cardiac arhythmias.

Tranquilizers

The major tranquilizers, with the exception of Haldol®, are not commonly abused. However, abuse of minor tranquilizers, such as Valium®, Librium®, and other sedative-hypnotics like methaqualone, is fairly common. An overdose is not as dangerous as the barbiturates, unless the person has taken another central nervous system depressant like alcohol. If a dose larger than the maximum recommended dose of that particular tranquilizer was taken within the past hour or so, get the person to vomit. Keep the person warm, watch for respiratory depression, and consult a physician.

Volatile Substances

Volatile substances can be dangerous. Some volatile substances cause death from cardiac arhythmias; most can cause respiratory failure. Remove the source of vapor, and check the airway, breathing, and pulse. Do cardiopulmonary resuscitation if there is no pulse, or mouth-to-mouth resuscitation if the heart is still going but the victim is not breathing on his or her own. Less serious intoxications can be treated simply by removing the source of vapor. Most abused volatile substances are not metabolized but are removed from the body by exhalation comparatively quickly. Once the user's confusion and disorientation clears, there is little risk of relapse into coma unless he or she has taken something else as well.

FIRST AID FOR WITHDRAWAL

Withdrawal symptoms from drugs that induce physical dependence, and "crashing" from high doses of drugs that induce psychological dependence, may need first aid followed by medical assistance. Withdrawal and "crashing" symptoms (Table 18-2) are usually the opposite of the effects of the drug in question. Withdrawal from depressants, such as alcohol, barbiturates, minor tranquilizers, and narcotics causes symptoms of tremors, runny nose, teary eyes, cramps, irritability, depression, hallucinations, and risk of convulsions. Not all patients will have the full range of symptoms with great severity. It depends on the individual, the dosage, and which depressant the person was on. A heavy dependence on alcohol and the barbiturates requires specific medical treatment for the best chance of survival. Often an alcoholic will not realize he or she is physically dependent. This person has not accepted the fact that he or she is an alcoholic and will try to prove that he or she can "take it or leave it." The minor tranquilizer dependency is in some ways more insidious, because dependent persons may have been taking a prescription as prescribed. Then when they are away from home and the prescription runs out, they are in trouble, because they had no idea they were physically dependent.

Specific first aid measures for withdrawal from the various drugs are covered in previous sections under the appropriate category.

"Crashing" from stimulants leads to marked exhaustion and depression. The person may be suicidal. The only treatment usually necessary is supportive care, reassurance, and rest.

MOUTH-TO-MOUTH RESUSCITATION AND CARDIOPULMONARY RESUSCITATION TECHNIQUES

These important, life-saving techniques should be learned and practiced under professional supervision. Instruction is generally available through local chapters of the Red Cross or the American Heart Association. Sometimes the local police, fire department, or hospital will sponsor the classes. The resuscitation methods are quite simple once you learn what to do and which technique is appropriate. The Red Cross recommends that people get training in cardiopulmonary resuscitation and learn how to activate the local Emergency Medical Services (EMS) system by telephoning 911, 0, or the local EMS number.

Before beginning mouth-to-mouth resuscitation, check to see if the person is conscious by speaking to him or her or tapping his or her shoulder; do not shake the person if there is any chance of head, neck, or back injury. If the person is unconscious, check to see if you can attract someone else's attention quickly, so he or she can go get help while you check for breathing. Roll the unconscious person over on his or her back (assuming no neck or back injury). Check the airway to verify that there is nothing (like a swallowed tongue or slipped dentures) preventing the person from breathing. First tip the head back until the chin points up; one way to do this is to apply pressure with one hand on the person's forehead while gently lifting the back of the neck with the other. As you are lifting, put your ear close to the person's mouth and watch his or her chest. If he or she is breathing, you will see the chest rise and fall, and feel the expired air on your face. Keep checking for about five seconds.

There is no time to be lost. If the person does not appear to be breathing after you have tipped his or her head, give four quick, full breaths by mouth to mouth (or mouth to nose if you cannot get a good seal on the mouth). After giving four quick breaths without pausing, check the carotid pulse and check for breathing again for at least five but not more than ten seconds. The carotid pulse is checked by locating the Adam's apple and sliding your fingers into the groove at the side of the neck nearby. You should feel the pulsation of the carotid artery if the heart is beating. The Red Cross calls this A Quick Check, which helps remind you of Airway, four Quick breaths, and Check for breathing and pulse.

If the victim is still not breathing but has a pulse, continue with mouth-to-mouth resuscitation until he or she starts breathing independently, or until someone else can take over, emergency medical personnel arrive, or you cannot continue any longer. Breaths should be given once every five seconds. Stop every few minutes for five seconds to check again for pulse and breathing.

If the person is not breathing and has no detectable pulse, he or she needs cardiopulmonary resuscitation (CPR) and emergency medical service. If you are not trained to give CPR, it is still worthwhile to try mouth-to-mouth resuscitation. There is a chance that the heart may be beating weakly, and your breathing for the victim may keep him or her alive. Continue making quick scans for someone to get help or someone who knows CPR. Breathe air into the victim about once per five seconds, and check for a pulse and breathing every few minutes, until it is clear the person is dead. (Actually, only a physician or other authorized person can declare a person legally dead.)

IDENTIFICATION OF DRUG ABUSERS

We have described first aid for drug emergencies in this chapter and medical treatment to a limited extent in other chapters. One of the first things one does before or during an emergency is identify the person with a drug problem. We mentioned some of the difficulties associated with diagnosing alcoholism in Chapter 11. The Pharmaceutical Manufacturers Association has developed a list of the signs and symptoms associated with drug abuse of other types.

Common Symptoms of Drug Abuse

The following is a list of changes or symptoms commonly seen in drug abusers.

1. Abrupt changes in attendance at school or work, quality of work, and discipline.
2. Unusual flare-ups or outbursts of temper.
3. Deterioration of physical appearance.
4. Furtive behavior about personal possessions, such as a backpack or contents of a locker.
5. Wearing sunglasses when no one else is.
6. Wearing long-sleeved garments in hot weather.
7. Association with known drug abusers.
8. Unusual borrowing of money from relatives or associates.
9. Stealing items that can be readily pawned or sold.
10. Withdrawal socially and from responsibility.
11. Changed frequency of going to basement, storage room, closet, or bathroom.

Symptoms Related to Specific Types of Drugs

The lists on the following pages indicate some of the changes or symptoms specifically related to particular drugs.

Depressants abuser

1. May seem intoxicated, but no alcohol odor on breath.
2. Staggering or stumbling movements.
3. Falling asleep in class (even if interested in subject!) or at work.
4. Loses interest in former activities.

Hallucinogen abuser

1. Often appears to be daydreaming or in a trance-like state.
2. May touch objects and examine everyday things carefully for long periods.
3. Body image and senses may be distorted, causing the person to panic.

Marijuana abuser

1. Odor of burned marijuana on clothes.
2. Whites of eyes may appear irritated.
3. May behave more quietly than previously.

Narcotics abuser

1. May have raw, red nostrils if sniffing; needle tracks if "shooting up."
2. Lethargic, drowsy behavior when high; purposive when obtaining money or locating source of drug.
3. Needs money to support habit, more so than other drugs.

Phencyclidine (PCP) abuser

1. Dazed, blank-stare expression; side-to-side eye movements.

2. Poor physical coordination as if drunk, but no odor of alcohol.
3. Sweating, flushed skin, and excess salivation.

Stimulants abuser

1. Pupils may be dilated.
2. Excessive activity, irritability, nervousness, and aggression.
3. Mouth and nose dry; bad breath; user licks lips frequently.

4. Thin; goes long periods without eating or sleeping.
5. May have needle marks if "shooting up."

Volatile substances abuser

1. Odor of substance on clothes, breath.
2. Runny nose.
3. Irritation and ulcerations around mouth.
4. Watery eyes.
5. Poor muscular coordination; drowsiness.

CHAPTER 19

DRUGS AND THE LAW

1. Discuss the three issues that have influenced the formation of drug laws.
2. What were the inconsistencies in reasoning behind passage of the Opium Exclusion Act and the Harrison Act?
3. List the sequence of U.S. laws and the year in which they were passed that (a) required accurate labeling of dependence-producing substances, (b) made fraudulent claims illegal, (c) required proof that a particular formulation of a drug was safe if taken as directed, and (d) required proof that the drug was effective.
4. Define and give an example of each: Schedule I, II, III, IV, and V drugs.
5. Defend the following statement: The net effect of drug laws passed since the mid-19th century has been to take from the consumer the right to select and to purchase drugs legally. Describe whether or not this process has been generally beneficial or detrimental.
6. Describe the constitutional protections a person has in regard to criminal drug offenses.
7. Give reasons why drug abuse laws do not work effectively.

BASIS FOR DRUG LAWS

Throughout history people have tried to regulate the use of drugs by various laws or codes of conduct. Most laws have moral and sociological implications—for example, it is wrong to lose control of body and mind, to harm society, or to upset the prescribed code of conduct. It is wrong to become dependent, to become unproductive or a drag on the community, or to be antisocial by stealing to obtain drugs, alcohol, and so on. The enactment of laws depends on the prevalent moral and social codes and customs of the times. What may seem like a repressive law today may very well be changed over a period of time or be replaced with a light penalty or even be repealed. Again, this depends on the desires of the people involved and on the events that occur in a changing world.

Coffee, tea, tobacco, alcohol, marijuana, hallucinogens, depressants like barbiturates, and narcotics have been subject to a wide range of controls, from none to rigid. In earlier parts of this book we described such severe penalties as strangulation for smoking tobacco or opium and strict bans on alcohol in Islamic countries. In other countries these substances were legal or sanctioned at the same time or at different times, depending on the situation and the desires of the population. Often the laws were changed because so many people used a particular drug that it would have been impossible to enforce a ban, or because the government needed the tax revenue.

There are three issues that have had a particular influence on drug laws:

1. If a person abuses a drug, should he or she be treated as a criminal or as a sick person with a type of disease?
2. How do we distinguish the user from the pusher of a particular drug, and who should be treated more harshly?
3. Is the law effective in deterring drug use or abuse, and how is effectiveness determined?

In regard to the first issue, drug abuse may be considered both an illness and a crime. It is an illness (abnormal functional state) when a person cannot stop using the drug, and a crime because the law, reflecting societal opinion, has made the abuse a crime. There clearly are health issues involved, because uncontrolled abuse of almost any drug can lead to physical and/or psychological damage. Because the public has to foot the bill for health care costs or societal damage, the laws have tried to prevent or treat drug abuse.

As concerns the second issue, drug laws have always been more lenient for the user than for the seller of a particular drug. However, it is often hard to separate user from pusher, because most drug abusers are both. Because there can be a lot of profit involved, some people may not use the drugs they peddle, and they are purely pushers. The law tries to deter use of drugs by concentrating on these persons, but again with questionable success. Organized crime is involved in major drug operations, and these "drug rings" have proven hard to break up.

In regard to the third issue, all available evidence indicates that the criminal law is a failure at deterring drug usage, at least in the United States. Reasonable estimates indicate there are over 300,000 narcotics addicts, millions of heavy marijuana users, and many heavy users of a variety of other illegal drugs in this country.

REGULATION OF SELF-MEDICATION

The "Chinese Problem"

Most people nowadays do not realize how recently it was common to eat or smoke opium in the

United States. The opium "eaters" were typically middle-class, White people who had become hooked on opiates in patent medicines. Because of the state of the art of medicine in the 1800s, the opiates provided an important form of relief from pain. Physicians at the time believed an opiate dependency was better than alcoholism and encouraged transference from the one drug to the other. Some became addicted to morphine as a result of the use of this drug during the Civil War to treat dysentery, pain, and fatigue, and took the needle habit home when the war was over. Dependence on opium or morphine was considered undesirable and not respectable, but, because the drugs were legal and their moderate use did not disrupt the user's life, it caused no serious concern. The only restriction on importation was a tax, passed in 1842 on all opiates brought into the United States.

Although concern would probably have developed sooner or later because of the growing extent of opiate addiction among the White middle class, the first restrictions centered on opium smoking among Chinese immigrants. Tens of thousands of Chinese laborers were brought to the United States in the 1850s–1860s to work on the railroad construction crossing the West. They brought their custom of smoking opium for relaxation. Labor contractors actually offered an allowance of half a pound of smoking opium a month as a bonus to recruit Chinese immigrant laborers. This worked fine until there was an economic depression that affected areas with large concentrations of Chinese immigrants. Unemployed American workers (there were no unemployment checks or welfare benefits then) unfairly blamed the Chinese laborers as the cause of their problems. The opium dens became a convenient scapegoat. White women and girls supposedly were induced to visit the opium dens, whereupon they were ruined and became depraved dope fiends.

It was possible in many states to buy smoking-grade opium in pharmacies and even in general stores. The state of Nevada, in 1877, was the first to prohibit retail sales of smoking opium. Twenty states, mostly in the West with substantial immigrant Chinese populations, passed statutes to prohibit operation of opium dens or the smoking and possession of opium. The actual importation and selling of opium remained legal until 1887, when importation of opium by Chinese (but not by Americans!) was forbidden. The effect of this restriction was to stimulate smuggling by organized groups. The tariff was increased further in 1890 and then halved in 1897 to discourage the smuggling and illegal manufacture by Chinese. In 1909 the Smoking Opium Exclusion Act banned the importation of smoking-grade opium, again with inflammatory anti-Chinese publicity about American girls and boys who were lured into addiction and "doomed, hopelessly doomed, beyond the shadow of redemption" (Austin, 1978). This hysterical attack on smoking opium is difficult to reconcile with the extensive use of laudanum and injected morphine by Americans at that time. In 1914, the tax was increased to $400 per pound on opium prepared in the United States, and the Harrison Act, also passed in 1914, increased penalties for illegal use of opiates even further.

The Great American Fraud: Patent Medicines

In the late 1800s and early 1900s the sales of medicines sold without controls flourished and became widespread. These medicines were called patent medicines, which signified that the ingredients were secret, not that they were patented. The law seemed to be more concerned with someone's recipe being stolen than with preventing possible damage from toxic ingredients, such as acetanilid in Bromo-Seltzer and

Orangeine, or prussic (hydrocyanic) acid in Shiloh's Consumption Cure. The patent medicines, or at least those that were later analyzed, appear to have been composed largely of either colored water or alcohol. Hostetter's Stomach Bitters, with 44% alcohol, could easily have been classified as liquor. Sale of Peruna (28% alcohol) was prohibited to Native Americans! Birney's Catarrh Cure contained 4% cocaine. Wistar's Balsam of Wild Cherry (Figure 19-1), Dr. King's Discovery for Consumption, Mrs. Winslow's Soothing Syrup, and many others contained opiates as well as alcohol.

In 1905 *Collier's Magazine* ran a series of articles, called the "Great American Fraud," against the abuse of patent medicines, which brought the problem to the attention of the public (Adams, 1905). Collier's coined the phrase *dope fiend* from *dope*, an African word meaning intoxicating substance. The American Medical Association, which had been ineffectually wrestling with the contradiction that the AMA accepted advertisements for patent medicines that physicians knew were addicting, joined in and distributed reprints of the Collier's story widely to inform the public about the dangers of these medicines. The publicity caused mounting pressure on Congress and on President Roosevelt to do something about it. In 1905 the president proposed that a law be enacted to regulate interstate commerce in misbranded and adulterated foods, drinks, and drugs. This received further impetus when Upton Sinclair's book *The Jungle* was published in 1906—a nauseatingly realistic exposé describing in detail the filth, disease, and putrefaction in the Chicago stockyards.

The 1906 Pure Food and Drug Act started the decline of patent medicines (although in itself it was not a strong law), because it required the manufacturer to print on the label the amount of alcohol, morphine, opium, cocaine, heroin,

FIGURE 19-1

This is a poster of one of the patent medicines that contained liberal doses of opium and a high concentration of alcohol. This medicine was widely used to treat tuberculosis ("consumption") around the turn of this century, when over 25% of all adult deaths were from this disease. The U.S. government finally forced the remedy off the market by 1920.

or marijuana extract in each container. It became obvious at this time that many of the drugs on the market labeled as nonaddictive were in fact potentially as addictive as the known addictive drugs. However, most of the governmental interest centered on regulation of the food industry, not drugs. Federal drug regulation was based on the free market idea that consumers would select for themselves and needed the information on possible dependence-producing drugs to ensure that they received a fair value for their money. The Pure Food and Drug Act made misrepresentations illegal, so that a patent drug could not be advertised as nonaddicting if it was. This law had the effect of lowering the narcotic content of patent medicines. Part of the decline in alcohol content in these medicines can be credited to the Internal Revenue Service, which taxed alcoholic patent medicines, and part to the Harrison Act, which separated control of narcotics from other drugs.

The Pure Food and Drug Act was modified, although not in a consumer-protective manner, by the Sherley Amendment in 1912. The shipper of a cancer "remedy" claimed on the label that the contents were effective, and was indicted. The case was decided in the Supreme Court in 1911. Justice Holmes, writing for the majority opinion, said that based on the 1906 Act the company was legally correct, because it did accurately state the contents and their strength and quality. Congress took the hint and passed the Sherley Amendment to add to the existing law the requirement that labels should not contain "any statement . . . regarding the curative or therapeutic effect . . . which is false and fraudulent." However, the government had to prove fraud, which turned out to be difficult. All this amendment did was to make the pharmaceutical companies' ads more vague (Temin, 1980).

Controls over Opium and Other Narcotics

The Harrison Narcotics Act

For irrelevant reasons, such as anti-Chinese sentiment, several important laws were passed in the United States that had a significant impact on the use of opiates and other drugs legally defined as *narcotics*. In 1909 Congress passed the Smoking Opium Exclusion Act, which forbade the importation of opium for nonmedical use. However, it was still legal to use and even to manufacture opium for nonmedical use.

By 1914 it was still possible to purchase opiates legally in the form of patent medicines or of smoking opium (provided you were a White American) in a number of states, although there were 28 state laws against smoking opium. For some time, the United States had been attempting to improve trade relations with China. The Harrison Act was passed as much in the spirit of impressing the Chinese government that we were willing to regulate opiate use here and help them control their own serious opium addiction problem, as addressing the problem of opiate addiction. Again, *Collier's* and also *Harper's Magazine* had helped to create public pressure for antidrug legislation by publishing articles about the use of dope, vividly illustrated with pictures and cartoons of opium dens and drug abuse. In 1914 there were an estimated 200,000 addicted Americans, as much as 1 person in 400 (see Figure 12-6 on p. 238).

The Harrison Act was a tax bill, rather than a drug regulatory bill. It controlled dispensing and dealing in narcotics. All dealers in narcotics, such as physicians, veterinarians, and dentists, were required to register with the Bureau of Internal Revenue, which was to enforce the law. The medical groups were upset because of interference with their freedom to prescribe.

Supreme Court Decisions on Narcotics

In 1919 the Supreme Court ruled in the Webb case that it was illegal to give drugs to an addict simply to prevent withdrawal. In the Behrman case in 1922 the Court ruled that it was unlawful to use drugs for a cure program.

The Narcotic Drugs Import and Export Act of 1922

This legislation limited imports to crude opium and coca leaves for medical purposes. Also called the *Jones-Miller Act,* it doubled penalties for dealing in narcotics to a $5000 fine and ten years in prison. It further specified conviction for mere possession of illegal drugs.

The Heroin Act of 1924

This law made it illegal to manufacture heroin or to possess the drug for any purpose other than government-controlled research.

Federal Narcotics Hospitals

In 1928 over one-third of all prisoners in the United States were serving sentences for drug-related offenses. Mescaline and marijuana were classified as narcotics at that time, and nearly half of these prisoners were convicted for use of these drugs. In 1929 the federal government authorized the establishment of two narcotics hospitals, or treatment facilities: one at Lexington, Kentucky, which opened in 1935, and the other at Fort Worth, Texas, which opened in 1938. They were closed in the early 1970s, partly because the programs they had were ineffectual. Of the narcotics addiction patients, over 90% of those released were using the same drugs within six months, and only 5% remained drug free

over an extended period of time. With the advent of methadone treatment and investigation of other treatment modalities, the time had come to close the centers.

The Marijuana Tax Act

As described in the chapter on marijuana, this plant was the center of controversy in the early 1930s because of the increasing use of the plant for smoking. In 1937, after a strong publicity campaign by papers and magazines, the Marijuana Tax Act was passed. This law provided controls over marijuana similar to the controls the Harrison Act had imposed on narcotics. A tax was levied on all transactions connected with marijuana. The law was never very effective, and gradually use of marijuana became more widespread. In 1969, the Supreme Court ruled that punishment for nonpayment of the tax was unconstitutional, because of self-incrimination. It was comparable to the leading question "When did you stop beating your wife?" Marijuana was still controlled by the federal narcotics laws and was legally considered a narcotic until 1971.

The Opium Poppy Control Act

In 1942 this law was passed to license the growing of opium poppies in the United States, because supplies from abroad had been cut off by World War II. Opium was a necessity for use in medicine. There was also a demand for poppy seeds, which are used in baked goods. There is no opium in the seeds, which are sterilized so they will not germinate.

The Boggs Amendment

This legislation was passed in 1951 as an amendment to the Harrison Narcotics Act; it established minimum mandatory sentences for all narcotic and marijuana offenses. This was the beginning of a new program of hard-line control of addictive drugs and of marijuana.

Narcotic Drug Control Act of 1956

In 1955 a report by a subcommittee of the Senate Judiciary Committee stated that drug addiction was responsible for 50% of crime in urban areas and 25% of all reported crimes. It was also reported that Communist China planned to demoralize the people of the United States by encouraging drug addiction. In view of the subcommittee's report, Congress passed an even tougher law, the Narcotic Drug Control Act of 1956. This act imposed very stiff penalties for narcotics and marijuana use. It prohibited suspended sentences, probation, or parole for all narcotic offenses except a first conviction for possession. Under the law a convicted seller or distributor of illegal narcotics was to be sentenced to prison. In most federal cases an individual who possessed over a few ounces of narcotics or marijuana was assumed to be a pusher and was treated as such. This law also provided for execution of a pusher selling heroin to a person under 18.

The Single Convention Treaty

This agreement replaced and consolidated parts of eight previous international agreements on narcotics. It was sponsored by the United Nations World Health Organization. It became effective in 1964, although the U.S. Senate did not ratify participation in it until 1967, because it thought parts of the treaty were weaker than an earlier (1953) treaty. It regulates the production, manufacture, import, export, trade, distribution, use, and possession of products from the opium poppy, coca plant, and cannabis plant. It does not cover the depressant, stimulant, and hallucinogenic drugs. Signatory parties must plan to phase out quasi-medical use of opium smoking (within 15 years of signing), and coca leaf chewing and the nonmedical use of cannabis (within 25 years of signing). In order to legalize marijuana in the United States it would be necessary to abrogate this treaty. This can be done by announcing the intent to withdraw from the treaty six months in advance.

The Narcotic Addict Rehabilitation Act (NARA)

This act, passed in 1966, gave states the opportunity to put pressure on addicts to go through treatment programs or go to jail. The law provided for easing a sentence if progress could be shown in treatment and rehabilitation.

Methadone Control Act

In 1972 the Food and Drug Administration released methadone to be used in treatment of opiate addiction. It had only been used experimentally up to that time. Because of poor administration and coordination of some early methadone maintenance programs, abuse of the drug on the street had increased. The Methadone Control Act of 1973 put controls on the dispensing and monitoring of methadone to help keep the drug off the streets.

The Heroin Trafficking Act of 1973

This law tightened up penalties for traffickers so that bail making could not be continually abused.

The Food, Drug, and Cosmetic Act*

The distinction between prescription and over-the-counter (OTC) drugs is relatively new to the pharmaceutical industry. All nonnarcotic drugs were available OTC until just before World War II. It was not until a drug company unwittingly produced a toxic product that killed over 100 people that the Food and Drug Administration (FDA) was given control over drug safety in the 1938 Federal Food, Drug, and Cosmetic Act. The bill had been debated for several years in Congress and showed no promise of passage. Then a pharmaceutical company wanted to sell a liquid form of a sulfa drug (the first antibiotic) and found that the drug would dissolve well in a chemical solvent, diethylene glycol. They marketed the antibiotic as Elixir Sulfanilamide without testing the solvent for toxicity. Under the 1906 Pure Food and Drug Act, the company could not be prosecuted for the toxicity of this form of drug or for not testing the formulation of the drug on animals first. They could only be prosecuted for mislabeling the product on the technicality that "elixir" refers to a solution in alcohol, not a solution in diethylene glycol.

The 1938 act differs from the 1906 law in several ways. It is organized by the regulated commodity (food, drug, or cosmetic) rather than by the type of violation. It defined drugs to include products affecting bodily structure or function in the absence of disease. Companies had to file applications with the government for all new drugs showing that they were safe (not effective, just safe!) for use as described. The drug label had to include all ingredients and the quantity of each, as well as instructions regarding correct use of the drug and warnings about

its dangers. Significantly, all this information was supposed to be written in language the average person would not understand, and it did not have to be passed along to the patient.

Prior to passage of the 1938 act, a person could go to a doctor and get a prescription for any nonnarcotic drug *or to the pharmacy directly* if he or she had already decided what was needed. The effect of the labeling requirement in the 1938 act was to allow the drug companies to create a class of drugs that could not be sold legally without a prescription. Although it is not certain, it is possible the FDA's actions were motivated by the way people used two classes of drug developed prior to passage of the 1938 law— the sulfa antibiotics and the barbiturates. They took too little of the antibiotics to cure an infection and too much of the barbiturates and became addicted.

Humphrey-Durham Amendment

The 1938 Food, Drug, and Cosmetic Act allowed the manufacturer to determine whether a given drug was to be labeled prescription or nonprescription. The same drug could be sold as prescription by one company and as an OTC by another! After the Humphrey-Durham amendment was passed in 1951, almost all new drugs were placed in the prescription-only class. The drugs that were patented and marketed after World War II included the potent new antibiotics and the phenothiazine tranquilizers such as Thorazine®. The FDA and the drug firms thought these were potentially too dangerous to sell OTC.

Kefauver-Harris Amendments

Senator Kefauver's hearings, which began in 1959, initially were concerned with the drug companies' enormous profit margins because of

---

* This section is largely from Temin, 1980.

"THE GENERIC NAME FOR MERLOSUTRICIN?
SNAKE-SKIN OIL."

the lack of competition in the market for new, patented drugs. Testimony by physicians revealed that an ordinary doctor in clinical practice was not able to evaluate the efficacy of the drugs he or she prescribed. Both Kefauver's bill and Harris's bill in the House showed no likely signs of becoming law until the thalidomide tragedy occurred. The 1938 law did not give the FDA authority to supervise clinical testing of drugs. Thalidomide was used in Europe and distributed on a small scale in the United States as a tranquilizer. There are two approximately 24-hour intervals early in pregnancy when thalidomide can affect the development of the embryo's arms and legs. If the woman took thalidomide on one or both of those days, the infant was born with rudimentary arms and/or legs (*phocomelia*, from the Greek words for *flippers*, or *seal-shaped limbs*).

Although standard testing probably would not have detected this effect of thalidomide, and the tragedy would have occurred anyway, these pathetic babies stimulated passage of the 1962 amendments. They strengthened the government's regulation of both the introduction of new drugs and the production and sale of existing drugs. For the first time, the FDA was empowered to withdraw approval of a drug from the market. The drug company had to have approval of its testing procedures before it could start testing, and it had to adhere to standards of good manufacturing practice.

To evaluate the effectiveness of the over 4000 drugs that had been introduced between 1938 and 1962, the FDA contracted the Drug Efficacy Study to the National Research Council. This investigation started in 1966 and ran for three years. The Council was asked to rank drugs as either effective or ineffective, but they ended up with six classifications: (1) effective, (2) effective but less so than another, (3) probably effective, (4) possibly effective, (5) ineffective as a fixed combination, and (6) ineffective. Unfortunately, although the study was supposed to be based on scientific evidence, this often was not available, and so its conclusions were sometimes founded on the clinical experience of the physicians on each panel. (The study had been initiated because physicians in practice were admittedly unable to make such decisions!)

The legal challenge that resulted when the FDA took an "ineffective in a fixed combination" drug off the market and the company sued, finally forced the FDA to define what constituted an adequate and well-controlled investigation. Adequate, documented clinical experience was no longer in good standing as proof that a drug was safe and effective. Each new drug application now had to include information about the drug's performance in comparison to that of a carefully defined control group. The drug could be compared with (1) a placebo, (2) another drug known to be active based on

previous studies, (3) the established results of no treatment, or (4) historical data on the course of the illness without the use of the drug in question. In addition, a drug marketed before 1962 could no longer be "grandfathered in." If the company could not prove the drug had the qualifications to pass the post-1962 tests for a new drug, it was considered as a new, unapproved drug and could not legally be sold.

Drug Abuse Control Amendments (DACA) of 1965

In the early 1960s the use of illegal drugs rose sharply and a shift in the types of drug being used took place. Large numbers of people were experimenting with drugs that altered mood and state of consciousness. Along with these new drugs came a rash of bad trips, medical complications, and drug emergency cases. Publicity on adverse reactions caused by these new varieties of street drugs roused the public to bring pressure on Congress to put controls on them. By the end of 1965 Congress passed a new series of laws, the Drug Abuse Control Amendments (DACA).

These laws, which excluded narcotics and marijuana, brought three classes of drugs under federal control: (1) the amphetamines, (2) the barbiturates, and (3) a group of drugs that had a potential for abuse because of their psychedelic or hallucinogenic effects. For the first time lysergic acid and lysergic acid amide were placed in a controlled substance group, because LSD could be made from these acids without much difficulty. However, these laws did allow the use of peyote by members of the Native American Church in their religious ceremonies. Some of the key regulations in the 1965 amendments are (1) no prescription could be filled or refilled after six months from date of issue or refilled more than five times; (2) manufacturers had to keep records of sales for three years; and (3) penalties for violation of the regulations ranged up to one year and a $1000 fine for a first offense and up to three years and a $10,000 fine for a second offense. Penalties were much higher for selling to anyone under 21 years of age. In 1968 an amendment to the DACA established that the sentence was to be suspended for a first conviction. If there was no conviction in the one-year probationary interlude, the first conviction was to be erased from the record.

Comprehensive Drug Abuse Prevention and Control Act of 1970

The Comprehensive Drug Abuse Prevention and Control Act was passed by Congress in 1971. President Nixon had proposed a broader education, research, and rehabilitation program to be covered by new drug laws, but after a great deal of political hassling Congress made it primarily a law enforcement bill, with some provision for treatment and education. This act:

1. Expanded community mental health centers and the Public Health Service Hospitals for drug abusers, and authorized drug education workshops and material for professional workers and public schools.

2. Set up a Commission on Marijuana and Drug Abuse to study these drugs for two years and to submit a report and make recommendations.

3. Excluded alcohol and tobacco from the group of drugs under study.

4. Determined that there would be no mandatory federal sentence for a first offense of illegal possession of any controlled drugs, and decreed that the possible sentences could be a year's imprisonment and/or a $5000 fine, or one year's probation. If probation is not violated the conviction is to be erased from the person's record (first offense only).

5. Determined that any person over 18 selling drugs to anyone under 21 should receive twice the first offense penalty and three times the penalty for a second or subsequent offense.

6. Decreed that any individual caught selling as part of a group of five or more (such a group is considered a drug ring) may receive a penalty of at least ten years and not more than a $100,000 fine for the first offense. A second offense has a penalty of not less than 20 years and not more than a $200,000 fine, or life imprisonment.

7. Divided drugs with actual or relative potential for abuse into five categories called *schedules*:
    a. Schedule I substances have a high potential for abuse and have no currently accepted medical use in treatment in the United States (heroin, LSD, peyote).
    b. Schedule II substances have a high potential for abuse, with severe psychic or physical dependence potential. They have some currently accepted medical uses in the United States, but their availability is tightly restricted. Amphetamines, opium, cocaine, and pentobarbital are in Schedule II.
    c. Schedule III substances have less potential for abuse than I or II, and they have current medical use in the United States. They have low to moderate potential for physical addiction, but a high potential for psychological dependence. Examples of Schedule III drugs include limited quantities of certain opioid drugs, some depressants such as glutethimide (Doriden®), paregoric, and certain barbiturates (except those listed in another schedule).

d. The Schedule IV drugs have low potential for abuse relative to drugs in Schedule III, have a currently accepted medical use in the United States, and have a limited potential for psychological or physical addiction compared to Schedule III drugs. Phenobarbital, chloral hydrate, diazepam (Valium®), and propoxyphene (Darvon®) are in this schedule.

e. The Schedule V substances have a low potential for abuse relative to Schedule IV drugs and have a currently accepted medical use in the United States. Abuse of this class may lead to limited physical or psychological dependence relative to Schedule IV drugs. Lomotil® and small amounts of codeine in cough preparations and analgesics are narcotics in Schedule V.

Prescription orders are written for drugs in Schedules II–IV, and sometimes V. Schedule V drugs may be distributed without prescription, subject to state regulation, by a pharmacist.

DRUG ABUSE REGULATORY AGENCIES

Drug Enforcement Administration (DEA)

In 1930 Congress authorized the establishment of the Bureau of Narcotics in the Treasury Department. It remained in that department until 1968, when it became part of a new group in the Justice Department, the Bureau of Narcotics and Dangerous Drugs. Harry Anslinger was appointed head of the bureau from its begin-

ning until 1962 when he retired. Anslinger was an agent during Prohibition, and later as head of the Bureau he played an important role in getting marijuana outlawed by the federal government. In 1973, the Bureau of Narcotics and Dangerous Drugs became the Drug Enforcement Administration (DEA). Today the DEA has the responsibility of infiltrating and breaking up illegal drug traffic in the United States.

Special Action Office for Drug Abuse Prevention (SAODAP)

In 1971 President Nixon set up a temporary agency, SAODAP, to get short-term and long-term planning of programs started and coordinate drug programs with the states, so that proper funding procedures and policies were followed. This office was in the White House and was supposed to advise the president. One of the major reasons for establishing such an office was the initial report of a high heroin addiction rate in returning Vietnam veterans. This program was supposed to actively fight the increase in addiction in the United States. SAODAP was abolished, as planned, with most of its education, research, treatment, and rehabilitation functions going to the new agency, the National Institute on Drug Abuse (NIDA). An expert on the staff of advisors to the president, the Domestic Policy staff, assumed the duties of advising the president on drug-related matters and drug abuse programs. The advisor is to keep track of budgets for drug programs and coordinate policy with law enforcement groups. Under the Reagan administration further changes have been proposed. As you have probably noticed by now, control and management of drug programs in the United States change with each new "crisis."

The Alcohol, Drug Abuse, and Mental Health Administration (ADAMHA)

In 1973, a new agency was formed after Health, Education, and Welfare Secretary Weinberger stripped the alcohol and drug abuse sections from the National Institute of Mental Health (NIMH). This action formed the National Institute of Alcohol Abuse and Alcoholism (NIAAA) and the new NIDA (see previous section). NIAAA, NIDA, and NIMH are under the new agency, ADAMHA. This shuffling and redesign was part of the federal attempts to bring the post-Vietnam heroin crisis under control and address the perennial problems of alcoholism and dependence on other drugs.

Drug Abuse Office and Treatment Acts

Starting with the increased publicity on drug use by servicemen in Vietnam, new policies were formed to try to control the situation and to try new techniques in treatment that had never been funded before. In 1972 the Drug Abuse Office and Treatment Act was signed; in 1974 and 1978 amendments were made to improve the law. This law has provided money for treatment slots for addicts. Many of the treatment slots are for methadone clinics and also for experimental programs discussed in Chapter 20.

At the same time, the moneys given to the Veterans' Administration hospitals were greatly increased to handle addiction in the military. All military branches became more attentive to the drug problem and started to form drug information and treatment programs. One of the significant advances made was the recognition of alcoholism as a drug problem. The military had largely ignored alcoholism previously, even though it was a visible and common problem. The Veterans' Administration hospitals now devote more effort to the treatment of alcoholism problems than they do to problems caused by all the other drugs.

Alcohol and Drug Abuse Education Amendments

In 1978 several amendments set up an Office of Alcohol and Drug Abuse Education in the Office of Education. These laws gave more emphasis to drug abuse in rural areas and helped to coordinate federal, state, and local programs in education and prevention training.

The federal laws controlling drug use and attempting to prevent drug abuse are summarized in Tables 19-1 and 16-1 (see p. 296). It is certain that new laws will be passed in the future with the intent of solving problems caused by drug abuse. Unless experts in the fields of prevention and treatment are heeded and funding given to them to set up programs that have been proven, it is hard to see how the new laws will have any more deterrent effects on drug abuse than present laws. Funds should be provided to those experts willing and capable of setting up well-controlled and well-analyzed studies on the best methods of prevention, treatment, and rehabilitation. At present there is no consensus on what methods or programs are the best or that will yield the best results. The most successful programs in the past decade seem to have been comprehensive ones that impact on drug abuse at many levels. However, the need for further research comes to us at a time when there is a strong interest in reducing federal and state budgets, so the next several years may not bring much progress in solving drug abuse problems.

TABLE 19-1 Federal laws for the control of narcotic and other abused drugs

Name of legislation	Date	Summary of coverage and intent of legislation
Harrison Act	1914	First federal legislation to regulate and control the production, importation, sale, purchase, and free distribution of opium or drugs derived from opium.
Narcotic Drug Import and Export Act	1922	Legislation intended to eliminate the use of narcotics except for medical and other legitimate purposes.
Heroin Act	1924	Made it illegal to manufacture heroin.
Marijuana Tax Act	1937	Provided controls over marijuana similar to the Harrison Act over narcotics.
Opium Poppy Control Act	1942	Prohibits the growing of opium poppies in the United States except under license.
Boggs Amendment to the Harrison Narcotics Act	1951	Establishes severe mandatory penalties for conviction on narcotics charges.
Narcotics Control Act	1956	Legislation intended to impose very severe penalties for those convicted of narcotics or marijuana charges.
Drug Abuse Control Amendments (DACA)	1965	Adopts strict controls over amphetamines, barbiturates, LSD, and similar substances with provisions to add new substances as the need arises.
Narcotic Addict Rehabilitation Act (NARA)	1966	Allows treatment as an alternative to jail.
DACA Amendments	1968	Sentence may be suspended and record is erased if not convicted for another violation for one year.
Comprehensive Drug Abuse Prevention and Control Act	1970	Replaces or updates all other laws concerning narcotics and dangerous drugs.
Drug Abuse Office and Treatment Act	1972	Establishes $1.1 billion over three years to combat drug abuse and start treatment programs.
Methadone Control Act	1973	Places controls on methadone licensing.
Heroin Trafficking Act	1973	Increases penalties for traffickers and makes bail procedures more stringent.
Alcohol, Drug Abuse, and Mental Health Administration (ADAMHA)	1973	Consolidates NIMH, NIAAA, and NIDA under ADAMHA.

TABLE 19-1 *(continued)*

Name of legislation	Date	Summary of coverage and intent of legislation
Drug Enforcement Administration (DEA)	1973	Bureau of Narcotics and Dangerous Drugs is remodeled to become the DEA.
Drug Abuse Prevention, Control, and Treatment Amendments	1974 and 1978	Extends the 1972 law.
Alcohol and Drug Abuse Education Amendments	1978	Sets up Office of Alcohol and Drug Abuse Education in the Department of Education. More emphasis on drug abuse in rural areas and on coordination at the federal-state level.

REGULATION OF DRUG ABUSE AT THE STATE LEVEL

States passed the first laws to control the abuse or misuse of drugs; federal laws were developed later, after the federal government gained more control over the well-being and lives of the citizens. Early state laws banned the use of smoking opium, regulated the sale of various psychoactive drug substances, and in a few instances set up treatment programs. There was no effort to prevent drug abuse. Drug abuse was controlled to a great extent by social pressure rather than by law. It was considered morally wrong to be an alcoholic or an addict to opium or some other drug.

State and local laws often developed from ordinances that originated in the pulpit. Some offenses were declared far worse than others under state and federal law. Those considered to be serious crimes were designated as felonies, and the sentence for committing a felony was usually over a year. Offenses of a lesser nature were designated as misdemeanors, which had sentences of under a year.

The drug laws in 1932 varied considerably from state to state, so the National Conference of Commissioners on Uniform State Laws set up the Uniform Narcotic Drug Act (UNDA), which was later adopted by nearly all states. The UNDA provided for the control of possession, use, and distribution of opiates and cocaine. In 1942 marijuana was included as a narcotic.

In 1967 the Food and Drug Administration proposed the Model Drug Abuse Control Act and urged the states to adopt it on a uniform basis. This law extended controls over depressant, stimulant, and hallucinogenic drugs similar to the 1965 federal law. Many of the states set up laws based on this model.

The federal Controlled Substances Act of 1970 stimulated the National Conference of Commissioners to propose a new Uniform Controlled Substances Act (UCSA). The UCSA permits enactment of a single state law regulating the illicit possession, use, manufacture, and dispensing of controlled psychoactive substances. At this time most states have enacted the UCSA or modifications of it.

CONSTITUTIONAL PROTECTIONS

The most common defense used in drug-related criminal proceedings are individual liberty guarantees based on the Bill of Rights and the 14th Amendment of the U.S. Constitution, and additional individual liberty guarantees in a particular state's constitution. These may be invoked by criminal defendants (those accused of and being prosecuted for a criminal act). The defenses most commonly used in drug cases are: defense of pharmacological duress; the right to privacy; the freedom of religion; the cruel and unusual punishment defense; the double jeopardy defense; and the sanity defense. The law works for the protection of the individual, and it often works more smoothly for those who can pay for the best legal assistance. It is difficult for the average citizen and criminal justice worker to see a guilty person released on a technicality. Nevertheless, it is better to err in releasing some violators than to imprison someone who is innocent.

The following are the articles of the Bill of Rights and the 14th Amendment of the Constitution that have played a major role in criminal defenses.

1.   Amendment I: "Congress shall make no law . . . prohibiting the free exercise of religion or abridging the freedom of speech." This has been the basis for allowing the Native American Indian Church to use peyote.

2.   Amendment IV guarantees the right to be secure in one's own home, sometimes called the right to privacy in one's own home, and to have protection against unauthorized search and seizure. This amendment is the basis for many successful drug defenses. Legal authorities cannot search someone's home without just cause, but must have a search warrant or other permission to do so. If a person is stopped while driving a car, and the car is searched and a hidden drug found, this could not be admissible as evidence unless the officer could demonstrate there was a reason, such as erratic driving, to stop that particular driver.

3.   Amendment V: the double jeopardy limitation. A person cannot be charged twice for the same crime, and once released cannot be recharged for the same crime. This is sometimes called the *due process amendment,* because it further says one cannot be deprived of life, liberty, or property without due process of law.

4.   Amendment VIII: the cruel and unusual punishment limitation. Sentences that are clearly out of line with the norm for the times can be successfully appealed.

5.   Amendment XIV: Each person is to have equal protection under the law. This amendment also guarantees due process.

The insanity defense is used in some proceedings. The 5th and 14th Amendments provide due process, but persons are excluded from criminal responsibility if they carried out the act as a result of insanity or the inability to tell right from wrong. The American Psychiatric Association has declared that drug addiction is a nonpsychotic mental disorder, so persons can claim they are not able to control their actions but at the same time must show they were insane at the time of the crime (which is difficult). Addicts are often given leniency if they agree to enroll in treatment or rehabilitation programs. If a person commits a serious crime while under the influence of the drug, the defense is much more complex.

THE EFFECT OF LAWS ON DRUG USE

From descriptions in earlier chapters and this chapter, drug laws and enforcement of the laws are not deterring people from using drugs. People have used drugs as long as history has been recorded and very likely will continue to do so. Brecher (1972) believes there is evidence to show that the rise in drug use in the 1960s was stimulated in four ways:

1. There is always a certain amount of deviant behavior in any society, from ancient Greece and Rome to the present day, but our many forms of modern communication have heavily stressed drug abuse as the major form of deviant behavior. This probably influenced susceptible people in this direction.

2. Because of the publicity surrounding marijuana, LSD, psychotropic drugs, amphetamines, barbiturates, and others, the entire generation was made aware of the particular drugs to choose from.

3. Many drug warnings actually work as lures for many potential users. There is a saying in advertising: "I don't care what you say about me, as long as you keep mentioning my name." Many people hear of something new and want to try it to get a new feeling, to impress peers, to take a risk, and so on.

4. There was an incredible conflict of information on drugs. In the information that was supposed to guide and inform young people, many quoted "facts" were obviously not true or were incorrectly emphasized. This led to a cynical attitude.

In reviewing developments since the 1950s, as a variety of drugs became popular, we think that the huge amount of misinformation about new drugs influenced many people to try them.

If a drug was said to be an aphrodisiac, or to give a different and special high, or to give insight into the meaning of life, many people believed this and wanted to try it. This type of attraction has existed as long as information has been recorded about mind-altering substances. Similar claims have been made for opium, methaqualone, ether, nitrous oxide, hashish, peyote, and just about every other substance taken by humans to alter the state of consciousness.

As the amount of addiction increased during the mid-1960s, many poor programs and laws were instituted with little investigation into the underlying reasons for the increase in drug use. Restrictive laws never seem to work if the majority of people do not believe in them. As laws became more restrictive there was no decrease in the levels of addiction; in fact, the numbers grew. During this time people sold drugs at all levels—high school, college, and probably in every community. In the early 1980s there are increasingly large volumes of drugs being sold throughout the United States. Billions of dollars are being paid for those drugs. Although no one knows how much money is being exchanged, it may approach $80 to $100 billion a year for all illegal drugs, of which the two biggest categories are an estimated $30 billion for cocaine and $24 billion for marijuana. Because of the large sums of money involved, there has been corruption at all levels. Notorious examples of this include the loss of millions of dollars of contraband heroin and cocaine held as evidence in police vaults in New York City, the indictment of a number of detectives in the homicide division of Miami for selling drugs and taking large bribes, and the claim that there were direct links between drug dealers and the governments of Colombia and Bolivia. Some law enforcement agencies have said that drugs are the largest export item from these countries. It is known that Miami is the key point of entry for both cocaine and marijuana into the United States and that money is "laundered" in businesses set up as fronts. In 1981 it was reported that the Miami Branch of the Federal Reserve Bank of Atlanta was the only branch bank in the U.S. Reserve System to show a cash surplus—$4.74 billion in 1980.

Because of insufficient law enforcement personnel and inadequate detention facilities, much drug traffic goes unchecked. In addition, the judiciary system cases get so backlogged that many never get to court. Plea bargaining is almost the rule in order to clear the court docket. Often dealers and traffickers are back in business the same day they are arrested. This seriously damages the morale of law enforcement people, the legislative branches of the various governmental agencies, and the average citizen.

It is estimated that there are nearly 500,000 drug-related arrests each year. This is a tremendous cost to society in damaged lives and family relationships, and such an arrest seriously jeopardizes one's opportunity for a normal life. Drug taking is closely tied to societal problems, and it will remain a problem unless society provides more meaningful experiences to those most susceptible to drug abuse. Improved education and increased support should be given to preteens, because that is the age when deviant behavior starts. In cases where drug-education programs have been successful in involving students, the amount of drug taking and illegal activity seems to go down (see Chapter 20).

COSTS OF DRUG ADDICTION TO SOCIETY

Society pays a high price for drug addiction. Many of the costs are immeasurable—for example, broken homes, illness, shortened lives, and loss of good minds to industry and professions. The dollar costs are also great. The National Institute on Drug Abuse has estimated that the typical narcotics habit costs the user $100 a day or more to maintain, depending on location, availability of narcotics, and other factors. Let us assume that a given heroin addict has a $50-a-day habit, about right for four bags a day. This addict would need $18,250 a year just to keep him- or herself in drugs. It is impossible for most addicts to get this amount of money legally, so many of them resort to criminal activity.

Most crimes related to drugs involve theft of personal property—primarily burglary and shoplifting—and less commonly assault and robbery (mugging). It is estimated that a heroin addict has to steal three to five times the actual cost of the drugs to maintain the habit. This means he or she would have to steal about $80,000 to $90,000 a year. A number of addicts resort to pimping and prostitution. No accurate figures are available on the costs of drug-related prostitution, although some law enforcement officials have estimated that prostitutes take in a total of $10 to $15 billion a year. It has also been estimated that nearly one out of every three or four prostitutes in major cities has a serious heroin dependency.

The costs to society continue after addicts are caught, because it takes from $20 to $50 a day to incarcerate each of them. To support programs like methadone maintenance costs much less. New York officials estimate that methadone maintenance programs cost about $2000 a year per patient. Some outpatient programs, such as in Washington, D.C., claim a cost as low as $5 to $10 a day (not counting cost of staff and facilities), much less than incarceration.

THE FUTURE OF DRUG LAWS

It is always hard to predict trends in any area, and the law is no exception. There appear to be three trends in various states and at the federal level that may result in new drug laws. These trends are: (1) decriminalization of possession of marijuana for personal use; (2) a series of laws aimed at getting tough with certain types of drug offense, like trafficking; and (3) a voluntary civil commitment option for all drug-dependent persons entering the criminal justice system.

Decriminalization was first recommended by the National Commission on Marijuana and Drug Abuse in 1973. A majority of states have followed through with laws that make possession of marijuana for personal use a misdemeanor. Until about 1973 nearly 500,000 youngsters a year were being arrested, and the laws varied so that in some states marijuana possession was a serious offense that stigmatized the person permanently. Some states separate private versus public possession, with the latter being more serious.

New York was one of the first states to set up "get tough" laws aimed primarily at drug trafficking. Indiana, New Jersey, New Hampshire, and Ohio followed. The drug laws of New York require lengthy mandatory minimum prison sentences followed by mandatory parole terms on release from prison. Postindictment plea bargaining (giving a lesser sentence if the person pleads guilty) is prohibited in all but a very few circumstances, thus ensuring prison sentences if a guilty verdict is returned. The New York law, put into effect in 1973, has not been a deterrent

to trafficking or drug use. Instead it encouraged dealers to move across state lines, sell smaller doses, and use minors as distributors. It may even have encouraged law enforcement personnel to make fewer drug busts, because a small drug dealer would get the same prison term as a murderer. Harsh laws in themselves have never been very effective unless they were backed by society and had a total commitment from all parts of the criminal justice system. In addition, cooperation with pharmaceutical companies to prevent overproduction and diversion to illicit markets is essential.

The third trend is in its infancy: creating a voluntary civil commitment option for all drug-dependent persons entering the criminal justice system. In 1973 the Uniform Drug Dependence Treatment and Rehabilitation Act was developed by the National Conference of Commissioners on Uniform State Laws. The act mandates an alternative of voluntary diversion of drug-dependent persons under criminal justice jurisdiction, but the period of required treatment cannot be less than the length of the sentence that would have been imposed. This act would balance society's interest in supervision or control of drug-dependent offenders and its goal of getting the drug-dependent person off the drugs and into society's mainstream. The object of the law is supposed to be rehabilitation rather than punishment alone.

CHAPTER 20

TREATMENT, REHABILITATION, AND PREVENTION

CHAPTER OBJECTIVES

1. List reasons why a person may become an addict.
2. Compare and contrast detoxification, methadone maintenance, opiate antagonist, and therapeutic community treatment programs.
3. Discuss treatment and rehabilitation criteria and their limitations in determining whether or not a given program is "successful."
4. List elements of successful primary prevention programs.
5. Explain why the desire to alter the state of consciousness may be inherent in human nature.
6. List the four assumptions on which the alternatives approach to prevent drug abuse is based.
7. List three ways altered states of consciousness may be caused, and give examples of each.
8. List effects on the mind when the person is in an altered state of consciousness.
9. Describe the altered states of consciousness that occur as a person moves from the typical waking state toward the extreme states of hyperarousal and hypoarousal.
10. Explain how the hyperaroused and the hypoaroused states are related to processing of sensory input in the brain.
11. Describe some of the physiological changes that occur in the relaxation response, or meditative state.

The United States has always had to deal with various types of drug dependence from the earliest days of its founding, and there have been conflicting views about the seriousness of the problem. Drug dependence has been considered a moral violation, a criminal act, and an illness. The laws passed in the country reflected the moral codes of the times. In the early days, alcoholism was rampant, and there were some pockets of opiate dependence. The Pilgrims and Puritans did not forbid drinking, only overindulgence. In the period after the Revolutionary War, people continued to accept heavy drinking as a normal way of life, although many believed it was morally wrong to drink to excess. So many Americans were addicted to alcohol that Presidents Washington and Jefferson stated it would be better to switch from distilled spirits to beer and wine, in order to reduce the disruptive influence of alcoholism. From that time until into the early 1900s opiate addiction grew, because it was legal to smoke and use these drugs and because they were widely available. The patent medicines, tonics, and elixirs had liberal amounts of the opiates as well as alcohol, and this compounded the increase in drug dependence. Barbiturates became available in the early 1900s. Some people became addicted to them, but little attention was given to this problem because it was possible to obtain supplies through medical channels. Amphetamine dependence was likewise managed medically. Barbiturates and amphetamines were not restricted by federal laws until 1965.

The World Health Organization of the United Nations has defined *addiction* as a "state of periodic or chronic intoxication detrimental to the individual and society, which is characterized by an overwhelming desire to continue taking the drug and to obtain it by any means." There are conflicting views on the nature of drug addiction, or drug dependence, as the WHO today prefers to call addiction. The two most prevalent views have been that drug dependence is a crime, or that it is a disease. The U.S. Supreme Court ruled in 1962 that the labeling of drug dependence as a crime is unconstitutional. Like alcoholism, drug dependence was to be regarded as a disease rather than the result of moral weakness. However, law enforcement groups maintain that considering drug dependence as a disease should not release the addict from the responsibility of criminal action to obtain drugs.

The disease model of drug dependence has had an effect on the approaches taken to prevent drug dependence and to treat and rehabilitate addicts. The disease model seems appropriate when one considers that drug dependence usually spreads like a disease, with points of contagion.

Chapter 12 noted that the majority of narcotic addicts exhibited antisocial behavior long before they started using drugs. They were poor or failing students and in trouble with the law. Eighty percent had preaddiction arrest records, and 40% had preaddiction convictions (Nurco, 1979). Many dropped out of middle or high school. They never learned a vocational skill or completed the minimal educational levels to get a job so they could support themselves, and thus for all intents and purposes they removed themselves from productive society. They were driven further into antisocial behavior in the form of crime as a way of life in order to make enough money to buy drugs. It is obvious that, even when drug dependence is considered to be a disease, it is also a social problem in that it is clearly linked to social and economic conditions in the community. When a person's emotional stability is disturbed by frustrations and rejections, he or she may seek the psychological and/or chemical means that are available for a measure of relief. For some this leads to delinquency; for others, drug dependence; and for many, a combination of these results. Because of the complex nature of drug dependence, nothing less than a comprehensive prevention and treatment program can deal with the multifaceted nature of drug dependence.

Nurco (1979) describes six reasons why individuals become drug addicts. These are:

1. They are easily frustrated and deal with frustration by aggression. Narcotics provide a way to safely handle the dangers of aggression and provide an escape.

2. Addicts were deprived as children, when they were dependent, and they still have the feeling they must have gratification immediately. Drugs provide this.

3. Addicts have inadequate sexual identification. They are expected to perform as heterosexuals, but it is less demanding to use drugs to reduce their libido.

4. Society often does not provide enough legitimate ways to achieve goals, so they use illegitimate methods.

5. Addicts are risk takers. They take more dares and fight to prove themselves. Taking narcotics is a risky business, and it satisfies their need to prove themselves.

6. Addicts are bored easily. Being addicted to narcotics is a full-time occupation, and there is no time for boredom.

TREATMENT AND REHABILITATION OF THE ADDICT

There has been a wide variety of drug-addiction treatment programs in the United States over the years. The first explicit commitment to make treatment readily available was the formation of the Special Action Office for Drug Abuse Prevention (SAODAP) in June 1971. This included a recommendation for additional support for increased efforts to control the availability of illicit drugs. Special problems in the military were addressed when President Nixon further directed the Secretary of Defense that drug use would no longer be a court martial offense. This humanitarian but practical action was necessary because of the widespread use of heroin and other drugs by American servicemen in Vietnam. In 1972 the Drug Abuse Office and Treatment Act added financial backing to the treatment programs. It is fair to say the 1970s were the "golden years" for development of new programs. It was also a period of time when billions of dollars helped support treatment and rehabilitation services in every state and in most medium and large cities (Jaffe, 1979).

The following list of treatment methods is arranged as a series of opposing pairs to show the range of techniques that have been developed:

1. Drug-free or maintenance programs. Drug-free programs start with the time of withdrawal from the drug, whereas maintenance programs are longer and may not deal with withdrawal at all. In the latter instance, the person is allowed to continue on a drug substitute for a predetermined or indefinite period of time.

2. Residential or ambulatory. In residential programs the drug-dependent person remains in the treatment facility, such as a hospital ("inpatient") or therapeutic community. Ambulatory ("outpatient") programs are based on the patient visiting the treatment facility at certain intervals.

3. Medical or nonmedical. The staff that runs the program may be composed of medical or nonmedical personnel—for example, former addicts.

4. Selective or nonselective. Selective programs screen prospective "clients" and accept only those who they judge are likely to benefit. The nonselective programs accept virtually all

with drug-dependence problems who apply or who are sent there, with the exception of the psychotic and violently assaultive.

5. Voluntary or involuntary. Practically all drug treatment involves some degree of coercion, if only from family or employer. However, involuntary usually refers to a legal requirement as part of the legal system's way of dealing with a drug addict. The person is required to enter some form of treatment and remain in it for a period of time or until he or she can demonstrate progress. In 1966 the federal government passed the Narcotic Addict Rehabilitation Act (NARA), which established national rules for admission to treatment and rehabilitation at federal centers. Addicts have the opportunity to have their sentences reduced or charges dismissed if they go for treatment.

Goals of Treatment

The goals of treatment are straightforward. Society wants the addict to stop using the drug or drugs in question and to stop committing crimes. At the same time, the addict is expected to find a job, stabilize his or her personal life, and to become a useful and productive citizen. Over the past 20 years or more that active treatment programs have functioned, it has become apparent that there is a serious problem in determining the effectiveness of the various treatment modalities. What measures should be used to determine success in treatment? Should it be keeping off of drugs, holding a job, buying a home, or what? Treatment success has been based on how long the person remains free from drug dependence. This criterion is not necessarily valid, because there are many who relapse and try drugs again before establishing a drug-free life. Criminality cannot always be used as a criterion either, because the ex-addict may con-

tinue to commit crimes, but to a lesser extent. Is this also a successful treatment outcome? Another problem that may be ignored is the substitution of other drugs for the original. If barbiturate, heroin, or methadone addicts go off those drugs, but become alcoholics, this is a dubious bargain.

In summary, there are a range of possible benefits and adverse effects that can be produced by treatment programs. To evaluate the success of treatment and rehabilitation programs there should be a variety of measuring devices, rather than success (total abstinence) or failure (remaining on the addicting drug or substituting other drugs). Success in a treatment program might therefore be based on many factors: abstinence from illegal drugs, abstinence from all addicting drugs, stabilization on a maintenance drug like methadone, employment, decreased or noncriminal conduct, support of a family, and improved physical health and psychological functioning. Any or all of these might show partial success and should be so considered (DeLong, 1972).

Detoxification and Abstinence Programs

One straightforward approach to drug dependence is to reduce the drug intake to zero and give the addict medical and psychological assistance through withdrawal. Opiate addicts can be withdrawn in this manner, with careful management, in five to ten days. This approach is not usually taken for alcohol or barbiturate dependencies, because withdrawal from heavy depressant dependence can be life threatening. Instead, the addict is stabilized on a long-acting depressant and withdrawn gradually (Chapter 10). Detoxification has several obvious benefits for both the addict and society. Even if the addict does not intend to stay off drugs, it reduces his or her habit and decreases its costs. This spares the addict the hassle, and society the crime costs, of his or her drug dependence for a period of time after detoxification. For a number of addicts it is a step toward rehabilitation. Detoxification alone does not have a high long-term success rate.

The goals and procedures of detoxification programs vary greatly. Most of them use no drugs for support after detoxification, although some use methadone maintenance and a variety of drug backups, like tranquilizers. These programs can be residential, where the patient lives in a hospital, clinic, or therapeutic community; or ambulatory, where the addict comes by for professional help and sometimes methadone or other support drugs. Some outpatient settings require attendance of programs and therapies during the day.

Maintenance Programs

Maintenance programs are based on the principle that past treatment programs have not been successful, so "incurable" addicts should be able to register and receive narcotics under supervision. Proponents contend that many addicts who are now forced into a life of crime to support their habits could become law-abiding and useful citizens if they received narcotics legally and that the illicit narcotics trade would be eliminated by automatic loss of customers. The opponents of such programs say that there are proper treatment programs that can cure many addicts and that providing an addict with a substitute narcotic is not solving the basic problem causing the drug dependence. Others have said that if we worked on providing a meaningful life for all people and improved the social and psychological climate, drug dependence would

disappear. It is difficult to assess the validity of those opposing views. It would also be difficult to implement goals such as providing a meaningful life for everyone. What is meaningful for one person will be boring for another.

In any case, the concept of maintenance on a noneuphoric opiate is now widely accepted in the United States as one way to help a significant proportion of addicts. This has not always been true.

Morphine Maintenance

After passage of the Harrison Narcotics Act in 1914, there were between 200,000 and 300,000 opiate addicts who were no longer able to obtain drugs legally except through physicians. After 1918, more than 40 morphine maintenance clinics opened. However, public opinion was against maintenance, and the last clinic closed in 1923. The Narcotics Division maintained a very tough attitude toward physicians who advocated maintenance and prescribed opiates for their patients. By 1938, about 25,000 doctors had been arrested for this, and of these about 5000 went to jail (DeLong, 1972).

Methadone and LAAM Maintenance

Drs. Vincent Dole and Marie Nyswander were the first to use the synthetic narcotic, methadone, in a rehabilitation program with heroin addicts in the mid-1960s. As of 1980, there were an estimated 70,000–75,000 addicts on methadone maintenance. The drug is used to alleviate narcotic craving and to prevent the occurrence of withdrawal symptoms. The advantages of methadone over other forms of maintenance therapy are (1) the drug can be administered orally; (2) it has a duration of action in the body of 24 to 36 hours, compared to heroin's action of four to eight hours; (3) no serious side effects are seen at maintenance doses; (4) at sufficient dose levels methadone will almost completely block the effects of heroin; and (5) when taken orally, it does not produce euphoric effects of its own. Disadvantages of methadone maintenance include (1) the person taking it will now have a drug dependence on methadone; and (2) it will not prevent the addict from taking other drugs that may interfere with treatment and rehabilitation. Some clinics require urine samples to test for heroin and other drugs periodically during treatment.

Once stabilized on methadone, the client faces a crucial period of adjustment: a life once devoted to maintaining a heroin habit, 24 hours a day, 365 days a year, must be transformed into a self-supporting, socially acceptable one. Methadone maintenance establishes the potential for such a change in life-style, but it is the person's motivation and capabilities that determine the success of the rehabilitation effort. A range of medical, psychiatric, social, and vocational services should be available during this phase of treatment.

Some drug abuse workers believe that both heroin addicts and addicts currently on methadone maintenance use alcohol extensively. Although data are limited, the prevalence of alcoholism is probably no greater among heroin addicts or addicts on methadone maintenance than it is among nonaddicted individuals from comparable socioeconomic backgrounds. In other words, the alcoholic former heroin addict did not turn to a combination of methadone plus alcohol as a substitute: he or she had always used alcohol. Nevertheless, excessive use of alcohol hinders progress in a methadone maintenance program. The treatment should be designed to bring the alcohol use under control as well as help the person learn to get away from heroin (Stimmel, 1980).

There have been numerous criticisms of the use of methadone, especially from proponents of therapeutic communities like Synanon, Narco, Daytop Village, Odyssey House, and others. Some critics have said that giving methadone is like switching an alcoholic from bourbon to wine. Methadone is not a perfect answer by any means. Former heroin addicts who had large habits may have to be maintained indefinitely on methadone. They are likely to relapse to heroin use if detoxified from methadone. They may never be rehabilitated in the conventional sense, because their backgrounds are such that they were never "habilitated" to begin with; they never had anything that approximated a so-called normal life. To create a normal life for these people may be too much to expect.

On the other hand, detoxification from methadone is a good possibility for methadone maintenance patients who were not addicted to heroin for a long period of time and who did not have an extensive background of criminal activity. Detoxification is not an automatic process in methadone maintenance. But, of those who completed detoxification, as many as 35% were narcotic-free and doing well up to six years later (Sells, 1979). Use of the nonopiate drug clonidine may help those who wish to stop taking methadone. It suppresses the signs and symptoms of opiate withdrawal and reduces the anxiety and irritability experienced by these patients during the difficult withdrawal step (Gold, Pottash, Sweeney, & Kleber, 1980).

The new long-acting methadone analog, levo-alpha-acetylmethadol (LAAM), need only be taken three times a week and is being experimented with in a number of programs. Because of the complexity of social and vocational problems the narcotic addict faces, he or she will progress faster through daily participation in intensive counseling. The addict stays close to the program for initial work and then later comes in for the maintenance drug and follow-up treatment less frequently. An addict might be treated with daily methadone first to increase the probability that he or she will at least attend counseling sessions, and then be switched to LAAM when he or she reaches an appropriate point in the program.

Heroin Maintenance

Great Britain set up heroin maintenance clinics for the treatment of its addicts in the early 1970s. The basis for this was both humanitarian and economic. It was argued that prescription heroin for proven addicts would save lives, eliminate illicit narcotics dealing, and at the same time clean up the crime that had been associated with the addict's need for money to buy heroin. At first there were problems because of lax controls, and heroin was being sold on the street that had been "ripped off" from the program. Later on, better controls were set up over heroin; also methadone began to be used in many clinics. It was estimated that there were less than 6000 opiate addicts in the whole of Great Britain in 1975, with no appreciable increase by 1980. Some have advocated the legal use of heroin in comparable maintenance programs in the United States. It is highly unlikely that this will be implemented, because methadone has advantages over heroin and also because heroin use in the United States has an unsavory history.

Opiate Antagonists

An antagonist is a compound that suppresses actions of a drug. Narcotic antagonists have properties that make them important tools in the clinical treatment of narcotic drug dependence and as therapeutic agents that reduce drug dependence. Another valuable property of antagonists is that they counteract the central nervous system depressant effects in opioid drug overdoses (Chapter 12).

Development of the antagonists was a by-product of research in analgesics. Scientists were interested in dissociating the dependence-producing properties and the necessary pain-relieving properties of substances that could replace morphine. This led to the development of nalorphine, the first specific opiate antagonist. Its short duration of action and high incidence of unpleasant side effects limited its clinical usefulness, but its properties stimulated further research on this class of drugs (Archer, 1981).

Cyclazocine was the next important antagonist to be developed. It is a more potent antagonist with a longer duration of action than nalorphine, but it also induces some unpleasant side effects, such as sedation, visual distortions, and racing thoughts. Tolerance to the side effects develops if the dose is increased gradually over several weeks. Because of these psychotomimetic side effects cyclazocine is not being used much at present.

Naloxone is a pure antagonist without analgesic properties. It does not have the unpleasant side effects that nalorphine and cyclazocine do, but it has a shorter duration of action and is less active if taken orally than desired for narcotic antagonist treatment programs. Nevertheless, it is valuable in treating toxic or near-lethal doses of narcotics (it is five to eight times more antagonistic than nalorphine). The drug seems to block narcotics from binding the opiate receptors in the brain, thus relieving depression of breathing and heartbeat.

Naltrexone is a chemical modification of naloxone that was synthesized in an effort to find a longer acting, more potent antagonist. It has low toxicity with few side effects, and a single dose provides an effective opiate blockade for up to 72 hours. Taking naltrexone three times a week is sufficient to maintain a fairly high level of opioid blockade. Starting in 1971, Congress mandated a large-scale increase in research on narcotic antagonistic drugs, and naltrexone seems to be the best that has been developed to this point. It has been used widely in experimental narcotic antagonist treatment programs (Archer, 1981).

Simple detoxification has not proved to be an effective means of treating heroin dependence, because a high proportion of addicts return to heroin use. Heroin dependence is more than a pharmacological problem. The detoxified person who returns to his or her home environment is challenged with conditioned responses, pressure from peers, the social frustrations that contributed to the heroin dependence originally, and the intense craving associated with prolonged abstinence. Methadone or LAAM maintenance decreases craving, eliminates abstinence symptoms, and frees the person from the constant drug-related activity associated with keeping up with a heroin habit, but it does substitute one narcotic for another. Methadone or LAAM is not suitable for the heroin addict who wishes to stay off all narcotics. The motivated abstinent addict is more likely to do well on a narcotic antagonist treatment program. The antagonist blocks the euphoria and the other effects of heroin, and provides the support the person may need to resist returning to heroin.

Clinical tests with heroin addicts in treatment have shown that addicts on naltrexone will try heroin or methadone once or twice, early in treatment, and then stop, compared to addicts on placebo, who continue to use illicit methadone or heroin sporadically. The naltrexone group also reported significantly less craving for heroin than the placebo group.

Naltrexone is not a complete treatment, any more than methadone or LAAM maintenance. It facilitates changing the addict's life through interaction between that person and the clinical staff. Naltrexone is best suited for adolescent heroin users with relatively short experience with heroin, for recently paroled prisoners who have been abstinent while incarcerated, and for persons who have been on methadone mainte-nance who wish to go off, but who are afraid of relapsing to heroin. Unless there is some means of enforcing compliance, such as requiring urine samples, or unless the person is highly motivated, narcotic antagonist treatment programs do not work well. This is partly because the narcotic antagonist drug does nothing positive for the person. It simply blocks the effects of heroin or methadone if the person takes these drugs up to three days after his or her last dose of naltrexone (Renault, 1981).

Therapeutic Communities

Therapeutic communities, or self-regulating communities, operate on the hypothesis that drug use is a symptom of an underlying character disorder or emotional immaturity. The programs at the various communities thus have as a main goal a complete change in life-style: abstinence from drugs, elimination of criminal behavior, and development of employable skills, self-reliance, and personal honesty. The first therapeutic community (TC) for drug addicts was Synanon, which was based on a TC for psychiatric patients. This venture was started by Dederich, a former alcoholic, to treat alcoholics, and it later expanded to include drug addicts. As soon as drug addicts came into the program, the alcoholics left, because they felt associating with addicts was degrading! Synanon was started in Santa Monica, California, in 1958. Many branches were founded on the same philosophy—for example, Daytop Village and Phoenix House.

As of 1980, there were over 300 residential therapeutic communities serving drug abusers, criminal offenders, and other socially dislocated persons. These programs are quite diverse, ranging in size from 35 to 500 beds, and they serve a variety of clients. Synanon and Daytop Village have been used as models for a number of these programs, with modifications based on the circumstances in each community. The TCs have had a major impact on drug abuse treatment.

The TC program includes encounter group therapy, various levels of educational programs, assigned jobs within the community, and, in the later stages, conventional jobs in a living-out situation. The primary staff are former drug abusers who have been rehabilitated in TC programs. TCs use self-government and group pressures, instead of relying on a professional therapeutic staff, to change the individual's immature behavior. This is based on the belief that only an ex-addict can truly understand and deal effectively with an addict. Some TCs have professionals with training in vocational guidance, education, medicine, and mental health who are paid or who may donate their services. Residents of the traditional TC stay at least 15 months before they return to the community. Several TCs have been experimenting with shorter resident times, ranging from two to nine months, based on individual client needs and progress.

There is a high rate of failure to complete the required length of treatment. Admission criteria to the TCs are minimal and usually exclude only obviously psychotic or violent individuals. People leave without completing the program for a variety of reasons: (1) they may not be ready to deal with the complete change in lifestyle demanded by the TC; (2) they may progress to a certain point and become bored or frustrated with the TC; and (3) they may relapse and return to the TC at some future point. It should be noted that, in all varieties of mental health treatment, relapse is the rule. TCs for drug abuse are no exception. Treatment should not be counted a complete failure if the person stayed in the TC for a while, abstinent from drugs and the criminal activity to support the

habit, relapsed to heroin, and then entered long-term methadone maintenance rather than go back to the TC. Estimates of readmission to the TC or another form of treatment range from 30% to 60% (De Leon & Rosenthal, 1979).

Treatment Effectiveness

When federal funds became available to treat drug addiction in the late 1960s, four major treatment modalities evolved: methadone maintenance, therapeutic communities, outpatient drug-free programs, and short-term detoxification. These are the treatment modalities most frequently compared. Criteria for comparison include: later use of narcotics and other drugs, arrest record or criminality, employment record, follow-up treatment required, and so on.

Assessment of success depends on the criteria selected. "Graduates" of TCs (those who complete the community's residential treatment program) constitute a small proportion (10% to 15%) of all admissions. Five to ten years after "graduation," these former addicts have stable life-styles, are employed, and are not using opiates or engaging in criminal activity. Less improvement is shown by the majority who drop out of the TC program before completion, and, as might be expected, the extent of improvement is directly correlated to the length of residence in the TC (Figures 20-1 and 20-2). The greatest proportion of dropouts leave during the first 30 days of residence; the rate declines rapidly thereafter. The attrition for TC programs is not especially different from other drug abuse treatment programs (De Leon & Rosenthal, 1979).

Methadone maintenance has been operated on an outpatient basis and combined with a rehabilitation-oriented therapy program. Drug-

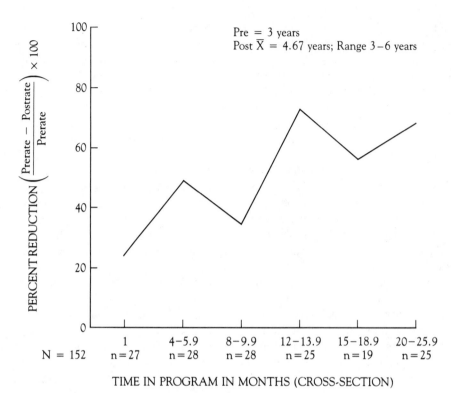

FIGURE 20-1
Percent reduction in arrest rate of dropouts from therapeutic communities (age at entry 19 and older) (De Leon & Rosenthal, 1979).

free programs are outpatient, intended primarily for nonopiate users. They range from highly demanding, socialization-oriented, daytime TCs to relaxed programs that offer rap sessions and support on request. There is an even higher rate of loss of patients from drug-free programs than from TCs. As described earlier, detoxification programs are usually short term, not over 21 days, and may be inpatient or outpatient depending on the drug and degree of dependence. Their primary goal is elimination of physiological dependence. Taking into consideration the variability in treatment approaches and in selection of patients, we can say that methadone maintenance, therapeutic communities, and drug-free programs have approximately the same success rate, whereas opiate antagonist and detoxification-only programs have appreciably lower success rates (Sells, 1979).

Innovative Treatments[*]

The addictive process is shaped by conditioned responses. Drugs shape behavior by their direct, pleasant effects (positive reinforcement, which

---

[*] This section is taken largely from O'Brien and Ng, 1979.

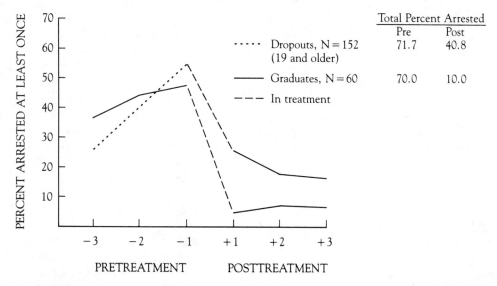

FIGURE 20-2
Percent of therapeutic-community dropouts and graduates arrested year by year (De Leon & Rosenthal, 1979).

produces primary psychological dependence) or by relieving withdrawal (negative reinforcement, which produces secondary psychological dependence). Wikler observed that former addicts who were free of drugs often developed tearing and yawning (opiate withdrawal signs) when they discussed drugs in group therapy. He and others later showed that conditioned withdrawal responses can be produced in animals and in humans. These conditioned withdrawal responses are thought to be partly caused by simple pairing of pharmacological withdrawal with environmental cues. Eventually the environmental stimuli, such as talking about drugs or showing pictures of drugs, could elicit a conditioned withdrawal. This would explain why former addicts yawned or formed tears when talking about drugs or when they returned to the environment in which they had previously used drugs. Not only do they develop drug craving during conditioned withdrawal, but they show

actual physical signs of sickness. Some addicts get conditioning cues from the injection procedure alone, and may even experience withdrawal relief when told they are getting an opiate, although they are actually getting a placebo. These persons are sometimes called "needle freaks." When they find the substance is a placebo, it no longer works.

Treatment methods have been developed based on our knowledge of the influence of conditioning in drug dependence. Some of these treatments block the conditioning process, whereas others may decondition or even enhance the conditioning to get off the drug in question.

Counterconditioning (Sensitization)

These procedures involve imagining scenes during therapy. As the patient develops a craving for drugs, he or she is asked to visualize as clearly as possible each link in the chain of events leading to drug taking. Then the patient is supposed to imagine becoming severely ill, in vivid terms, as a consequence of the drug. When the patient focuses on the avoidance of drugs, he or she is told to imagine pleasant scenes. This method has been used in several experimental programs, but not on a large scale. It is best suited for a motivated, cooperative patient who is doing well in a therapeutic community or a narcotic antagonist program.

Biofeedback Relaxation Therapy

Biofeedback involves control of the body by a series of mental conditioning exercises. In order for biofeedback therapy to be successful, there must be some means of making the person aware of the physiological process being regulated and of the occurrence of desired changes in this process. Often this means is a signal triggered by the dominant activity going on in the brain. The cerebral cortex of the brain is made up of two hemispheres that collect and respond to sensory stimulation. Each hemisphere has four major lobes that perform different cerebral functions: the *frontal, temporal, parietal,* and *occipital lobes.* The neurons that comprise these lobes generate small electrical currents, called *brain waves,* that can be detected with an instrument called the *electroencephalograph* (EEG) (literally, the graph of the electricity in the head).

There are four major types of brain wave classified according to their frequency: *beta, alpha, theta,* and *delta waves.* These are measured and identified in units called *Hertz* (Hz); one Hertz is equal to one cycle per second of frequency. Beta waves have frequencies of more than 14 Hz and are the fastest; they are usually related to stimulation, anxiety, increased attention, and mental concentration. Beta waves comprise the majority of the brain waves as we carry out normal waking activities. The alpha waves are 8 to 13 Hz and are apparently related to relaxed mental states, to the shutting out of sensory input, and even to the closing of the eyelids. Theta waves range from 4 to 7 Hz and are associated with the functioning of the thalamic portion of the reticular activating system (see Figure 2-5 on p. 28) and emotional stress. (Contrary to claims, an association between theta waves and creativity has not been proven.) Delta waves are the slowest and the largest, less than 4 Hz, and are prominent in the deep sleep stage where no dreaming occurs.

In the early 1970s there was great interest in alpha feedback training. It was found that a person could learn how to increase the output of alpha waves using a simple biofeedback instrument. (Many of these inexpensive instruments did not work well and interest declined.) Investigators with good instruments claimed an increase in alpha waves caused a feeling of calm alertness, whereas others claimed that tension was reduced and insights or creativity were increased. Many of the claims have not been supported with subsequent research. Although some of these experiments indicate that people can learn to relax, such an occurrence could be a side effect of muscle relaxation processes rather than a result of alpha wave increases.

Therapeutic use of biofeedback is based on two distinct models: the learning theory model and the relaxation model. In the learning theory model, the person learns to control a physiological process, such as blood pressure regulation, with an appropriate monitoring device to let him or her know when the blood pressure is changing in the desired direction—usually down. The relaxation, or antistress, model is based on the concept that stress exacerbates psychosomatic problems and may cause such disorders as hypertension, headaches, and anxiety. The biofeedback is directed at general muscular or cortical relaxation, with the idea that, when

"MY PROBLEM HAS ALWAYS BEEN AN OVERABUNDANCE OF ALPHA WAVES."

in a stressful situation, the patient will use what he or she has learned. One positive aspect of using biofeedback therapy in a treatment package is that it shifts the responsibility of "cure" from the doctor to the patient. The patient must become involved and actively work toward his or her own health, which should help the person to retain it afterwards. If a biofeedback method is to be used therapeutically, it should meet the following criteria: (1) it must have an effect greater than the placebo effect in controlled studies; (2) it must produce effects that are clinically significant, rather than just statistically significant; (3) the procedure must be effective in the person's normal environment, not just in the clinic; and (4) the benefits must continue past the end of formal treatment (Ray, Raczynski, Rogers, & Kimball, 1979).

Biofeedback-assisted relaxation procedures have been used as part of the therapeutic approach with alcoholics and methadone-maintenance addicts. Carefully controlled studies using muscular relaxation techniques and alpha EEG training in helping addicts withdraw have not produced clinical improvement. Unfortunately for people who had great expectations, the various types of biofeedback have not been shown to be better than general relaxation procedures (Ray et al., 1979).

Relaxation training has proved valuable as a nondrug coping device that the drug user can call on when in a situation that evokes feelings of anxiety, tension, or drug craving: the abuser can counter the feelings with relaxation rather than a drug. Although patients trained with biofeedback report that they feel it has helped them, biofeedback patients actually do not have significantly better outcomes than those on methadone maintenance or detoxification alone. In other words, the "improvement" appears to be a placebo effect.

Contingency Management Techniques

One of the best known of these techniques is the "token economy" system, which has been used successfully to treat prisoners and mental patients. Through this system, the rewards and punishments in the addict's environment are identified and then manipulated to redirect his or her responses. Subjects gain points if they perform certain tasks that are beneficial to the treatment program, such as participation in group therapy and educational situations, doing a special job of benefit to the group, or making a special contribution. The accumulated points can be used to "buy" an early release or to get special privileges or other rewards. The addicts in such a program show greatly increased participation in therapeutic and educational activities. They also report generalization to other socially desirable behaviors, such as improved communication and decreased hostility.

In an outpatient methadone program it was found that "take home" doses of methadone were desired reinforcers. Attendance at counseling sessions increased markedly when "take home" privileges were made contingent on attendance. In other programs rewards are given if the participants' urine tests are negative for illicit drugs. Contingency management techniques are most appropriate for structured treatment programs such as methadone maintenance and inpatient settings. Assessments of long-term change and comparisons to other techniques need to be made.

Hypnosis

This procedure has been used to link drug-taking behavior with negative consequences such as nausea, anxiety, and so on. It has also been used to produce imagery of a previous "good trip" or a happy drug experience. Advantages of such an approach (remembering a good drug experience) are that they are free, under the subject's control, and not against the law. Subjects can be taught to hypnotize themselves, thus giving them further control when they feel temptation to use drugs. Hypnosis can also be used to help in attaining relaxation, similar to biofeedback. There is too little evidence at present to say if hypnosis is an effective treatment program for drug abuse.

Acupuncture

This scientific use of needles has been practiced in China for 5000 years or more and is still used there as an anesthetic or an aid to anesthesia for surgery. When the method was tried in 1972 in Hong Kong on opium addicts having neurosurgery, the addicts claimed they felt relief from withdrawal symptoms, although the acupuncture was intended only as an anesthetic. Later, a combination of acupuncture and electrical stimulation was used on heroin and opium addicts. Fine acupuncture needles were placed subcutaneously in the outer ear and connected to an electrical stimulator for about 30 minutes. The investigators reported that symptoms of tearing, runny nose, aching bones, cramps, and irritability usually disappeared after about 10 to 15 minutes. While under stimulation, the patients' craving for the narcotic drug ceased, and they began to feel more relaxed. Since that time other researchers in the United States and abroad have given acupuncture treatments to addicts, with variation in the numbers of needles and types of needle stimulation (manual, with heating, or with electricity). Encouraging results have been reported. Clearly, more controlled research needs to be done with this method to see if it is effective (as opposed to a placebo effect) and how it works. It seems possible that acupuncture might release endorphins, the natural opiates of the body.

DRUG-ABUSE AND ADDICTION PREVENTION PROGRAMS*

Because of the various kinds of drug dependence, many different prevention programs have been founded on the various approaches previously described. This section will discuss some of these prevention programs.

Approaches to drug abuse depend on the state of the individual affected, and they include prevention, intervention, and treatment. The differences among primary, secondary, and tertiary prevention are summarized in Table 20-1. The idea of primary prevention is a complex one that may include alternatives to drugs, personal and social growth of the person, mental health promotion, and overall stimulation of an individual to reach a high level of functioning, which theoretically will prevent problems associated with drug abuse from occurring.

The concept of primary prevention may mean different things to different people in the various professions. The medical profession has defined *abuse* as occurring when a person fails to follow prescription directions or engages in self-medication, such as using a drug prescribed for someone else. Law enforcement professionals define *abuse* as any use of illicit drugs, and the social scientists define *abuse* as use that is harmful to the individual or to society. We will be referring to the social definition. The term *harmful* may also mean various things. It may mean illness and death, acute behavioral effects, behavioral impairment, barriers to social acceptance, removal from society as a functional person, and so on.

In the past several years, the majority of drug-abuse prevention specialists have adopted the idea of emphasizing personal and social development of the individual as a means of preventing harmful consequences of drug abuse. These programs usually are built around three themes: (1) increased self-understanding and acceptance through activities such as values clarification, sensory awareness, decision making, and so on; (2) improved interpersonal relations through activities such as communication training, peer counseling, assertiveness training, and so forth; and (3) increased ability to meet one's needs through social institutions, such as family, church and community affiliations, and the like.

The U.S. federal government directs many

---

*This section is largely from Swisher, 1979.

TABLE 20-1 Differences among primary, secondary, and tertiary drug-abuse and addiction prevention[*]

Timing	Activities	Terminology
Before abuse	Education Information Alternatives Personal and social growth	Primary prevention
During early stages of abuse	Crisis intervention Early diagnosis Crisis monitoring Referral	Secondary prevention
During later stages of abuse	Treatment Institutionalization Maintenance Detoxification	Tertiary prevention

[*]Swisher, J. D. 1979. Prevention issues. In R. L. DuPont; A. Goldstein, and J. O'Donnell, eds. *Handbook on Drug Abuse.* Washington, D.C.: National Institute on Drug Abuse, Department of Health, Education, and Welfare.

of the programs that are useful in helping drug-abuse prevention, but they are very diverse, from treatment of delinquency, to mental health activities, to truancy, to a wide range of activities developed by groups funded by the National Institute on Drug Abuse—such as alternatives to drugs, drug information, and direction to social help agencies. At the present time, the necessary coordinating effort is not being made for these programs to have a major impact in the area of primary prevention. The following assumptions should be in back of all primary prevention programs:

1. A reasonable goal for drug-abuse prevention should be to educate people of all ages toward responsible decision making regarding the use of all drugs, licit and illicit.

2. Responsible decisions regarding personal use of drugs should result in fewer negative consequences for the individual.
3. The most effective approach to achieve the preceding goals would be a program that increases self-esteem, interpersonal skills, and participation in alternatives to drug use.

Because a large number of local, state, and federal agencies have similar goals and assumptions for dealing with other forms of social problem behaviors, there should be a unified governmental effort that would result in the mutual funding of the development, implementation, and evaluation of a multidimensional prevention effort.

The National Institute on Drug Abuse and several individual researchers have evaluated the multitude of drug-abuse prevention programs in the United States. The general conclusions of these studies are: (1) very few programs have demonstrated clear success or have incorporated adequate evaluative designs; and (2) the relationship among (a) information about drugs, (b) attitudes toward use, and (c) actual use of drugs, is unclear in these programs. Elements in the few successful primary prevention programs included the following:

1. They resulted from the combined efforts of schools, families, and community projects. This means that prevention should be a major coordinated effort at many levels to ensure success.

2. They combined information on personal and social growth with drug information. Just getting drug information alone has little effect in the long run.

3. The programs were integrated into the ongoing activities of schools, families, and community organizations rather than being simply additions in any setting. A major problem, even in communities where there are obvious drug problems, is how to convince schools, families, and community groups that they should make time for a prevention program. Programs that are integrated into current activities are more likely to have a longer life and to accomplish their goals than those that are added on or provided in a series of assemblies or as a short, special project.

4. Programs that synthesized and extracted various valuable components from different prepackaged materials and integrated them into existing programs were more likely to be successful. There have been a great number of fads and many experimental programs in this field; however, not enough effort has been made to evaluate and extract what is good.

ALTERNATIVES TO DRUGS: THE JOURNEY BEYOND TRIPS

There is no single reason why people take drugs. There are many underlying reasons and motivations, and they are usually quite complex. A person may try to alter the normal state of mind by taking a psychoactive drug, a substance that has some effect on the normal sensory input and interpretation of that input in the nervous system. Reasons for trying these modifications are curiosity (an important feature of the human personality), avoidance of boredom or stress, search for pleasure and new experiences, and, for some, a search for identity or to satisfy personal need. If the drug experience did not fill some need, give relief, or give a positive reward, use of it probably would not continue. If use were continued without satisfying a need or giving a reward, it would be less likely to cause a problem.

Part of the reason programs for the prevention and treatment of drug abuse have not been successful is due to the false impression on which these programs have been based. A great number of people still believe that only an abnormal minority uses a lot of drugs or drugs that are considered illegal. However, by this point you should realize that virtually all people use psychoactive drugs. A great number of people either use what are considered illegal drugs, or they abuse legal drugs. The majority of the population uses psychoactive drugs to alter their state of consciousness—yes, even to "get high." All the evidence points to the fact that drug use is now a social norm (although people may not be willing to recognize alcohol and tobacco use as drug use). This means that we now consider drug taking the normal thing to do, and it is done all the time by almost everyone in varying degrees and with varying methods.

It is possible to reduce the abuse of many drugs by making them hard to get and by putting a large number of abusers away. Not only are these procedures impractical, but, more important, they ignore the underlying motives for using drugs, which are central to the drug-abuse problem. According to Weil (1972) and others, taking drugs is part of a pattern, not a cause, of behavior. He puts this into perspective as follows: "We are spending much time, money, and intellectual energy trying to find out why people are taking drugs, but, in fact, what we are doing is trying to find out why some people are taking some drugs we disapprove of." In other words, we are not being honest with ourselves if we discuss marijuana or even heroin abuse while sipping on a cocktail and smoking cigarettes, without clearly recognizing that we are exhibiting the same behavior.

Part of the basis for believing there is an innate need to alter one's conscious state is based on the observation that preschool age children deliberately, as part of their normal play, whirl themselves dizzy and even choke each other voluntarily to lose consciousness. They usually have discovered chemical ways, such as sniffing shoe polish or gasoline, to alter consciousness before they are six years old and have also learned to be very secretive about this behavior. They learn to be circumspect while altering consciousness, or they come to feel guilty and repress the desire to alter consciousness when adults catch them in these activities. If this desire to alter the state of consciousness is inherent in human nature, then the use of psychoactive drugs, legally or illegally, in adulthood is a logical continuation of a developmental sequence that goes back to early childhood (Carroll, 1977b; Weil, 1972).

People who do not abuse psychoactive drugs apparently have found positive alternatives to fill the need to alter consciousness, so that there is no perceived need to take substances for this purpose. Workers in the drug abuse field tend to agree, by noting that young ex-abusers of common illicit drugs stopped using them more because of satisfaction gained in exploring positive alternatives, rather than from a fear of consequent harm. No doubt some young people avoid drugs because they are afraid they might be harmed, but the majority do not let it deter them. At that age, the majority have a sense of invulnerability, almost of immortality. Coma and brain damage from over-the-counter diet pills, lung cancer from tobacco or marijuana, heart and liver damage from alcohol, could not possibly happen to them. Or if they do happen 20 to 30 years later, by then medical science will have a cure.

The law has not been much of a deterrent for drug use and abuse, because it does not provide viable alternatives to the underlying motives for using psychoactive drugs to achieve the high or altered state of consciousness. Most laws, and moral codes that preceded the laws, frown on getting high on anything but socially approved substances.

In rehabilitation and treatment of drug abusers, the alternatives should be tailored to the type of drug abused, or rehabilitation will not succeed. For example, in treating heroin addiction, methadone represents an alternative to the physical component of the addict's needs, but it does not provide a high. Heroin addicts turn to methadone programs only when they are so tired of the heroin hustle that they are willing to give up the heroin effects, and they may stay in methadone maintenance only long enough to recuperate. It is in that interval that the treatment staff must convince the addict of the value of nondrug highs. What the straight person thinks of as rewarding may not be available to the methadone-maintenance addict without years of effort—for example, having even a small retreat cottage in the country or by the seashore to which the straight person loves to go and relax takes money, which usually means a regular job at fairly high pay, which requires extensive and expensive education, and so on. The positive alternative for the addict has to be something realistic in terms of his or her life.

Drug-Abuse Prevention Strategies*

In the 1970s a series of new intellectual and educational trends were expanded to address drug abuse and misuse. These trends have greatly influenced the field of prevention at the present. Some of these were:

1. The human potential movement. New approaches to human development and methods of psychotherapy emphasized the importance of the individual, who has needs and desires that can be used in prevention programs. The work of Abraham Maslow (Chapter 1) and others influenced the programs that evolved from this movement.

2. Dissatisfaction with traditional forms of schooling. The public schools were widely criticized as not meeting the needs of many students. This dissatisfaction led to the popularity of the "affective education" movement. Affective education emphasizes personalized classroom activities designed to bring students in touch with their feelings, values, and attitudes. Some of the methods of affective education involve nonverbal communication exercises and enhanced interpersonal relationships. Alternative schools were started to reach potential drug abusers and others not having successful

---

*This section is largely from Resnik, 1979.

educational experiences under the traditional methods. These schools have been controversial in some communities.

3. The concept of alternatives as a way to enrich people's lives and guide them into programs where they can fulfill personal needs and drives. Alternatives can come from within and without the typical educational routine; they also can be adapted to existing curricula. An alternative can be virtually anything that would be more attractive than drugs. You can understand why some educators and parents have not encouraged incorporation of alternatives into the typical curriculum: they were afraid the teaching of alternatives would dilute what they felt was the goal of the traditional curriculum (reading, writing, and calculation skills). Of course, it is possible to go overboard and give high school diplomas to students who have high self-esteem but cannot read and calculate well enough to get and hold a job—but this would not do much for self-esteem in the long run.

The Alternatives Approach to Prevent Drug Abuse

The alternatives approach can be used immediately with high-risk populations. It requires no particular training and is one of the easiest, most practical strategies to implement. Nevertheless, it is a complex undertaking that requires a long-term commitment and unusual organizing skills to be successful. It is based on several assumptions about drug-using behavior in people:

1. People use drugs voluntarily to fill a need or basic drive.

2. Most people use drugs for "negative" reasons. This might be to deal with negative feelings or situations, such as relief of boredom, anxiety, depression, tension, or other unpleasant emotional and psychological states. The

person may be rebelling against authority, trying to escape from feelings of loneliness or inadequacy, or trying to be accepted by peers. Peer pressure is extremely important as an inducing force.

3. Some people use drugs for what might be considered "positive" or "healthy" reasons. These may be enhancement of sensual experiences—for example, listening to music, achieving altered states of consciousness, or simply experiencing a sense of adventure. Some people may want to explore their own consciousness and reasons for being.

4. Whether the reasons are positive or negative, the same effects can be achieved through alternative, nondrug means. The nondrug means are preferable and more constructive, because the person is not relying on a psychoactive substance for satisfaction but is finding satisfaction based on his or her own achievements. Ideally, this should lead to a lifetime of constructive sources of self-satisfaction.

Table 20-2 lists a variety of levels of experience, the motives for such experiences, the probable associated drugs of abuse, and alternatives to these drugs. As shown in the table, any constructive activity could be considered an alternative to drug abuse. The difference between a city's summer arts and crafts program and an arts and crafts program labeled "drug abuse prevention" is primarily a difference in context. In the former, the children do little projects they enjoy, perhaps visit a museum or two, and give mothers a break; in the latter, the children are learning that there are satisfying things to do besides watch TV and hang out. Summer camp is similar. Some parents send their children to camp because they were sent to camp and enjoyed it; others send their children to camp to increase their self-confidence. The latter is the use of

alternative activities as drug abuse prevention, even if the parents never actually realize this.

Familiarity with prevention strategy gives parents and youth workers the advantage that they can place the child's or young person's behavior in a context that allows them to decide what kinds of experiences might be more helpful than others. For example, from Table 20-2 you can see that a young person who needs an outlet for increased physical energy might respond better to dance and movement training, tai chi, judo, karate, or a project in preventative medicine than to work on ecological projects.

Most communities have a range of youth organizations, such as scouting, 4-H clubs, and school clubs. The problem is that the young people who participate in these readily are those at low risk of becoming drug abusers. They already have developed self-confidence and self-esteem. The traditional organizations have few ways of reaching out to the high-risk youth who need their help much more. This is where the paradox of the alternatives approach becomes apparent. Much of the approach is already in place (school band and athletics, scouting, and so on), but an effective drug abuse prevention program requires a leader who has community commitment to back him or her and the organizational skills to get the high-risk young people to use alternatives.

The alternative activities that young people have become involved in have been extremely broad. In a large alternatives program in Idaho, the following activities were part of the program during one particular month: arts and crafts, karate, reforestation, backpacking, a Humane Society dog show, horseback riding, artwork for posters for the various programs, astrology, camping, and volunteering in a local hospital. In southeastern Ohio, teenagers from nine area high schools researched the history of coal mining and the canal in a three-county area. Pub-

TABLE 20-2 Experiences, motives, and possible alternatives for a drug abuser[*]

Experience	Corresponding motives	Drugs abused	Possible alternatives
Physical	Desire for physical well-being: physical relaxation, relief from sickness, desire for more energy.	Alcohol, tranquilizers, stimulants, marijuana.	Athletics, dance, exercise, hiking, diet, carpentry, outdoor work, swimming, hatha yoga.
Sensory	Desire to magnify sensorium: sound, touch, taste, need for sensual/sexual stimulation.	Hallucinogens, marijuana, alcohol.	Sensory awareness training, sky diving, experiencing sensory beauty of nature, SCUBA diving.
Emotional	Relief from psychological pain: attempt to resolve personal problems, relief from bad mood, escape from anxiety, desire for emotional insight, liberation of feeling and emotional relaxation.	Narcotics, alcohol, barbiturates, tranquilizers.	Competent individual counseling, well-run group therapy, instruction in psychology of personal development.
Interpersonal	To gain peer acceptance, break through interpersonal barriers, "communicate"; defiance of authority figures.	Any, especially alcohol, marijuana.	Expertly managed sensitivity and encounter groups, well-run group therapy, instruction in social customs, confidence training, emphasis on assisting others—for example, YMCA or YWCA volunteer.
Social	To promote social change, find identifiable subculture, tune out intolerable environmental conditions—for example, poverty.	Marijuana, psychedelics.	Social service community action in positive social change; helping the poor, aged, infirm, young; tutoring handicapped; ecology action; YMCA or YWCA Big Brother/Sister programs.

(continued)

[*]Cohen, A. Y. 1973. *Alternatives to Drug Abuse: Steps Toward Prevention.* Washington, D.C.: National Institute on Drug Abuse no. 14, Department of Health, Education, and Welfare.

TABLE 20-2 (continued)

Experience	Corresponding motives	Drugs abused	Possible alternatives
Political	To promote political change (out of desperation with the social-political order) and to identify with antiestablishment subgroup.	Marijuana, psychedelics.	Political service, lobbying for nonpartisan projects—for example, Common Cause; field work with politicians and public officials.
Intellectual	To escape boredom, out of intellectual curiosity, to solve cognitive problems, gain new understanding in the world of ideas, research one's own awareness.	Stimulants, sometimes psychedelics.	Intellectual excitement through reading, debate, and discussion; creative games and puzzles; self-hypnosis; training in concentration.
Creative-aesthetic	To improve creative performance, enhance enjoyment of art already produced—for example, music; enjoy imaginative mental productions.	Marijuana, stimulants, psychedelics.	Nongraded instruction in producing and/or appreciating art, music, drama, and creative hobbies.
Philosophical	To discover meaningful values, find meaning in life, help establish personal identity, organize a belief structure.	Psychedelics, marijuana, stimulants.	Discussions, seminars, courses on ethics, the nature of reality, relevant philosophical literature; explorations of value systems.
Spiritual-mystical	To transcend orthodox religion, develop spiritual insights, reach higher levels of consciousness, augment yogic practices, take a spiritual shortcut.	Psychedelics, marijuana.	Exposure to nonchemical methods of spiritual development; study of world religions, mysticism, meditation, yogic techniques.

lication of their report, which they produced themselves as part of the Youth Alternatives Program, was funded by a grant from the National Endowment for the Humanities. The students were justifiably proud of a job well done and clearly got a good deal of pleasure from it as well as learning some local history.

Part-time job placement is extremely important as one of the alternative approaches. When a young person gets his or her first job and has earned money, it really helps build feelings of self-worth and confidence.

The Altered
State of Consciousness
and the Drug High

Most people may not be aware how common it is to modify the conscious state of mind. Sleeping, daydreams, meditation, anesthesia, and psychoses are examples of conditions that produce such a state. The complex brain of *Homo sapiens* is capable of processing millions of pieces (or bits) of information each minute, and yet much of this processing is relegated to the unconscious mind. Under the influence of stress, drugs, and internal and external factors, the input may be modified and interpretation in the brain changed. This is called altering the conscious state. Levels of stimulation above or below the normal range can cause modifications, or an altered state of consciousness. Examples of causes of altered states of consciousness include:

1. Reduction of sensory input. There are procedures or substances that reduce stimulation or motor activity, such as solitary confinement, floating on warm water in a darkened chamber, extreme muscle relaxation, biofeedback inducing an increase in alpha or theta brain wave rhythms, meditation, and use of some depressant drugs.

2. Increasing the sensory input. Procedures or substances that increase sensory input might be religious ceremonies (revival meetings), long periods of tension (truck driving, flying, or sentry duty, video games, long-distance running), or hallucinogens and stimulant drugs.

3. Modification of body chemistry, thus influencing input and interpretation. Causes are: dehydration, fever, sleep deprivation, anesthesia, modification of acid-base balance in the blood (for example, by hyperventilation), hypoglycemia, or drugs such as hallucinogens, depressants, and stimulants. This category is separate because it can include either or both of the first two.

As you can see, causes of altered states of consciousness can be quite complex. There are a number of effects on the mind when a person is in the altered state. A brief list of these is:

1. Distortion in perception. This may result in increased visual imagery or hallucinations. Many mystics and religious persons have reported distortions without using drugs, although some used psychoactive substances.

2. A blurred distinction between cause and effect, which makes it difficult to tell what is real and what is not.

3. A change in the meaning or significance of ideas or occurrences compared to their significance in the normal state.

4. Modification of memory or change in ability to concentrate or remember.

5. A feeling of reduced inhibitions or of losing self-control.

6. Modification in time sense. This may be a feeling that time is slowing down or speeding

up. Ability to estimate the passage of time becomes impaired.

7. A feeling of increased suggestibility, which may be the result of certain drugs as well as the nondrug causes of altered states. This condition is used by interrogators and brainwashers to get information or mold opinion.

All of the preceding effects, plus alterations in the autonomic nervous system (heart rate, perspiration rate, and so on) that cause changed sensations in the body, make up what is called the "high," sometimes called *euphoria* (which means good feelings). Whether the high is good or bad is a subjective experience depending on set and setting.

Many people, such as the philosopher William James, have taken drugs because they thought they could develop insight while in that state. While under the influence of nitrous oxide, James believed he understood the ultimate mystery of life and recorded his thoughts on paper. After he returned to the normal state, he eagerly consulted the piece of paper on which he had scrawled the Great Message. It read:

Hogamous, Higamous
Man is polygamous.
Higamous, Hogamous,
Woman is monogamous.

[De Ropp, 1968]

The famous jurist Oliver Wendell Holmes had similar experiences with ether. While sniffing it he wrote down what he thought was an insight into the reason for human existence. Later, he found he had written "Ether stinks." (We hope there is more to the ultimate mystery of life than that!) James also praised alcohol because of what

he described as its "liberating power." This was probably a reference to alcohol's ability to reduce inhibitions.

Using the Mind for Nondrug Highs

One area of considerable interest in the area of alternatives to drug use involves the mind. Ever since people have had time to sit and think about life, they have been deeply interested in and curious about the mind. However, we still understand very little about the mind. We know that we have locked up in our minds abilities that we rarely use. Many people are interested in the possibilities of mind-body interactions and control through biofeedback systems. By using the mind it is possible to lower blood pressure, modify temperature in selected parts of the body, modify the output of brain waves, and alter many aspects of the autonomic nervous system. These techniques are now being used in medicine and by interested persons wanting to control their bodies.

Experimental psychiatrists, neurophysiologists, psychologists, and physicians are investigating the mind. Some of the most intriguing work is being done on the state of the mind during meditation. Countries like India have long histories linked to people who were able to achieve certain goals through meditation. The word *yoga* is derived from the Sanskrit word for *union*, or *yoking*, meaning the process of discipline by which a person attains union with the Absolute. In a sense, it refers to the use of the mind to control itself and the body. Various systems of mind control have been used for thousands of years to find peace and contentment within. To conclude our discussion of alternatives, we will describe in some detail a map of inner space, to show where some mind-control systems are believed to fit in. These have value in achieving "highs" without drugs.

The Conscious States of Mind

Dr. Roland Fischer is one of the researchers who has probed the ability and powers of the conscious and subconscious mind. Figure 20-3 shows his representation of the varieties of conscious states, in which he explains some of the abilities of the mind (Fischer, 1971). Notice in the figure that there are three major conscious states. The one in the middle is the normal waking state of mind that focuses on stimuli in normal life. This state of the conscious mind (called the *I* portion) is active during the daily routine. The state on the right represents the lowered sensory input into the brain that occurs as a person relaxes; conversely, the state on the left represents increased sensory input from activity, or a removal of filters to sensory input. The change in alertness may be measured by the types of brain wave and their intensity, as may be noted on the small semicircle in the center of the diagram.

The term *ergotropic*, referring to the arousal state shown on the left of Figure 20-3, means inciting to activity. It is characterized by increased activity of the sympathetic nervous system and an activated psychic state. The ergotropic state has more than normal amounts of sensory input coming into the brain. As one moves from the *aroused*, to *hyperaroused*, and finally the *ecstatic* stages, the stimuli coming into the brain increase so the person's nervous system gets more excited and aroused. This is very much like removing filters in the brain, which is probably one of the best ways to explain the increased activity.

As the brain evolved, the sensory detection organs in and on the exterior of the body sent in so much nerve impulse information that much

of the processing of the information was delegated to the subconscious. For instance, perhaps ten times as many impulses are transmitted to the brain from internal sensory organs as are transmitted from outside the body. All the internal organs—the pulsating heart, the contracting stomach and intestines, the bladder, and the skeletal muscles—continuously transmit impulses to the brain. These impulses are interpreted subconsciously, so we are usually unaware of them until a threshold is exceeded. As Huxley (1954) put it, "The function of the brain is to protect us from being overwhelmed . . . by this mass of largely useless and irrelevant knowledge, by shutting out most . . . and leaving only that . . . special selection which is likely to be practically useful." Thus violent contractions of the intestine or stomach, a full bladder, or muscular cramps are noted by the conscious mind. If the filtering process allows more impulses to enter the higher brain centers or filters out fewer impulses than is normally the case, the brain can be flooded with more data than we are used to. This flooding may arouse feelings we may not know how to handle.

The first part of the ergotropic state, the *aroused* stage, shows the effects of increased input into the conscious mind. In this stage sensitivity, creativity, and anxiety, in that order, are signs that the level of arousal in the brain is increasing. This may be the stage where people get inspirations or new ideas and feelings, and where they become anxious about things. All people have anxieties; it is this type of anxiety that gives a person the drive to get things done. If the person cannot handle anxiety, psychological and physical problems result. These effects occur without drugs, but drugs can speed up the process tremendously, and often unpredictably.

As input increases into the conscious brain, we reach the *hyperaroused* ergotropic stage. If

VARIETIES OF CONSCIOUS STATE

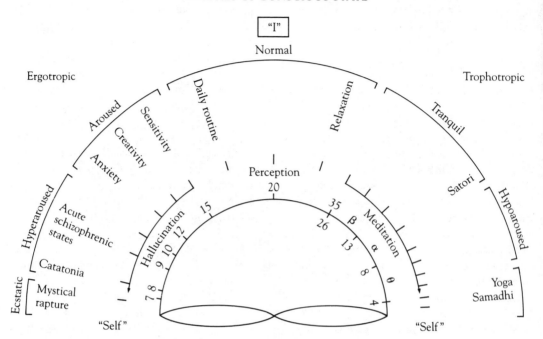

FIGURE 20-3

Varieties of conscious states mapped on a continuum of increasing *ergotropic* arousal (left) or *trophotropic* arousal (right) from normal waking consciousness (*I*). These levels of hyper- and hypoarousal are interpreted as normal, creative, psychotic, and ecstatic states (left), and satori and samadhi (right). The loop connecting the two "Self" extremes represents the rebound from ecstasy to samadhi, which is observed in response to intense ergotropic excitation. The numbers 35 to 7 on the perception-hallucination continuum are Goldstein's coefficient of variation, specifying the increase in variability of the EEG amplitude with increasing ergotropic arousal. The numbers 26 to 4 on the perception-meditation continuum refer to those beta, alpha, and theta EEG waves that predominate during, but are not specific to, these states. (From "A Cartography of the Ecstatic and Meditative States," by R. Fischer, Science, *174*(26), pp. 897–904. Copyright 1971 by the American Association for the Advancement of Science. Reprinted by permission.)

this persists long it may cause overanxiety and, in some people, a condition called *schizophrenia.* It is at this stage that the person may hallucinate, as normal processing of input fails. Hallucinations are states in which images of things are perceived as objective facts or sensations.

The person may hear sounds or voices and see visual images that may appear quite real. Often unhappy past experiences may be reexperienced in a surrealistic sense. The brain is not able to process all the information properly; thus the sensory input is scrambled and mixed up with memories in peculiar ways. For some this may result in visions or a feeling of seeing cosmic truth or deities. People have known about visions as long as we have had written and oral records. Some societies have regarded seeing visions as a holy experience. Those whom we might label *schizophrenic* were looked on as the holy ones of the tribe and venerated as such, because it was believed that they could see and communicate with the spirits that were invisible to all others. In other cases, it was believed that such people were possessed by demons or the devil, and the society dealt with them according to the cultural beliefs.

In the most aroused part of the hyperaroused stage, there is so much input that the nervous system can no longer handle or process all the data, so the person becomes *catatonic*. Sometimes the catatonic phase is called the "jammed computer" phase, which means the brain is so swamped with input that the individual freezes into a trance-like state of consciousness in which the limbs are rigidly fixed. Note in Figure 20-3 that hallucinations do not occur in the catatonic phase as far as we know.

The next stage of increasing sensory input is known as *mystical rapture*. Mysticism, like hallucination, has been described in our earliest records. St. Teresa of Avila and other mystics from various religious traditions wrote about their feelings of mystical rapture in their religious experiences. Some persons reach the most intense level of input and yet somehow have learned to handle it without becoming catatonic or without damage to the conscious mind. These are the mystics in the world's literature who induced ecstatic feelings through inner focusing of all input. In many instances the mystic learns to do this without hallucinating, although scholars believe that visions, dreams, and religious and transcendental experiences may occur at this

stage. There are also those who claim that they can reach this mystical stage with drugs like LSD, psilocybin, or mescaline.

Now let us look at the right side of Figure 20-3 to examine the *trophotropic* portion, where there is less sensory input coming into the brain. Fischer states that trophotropic arousal results from an integration of the parasympathetic nervous system with skeletal muscular activity to produce behavioral patterns that conserve and restore energy. This produces a decrease in sensitivity to external stimuli, and sedation. There are two of these stages on the trophotropic side: the *tranquil* and the *hypoaroused* stages. The technique of meditation works by reducing the amount of sensory input, as seen in the diagram, and can be detected by a shift in the pattern of brain waves from beta to alpha and then to more theta. We will describe the relationship of brain wave patterns to meditation in the next section.

As the brain filters out or blocks input into the conscious mind, the person first reaches a feeling of tranquility or deep relaxation. No one has explained how the brain can filter out sensory input to a greater extent than usual. Some people who meditate reach a deep state of relaxation and tranquility that is called *satori*, after the Zen Buddhist tradition. *Meditation* may be defined as a constant and continuous flow of awareness of one chosen object, attained by emptying the mind of its contents and maintaining a thought-free state. This systematized practice is what yoga, Sufism, Zen Buddhism, and other spiritual paths are about.

The *hypoaroused* stage is the second level of the trophotropic portion of the diagram. At this stage the sensory input has been shut out until the arousal level is very low. The relative activity of alpha and theta brain waves is increased, as shown in the figure. The highest level of the hypoaroused stage, the *yoga samadhi* stage, is the ultimate in lowered input from the senses. It takes many years to achieve the mind and body control that characterize this stage, at which the person is in complete union with the Self, or the Absolute.

Note that this stage of complete union with the Self, or Absolute, occurs at two points—mystical rapture and yogic samadhi. There is a loop, resembling the mathematical symbol for infinity, between the extremes of the ergotropic and trophotropic states. Fischer and others believe it is possible to move from samadhi into ecstasy and vice versa. This means that an experienced meditator may spontaneously move into total ecstasy, and the person in mystical rapture may spontaneously move into total calm and peace. (In a later version of his diagram, Fischer uses a circular arrangement instead of an ergotropic and a trophotropic side joined by this loop.)

One final note: Fischer's interesting map of inner space is hypothetical. It should not be interpreted as a literal representation of data obtained on the human brain.

The Relaxation Response

It seems that technologically oriented Westerners are rediscovering, to their surprise, what other cultures have accepted for millennia. Somehow a concept only becomes real for Western scientists when they can measure it. Patient yogis and Zen monks (with a trace of amusement?) have permitted themselves to be wired up with electrodes to their scalps to measure brain waves, strain gauges around their rib cages to measure respiration, electrodes on their skin to measure skin resistance based on perspiration, masks covering their mouths and noses to measure oxygen consumption, and rectal probes to measure their core temperatures. Then they enter meditation. Both types (Zen and yogi) develop

a predominance of alpha waves (increased amplitude and regularity) during meditation. They decrease their oxygen consumption within a matter of minutes as much as 20%, a level usually reached only after four to five hours of sleep in the nonmeditator. However, meditation is physiologically different from sleep, based on the EEG pattern and rate of decline of oxygen consumption (although some people do fall asleep during meditation) (Pagano, Rose, Stivers, & Warrenburg, 1976). Along with the decreased metabolic rate and changes in EEG there is a marked decrease in blood lactate. Lactate is produced by metabolism of skeletal muscle, and the decrease is probably due to the reduced activity of the sympathetic nervous system during meditation. Heart rate and respiration are also slowed.

Benson (1975) has dubbed this sequence of changes "the relaxation response" in a readable little book by the same title. He was interested in applying nondrug means of treating his hypertensive patients to bring down their blood pressure. With the assistance of Maharishi Mahesh Yogi and volunteers from Transcendental Meditation, a Westernized form of yoga, he worked out a clinical approach he has used for hypertension (Benson, 1977). It is an excellent starting point for someone who does not want anything to do with Eastern mysticism. The four basic conditions to elicit a relaxation response are: (1) a passive attitude (probably the most important condition), (2) a quiet environment, (3) an object to dwell on, such as a word or sound repetition, and (4) a comfortable position, such as sitting, in which the person is not as likely to fall asleep during the 20-minute session as if he or she lies down. He recommends using the word "one" to concentrate on, or a simple prayer from one's own religious tradition. The relaxation response is elicited twice daily for 10 to 20 minutes each time. Benson and his coworkers recommend what yogis and Zen Buddhists have known for a long time—the procedure works best on an empty stomach. The relaxation response is a most useful way of reducing the effects of stress on the body and mind.

The Natural Mind

The category of people who take drugs as part of their search for the meaning of life eventually look for other methods of maintaining the valuable parts of the drug experience. Such people learn to value the meditation "high" and abandon drugs. They describe their drug experiences as having given them a taste of their potential, as something they grew out of now that they are established in the real thing. As Weil (1972) put it, "One does not see any long-time meditators give up meditation to become acid heads." Chemical highs, although they are effective means of altering the state of consciousness, interfere with the most worthwhile states of altered consciousness, because they reinforce the illusion that highs come from external, material agents rather than from within one's own nervous system. People who have not yet learned to meditate effectively continue to use drugs, because they seem to work *immediately*, whereas meditation requires regular, daily practice and some discipline, especially at first. It takes effort over a period of time to get a natural high on meditation and more focused practice to maintain that high throughout the day, dealing with the world as it is. Nevertheless, it is within everyone's potential to do so.

In conclusion, the alternative technique selected to prevent drug abuse or misuse should correlate with the person's needs or motives for abusing drugs, or potential for doing so (Table 20-2). The person who desires physical well-being and who turns, or might be predicted to turn, to alcohol, tranquilizers, or marijuana might respond well to biofeedback designed to relax him or her or to hatha yoga. In fact, most people who use depressant drugs could probably benefit from relaxation techniques. Those who select the psychedelics, especially for spiritual and mystical experiences, might find greater appeal in studies of mysticism and meditation. An extensive list of readings is available through the Vedanta Society's catalog of 600 selected books from the world's great spiritual and mystical literature. (This nonprofit organization's address is P. O. Box 2508, Hollywood CA 90028.)

STRUCTURES OF NEUROTRANSMITTERS AND REPRESENTATIVE PSYCHOACTIVE SUBSTANCES

APPENDIX A.1

$$CH_3-\overset{\overset{\displaystyle O}{\|}}{C}-O-CH_2-CH_2-N^+-(CH_3)_3$$

Acetylcholine

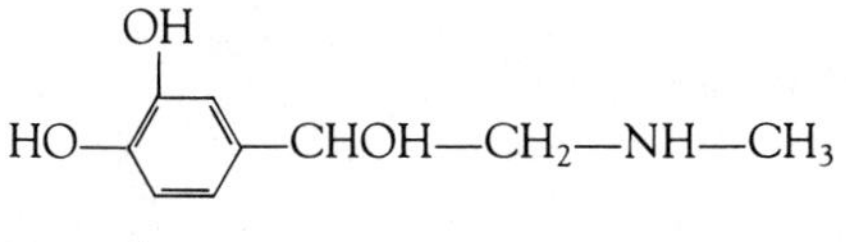

Epinephrine

$$HO-C_6H_3(OH)-CHOH-CH_2-NH-CH_3$$

Epinephrine

$$HOOC-CH_2-CH_2-CH_2-NH_2$$

Gamma aminobutyric
acid (GABA)

$$HOOC-CH_2-CH(NH_2)-COOH$$

Aspartic acid

$$HOOC-CH_2-CH_2-CH(NH_2)COOH$$

Glutamic acid

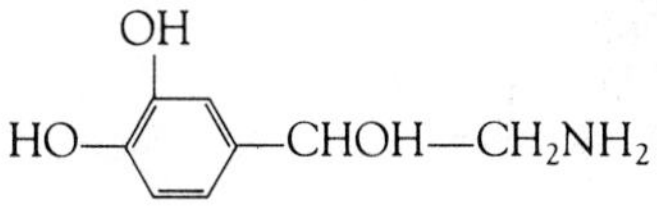

Norepinephrine

$$HO-C_6H_3(OH)-CHOH-CH_2NH_2$$

Norepinephrine

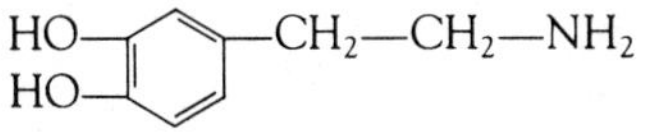

$$HO-C_6H_3(OH)-CH_2-CH_2-NH_2$$

Dopamine

$$HO-C_6H_3(OH)-CH_2-CH_2-NH_2$$

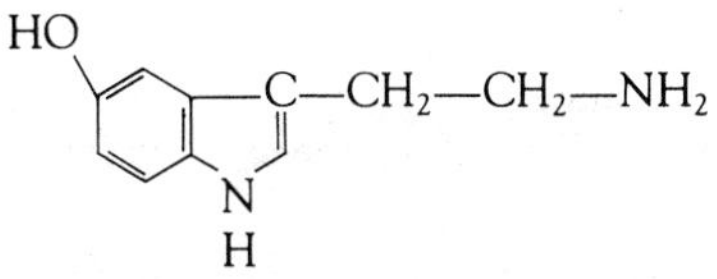

5-Hydroxytryptamine
(serotonin)

APPENDIX A.2

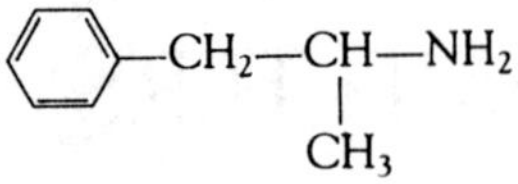

Amphetamine

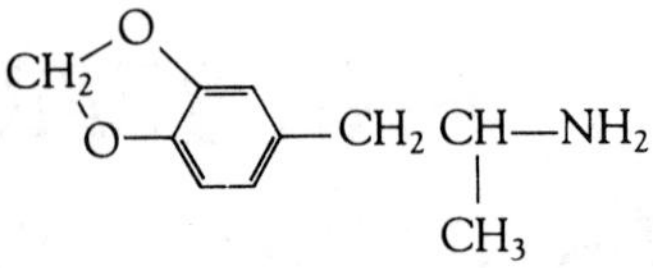

MDA
3, 4-Methylenedioxyamphetamine

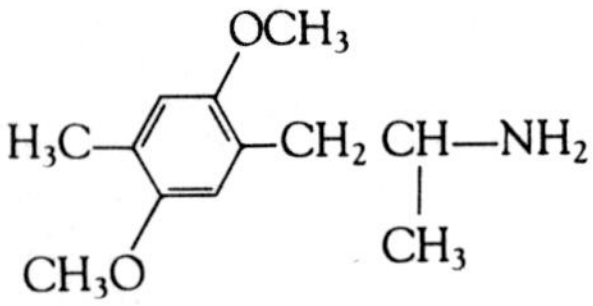

DOM (STP)
2,5-Dimethoxy-4-
methylamphetamine

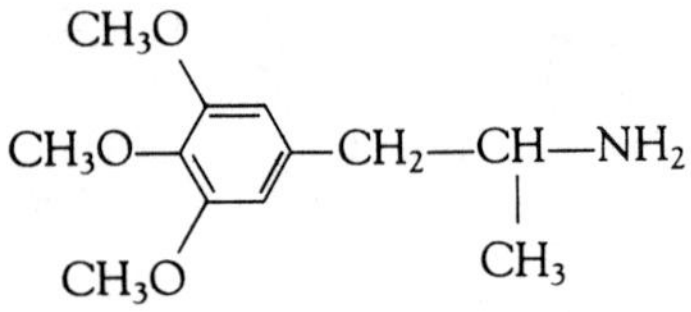

a-Methylmescaline

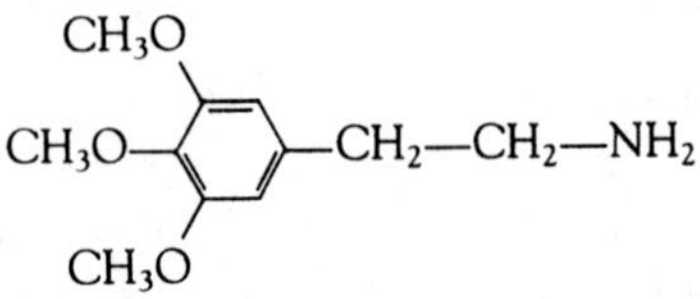

Mescaline
3, 4, 5-Trimethoxyphenethylamine

APPENDIX A.3

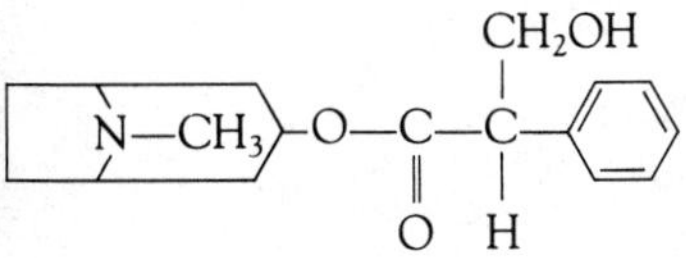

Atropine (*dl*-hyoscyamine)

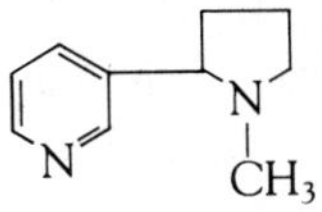

Nicotine

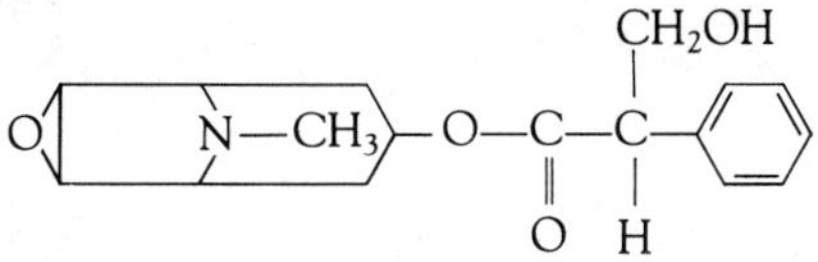

Scopolamine (*l*-hyoscine)

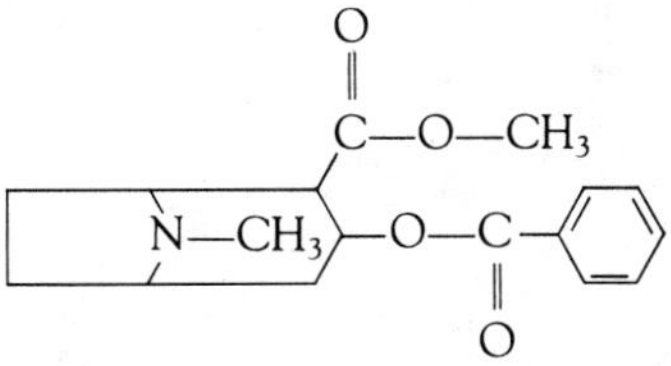

Cocaine

APPENDIX A.4

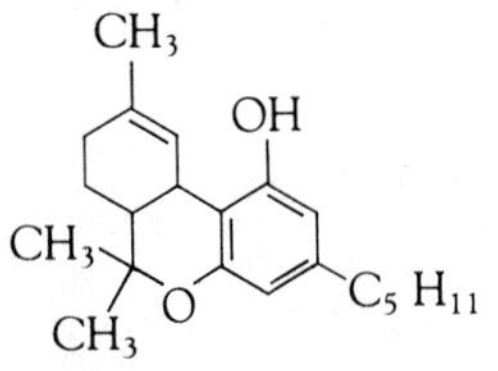

$\Delta^9 - THC$

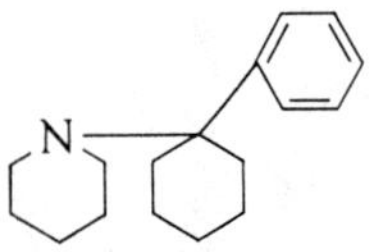

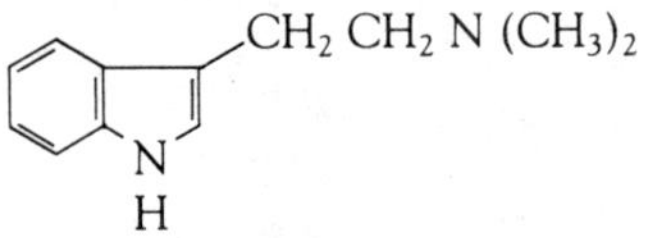

N, N-dimethyltryptamine (DMT)

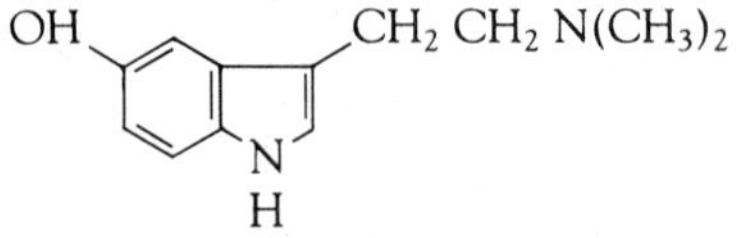

Phencyclidine

Bufotenin

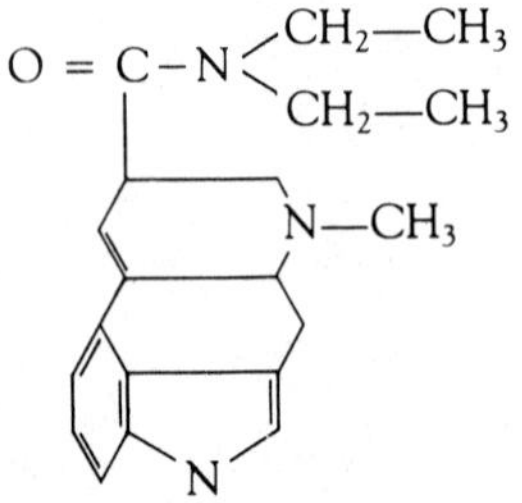

d-lysergic acid diethylamide (LSD)

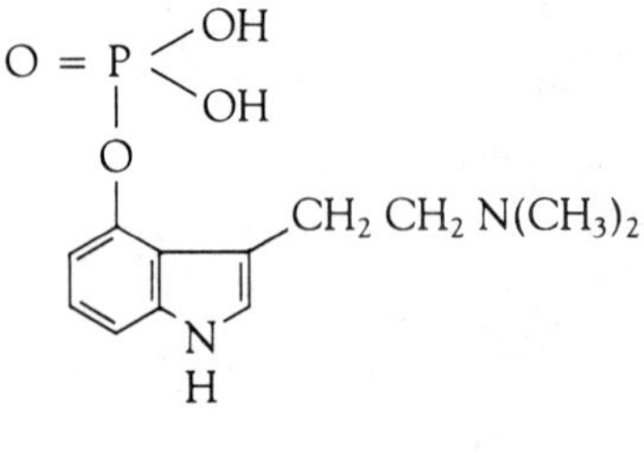

Psilocybin

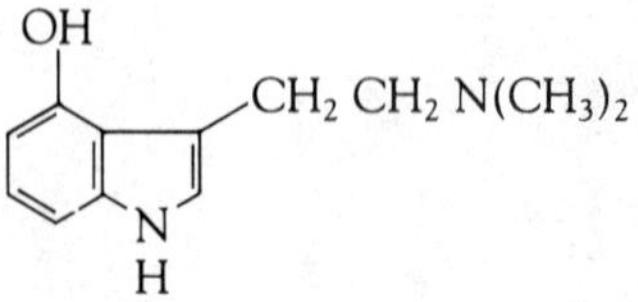

Psilocin

APPENDIX A.5

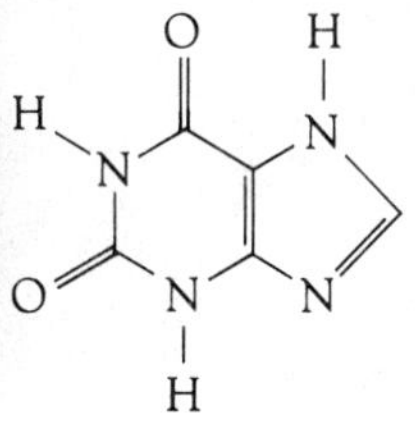

Xanthine

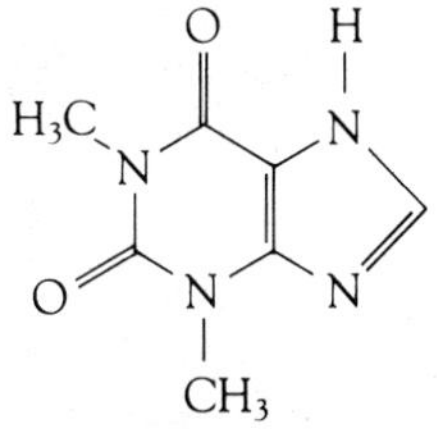

Theophylline

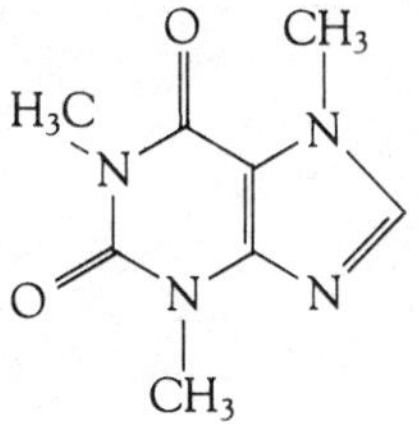

Caffeine

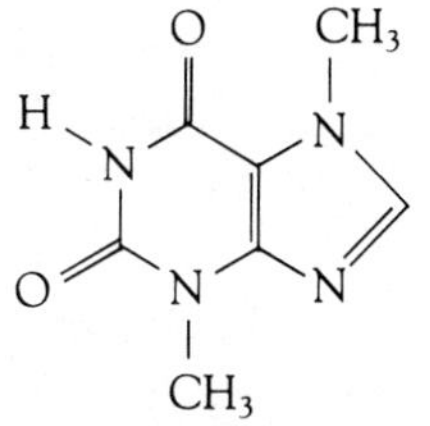

Theobromine

APPENDIX A.6

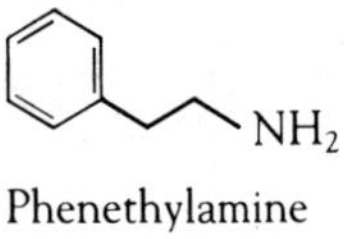

Phenethylamine

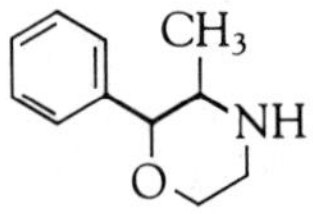

Phenmetrazine

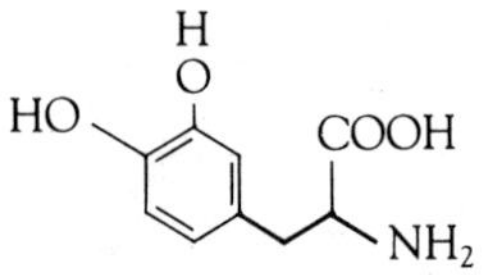

L-Dopa

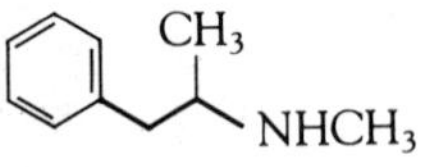

Methamphetamine

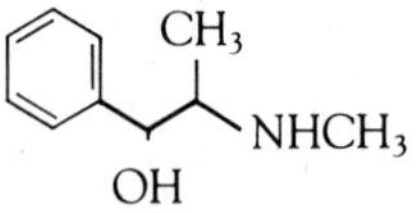

Ephedrine

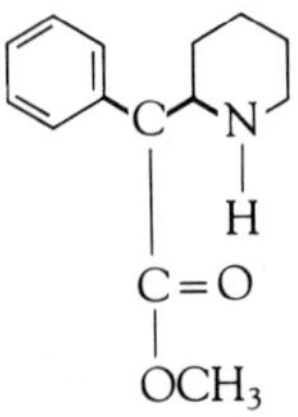

Methylphenidate

APPENDIX A.7

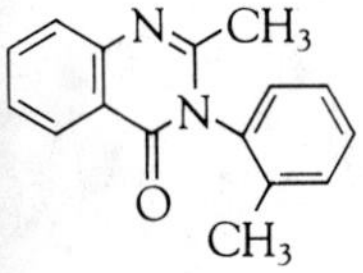

Methaqualone

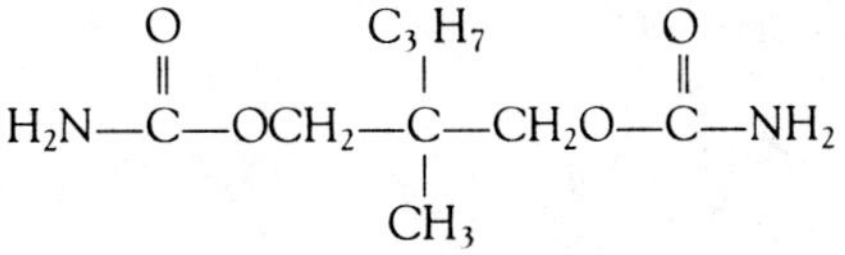

Meprobamate

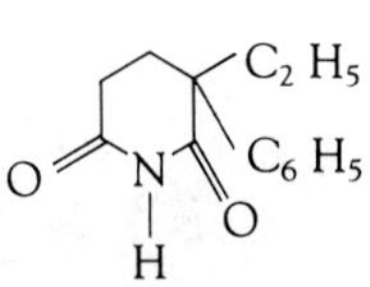

Glutethimide

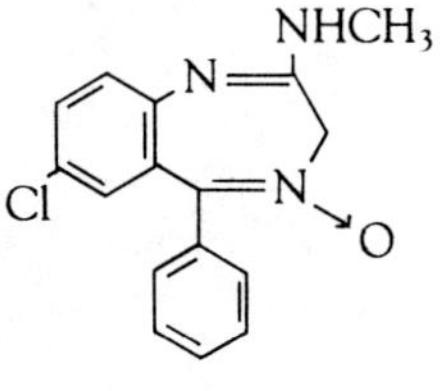

Chlordiazepoxide (Librium®)

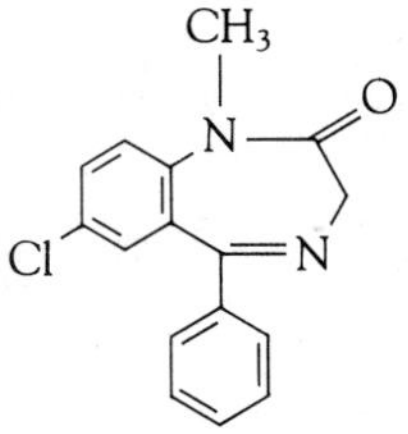

Diazepam (Valium®)

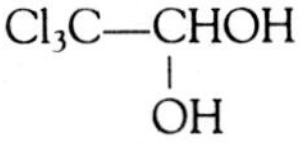

$$Cl_3C—CHOH$$
$$|$$
$$OH$$

Chloral hydrate

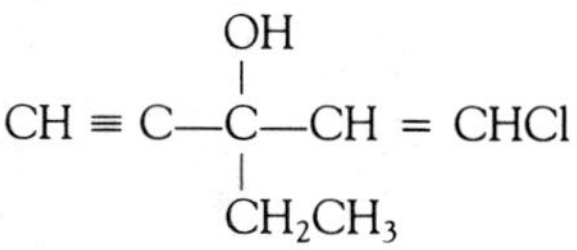

Ethchlorvynol

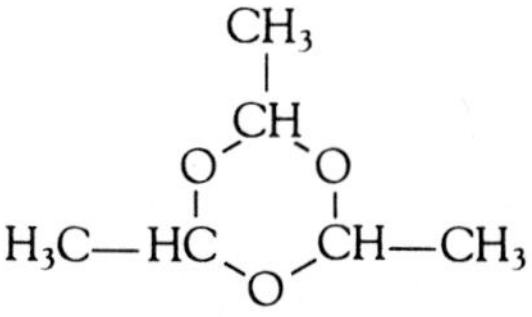

$$CH \equiv C—C—CH = CHCl$$

Paraldehyde

APPENDIX A.8

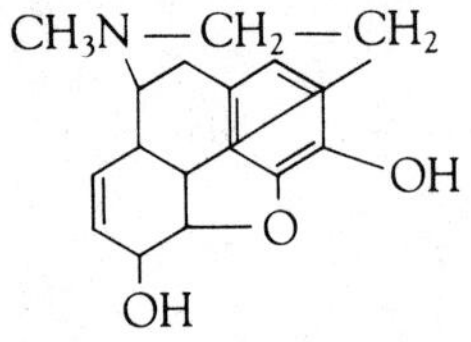

$CH_3N - CH_2 - CH_2$

Morphine

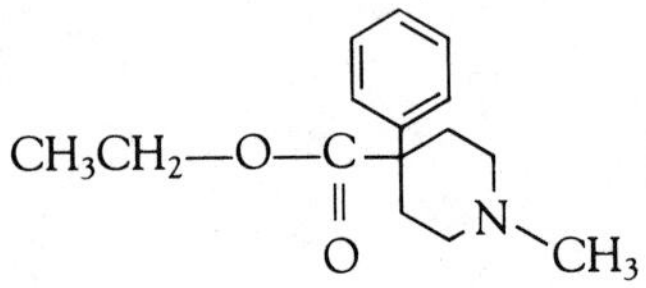

Meperidine

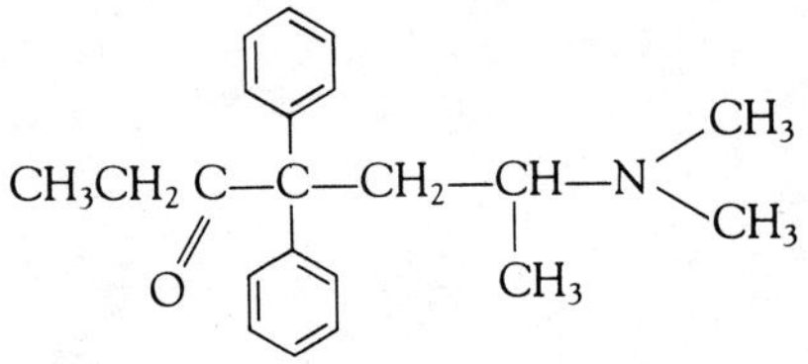

Methadone

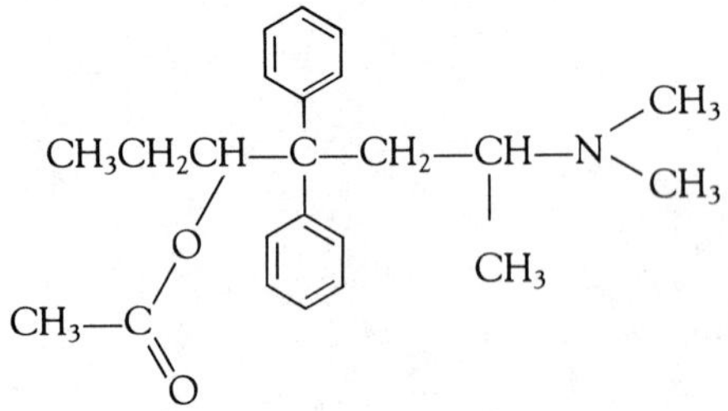

Acetylmethadol

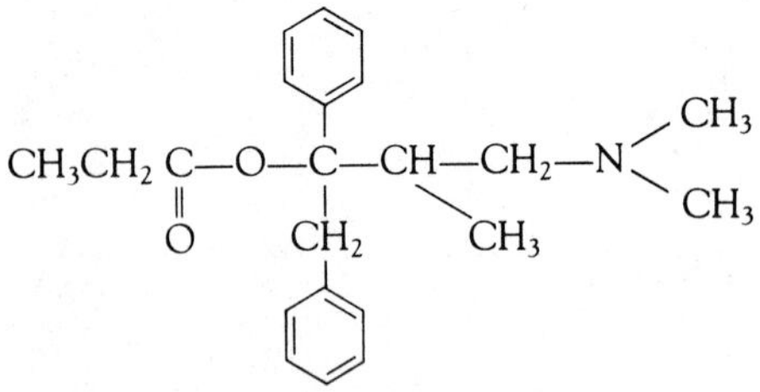

Propoxyphene

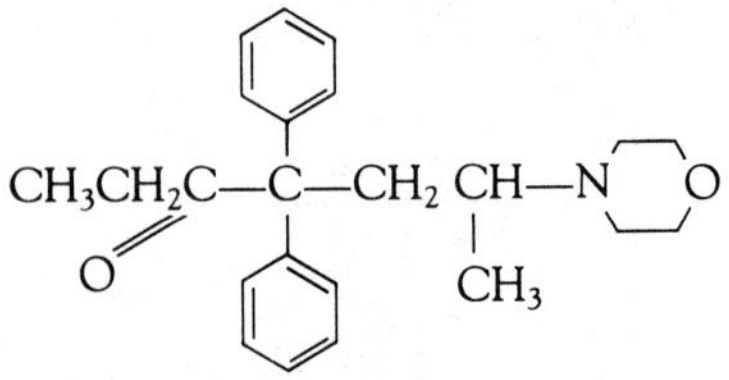

Phenadoxone

COMMON WEIGHT MEASUREMENTS FOR DRUGS

Term	Measurement
Nanogram (ng)	One billionth of a gram
Microgram (mcg)	One millionth of a gram
Milligram (mg)	One thousandth of a gram
Grain	65 mg (not a metric unit)
Gram (g)	One thousandth of a kilogram (kg)
Ounce (oz)	Twenty-eight grams; one-sixteenth of a pound (not a metric unit)

GLOSSARY

A-delta fiber Type of nerve fiber that transmits rapidly and leads to the sensation of sharp, pricking pain; see also *C-fiber.*

Absorbent Agent that takes up water or fluid and increases in bulk; compare to *Adsorbent.*

Acetaldehyde Toxic breakdown product of ethyl alcohol.

Acetylcholine A neurotransmitter in the parasympathetic nervous system, also abbreviated Ach or ACh.

Acupuncture Method of analgesia in which needles are inserted in the skin at special points and a stimulus applied by twirling, vibration, or an electrical charge.

Acute effect The immediate, short-term response to a single dose of drug; compare to *Chronic effect.*

Addiction Defined in 1957 by the World Health Organization as a state of periodic or chronic intoxication produced by the repeated consumption of a drug. Its characteristics include (1) an overpowering desire or compulsion to continue taking the drug and to obtain it by any means; (2) a tendency to increase the dose; (3) a psychic (psychological) and generally a physical dependence on the effects of the drug; (4) an effect detrimental to the individual and to society; see also *Drug dependence, Habituation, Physical dependence,* and *Psychological dependence.*

Adrenergic blocker Drug acting at sympathetic nerve endings to reduce the effective concentration of norepinephrine—for example, guanethidine, methyldopa. Different drugs can block the alpha, beta-1, or beta-2 functions selectively.

Adsorbent Agent that binds chemical substances to its surface, such as charcoal; compare to *Absorbent.*

Adulterant Cheap substitute mixed with a pure drug—for example, heroin diluted with quinine.

Agonist Drug that mimics the action of a normally present biological compound, such as a neurotransmitter or hormone.

Akathesia Side effect of major tranquilizers that causes the person to be restless and possibly unable to sit or lie down quietly, or sleep.

Alkaloid Any member of a very diverse group of organic compounds containing a nitrogen atom in a ring structure, such as morphine, nicotine, and cocaine. The chemically basic molecule is unstable and is usually prepared in the more stable salt form; see *Free basing.*

Allergenic reaction Hypersensitivity to a drug or other substance due to an unwanted immune-system response.

Alpha receptor Postjunctional receptor site that responds primarily to norepinephrine.

Anabolic steroid Steroid hormone that promotes general body growth (anabolism), such as testosterone or one of the synthetic androgens.

Analeptic A drug that stimulates the central nervous system.

Analgesic Drug that produces relief from pain without loss of consciousness—for example, the opiates, phenacetin.

Anaphylactic shock Serious, often fatal allergenic reaction occurring in a previously sensitized person, starting within minutes after administration

GLOSSARY

of a foreign serum or certain drugs—for example, typhoid vaccine, penicillin.

Androgen Class of chemical compounds, some of which are synthetic, that are similar to testosterone in action; masculinizing hormone.

Anesthetic Drug that causes loss of sensation or feeling, especially pain, by its depressant effect on the nervous system.

Angina pectoris Severe chest pain caused by inadequate blood supply to the heart muscle, brought on by exertion or excitement.

Anorexia State of not feeling hungry; a blocked hunger center caused by some drugs and psychological factors.

Anorexiant Anorectic; drug that causes loss of appetite.

Antabuse syndrome Accumulation of the toxic metabolite of alcohol, acetaldehyde, due to Antabuse® or a genetic deficiency, which causes unpleasant symptoms: intense throbbing in head and neck, a pulsating headache, difficulty in breathing, nausea, copious vomiting, sweating, thirst, and chest pain.

Antagonist Drug that blocks or interferes with the action of a normally present biological compound, such as a neurotransmitter or hormone, or of another drug, such as a narcotic antagonist.

Anthropometry The measurement of the size, weight, and proportions of the body.

Anticholinergic Cholinergic blocking agent—for example, atropine, nicotine; prevents acetylcholine from stimulating the receptor.

Anticoagulant Substance that slows the rate of blood-clot formation.

Antidepressant Group of drugs used to elevate mood in severely depressed persons—for example, Tofranil®.

Antigen Substance that stimulates production of antibodies, such as penicillin; see also *Hapten*.

Antihistamine Drug that prevents or antagonizes the action of histamine—for example, chlorpheniramine, isoproterenol.

Antihypertensive Drug used to reduce hypertension, or high blood pressure.

Anti-inflammatory Drug that reduces inflammation—for example, cortisone.

Antimuscarinic An anticholinergic drug that affects the muscarinic type of receptor, not the nicotinic—for example, belladonna.

Antipsychotic (neuroleptic) Drugs that produce an effect of emotional quieting and relative indifference to one's surroundings; also called *major tranquilizers*.

Antipyretic Drug that reduces fever—for example, aspirin.

Aphrodisiac Substance that will produce a sexually enhancing effect in a person who does not expect this result.

Ataraxic Any drug that creates a feeling of calmness; the tranquilizers.

Autonomic nervous system Motor system consisting of the nerves that control heart muscle, glands, and smooth muscle. It has two major divisions: the sympathetic (thoracolumbar) and the parasympathetic (craniosacral).

Axon Extension from neuron; usually carries impulses away from the cell body; may have an insulating myelin sheath.

Basal ganglia Interconnected structures in the forebrain that direct involuntary muscle function that is not under conscious control, including maintenance of muscle tone and posture; dopamine is probably the neurotransmitter involved.

Basal metabolic rate Rate at which the body uses oxygen for energy required to maintain homeostasis; measured in the quietly resting person, at least 12 hours after the latest meal, to obtain lowest essential level.

Behavioral tolerance The learning of control over some drug effects over a period of time; thought to be a subtype of pharmacodynamic tolerance.

Behavioral stereotypy Getting "hung up" in a meaningless repetition of a simple activity for hours at a time; characteristic of amphetamine abuse and paranoid schizophrenia.

Beta receptor Postjunctional receptor site that responds primarily to epinephrine; divided into beta-1 and beta-2 types based on the response to sympathomimetic drugs.

Biofeedback Use of a signal, such as muscle tension or brain waves, to control a normally involuntary physiological process.

Biological half-life The amount of time required to remove half of the original amount of a drug from the body.

Biotransformation Process of metabolism of drugs in the body, usually in the liver; see also *Detoxification.*

Blood-brain barrier Selective filtering system that permits ready passage of oxygen, glucose, and other nutrients into neurons but largely excludes proteins, ionized molecules, and nonfat-soluble substances.

Blood-placental barrier The placenta, the organ that interfaces between the mother's blood supply and the fetal blood supply, excludes transfer of some water-soluble substances to the fetus. Most lipid-soluble drugs and many water-soluble drugs will transfer to the fetal blood.

Blue Velvet Mixture of paregoric, a tincture of opium, and tripelennamine (pyribenzamine), an antihistamine.

Bradykinin One of a group of naturally present peptides that acts on blood vessels, smooth muscles, and nociceptors; no known function.

Brainstem (hindbrain) The enlarged extension of the spinal cord; it includes the medulla oblongata, the pons, and the cerebellum.

Brompton's cocktail (mixture) An alcoholic solution of an opioid, usually heroin or morphine; and cocaine, amphetamine, or a phenothiazine tranquilizer; used to control severe pain in terminal cancer patients.

Bronchitis Inflammation of the bronchial tubes in the lungs, causing difficulty in breathing.

Bursitis Inflammation, causing pain, of the fluid-filled sac between a tendon and a bone, such as in the shoulder or elbow.

C-fiber Type of nerve fiber that transmits slowly and gives rise to the sensation of dull, diffuse, or burning pain; see also *A-delta fiber.*

Carcinogen Agent or factor that causes cancer.

Cardiac arhythmia Disturbance of the normal synchronized rhythm of the heartbeat so that the heart does not pump blood; fatal if not reversed.

Catatonia Condition of muscular rigidity in which the person remains in whatever position he or she is placed; occurs in schizophrenia and in PCP and LSD psychoses; also called *catalepsy*; catatonic seizure.

Catecholamine Class of biochemical compounds including the neurotransmitters dopamine, norepinephrine, and epinephrine.

Central nervous system The neurons that are located in the brain and spinal cord; see also *Peripheral nervous system.*

Cerebellum Part of the brainstem; concerned especially with the coordination of muscles and bodily equilibrium.

Cerebrum (cerebral cortex) The convoluted layer of gray matter that forms the largest part of the brain in humans; the highest neural center for coordination and interpretation of external and internal stimuli; contains sensory, motor, and association areas.

Chipper Controlled, nonaddicted heroin user.

Cholinergic Neuron that uses acetylcholine (Ach) as a neurotransmitter.

Cholinoceptive site Postjunctional receptor for acetylcholine, also affected by the agonists muscarine and nicotine.

Chronic effect The long-term response to repeated doses of a drug; compare to *Acute effect.*

Cirrhosis Pathological changes taking place in the liver after long-term alcoholism, causing altered liver metabolism that includes decreased testosterone and increased estrogen in the male.

Climacteric The sum of all the physiological changes that occur as part of the natural aging process, as the pituitary-gonad relationship diminishes in men and women; see also *Menopause.*

Combination pill (oral contraceptive) Contains a fixed proportion of synthetic progestin and estrogen.

Complex The combination of a molecule of a drug, hormone, or neurotransmitter with a particular protein, in the blood or in association with a cell. Some complexes function as transport units; in others, the protein changes shape because of the interaction, initiating a metabolic change; see also *Protein binding.*

Congener Nonalcoholic constituents in alcoholic beverages, from the fermentation process, storage, the original plant material, or added substances.

Conjunctival injection Reddened, irritated appearance of the whites of the eyes, such as from marijuana.

Contraceptive Any means that prevents pregnancy, including substances or devices that prevent ovulation, fertilization, or implantation.

Convulsion An involuntary, violent, and irregular series of contractions of the skeletal muscles.

Counterirritant Preparation containing an irritant applied to the skin to stimulate sensory receptors, increase blood flow, and induce a sensation of warmth (oil of mustard); may have an analgesic action (methyl salicylate).

Cross-dependence Different drugs, like barbiturates and alcohol, may cause physical dependence because of their similar pharmacological activity and can be used interchangeably to prevent withdrawal symptoms.

Cross-tolerance Development of tolerance to one drug can accelerate the metabolism of, and reduce the nervous system's response to, other drugs that act by the same mechanism—for example, LSD and mescaline, or alcohol and tranquilizers.

DAWN (Drug Abuse Warning Network) Federal program designed to identify drugs currently abused and the patterns of abuse in selected metropolitan areas from medical records of emergency room patients and morgues.

Delirium A condition characterized by mental excitement, confusion, disordered speech, and, often, hallucinations.

Dendrite Thin, cellular extension from a neuron; serves as reception area (postsynaptic) for signals coming to the neuron from other neurons.

Depressant Any of several drugs that sedate by acting on the central nervous system; medical uses include the treatment of anxiety, tension, and high blood pressure.

Detoxification The biological process by which toxins (poisons), drugs, and hormones are modified into less toxic, or more readily excretable, substances, usually in the liver; see also *Biotransformation* and *Enzyme induction*.

Diethylstilbestrol (DES) Synthetic compound with estrogenic activity; is carcinogenic in animals; sometimes used as a "morning-after" birth control method.

Diuretic Drug used to increase the excretion of water by the kidneys, with a concurrent loss of sodium.

Dol Unit of pain intensity based on a sequence of just-noticeable-difference steps in stimulus intensity.

Dose-response (dose-effect) relationship The intensity and character of response to a drug depends on the amount administered and individual variability; see also *Effective dose* and *Threshold dose*.

Double-blind, placebo-controlled Testing setup to show whether a drug's effects are due to it or the patient's expectations. Neither the physician nor the research volunteer subject knows whether he or she is getting a "real" drug or a placebo until the study is over.

Drug dependence Defined by the World Health Organization as a "state arising from repeated administration of a drug on a periodic or continuous basis." It is subdivided by types—for example, drug dependence of the morphine type, of the cocaine type, of the cannabis type, of the barbiturate type, and so on; see also *Physical dependence* and *Psychological dependence*.

Drug disposition tolerance The state in which enzyme systems in the liver increase their capacity to metabolize a drug, so the body disposes of the drug faster.

Drug interaction When a drug action is modified by another substance, it may (1) add to, (2) inhibit, or (3) be enhanced; see also *Potentiation*.

EEG See *Electroencephalogram*.

Effective dose The dose that is effective therapeutically. ED-50 would mean that the dose given causes the response in 50% of the test animals; see also *Therapeutic index*.

Electroencephalogram A recording of the small electrical currents (brain waves) generated by groups of neurons in the several lobes of the brain.

Emphysema A disease in which the lungs are inelastic, causing oxygen and carbon dioxide exchange to be impaired; heart action is often impaired as well.

End bulb, or presynaptic terminal Part of the axon of the neuron where neurotransmitters are released

Endocrine system One of the two major control systems of the body for homeostasis. Endocrine glands secrete biochemical messengers called *hor-*

mones into the bloodstream or cerebrospinal fluid, which, when they reach their target tissue, adjust the target tissue's activity.

Endorphin Class of peptides from the pituitary gland and nervous tissue with action similar to morphine; see also *Enkephalin.*

Enkephalin A small peptide produced by the brain, similar in action to morphine; see also *Endorphin.*

Enteral Refers to a drug that is taken orally.

Enzyme induction An increase in the metabolic capacity of an enzyme system (usually in the liver) to detoxify, or metabolize, substances and clear them from the body; see also *Biotransformation.*

Ergotism Condition caused by the vasoconstrictive action of the chemicals in ergot fungus, related to LSD; can cause delirium, hallucinations, convulsions, and gangrene; also called *St. Anthony's fire.*

Ergotropic That which incites to activity; hyperaroused; compare to *Trophotropic.*

Estrogen Class of chemical compounds, some of which are synthetic and taken orally, that are similar to ovarian estradiol in action; used in oral contraceptives.

Eunuchoid Similar to a eunuch, a castrated male, in appearance.

Euphoria Elevation of mood; a stimulant drug may cause a sensation of euphoria.

Expectorant Compounds that enhance the removal of respiratory tract fluids by coughing—for example, ipecac.

Fermentation Biochemical process in which yeast converts sugar into alcohol.

Fetal alcohol syndrome An associated group of symptoms such as mental retardation, impairment of growth, and facial deformities caused by prenatal exposure to alcohol.

Flashback Unexpected return, without having taken the drug, of the subjective sensations from a hallucinogenic drug experience.

Formication "Cocaine bugs," a sensation of insects crawling underneath the skin, caused by stimulants such as cocaine and amphetamine.

Free basing Conversion of the stable salt form of an alkaloid, like cocaine, into the less chemically stable but more biologically potent basic form "freed" of the ionic salt; also, using a drug in this form.

FSH (follicle stimulating hormone) A gonadotropin from the pituitary gland; it directs the ovary to mature follicles in preparation for ovulation, and the testis to continue spermatogenesis.

Galactorrhea Excessive or spontaneous flow of milk when not physiologically appropriate, such as a side effect of a drug.

Ganglia Groups of nerve cell bodies outside the central nervous system, such as along the spinal cord.

Gastritis Inflammation of the stomach, causing damage to the blood vessels and erosion of stomach tissue; the beginning of peptic ulcer.

Glial cell Cells that surround the neurons in the brain and that help form the blood-brain barrier; also called *astrocytes.*

Gonadotropin Hormone from the pituitary gland that directs the gonad (testis or ovary) in the male or female reproductive cycle. The two pituitary gonadotropins are FSH (follicle stimulating hormone) and LH (luteinizing hormone).

GRAS (Generally Recognized As Safe) List List of food additives exempted from the FDA's present requirements for toxicological tests because they had been used in foods for many years without problems before the requirement for testing went into effect.

Gynecomastia Development of the breasts when physiologically inappropriate, such as in men; see also *Galactorrhea.*

Habituation As defined in 1957 by the World Health Organization, a condition resulting from the repeated consumption of a drug, which includes these characteristics: (1) a desire (but not compulsion) to continue taking the drug for the sense of improved well-being that it engenders; (2) little or no tendency to increase the dose; (3) some degree of psychic dependence on the effect of the drug, but absence of physical dependence and hence no abstinence syndrome; (4) a detrimental effect, if any, primarily on the user; see *Psychological dependence.*

Hallucinogen Any of several drugs, popularly called *psychedelics*, that produce sensations such as distortions of time, space, sound, color, and other bizarre effects. Although they are pharmacologically nonnarcotic, some of these drugs have been regulated under federal narcotic laws (Schedule I).

Hapten   A substance that does not stimulate anti-body formation itself but that will combine with a carrier antigen to stimulate antibody formation.

Histamine   Biochemical substance (in the amine class) stored in mast cells and released by tissue injury, including allergic reactions; no known functional role, but may be a neurotransmitter.

Homeostasis   Maintenance of a stable biochemical environment within the body's cells and the fluid bathing the cells, in response to constant internal and external fluctuations, such as variations in nutrient supply and demands on organs like the liver and kidney to metabolize and excrete natural and foreign substances.

Hormone   A biochemical substance produced and secreted by an endocrine gland that brings about an adjustment in or development of a target tissue.

Hyperkinesis   Hyperactivity; a behavioral disorder in which the person, usually a child, is abnormally and uncontrollably active.

Hyperpyrexia   Abnormally elevated body temper-ature, as from a fever or activation of the sym-pathetic nervous system due to a drug like amphetamine.

Hypertension   Blood pressure elevated over normal values for age and sex; classified as mild, moderate, or severe.

Hypnotic   A central nervous system depressant that induces sleep; see also *Sedative.*

Hypoglycemia   Low blood sugar (glucose).

Hypothalamus   Region of the forebrain below the thalamus that is the major central control of the autonomic nervous system and is important in the regulation of blood pressure, heart rate, mainte-nance of body temperature, metabolism, and the endocrine system.

Hypothyroidism   Inadequate secretion of the thy-roid gland's hormone; causes slowed reflexes, impaired metabolism, and psychological dis-turbances.

Iatrogenic   Disorder caused by the treatment process, as in "iatrogenic disease."

Implantation   The process in which a fertilized human egg burrows into the uterine lining to obtain nutrients and exchange waste; marks the begin-ning of pregnancy.

Impotence   Condition in which the affected man is unable to achieve and maintain an erection.

IND (Investigational New Drug) number   An FDA-assigned code number used during human clinical tests of a new drug prior to the granting of per-mission to market it.

Injection   Dosage form in which the drug is admin-istered intravenously (IV), intramuscularly (IM), intraperitoneally (IP, into the abdominal cavity); subcutaneously (SC, under the skin).

Inositol   Vitamin in the B complex found as an adulterant in street cocaine.

Intrauterine device (IUD)   Foreign object placed into the uterus for contraceptive purposes.

Khat (Catha)   A shrub native to Africa and Arabia; the leaves and twigs are chewed, brewed like tea, or fermented with honey. Causes a stimulatory, euphoric effect and a particular type of drug dependence.

Lethal dose, or LD   The dosage that will kill; LD-50 means that this dose would be lethal to 50% of the test animals. See also *Therapeutic index.*

LH (luteinizing hormone)   A gonadotropin from the pituitary gland that directs the testis to secrete testosterone and the ovary to ovulate and to form the corpus luteum.

Libido   Sexual drive; desire.

Life expectancy at birth   The number of years a newborn infant can expect to live, figured accord-ing to the levels of mortality prevailing in the year of its birth.

Limbic system   Neurons in the hippocampus, amygdala, and other structures integrating the cerebral cortex with the hypothalamus; concerned with emotion and motivation; probably uses dopa-mine as the neurotransmitter.

Lipid   Fat-soluble molecule.

Lipophilic   Drug or other substance that is more soluble in lipid (fat) than in water.

Liver induction   See *Enzyme induction.*

Main effect   A drug's desired effect; no known drug has only a main effect; see also *Side effect.*

Mainline   Injection of a drug intravenously.

Mandrake   European herb whose roots may resem-ble the human form; contains hallucinogenic bel-ladonna compounds.

Manic depressive   Mental disorder characterized by alternating extremes of excitement and depression.

Mannitol   Mannite; a white, powdery type of sugar found as an adulterant in street cocaine and heroin.

Margin of safety   Dosage range between an ineffective (threshold) amount and a lethal amount of a drug; see also *Therapeutic index*.

Medial forebrain bundle   Group of nerve fibers connecting the forebrain, midbrain, and hypothalamus; location of the pleasure (reward) center; probably uses norepinephrine as a neurotransmitter.

Meditation   A state of constant and continuous flow of awareness of one chosen object, created by maintaining a thought-free state of mind.

Medulla oblongata   Part of the hindbrain (brainstem) between the spinal cord and pons; controls many vital functions, such as respiration, heart rate, and blood pressure; many depressant drugs have secondary toxic effects on the medulla.

Menopause   Cessation of menstrual cycles; part of the female climacteric.

Midbrain   Component of the brain between the brainstem and the forebrain; has tracts from the spinal cord and the medulla oblongata going to the higher cortical centers and has relays that control vision and hearing.

Miosis   Constriction of the pupils of the eyes; compare to *Mydriasis*.

Morning-after (postcoital) contraceptive   Oral or injectable estrogens and injectable progestins used to prevent pregnancy if no other contraceptive means were used and avoidance of pregnancy is medically preferable to abortion later, such as a possibility of pregnancy after rape.

Mortality ratio   The number obtained by dividing the death rate in one group of people, such as drug users, by a matched group of people who do not use that drug, in order to estimate what contribution to the death rate is made by the drug.

Muscarinic cholinoceptive site   Postjunctional receptor for acetylcholine; also affected by muscarine.

Mutagen   Chemical or physical agent that causes genetic mutations.

Mydriasis   Dilation of the pupils of the eyes; compare to *Miosis*.

Narcolepsy   A condition in which the person falls into brief, deep sleep spontaneously and without warning.

Narcotic   Numbness producer; this term has two definitions. Medically, a narcotic is any drug that produces sleep or stupor and also relieves pain; legally, a narcotic means any drug regulated under the Harrison Act and other federal narcotic laws.

Nerve block   Method of analgesia in which a nerve-destroying agent is injected close to the troublesome nerve.

Nervous system   One of the two major control systems of the body for homeostasis. The nervous system receives and interprets stimuli and transmits impulses to effector organs; see also *Autonomic*, *Central*, and *Peripheral nervous systems*.

Neuralgia   Sharp, paroxysmal pain along the path followed by a nerve.

Neuroleptic   See *Antipsychotic*.

Neuron   Functional unit of the nervous system; a nerve cell; it has specialized structures to receive and transmit information; see also *Axon*, *Dendrite*, *End bulb terminal*, *Receptor*, and *Synapse*.

Neurotransmitter   Biochemical substance, released from the end bulb into the synapse between neurons, that affects the receiving neuron, either to excite it and continue the neurotransmission or, if appropriate, to inhibit the receiving neuron.

Nicotinic cholinoceptive site   Postjunctional receptor for acetylcholine; also affected by nicotine.

Nociceptor   A sensory receptor that transmits a pain signal when sufficiently stimulated.

Norepinephrine   A neurotransmitter in the sympathetic nervous system; also called *NE*.

Nystagmus   A rapid, involuntary oscillation of the eyeballs, usually side-to-side.

Operant pain   Learned pain behavior that may respond to behavioral modification; see also *Respondent pain*.

Oral contraceptive (The Pill)   Oral synthetic progestin or a combination of oral progestin and estrogen used to prevent pregnancy; see also *Estrogen*, *Progestin*.

Over-the-counter (OTC, patent) drug   Pharmaceutical substance that can be purchased without a prescription—for example, aspirin; claims for its effectiveness are regulated to some extent by the Food and Drug Administration; compare to *Prescription drug.*

Ovulation Process by which the eggs, or female germ cells, are released from the ovary.

Pain Perception of a sensation as physically extremely uncomfortable; a signal of possible damage to the body. Subclassified as *visceral* (nonskeletal) or *somatic* (skeletal muscle and bone), and *sharp* (carried by A-delta fibers) or *dull* (carried by C-fibers).

Pain gate Hypothetical system in the spinal cord thought to account for varying perception of pain by modulating signals ascending into the brain. The "gate" can be "closed" by acupuncture and hypnosis, which may work by activating higher centers to send inhibitory signals back down the spinal cord.

Pain threshold That level at which a stimulus is first recognized as unpleasant; see also *Pain tolerance.*

Pain tolerance The level of painful stimulation at which the person says he or she cannot bear any more; psychological factors are important in determining pain tolerance.

Parachlorophenylalanine (PCPA) Drug that blocks serotonin synthesis and produces a deficiency of that neurotransmitter.

Parasympathetic (craniosacral) nervous system Part of the autonomic nervous system; stimulates those organs generally concerned with the acquisition and conservation of energy.

Parenteral Taking a drug other than orally—for example, by injection, topically, and so on.

Parkinson's disease Progressive degenerative disease of the nervous system's motor control center in the basal ganglia, causing muscular tremors, stiffness, and difficulty in moving.

Pelvic inflammatory disease (PID) Inflammation of the pelvic organs following infection of the urethra and/or of the vagina by gonorrhea or a variety of other organisms; these migrate upwards to infect the cervix, uterus, fallopian tubes, ovaries, and other tissues in the abdominal cavity.

Peptide Biochemical polymer of two or more amino acids linked between the amine group of one and the carboxyl group of the next amino acid; a chain of more than 100 amino acids is usually called a *protein.*

Peripheral nervous system All the neurons located outside the brain and spinal cord; see also *Central nervous system.*

Periventricular system Group of neurons in the hypothalamus and thalamus; location of the punishment (avoidance) center; probably uses acetylcholine as neurotransmitter.

Phagocyte Type of white blood cell that attacks and engulfs foreign objects such as bacteria and sperm. Once inside the phagocyte, the foreign objects are broken down by enzymes.

Phantom pain Pain experienced by some amputees "in" a missing limb.

Pharmacodynamic tolerance The state in which a drug's target tissue, such as the brain, has adapted to the drug gradually, over a period of weeks to months, by an unknown mechanism, so that the same concentration of drug produces a decreased response.

Physical addiction See *Physical dependence.*

Physical dependence Physiological adaptation of the body to the presence of a drug. In effect, the body develops a continuing need for the drug. Once such dependence has been established, the body reacts with predictable symptoms if the drug is abruptly withdrawn. The nature and severity of withdrawal symptoms depend on the drug being used and the daily dosage level attained.

Piloerection Hair standing up, as during the skin's response to cold.

Pituitary gland Important endocrine gland situated at the base of the hypothalamus and directed by it; secretes (among many other hormones) the gonadotropins.

Placebo An inert substance, such as a sugar tablet or an injection of sterile water, given as if it were a real medication; also an ineffective dose of an active drug. Can be highly effective.

Polypharmacy The giving of more than one drug concurrently.

Pore (transport channel) Place in a cell membrane involved in transport of a substance across the membrane barrier.

Postjunctional receptor site Receptor for a neurotransmitter on the receiving neuron.

Potency The absolute amount of a drug required to produce a given pharmacological effect; see also *Therapeutic index.*

Potentiation See *Synergism.*

Precursor In a metabolic sequence of reactions, a precursor is a compound that gives rise to the next compound; for example, choline is the precursor for the neurotransmitter acetylcholine.

Prescription (ethical; legend) drug Pharmaceutical substance whose prescription order is regulated by law to a licensed person, such as a physician; classified in one of the Schedules II–IV of Controlled Substances; see also *Schedule II,* and so on.

Pressor Substance that elevates blood pressure—for example, tyramine.

Presynaptic terminal See *End bulb.*

Priapism An uncomfortable, prolonged penile erection caused by a pathological condition or a drug—for example, Spanish fly.

Progestin Class of chemical compounds, some of which are synthetic and administered orally, that are similar to ovarian progesterone in action; used in oral contraceptive pills, injectable contraceptives, and medicated intrauterine devices.

Prolactin Hormone from the pituitary gland that acts on the breasts to stimulate secretion of milk; see also *Galactorrhea.*

Prostate One of the secondary male sex organs; a three-lobed organ near the urinary bladder whose secretions make up much of the volume of the ejaculate.

Protein binding Drugs and hormones may circulate in blood bound to carrier proteins; the proportion of bound to unbound (free) protein varies with the drug's structure.

Psychedelic Mind-manifesting; group of drugs producing a mental state of great calm and intensely pleasurable perception.

Psychoactive (psychotropic) drug One that affects mood and/or consciousness; may be a prescription (Valium ®) or a nonprescription (marijuana) drug.

Psychological addiction See *Psychological dependence.*

Psychological dependence, primary An attachment to drug use that arises from a drug's ability to satisfy some emotional or personality need; see also *Habituation.*

Psychological dependence, secondary Taking a drug to avoid the withdrawal symptoms once physical dependence has developed; also called *aversive reinforcement.*

Psychosis A major mental derangement; the deeper, more far-reaching and prolonged behavioral disorders. (Compare to "insanity," which is a social and legal term referring to a mental derangement.)

Psychotomimetic Mimicking a psychosis; compounds capable of producing hallucinations, sensory illusions, and bizarre thoughts; see also *Hallucinogen, Psychedelic.*

Psychotoxic Drugs, including therapeutic and abused, that can produce a (1) psychosis (psychotogenic drugs), a (2) mood change, or (3) anxiety. The psychotogenic drugs can produce euphoria in low doses but in higher doses can produce a psychotic state—for example, amphetamine, LSD, marijuana.

Quasi-medical Having the characteristics of medical use but not accepted in usual modern medical practice.

Quinine White alkaloid with a bitter taste, found as an adulterant in street heroin.

Rebound (paradoxical) effect State of agitation that occurs when a person who has developed tolerance and physical dependence withdraws from a depressant drug; the rebound symptoms during withdrawal are often the opposite of the effects of the drug.

Receptor Special protein on the membrane or in the cytoplasm of a target cell with which a drug, a neurotransmitter, or a hormone interacts; see also *Alpha receptor, Beta receptor, Cholinoceptive site,* and *Postjunctional receptor site.*

Recidivism Return or relapse to a type of behavior, such as drug taking.

Reflex action An automatic response to a stimulus during which a nerve impulse from a receptor passes to a nerve center, such as the spinal cord, and then outward to an effector without reaching the level of conscious action.

REM (Rapid Eye Movement) sleep There are four stages of sleep, as characterized by brain-wave recordings. REM sleep occurs during stage 1, light sleep, and is associated with dreaming.

Respondent pain Pain with a definite physical cause; see also *Operant pain.*

Reticular activating system Network of nerve fibers located in the central portion of the brainstem with neural connections to the cerebral cortex. Its function is to arouse the cortex and maintain a state of consciousness; suppressed by most general anesthetics.

Rubefaction Condition of inducing increased blood flow and a redness to the skin, without blistering, such as with a counterirritant drug.

Schedule I Substances Drugs that have no accepted medical use in the United States and that have a high abuse potential—for example, heroin, LSD, marijuana, psilocybin.

Schedule II Substances Drugs considered to have a high abuse potential with severe psychological or physical dependence liability—for example, amphetamine, methaqualone, morphine. The physician must write the prescription in ink or type it, and sign it, and it cannot be refilled.

Schedule III Substances Drugs considered to have less abuse potential than Schedule II substances, including compounds with limited quantities of certain narcotic drugs, and nonnarcotic drugs—for example, glutethimide (Doriden®), nalorphine. The prescription may be written or given orally to the pharmacist, and it can be refilled if this is specified.

Schedule IV Substances Drugs considered to have less abuse potential than Schedule III substances—for example, phenobarbital, Valium®.

Schedule V Substances Drugs that have an abuse potential less than Schedule IV substances and that consist of preparations containing limited quantities of certain narcotic drugs for antitussive (cough) and antidiarrheal purposes—for example, Robitussin®, Lomotil®. These may be dispensed (subject to state law) without a prescription by a phar-

macist, who is required to maintain a record book of these purchases.

Secondary sex organs See *Prostate* and *Seminal vesicles.*

Sedative Psychoactive drug that decreases excitability and anxiety as part of its general depressant action; higher doses may be hypnotic (sleep inducing).

Seminal vesicles Secondary male sex organs; a pair of sacs located on both sides of the urinary bladder that contribute substances and fluid to the ejaculate.

Serotonin A neurotransmitter found primarily in the upper brainstem; also called 5-hydroxytryptamine, or 5-HT. May prevent overreaction to various stimuli; regulates release of hypothalamic hormones, which in turn regulate the pituitary's release of gonadotropins.

Set Psychological makeup or behavior of drug user. If a good result is expected, it is more likely to occur.

Setting The physical surroundings in which a drug is taken. A pleasant environment is often important in determining the effects of a hallucinogen.

Side effect A given drug may have many actions; usually one or two of the more prominent will be medically useful. The others, usually weaker effects, are called side effects; they are not necessarily harmful but may be annoying; see also *Main effect.*

Skin popping Injection of a drug subcutaneously.

Snorting Application of a drug, like cocaine, to the nasal mucosa or membranes by inhaling.

Solution Dosage form in which the drug is dissolved in a liquid.

Spanish fly A preparation of the irritating substances, the cantharides, from blister beetles; used as an aphrodisiac. Produces an inflammation of the lining of the urinary bladder and the urethra in both male and female.

Speed Methamphetamine or other amphetamine in an injectable form.

Speedball Combination of heroin and cocaine or amphetamine.

Spermatogenesis Production of sperm, or male gametes; one of the functions of the testis.

Spermicidal jelly Contraceptive agent in the form of a gel with a chemical ingredient to kill sperm.

Steady state The situation that exists when the rate of elimination of a drug equals the rate of its intake.

Stimulant Any of several drugs that act on the central nervous system to produce excitation, alertness, and wakefulness. Medical uses include the treatment of hyperkinesia and narcolepsy.

Substance P Peptide found in nerves that transmit pain signals; may be a pain neurotransmitter.

Suppository Dosage form of a drug that is placed in an orifice, such as the anus or vagina.

Suspension Dosage form in which particles of an insoluble drug are suspended in a liquid.

Sympathetic (thoracolumbar) nervous system Part of the autonomic nervous system; stimulates structures generally concerned with the expenditure of body energy.

Sympathomimetic Drug that affects postjunctional receptor sites for norepinephrine and epinephrine, the intensity depending on the receptor type (alpha, beta-1, or beta-2).

Synapse Gap between end bulb (presynaptic terminal) of axon from first neuron to dendrite (postsynaptic membrane) of second, communicating, neuron, across which the neurotransmitter molecules diffuse.

Synaptic vesicle Membrane-enclosed package of neurotransmitter found in the end bulb.

Synergism (potentiation) The combined action of two or more drugs is greater than the sum of the effects of each drug taken alone.

Synesthesia Cross-sensing; the brain interprets a sensation incorrectly, such as "hearing" colors.

Tachycardia Rapid heartbeat, such as from stress or stimulant drugs.

Tardive dyskinesia Long-term side effect of major tranquilizers in which, after years of treatment, the person has difficulty controlling voluntary movement, especially of the lips and tongue.

Teratogen An agent or factor that causes physical defects in a developing embryo.

Testosterone Sex hormone from the testis that maintains libido and the male characteristics—for example, beard, musculature. Naturally occurring compound in the class of androgens (masculinizing hormones).

Thalamus Portion of the forebrain where sensations such as pain are interpreted and relayed to appropriate areas of the cerebral cortex; important in emotional responses associated with feelings of pleasantness and unpleasantness.

Therapeutic index Relative margin of safety of a drug; the dose required to produce toxic effects divided by the dose required to produce therapeutic effects, or LD/ED. See also *Effective dose* and *Lethal dose.*

Threshold dose The least amount of drug that shows any therapeutic effect.

Thromboembolism Obstruction of a blood vessel by a thrombus (blood clot) that has broken loose and moved from its site of formation.

Thrombosis Formation or presence of a blood clot (thrombus).

Thyroid gland Endocrine gland situated in the neck that secretes thyroid hormone, which regulates many aspects of metabolism, including maintenance of reproductive function.

Tinnitus Sensation of ringing sound in head; can be caused by aspirin or caffeine.

Tolerance With many drugs, a person must keep increasing the dosage to maintain the same effect. Tolerance develops with the barbiturates, amphetamines and related compounds, and opiates; see *Behavioral tolerance, Drug disposition tolerance,* and *Pharmacodynamic tolerance.*

Topical Dosage form in which the drug is applied to an external surface.

Toxicity Degree of poisonousness; any substance in excessive amounts can act as a poison or toxin. With drugs, the margin between the dosage that produces beneficial effects and the dosage that produces toxic or poisonous effects varies with the drug and the person receiving it; see also *Lethal dose.*

Tranquilizers, major Drugs used to relieve symptoms of severe psychosis—for example, Thorazine®.

Tranquilizers, minor Psychoactive drugs with sedative and antianxiety effects; also used as anticonvulsants and muscle relaxants (Valium®).

Trophotropic   That which characterizes a tranquil, restorative, nourishing state; hypoaroused; compare to *Ergotropic.*

Tryptaminergic   Neuron that uses 5-hydroxytryptamine (serotonin) as a neurotransmitter.

Ts and Blues   Mixture of pentazocine (Talwin®), a narcotic analgesic, and tripelennamine (pyribenzamine), an antihistamine; and used as a heroin substitute.

Vasocongestion   Engorgement of blood vessels: more blood flows into particular tissues than leaves, resulting in vasocongestion. Pelvic vasocongestion causes penile erection or vaginal lubrication.

Vasodilatation   Increase in diameter of blood vessels, causing increased volume of flow in that vessel.

Withdrawal (abstinence) syndrome   Cluster of symptoms that occur after a drug that causes physical dependence is no longer taken; divided into *morphine type* and *alcohol-barbiturate type.*

Woman-year   The pregnancy rate per woman-year is a means of comparing the effectiveness of different contraceptive methods. It assumes that a woman is having intercourse regularly and that she has 13 ovulatory menstrual cycles per year in which to become pregnant.

Xanthine   Biochemical substance in the alkaloid family with stimulant properties—for example, caffeine.

Yoga   *Union;* the process of discipline by which a person attains unity with the Supreme Being, or Absolute.

REFERENCES

Abel, E. L. 1980. *Marijuana: The First Twelve Thousand Years.* New York: Plenum Press.

Adams, S. H. 1905–1906. The great American fraud. *Collier's* **36**:17–18 (no. 5), 16–18 (no. 10), and 18–20 (no. 16).

Africa, T. W. 1961. The opium addiction of Marcus Aurelius. *Journal of the History of Ideas* **22**:97–102.

Altura, B. T. and B. M. Altura. 1981. Phencyclidine, lysergic acid diethylamide, and mescaline: cerebral artery spasms and hallucinogenic activity. *Science* **212**:1051–1052.

American Medical Association Committee on Alcoholism and Addiction. 1965. Dependence on barbiturates and other sedative drugs. *Journal of the American Medical Association* **193**:673–677.

American Red Cross. 1980. *Respiratory and Circulatory Emergencies.*

Anslinger, H. J. and C. R. Cooper. 1937. Marijuana: assassin of youth. *The American Magazine* **124**: 18–19, 150–153 (July).

Archer, S. 1981. Historical perspective on the chemistry and development of naltrexone. In R. E. Willette and G. Barnett, Eds., *Narcotic Antagonists: Naltrexone Pharmacochemistry and Sustained-Release Preparations.* Washington, D.C.: National Institute on Drug Abuse Research Monograph 28, Department of Health and Human Services, pp. 3–10.

Ariel, G. and W. Saville. 1972. Anabolic steroids: the physiological effects of placebos. *Medicine and Science in Sports* **4**:124–126.

Aronow, L. 1980. *Alcoholism, Alcohol Abuse, and Related Problems: Opportunities for Research.* Institute of Medicine, National Academy of Sciences. Washington, D.C.: National Academy Press.

Austin, G. A. 1978. *Perspectives on the History of Psychoactive Substance Use.* Washington, D.C.: National Institute on Drug Abuse Research Issues 24, Department of Health, Education, and Welfare.

Azizi, F., A. G. Vagenakis, C. Longcope, S. H. Ingbar, and L. E. Braverman. 1973. Decreased serum testosterone concentration in male heroin and methadone addicts. *Steroids* **22**:467–472.

Baldessarini, R. J. 1980. Drugs and the treatment of psychiatric disorders. In A. G. Gilman, L. S. Goodman, and A. Gilman, Eds., *The Pharmacological Basis of Therapeutics*, 6th ed. New York: Macmillan, pp. 391–447.

Barchas, J. D., P. A. Berger, S. Matthysse, and R. J. Wyatt. 1978. The biochemistry of affective disorders and schizophrenia. In W. G. Clark and J. del Giudice, Eds., *Principles of Psychopharmacology.* New York: Academic Press, pp. 105–131.

Baudelaire, C. 1971. *Artificial Paradise: On Hashish and Wine as Means of Expanding Individuality* [translated by Ellen Fox]. New York: Herder and Herder, pp. 45–56.

Beecher, H. K. 1975. Quantification of the subjective pain experience. In M. Weisenberg, Ed., *Pain: Clinical and Experimental Perspectives.* St. Louis: C. V. Mosby Co., pp. 56–66.

Benson, H. 1975. *The Relaxation Response.* New York: Wm. Morrow & Co., Inc.

Benson, H. 1977. Systemic hypertension and the relaxation response. *New England Journal of Medicine* **296**:1152–1156.

Beverly, R. 1705/1947. *The History and Present State of Virginia.* Chapel Hill: University of North Carolina Press, p. 139.

Bianchine, J. R. 1980. Drugs for Parkinson's disease: centrally acting muscle relaxants. In A. G. Gilman, L. S. Goodman, and A. Gilman, Eds., *The Pharmacological Basis of Therapeutics,* 6th ed. New York: Macmillan, pp. 475–493.

Billups, N. F. and S. M. Billups. 1981. *American Drug Index 1981.* Philadelphia: J. B. Lippincott Co.

Blackshear, P. J. 1979. Implantable drug-delivery systems. *Scientific American* **241**(6):66–73.

Blaschke, T. F. and K. L. Melmon. 1980. Antihypertensive agents and the drug therapy of hypertension. In A. G. Gilman, L. S. Goodman, and A. Gilman, Eds., *The Pharmacological Basis of Therapeutics,* 6th ed. New York: Macmillan, pp. 793–818.

Block, M. A. 1980. Motivating the alcoholic patient. In S. E. Gitlow and H. S. Peyser, Eds., *Alcoholism: A Practical Treatment Guide.* New York: Grune & Stratton, pp. 47–71.

Blum, R. and L. Richards. 1979. Youthful drug use. In R. L. DuPont, A. Goldstein, and J. O'Donnell, Eds., *Handbook on Drug Abuse.* Washington, D.C.: National Institute on Drug Abuse, Department of Health, Education, and Welfare, pp. 257–269.

Bok, S. 1977. The ethics of giving placebos. In R. Hunt and J. Arras, Eds., *Ethical Issues in Modern Medicine.* Palo Alto, Calif.: Mayfield Publishing Co., pp. 278–290.

Bond, M. R. 1979. *Pain: Its Nature, Analysis, and Treatment.* New York: Churchill Livingstone.

Bourne, P. G., Ed. 1976. *Acute Drug Emergencies. A Treatment Manual.* New York: Academic Press.

Bozzetti, L. P. and J. P. MacMurray. 1977. Drug misuse among the elderly: a hidden menace. *Psychiatric Annals* **7**:155–161.

Brecher, E. M. 1972. *Licit and Illicit Drugs.* Boston: Little, Brown & Co.

Bressler, R. 1982a. Adverse drug reactions. In K. A. Conrad and R. Bressler, Eds., *Drug Therapy for the Elderly.* St. Louis: C. V. Mosby Co., pp. 64–85.

Bressler, R. 1982b. Neuroleptic agents. In K. A. Conrad and R. Bressler, Eds., *Drug Therapy for the*

Elderly. St. Louis: C. V. Mosby Co., pp. 277–294.

Bridger, W. H., G. A. Barr, J. L. Gibbons, and D. A. Gorelick. 1978, Dual effects of LSD, mescaline, and DMT. In R. C. Stillman and R. E. Willette, Eds., *The Psychopharmacology of Hallucinogens.* New York: Pergamon Press, pp. 150–180.

Briggs, K. M. 1962. *Pale Hecate's Team.* New York: Humanities Press, p. 81.

Brooks, J. E. 1952. *The Mighty Leaf: Tobacco through the Centuries.* Boston: Little, Brown & Co.

Brown, B. S. and A. H. Pilch. 1972. The effects of exercise and Dianabol upon selected performances and physiological parameters in the male rat. *Medicine and Science in Sports* **4**:159–165.

Brown, N. A., E. H. Goulding, and S. Fabro. 1979. Ethanol embryotoxicity: direct effects on mammalian embryos in vitro. *Science* **206**:573–575.

Brown, S. C. 1978. Beers and wines of Old New England. *American Scientist* **66**:460–467.

Byck, R. 1975. Drugs and the treatment of psychiatric disorders. In L. S. Goodman and A. Gilman, Eds., *The Pharmacological Basis of Therapeutics,* 5th ed. New York: Macmillan, pp. 152–200.

Byck, R. and C. Van Dyke. 1977. What are the effects of cocaine in man? In R. C. Petersen and R. C. Stillman, Eds., *Cocaine: 1977.* Washington, D.C.: National Institute on Drug Abuse Research Monograph Series No. 13, Department of Health, Education, and Welfare, pp. 97–117.

Cahn, S. 1970. *The Treatment of Alcoholics: An Evaluative Study.* New York: Oxford University Press.

Caminos-Torres, R., L. Ma, and P. J. Snyder. 1977. Gynecomastia and semen abnormalities induced by spironolactone in normal men. *Journal of Clinical Endocrinology* **45**:255–260.

Caporael, L. R. 1976. Ergotism: the Satan loosed in Salem? *Science* **192**:21–26.

Carroll, E. 1977a. Coca: The plant and its use. In R. C. Petersen and R. C. Stillman, Eds., *Cocaine: 1977.* National Institute on Drug Abuse Research Monograph 13. Washington, D.C.: Department of Health, Education, and Welfare, pp. 35–45.

Carroll, E. 1977b. Notes on the epidemiology of inhalants. In C. W. Sharp and M. L. Brehm, Eds., *Review of Inhalants.* National Institute on Drug Abuse

Research Monograph 15. Washington, D.C.: Department of Health, Education, and Welfare, pp. 14–27.

Chambers, C. D. and M. S. Griffey. 1975. Use of legal substances within the general population: the sex and age variables. *Addictive Diseases* 2:7–19.

Chenoweth, M. B. 1977. Abuse of inhalation anesthetic drugs. In C. W. Sharp and M. L. Brehm, Eds., *Review of Inhalants*. National Institute on Drug Abuse Research Monograph 15. Washington, D.C.: Department of Health, Education, and Welfare, pp. 102–111.

Cicero, T. J., R. D. Bell, W. G. Wiest, J. H. Allison, K. Polakoski, and E. Robins. 1975. Function of the male sex organs in heroin and methadone users. *New England Journal of Medicine* 292:882–887.

Cicero, T. J., E. R. Meyer, R. D. Bell, and G. A. Koch. 1976. Effects of morphine and methadone on serum testosterone and luteinizing hormone levels and on the secondary sex organs of the male rat. *Endocrinology* 98:367–372.

Claus, E. P., V. E. Tyler, and L. R. Brady. 1970. *Pharmacognosy*, 6th ed. Philadelphia: Lea & Febiger.

Cohen, A. Y. 1973. *Alternatives to drug abuse: steps toward prevention*. National Institute on Drug Abuse Monograph 14. Washington, D.C.: Department of Health, Education, and Welfare.

Cohen, P. J. 1975. History and theories of general anesthesia. In L. S. Goodman and A. Gilman, Eds., *The Pharmacological Basis of Therapeutics*, 5th ed. New York: Macmillan, pp. 53–59.

Cohen, S. 1976. The 94-day cannabis study. *Annals New York Academy of Sciences* 282:211–220.

Cohen, S. 1978. Psychotomimetics (hallucinogens) and cannabis. In W. G. Clark and J. del Giudice, Eds., *Principles of Psychopharmacology*, 2nd ed. New York: Academic Press, pp. 357–369.

Cohen, S. 1980. Therapeutic aspects. In R. C. Petersen, Ed., *Marijuana Research Findings: 1980*. Washington, D.C.: National Institute on Drug Abuse Research Monograph 31, Department of Health and Human Services, pp. 199–221.

Coleman, S. and P. T. Piotrow. 1979. Spermicides— simplicity and safety are major assets. Population

Reports Series H, no. 5 (September). Baltimore, Md.: Johns Hopkins University.

Coleman, S., P. T. Piotrow, and W. Rinehart. 1979. Tobacco: hazards to health and human reproduction. *Population Reports series L*, no. 1 (March).

Collins, M. A., W. P. Nijm, G. F. Borge, G. Teas, and C. Goldfarb. 1979. Dopamine-related tetraisoquinolines: significant urinary excretion by alcoholics after alcohol consumption. *Science* 206:1184–1186.

Comstock, E. G. and B. S. Comstock. 1977. Medical evaluation of inhalant abusers. In C. W. Sharp and M. L. Brehm, Eds., *Review of Inhalants*. National Institute on Drug Abuse Research Monograph 15. Washington, D.C.: Department of Health, Education, and Welfare, pp. 54–80.

Conrad, K. A. 1982. Antianxiety agents and hypnotics. In K. A. Conrad and R. Bressler, Eds., *Drug Therapy for the Elderly*. St. Louis: C. V. Mosby Co., pp. 262–276.

Cormier, J. F. and B. G. Bryant. 1979. Cold and allergy products. In *Handbook of Nonprescription Drugs*, 6th ed. Washington, D.C.: American Pharmaceutical Association, pp. 73–114.

Corti, E. C. 1931. *A History of Smoking*. London: G. G. Harrap & Co., Ltd.

Darlington, R. C. and C. E. Curry, Jr. 1979. Laxative products. In *Handbook of Nonprescription Drugs*, 6th ed. Washington, D.C.: American Pharmaceutical Association, pp. 37–54.

Daughaday, W. H. 1974. The adenohypophysis. In R. H. Williams, Ed., *Textbook of Endocrinology*, 5th ed. Philadelphia: Saunders, pp. 31–79.

Davison, W. 1978. The hazards of drug treatment in old age. In J. C. Brocklehurst, Ed., *Textbook of Geriatric Medicine and Gerontology*, 2nd ed. New York: Churchill Livingstone, pp. 651–669.

De Leon, G. and M. S. Rosenthal. 1979. Therapeutic communities. In R. L. DuPont, A. Goldstein, and J. O'Donnell, Eds., *Handbook on Drug Abuse*. Washington, D.C.: National Institute on Drug Abuse, Department of Health, Education, and Welfare, pp. 39–47.

DeLong, J. V. 1972. Treatment and rehabilitation.

In *Dealing with Drug Abuse: A Report to the Ford Foundation.* New York: Praeger, pp. 173–254.

De Ropp, R. S. 1957. *Drugs and the Mind.* New York: Grove Press.

De Ropp, R. S. 1968. *The Master Game: Pathways to Higher Consciousness beyond the Drug Experience.* New York: Delacorte Press.

Diaz, J. and H. H. Samson. 1980. Impaired brain growth in neonatal rats exposed to ethanol. *Science* 208:751–753.

Dishotsky, N. I., W. D. Loughman, R. E. Mogar, and W. R. Lipscomb. 1971. LSD and genetic damage. *Science* 172:431–440.

Doyle, A. C. 1938. The Sign of Four. In *The Complete Sherlock Holmes.* Garden City, N.Y.: Doubleday.

Earnest, D. L. and I. L. MacGregor. 1982. Therapy for gastrointestinal disease. In K. A. Conrad and R. Bressler, Eds., *Drug Therapy for the Elderly.* St. Louis: C. V. Mosby Co., pp. 159–209.

Edmondson, H. A., B. Henderson, and B. Benton. 1976. Liver-cell adenomas associated with use of oral contraceptives. *New England Journal of Medicine* 294:470–472.

Eisdorfer, C. and M. M. Basen. 1979. Drug misuse by the elderly. In R. L. DuPont, A. Goldstein, and J. O'Donnell, Eds., *Handbook on Drug Abuse.* Washington, D.C.: National Institute on Drug Abuse, Department of Health, Education, and Welfare, pp. 271–276.

Ellinwood, E. H., Jr. 1974. The epidemiology of stimulant abuse. In E. Josephson and E. E. Carroll, Eds., *Drug Use—Epidemiological and Sociological Approaches.* Washington, D.C.: Hemisphere Publishing Co., pp. 303–329.

Evans, F. J. 1977. The power of a sugar pill. In R. Hunt and J. Arras, Eds., *Ethical Issues in Modern Medicine.* Palo Alto, Calif.: Mayfield Publishing Co., pp. 271–277.

Everett, G. M. 1975. Role of biogenic amines in the modulation of aggressive and sexual behavior in animals and man. In M. Sandler and G. L. Gessa, Eds., *Sexual Behavior: Pharmacology and Biochemistry.* New York: Raven Press, pp. 81–84.

Fingl, E. and D. M. Woodbury. 1975. General Principles. In L. S. Goodman and A. Gilman, Eds., *The Pharmacological Basis of Therapeutics,* 5th ed. New York: Macmillan, pp. 1–46.

Fischer, R. 1971. A cartography of the ecstatic and meditative states. *Science* 174:897–904.

Fordyce, W. E. 1976. *Behavioral Methods for Chronic Pain and Illness.* St. Louis: C. V. Mosby Co.

Franz, D. N. 1980. Central nervous stimulants. In A. G. Gilman, L. S. Goodman, and A. Gilman, Eds., *The Pharmacological Basis of Therapeutics,* 6th ed. New York: Macmillan, pp. 585–591.

Fratta, W., G. Biggio, and G. L. Gessa. 1977. Homosexual mounting behavior induced in male rats and rabbits by a tryptophan-free diet. *Life Sciences* 21:379–384.

Freed, D. L. J., A. J. Banks, D. Longson, and D. M. Burley. 1975. Anabolic steroids in athletics: crossover, double-blind trial on weight lifters. *British Medical Journal* 2:471–473 (31 May).

Garattini, S. and P. L. Morselli. 1978. Metabolism and pharmacokinetics of psychotropic drugs. In W. G. Clark and J. del Giudice, Eds., *Principles of Psychopharmacology,* 2nd ed. New York: Academic Press, pp. 169–182.

Garnett, W. R. 1979. Antacid products. In *Handbook of Nonprescription Drugs,* 6th ed. Washington, D.C.: American Pharmaceutical Association, pp. 1–18.

Gay, G. R., J. A. Newmeyer, R. A. Elion, and S. Wieder. 1975. Drug-sex practice in the Haight-Ashbury or "the sensuous hippie." In M. Sandler and G. L. Gessa, Eds., *Sexual Behavior: Pharmacology and Biochemistry.* New York: Raven Press, pp. 63–79.

Gessa, G. L. and A. Tagliamonte. 1975. Role of brain serotonin and dopamine in male sexual behavior. In M. Sadler and G. L. Gessa, Eds., *Sexual Behavior: Pharmacology and Biochemistry.* New York: Raven Press, pp. 117–128.

Gold, M. S., A. C. Pottash, D. R. Sweeney, and H. D. Kleber. 1980. Opiate withdrawal using clonidine. *Journal of the American Medical Association* 243:343–346.

Goldberg, S. R., R. D. Spealman, and D. M. Goldberg. 1981. Persistent behavior at high rates maintained by intravenous self-administration of nicotine. *Science* 214:573–575.

Goldstein, A. 1979. Recent advances in basic research relevant to drug abuse. In R. L. DuPont, A. Goldstein, and J. O'Donnell, Eds., *Handbook on Drug Abuse*. Washington, D.C.: National Institute on Drug Abuse, Department of Health, Education, and Welfare, pp. 439–446.

Goldzieher, J. W., L. E. Moses, E. Averkin, C. Scheel, and B. Z. Taber. 1971. Nervousness and depression attributed to oral contraceptives: a double-blind, placebo-controlled study. *American Journal of Obstetrics and Gynecology* 111:1013–1020.

Goodwin, D. W. 1979. Alcoholism and heredity: a review and hypothesis. *Archives of General Psychiatry* 36:57–61.

Gordon, G. G., K. Altman, A. L. Southren, E. Rubin, and C. S. Lieber. 1976. Effect of alcohol (ethanol) administration on sex-hormone metabolism in normal men. *New England Journal of Medicine* 295:793–797.

Gotz, B. E. and V. P. Gotz. 1978. Drugs and the elderly. *American Journal of Nursing* 78:1347–1351.

Graedon, J. 1976. *The People's Pharmacy*. New York: St. Martin's Press, Inc.

Greenberg, J. 1979. Psyching out pain. *Science News* 115:332–333.

Grinspoon, L. and J. B. Bakalar. 1979. Cocaine. In R. L. DuPont, A. Goldstein, and J. O'Donnell, Eds., *Handbook on Drug Abuse*. Washington, D.C.: National Institute on Drug Abuse, Department of Health, Education, and Welfare, pp. 241–247.

Grof, S. 1976. *Realms of the Human Unconscious: Observations from LSD Research*. New York: E. P. Dutton.

Grunt, J. A. and W. C. Young. 1952. Differential reactivity of individuals and the response of the male guinea pig to testosterone propionate. *Endocrinology* 51:237–248.

Gulevich, G. D. 1977. Psychopharmacological treatment of the aged. In J. D. Barchas, P. A. Berger, R. D. Ciaranello, and G. R. Elliott, Eds., *Psychopharmacology: From Theory to Practice*. New York: Oxford University Press, pp. 448–465.

Hall, R. C. W., S. K. Stickney, and M. K. Popkin.

1978. Physician drug abuser. *Journal of Nervous and Mental Disease* 166:787–793.

Harclerode, J. 1980. The effect of marijuana on reproduction and development. In R. C. Petersen, Ed., *Marijuana Research Findings: 1980*. Washington, D.C.: National Institute on Drug Abuse Research Monograph 31, Department of Health and Human Services, pp. 137–166.

Harvey, S. C. 1980. Hypnotics and sedatives. In A. G. Gilman, L. S. Goodman, and A. Gilman, Eds., *The Pharmacological Basis of Therapeutics*, 6th ed. New York: Macmillan, pp. 339–375.

Hatcher, R. A., G. K. Stewart, F. Stewart, F. Guest, P. Stratton, and A. H. Wright. 1978. *Contraceptive Technology 1978–1979*, 9th ed. New York: Irvington Publishers.

Hecht, A. 1980. Inhalants: quick route to danger. *FDA Consumer* (May). Washington, D.C.: Department of Health and Human Services.

Heimann, R. K. 1960. *Tobacco and Americans*. New York: McGraw-Hill.

Hekimian, L. J. and S. Gershon. 1968. Characteristics of drug abusers admitted to a psychiatric hospital. *Journal of the American Medical Association* 205:125–130.

Himes, N. E. 1963. *Medical History of Contraception*. New York: Schocken Books.

Hofmann, A. 1968. Psychotomimetic agents. In A. Burger, Ed., *Drugs Affecting the Central Nervous System*, Vol. 2. New York: Marcel Dekker, pp. 169–235.

Hollister, L. E. 1973. Human pharmacology of drugs of abuse with emphasis on neuroendocrine effects. In E. Zimmerman, W. H. Gispen, B. H. Marks, and D. DeWied, Eds., *Drug Effects on Neuroendocrine Regulation. Progress in Brain Research* 39: 373–381.

Hollister, L. E. 1975. Drugs and sexual behavior in man. *Life Sciences* 17:661–668.

Holmstedt, B. 1967. Historical survey. In D. H. Efron, Ed., *Ethnopharmacologic Search for Psychoactive Drugs*. Public Health Service Publication no. 1645. Washington, D.C.: U.S. Government Printing Office, pp. 3–32.

Hughes, J. 1975. Isolation of an endogenous compound from the brain with pharmacological properties similar to morphine. *Brain Research* **88**: 295–308.

Huisking, C. L. 1968. *Herbs to Hormones.* Essex, Conn.: Pequot Press, Inc., p. 138.

Huxley, A. 1954. *The Doors of Perception.* New York: Harper & Bros.

Hyyppä, M. T., S. Falck, H. Aukia, and U. K. Rinne. 1975. Neuroendocrine regulation of gonadotropin secretion and sexual motivation after L-tryptophan administration in man. In M. Sandler and G. L. Gessa, Eds., *Sexual Behavior: Pharmacology and Biochemistry.* New York: Raven Press, pp. 307–314.

Institute of Medicine, National Academy of Sciences. 1982. *Marijuana and Health.* Washington, D.C.: National Academy Press.

Iversen, L. L. 1979. The chemistry of the brain. *Scientific American* **241**(3):134–149.

Jacobs, B. L. and M. E. Trulson. 1979. Mechanisms of action of LSD. *American Scientist* **67**:396–404.

Jaffe, J. H. 1979. The swinging pendulum: the treatment of drug users in America. In R. L. DuPont, A. Goldstein, and J. O'Donnell, Eds., *Handbook on Drug Abuse.* Washington, D.C.: National Institute on Drug Abuse, Department of Health, Education, and Welfare, pp. 3–16.

Jaffe, J. H. 1980. Drug addiction and drug abuse. In A. G. Gilman, L. S. Goodman, and A. Gilman, Eds., *The Pharmacological Basis of Therapeutics,* 6th ed. New York: Macmillan, pp. 535–584.

Jaffe, J. H. and M. Kanzler. 1979. Smoking as an addictive disorder. In N. A. Krasnegor, Ed., *Cigarette Smoking as a Dependence Process.* Washington, D.C.: National Institute on Drug Abuse Research Monograph 23, Department of Health, Education, and Welfare, pp. 4–23.

Jaffe, J. H. and W. R. Martin. 1980. Opioid analgesics and antagonists. In A. G. Gilman, L. S. Goodman, and A. Gilman, Eds., *The Pharmacological Basis of Therapeutics,* 6th ed. New York: Macmillan, pp. 494–534.

Jarvik, M. E. 1979. Biological influences on cigarette smoking. In N. A. Krasnegor, Ed., *The Behavioral Aspects of Smoking.* Washington, D.C.: National

Institute on Drug Abuse Research Monograph 26, Department of Health, Education, and Welfare, pp. 7–45.

Jellinek, E. M. 1952. Phases of alcohol addiction. *Quarterly Journal of Studies on Alcohol* **13**:673–684.

Jick, H., A. M. Walker, K. J. Rothman, J. R. Hunter, L. B. Holmes, R. N. Watkins, D. C. D'Ewart, A. Danford, and S. Madsen. 1981. Vaginal spermicides and congenital disorders. *Journal of the American Medical Association* **245**:1329–1332.

Johnson, D. N. and M. Diamond. 1969. Yohimbine and sexual stimulation in the male rat. *Physiology and Behavior* **4**:411–413.

Johnson, E. M., Jr., R. A. Macia, and T. O. Yellin. 1977. Marked difference in the susceptibility of several species to guanethidine-induced chemical sympathectomy. *Life Sciences* **20**:107–112.

Jones, B. M. and A. Paredes. 1974. Circadian variation of ethanol metabolism in alcoholics. *British Journal of Addiction* **69**:3–10.

Jones, R. T. 1980. Human effects: an overview. In R. C. Petersen, Ed., *Marijuana Research Findings: 1980.* Washington, D.C.: National Institute on Drug Abuse Research Monograph 31, Department of Health and Human Services, pp. 54–80.

Jones, R. T., T. R. Farrell III, and R. I. Herning. 1978. Tobacco smoking and nicotine tolerance. In N. A. Krasnegor, Ed., *Self-Administration of Abused Substances: Methods for Study.* Washington, D.C.: National Institute on Drug Abuse Research Monograph 20, Department of Health, Education, and Welfare, pp. 202–208.

Jones, W. H. S. 1956. *Natural History.* Cambridge, Mass.: Harvard University Press.

Kaij, L. and J. Dock. 1975. Grandsons of alcoholics: a test of sex-linked transmission of alcohol abuse. *Archives of General Psychiatry* **32**:1379–1381.

Kaplan, H. S. 1974. *The New Sex Therapy.* New York: Brunner/Mazel.

Keller, M. 1958. Alcoholism: nature and extent of the problem. In S. D. Bacon, Ed., *Understanding Alcoholism. Annals American Academy Political and Social Science* **315**:1–11.

Koelle, G. B. 1975. Neurohumoral transmission and the autonomic nervous system. In L. S. Goodman and A. Gilman, Eds., *The Pharmacological Basis of Therapeutics*, 5th ed. New York: Macmillan, pp. 404–444.

Kolata, G. B. 1979. New drugs and the brain. *Science* 205:774–776.

Kolodny, R. C., W. H. Masters, R. M. Kolodner, and G. Toro. 1974. Depression of plasma testosterone levels after chronic intensive marijuana use. *New England Journal of Medicine* 290:872–874.

Krasnegor, N. A. 1979. Introduction. In N. A. Krasnegor, Ed., *The Behavioral Aspects of Smoking*. Washington, D.C.: National Institute on Drug Abuse Research Monograph 26, Department of Health, Education, and Welfare, pp. 1–6.

La Barre, W. 1970. *The Peyote Cult*. Hamden, Conn.: The Shoe String Press.

La Barre, W., D. P. McAllester, J. S. Slotkin, O. C. Stewart, and S. Tax. 1951. Statement on peyote. *Science* 114:582–583.

Lamy, P. P. 1980. *Prescribing for the Elderly*. Littleton, Mass.: PSG Publishing Co., Inc.

Leary, T., R. Metzner, and R. Alpert. 1964. *The Psychedelic Experience*. New Hyde Park, N.Y.: University Books.

Lee, D. 1976. *Cocaine Consumer's Handbook*. Berkeley, Calif.: And/Or Press.

Lee, H. 1963. *How Dry We Were: Prohibition Revisited*. Englewood Cliffs, N.J.: Prentice-Hall.

Lemberger, L., N. R. Tamarkin, J. Axelrod, and I. J. Kopin. 1971. Delta-9-tetrahydrocannabinol: metabolism and disposition in long-term marihuana smokers. *Science* 173:72–74.

Lemere, F. and J. W. Smith. 1973. Alcohol-induced sexual impotence. *American Journal of Psychiatry* 130:212–213.

Lerner, S. E. and R. S. Burns. 1978. Phencyclidine use among youth: history, epidemiology, and acute and chronic intoxication. In R. C. Petersen and R. C. Stillman, Eds., *Phencyclidine (PCP) Abuse: An Appraisal*. Washington, D.C.: National Institute on Drug Abuse Research Monograph 21, Department of Health, Education, and Welfare, pp. 66–118.

Lettieri, D. J., M. Sayers, and H. W. Pearson, Eds. 1980. *Theories on Drug Abuse: Selected Contemporary Perspectives*. Washington, D.C.: National Institute on Drug Abuse Research Monograph 30, Department of Health and Human Services.

Lewin, L. 1931. *Phantastica: Narcotic and Stimulating Drugs*. London: Routledge & Kegan Paul (reprinted 1964).

Lieber, C. S. 1976. The metabolism of alcohol. *Scientific American* 234(3):25–33.

Ling, W. and J. D. Blaine. 1979. The use of LAAM in treatment. In R. L. DuPont, A. Goldstein, and J. O'Donnell, Eds., *Handbook on Drug Abuse*. Washington, D.C.: National Institute on Drug Abuse, Department of Health, Education, and Welfare, pp. 87–96.

Longe, R. L. 1979. Antidiarrheal and other gastrointestinal products. In *Handbook of Nonprescription Drugs*, 6th ed. Washington, D.C.: American Pharmaceutical Association, pp. 25–36.

Loomis, T. A. 1978. *Essentials of Toxicology*, 3rd ed. Philadelphia: Lea & Febiger.

Lowinson, J. H. and R. B. Millman. 1979. Clinical aspects of methadone maintenance treatment. In R. L. DuPont, A. Goldstein, and J. O'Donnell, Eds., *Handbook on Drug Abuse*. Washington, D.C.: National Institute on Drug Abuse, Department of Health, Education, and Welfare, pp. 49–56.

Luisada, P. V. 1978. The phencyclidine psychosis: phenomenology and treatment. In R. C. Petersen and R. C. Stillman, Eds., *Phencyclidine (PCP) Abuse: An Appraisal*. Washington, D.C.: National Institute on Drug Abuse Research Monograph 21, Department of Health, Education, and Welfare, pp. 241–253.

Madsen, K. B. 1974. *Modern Theories of Motivation*. New York: John Wiley & Sons.

Marihuana menaces youth. 1936. *Scientific American* 154:150–151.

Marks, V. and J. Chakraborty. 1973. The clinical endocrinology of alcoholism. *Journal of Alcoholism* 8:94–103.

Marquardt, G. M., V. DiStefano, and L. L. Ling. 1978. Pharmacological effects of (±)-, (S)-, and (R)-MDA. In R. C. Stillman and R. E. Willette, Eds., *The Psychopharmacology of Hallucinogens*. New York: Pergamon Press, pp. 84–104.

REFERENCES

Martin, E. W. 1971. *Hazards of Medication.* Philadelphia: J. B. Lippincott.

Martin, W. R. 1978. Multiple receptors: speculations about receptor evolution. In J. Fishman, Ed., *The Bases of Addiction.* Berlin: Dahlem Konferenzen, pp. 395–409.

Marx, J. L. 1979. Brain peptides: is substance P a transmitter of pain signals? *Science* **205**:886–889.

Maslow, A. H. 1973. A theory of human motivation. In R. J. Lowry, Ed., *Dominance, Self-Esteem, Self-Actualization: Germinal Papers of A. H. Maslow.* Monterey, Calif.: Brooks/Cole Publishing Co., pp. 153–173.

McConnell, R. F., Jr., E. Dupree, and G. S. Parcel. 1977. Poisoning and toxic reactions. In G. S. Parcel, Ed., *First Aid in Emergency Care.* St. Louis: C. V. Mosby Co., pp. 97–115.

McGlothin, W., S. Cohen, and M. S. McGlothin. 1967. Long lasting effects of LSD on normals. *Archives of General Psychiatry* **17**:521–532.

McLean, B. K., A. Rubel, and M. B. Nikitovitch-Winer. 1977. The differential effects of exposure to tobacco smoke on the secretion of luteinizing hormone and prolactin in the proestrous rat. *Endocrinology* **100**:1566–1570.

Mendelson, J. H., J. Kuehnle, J. Ellingboe, and T. F. Babor. 1974. Plasma testosterone levels before, during, and after chronic marijuana smoking. *New England Journal of Medicine* **291**:1051–1055.

Meyer, H. 1954. *Old English Coffee Houses.* Emmaus, Penn.: The Rodale Press.

Mishara, B. L. and R. Kastenbaum. 1980. *Alcohol and Old Age.* New York: Grune & Stratton.

Monroe, R. R. and H. J. Drell. 1947. Oral use of stimulants obtained from inhalers. *Journal of the American Medical Association* **135**:909–915.

Moreau, J. J. 1845/1973. *Hashish and Mental Illness* [*Du Hachish et de l'Alienation Mentale; Etudes Psychologiques;* translated by G. J. Barnett]. New York: Raven Press.

Murad, F. and R. C. Haynes. 1980. Androgens and anabolic steroids. In A. G. Gilman, L. S. Goodman, and A. Gilman, Eds., *The Pharmacological Basis of Therapeutics,* 6th ed. New York: Macmillan, pp. 1448–1465.

Naranjo, C., A. T. Shulgin, and T. Sargent. 1967. Evaluation of 3,4-methylenedioxyamphetamine (MDA) as an adjunct to psychotherapy. *Medicina et Pharmacologia Experimentalis* **17**:359–364.

National Institute on Alcohol Abuse and Alcoholism. 1980. *Facts about Alcohol and Alcoholism.* Washington, D.C.: U.S. Government Printing Office, 329–919/6640.

Nauta, W. J. H. and M. Feirtag. 1979. The organization of the brain. *Scientific American* **241**(3):88–111.

Newmeyer, J. A. 1974. The Watergate-era junkie: observations on the changing face of heroin addiction in San Francisco. *Report of the 36th Annual Scientific Meeting,* Committee on Problems of Drug Dependence, National Research Council, National Academy of Sciences. Mexico City, March 10–14, pp. 1065–1073.

Nichols, J. R. and S. Hsiao. 1967. Addiction liability of albino rats: breeding for quantitative differences in morphine drinking. *Science* **157**:561–563.

Nickerson, M. and B. Collier. 1975. Drugs inhibiting adrenergic nerves and structures innervated by them. In L. S. Goodman and A. Gilman, Eds., *The Pharmacological Basis of Therapeutics,* 5th ed. New York: Macmillan, pp. 533–564.

Nilsson, S. and K.-G. Nygren. 1979. Transfer of contraceptive steroids to human milk. *Research in Reproduction* **11**:1–2 (January).

Notermans, S. L. H. and M. M. W. A. Tophoff. 1975. Sex difference in pain tolerance and pain apperception. In M. Weisenberg, Ed., *Pain: Clinical and Experimental Perspectives.* St. Louis: C. V. Mosby Co.

Nurco, D. N. 1979. Etiological aspects of drug abuse. In R. L. DuPont, A. Goldstein, and J. O'Donnell, Eds., *Handbook on Drug Abuse.* Washington, D.C.: National Institute on Drug Abuse, Department of Health, Education, and Welfare, pp. 315–324.

O'Brien, C. P. and L. K. Y. Ng. 1979. Innovative treatments for drug addiction. In R. L. DuPont, A. Goldstein, and J. O'Donnell, Eds., *Handbook on Drug Abuse.* Washington, D.C.: National Institute on Drug Abuse, Department of Health, Education, and Welfare, pp. 193–201.

Odell, W. D. and M. E. Molitch. 1974. The pharmacology of contraceptive agents. *Annual Review of Pharmacology* **14**:413–434.

Pagano, R. R., R. M. Rose, R. M. Stivers, and S. Warrenburg. 1976. Sleep during transcendental meditation. *Science* **191**:308–310.

Pahnke, W. N., A. A. Kurland, S. Unger, C. Savage, and S. Grof. 1970. The experimental use of psychedelic (LSD) psychotherapy. In J. R. Gamage and E. L. Zerkin, Eds., *Hallucinogenic Drug Research: Impact on Science and Society*. Beloit, Wisc.: Stash Press, pp. 48–68.

Pahnke, W. N. and W. A. Richards. 1966. Implications of LSD and experimental mysticism. *Journal of Religion and Health* **5**:175–208.

Panikkar, R. 1977. *The Vedic Experience*. Berkeley: University of California Press, p. 367.

Petersen, D. M. and F. J. Whittington. 1977. Drug use among the elderly: a review. *Journal of Psychedelic Drugs* **9**:25–37.

Petersen, R. C. 1974. In L. Messolonghites, Ed., *Alternative Pursuits for America's 3rd Century*. Washington, D.C.: National Institute on Drug Abuse, Department of Health, Education, and Welfare Publication No. (HSM) 73–9158.

Petersen, R. C. 1980. Marijuana and health. In R. C. Petersen, Ed., *Marijuana Research Findings: 1980*. Washington, D.C.: National Institute on Drug Abuse Research Monograph 31, Department of Health and Human Services, pp. 1–53.

Petersen, R. C. and R. C. Stillman. 1978. Phencyclidine: an overview. In R. C. Petersen and R. C. Stillman, Eds., *Phencyclidine (PCP) Abuse: An Appraisal*. Washington, D.C.: National Institute on Drug Abuse Research Monograph 21, Department of Health, Education, and Welfare, pp. 1–17.

Petrakis, N. L., L. D. Gruenke, T. C. Beelen, N. Castagnoli, Jr., and J. C. Craig. 1978. Nicotine in breast fluid of nonlactating women. *Science* **199**:303–305.

Piland, B. 1979. The aging process and psychoactive drug use in clinical treatment. In *The Aging Process and Psychoactive Drug Use*. Washington, D.C.: National Institute on Drug Abuse, Department of Health, Education, and Welfare, pp. 1–16.

Piotrow, P. T., W. Rinehart, and J. C. Schmidt. 1979. IUDs—update on safety, effectiveness, and research. Population Reports Series B, no. 3 (May). Baltimore, Md.: Johns Hopkins University.

Planas, G. M. and J. Kuć. 1968. Contraceptive properties of Stevia rebaudiana. *Science* **162**:1007.

Pomerleau, O. F. 1979. Behavioral factors in the establishment, maintenance, and cessation of smoking. In N. A. Krasnegor, Ed., *The Behavioral Aspects of Smoking*. Washington, D.C.: National Institute on Drug Abuse Research Monograph 26, Department of Health, Education, and Welfare, pp. 47–67.

Prentice, R. 1979. Patterns of psychoactive drug use among the elderly. In *The Aging Process and Psychoactive Drug Use*. Washington, D.C.: National Institute on Drug Abuse, Department of Health, Education, and Welfare, pp. 17–41.

Procacci, P., M. Della Corte, M. Zoppi, S. Romano, M. Maresca, and M. R. Voegelin. 1974. Pain threshold measurements in man. In J. J. Bonica, P. Procacci, and C. A. Pagni, Eds., *Recent Advances on Pain: Pathophysiology and Clinical Aspects*. Springfield, Ill.: Charles C Thomas, pp. 105–147.

Rall, T. W. 1980. Central nervous system stimulants. In A. G. Gilman, L. S. Goodman, and A. Gilman, Eds., *The Pharmacological Basis of Therapeutics*, 6th ed. New York: Macmillan, pp. 592–607.

Ray, W. J., J. M. Raczynski, T. Rogers, and W. H. Kimball. 1979. *Evaluation of Clinical Biofeedback*. New York: Plenum Press.

Renault, P. F. 1981. Treatment of heroin-dependent persons with antagonists: current status. In R. E. Willette and G. Barnett, Eds., *Narcotic Antagonists: Naltrexone Pharmacochemistry and Sustained-Release Preparations*. Washington, D.C.: National Institute on Drug Abuse Research Monograph 28, Department of Health and Human Services, pp. 11–22.

Resnik, H. S. 1979. *It Starts with People: Experiences in Drug Abuse Prevention*. Washington, D.C.: National Institute on Drug Abuse, Department of Health, Education, and Welfare Publication No. (ADM) 79-590.

Rinehart, W. and P. T. Piotrow. 1979. OCs—update on usage, safety, and side effects. Population Reports Series A, No. 5 (January). Baltimore, Md.: Johns Hopkins University.

Ritchie, J. M. 1980. The aliphatic alcohols. In A. G. Gilman, L. S. Goodman, and A. Gilman, Eds., *The Pharmacological Basis of Therapeutics*, 6th ed. New York: Macmillan, pp. 376–390.

Ross, D. H., M. A. Medina, and H. L. Cardenas. 1974. Morphine and ethanol: selective depletion of regional brain calcium. *Science* 186:63–65.

Roueché, B. 1960. *The Neutral Spirit: A Portrait of Alcohol.* Boston: Little, Brown and Co.

Rubin, E. and C. S. Lieber. 1971. Alcoholism, alcohol, and drugs. *Science* 172:1097–1102.

Rumbaugh, C. L. 1977. Small vessel cerebral vascular changes following chronic amphetamine intoxication. In E. H. Ellinwood, Jr., and M. M. Kilbey, Eds., *Cocaine and Other Stimulants.* New York: Plenum Press, pp. 241–251.

Santen, R. J., J. Sofsky, N. Bilic, and R. Lippert. 1975. Mechanism of action of narcotics in the production of menstrual dysfunction in women. *Fertility and Sterility* 26:538–548.

Schaeffer, J., T. Andrysiak, and T. J. Ungerleider. 1981. Cognition and long-term use of ganja (cannabis). *Science* 213:465–466.

Schleiffer, H. 1979. *Narcotic Plants of the Old World.* Monticello, N.Y.: Lubrecht & Cramer.

Schuckit, M. A. and V. Rayses. 1979. Ethanol ingestion: differences in blood acetaldehyde concentrations in relatives of alcoholics and controls. *Science* 203:54–55.

Schultes, R. E. 1970. The plant kingdom and hallucinogens (part III). *Bulletin on Narcotics* 22(1):25–53.

Schultes, R. E. 1978. Ethnopharmacological significance of psychotropic drugs of vegetal origin. In W. G. Clark and J. del Giudice, Eds., *Principles of Psychopharmacology*, 2nd ed. New York: Academic Press, pp. 41–70.

Schultes, R. E. and A. Hofmann. 1973. *The Botany and Chemistry of Hallucinogens.* Springfield, Ill.: Charles C Thomas.

Scott, J. M. 1969. *The White Poppy: A History of Opium.* New York: Funk & Wagnalls.

Seashore, R. H. and A. C. Ivy. 1953. The effects of analeptic drugs in relieving fatigue. *Psychological Monographs* 67:1–16 (no. 15).

Seevers, M. H. 1968. Psychopharmacological elements of drug dependence. *Journal of the American Medical Association* 206:1263–1266.

Segovia-Riquelme, N., A. Hederra, M. Anex, O. Barnier, I. Figuerola-Campo, I. Campos-Hoppe, N. Jara, and J. Mardones. 1970. Nutritional and genetic factors in the appetite for alcohol. In R. E. Popham, Ed., *Alcohol and Alcoholism.* Toronto: University of Toronto Press, pp. 86–96.

Seixas, F. A. 1980. The medical complications of alcoholism. In S. E. Gitlow and H. S. Peyser, Eds., *Alcoholism: A Practical Treatment Guide.* New York: Grune & Stratton, pp. 165–180.

Sellers, E. M. and H. Kalant. 1978. Pharmacotherapy of acute and chronic alcoholism and alcohol withdrawal syndrome. In W. G. Clark and J. del Giudice, Eds., *Principles of Psychopharmacology*, 2nd ed. New York: Academic Press, pp. 721–740.

Sells, S. B. 1979. Treatment effectiveness. In R. L. DuPont, A. Goldstein, and J. O'Donnell, Eds., *Handbook on Drug Abuse.* Washington, D.C.: National Institute on Drug Abuse, Department of Health, Education, and Welfare, pp. 105–118.

Sleator, E. K. and R. L. Sprague. 1978. Pediatric psychopharmacology. In W. G. Clark and J. del Giudice, Eds., *Principles of Psychopharmacology*, 2nd ed. New York: Academic Press, pp. 573–591.

Smith, D. E., D. R. Wesson, and R. B. Seymour. 1979. The abuse of barbiturates and other sedative-hypnotics. In R. I. DuPont, A. Goldstein, and J. O'Donnell, Eds., *Handbook on Drug Abuse.* Washington, D.C.: National Institute on Drug Abuse, Department of Health, Education, and Welfare, pp. 233–240.

Smith, G. M. and H. K. Beecher. 1959. Amphetamine sulfate and athletic performance. I. Objective effects. *Journal of the American Medical Association* 170:542–557.

Smith, R. G., N. F. Besch, P. K. Besch, and C. G. Smith. 1979. Inhibition of gonadotropin by delta-9-tetrahydrocannabinol: mediation by steroid receptors? *Science* 204:325–327.

REFERENCES

Snyder, S. H. 1977. Opiate receptors in the brain. *New England Journal of Medicine* **296**:266–271.

Solomon, D., Ed. 1966. *The Marihuana Papers.* New York: New American Library, pp. 277–410.

Soulairac, M.-L. and A. Soulairac. 1975. Monoaminergic and cholinergic control of sexual behavior in the male rat. In M. Sandler and G. L. Gessa, Eds., *Sexual Behavior: Pharmacology and Biochemistry.* New York: Raven Press, pp. 99–116.

Spark, R. F., R. A. White, and P. B. Connolly. 1980. Impotence is not always psychogenic. Newer insights into hypothalamic-pituitary-gonadal dysfunction. *Journal of the American Medical Association* **243**: 750–755.

Spotts, J. V. and C. A. Spotts, Eds. 1980. *Use and Abuse of Amphetamine and Its Substitutes.* Washington, D.C.: National Institute on Drug Abuse Research Issues No. 25, Department of Health, Education, and Welfare.

Statistical Abstracts of the United States. 1980. 101st ed. Washington, D.C.: U.S. Department of Commerce, Bureau of the Census.

Stevens, C. F. 1979. The neuron. *Scientific American* **241(3)**:55–65.

Stimmel, B. 1980. Methadone maintenance and alcohol use. In S. E. Bardner, Ed., *Drug and Alcohol Abuse. Implications for Treatment.* Washington, D.C.: National Institute on Drug Abuse Treatment Research Monograph, Department of Health and Human Services, pp. 57–71.

Streissguth, A. P., S. Landesman-Dwyer, J. C. Martin, and D. W. Smith. 1980. Teratogenic effects of alcohol in humans and laboratory animals. *Science* **209**:353–361.

Sulser, F. and E. Sanders-Bush. 1971. Effects of drugs on amines in the CNS. *Annual Reviews of Pharmacology* **11**:209–230.

Surgeon General. 1979. *Smoking and Health: A Report of the Surgeon General.* Washington, D.C.: U.S. Department of Health, Education, and Welfare Publication No. (PHS) 79-50066.

Surgeon General. 1981. *The Changing Cigarette.* Washington, D.C.: U.S. Department of Health, Education, and Welfare Publication No. (PHS) 81-50156.

Swisher, J. D. 1979. Prevention issues. In R. L. DuPont, A. Goldstein, and J. O'Donnell, Eds., *Handbook on Drug Abuse.* Washington, D.C.: National Institute on Drug Abuse, Department of Health, Education, and Welfare, pp. 423–435.

Tallman, J. F., S. M. Paul, P. Skolnick, and D. W. Gallagher. 1980. Receptors for the age of anxiety: pharmacology of the benzodiazepines. *Science* **207**:274–281.

Taylor, P. 1980. Ganglionic stimulating and blocking agents. In A. G. Gilman, L. S. Goodman, and A. Gilman, Eds.; *The Pharmacological Basis of Therapeutics,* 6th ed. New York: Macmillan, pp. 211–219.

Temin, P. 1980. *Taking Your Medicine: Drug Regulation in the United States.* Cambridge, Mass.: Harvard University Press.

Terry, C. E. and M. Pellens. 1928. *The Opium Problem.* Bureau of Social Hygiene. Reprinted 1970, Patterson Smith, Montclair, N.J.

33rd annual report on consumer spending. 1981. *Drug Topics 125,* no. 13. Oradell, N.J.: Medical Economics Co., Inc.

Tolis, G., J. Hickey, and H. Guyda. 1975. Effects of morphine on serum growth hormone, cortisol, prolactin, and thyroid stimulating hormone in man. *Journal of Clinical Endocrinology and Metabolism* **41**:797–800.

Trice, H. M. 1979. Job-based alcohol and drug abuse programs: recent program developments and research. In R. L. DuPont, A. Goldstein, and J. O'Donnell, Eds., *Handbook on Drug Abuse.* Washington, D.C.: National Institute on Drug Abuse, Department of Health, Education, and Welfare, pp. 181–191.

Turner, C. E. 1980. Chemistry and metabolism. In R. C. Petersen, Ed., *Marijuana Research Findings: 1980.* Washington, D.C.: National Institute on Drug Abuse Research Monograph 31, Department of Health and Human Services, pp. 81–97.

Ullman, A. D. 1958. Sociocultural backgrounds of alcoholism. In S. D. Bacon, Ed., *Understanding Alcoholism. Annals American Academy Political and Social Science* **315**:48–54.

Van Dyke, C., P. Jatlow, J. Ungerer, P. G. Barash, and R. Byck. 1978. Oral cocaine: plasma concentrations and central effects. *Science* **200**:201–213.

Van Thiel, D. H., J. Gavaler, and R. Lester. 1974. Ethanol inhibition of vitamin A metabolism in the testes: possible mechanism for sterility in alcoholics. *Science* **186**:941–942.

Van Thiel, D. H. and R. Lester. 1976. Sex and alcohol: a second peek. *New England Journal of Medicine* **295**:835–836.

Van Tyle, W. K. 1979. Internal analgesic products. In *Handbook of Nonprescription Drugs*, 6th ed. Washington, D.C.: American Pharmaceutical Association, pp. 125–140.

Volle, R. L. and G. B. Koelle. 1975. Ganglionic stimulating and blocking agents. In L. S. Goodman and A. Gilman, Eds., *The Pharmacological Basis of Therapeutics*, 5th ed. New York: Macmillan, pp. 565–574.

Vorhees, C. V., R. L. Brunner, and R. E. Butcher. 1979. Psychotropic drugs as behavioral teratogens. *Science* **205**:1220–1225.

Warner, K. E. 1981. Cigarette smoking in the 1970's: the impact of the antismoking campaign on consumption. *Science* **211**:729–731.

Way, E. L. 1978. Common and selective mechanisms in drug dependence. In J. Fishman, Ed., *The Bases of Addiction*. Berlin: Dahlem Konferenzen 1978, pp. 333–352.

Weil, A. 1972. *The Natural Mind*. Boston: Houghton Mifflin Co.

Weiner, N. 1980a. Norepinephrine, epinephrine, and the sympathomimetic amines. In A. G. Gilman, L. S. Goodman, and A. Gilman, Eds., *The Pharmacological Basis of Therapeutics*, 6th ed. New York: Macmillan, pp. 138–175.

Weiner, N. 1980b. Drugs that inhibit adrenergic nerves and block adrenergic receptors. In A. G. Gilman, L. S. Goodman, and A. Gilman, Eds., *The Pharmacological Basis of Therapeutics*, 6th ed. New York: Macmillan, pp. 176–210.

Weiss, B. 1969. Enhancement of performance by amphetamine-like drugs. In F. Sjoqvist and M. Tottie, Eds., *Abuse of Central Stimulants*. New York: Raven Press, pp. 31–60.

Weiss, B. and V. G. Laties. 1962. Enhancement of human performance by caffeine and the amphetamines. *Pharmacological Review* **14**:1–36.

Wesson, D. R. and D. E. Smith. 1977. Cocaine: its use for central nervous system stimulation including recreational and medical uses. In R. C. Petersen and R. C. Stillman, Eds., *Cocaine: 1977*. Washington, D.C.: National Institute on Drug Abuse Research Monograph Series No. 13, Department of Health, Education, and Welfare, pp. 137–152.

Whalen, R. E., B. B. Gorzalka, and J. F. DeBold. 1975. Methodological considerations in the study of animal sexual behavior. In M. Sandler and G. L. Gessa, Eds., *Sexual Behavior: Pharmacology and Biochemistry*. New York: Raven Press, pp. 33–44.

Wolfe, T. 1968. *The Electric Kool-Aid Acid Test*. New York: Farrar, Straus, and Giroux.

World Health Organization Expert Committee on Addiction-Producing Drugs. 1964. Terminology in regard to drug abuse. *World Health Organization Technical Report* **273**:9–10.

Ylikahri, R. and M. Huttunen. 1974. Low plasma testosterone values in men during hangover. *Journal of Steroid Biochemistry* **5**:655–658.

Zinsberg, N. E. 1979. Nonaddictive opiate use. In R. L. DuPont, A. Goldstein, and J. O'Donnell, Eds., *Handbook on Drug Abuse*. Washington, D.C.: National Institute on Drug Abuse, Department of Health, Education, and Welfare, pp. 303–313.

INDEX